Management Information Systems

FOR THE INFORMATION AGE

Management Information Systems

FOR THE INFORMATION AGE

SIXTH EDITION

Stephen Haag

DANIELS COLLEGE OF BUSINESS

UNIVERSITY OF DENVER

Maeve Cummings

COLLEGE OF BUSINESS

PITTSBURG STATE UNIVERSITY

Amy Phillips

DANIELS COLLEGE OF BUSINESS

UNIVERSITY OF DENVER

McGraw-Hill
Irwin

Boston   Burr Ridge, IL   Dubuque, IA   Madison, WI   New York   San Francisco   St. Louis
Bangkok   Bogotá   Caracas   Kuala Lumpur   Lisbon   London   Madrid   Mexico City
Milan   Montreal   New Delhi   Santiago   Seoul   Singapore   Sydney   Taipei   Toronto

Irwin

MANAGEMENT INFORMATION SYSTEMS FOR THE INFORMATION AGE

Published by McGraw-Hill/Irwin, a business unit of The McGraw-Hill Companies, Inc., 1221 Avenue of the Americas, New York, NY, 10020. Copyright © 2007 by The McGraw-Hill Companies, Inc. All rights reserved. No part of this publication may be reproduced or distributed in any form or by any means, or stored in a database or retrieval system, without the prior written consent of The McGraw-Hill Companies, Inc., including, but not limited to, in any network or other electronic storage or transmission, or broadcast for distance learning.

Some ancillaries, including electronic and print components, may not be available to customers outside the United States.

This book is printed on acid-free paper.

1 2 3 4 5 6 7 8 9 0 WCK/WCK 0 9 8 7 6 5

ISBN-13: 978-0-07-110610-8
ISBN-10: 0-07-110610-3

www.mhhe.com

For Indy. He passed on to a far greater life after filling ours with 15 wonderful years.

Stephen Haag

To Harry; In the successes of your life may you find joy and fulfillment: in your failures, humor and wisdom.

Maeve Cummings

To my father, J. Dale McLeod, with love. Thank you for being a part of my life.

Amy Phillips

BRIEF CONTENTS

CHAPTER ONE   2
The Information Age in Which You Live:
Changing the Face of Business

CHAPTER TWO   70
Major Business Initiatives:
Gaining Competitive Advantage with IT

CHAPTER THREE   122
Databases and Data Warehouses:
Building Business Intelligence

CHAPTER FOUR   178
Decision Support and Artificial
Intelligence: Brainpower for Your Business

CHAPTER FIVE   238
Electronic Commerce:
Strategies for the New Economy

CHAPTER SIX   278
Systems Development:
Phases, Tools, and Techniques

CHAPTER SEVEN   316
Enterprise Infrastructure and Integration:
Building the Dynamic Enterprise

CHAPTER EIGHT   354
Protecting People and Information:
Threats and Safeguards

CHAPTER NINE   432
Emerging Trends and Technologies:
Business, People, and Technology Tomorrow

EXTENDED LEARNING MODULE A   38
Computer Hardware and Software

EXTENDED LEARNING MODULE B   102
The World Wide Web and the Internet

EXTENDED LEARNING MODULE C   160
Designing Databases and Entity-
Relationship Diagramming

EXTENDED LEARNING MODULE D   218
Decision Analysis with Spreadsheet
Software

EXTENDED LEARNING MODULE E   276
Network Basics

EXTENDED LEARNING MODULE F   314
Building a Web Page with HTML

EXTENDED LEARNING MODULE G   352
Object-Oriented Technologies

EXTENDED LEARNING MODULE H   390
Computer Crime and Forensics

EXTENDED LEARNING MODULE I   454
Building an E-Portfolio

EXTENDED LEARNING MODULE J   494
Implementing a Database with Microsoft
Access

EXTENDED LEARNING MODULE K   496
Careers in Business

EXTENDED LEARNING MODULE L   498
Building Web Sites with FrontPage

EXTENDED LEARNING MODULE M   500
Programming in Excel with VBA

Group Projects   502

TABLE OF CONTENTS

Preface   *xvi*

CHAPTER ONE   2

The Information Age in Which You Live: Changing the Face of Business

OPENING CASE STUDY: DISRUPTIVE TECHNOLOGIES
DISRUPT BLOCKBUSTER LATE FEES   3

INTRODUCTION   4

INFORMATION AS A KEY RESOURCE   6

Data, Information, and Business Intelligence   6
Personal Dimensions of Information   6
Organizational Dimensions of Information   8

PEOPLE AS THE KEY RESOURCE   10

Information and Technology Literacy   10
Your Ethical Responsibilities   13

INFORMATION TECHNOLOGY AS A KEY RESOURCE   14

Key Technology Categories   15
Ubiquitous Computing: Decentralized Computing, Shared Information, Mobile Computing, and a Whole Lot More   17

CREATING THE BUSINESS VISION FOR INFORMATION
TECHNOLOGY   18

Top Line versus Bottom Line   18
Databases in Support of Competitive Advantages   20
Supporting Decision Making for Competitive Advantage   21
Pursuing Major Business Initiatives for Competitive Advantage   24
Run, Grow, and Transform   25

INFORMATION TECHNOLOGY IN YOUR LIFE   26

Your Career   26
Ethics, Security, and Privacy   27

Closing Case Study One: You and
Your Information   30

Closing Case Study Two: Technology Metrics—
Measuring Efficiency and Effectiveness   32

Electronic Commerce: Using the Internet
as a Tool to Find a Job   36

EXTENDED LEARNING MODULE A   38

Computer Hardware and Software

INTRODUCTION   39

A QUICK TOUR OF TECHNOLOGY   40

CATEGORIES OF COMPUTERS BY SIZE   42

Personal Digital Assistants (PDAs)   42
Tablet PCs   42
Notebook Computers   43
Desktop Computers   43
Minicomputers, Mainframe Computers, and Supercomputers   44

SOFTWARE: YOUR INTELLECTUAL INTERFACE   45

Application Software   45
System Software   48

HARDWARE: YOUR PHYSICAL INTERFACE   51

Common Input Devices   52
Common Output Devices   54
Common Storage Devices   56
CPU and RAM   59
Connecting the Hardware Outside to the Hardware Inside   61

CHAPTER TWO   70

Major Business Initiatives: Gaining Competitive Advantage with IT

OPENING CASE STUDY: BUSINESS INTELLIGENCE IS KEY
TO THE SUCCESS OF THE MIAMI DOLPHINS   71

INTRODUCTION   72

PORTER'S FIVE FORCES MODEL   72

Buyer Power   73
Supplier Power   73
Threat of Substitute Products or Services   74
Threat of New Entrants   75
Rivalry among Existing Competitors   75

THE VALUE CHAIN   76

Identifying Processes That Add Value   77
Identifying Processes That Reduce Value   77

SUPPLY CHAIN MANAGEMENT   78

Strategic and Competitive Opportunities with SCM   80
IT Support for Supply Chain Management   81

CUSTOMER RELATIONSHIP MANAGEMENT   81

*Strategic and Competitive Opportunities
with CRM   83*

*IT Support for Customer Relationship
Management   84*

BUSINESS INTELLIGENCE   85

*Strategic and Competitive Opportunities
with BI   86*

IT Support for Business Intelligence   87

INTEGRATED COLLABORATION ENVIRONMENTS   88

*Strategic and Competitive Opportunities
with ICEs   90*

*IT Support for Integrated Collaboration
Environments   90*

BACK TO THE BEGINNING   92

**Closing Case Study One: If We Don't Have It,
You Get It for Free**   95

**Closing Case Study Two: The Restaurant Business
Eats Up Business Intelligence**   96

Electronic Commerce: Ordering Products
and Services on the Internet   100

EXTENDED LEARNING MODULE B   102
The World Wide Web and the Internet

INTRODUCTION   103

WORLD WIDE WEB   104

Web Sites, Addresses, and Pages   104
Understanding Addresses   105
Using Web Browser Software   106

SEARCH ENGINES   108

Using a Directory Search Engine   108
Using a True Search Engine   110

INTERNET TECHNOLOGIES   111

The Internet Backbone   111
Internet Servers   112
Communications Protocols   113

CONNECTING TO THE INTERNET   114

Communications Software   115
Telecommunications Hardware   116

CHAPTER THREE   122
**Databases and Data Warehouses: Building
Business Intelligence**

**OPENING CASE STUDY: KRISPY KREME—SEVEN
DOUGHNUTS FOR EVERY MAN, WOMAN, AND CHILD
IN THE UNITED STATES EVERY YEAR**   123

INTRODUCTION   124

THE RELATIONAL DATABASE MODEL   126

Collections of Information   126
Created with Logical Structures   126
With Logical Ties within the Information   128
With Built-In Integrity Constraints   129

DATABASE MANAGEMENT SYSTEM TOOLS   130

Data Definition Subsystem   131
Data Manipulation Subsystem   132
Application Generation Subsystem   136
Data Administration Subsystem   136

DATA WAREHOUSES AND DATA MINING   140

What Is a Data Warehouse?   140
What Are Data-Mining Tools?   141
Data Marts: Smaller Data Warehouses   143
Data Mining as a Career Opportunity   144
*Important Considerations in Using a Data
Warehouse   145*

INFORMATION OWNERSHIP   146

Strategic Management Support   146
The Sharing of Information with Responsibility   147
Information Cleanliness   148

**Closing Case Study One: Ben & Jerry's, Bigelow Teas,
and Business Intelligence**   150

Closing Case Study Two: Mining Dining Data   152

Electronic Commerce: Searching Online
Databases and Information Repositories   157

EXTENDED LEARNING MODULE C   160
**Designing Databases and Entity-
Relationship Diagramming**

INTRODUCTION   161

DESIGNING AND BUILDING A RELATIONAL DATABASE   161

*Step 1: Defining Entity Classes and Primary
Keys   163*
*Step 2: Defining Relationships among the Entity
Classes   164*
*Step 3: Defining Information (Fields) for Each
Relation   172*
*Step 4: Using a Data Definition Language
to Create Your Database   175*

CHAPTER FOUR   178
**Decision Support and Artificial
Intelligence: Brainpower for Your Business**

**OPENING CASE STUDY: DECISION SUPPORT SYSTEM—
THE RESIDENT SECOND OPINION**   179

INTRODUCTION 180

DECISIONS, DECISIONS, DECISIONS 181
How You Make a Decision 181
Types of Decisions You Face 182

DECISION SUPPORT SYSTEMS 183
Components of a Decision Support System 184

GEOGRAPHIC INFORMATION SYSTEMS 187

ARTIFICIAL INTELLIGENCE 189

EXPERT SYSTEMS 190
What Expert Systems Can and Can't Do 192

NEURAL NETWORKS AND FUZZY LOGIC 193
Inside a Neural Network 195
Fuzzy Logic 197

GENETIC ALGORITHMS 197

INTELLIGENT AGENTS 200
Information Agents 200
Monitoring-and-Surveillance Agents 201
Data-Mining Agents 202
User Agents 203

MULTI-AGENT SYSTEMS AND AGENT-BASED MODELING 204
Ant Colonies and Swarm Intelligence 204

Closing Case Study One: Shuttle Debris, Trees, and Sniper Attacks 210

Closing Case Study Two: Using Neural Networks to Categorize People 211

Electronic Commerce: Finding Investment Opportunities on the Internet 216

EXTENDED LEARNING MODULE D 218
Decision Analysis with Spreadsheet Software

INTRODUCTION 219

LISTS 220

BASIC AUTOFILTER 222

CUSTOM AUTOFILTER 224

CONDITIONAL FORMATTING 226

PIVOT TABLES 228

BACK TO DECISION SUPPORT 235
AutoFilter 235
Conditional Formatting 235
Pivot Table 235

CHAPTER FIVE 238
Electronic Commerce: Strategies for the New Economy

OPENING CASE STUDY: IS AMERICA ONLINE (AOL) INCHING TOWARD BECOMING AN INTERNET BANK? 239

INTRODUCTION 240

E-COMMERCE BUSINESS MODELS 242

UNDERSTAND YOUR BUSINESS, PRODUCTS, SERVICES, AND CUSTOMERS 244
Who Are Your Customers? 244
What Is the Value of Your Products and Services as Perceived by Your Customers? 245

FIND CUSTOMERS AND ESTABLISH RELATIONSHIPS 250
Business to Consumer 250
Business to Business 252

MOVE MONEY EASILY AND SECURELY 254
Business to Consumer Payment Systems 254
Business to Business Payment Systems 256
Security: The Pervading Concern 258

THE BROADENING OF E-GOVERNMENT 261
Government to Government (G2G, intra-G2G) 262
Government to Business 262
Government to Consumer 263
International Government to Government (inter-G2G) 264
Government Spending on Information Technology 264

Closing Case Study One: When You're Big, You Can Be Your Own B2B E-Marketplace 267

Closing Case Study Two: Toting the E-Commerce Line with eBags 269

Electronic Commerce: Getting Your Business on the Internet 274

EXTENDED LEARNING MODULE E 276
Network Basics (on CD)

CHAPTER SIX 278
Systems Development: Phases, Tools, and Techniques

OPENING CASE STUDY: MERCEDES-BENZ ONLINE BUILT-TO-ORDER TRUCKS 279

INTRODUCTION 280

THE SYSTEMS DEVELOPMENT LIFE CYCLE   280

    Phase 1: Planning   280
    Phase 2: Analysis   282
    Phase 3: Design   283
    Phase 4: Development   284
    Phase 5: Testing   285
    Phase 6: Implementation   286
    Phase 7: Maintenance   286

SYSTEMS DEVELOPMENT METHODOLOGIES   287

    Waterfall Methodology   288
    Rapid Application Development Methodology   288
    Extreme Programming Methodology   289
    Agile Methodology   290

OUTSOURCING   290

    Outsourcing Options   293
    The Advantages and Disadvantages of
       Outsourcing   295
    Business Process Outsourcing (BPO)   297

PROTOTYPING   298

    The Prototyping Process   300
    The Advantages of Prototyping   301
    The Disadvantages of Prototyping   301

END-USER DEVELOPMENT   302

    Which Applications for IT to Offload   303
    The Right Tool for the Job   303

**Closing Case Study One: Getting Software
Development Right**   305

**Closing Case Study Two: To Outsource or Not
to Outsource**   306

Electronic Commerce: Finding Freeware and
Shareware on the Internet   311

EXTENDED LEARNING MODULE F   314
Building a Web Page with HTML (on CD)

CHAPTER SEVEN   316
**Enterprise Infrastructure and Integration:
Building the Dynamic Enterprise**

**OPENING CASE STUDY: ONE VIEW
FOR DEL MONTE FOODS**   317

INTRODUCTION   318

ENTERPRISE SYSTEMS   318

    What Are Enterprise Systems?   318
    Enterprise Resource Planning (ERP) Systems   320
    The Evolution of ERP Systems   323
    ERP Vendors and Market Trends   324

DEVELOPING AGILE IT SYSTEMS   326

    Availability   326
    Accessibility   326
    Reliability   327
    Scalability   327
    Flexibility   327
    Performance   327
    Capacity Planning   328

INFORMATION SYSTEMS INFRASTRUCTURE   328

    Why Architecture Matters   330
    Why Infrastructure Matters   330

INFORMATION TECHNOLOGY INFRASTRUCTURE   332

    Decentralized Infrastructure   332
    Centralized Infrastructure   333
    Distributed Infrastructure   334
    Client/Server Infrastructure   334
    Other Types of Infrastructures   335
    The Infrastructure Investment   336
    Supporting an IT Infrastructure   337
    Real World IT Infrastructures   338

INTEGRATING THE ENTERPRISE   339

    Why Integration Is Necessary   340
    Motives for Integration   341
    Benefits of Integration   342
    Integration Obstacles   342

**Closing Case Study One: Linux Supports
an Infrastructure**   344

**Closing Case Study Two: Netflix—Transforming the
Entertainment Industry**   345

Electronic Commerce: Living Life
on the Internet   349

EXTENDED LEARNING MODULE G   352
Object-Oriented Technologies (on CD)

CHAPTER EIGHT   354
**Protecting People and Information:
Threats and Safeguards**

**OPENING CASE STUDY: THEY KNOW ABOUT
96 PERCENT OF AMERICAN HOUSEHOLDS**   355

INTRODUCTION   356

ETHICS   356

    *Two Factors That Determine How You Decide
       Ethical Issues*   357
    Guidelines for Ethical Computer System Use   358
    Intellectual Property   359

PRIVACY   361

    Privacy and Other Individuals 362
    Identity Theft 362
    Privacy and Employees 364
    Privacy and Consumers 367
    Privacy and Government Agencies 371
    Laws on Privacy 373

SECURITY   374

    Security and Employees 374
    Security and Outside Threats 376
    Security Precautions 378

**Closing Case Study One: Cautionary Tales
of Indiscreet E-Mail**   383

**Closing Case Study Two: The Problem of
Information Protection**   384

Electronic Commerce: **Making Travel
Arrangements on the Internet**   388

EXTENDED LEARNING MODULE H   390
Computer Crime and Forensics

INTRODUCTION   391

COMPUTER CRIME   392

    Outside the Organization 392
    Web Defacing 399
    The Players 400
    Inside the Organization 403

COMPUTER FORENSICS   403

    The Collection Phase 405
    The Analysis Phase 408

RECOVERY AND INTERPRETATION   409

    Places to Look for Useful Information 409
    Ways of Hiding Information 412

WHO NEEDS COMPUTER FORENSIC INVESTIGATORS?   415

    *Proactive Computer Forensic Education for
       Problem Prevention* 415
    *Reactive Computer Forensics for Incident
       Response* 416
    *A Day in the Life of a Computer Forensic
       Expert* 417

CHAPTER NINE   422
**Emerging Trends and Technologies:
Business, People, and Technology Tomorrow**

**OPENING CASE STUDY: THE FUTURE: TECHNOLOGY OUT,
PRINGLES IN**   423

INTRODUCTION   424

THE CHANGING INTERNET   425

    Software-as-a-Service 425
    *Push, Not Pull, Technologies and
       Personalization* 426
    Voice over Internet Protocol (VoIP) 428

PHYSIOLOGICAL INTERACTION   428

    Automatic Speech Recognition 429
    Virtual Reality 429
    Cave Automatic Virtual Environments 431
    Biometrics 432

INCREASING PORTABILITY AND MOBILITY   435

    Digital Cash 436
    Wearable Computers 437
    *Multi-State CPUs and Holographic Storage
       Devices* 438

THE WIRELESS ARENA   439

    *The Next Generation of Cell Phone
       Technology* 439
    RFID (Radio Frequency Identification) 440

MOST IMPORTANT CONSIDERATIONS   442

    The Necessity of Technology 443
    Closing the Great Digital Divide 443
    Technology for the Betterment of Society 444
    Exchanging Privacy for Convenience 444
    Ethics, Ethics, Ethics 445

**Closing Case Study One: Wildseed—A Cell Phone
for Every Fashion**   446

**Closing Case Study Two: T2C—Not Another New
E-Commerce Business Model**   448

Electronic Commerce: **Continuing Your
Education Through the Internet**   452

EXTENDED LEARNING MODULE I   454
Building an E-Portfolio

INTRODUCTION   455

**THE ELECTRONIC JOB MARKET—EXTENDING
YOUR REACH**   455

**CONVERGENCE OF ONLINE NETWORKING
AND RÉSUMÉ DEVELOPMENT**   457

    Start to Network 457
    Perform a Self-Assessment 459
    Research Careers, Industries, and Companies 459

RÉSUMÉ BUILDING—A LIFELONG PROCESS   461

    Content, Content, Content 462
    Electronic File Formats 467
    What Is the Right Résumé Style? 472

DEVELOPING YOUR JOB SEARCH E-PORTFOLIO   473

Self-Promotion   473
Give Them What They Want   474
The Shape of an E-Portfolio   475
E-Gallery   475

WEB DESIGN CONSIDERATIONS   476

Basic Web Design Principles   476
Design Your Homepage   481

PREPARING WEB CONTENT   484

HTML versus Generated Code   485
Test, Test, Test   488

EXTENDED LEARNING MODULE J   494
Implementing a Database with Microsoft Access (on CD)

EXTENDED LEARNING MODULE K   496
Careers in Business (on CD)

EXTENDED LEARNING MODULE L   498
Building Web Sites with FrontPage (on CD)

EXTENDED LEARNING MODULE M   500
Programming in Excel with VBA (on CD)

Glossary   526
Notes   540
Photo Credits   547
Index   548

FEATURES

On Your Own Projects

E-Mail: Electronic Mail or Expensive Mail?   14

Researching Your Career and Information Technology   27

Understanding Supply Chain Management within Your Business Strategy   81

Understanding Customer Relationship Management in Your Business Strategy   84

Using a Web Portal   113

Researching Personal DBMSs   138

CRUD: Defining Information Ownership   148

Creating the Final Structure for Your School   175

Traffic Lights Revisited   193

Go Bargain Hunting Online   203

Lists, List Definition Tables, and Using AutoFilter   223

Creating a Two-Dimensional Pivot Table   232

Your Perception of Product and Service Value   246

Developing a Marketing Mix Strategy for Monster.com   253

How Is a Server Different from a Client Computer? (on CD)   E.29

Analyzing Business Requirements   283

Build vs. Buy   304

Creating a Basic Web Site (on CD)   F.10

Creating Your Own Web Site (on CD)   F.19

The Future of Client/Server   333

Do You Have a Backup?   339

Identifying Object-Oriented Concepts (on CD)   G.8

Trace the Route of Your Journey to a Web Site   361

Find Firewall Protection   381

Digital Signatures and Certificates   403

How Much Do You Know?   416

Where Should the Decision Rest?   428

Necessity, Convenience, and Privacy   445

Build Your 30-Second Commercial   458

Start Your Research   461

Write Your Own Objective Statement   463

Build Your Résumés and Visit E-Portfolio Sites   480

Use Excel to Create and Populate a Table (on CD)   J.16

Create an Accounts Receivable Report (on CD)   J.33

If You Build It, They Will Come (on CD)   L.20

You Should Be in Pictures (on CD)   L.24

Links, Links, Links (on CD)   L.26

It's All about Me! (on CD)   L.32

Welcome to Your Theme Park (on CD)   L.36

Micro Macro (on CD)   M.13

Function, Function . . . What's Your Function? (on CD)   M.19

Let's Make a Decision (on CD)   M.21

Team Work Projects

Identifying Hardware and Software   16

Developing Strategies for Protecting Yourself Against Identity Theft   28

Buying Personal Productivity Software Suites   47

Evaluating Utility Software Suites   49

Using Porter to Evaluate the Movie Rental Industry   75

Do You Want Spoke Poking Around?   91

Finding and Using Search Engines   111

Evaluating ISP Options   116

Primary Keys, Foreign Keys, and Integrity Constraints   129

How Up-to-Date Should Data Warehouse Information Be?   145

Defining Entity Classes and Primary Keys   164

Defining Relationships among Entity Classes   166

Defining the Cardinality among Entity Classes   168

Creating an Intersection Relation   171

How Would You Classify People?   194

Be a Genetic Algorithm and Put Nails in Boxes   199

Using Custom AutoFilters   226

Conditional Formatting   228

Defining Your Business to Consumer E-Commerce Business   260

Exploring the World of E-Government   265

What's the Big Deal with Frequencies? (on CD)   E.17

What Sort of Computer Network Does Your School Have? (on CD)   E.25

Writing Test Conditions   285

How Many Are There?   296

Creating a Web Site with Links and Images (on CD)   F.15

Creating a Web Site with Lists (on CD)   F.18

Ranking the "ilities"   328

Infrastructure Components   340

Can You Find the Errors in this Class Diagram? (on CD)   G.13

Designing a Banking System (on CD)   G.21

What Would You Do?   366

How Protected Are Computers in Your Part of the World?   380

Make Up a Good Password   402

Finding Applications of Virtual Reality   430

How Many Computers Do You Rely on in a Week?   443

Feedback, Feedback, Feedback!   465

Create the Other Tables (on CD)   J.10

Find All the Orders for Premier Shell Concrete (on CD)   J.22

Building a Storyboard (on CD)   L.5

Graphically Pleasing (on CD)   L.23

GROUP PROJECTS

1. ***Assessing the Value of Customer Relationship Management: Trevor Toy Auto Mechanics***
Use spreadsheet software to help determine how to improve customer service and personalization for customers of an auto mechanics business 502

2. ***Analyzing the Value of Information: Affordable Homes Real Estate***
Use spreadsheet software to evaluate 600 real estate transactions and help Affordable Homes determine in which area to concentrate its future sales efforts 503

3. ***Executive Information System Reporting: Political Campaign Finance***
Use spreadsheet software to build reports within an executive information system (EIS) that illustrates the concept of "drilling down" 504

4. ***Building Value Chains: Helping Customers Define Value***
Use database management system software to evaluate customer survey responses and determine which processes are value adding and which are value reducing 505

5. ***Using Relational Technology to Track Projects: Foothills Construction***
Use database management system software and employ the rules of normalization to build a database that tracks construction projects 507

6. ***Building a Decision Support System: Creating an Investment Portfolio***
Use spreadsheet software to build a decision support system that will help you determine which of 10 different stocks to include in your investment portfolio 508

7. ***Advertising with Banner Ads: HighwaysAndByways.com***
Use spreadsheet software to evaluate Web site traffic and help determine how best to take advantage of implementing banner ads 509

8. ***Assessing the Value of Outsourcing Information Technology: Creating Forecasts***
Use spreadsheet software to develop growth, trend, and forecast analyses to help Innovative Software determine how to outsource some of its information technology functions 510

9. ***Demonstrating How to Build Web Sites: With HTML***
Use presentation software to create a dynamic and exciting presentation that illustrates how to build a Web site using HTML and good design guidelines 511

10. ***Making the Case with Presentation Software: Information Technology Ethics***
Use presentation software to convert a word processing document into a powerful, exciting, and dynamic presentation on information technology ethics 512

11. ***Building a Web Database System: Web-Based Classified System***
From a single screen capture and discussion of business processes, design and implement a database to support an online auction 513

12. ***Creating a Decision Support System: Buy versus Lease***
Use spreadsheet software to help a leading supplier of wine grapes determine whether to buy or lease its delivery and service vehicle fleet 514

13. ***Developing an Enterprise Resource Planning System: Planning, Reporting, and Data Processing***
Use spreadsheet software to develop a series of budget reports for the Higher Educational System of Colorado 515

14. ***Assessing a Wireless Future: Emerging Trends and Technology***
Use presentation software to develop an insightful presentation that describes the innovative wireless products currently under development by two manufacturers 516

15. ***Evaluating the Next Generation: Dot-Com ASPs***
Use spreadsheet software to help Front Range Car Rental evaluate the cost benefits of developing a system internally or outsourcing to an application service provider (ASP) 517

16. ***Analyzing Strategic and Competitive Advantage: Determining Operating Leverage***
Use spreadsheet software to help a coffee boutique determine whether or not to move its office operations based on such factors as driving distance, breakeven, and earnings before interest and taxes (EBIT) 519

17. ***Building a Decision Support System: Break-Even Analysis***
Use spreadsheet software to develop a break-even analysis to support a ski manufacturer in selling a new line of skis 520

18. ***Creating a Financial Analysis: Qualification and Amortization Worksheets***
Use spreadsheet software to complete a mortgage qualification worksheet which will be used to create a mortgage amortization analysis worksheet 521

19. ***Building a Scheduling Decision Support System: Airline Crew Scheduling***
Use spreadsheet software to assist Rockies Airline in finding the minimum cost for scheduling its flight crew 522

20. ***Creating a Database Management System: Mountain Bike Rentals***
Use database management system software to design and implement a database to support a mountain bike rental company 522

21. ***Evaluating the Security of Information: Wireless Network Vulnerability***
Use presentation software to report on the tips, techniques, and best practices to protect against amateur hacking, such as "PringlesCantenna" 524

22. ***Assessing the Value of Supply Chain Management: Optimizing Shipments***
Use spreadsheet software to determine the most cost-effective method of shipping golf clubs from three production plants to five warehouses 525

PREFACE

The sixth edition of *Management Information Systems for the Information Age* provides you the ultimate in flexibility to tailor content to the exact needs of your MIS or IT course. The nine chapters and thirteen Extended Learning Modules may be presented in logical sequence, or you may choose your own mix of technical topics and business/managerial topics.

The nine chapters form the core of material covering business and managerial topics, from strategic and competitive technology opportunities to the organization and management of information using databases and data warehouses. If you covered only the chapters and none of the modules, the focus of your course would be MIS from a business and managerial point of view.

The thirteen Extended Learning Modules provide a technical glimpse into the world of IT, covering topics ranging from building a Web site, to computer crimes and forensics, to how to use Microsoft Access. If you chose only the modules and none of the chapters, the focus of your course would be on the technical and hands-on aspects of IT.

Each module follows its corresponding chapter, but chapters and modules may usefully be presented independently. For example, Module H on computer crime and forensics follows logically after Chapter 8 on protecting people and information. But you can cover Chapter 8 and omit Module H—that's completely up to you. On the other hand, you can omit Chapter 8 and cover Module H—you have flexibility to do what suits your needs.

You can easily select a course format that represents your own desired blend of topics. While you might not choose to cover the technologies of networks, for example, you might require your students to build a small database application. In that case, you would omit Module E (Network Basics) and spend more time on Module C (Designing Databases and Entity-Relationship Diagramming) and Module J (Implementing a Database with Microsoft Access).

On the facing page, we've provided a table of the chapters and the modules. As you put your course together and choose the chapters and/or modules you want to cover, we would offer the following:

- Cover any or all of the chapters as suits your purposes.
- Cover any or all of the modules as suits your purposes.
- If you choose a chapter, you do not have to cover its corresponding module.
- If you choose a module, you do not have to cover its corresponding chapter.
- You may cover the modules in any order you wish.

Please note that your students will find Modules E, F, G, J, K, L, and M on the CD that accompanies the textbook. In the book, we provide a two-page introduction to these modules. All your students have to do is go to the CD to read the full modules.

The unique organization of this text gives you **complete flexibility** to design your course as you see fit.

THE CHAPTERS	THE EXTENDED LEARNING MODULES
CHAPTER 1	**Extended Learning Module A**
The Information Age in Which You Live	Computer Hardware and Software
CHAPTER 2	**Extended Learning Module B**
Major Business Initiatives	The World Wide Web and the Internet
CHAPTER 3	**Extended Learning Module C**
Databases and Data Warehouses	Designing Databases and Entity-Relationship Diagramming
CHAPTER 4	**Extended Learning Module D**
Decision Support and Artificial Intelligence	Decision Analysis with Spreadsheet Software
CHAPTER 5	**Extended Learning Module E***
Electronic Commerce	Network Basics
CHAPTER 6	**Extended Learning Module F***
Systems Development	Building a Web Page with HTML
CHAPTER 7	**Extended Learning Module G***
Enterprise Infrastructure and Integration	Object-Oriented Technologies
CHAPTER 8	**Extended Learning Module H**
Protecting People and Information	Computer Crime and Forensics
CHAPTER 9	**Extended Learning Module I**
Emerging Trends and Technologies	Building an e-Portfolio
	Extended Learning Module J*
	Implementing a Database with Microsoft Access
	Extended Learning Module K*
	Careers in Business
	Extended Learning Module L*
	Building Web Sites with FrontPage
	Extended Learning Module M*
	Programming in Excel with VBA

*The complete text for modules E, F, G, J, K, L, and M are on the CD that accompanies this text.

- Management Focus—By focusing on the chapters, your class will take a managerial approach to MIS.
- Technical Focus—If hands-on, technical skills are more important, focus your MIS course on the modules.

Organization—The Haag Advantage

The separation of content between the chapters and the Extended Learning Modules is very simple. We can sum it up by saying:

- The **chapters** address what you want your students **to know.**
- The **modules** address what you want your students **to be able to do.**

Together, both combine to provide a well-balanced repository of important information aimed at developing a prospective business professional equipped with both foundational knowledge and application experience, ready to take on today's highly competitive job market.

Each chapter and module contains full pedagogical support:

- Student Learning Outcomes
- On Your Own Projects
- Team Work Projects
- Summary
- Key Terms and Concepts
- Short-Answer Questions
- Assignments and Exercises

> The **chapters** focus on the *business and managerial* applications of MIS and information technology.

Figure 3.8
A Multidimensional Data Warehouse with Information from Multiple Operational Databases

ligence, many organizations are building data warehouses and providing data-mining tools. A data warehouse is simply the next step (beyond databases) in the progression of building business intelligence. And data-mining tools are the tools you use to mine a data warehouse and extrapolate the business intelligence you need to make a decision, solve a problem, or capitalize on an opportunity to create a competitive advantage.

WHAT IS A DATA WAREHOUSE?

A ***data warehouse*** is a logical collection of information—gathered from many different operational databases—used to create business intelligence that supports business analysis activities and decision-making tasks (see Figure 3.8). Sounds simple enough on the surface, but data warehouses represent a fundamentally different way of thinking about organizing and managing information in an organization. Consider these key features of a data warehouse, detailed in the sections that follow.

DATA WAREHOUSES ARE MULTIDIMENSIONAL
In the relational database model, information is represented in a series of two-dimensional files or tables. Not so in a data warehouse—most data warehouses are multidimensional, meaning that they contain layers of columns and rows. For this reason, most data warehouses are really *multidimensional databases.* The layers in a data warehouse represent information according to different dimensions. This multidimensional representation of information is referred to as a *hypercube.*

> The **modules** focus on giving your students real *hands-on-knowledge* they can apply in both their personal and professional experiences.

Figure C.3
Reading an Entity-Relationship (E-R) Diagram

Once you determine that a relationship does exist, you must then determine the numerical nature of the relationship, what we refer to as "minimum and maximum cardinality." To describe this, you use a | to denote a single relationship, a 0 to denote a zero or optional relationship, and/or a crow's foot (◄) to denote a multiple relationship. By way of illustration, let's consider the portion of your E-R diagram in Figure C.3 above. To help you read the symbols and diagram, we've added blue lines and arrows. Following the line marked A, you would read the E-R diagram as:

"A *Supplier* may not provide any Raw Material (denoted with the 0) but may provide more than one *Raw Material* (denoted with the crow's foot)."

So, that part of the E-R diagram states that the logical relationship between *Supplier* and *Raw Material* is that a *Supplier* may provide no *Raw Material* currently in inventory but may provide more than one *Raw Material* currently in inventory. This is exactly what business rule 4 (on page 163) states.

Following the blue line marked B, you would read the E-R diagram as:

Student Learning Outcomes and Summary

Student learning outcomes drive each chapter and module. We then summarize each chapter and module by revisiting the student learning outcomes. It's the old adage . . .

1. Tell them what you're going to tell them.
2. Tell them.
3. Tell them what you told them.

At the beginning of each chapter and module, you'll find a list of **Student Learning Outcomes,** providing your students with a road map of what they should learn and accomplish while reading a chapter or module.

CHAPTER TWO OUTLINE

STUDENT LEARNING OUTCOMES

1. Describe how to use Porter's Five Forces Model to evaluate the relative attractiveness of an industry.
2. Describe the role of value chains in identifying value-added and value-reducing processes.
3. Define supply chain management (SCM) systems and describe their strategic and competitive opportunities and IT support.
4. Define customer relationship management (CRM) systems and describe their strategic and competitive opportunities and IT support.
5. Define business intelligence (BI) systems and describe their strategic and competitive opportunities and IT support.
6. Define integrated collaboration environments (ICEs) and describe their strategic and competitive opportunities and IT support.

Summary: Student Learning Outcomes Revisited

1. **Describe business intelligence and its role in an organization.** *Business intelligence* is knowledge—knowledge about your customers, your competitors, your partners, your competitive environment, and your own internal operations—that gives you the ability to make effective, important, and often strategic business decisions. Business intelligence is much more than just a list of your products or to whom you've sold them. It might combine your product information with your advertising strategy information and customer demographics, for instance, to help you determine the effectiveness of various advertising media on demographic groups segmented by location.

2. **Differentiate between databases and data warehouses with respect to their focus on online transaction processing and online analytical processing.** A *database* is a collection of information that you organize and access according to the logical structure of that information. Databases support both online transaction processing (OLTP) and online analytical processing (OLAP). Databases that support OLTP are often referred to as *operational databases*. These databases contain detailed information about transactions that have taken place. And using various data manipulation tools, you can query a database to extract meaningful information. A *data warehouse* is a collection of information—gathered from many different operational databases—used to create business intelligence that supports business analysis activities and decision-making tasks. So, data warehouses support only OLAP, not OLTP.

3. **List and describe the key characteristics of a relational database.** The *relational database* model uses a series of logically related two-dimensional tables or files to store information in the form of a database. Key characteristics include
   - A collection of information—Composed of many files or tables of information that are related to each other
   - Contain logical structures—You care only about the logical information and not about

how it's physically stored or where it's physically located
   - Have logical ties among the information—All the files in a database are related in that some primary keys of certain files appear as foreign keys in others
   - Possess built-in integrity constraints—When creating the data dictionary for a database, you can specify rules by which the information must be entered (e.g., not blank, etc.)

4. **Define the five software components of a database management system.** The five software components of a database management system include
   - *DBMS engine*—Accepts logical requests from the various other DBMS subsystems, converts them into their physical equivalent, and actually accesses the database and data dictionary as they exist on a storage device
   - *Data definition subsystem*—Helps you create and maintain the data dictionary and define the structure of the files in a database
   - *Data manipulation subsystem*—Helps you add, change, and delete information in a database and query it for valuable information
   - *Application generation subsystem*—Contains facilities to help you develop transaction-intensive applications
   - *Data administration subsystem*—Helps you manage the overall database environment by providing facilities for backup and recovery, security management, query optimization, concurrency control, and change management

5. **List and describe the key characteristics of a data warehouse.** The key characteristics of a data warehouse include
   - Multidimensional—While databases store information in two-dimensional tables, data warehouses include layers to represent information according to different dimensions
   - Support decision making—Data warehouses, because they contain summarized information, support business activities and decision-making tasks, not transaction processing

A **Summary** of these outcomes appears with the EOC elements per chapter/module, providing an invaluable tool for your students as they prepare to take an exam.

Case Studies

Opening Case

Each chapter begins with a one-page opening case study, highlighting how an organization has successfully implemented many of that chapter's concepts.

NETFLIX—TRANSFORMING THE ENTERTAINMENT INDUSTRY

The online DVD rental pioneer Netflix is transforming the movie rental business with its unique business model, streamlined shipping strategy, and efficient application infrastructure. Netflix is quickly becoming one of Hollywood's most promising new business partners and is experiencing staggering growth with over 2 million subscribers, accounting for 3 to 5 percent of all U.S. home video rentals.

Typically, video rental stores focus on major films and ignore older movies and smaller titles with niche audiences. With over 35,000 DVD titles, Netflix is turning that idea upside down by offering a serious market for every movie, not just blockbusters. How? Netflix at...

flix's unique application infrastructure allows it to track, monitor, and maintain detailed information on each of its discs, customers, and shippers. At any point in time the company can tell you the exact location of each of its discs, a critical component for Netflix's business model.

To handle the rental logistics for its 5.5 million DVD library the company created several proprietary applications. One of its most successful systems is its Web-based supply chain management system. The system works by having operators scan a bar code on each label for every single disc that arrives in its warehouses. The software then retrieves the name and address of ... DVD, prints out ... to the mail. The ... etflix to slow hir... ent, and the vast ... ehouse shelf. On ... titles in Netflix's ... tomers.[19]

CHAPTER ONE

The Information Age in Which You Live
Changing the Face of Business

OPENING CASE STUDY:
DISRUPTIVE TECHNOLOGIES DISRUPT BLOCKBUSTER LATE FEES

The term "disruptive technologies" almost makes technology sound like a bad thing, but it isn't. A disruptive technology is any technology that causes a business (or person) to dramatically change the way that it (or she or he) works. The recording industry, for example, is undergoing significant transformation because of technological advances. Fewer people are buying complete CDs or albums, in favor of purchasing only music selections and songs they want via the Internet. The Internet, peer-to-peer file sharing systems, and Web sites such as Apple's iTunes (www.apple.com/itunes) are disruptive technologies causing the recording industry to rethink ... d sells music. ... h the video ... dominated ... 32 percent ... e of disrup-

And don't forget Netflix. Its Internet model of renting videos to people for as long as they want with no late fees is definitely affecting Blockbuster. Netflix predicted that it would have 2.65 million customers by the end of 2004.

What is Blockbuster doing to save its market share? A Blockbuster initiative in January 2004 was to no longer assess late fees if a customer returns a movie anytime within a week. After a week, Blockbuster automatically sells the movie to the customer at retail price minus the rental fee. If the customer doesn't want to buy it though and returns the movie after a week, Blockbuster charges only a $1.25 restocking fee.

All types of new and disruptive technology challenge organizations (1) to rethink how they do business and (2) to embrace the technology and determine how best to use it to create a competitive advantage.

That's the focus of this text. We will introduce you to a wide array of technology terms and concepts and teach you the technology, but we want you always to keep in mind the essential challenge of how to apply the technology to create a

TOTING THE E-COMMERCE LINE WITH EBAGS

For a true e-commerce success story you don't have to look any further than eBags (www.ebags.com). While many pure-play e-commerce Web sites have fallen by the wayside, eBags is not only surviving, it is thriving. It is the world's leading online provider of bags and accessories for all lifestyles. With 180 brands and over 8,000 products, eBags has sold more than 2.5 million bags since its launch in March 1999. It carries a complete line of premium and popular brands, including Samsonite, JanSport, The North Face, Liz Claiborne, and Adidas. You can buy anything from backpacks and carry-ons to computer cases and handbags at extremely competitive prices from its Web site.

eBags has received several awards for excellence in online retailing, among them:

- Circle of Excellence Platinum Award, Bizrate.com
- Web Site of the Year, *Catalog Age Magazine* (for the second year in a row)
- Email Marketer of the Year, ClickZ.MessageMedia
- Marketer of the Year, Colorado AMA
- Rocky Mountain Portal Award
- Gold Peak Catalog, Colorado AMA
- Entrepreneur of the Year—Rocky Mountain Region, Ernst and Young
- E-Commerce Initiative Award of Merit, Colorado Software and Internet Association
- Best of Show, eTravel World Awards
- 50 Essential Web Sites, *Condé Naste Traveler*
- Internet Retailer's Best of the Web

A good part of the reason for eBags's success is its

For the past several years, eBags has outsourced both the handling of phone orders and customer service calls to Finali Corporation (www.finali.com). "The call center is often the only human contact customers have with our brand," says eBags CEO Jon Nordmark. "By maintaining a call center staff that can think on its feet, Finali delivers real value to our customers and a measurable return on our call center investment."

Typically, the conversion rate of inbound customer calls to sales at the call center has been about 25 percent. But during the 2001 holiday season, special training and incentives for Finali call center reps servicing the eBags Web site helped raise that number to 44 percent. In addition, the average size of orders placed through the call center hit $100, topping the average Web order of just over $75. The increased conversion rates and order size meant that for every dollar eBags spent with Finali, Finali generated $3.79 in sales.

eBags's many online services also distinguish it from the rest of the online marketplace. eBags's Laptop Finder searches for compatible laptop cases based on the brand and model number of your computer. And eBags's Airline Approved Carry-On Finder will show you all the carry-on bags that fit in each airline's overhead bins. eBags has also tightly integrated its systems with those of UPS to provide accurate estimated arrival dates and free returns.

eBags announced profits for the first time in December 2001, posting 5.4 percent earnings before interest, taxes, depreciation, and amortization. "Part of that achievement was due to smart outsourcing like the call center," says eBags CFO Eliot Cobb. As of early ...

Closing Cases

To help your students apply what they have just learned, you'll find two closing case studies at the end of each chapter. Each case has a set of questions that are great for class discussion.

Team Work and On Your Own Projects

There are now 82 Team Work and On Your Own projects spread throughout the text, in both the chapters and modules. Many of these can be used as break-out exercises, and just as many can be assigned as homework. In the Instructor's Manual, you'll find our discussions of and solutions to each of these projects.

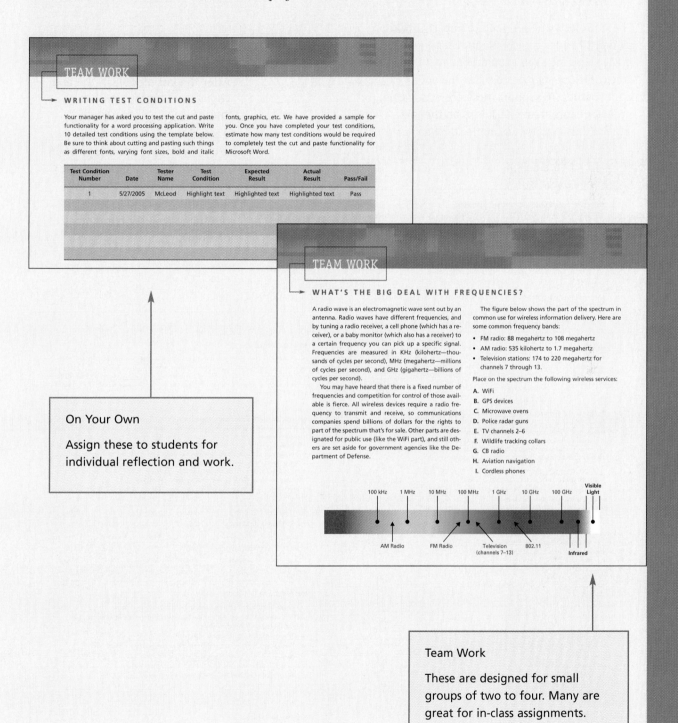

TEAM WORK

WRITING TEST CONDITIONS

Your manager has asked you to test the cut and paste functionality for a word processing application. Write 10 detailed test conditions using the template below. Be sure to think about cutting and pasting such things as different fonts, varying font sizes, bold and italic fonts, graphics, etc. We have provided a sample for you. Once you have completed your test conditions, estimate how many test conditions would be required to completely test the cut and paste functionality for Microsoft Word.

Test Condition Number	Date	Tester Name	Test Condition	Expected Result	Actual Result	Pass/Fail
1	5/27/2005	McLeod	Highlight text	Highlighted text	Highlighted text	Pass

TEAM WORK

WHAT'S THE BIG DEAL WITH FREQUENCIES?

A radio wave is an electromagnetic wave sent out by an antenna. Radio waves have different frequencies, and by tuning a radio receiver, a cell phone (which has a receiver), or a baby monitor (which also has a receiver) to a certain frequency you can pick up a specific signal. Frequencies are measured in KHz (kilohertz—thousands of cycles per second), MHz (megahertz—millions of cycles per second), and GHz (gigahertz—billions of cycles per second).

You may have heard that there is a fixed number of frequencies and competition for control of those available is fierce. All wireless devices require a radio frequency to transmit and receive, so communications companies spend billions of dollars for the rights to part of the spectrum that's for sale. Other parts are designated for public use (like the WiFi part), and still others are set aside for government agencies like the Department of Defense.

The figure below shows the part of the spectrum in common use for wireless information delivery. Here are some common frequency bands:

- FM radio: 88 megahertz to 108 megahertz
- AM radio: 535 kilohertz to 1.7 megahertz
- Television stations: 174 to 220 megahertz for channels 7 through 13.

Place on the spectrum the following wireless services:

A. WiFi
B. GPS devices
C. Microwave ovens
D. Police radar guns
E. TV channels 2–6
F. Wildlife tracking collars
G. CB radio
H. Aviation navigation
I. Cordless phones

On Your Own

Assign these to students for individual reflection and work.

Team Work

These are designed for small groups of two to four. Many are great for in-class assignments.

Electronic Commerce and Group Projects

Electronic Commerce

These projects are designed to impart to your students hands-on technological experiences, many requiring Web exploration. You'll find an Electronic Commerce project at the end of each chapter. To support these projects, we've provided more than 1,000 links on the Web site for this text at www.mhhe.com/haag.

Group Projects

After the last module in the text, you'll find 22 Group Projects. These require your students to use technology to solve a problem or take advantage of an opportunity. A quick warning to instructors: Some of these take an entire weekend to solve. Be careful not to assign too many at one time.

Electronic | COMMERCE

Searching Online Databases and Information Repositories

As you find sites on the Internet that provide information, many of them will do so in the form of a database—a searchable grouping of information that allows you to find specific information by entering key words and key phrases. These words and phra[...] fact, some sort of keys (similar to primary and foreign keys we discussed in th[...] that are used as matching criteria in a field of the database.

In this section, you'll explore a variety of information topics that you can f[...] Internet. To help you, we've included a number of Web sites related to search[...] database and information repositories. On the Web site that supports [...] (www.mhhe.com/haag), we've provided direct links to all these Web sites [...] many, many more. These are a great starting point for completing this Electr[...] merce section.

FINANCIAL AID RESOURCES

On the Internet, you can find valuable databases that give you access to finan[...] sources as you attend school. These resources can be in the form of sch[...] money you don't have to pay back—and standard student loans. And there a[...] of financial aid lenders, ranging from traditional banks, the government, and p[...] ties wanting to give something back to society. Find at least three Web sites th[...] a financial aid database and answer the following questions for each.

A. Do you have to register as a user to access information?
B. Do you have to pay a fee to access information?
C. Can you build a profile of yourself and use it as you search?
D. Can you apply for aid while at the site or must you request paper app[...] that you need to complete and return?
E. By what sort of categories of aid can you search?

CASE 19:
BUILDING A SCHEDULING DECISION SUPPORT SYSTEM

AIRLINE CREW SCHEDULING

Rockies Airline is a new airline company that maintains a schedule of two daily flights between Salt Lake City, Denver, and Chicago. Rockies Airline took to the air on February 11, 2004, with the inauguration of service between Denver International Airport and Salt Lake City. Every Rockies Airline aircraft is outfitted with roomy all-leather seats, each equipped with 24 channels of DIRECTV programming.

Rockies Airline must strategically position itself as a low-cost provider in a very volatile industry. Therefore, it must work toward finding a minimum cost assignment of flight crews to a given flight schedule while satisfying restrictions dictated by the Federal Aviation Administration. Rockies Airline needs to solve the crew scheduling problem that is an involved and time-consuming process.

To begin, you will want to figure out all the possible crew rotations. You will want to find an approximate expected cost of each combination and then solve the traditional crew scheduling problem by using these costs. Second, you will want to calculate the crew constraints in order to determine the decision variables, constraints, and objectives.

You have been given Rockies Airline flight schedule as follows:

From	To	Departure	Arrival	Departure	Arrival
Salt Lake City	Denver	9:00 AM	12:00 PM	2:00 PM	5:00 PM
Salt Lake City	Chicago	10:00 AM	2:00 PM	3:00 PM	7:00 PM
Denver	Salt Lake City	8:00 AM	11:00 AM	2:00 PM	5:00 PM
Denver	Chicago	9:00 AM	11:00 AM	3:00 PM	5:00 PM
Chicago	Salt Lake City	8:00 AM	12:00 PM	2:00 PM	6:00 PM
Chicago	Denver	10:00 AM	12:00 PM	4:00 PM	6:00 PM

SOME PARTICULARS YOU SHOULD KNOW

1. A crew that leaves a city in the morning has to return there at night.
2. The crew can be brought back on another airline. This would always be on an 8 PM flight. There are 6 airplanes in use.
3. When a crew is flying, the cost is $200 per hour.
4. When a crew is waiting or being flown back, the cost is $75 per hour.
5. How should the company schedule its crews to minimize cost?
6. *Hint:* You will want to install the Solver Add-in to assist with this.
7. File: **CREWSCHEDULING.xls** (Excel file).

CASE 20:
CREATING A DATABASE MANAGEMENT SYSTEM

MOUNTAIN BIKE RENTALS

Vail Resort in Vail, Colorado, is internationally known as one of the best places in North America for mountain biking. Since 1973, Slopeside Bike Rentals has been a tradition in the area. At Slopeside Bike Rentals customers will find the largest selection of bikes, parts, accessories, books, maps, clothing, shocks, helmets, eyewear, shoes, car racks, and touring gear in the area with every-

End-of-Chapter Elements

Discussion Questions

1. IT infrastructures often mimic organizational hierarchies. Describe two different types of organizational hierarchies and how the IT infrastructure would be built in order to support them.

2. IT infrastructure features can include anything from software to strategic functions. After reading this chapter and learning about a few of the primary features of IT infrastructure, explain why a company's IT infrastructure can have so many different features.

3. Organizations spend a great deal of time determining their primary goals, objectives, structures, and strategies. Define your school's goals, and then define your school's objectives, structure, and strategies that support those

Key Terms and Concepts

1-tier infrastructure, 336
2-tier infrastructure, 336
3-tier infrastructure, 336
Architecture, 329
Backup, 337
Benchmark, 327
Benchmarking, 327
Business process reengineering (BPR), 341
Capacity planning, 328
Centralized infrastructure, 333
Client/server infrastructure, 334
Cold site, 338
Collocation facility, 338
Decentralized infrastructure, 332
Disaster recovery cost curve, 338
Disaster recovery plan, 338

Distributed infrastructure, 334
Enterprise resource planning (ERP) system, 320
Enterprise system (ES), 318
Hot site, 338
Infrastructure, 329
Integration, 339
Legacy information system (LIS), 320
N-tier infrastructure, 336
Performance, 327

Short-Answer Quest

1. What is an enterprise system?
2. What are the core functions of an e resource planning system?
3. Describe the evolution of ERP system
4. What is a legacy information system
5. Name three of the "ilities."
6. What is IT architecture?
7. What is IT infrastructure?
8. What are the primary differences a 2-tier, 3-tier, and n-tier infrastructure
9. Why do you need a backup of infor
10. Why would you need to recover info
11. Why does a business need a disaster plan?

Assignments and Exercises

1. **IT INFRASTRUCTURE SPONSOR** To build a solid IT infrastructure you must have executive sponsorship. Your current boss doesn't understand the importance of building a solid IT infrastructure. In fact, your boss doesn't even understand the term IT infrastructure. First, explain to your boss what an IT infrastructure is and why it is critical for any organization. Second, explain three primary components of an IT infrastructure.

2. **IT INFRASTRUCTURE COMPONENTS AND THE REAL WORLD** Throughout this chapter we discussed many IT infrastructure concepts, features, and trends including client/server infrastructure and the concept of integration, among others. Pick two of them and find business examples of how companies are using them in the real world. Search the Internet to see if you can find two additional IT infrastructure concepts, components, or features that were not discussed in this chapter along with business examples of how businesses are using them in the real world.

3. **CREATING THE IDEAL INFRASTRUCTURE** This chapter focused on many different IT infrastructure concepts and components. Choose three of them and explain how you could use them to improve the IT infrastructure at your school. Be sure to think of current requirements as well as future requirements for the IT infrastructure.

4. **INTEGRATING INFORMATION** Imagine you are working for a large cookie manufacturing company. The company is 75 years old and is just starting to implement technology to help improve operations. Your direct manager has asked you to put together a presentation discussing integration. In your presentation you must include the definition of integration along with an example of the problems associated with nonintegrated systems as relating to cookie manufacturing.

5. **CREATING A CAMPUS IT INFRASTRUCTURE** You have been assigned the role of student IT infrastructure manager. Your first assignment is to approve the designs for the new on-campus Internet infrastructure. You're having a meeting at 9:00 A.M. tomorrow morning to review the designs with the student IT employees. To prepare for the meeting, you must understand the student requirements and their current use of the Internet, along with future requirements. The following is a list of questions you must answer before attending the meeting. Provide an answer to each question.

   • Do you need to have a disaster recovery plan? If so what might it include?
   • Does the system require backup equipment?
   • When will the system need to be available to the students?
   • What types of access levels will the students need?
   • How will you ensure the system is reliable?
   • How will you build scalability into the system?
   • How will you build flexibility into the system?
   • What are the minimum performance requirements for the system?
   • How will the system handle future growth?

Each chapter and module contains complete pedagogical support in the form of:

- **Summary of Student Learning Outcomes** These mirror the chapter's or module's opener.

- **Two Closing Case Studies** Reinforcing important concepts with prominent examples from businesses and organizations (chapters only).

- **Key Terms and Concepts** With page numbers where discussions of them are found.

- **Assignments and Exercises** One full page of problems designed to give your students the chance to apply key concepts of the text.

- **Discussion Questions** Challenging questions aimed at promoting an atmosphere of critical thinking in your classroom (chapters only).

Changes for the Sixth Edition

The content changes for the sixth edition were driven by:

- Instructor feedback from the fifth edition.
- Changes that have occurred in the business world.
- Advances that have occurred in the technology arena.
- Changes made by our competitors.

As a group of authors and contributors working together, we carefully sifted through all the competitive scanning information we could gather to create a sixth edition that builds on the success of the fifth edition.

Throughout the text, you'll find new or updated opening and closing case studies, Industry Perspectives, Global Perspectives, Group Projects, and Team Work and On Your Own projects, as well as new or expanded coverage of such topics as:

- Ubiquitous computing
- Top-line versus bottom-line considerations
- Run-Grow-Transform (RGT) framework
- Value chains
- Inter-modal transportation
- Fuzzy logic
- Biomimicry
- Agent-based modeling
- Swarm intelligence

- E-government
- Onshore outsourcing
- Nearshore outsourcing
- Offshore outsourcing
- ERP systems
- Business process outsourcing
- Pfishing
- RFID
- Software-as-a-service
- F2b2C
- Haptic interfaces

Most important, we're pleased to have been able to respond to reviewer suggestions and provide the following:

- More IT and business strategy integration issues by covering top-line versus bottom-line considerations, the run-grow-transform (RGT) framework, Porter's Five Forces Model, and value chains in Chapters 1 and 2.
- New *Extended Learning Module L* on using FrontPage to build Web sites.
- New *Extended Learning Module M* on programming in Excel with VBA.
- Updated Chapter 4 on decision support and artificial intelligence with more focus on agent-based modeling and swarm intelligence.
- Updated *Extended Learning Module E* on networks including such topics as T1 and DS3 lines.
- Updated Chapter 5 on electronic commerce with expanded coverage of e-government.
- Updated Chapter 6 on systems development with expanded coverage of onshore, nearshore, and offshore outsourcing.
- Updated Chapter 7 on infrastructures and architectures with more focus on enterprise and ERP systems.
- Updated Chapter 9 on emerging trends and technologies including software-as-a-service and RFID technologies.

The Support Package

We realize that no text is complete without a well-rounded and value-added support package. Our support package is designed to ease your teaching burden by providing you with a Web site full of valuable information, a test bank with more than 2,000 questions and easy-to-use test generating software, an Instructor's Manual that walks you through each chapter and module and provides value-added teaching notes and suggestions, and PowerPoint presentations.

ONLINE LEARNING CENTER AT WWW.MHHE.COM/HAAG

As in previous editions, the Web site for the sixth edition contains a wealth of valuable information and supplements for both the instructor and the student.

INSTRUCTOR'S MANUAL

The Instructor's Manual is provided to you in an effort to help you prepare for your class presentations. In its new format, you will find a separate box for each PowerPoint slide. In that box, you will find an overview of the slide and a list of key points to cover. This presentation enables you to prepare your class presentation by working solely with the Instructor's Manual because you also see the PowerPoint slide presentations. We've also provided embedded links within each Instructor's Manual document to the various in-text pedagogical elements including:

- **On Your Own** and **Team Work projects**—when to use them, how to grade them, how long they should take, etc.
- **The Global** and **Industry Perspectives boxes**—how to introduce them, key points to address, possible discussion questions to ask, etc.

At the beginning of each Instructor's Manual document you'll find other useful information including the appropriate author to contact if you have questions or comments, a list of the Group Projects that you can cover, and a list of any associated data files.

We've provided the Instructor's Manual files in Word format and placed them on both the Instructor's CD and the text's Web site.

TEST BANK

For each chapter and module, there are approximately 125 multiple-choice, true/false, and fill-in-the-blank questions aimed at challenging the minds of your students. McGraw-Hill's EZ Test is a flexible and easy-to-use electronic testing program. The program allows instructors to create tests from book-specific items. It accommodates a wide range of question types and instructors may add their own questions. Multiple versions of the test can be created and any test can be exported for use with course management systems such as WebCT, BlackBoard, or PageOut. EZ Test Online is a new service and gives you a place to easily administer your EZ Test–created exams and quizzes online. The program is available for Windows and Macintosh environments.

POWERPOINT PRESENTATIONS

The PowerPoint presentations are ready for you to use in class. In preparing to use these, you simply work through the Instructor's Manual which includes thumbnails of each slide and important points to cover. Of course, we realize that you'll probably want to customize some of the presentations. So, we've made available to you most of the images and photos in the text. You can find these on your Instructor's CD as well as the text's Web site at www.mhhe.com/haag.

Supplements:

- Online Learning Center
- Instructor's Manual
- Test Bank
- PowerPoint Presentations
- Student CD
- MISource CD
- Classroom Performance System
- Problem Solving Video Vignettes
- MBA MIS Cases
- Application Cases for MIS

Empowered Instruction

Classroom Performance System

Engage students and assess real-time lecture retention with this simple yet powerful wireless application. You can even deliver tests that instantly grade themselves.

Instructor Resource CD

Everything you need on one CD: PowerPoint slides, Test Item File (in Word and Diploma format), Solutions to end-of-chapter exercises and real world case questions, and much more.

PowerPoint Presentation

Robust, detailed, and designed to keep students engaged.

MISOURCE

Software Skills & Computer Concepts

MISource provides animated tutorials and simulated practice of the core skills in Microsoft Excel, Access, and PowerPoint. MISource also animates 47 important computer concepts.

Spend less time reviewing software skills and computer literacy. Each text includes a copy of MISource.

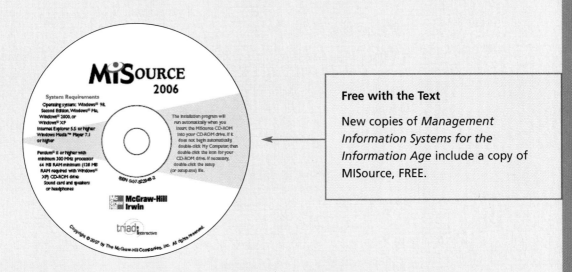

Free with the Text

New copies of *Management Information Systems for the Information Age* include a copy of MISource, FREE.

PROBLEM SOLVING VIDEO VIGNETTES

Three separate segments show how a growing beverage company comes to terms with problems and opportunities that can be addressed with database systems, telecommunications technology, and system development. Use the questions that follow each segment to inspire discussion or test students' critical thinking skills.

POWERWEB

PowerWeb is dynamic and easy to use. It automatically finds and delivers newly published supplemented MIS-specific content. PowerWeb is the first online supplement to offer your students access to

- Course-specific current articles refereed by content experts
- Course-specific real-time news
- Weekly course updates
- Interactive exercises and assessment tools
- Student study tips
- Web research tips and exercises
- Refereed and updated research links
- Daily news
- Access to the Northernlight.com Special Collection™ of journals and articles

MBA MIS CASES

Developed by Richard Perle of Loyola Marymount University, these 14 comprehensive cases allow you to add MBA-level analysis to your course. Visit our Web site to review a sample case.

ONLINE LEARNING CENTER

Visit www.mhhe.com/haag for additional instructor and student resources.

ONLINE COURSES

Content for the Sixth Edition is available in WebCT, Blackboard, and PageOut formats to accommodate virtually any online delivery platform.

EXTENDED LEARNING MODULE CD-ROM

This text is packaged with a student CD (0072962593) that contains seven *Extended Learning Modules* (E, F, G, J, K, L, and M). There is a two-page introduction to each module in the book itself. All your students have to do is go to the CD to read the full module.

ACKNOWLEDGMENTS

As we present our sixth edition of this text, we remember how things began and the people who have helped us along the way. In 1995, the Web was very much in its infancy, cell phones were used only in case of an emergency, and terms such as pfishing and pfarming had yet to be invented. It's been a fast 10 years and we have many people to thank.

McGraw-Hill's strategic management is simply second to none. We gratefully acknowledge the dedicated work and leadership of Ed Stanford, J.P. Lenney, Kevin Kane, and David Littlehale. Their guidance is invaluable.

EDP includes all those people who take our thoughts on paper and bring them to life in the form of an exciting and engaging book. Merrily Mazza leads this wonderful group of people, including Mary Conzachi (the book's project manager), Peter de Lissovoy (our manuscript editor), Jeremy Cheshareck (photo research coordinator), and Mary Kazak (cover and interior design specialist).

The editorial group comprises those people who determine which projects to publish, and they have guided us every step of the way with a wealth of market intelligence. Stewart Mattson (publisher) leads the editorial group that includes Paul Ducham (our senior sponsoring editor) and Kelly Delso (the book's developmental editor). We are indebted to them for leading the way.

We would also like to acknowledge the dedicated work of the following people at McGraw-Hill: Greg Bates (media producer), Rose Range (supplement producer), and Sankha Basu (marketing manager). Without Greg and Rose, our text would be just a text, with no supplements or great supporting Web site. Without Sankha, you might never know we created this text.

We wish to acknowledge the wonderful efforts of our contributor team: Dan Connolly, David Cox, Kathleen Davisson, Jeff Engelstad, Syl Houston, and Keith Neufeld. Each has brought to the table unique talents and knowledge indispensable to the success of this text.

Last, but certainly not least, we offer our gratitude to our reviewers, who took on a thankless job that paid only a fraction of its true worth. We had the best. They include

John Aje
University of Maryland University College

Noushin Ashrafi
University of Massachusetts–Boston

Jack D. Becker
University of North Texas

Jerry Carvalho
University of Utah

Casey Cegielski
Auburn University

Syama Chaudhuri
University of Maryland University College

David J. Cohen
University of Maryland University College

Vance Cooney
Eastern Washington University

Mohammad Dadashzadeh
Oakland University

Frederick Fisher
Florida State University

Fred Hughes
Faulkner University

Wade M. Jackson
Fogelman College

Jack T. Marchewka
Northern Illinois University

Ram Misra
Montclair State University

Lawrence S. Orilia
Nassau Community College

Leslie Pang
University of Maryland University College

Leonard Presby
William Paterson University

Keng Siau
University of Nebraska–Lincoln

Andrew Targowski
Western Michigan University

Jyhhorng Michael Tarn
Haworth College of Business, Western Michigan University

Sameer Verma
San Francisco State University

Robert Wurm
Nassau Community College

James E. Yao
Montclair State University

FROM THE AUTHORS

FROM STEPHEN HAAG   To the entire author team—coauthors and contributors alike—I commend you for all your efforts. I specifically acknowledge the work of Maeve and Amy, who make writing a true pleasure.

I am also grateful to the many people who helped me along the career path of writing books. They include Peter Keen, Dr. L. L. Schkade, JD Ice, Rick Williamson, and a host of people still working at McGraw-Hill.

My colleagues in the Daniels College of Business at the University of Denver also provide support. I wish I could name all of you, but there isn't enough room. To James Griesemer (Dean Emeritus), Karen Newman (Dean), and Glyn Hanbery (Senior Associate Dean), I thank you all.

And my writing efforts would not be successful nor would my life be complete without my family. My mother and father live just a few minutes away from me and give me unending support. My two sons—Darian and Trevor—make me smile after long nights of working. My four-legged son—Zippy—doesn't really care that I write books; he offers me unconditional love. Finally, my wife, Pam, should be listed as a coauthor on many of my books. Her work is never done, and she loves every minute of it.

FROM MAEVE CUMMINGS   My sincere thanks goes to the many people who helped directly and indirectly with this edition and the previous five. Thanks to Steve, who is every bit as good a friend as he is a lead author. Thanks to Amy, who is great to work with. Thanks to all the people at McGraw-Hill who put in long hours and a lot of work to bring this book to completion.

A special thanks to Keith Neufeld, who is an expert on networks and generous with his knowledge, and to Lanny Morrow, who keeps me in touch with the fascinating world of computer forensics. Felix Dreher and Barbara Clutter were, and always have been, unwaveringly supportive and helpful.

Thanks to the Holy Faith and Loreto nuns who gave me an excellent early education, which served as a solid foundation on which I was able to build. These were exceptionally dedicated teachers and I learned much more from them than the basics of reading, writing, and arithmetic. Much credit goes to Jan Guynes Clark, who helped me through several exhilarating and terrifying years at the University of Texas at Arlington.

As always, I want to thank my great family: my parents (Dolores and Steve), sisters (Grainne, Fiona, and Clodagh), and brother (Colin). And last, but by no means least, thanks to my husband, Slim, for making everything I do possible.

FROM AMY PHILLIPS   No one ever said writing was easy, but thanks to Stephen and Maeve, writing this edition has been a true pleasure and wonderful experience.

I am extremely appreciative of all my colleagues in the ITEC department in the Daniels College of Business at the University of Denver. What a wonderful group of people you are. This has been a great ride.

A special thanks goes to my very close friend of 20 years, Deborah Jean, who is always at the end of a phone or e-mail message to listen, process, or just remind me to laugh. You are a true gem, Deborah. Thanks to the wonderful, dedicated folks at McGraw-Hill, Paul, Mary, and Liz. You have made this whole process very rewarding.

Finally, thanks to my family. My mother, Jane, who is the center and light of my life. My brother, Glenn, and his family, for anchoring my mother. My nephew, Mike, for realizing that being a teenager is a difficult thing. My dog, Gabby, who sits happily beside me night after night as I type away. Don't worry Gabs, summer is approaching, and we will return to our daily hikes, I promise!

STEPHEN HAAG is the Associate Dean of Graduate Programs and Director of the MBA program in the Daniels College of Business at the University of Denver. Prior to being Associate Dean, Stephen served as Chair of the Department of Information Technology and Electronic Commerce and Director of the Master of Science in Information Technology program. Stephen holds a B.B.A. and M.B.A. from West Texas State University and a Ph.D. from the University of Texas at Arlington.

Stephen is the author/coauthor of numerous books including *Computing Concepts in Action* (a K-12 textbook), *Interactions: Teaching English as a Second Language* (with his mother and father), *Information Technology: Tomorrow's Advantage Today* (with Peter Keen), *Excelling in Finance, Business Driven Technology,* and more than 40 books within the *I-Series.* He has also written numerous articles appearing in such journals as *Communications of the ACM, Socio-Economic Planning Sciences,* the *International Journal of Systems Science, Managerial and Decision Economics, Applied Economics,* and the *Australian Journal of Management.* Stephen lives with his wife, Pam, and their three sons—Darian, Trevor, and Zippy—in Highlands Ranch, Colorado.

MAEVE CUMMINGS is a professor of Information Systems at Pittsburg State University. She holds a B.S. in Mathematics and Computer Science and an M.B.A from Pittsburg State and a Ph.D. in Information Systems from the University of Texas at Arlington. She has published in various journals including the *Journal of Global Information Management* and the *Journal of Computer Information Systems.* She serves on various editorial boards and is a coauthor of *Case Studies in Information Technology* and the concepts books of the *I-Series,* entitled *Computing Concepts.* Maeve has been teaching for 20 years and lives in Pittsburg, Kansas, with her husband, Slim.

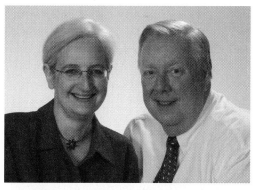

AMY PHILLIPS teaches in the Department of Information Technology and Electronic Commerce in the Daniels College of Business at the University of Denver. Amy's main teaching and research areas involve Internet and mobile technologies. With her MCT certification, Amy works with developing training material for Microsoft's Web Services platform, .NET. With more than 22 years teaching experience, Amy has coauthored several textbooks, including *Business Driven Technology, Internet Explorer 6.0,* and *PowerPoint 2003.*

KEITH NEUFELD is the lead network engineer in University Computing and Telecommunications Services at Wichita State University. Keith has been working in information technology for 15 years, including 13 years as a Unix system administrator and 8 years with increasing network design and support responsibilities.

Before moving into higher education, he worked for 10 years in nonprofit healthcare and for 3 years at Cessna aircraft. Keith's interests include resilient network design, open-source software development, and vintage video arcade game collecting and restoration.

Careers in Business Contributors are the people who offered great insight into Module K on Careers in Business. No single person could have compiled information on the many business careers that appear in that module. The contributor team includes:

- Dan Connolly (Hospitality and Tourism Management)
- David Cox (Finance)
- Kathleen Davisson (Accounting)
- Jeff Engelstad (Real Estate and Construction Management)
- Syl Houston (Management)

Management Information Systems

FOR THE INFORMATION AGE

CHAPTER ONE OUTLINE

STUDENT LEARNING OUTCOMES

1. Define management information systems (MIS) and information technology (IT) and describe their relationship.

2. Validate information as a key resource and describe both personal and organizational dimensions of information.

3. Explain why people are the most important organizational resource, define their information and technology literacy challenges, and discuss their ethical responsibilities.

4. Describe the important characteristics of information technology (IT) as a key organizational resource.

5. Define competitive advantage and illustrate the role of information technology in supporting competitive advantages and business vision.

6. Discuss the impacts information technology can and will have on your life.

INDUSTRY PERSPECTIVES

10 Timely Information: From 48 Hours to Just 20 Minutes

12 Always Remember: Business Drives Technology

19 A More "Customer-Oriented" Internal Revenue Service

23 Using Technology When Millions of Possible Solutions Exist

FEATURES

7 Global Perspective
Overcoming Language Barriers on the Internet

14 On Your Own
E-Mail: Electronic Mail or Expensive Mail?

16 Team Work
Identifying Hardware and Software

22 Global Perspective
Managing Knowledge with a Knowledge Management System

27 On Your Own
Researching Your Career and Information Technology

28 Team Work
Developing Strategies for Protecting Yourself against Identity Theft

36 Electronic Commerce
Using the Internet as a Tool to Find a Job

WEB SUPPORT

www.mhhe.com/haag

- Job databases
- Electronic résumés
- Locating internships
- Interviewing and negotiating tips

CHAPTER ONE

The Information Age in Which You Live
Changing the Face of Business

OPENING CASE STUDY:
DISRUPTIVE TECHNOLOGIES DISRUPT BLOCKBUSTER LATE FEES

The term "disruptive technologies" almost makes technology sound like a bad thing, but it isn't. A disruptive technology is any technology that causes a business (or person) to dramatically change the way that it (or she or he) works. The recording industry, for example, is undergoing significant transformation because of technological advances. Fewer people are buying complete CDs or albums, in favor of purchasing only music selections and songs they want via the Internet. The Internet, peer-to-peer file sharing systems, and Web sites such as Apple's iTunes (www.apple.com/itunes) are disruptive technologies causing the recording industry to rethink and reshape the way it packages and sells music.

The same thing is happening in the video rental market. In 2003, Blockbuster dominated the video rental market, controlling 32 percent of it. That is quickly changing because of disruptive technologies.

In 2004, 12.5 million homes in the United States had access to video-on-demand movies. This means families in those homes no longer have to go to a video rental store to rent a movie.

You can rent videos at kiosks, which look very similar to ATMs. You swipe your credit card, select a movie, and take it with you. Some kiosks require you to return the movie to the same kiosk, while others let you drop it in the mail for return. These kiosks are popping up on college campuses, in McDonald's, at shopping malls, and in many other food and retail outlets.

And don't forget Netflix. Its Internet model of renting videos to people for as long as they want with no late fees is definitely affecting Blockbuster. Netflix predicted that it would have 2.65 million customers by the end of 2004.

What is Blockbuster doing to save its market share? A Blockbuster initiative in January 2004 was to no longer assess late fees if a customer returns a movie anytime within a week. After a week, Blockbuster automatically sells the movie to the customer at retail price minus the rental fee. If the customer doesn't want to buy it though and returns the movie after a week, Blockbuster charges only a $1.25 restocking fee.

All types of new and disruptive technology challenge organizations (1) to rethink how they do business and (2) to embrace the technology and determine how best to use it to create a competitive advantage.

That's the focus of this text. We will introduce you to a wide array of technology terms and concepts and teach you the technology, but we want you always to keep in mind the essential challenge of how to apply the technology to create a competitive advantage. Technology is a set of tools you use to work with information. The competitive advantage of technology really lies in how you and your organization decide to respond to technology and use it. As is the case with Blockbuster, many times you'll find it necessary to transform what you do to meet the changing needs and desires of customers. Responding to changes in its market caused by technology, Blockbuster expects to forgo almost $300 million in late fees in 2005, but it hopes to offset that loss with increased sales and more loyal customers because of the "no late fee" concept.[1,2,3]

Introduction

It is the ***information age***—a time when knowledge is power. Today, more than ever, businesses are using information (and information technology) to gain and sustain a competitive advantage. You'll never find a successful business whose slogan is "What you don't know can't hurt you." Businesses understand that what they don't know can become an Achilles' heel and a source of advantage for the competition.

Whether your major is marketing, finance, accounting, human resource management, or any of the many other specializations in a business program, you're preparing to enter the business world as a *knowledge worker*. Simply put, a ***knowledge worker*** works with and produces information as a product. According to *U.S. News & World Report* in 1994, knowledge workers in the United States outnumbered all other workers by a four-to-one margin.[4] Today, that margin is even greater, probably five-to-one or six-to-one.

In the information age, *management information systems* and *information technology* are vitally important tools and topics. Why? Because management information systems deals with the coordination and use of three very important organizational resources—information, people, and information technology. Formally, we define management information systems and information technology as follows:

- ***Management information systems (MIS)*** deals with the planning for, development, management, and use of information technology tools to help people perform all tasks related to information processing and management.

- ***Information technology (IT)*** is any computer-based tool that people use to work with information and support the information and information-processing needs of an organization.

Statistically, there are any number of ways to validate the impact technology is having on the business world. Consider the graph in Figure 1.1, which shows that in 2003 $46 billion (20 percent) of all U.S. travel revenue derived from online bookings. As

Figure 1.1

Online Versus Non-Online Travel Booking Revenues through 2009[5]

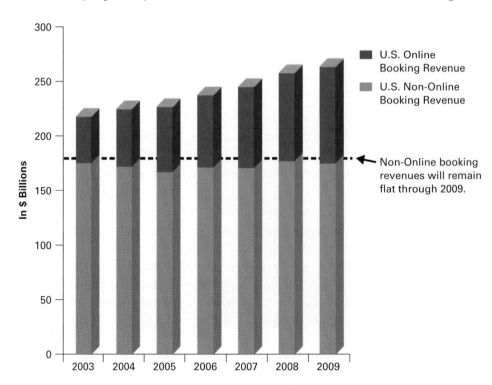

In $ Billions

■ U.S. Online Booking Revenue

■ U.S. Non-Online Booking Revenue

← Non-Online booking revenues will remain flat through 2009.

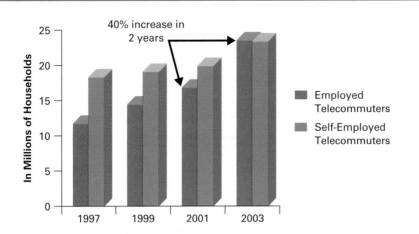

Figure 1.2

Telecommuting on the Rise[6]

shown in the figure, it is estimated that $91 billion (33 percent) of all U.S. travel revenue will come from online bookings in 2009. Those should be eye-opening statistics for the travel agent industry. As we discussed in the opening case study, disruptive technologies cause businesses to rethink and reshape their operations, and the travel agent industry will definitely be impacted by the increased use of online booking sites such as Travelocity (www.travelocity.com). For example, while revenue from online bookings is expected to grow from $46 billion in 2003 to $91 billion in 2009, revenue from non-online bookings is expected to remain flat over the same period of time ($184 billion in 2003 and $185 billion in 2009).

Think about your future job. It may include ***telecommuting,*** the use of communications technologies (such as the Internet) to work in a place other than a central location. In Figure 1.2, you can see that telecommuting among employed workers in the United States rose to 23.5 million in 2003, a more than 100 percent increase from 1997 and an almost 40 percent increase from 2001.

From a personal point of view, telecommuting presents wonderful "quality of life" opportunities. From a business point of view, it is also good but presents new challenges. Now more than ever businesses must consider the issue of security. With the advent of the Internet, wireless communications, and telecommuting, the security of information is a top priority. People working from home are more vulnerable to virus attacks than are workers at a central location behind company firewall hardware and software. Communications across the Internet (either wired or wireless) are more susceptible to interception than communications on a secure local area network in an office building. Management information systems (MIS) encompasses all of these issues and many more, as well as the enabling technologies.

This is an MIS book, but what you need to keep in mind is that technology is not the sole focus of MIS. Technology is a set of tools that enable you to work more efficiently and effectively with information. Pragmatically speaking, people and information are the most important resources within MIS, not technology. Of course, every organization today needs all three (and many others such as capital) to compete effectively in the marketplace.

In this first chapter, we will explore with you the three key resources of MIS—information, people, and information technology. We'll do so at a fairly high level in the interest of providing you with a solid understanding of the roles of each resource and their interrelationships. In subsequent chapters (and modules), we'll focus specifically on the strategic and competitive opportunities of IT (Chapters 2 and 5), provide you technology-centric coverage (the extended learning modules and Chapters 3, 4, 6, and 7), ask why protection is necessary for organizations and you in cyberspace (Chapter 8), and finally look at emerging trends that we see on the horizon (Chapter 9).

Information as a Key Resource

Information is crucially important today. We are in the "information age," a time when knowledge is power. Information is one of the three key components of management information systems (MIS) along with information technology and people. Knowledge comes from having timely access to information and knowing what to do with it, the province of MIS.

DATA, INFORMATION, AND BUSINESS INTELLIGENCE

To understand the nature of information and *business intelligence,* you must first understand another term—*data*. **Data** are raw facts that describe a particular phenomenon. For example, the current temperature, the price of a movie rental, and your age are all data. **Information** then is simply data that have a particular meaning within a specific context. For example, if you're trying to decide what to wear, the current temperature is information because it's pertinent to your decision at hand (what to wear); in this situation the price of a movie rental is not pertinent information.

Information may be data that have been processed in some way or presented in a more meaningful fashion. In business, for instance, the price of a movie rental may be information to a checkout clerk, although it may represent only data to an accountant who is responsible for determining net revenues at the end of the month.

Business intelligence is information "on steroids," so to speak. **Business intelligence (BI)** is knowledge—knowledge about your customers, your competitors, your business partners, your competitive environment, and your own internal operations—that gives you the ability to make effective, important, and often strategic business decisions. BI enables your organization to extract the true meaning of information to take creative and powerful steps to ensure a competitive advantage. So, business intelligence is much more than just a list of the products you sell. It could combine your product information with your advertising strategy information and customer demographics information to help you determine the effectiveness of various advertising media on demographic groups segmented by location. You'll learn more about business intelligence, how to gather it, how to use it, and how to use IT to generate it throughout this text, and especially in Chapters 2 and 3.

PERSONAL DIMENSIONS OF INFORMATION

As a knowledge worker, you work with and produce information. As you do, you can consider it from three points of view or dimensions: time, location, and form (see Figure 1.3).

THE TIME DIMENSION   The time dimension of information has two aspects: (1) having access to information when you need it, or *timeliness,* and (2) having information that describes the time period you're considering. Information, like many organizational resources, can become old and obsolete. For example, if you want to make a stock trade today, you need to know the price of the stock right now. If you have to wait a day to view stock prices, you may not survive in the turbulent securities market. It's no wonder that over one-third of all stock transactions today occur over the Internet.[7]

Figure 1.3

Personal Dimensions of Information

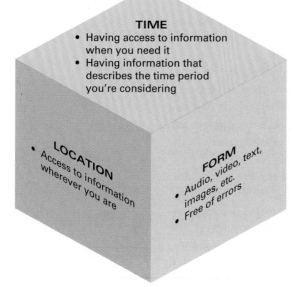

TIME
- Having access to information when you need it
- Having information that describes the time period you're considering

LOCATION
- Access to information wherever you are

FORM
- Audio, video, text, images, etc.
- Free of errors

OVERCOMING LANGUAGE BARRIERS ON THE INTERNET

The Internet is certainly a disruptive technology that has eliminated geographical and location barriers. With almost one-sixth of the world's population having access to the Internet, "location, location, location" in the physical world is becoming less and less and less important.

However, now we have new issues to deal with, notably, a language barrier. What happens if you connect to a site that offers information in a language you don't understand? How can you send an e-mail to someone in Japan who doesn't speak English?

One solution is language translation software, and one company leading the way in the development of language translation software is SYSTRAN. SYSTRAN offers a suite of software tools that enables you, among other things, to translate about 3,700 words per minute, translate e-mail, Web page, and pdf content, and display Asian fonts.

Is it perfect? Not according to SYSTRAN's disclaimer. It states specifics about what its products will do, but does encourage you to carefully review any translation before making it a part of your business communications.

Indeed, when Kentucky Fried Chicken wanted to translate its slogan "finger-lickin' good" into Chinese, it came out as "eat your fingers off." Now, KFC wasn't using SYSTRAN's software, but this example does illustrate the difficulty of translating idiomatic phrases from one language to another. Product names are another example. When General Motors (GM) tried to sell the Chevy Nova in South America, people didn't buy it. As it turns out, *No va* means "it won't go" in Spanish. GM subsequently changed the name to Caribe for its Spanish markets.

Experiment with this. Connect to SYSTRAN's Web site at www.systransoft.com. Type in a phrase and choose the language into which you would like it translated.

Your information is useful and relevant only if it describes the appropriate time period. For example, most utility companies provide you with a bill that not only tells you of your current usage and the average temperature but also compares that information to the previous month and perhaps the same month last year. This type of information can help you better manage your utilities or simply understand that this month's high utility bill was caused by inclement weather.

THE LOCATION DIMENSION Information is no good to you if you can't access it. The location dimension of information means having access to information no matter where you are. Ideally, in other words, your location or the information's location should not matter. You should be able to access information in a hotel room, at home, in the student center of your campus, at work, on the spur of the moment while walking down the street, or even while traveling on an airplane. This location dimension is closely related to mobile and wireless computing (and also ubiquitous computing) which we'll discuss in an upcoming section.

To keep certain information private and secure while providing remote access for employees, many businesses are creating intranets. An *intranet* is an internal organizational Internet that is guarded against outside access by a special security feature called a *firewall* (which can be software, hardware, or a combination of the two). So, if your organization has an intranet and you want to access information on it while away from the office, all you need is Web access and the password that will allow you through the firewall.

For example, Citigroup's Global Corporate and Investment Banking division uses an intranet to provide the entire IT staff with access to all IT projects under construction.[8] Available information includes project owner, delivery date, and numerous budget metrics. Just by making this information easily and securely available to all IT staffers via an intranet, Citigroup has realized an across-the-board 15 percent improvement in on-time delivery of IT projects.

THE FORM DIMENSION   The form dimension of information has two primary aspects. The first is simply having information in a form that is most usable and understandable by you—audio, text, video, animation, graphical, and others. The second is accuracy. You need information that is free of errors. Think of information as you would think of a physical product. If you buy a product and it's defective, you become an unsatisfied customer. Likewise, if you receive information that is incorrect, you're very unhappy as well.

ORGANIZATIONAL DIMENSIONS OF INFORMATION

Even if your choice in life is to be an entrepreneur, you need to consider various organizational dimensions of information. These include information flows, information granularity, what information describes, and how information is used (whether for transaction processing or analytical processing, which we'll discuss in an upcoming section).

INFORMATION FLOWS   Information in an organization flows in four directions: up, down, horizontally, and inward/outward. To consider these flows, let's briefly review the structure of an organization. Most people view a traditional organization as a pyramid with four levels and many sides (see Figure 1.4). From top to bottom, the levels are:

- *Strategic management,* which provides an organization with overall direction and guidance.
- *Tactical management,* which develops the goals and strategies outlined by strategic management.
- *Operational management,* which manages and directs the day-to-day operations and implementations of the goals and strategies.
- Nonmanagement employees, who actually perform daily activities, such as order processing, developing and producing goods and services, and serving customers.

If you consider your school as an example, strategic management might include the chancellor, president, and various vice presidents. Tactical management would include the deans. Operational management would include the department chairs and directors of academic programs. The final level would include instructors who are responsible for teaching your classes.

Figure 1.4

An Organization, Its Information Flows, and Information Granularity

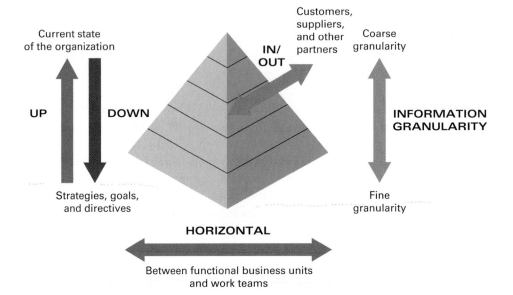

Information that flows upward, or the *upward flow of information*, describes the current state of the organization based on its daily transactions. When a sale occurs, for example, that information originates at the lowest level of the organization that then is passed up through various levels of management. Information that is gathered as a part of everyday operations is consolidated by information technology and passed upward to decision makers who monitor and respond to problems and opportunities.

The *downward flow of information* consists of the strategies, goals, and directives that originate at one level and are passed to lower levels. Many organizations are taking advantage of collaborative technologies and systems to share and move this type of information. You'll learn more about these types of technologies later in this chapter and in Chapter 2.

Information that flows horizontally, or the *horizontal flow of information*, is between functional business units and work teams. For example, at your school various departments are responsible for scheduling courses. That information is passed horizontally to the registrar's office, which creates a course schedule for your entire campus (which may be online—timely and accessible from anywhere by you). Again, collaborative technologies and systems support the horizontal flow of information.

Finally, the *outward and inward flows of information* consist of information that is communicated to customers, suppliers, distributors, and other partners for the purpose of doing business. These flows of information are really what electronic commerce is all about. Today, no organization is an island, and you must ensure that your organization has the right information technology to communicate with all types of business partners. We cover these important topics in Chapter 2 (on major business initiatives), Chapter 5 (on e-commerce), *Extended Learning Module E (Network Basics),* and Chapter 7 (IT infrastructures).

INFORMATION GRANULARITY   Figure 1.4 also illustrates another dimension of information—granularity. ***Information granularity*** refers to the extent of detail within the information. On one end of this spectrum is coarse granularity, or highly summarized information. At the other end is fine granularity, or information that contains a great amount of detail. As you might guess, people in the highest levels of the organization deal mainly with a coarse granularity of information, with sales by year being an example. People in the lowest levels of the organization, on the other hand, need information with fine granularity. If you consider sales again, nonmanagement employees need information in great detail that describes each transaction—when it occurred, whether by credit or cash, who made the sale, to whom that sale was made, and so on.

So, when transaction information originates at the lowest level of an organization (with fine granularity), it is consolidated by IT to a coarser granularity as it moves up through the organization (the upward flow of information).

WHAT INFORMATION DESCRIBES   Another organizational dimension of information is what the information describes. Information can be internal, external, objective, subjective, or some combination of the four.

1. ***Internal information*** describes specific operational aspects of an organization.
2. ***External information*** describes the environment surrounding the organization.
3. ***Objective information*** quantifiably describes something that is known.
4. ***Subjective information*** attempts to describe something that is unknown.

Consider a bank that faces a decision about what interest rate to offer on a CD. That bank will use internal information (how many customers it has who can afford to buy a CD), external information (what rate other banks are offering), objective information

In the fast-paced, high-volume, low-margin grocery retail industry, you need up-to-date information and you need it within minutes not days. Produce can spoil, competitors can change prices quickly and run loss-leader specials, and out-of-stock items mean that your customers will go elsewhere.

Big Y Foods, based in Springfield, Massachusetts, is one of the fastest growing grocery retail chains in the United States. It currently has 47 locations in central and western Massachusetts and throughout Connecticut. Organizing and managing information—including everything from inventory to profitability to labor—is no small task for Big Y Foods. And it must be done in a way that provides key decision makers with timely access to information.

Big Y Foods uses Cognos (www.cognos.com) software, a leader in the business intelligence market. According to Jim Beaudreault, Big Y Foods' financial re-

porting manager, "Before we started using Cognos, we were generating reports out of our mainframe. We would submit the reports to the report writer tool over the weekend because they would take so long to run." The following week, decision makers would download the mainframe reports into spreadsheet software, create a standardized report format, and eventually distribute the reports.

But you can't rely on days-old information in the grocery retail industry to make decisions. When Big Y Foods turned to Cognos, it was in the hope of reducing reporting time from 48 hours (the weekend) to just 20 minutes. And it succeeded. As Jim explains, "Now it takes no more than 20 minutes, so there was a significant time savings. The reduced reporting time means that key people within the organization are getting more timely information and you can't put a price tag on that."[9]

(what is today's prime interest rate), and subjective information (what prime interest rate is expected in the future). Actually, the rate other banks are offering is not only external information (it describes the surrounding environment) but objective information (it is quantifiably known). Information often has more than one aspect to it.

As a general rule, people in the lowest level of the organization deal mainly with internal and objective information (the price of a movie rental is an example). People in the highest levels of the organization, on the other hand, deal with all types of information.

People as the Key Resource

The single most important resource in any organization is its people. People set goals, carry out tasks, make decisions, serve customers, and, in the case of IT specialists, provide a stable and reliable technology environment so the organization can run smoothly and gain a competitive advantage in the marketplace. This discussion is all about you. You're preparing to be a knowledge worker.

INFORMATION AND TECHNOLOGY LITERACY

In business, your most valuable asset is <u>not</u> technology but rather your *mind*. IT is simply a set of tools that helps you work with and process information, but it's really just a *mind support* tool set. Technology such as spreadsheet software can help you quickly create a high-quality and revealing graph. But it can't tell you whether you should build a bar or a pie graph, and it can't help you determine whether you should show sales by territory or sales by salesperson. Those are your tasks, and that's why your business curriculum includes classes in human resource management, accounting, finance, marketing, and perhaps production and operations management.

Nonetheless, technology is an important set of tools for you. Technology can help you be more efficient and can help you dissect and better understand problems and opportunities. So, it's important for you to learn how to use your technology tool set. And it's equally important that you understand the information to which you're applying your technology tools.

A *technology-literate knowledge worker* is a person who knows how and when to apply technology. The "how" aspect includes knowing what technology to buy, how to exploit the many benefits of application software, and what technology infrastructure is required to get businesses connected to each other, just to name a few. From your personal perspective, we've provided many extended learning modules in this text to help you become a technology-literate knowledge worker. These include:

- *Extended Learning Module A*—basic computer hardware and software terminology.
- *Extended Learning Module B*—how to search and use the Web.
- *Extended Learning Modules C* and *J*—how to design and implement a database.
- *Extended Learning Module D*—advanced decision support tools in Excel including filtering, conditional formatting, and pivot tables.
- *Extended Learning Module E*—the basics of networks including how to set up a home network.
- *Extended Learning Module F*—how to write HTML to create a Web site.
- *Extended Learning Module I*—how to build an e-portfolio to advertise yourself on the Web.
- *Extended Learning Module L*—using FrontPage to create a Web site.
- *Extended Learning Module M*—writing VBA in Excel.

A technology-literate knowledge worker also knows "when" to apply technology. Unfortunately, in many cases, people and organizations have blindly decided to use technology to help solve some sort of business problem. What you need to understand is that technology is not a panacea. You can't simply apply technology to any given process and expect that process instantly to become more efficient and effective. Look at it this way— if you apply technology to a process that doesn't work correctly, then you'll only be doing things wrong millions of times faster. There are cases when technology is not the solution. Being a technology-literate knowledge worker will help you determine when and when not to apply technology.

Information-literate knowledge workers

- Can define what information they need.
- Know how and where to obtain that information.
- Understand the information once they receive it (i.e., can transform it into business intelligence).
- Can act appropriately based on the information to help the organization achieve the greatest advantage.

Consider a unique, real-life example of an information-literate knowledge worker.

Several years ago, a manager of a retail store on the East Coast received some interesting information: diaper sales on Friday evening accounted for a large percentage of total sales for the week. Most people in this situation would immediately jump to the

ALWAYS REMEMBER: BUSINESS DRIVES TECHNOLOGY

The key to success in any business is its people, or knowledge workers. Knowledge workers must be both information-literate and technology-literate. Regarding the latter, though, don't get too caught up in the "sizzle" of technology. Technology for the sake of technology is not a good thing. Your business initiatives should always drive your choices and uses of technology.

Consider this quote: "Business is not about technology; it is about using technology to make money. I find that most IT people simply do not understand this. They often look down on simple solutions and instead engage in complex, expensive projects that in the end don't deliver. Business needs solutions, not cool tech-

nology." That statement was made by Mike Hugos, CIO of Network Services. And Mike is an IT person. His job title of CIO, chief information officer, is one primarily held by IT people. Mike understands that business must drive technology, not the reverse.

Regardless of your career choice, always remember that business drives technology. Technology is a set of tools that can be an important and integral enabler of business efficiency, effectiveness, and innovation. But it can be successful as an enabler only if your choices and uses of technology are driven by your business initiatives.[10]

decision to ensure that diapers are always well stocked on Friday evenings or to run a special on diapers during that time to increase sales further, but not our information-literate knowledge worker. She first looked at the information and decided it was not complete. That is, she needed more information (business intelligence) before she could act.

She decided the BI she needed was *why* a rash of diaper sales (pardon the pun) occurred on Friday evenings and *who* was buying the diapers. That intelligence was not stored within the computer system, so she stationed an employee in the diaper aisle on Friday evening to record any information pertinent to the situation (i.e., she knew how and where to obtain information). The store manager learned that young businessmen purchased the most diapers on Friday evenings. Apparently, they had been instructed to buy the weekend supply on their way home from work. The manager's response was to stock premium domestic and imported beer near the diapers. Since then, Friday evening has been a big sale time not only for diapers but also for premium domestic and imported beer.

There are a couple of important lessons you can learn from this story. First, as we've already stated, technology is not a panacea. Although a computer system generated the initial report detailing the sale of diapers on Friday evenings, our retail store manager did not make any further use of technology to design and implement her innovative and highly effective solution. Second, this story can help you distinguish between information and business intelligence. In this case, the information was the sale of diapers on Friday evening. The business intelligence included:

- *Who* was making diaper purchases on Friday evening.
- *Why* those people were purchasing diapers on Friday evening.
- *What* complementary product(s) those people might also want or need.

As a good rule of thumb, when you receive information and need to make a decision based on it, ask yourself questions that start with who, what, when, why, where, and how. Answers to those questions will help you create business intelligence and make better decisions.

YOUR ETHICAL RESPONSIBILITIES

Your roles as a technology-literate and information-literate knowledge worker extend far beyond using technology and information to gain a competitive advantage in the marketplace for your organization. You must also consider your social responsibilities: This is where ethics become important. ***Ethics*** are the principles and standards that guide our behavior toward other people. Your ethics have consequences for you just as laws do. But ethics are different from laws. Laws either clearly require or prohibit an action. Ethics are more subjective, more a matter of personal or cultural interpretation, and thus a decision or an action might have—or be expected to have—an outcome that is right or wrong according to different people's ethics. Thus, ethical decision making can be complex. Consider the following examples:

1. Copying software you purchase, making copies for your friends, and charging them for the copies.

2. Making an extra backup of your software just in case both the copy you are using and the primary backup fail for some reason.

3. Giving out the phone numbers of your friends and family, without their permission, to a telecom provider of some sort of calling plan so you can receive a discount.

Each of these examples is either ethically (according to you or some people) and/or legally (according to the government) incorrect. In the second example, you might be ethically okay in making an extra backup copy (because you didn't share it with anyone), but according to most software licenses you're prohibited by law from making more than one backup copy. What do you think about the first and third examples? Illegal? Unethical? Both?

To help you better understand the relationship between ethical acts and legal acts, consider Figure 1.5. The graph is composed of four quadrants, and the complexity of ethical decisions about behavior is suggested by quadrant III (legal but unethical). Do any of the three examples above fall in quadrant III? Perhaps you can think of some other actions that although legal might still be unethical (how about gossiping?). You always want your actions to remain in quadrant I. If all your actions fall into that quadrant, you'll always be acting legally *and* ethically, and thus in a socially responsible way. Technology has further increased the complexity of ethics in our society because of the speed and casual ease with which people can access, distribute, and use information.

Being socially and ethically responsible in the information age involves not only the actions you initiate yourself but also what you do to protect yourself and your organization against the actions of others— that is, protecting yourself against cyber crimes. There are many types of cyber crimes—such as viruses, worms, identity theft, and Web defacing—performed by a variety of hackers such as black-hat hackers and cyberterrorists, and it is your responsibility to guard against them. It might even be considered an ethical lapse not to do so. We cannot stress enough how important it is for you to protect yourself and your organization's assets in cyberspace. We'll talk more about these issues later in this chapter, and we'll explore them in great detail in *Extended Learning Module H (Computer Crime and Forensics)* and Chapter 8 (Protecting People and Information).

Figure 1.5

Acting Ethically and Legally[11]

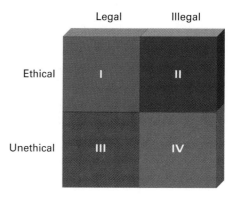

E-MAIL: ELECTRONIC MAIL OR EXPENSIVE MAIL?

In February 1995, an employee at Chevron came across what he thought was an interesting and funny list—"25 Reasons Why Beer Is Better Than Women." He quickly logged into his e-mail and distributed the list to many people. The only problem was that one of the people who received the e-mail was a woman, and she was offended by it. What followed was a lot of legal mumbo jumbo and an eventual out-of-court settlement worth $2 million that Chevron had to pay to the offended employee—definitely an example of when e-mail becomes expensive mail.

Most people agree that the original sender should not have distributed the list. It was mail that was potentially embarrassing and offensive to some people and, therefore, should not have been distributed as a matter of ethics. What people don't agree on, however, is whether or not the company was at fault for not monitoring and stopping the potentially offensive mail. What are your thoughts? Before you decide, follow the accompanying diagram and consider the consequences of your answers.[12]

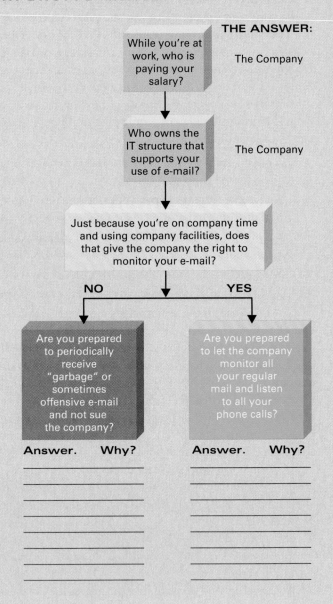

Information Technology as a Key Resource

Within management information systems (MIS), the third key resource is information technology. As we have already defined it, ***information technology (IT)*** is any computer-based tool that people use to work with information and support the information and information-processing needs of an organization. So, IT includes a cell phone or PDA that you might use to obtain stock quotes, your home computer that you use to write term papers, large networks that businesses use to connect to one another, and the Internet that almost one in every six people in the world currently uses.[13]

KEY TECHNOLOGY CATEGORIES

There are two basic categories of technology: hardware and software (see Figure 1.6). *Hardware* consists of the physical devices that make up a computer (often referred to as a *computer system*). *Software* is the set of instructions that your hardware executes to carry out a specific task for you. So, your PDA is the actual hardware; it contains software that you use to maintain your calendar, update your address book, and so on. Let's briefly look at hardware and software; for a more thorough discussion, read *Extended Learning Module A (Computer Hardware and Software)*, which follows this chapter.

TECHNOLOGY HARDWARE   All hardware falls into one of the following six categories:

1. *Input device*—tool you use to enter information and commands. Input devices include such tools as a keyboard, mouse, touch screen, game controller, and bar code reader.

Figure 1.6

Information Technology
Hardware and Software

2. *Output device*—tool you use to see, hear, or otherwise recognize the results of your information-processing requests. Output devices include such tools as a printer, monitor, and set of speakers.

3. *Storage device*—tool you use to store information for use at a later time. Storage devices include such tools as a hard disk, flash memory card, and DVD.

4. *Central processing unit (CPU)*—the hardware that interprets and executes the system and application software instructions and coordinates the operation of all the hardware. Popular personal CPUs include the Intel Pentium and Xeon product lines and the AMD Athlon series. *RAM,* or *random access memory,* is a temporary holding area for the information you're working with as well as the system and application software instructions that the CPU currently needs.

5. *Telecommunications device*—tool you use to send information to and receive it from another person or computer in a network. For example, if you connect to the Internet using a modem, the modem is a telecommunications device.

6. Connecting device—includes such things as a USB port into which you would connect a printer, connector cables to connect your printer to the USB port, and internal connecting devices on the motherboard.

TECHNOLOGY SOFTWARE There are two main types of software: application and system. *Application software* is the software that enables you to solve specific problems or perform specific tasks. Microsoft Word, for example, can help you write term papers. From an organizational perspective, payroll software, collaborative software, and inventory management software are all examples of application software.

System software handles tasks specific to technology management and coordinates the interaction of all technology devices. Within system software, you'll find operating system software and utility software. *Operating system software* is system software that controls your application software and manages how your hardware devices work together. Popular operating systems include Microsoft Windows (and all its variations), Mac OS, Linux (an open-source operating system), and Unix.

Utility software is software that provides additional functionality to your operating system software. Utility software includes anti-virus software, screen savers, uninstaller software (for properly removing unwanted software), file security software (which usually includes encryption), and a host of others. Again, in the extended learning module that follows this chapter, we discuss both hardware and software in greater detail.

UBIQUITOUS COMPUTING: DECENTRALIZED COMPUTING, SHARED INFORMATION, MOBILE COMPUTING, AND A WHOLE LOT MORE

The global business economy operates year-round, without regard to time, location, geographic boundaries, language, or culture. For any business to succeed, it must create a technology platform and infrastructure that operate in the same way. This has given rise to the notion of ***ubiquitous computing***—computing and technology support anytime, anywhere, with access to all needed information and all business partners always, both internal and external to the organization. Ubiquitous computing is not so much the technology; it is a concept about the technology, stressing that technology should enable you to work anywhere and anytime. To support the trend toward ubiquitous computing, the concepts of decentralized computing, shared information, and mobile computing are very important (see Figure 1.7).

Decentralized computing is an environment in which an organization distributes computing power and locates it in functional business areas as well as on the desktops of knowledge workers. This is possible because of the proliferation of less expensive, more powerful, and smaller systems including tablet PCs, notebooks, desktop computers, minicomputers, and servers. Equally important are technology infrastructures such as integrations and middleware that enable different computers and networks to communicate with each other and share information. You'll learn more about technology infrastructures in Chapter 7.

Shared information is an environment in which an organization's information is organized in one or more central locations, allowing anyone to access and use it as he or she needs to. Shared information enables people in the sales department, for example, to access work-in-progress manufacturing information to determine which products will be available to ship. At your school, the registrar's office can access the information within the financial aid office to determine how much of your tuition bill is covered by a scholarship or loan. To support shared information, most businesses organize information in the form of a database. In fact, databases have become the standard by which businesses organize their information and provide everyone access to it. We'll talk more about databases in a moment within the context of IT support for operational

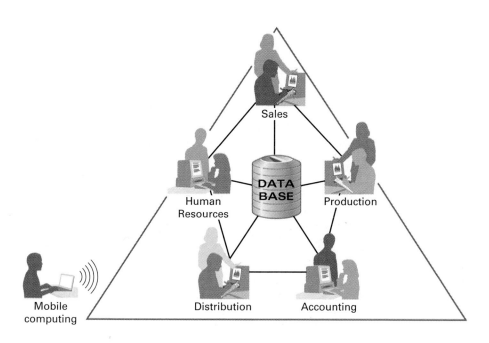

Figure 1.7

Decentralized Computing, Shared Information, and Mobile Computing excellence, and we've devoted all of Chapter 3, *Extended Learning Module C (Designing Databases and Entity-Relationship Diagramming)*, and *Extended Learning Module J (Implementing a Database with Microsoft Access)* to the topic of databases.

Finally, ***mobile computing*** is a broad term describing your ability to use technology to wirelessly connect to and use centrally located information and/or application software. Mobile computing is all about wireless connectivity. For example, ***m-commerce***, the term used to describe electronic commerce conducted over a wireless device such as a cell phone, PDA, or notebook, now gives you the ability to buy and sell stocks, check weather forecasts, download music, and read your e-mail while sitting in an airport waiting to catch a flight. Business is now global and knows no geographical boundaries. You need mobile computing and wireless access to information and software no matter where you are.

Creating the Business Vision for Information Technology

People, information, and information technology are the heart of management information systems. Your vision of how they will work together in a coordinated and integrated fashion will determine your organization's IT-enabled competitive advantage. A ***competitive advantage*** is providing a product or service in a way that customers value more than what the competition is able to do. IT can help you and your organization achieve and sustain competitive advantages. It is up to you to determine how to use IT in your organization to do so.

IT in and of itself is <u>not</u> a competitive advantage. IT can help your organization achieve a competitive advantage only when you place it and use it within the context of your business strategy and strategic vision. IT is an essential element—but only an element—of your strategic vision and the initiatives your organization chooses to undertake. You need to think carefully about the role of information technology in helping your organization achieve competitive advantage. It's up to you to decide what role information technology will play.

TOP LINE VERSUS BOTTOM LINE

A typical income statement for a business has two main parts: (1) revenues and (2) expenses (see Figure 1.8). Revenues are monies your organization receives from selling its

Figure 1.8

Competitive Advantage: Top Line versus Bottom Line

INCOME STATEMENT

Sales:		
_____	$_____	
_____	$_____	
_____	$_____	
Total Sales	$_____	

Top Line
Reach new customers, offer new products, cross-sell services, offer complementary products

Expenses:	
Cost of Goods Sold	$_____
Admin Expense	$_____
Payroll	$_____
Total Expenses	$_____

Bottom Line
Optimize manufacturing processes, decrease transportation costs, reduce cost of human capital, minimize errors in a process

A MORE "CUSTOMER-ORIENTED" INTERNAL REVENUE SERVICE

The Internal Revenue Service (IRS) of the United States is seldom seen as anyone's friend. IRS CIO Tom Grams wants to change that and has supervised numerous efforts over the past several years to become a "friend" to the taxpayer.

Most notably, Tom has led in several efforts to create customer self-service systems for taxpayers. In 2004 alone, the IRS Web site drew more than 800 million page visits, or approximately three visits for every man, woman, and child in the United States. In 2004, there were a total of 136.2 million individual tax returns filed with the IRS. Would you care to guess how many of those were filed online with the IRS's new self-service tax filing system? It may surprise you to learn that 52.7 million individual tax returns were filed online in 2004 (approximately 40 percent of all individual tax returns). Of that 52.7 million, 14.5 million were self-prepared by people with personal computers, with the remainder being filed by tax professionals. Tom hopes that percentage will top 80 percent in the year 2007. Those are astounding numbers, especially considering that tax filing online is still voluntary and will be so through 2007.

Another successful customer self-service system is called "Where's My Refund?" This self-service system allows taxpayers to track the status of their refund checks online. In 2004, the system handled almost 24 million inquiries online. According to Tom, "For every online inquiry about a refund, we've reduced the number of calls we would otherwise get by 1.5 to 2." That has allowed the IRS to redeploy those resources to more important issues and initiatives.

Booz Allen Hamilton, a consultant to the IRS, estimates that online filing in 2007—if the 80 percent number is achieved—could save the IRS and ultimately the taxpayers $243 million.[14]

products and services while expenses are the costs it incurs providing those products and services. From a competitive advantage point of view, you can use IT to focus on "top-line" (revenue) or "bottom-line" (cost) activities.

When focusing on the top line, your competitive advantage goal is to *increase revenues,* which can be achieved any number of ways—reaching new customer segments, offering new products, cross-selling related services, offering complementary products, just to name a few. Conversely, when focusing on the bottom line, your competitive advantage goal is to *minimize your expenses* in making your products or providing your services, which can be achieved in a number of ways as well—optimizing manufacturing processes, decreasing transportation costs, reducing the costs of human capital, minimizing errors in a process, again, just to name a few.

From an organizational point of view, you must form a business vision that addresses the role of IT in creating both top-line and bottom-line competitive advantages. You will never focus solely on one to the neglect of the other; rather, you will focus on some combination of the two, since they are means to the same end.

For example, you could use technology to implement a customer self-service system on the Web. A *customer self-service system* is an extension of a transaction processing system that places technology in the hands of an organization's customers and allows them to process their own transactions. (A *transaction processing system* or *TPS* is a system that processes transactions within an organization.) Online banking and ATMs are examples. With these bank customers have the ability to do their banking anywhere at anytime. They can check their account balances, move funds from one account to another, withdraw and deposit cash, pay bills electronically, and even request that the bank send a physical check to a business or another person.

Online banking and ATMs have allowed banks to minimize the costs associated with the delivery of these types of services. Thus, they have achieved bottom-line competitive advantages. At the same time, online banking and ATMs support top-line competitive advantage initiatives. Financial institutions use them to attract new customers. Many financial institutions now also offer various products such as stamps for sale through ATMs. Again, this is an example of using IT to focus on increasing revenues—by selling new products.

As you learn about various technologies in this book, ask yourself:

1. How can I apply these technologies in a business environment to help my organization focus on top-line competitive advantages?

2. How can I apply these technologies in a business environment to help my organization focus on bottom-line competitive advantages?

DATABASES IN SUPPORT OF COMPETITIVE ADVANTAGES

Minimizing costs, reducing costs, increasing market share, and offering new products and services all fall in the broad category of competitive advantages. In support of achieving these competitive advantages, all businesses use databases and database management systems (see Figure 1.9). Databases (which we focus on in Chapter 3, *Extended Learning Modules C* and *J*, and elsewhere) are large repositories of information that maintain tremendous detail on every transaction. Between databases and a TPS or customer self-service system is database management system (DBMS) software. DBMS software provides a bridge between a database (the information) and a software system (e.g., inventory management). It allows each different TPS and customer self-service system to access, use, and update the database information according to specific business rules.

Consider Amazon.com. Its world-renowned "1-Click ordering" customer self-service system on the Web provides a tremendous competitive advantage because of its ease of

Figure 1.9

Database Support for
Competitive Advantages

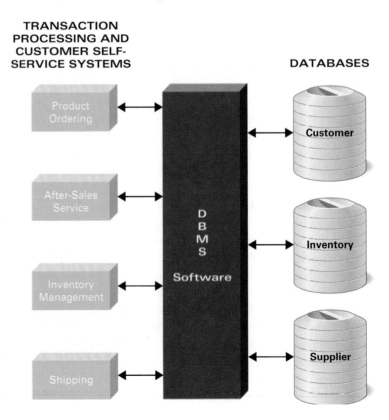

TRANSACTION PROCESSING AND CUSTOMER SELF-SERVICE SYSTEMS

DATABASES

Product Ordering

After-Sales Service

Inventory Management

Shipping

D B M S

Software

Customer

Inventory

Supplier

ordering, its filtering capabilities that match complementary products to your past purchases and that make recommendations concerning what might interest you, and its ability to maintain your billing and shipping information (so you're not forced to enter that information every time you make a purchase). Behind Amazon's customer self-service system is a large database that stores product information and information about your previous purchases along with DBMS software that gives you the ability to access and use that information.

Amazon has other systems as well—such as order fulfillment, inventory management, and supply chain management—that also use the DBMS software to access product and customer information. Together, all these systems provide Amazon with a competitive advantage in the fiercely competitive online retail environment.

Databases and DBMS software are not only tools for achieving organizational competitive advantage, they are vitally important tools for enabling your career success. If you read *Extended Learning Module K (Careers in Business),* you'll notice that a knowledge of databases, database design, and DBMS software is essential for almost every business discipline. So, it doesn't matter if you're majoring in finance, marketing, management, hospitality, or any other specialization, you need database and DBMS software skills. As educators, we believe that these tools are so important for your success that we've devoted the following parts of this textbook to databases and DBMS software:

- Chapter 3—databases and data warehouses.
- *Extended Learning Module C*—designing databases.
- *Extended Learning Module J*—implementing databases with Microsoft Access (on your CD).

In addition, you'll find that many of the Group Projects require you to build and/or use a database. We strongly encourage you to use this textbook to hone your skills in the area of databases.

SUPPORTING DECISION MAKING FOR COMPETITIVE ADVANTAGE

We have discussed transaction processing systems and customer self-service systems. These support the concept of *online transaction processing (OLTP),* the gathering of input information, processing that information, and updating existing information to reflect the gathered and processed information. The counterpart to OLTP is *online analytical processing (OLAP),* the manipulation of information to support decision making. Just as with the processing of transactions, information technology is an important enabler of the decision-making process in business.

Some business decisions are relatively easy to make while others are not. For example, deciding how many inventory units to reorder may be relatively easy (and structured using a reorder point algorithm), while deciding where to build a new distribution center may not be. In the case of the latter, you need to take into account numerous logistical issues, including proximity to major highways, proximity to a major airport, the workforce in a proposed area, tax incentives, and so on.

Technology to support decision making falls into one of two general categories: (1) systems that help you analyze a situation and then leave the decision entirely up to you and (2) systems that actually make some sort of recommendation concerning what action to take. The first category includes such IT tools as decision support systems and executive information systems. For example, an *executive information system (EIS)* is a highly interactive IT system that allows you to first view highly summarized information and then choose how you would like to see greater detail, which may alert you to potential

MANAGING KNOWLEDGE WITH A KNOWLEDGE MANAGEMENT SYSTEM

If you run a consulting business, you need any given consultant to know everything that all the other consultants know. As Peter Nevin, group information systems manager at Sinclair Knight Merz, explains it, "Our business demands we have a wealth of knowledge in our staff. If a consultant is facing a challenge, it's a fair bet somebody, somewhere in the company has come across a similar scenario before and can help."

Sinclair Knight Merz is one of Australia's leading global professional services consulting firms, with offices worldwide and up to 10,000 different active consulting jobs at any time. Peter realized that the company needed a Web-based knowledge management system, otherwise it would be almost impossible to identify the right people with the relevant past experience to provide knowledge on a new consulting project.

Sinclair Knight Merz's Web-based knowledge management system is called WiSE (Worldwide information Sharing Environment). WiSE allows any consultant to access the company's knowledge concerning previous projects. WiSE enables the company to support growth, share knowledge, increase and sustain its competitive advantage, and reduce project costs. Achieving those goals is what a knowledge management system is all about. If you can harness your organization's knowledge, you can succeed in the business world.[15]

problems or opportunities. In Figure 1.10, you can see three graphs that might appear in an EIS. The first one at the left shows sales by year. By clicking on a particular year, you can view sales by territory for that year. Then, by clicking on a particular territory, you can view sales by product line for that territory within a given year. These types of IT systems offer you great speed in massaging information, developing alternatives, and viewing information from various perspectives. They do not make a recommendation concerning what you should do, however.

When making important business decisions, the old adage of "two heads are better than one" definitely applies. In the business world, you'll work on a number of teams, performing processes and making decisions. In this instance, technology plays an important role by providing tools that allow teams of people to work together, sharing ideas and addressing problems and opportunities. Most notably, you'll be working with a *collaboration system,* a system that is designed specifically to improve the performance of teams by supporting the sharing and flow of information. Many of these systems support "anonymous voting." That is, you can post a possible alternative to solving a problem

Figure 1.10

Drilling Down with an Executive Information System (EIS)

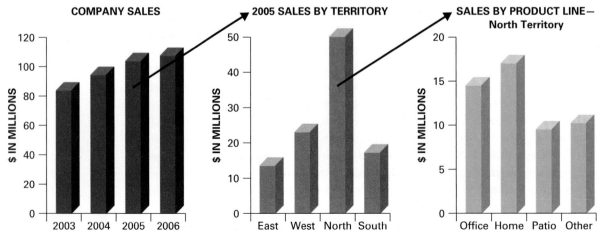

USING TECHNOLOGY WHEN MILLIONS OF POSSIBLE SOLUTIONS EXIST

Another important artificial intelligence tool is a genetic algorithm. A *genetic algorithm* is an artificial intelligence system that mimics the evolutionary, survival-of-the-fittest process to generate increasingly better solutions to a problem. Organizations apply genetic algorithms to problems for which (1) there are literally millions of possible solutions and (2) there is no appropriate problem-solving algorithm that will generate the perfect solution.

Consider the development of a new home area. Assume that someone has purchased a large parcel of land and intends to build 5,000 homes for residential sale. The task of laying out the design of the new home area is a daunting one. This is further complicated when having to determine how to optimally lay utility lines (fresh water lines, sewer lines, electrical lines, phone lines, gas lines, and cable TV lines). There are extensive sets of constraints concerning the laying of utility lines, but no simple algorithm that will help you find the right solution.

For example, depending on the grade of the terrain, fresh water and sewer lines must be sized to accommodate the slope of the terrain. And you can't run electrical or gas lines under a bridge. Furthermore, cable TV substations have to be positioned appropriately to ac-

commodate the use of high-speed cable TV modems. Those are just a few of the many considerations, never mind the most basic one of optimizing lot tracts to build the most homes while minimizing unused land.

Many residential home developers turn to a genetic algorithm for this problem. Once the genetic algorithm has been fed all the necessary information (maximum and minimum lot tract sizes, topographical information of the terrain, performance criteria for evaluating solutions, and so on), it sets out creating solutions. As it comes across a fairly good solution, it attempts to alter the solution (using evolutionary, survival-of-the-fittest processes such as crossover, selection, and mutation) to create a better one. Eventually, the genetic algorithm exhausts all possible solutions and makes a recommendation concerning the best one, given the constraints and performance criteria that were specified.

Of course, the decision is still yours to make. While a genetic algorithm can determine the best possible solution, you need to carefully analyze the solution and determine if it really is "best." Technology can make recommendations, but the ultimate decision is still yours. In the end, you receive either the credit for making a good decision or the reprimand for making a bad one.

and every team member can vote concerning whether they like the idea without specifying who they are. This helps teams develop innovative solutions and avoid such traps as "groupthink" or dominance by a particular team member. We'll talk more about EISs, collaboration systems, and other decision support technologies in Chapters 2 and 4.

The second category of decision support technologies (those that signal some action to take) includes technologies in the area of artificial intelligence. *Artificial intelligence (AI)* is the science of making machines imitate human thinking and behavior. For example, a neural network is an artificial intelligence system that is capable of finding and differentiating patterns within information. Your credit card company probably uses a neural network to monitor your card use and identify possible fraud in case someone else happened to steal your card and attempted to use it. In this instance, the neural network has been fed every single credit card transaction you've performed, and it has developed a pattern of how, when, and why you use your card. Then, when a transaction occurs that doesn't fit the pattern of your profile, the neural network alerts someone that your credit card may have been stolen. You may have, in fact, received a call from your credit card company to verify a transaction. If so, it was most likely a neural network that "sent up a red flag" concerning the transaction.

Artificial intelligence is growing in use every day in the business world. Although you may not be directly involved in the development of such tools, you will very likely use them sometimes. So, it's important that you understand to which situations you should apply each AI tool. We'll cover those issues and many more in Chapter 4.

PURSUING MAJOR BUSINESS INITIATIVES FOR COMPETITIVE ADVANTAGE

In creating a business vision for the use of IT, many organizations focus on major business initiatives such as customer relationship management, supply chain management, enterprise resource planning, sales force automation, and the like. These are all important and need IT support if they are to become competitive advantages for your organization.

Let's consider supply chain management. **Supply chain management (SCM)** tracks inventory and information among business processes and across companies. Therefore, a **supply chain management (SCM) system** is an IT system that supports supply chain management activities by automating the tracking of inventory and information among business processes and across companies. Consider the supply chain in Figure 1.11 and suppose your organization is a wholesaler of office furniture. You have customers—retail outlets such as Office Max and Office Depot. Those organizations have other customers, namely, businesses and individuals who purchase and use the office furniture. So, moving forward, your supply chain includes your customers and your customers' customers. Moving backward, your supply chain is even more extensive. You have distributing lines (e.g., truck and rail companies) that move products from manufacturers to you. You have manufacturers, and those manufacturers have suppliers of raw materials and suppliers of parts. So, your supply chain includes your suppliers and your suppliers' suppliers.

The goal of a comprehensive supply chain management system is to automate the flow of inventory and information across the entire supply chain. Ideally, your organization would use **electronic data interchange (EDI)**—the direct computer-to-computer transfer of transaction information contained in standard business documents, such as invoices and purchase orders, in a standard format—to order needed inventory from various manufacturers. Those electronic orders would trigger other systems within the manufacturing companies including the ordering of raw materials and parts from their suppliers and drop shipment schedules sent to the distributing lines. Likewise, when an end customer ordered furniture from a retail outlet, that retail outlet would communicate its needed inventory in similar fashion to your organization. To be effective and offer the greatest competitive advantage in the marketplace, all processes that move information (including the electronic transfer of funds to reconcile accounts) would be handled in an automated fashion by EDI within an SCM system.

Major business initiatives—including customer relationship management, supply chain management, business intelligence, and integrated collaboration environments—are the focus of Chapter 2.

Figure 1.11

Suppliers' Suppliers and Customers' Customers in a Supply Chain

RUN, GROW, AND TRANSFORM

A helpful conceptual framework for viewing the bigger organizational picture and determining the use of IT in support of competitive advantages is "Run-Grow-Transform" (RGT). The RGT framework allows you to allocate, in terms of percentages, how you will spend your IT dollars on various types of initiatives. If you're only interested in "business-as-usual," you would focus 100 percent of your IT dollars on "run" initiatives. If you wanted to transform your business in some way, you would allocate a certain percentage of your IT dollars to "transform" initiatives. The following are the aspects of the RGT framework:

- **Run**—optimizing the execution of activities and processes already in place.
- **Grow**—increasing market reach, product and service offerings, expanding market share, and so on.
- **Transform**—innovating business processes in a completely new way, moving into seemingly different markets, and so on.

You can consider "run" in the RGT framework to be very similar to bottom-line efforts and "grow" in the RGT framework to be very similar to top-line efforts toward achieving competitive advantage. Again, RGT is not technology but a way of thinking about how you can leverage technology.

The application of the RGT framework often depends on considerations of the maturity of the organization. A new venture start-up will often focus more of its efforts on the "grow" aspect, while a mature organization—with a well-defined and successful line of products and services—will often focus more of its efforts on the "run" aspect. In the latter instance, the organization may already be a market leader and want to ensure and sustain its competitive advantage through price and cost optimization.

Regardless of maturity, however, all organizations must focus on the *transformation* aspect. As you read in the opening case, information technology—specifically, disruptive technologies—often forces an entire industry to transform itself and the way it does business. Indeed, it will be interesting to watch as the recording industry transforms itself in the coming years from an album-based or CD-based music provider to a pay-per-tune music provider and as Blockbuster moves on from its "late fee" model.

Let's focus right now on just one organization—your organization—instead of an entire industry. In the business world, as is often said, if you're standing still, you're falling behind. It's a simple fact—your competition is always trying to do something better than you are. Therefore, your organization must constantly seek to evolve and, in most cases, to transform itself. Your organization can take a proactive approach to using technology to transform itself.

eBay is a good example. It was never content with being the world's premier online auction house. A few years ago, it acquired PayPal and began offering payment services to its buyers and sellers. In 2003, it began offering its own credit card, with its "Anything Points" program offering eBay members the ability to buy products and pay for seller services with points accumulated from using the credit card. The integration of PayPal into its auction format and the offering of a credit card are simply not possible without sophisticated IT systems.

General Motors (GM) is another good example. Many people believe that GM's core competency is production of automobiles. While that may be true, it makes more money financing automobiles (and other big-ticket items such as homes) than it does manufacturing them. Its financing business segment (GMAC) is now more profitable than the actual manufacturing and selling of automobiles. GM doesn't want you to pay cash for a car—it wants you to finance the purchase or lease the car through GMAC. Again, it requires extensive use of technology to create financing and leasing systems in the automotive industry.

AOL is another example. In March 2004, America Online (AOL) launched a streamlined new service for online bill payment.[16] Although it doesn't yet provide you with the capability to pay online bills directly through AOL, the initiative (called *AOL Bill Pay*) does seem to indicate that AOL is positioning itself to potentially transform itself from a pure Internet service provider (ISP) to an online bank in the future.

Like these examples, your organization too must constantly seek to transform itself. The highly competitive business environment necessitates this focus or evolving toward ever greater competitive advantage. IT can help.

Information Technology in Your Life

Information technology plays an important role in every aspect of your life. From a personal point of view, you probably use a home computer to surf the Web, talk through Instant Messaging to your friends all over the world, buy products, and search for information. In the business world, information technology is everywhere and inescapable. This text shows you what you need to know about information technology in the business world to effectively use it and manage it to be more efficient at what you do and to help your organization gain competitive advantage.

To help you better understand the types of technologies you will be dealing with in your future business career, we've created *Extended Learning Module K (Careers in Business)*. In *Module K*, we highlight the typical jobs in various functional areas such as accounting, finance, marketing, and real estate and construction management, and for every functional area we provide a list of the critical IT skills you need to gain while in school. *Extended Learning Module K* appears on the CD that accompanies your text. It's well worth your time to read through that module.

YOUR CAREER

No matter what career you choose, information technology will have a great impact. Just as no person or organization is an island, neither is any specific function within an organization ever isolated. All functions in an organization need to work together, sharing information to achieve the greatest possible competitive advantage.

Sharing information occurs through information technology, most notably decentralized computing, which we discussed in a previous section of the chapter. Powerful central information repositories or databases maintain a wealth of organizational information—everything from planned shipments of raw materials from suppliers to detailed information on customer inquiries, and perhaps complaints. If your customers consistently complain about the quality of a product, for instance, you need to be able to determine the cause of the problem, which may include looking at which supplier provided the raw materials that went into the production of the product, the production process itself such as which machines were used to produce the product, the salesperson who sold the product, and perhaps even how long the product sat in inventory before being sold.

So, clearly, you need to learn a variety of business information technology tools. Many of these tools (called *vertical market software*) are specific to a given industry, such as the health care industry. Others (called *horizontal market software*) are more general, including accounting software or customer relationship management which can be used in numerous industries.

As you work with organizational information, you'll have the opportunity to download parts of it to your personal technology environment. From there, you can explore

RESEARCHING YOUR CAREER AND INFORMATION TECHNOLOGY

To position yourself in the best possible way to succeed in the business world, you need to start researching your career right now. Here, we would like you to focus on the IT skills your career requires.

First, consider what career you want to have. Record that career in this box. Second, visit Monster.com (www.monster.com) and search for jobs that relate to

your career. Read through several of the job postings and determine what IT skills you need to acquire. Write down those skills in this box as well.

Finally, compare your findings to those of other students in your class interested in a similar career. Together, you should be able to create a comprehensive list of IT skills you need to be successful.

CAREER: _____

IT SKILLS

_____

_____

_____

_____

IT SKILLS

_____

_____

_____

_____

problems and opportunities by using personal productivity tools such as spreadsheet and database management system software. Your ability to use these personal productivity tools effectively will, in part, define your career success. We would encourage you to learn as much about these tools as you can. In this text, we've provided several extended learning modules to help you learn about the true productivity power of spreadsheet and database management system software.

In the business world, you'll be working with information technology, managing people, and most probably managing a budget. That doesn't mean you have to major in IT, human resource management, and finance. Information, people, and money pervade every aspect of business. You must learn to use and manage them well.

ETHICS, SECURITY, AND PRIVACY

As we close this first chapter, let's turn our attention back to ethics and to two extremely important IT topics—security and privacy.

We cannot stress enough how important it is for you to be ethical in your use of information and information technology. Even if you're not breaking the law, "shady" ethical acts can have a great impact on other people, and serious consequences for you. As a general rule of thumb when developing your ethical position, we encourage you to follow one simple rule—*Do unto others as you would have them do unto you.*

Unfortunately, you can't expect everyone to follow that rule, so you must be vigilant in protecting yourself, your information, and your technology tools. As we said earlier, the easy power of information tools today increases the odds they will be misused by some people, and not to guard your organization against bad actors out there is almost unethical in itself. You're probably familiar with viruses and worms, special types of software designed to do damage to your information and technology tools. You may also encounter *spyware* (also called *sneakware* or *stealthware*), malicious software that

DEVELOPING STRATEGIES FOR PROTECTING YOURSELF AGAINST IDENTITY THEFT

Identity theft is not something that happens to someone else. Almost 10 million people in the United States reported themselves as victims of identity theft in 2002—that's about one in every 29 people (even less when you take children out of the equation).

We ended the chapter with an initial short list of things you can do to protect yourself, your information, and your technology tools. As a group, focus on creating a comprehensive list of steps you can take to avoid identity theft. Write down the most important steps in the table provided below. To help you start, consider visiting these sites:

Federal Trade Commission—www.ftc.gov

Identity Theft Prevention and Survival—www.identitytheft.org

MSN's MoneyCentral—moneycentral.msn.com (search on Financial Privacy)

Identity Theft Resource Center—www.idtheftcenter.org

1.	6.
2.	7.
3.	8.
4.	9.
5.	10.

collects information about you and your computer and reports it to someone else without your permission. Spyware can invade your privacy, collect information about you, and send it—via the Internet—to an organization that might later sell that information. According to one study, the incidents of detected spyware (and *adware*, another type of menacing software) rose from about 500,000 in August 2003 to almost 11.5 million in March 2004.[17]

Perhaps the greatest threat today (and on the horizon) to your personal safety in cyberspace is identity theft. **Identity theft** is the forging of someone's identity for the purpose of fraud. If you become a victim of identity theft, the "thief" will steal and use your credit cards, driver's license, and numerous other forms of identification. In today's IT-based and often virtual world, the thief has only to steal the information associated with those forms of identifications, not the actual documents themselves.

In 2003, financial losses from identity theft were estimated to be approximately $100 billion in the United States and $300 billion worldwide. Those are astounding numbers, but pale in comparison to what many experts are predicting for 2005—$1.8 trillion in the United States and almost $5 trillion worldwide.[18]

It is crucially important that you protect yourself, your information, and your technology tools. For starters, here are a few things to keep in mind (there are many more):

- Keep your anti-virus software up to date.
- Use only secure Web sites when submitting personal or financial information.
- Never give out your personal information to enter a contest on the Internet.
- Change your passwords frequently and intersperse capital letters and digits in them.
- Never assume that everyone has the same ethical standards you do.

Summary: Student Learning Outcomes Revisited

1. **Define management information systems (MIS) and information technology (IT) and describe their relationship.** *Management information systems (MIS)* deals with the planning for, development, management, and use of information technology tools to help people perform all tasks related to information processing and management. *Information technology (IT)* is any computer-based tool that people use to work with information and support the information and information-processing needs of an organization. IT is one of the three key elements, along with people and information, of management information systems.

2. **Validate information as a key resource and describe both personal and organizational dimensions of information.** Information is one of the three key elements within MIS. We are in the "information age," a time when knowledge is power. Information is the foundation for business intelligence. The personal and organizational dimensions of information include

   - Personal
     - Time—Access to information when you need it and information that describes the time period you're considering
     - Location—Access to information no matter where you are
     - Form—Information in a form that is most usable and understandable and information that is free of errors
   - Organizational
     - Information flows—Up, down, horizontal, and inward/outward
     - *Granularity*—The extent of detail within information
     - What information describes—*Internal* (specific operational aspects), *external* (the surrounding environment), *objective* (quantifiably known), and *subjective* (something unknown)

3. **Explain why people are the most important organizational resource, define their information and technology literacy** challenges, and discuss their ethical responsibilities. People are the single most important resource in any organization, setting goals, carrying out tasks, and making decisions.

   - *Technology-literate knowledge workers* are people who know how and when to apply technology.
   - *Information-literate knowledge workers* (1) can define what information they need; (2) know how and where to obtain that information; (3) understand the information once they receive it; and (4) can act appropriately based on the information.
   - Most important, knowledge workers must be ethical. *Ethics* are the principals and standards that guide our behavior toward other people.

4. **Describe the important characteristics of information technology (IT) as a key organizational resource.** Information technology is a set of tools you use to work with information. All technology is either *hardware* (the physical devices that make up a computer) or *software* (the set of instructions that your hardware executes).

5. **Define competitive advantage and illustrate the role of information technology in supporting competitive advantages and business vision.** A competitive advantage results when you provide a product or service in a way that customers value more than what your competition is able to provide. IT support:

   - Top-line—increase revenues through IT
   - Bottom-line—decrease costs/expenses through IT
   - Databases and DBMS software—for tracking vast amounts of information
   - Support decision making—IT systems for analyzing situations and sometimes recommending a course of action
   - Major business initiatives—supporting supply chain management, customer relationship management, and others
   - Transformation—IT support enabling an organization to transform itself in dramatic ways

6. **Discuss the impacts information technology can and will have on your life.** Technology is everywhere in the business world. For your career, you need to learn to use technology tools specific to your job and industry and personal productivity tools. You also need to protect yourself, your technology, and your information in cyberspace. The issues of security and privacy are vitally important.

CLOSING CASE STUDY ONE

YOU AND YOUR INFORMATION

No matter what you do or where you go, your information travels with you and is eventually captured and stored by a number of organizations. In this all-encompassing information and IT environment, let's consider two issues: trust and accuracy. As you'll see, both are related.

First, answer the questions below (with a simple *yes* or *no*), which pertain to your everyday life.

1. Do you keep a paper record of all your long-distance phone calls—when you placed them by date and time, to whom, and the length—and then compare that list to your monthly phone bill?

   Yes ☐ No ☐

2. Do you meet with the meter reader to verify the correct reading of your water, gas, or electricity usage?

   Yes ☐ No ☐

3. As you shop, do you keep a record of the prices of your groceries and then compare that record to the register receipt?

   Yes ☐ No ☐

4. Do you frequently ask to see your doctor's medical record on you to ensure that it's accurate?

   Yes ☐ No ☐

5. When you receive a tuition bill, do you pull out your calculator, add up the amounts, and verify that the total is correct?

   Yes ☐ No ☐

6. Have you ever purchased a credit report on yourself to make sure your credit information is accurate?

   Yes ☐ No ☐

7. Have you ever called the police department to verify that no outstanding traffic violations have been inadvertently assigned to you?

   Yes ☐ No ☐

8. Do you count your coin change when you receive it from a store clerk?

   Yes ☐ No ☐

9. Do you verify your credit card balance by keeping all your credit card receipts and then matching them to charges on your statement?

   Yes ☐ No ☐

10. Do you keep all your paycheck stubs to verify that the amounts on your W-2 form at the end of the year are accurate?

    Yes ☐ No ☐

How many of these questions did you answer *yes?* How many did you answer *no?* More than likely, you probably answered no to almost all the questions (if not all of them). What does that say about your trust that organizations are maintaining accurate information about you? Well, it basically says that you trust organizations to keep accurate information about you. The real question is—Is that necessarily the case?

Now answer the following questions which relate to the level of confidence organizations have in the accuracy of information that *you* give *them.*

1. When interviewing with potential employers, do they take your word that you have a college degree?

   Yes ☐ No ☐

2. If you deposit several checks into your checking account at once, does the bank trust you to correctly add the amounts?

   Yes ☐ No ☐

3. When you register for a class that has a prerequisite, does your school assume that you have actually taken the prerequisite class?

   Yes ☐ No ☐

4. When you make a deposit at an ATM and enter the amount, does the bank assume that you entered the correct amount?

   Yes ☐ No ☐

5. When you're buying a house and negotiating a loan, does the bank assume that the price you're paying for the house is correct and not inflated?

   Yes ☐ No ☐

6. When insuring your car, does the insurance company assume that you have a good driving record?

   Yes ☐ No ☐

7. When you apply for a parking permit at your school, does it assume that the car belongs to you?

   Yes ☐ No ☐

8. When you file your taxes, does the IRS assume that you've correctly reported all your income over the past year?

   Yes ☐ No ☐

The answer to each of these questions is probably *no.* And what does that say about the extent to which organizations trust you to provide accurate information? In this instance, it may not be strictly a matter of trust. Organizations today can't afford to have dirty information—information that's not accurate. Because organizations base so many of their decisions on information, inaccurate information creates a real problem that may equate to inefficient processes and lost revenue.

So, on the one side, you're probably very trusting in your assumptions that organizations are maintaining accurate information about you. On the other side, organizations don't really depend on you to provide accurate information.

Questions

1. Should you really trust organizations to maintain accurate information about you? In many instances, is it even worth your time and energy to verify the accuracy of that information?

2. What other examples can you think of in which you simply trust that your information is accurate? What other examples can you think of in which specific organizations don't assume that you're providing accurate information?

3. What sort of impact will cyberspace business have on the issues of trust and accuracy? Will it become easier or more difficult for cyberspace business to assume that you're providing accurate information? Will you trust cyberspace business to maintain your information more accurately than traditional organizations?

4. What are the ethical issues involved in organizations sharing information about you? In some instances it may be okay and in your best interest. But what if the shared information about you is inaccurate? What damage could it cause? What recourse do you have, if any?

5. It's a real dilemma: Most people think that credit card offerers charge extremely high interest rates. But how many people do you know who actually go through the process of calculating their average daily balances, applying the interest rates, and then verifying that the interest charged on their accounts is correct? Why do people complain that they are being charged excessive interest rates and then fail to check the accuracy of the interest calculations?

6. What about the future? As more organizations maintain even more information about you, should you become more concerned about its accuracy? Why or why not?

CLOSING CASE STUDY TWO

TECHNOLOGY METRICS—MEASURING EFFICIENCY AND EFFECTIVENESS

The largest organization in the world undergoing transformation because of information technology is the U.S. government. According to the President's Management Agenda (PMA), one of the top five federal government initiatives is expanded electronic government, an initiative that focuses on transforming the government into a click-and-mortar enterprise.

According to Nielsen Net Ratings in August 2004, the U.S. government ranked sixth among the most popularly visited sites, behind Microsoft, Time Warner (AOL), Yahoo!, Google, and eBay but ahead of the likes of Lycos, Walt Disney, RealNetworks, Amazon, and even Ask Jeeves. With populations now flocking to various government sites, the U.S. government has turned its attention to transformational activities using information technology.

An important question that any organization must ask when undertaking transformation is the extent to which the transformation is successful. To address that, you must be able to measure the success. Here, you can use two different types of metrics—efficiency metrics and effectiveness metrics. *Efficiency* metrics deal with

measuring "doing things right," that is, how efficient you are in using resources, decreasing processing time, decreasing downtimes, decreasing costs, and decreasing errors. *Effectiveness* metrics deal with measuring "doing the right things," that is, how effective you are at achieving your initiatives, increasing your customer base, expanding your market share, and so on.

In 2002 and 2003, two interesting reports revealed dramatic differences in the efficiency and effectiveness of the U.S. government as it undertook its click-and-mortar transformation (see the accompanying table). The first report was presented by the United Nations, which ranked the United States first in terms of efficiency. Metrics here included number of computers per 100 citizens, number of Internet hosts per 1,000 citizens, the percentage of population online, the number of telephone lines per 100 citizens, a human development index (technology literacy of citizens), and an information access index (the ease with which government information can be found).

The second report was released by Accenture. Accenture's research focused on citizen satisfaction with the provision of government services via the Internet. Customer satisfaction is an important metric tool for measuring effectiveness. The research concluded that Canada ranked first and the United States third. Metrics here included the extent to which the government was performing customer relationship management, the maturity level of delivering services electronically, the number of multichannel service delivery options, and the extent to which agencies within the government shared citizen information.[19,20,21]

Comparing Governments by Efficiency and Effectiveness

Efficiency Rankings	Effectiveness Rankings
1. United States	1. Canada
2. Australia	2. Singapore
3. New Zealand	3. United States
4. Singapore	4. Denmark
5. Norway	5. Australia
6. Canada	6. Finland
7. United Kingdom	7. Hong Kong
8. Netherlands	8. United Kingdom
9. Denmark	9. Germany
10. Germany	10. Ireland

Questions

1. Consider the relationship between efficiency and effectiveness. In mathematical terms, efficiency is necessary and effectiveness is sufficient. That is, you must be efficient in your transformational activities but that efficiency doesn't necessarily mean that you'll be successful. As well, your transformational activities must be effective and can really only

be effective if you're also efficient. Discuss how the United States can be ranked first in terms of efficiency but only third in terms of effectiveness.

2. The portal for the United States government is FirstGov (www.firstgov.gov). Visit that site and review the services provided to citizens. What sort of services is the government providing online to its citizens? Were you aware that all of these services were available on the Internet? Which services are you currently using online? Which services do you see as being beneficial? Will you start to use them? Why or why not?

3. What must the United States government do to become more effective in its electronic delivery of services?

4. Using any of the Industry or Global perspectives in this chapter, develop a set of efficiency and effectiveness metrics for assessing the success of the discussed initiative. How could being efficient not necessarily imply that your chosen organization will be successful?

5. What metrics would you use to measure such concepts as "anywhere" and "anytime"? How could you gather information to use in support of the development of those metrics?

Key Terms and Concepts

Application software, 16
Artificial intelligence (AI), 23
Business intelligence (BI), 6
Central processing unit (CPU), 16
Collaboration system, 22
Competitive advantage, 18
Customer self-service system, 19
Data, 6
Decentralized computing, 17
Electronic data interchange (EDI), 24
Ethics, 13
Executive information system (EIS), 21
External information, 9
Genetic algorithm, 23
Hardware, 15
Identity theft, 28
Information, 6
Information age, 4
Information granularity, 9

Information-literate knowledge worker, 11
Information technology (IT), 4
Input device, 15
Internal information, 9
Intranet, 7
Knowledge worker, 4
Management information systems (MIS), 4
M-commerce, 18
Mobile computing, 18
Objective information, 9
Online analytical processing, (OLAP), 21
Online transaction processing (OLTP), 21
Operating system software, 16
Operational management, 18
Output device, 16
Random access memory (RAM), 16

Shared information, 17
Software, 15
Spyware (sneakware or stealthware), 27
Storage device, 16
Strategic management, 8
Subjective information, 9
Supply chain management (SCM), 24
Supply chain management (SCM) system, 24
System software, 16
Tactical management, 8
Technology-literate knowledge worker, 11
Telecommunications device, 16
Telecommuting, 5
Transaction processing system (TPS), 19
Ubiquitous computing, 17
Utility software, 16

Short-Answer Questions

1. How does a knowledge worker differ from other types of workers?
2. What are the three key resources of management information systems (MIS)?
3. What is telecommuting? What new challenges does telecommuting pose for businesses?
4. How are data, information, and business intelligence related?
5. What are the personal dimensions of information?

6. What are the four types of information flows in an organization?
7. What is information granularity? How does it relate to the levels of an organization?
8. What are the four types of information according to what information describes?
9. How are information-literate knowledge workers and technology-literate knowledge workers different and how are they similar?

10. What are ethics? Why are ethics so important?
11. What are the key categories of information technology?
12. What is ubiquitous computing? What is the relationship between decentralized computing and shared information?
13. What are mobile computing and m-commerce?
14. How do top-line and bottom-line focuses on competitive advantage differ? How can IT support them?
15. In what ways are the Run-Growth-Transform conceptual framework and top-line/bottom-line competitive initiatives similar to each other?
16. What are the roles of technology in support of decision making?
17. What is spyware and what is identity theft? How can you protect yourself, your technology, and your information in cyberspace?

Assignments and Exercises

1. **INTERNAL, EXTERNAL, OBJECTIVE, AND SUBJECTIVE INFORMATION** Consider a local video rental store. It must make a decision regarding how many copies of a new video rental release to carry in its inventory. In making this decision, the video rental store will use a variety of specific information, all of which will be internal, external, objective, subjective, or some combination of the four. Complete the table below by identifying specific pieces of information that the video rental store would use in making such a decision—list each piece of information in the left column. In the remaining four columns, place appropriate check marks to designate the information as internal, external, objective, subjective, or some combination of the four.

INFORMATION	INTERNAL	EXTERNAL	OBJECTIVE	SUBJECTIVE

2. **SURVEYING GLOBAL INFORMATION TECHNOLOGY** The Central Intelligence Agency (CIA) of the U.S. federal government gathers and publishes worldwide information on a variety of topics by country including information technology. Go to the CIA's Web site (www.cia.gov) and click on **The World Factbook**. On the page that appears, click on **Search** *The World Factbook* and enter **Internet Service Provider** as a search term. You will find a listing of every country in the world. Select 10 countries from different parts of the world and review the section for each called Communications. For each country, enter the number of Internet hosts, number of Internet service providers, and number of Internet users into a spreadsheet. If you wanted to become an ISP, which country would you choose? Why? Be creative here and use your spreadsheet software to perform different analyses of the information.

3. **CREATING A SAFE HAVEN FOR CHILDREN ON THE INTERNET** There is growing concern that children should be able to surf the Internet without danger of having their personal information collected and distributed without parental consent and/or knowledge. Connect to TRUSTe (www.truste.org) and review its Children's Privacy Seal Program requirements. Prepare a short report/presentation concerning the social responsibility of a Web site owner in not collecting and distributing information on children.

4. **REVIEWING THE 100 BEST COMPANIES TO WORK FOR** Each year *Fortune* magazine devotes an issue to the top 100 best companies to work for. Find the most recent issue of *Fortune* that does this (or visit its Web site at www.fortune.com). First, develop a numerical summary that describes the 100 companies in terms of their respective industries. Which industries are the most dominant? Pick one of the more dominant industries (preferably one in which you would like to work) and choose a specific highlighted company. Prepare a short class presentation on why that company is among the 100 best to work for.

Discussion Questions

1. Knowledge workers dominate today's business environment. However, many industries still need workers who do not fall into the category of knowledge workers. What industries still need skilled workers who are not knowledge workers? Can you see a time when these jobs will be replaced by knowledge workers? Can you envision circumstances that would actually cause an economy to do an "about-face" and begin needing more non–knowledge skilled workers than knowledge workers?

2. The three key resources in management information systems (MIS) are information, information technology, and people. Which of these three resources is the most important? Why? The least important? Why?

3. Telecommuting is like everything else: it has a good side and it has a bad side. What are some of the disadvantages or pitfalls of telecommuting? How can these be avoided?

4. As an information-literate knowledge worker for a local distributor of imported foods and spices, you've been asked to prepare a customer mailing list that will be sold to international cuisine restaurants in your area. If you do so, will you be acting ethically? Suppose you don't consider the proposal ethical. What will you do if your boss threatens to fire you if you don't prepare the list? Do you believe you would have any legal recourse if you didn't prepare the list and were subsequently fired?

5. Consider the ATM system that is now worldwide. How does it address your personal dimensions of time, location, and form? Besides just tracking what transactions you've completed using an ATM, what other information might your bank want to know and use concerning your use of the ATM system?

6. In addition to using neural networks to monitor credit card fraud, the same companies also use neural networks to determine whether or not you are creditworthy. By feeding in thousands of credit card applications, the neural network develops a pattern of who is and who isn't creditworthy. Basically, the neural network compares your credit application to those of past ones and recommends an action. What do you think about that? Should you be given or denied a credit card based on what others have done (or failed to do)? Why or why not?

7. Many schools use collaboration systems to offer distance learning classes. Instead of going to class, you communicate with your instructors and classmates via technology. Would you like to take distance learning classes? What are the advantages? Can you learn as much without going to class and personally interacting with your instructor and classmates? What might be some of the disadvantages of distance learning? Is there a happy medium? How about going to school for only one class session per week and then attending the others virtually via technology? Is distance learning a good or bad idea?

8. We often say that hardware is the *physical* interface to a technology system while software is the *intellectual* interface. How is your hardware your physical interface to your computer? How is your software your intellectual interface to your computer? Do you see technology progressing to the point that we may no longer distinguish between hardware and software and thus no longer perceive differing physical and intellectual interfaces?

Using the Internet as a Tool to Find a Job

Are you taking advantage of the Internet to find a job? Locate an internship? Learn about interviewing and negotiating skills? We'd like to help you learn how. Complete the project on this page and the next and visit the Web site for this text (www.mhhe.com/ haag, select "Electronic Commerce Projects") to find approximately 100 valuable links for using the Internet as a tool to find a job.

JOB DATABASES

There are, quite literally, thousands of sites that provide you with databases of job postings. Some are better than others. Some focus on specific industries, others offer postings for only executive managers.

Think for a moment about the job you want. What would be its title? In which industry do you want to work? In what part of the country do you want to work? Connect to a couple of different databases, search for your job, and answer the following questions for each database.

A. What is the date of the last update?

B. Are career opportunities abroad listed as a separate category or are they integrated with domestic jobs?

C. Can you search for a specific organization?

D. Can you search by geographic location? If so, how? By state? By city? By zip code?

E. Can you apply for a position online? If so, how do you submit your résumé?

CREATING AND POSTING AN ELECTRONIC RÉSUMÉ

Most, if not all, job databases focus on two groups: employers and employees. As a potential employee, you search to find jobs that meet your qualifications and desires. Likewise, employers search job databases that contain résumés so they can find people (like you) who meet their qualifications and desires. In this instance, you need to build an electronic résumé (or e-portfolio, which we discuss in *Extended Learning Module I*) and leave it at the various job database sites as you perform your searches. That way, organizations performing searches can find you.

Most job database sites give you the ability to create and post an electronic résumé. Visit two job database sites (different from those you visited to find a job). In each, go through the process of creating an e-résumé, posting it, and making some sort of modifications to it. As you do, answer the following questions for each of the sites.

A. Do you have to register as a user to build an e-résumé?

B. Once a potential employer performs a search that matches your e-résumé, how can that employer contact you?

C. What five valuable tips for building a good e-résumé are available?

D. Once you build your e-résumé, can you use it to perform a job search?

E. When you modify your e-résumé, can you update your existing e-résumé or must you delete the old one and create a new one?

F. How many key terms concerning your qualifications can you include in your e-résumé?

G. For what time frame does your e-résumé stay active?

LOCATING THAT "ALL IMPORTANT" INTERNSHIP

Have you ever noticed that a large number of jobs require expertise? That being the case, how does someone gain relevant experience through a job when experience is required to get the job? As it turns out, that has always been a perplexing dilemma for many college students, and one way to solve it is by obtaining an internship. Internships provide you with valuable knowledge about your field, pay you for your work, and offer you that valuable experience you need to move up in your career.

On the Web site for this text (www.mhhe.com/haag, select "Electronic Commerce Projects"), we have provided you with a number of Web sites that offer internship possibilities—visit a few of them. Do you find any internships in line with your career? What about pay? Do you find both paying and nonpaying internships? How do these internship sites compare to the more traditional job database sites you looked at earlier? Why do you think this is true?

INTERVIEWING AND NEGOTIATING

The Internet is a vast repository of information—no doubt more information than you'll ever need in your entire life. During the job search process, however, the Internet can offer you very valuable specific information. In the area of interviewing and negotiating, for example, the Internet contains more than 5,000 sites devoted to interviewing skills, negotiating tips, and the like.

Interviewing and negotiating are just as important as searching for a job. Once you line up that first important interview, you may still not land the job if you're not properly prepared. If you do receive a job offer, you may be surprised to know that you can negotiate such things as moving expenses, signing bonuses, and allowances for technology in your home.

We've provided Web sites for you that address the interviewing and negotiating skills you need in today's marketplace. Review some of these sites (and any others that you may find). Then, develop a list of do's and don'ts for the interviewing process. Finally, develop a list of tips that seem helpful to you that will increase your effectiveness during the negotiation process. Once you've developed these two lists, prepare a short class presentation.

EXTENDED LEARNING MODULE A

COMPUTER HARDWARE AND SOFTWARE

Student Learning Outcomes

1. DEFINE INFORMATION TECHNOLOGY (IT) AND ITS TWO BASIC CATEGORIES: HARDWARE AND SOFTWARE.

2. DESCRIBE THE CATEGORIES OF COMPUTERS BASED ON SIZE.

3. COMPARE THE ROLES OF PERSONAL PRODUCTIVITY, VERTICAL MARKET, AND HORIZONTAL MARKET SOFTWARE.

4. DESCRIBE THE ROLES OF OPERATING SYSTEM AND UTILITY SOFTWARE AS COMPONENTS OF SYSTEM SOFTWARE.

5. DEFINE THE PURPOSE OF EACH OF THE SIX MAJOR CATEGORIES OF HARDWARE.

Introduction

In this extended learning module, we cover the basics of computer hardware and software, including terminology, characteristics of various devices, and how all the parts work together to create a complete and usable computer system. If you've had a previous computing concepts course, this material will be a quick, solid review for you. If this is your first real exposure to hardware and software technologies, you'll definitely learn a great deal from this module.

Information technology (IT) is any computer-based tool that people use to work with information and support the information and information-processing needs of an organization. So information technology (IT) includes the Internet, a personal computer, a cell phone that can access the Web, a personal digital assistant you use for note taking and appointment scheduling, presentation software you use to create a slide show, a printer, a joystick or gamepad for playing video games . . . the list is almost endless (see Figure A.1).

Figure A.1

Information Technology (IT) Includes Many Tools

All of these technologies help you perform specific information-processing tasks. For example, a printer allows you to create a paper version of a document, the Internet connects you to people all over the world, a CD allows you to store information for use at a later time, and word processing software helps you create letters, memos, and term papers.

So, do you need all these various technologies? Yes and no. As you read this module, you'll see categories of both hardware and software. More than likely, you'll need something from each category. But you certainly won't need every one.

A Quick Tour of Technology

There are two basic categories of information technology: hardware and software. **Hardware** consists of the physical devices that make up a computer (often referred to as a *computer system*). **Software** is the set of instructions that your hardware executes to carry out a specific task for you. If you create a graph, you use various hardware devices such as a keyboard to enter information and a monitor to see the graph, and you use software such as Microsoft Excel to create the graph.

All hardware falls into one of six categories. Here's a quick summary (see Figure A.2).

Figure A.2

Six Categories of Computer Hardware

Mice and keyboards are the most popular input devices. This keyboard has a fingerprint scanner.

CDs are common storage media.

The Pentium M is a CPU.

A cable modem allows you to access the Internet.

A video card connects a monitor to the motherboard inside the system unit.

A monitor is an output device.

1. Input: *Input devices* are tools you use to enter information and commands.

2. Output: *Output devices* are tools you use to see, hear, or otherwise recognize the results of your information-processing requests.

3. Storage: *Storage devices* are tools you use to store information for use at a later time.

4. Processing: The *central processing unit (CPU)* is the actual hardware that interprets and executes the software instructions and coordinates the operation of all other hardware. *RAM,* or *random access memory,* is a temporary holding area for the information you're working with, as well as the system and application software instructions that the CPU currently needs.

5. Telecommunications: A *telecommunications device* is a tool you use to send information to and receive it from another person or computer in a network. Telecommunications, as a field, and its associated devices is so broad that we've devoted an entire module to the topic. Please read *Extended Learning Module E* to learn about cable and DSL modems, home networks, fiber optics, and much more.

6. Connecting: Connecting devices include such things as USB ports into which you would connect a printer and connector cords to connect your printer to the parallel port.

The two main types of software are application and system software. *Application software* is the software that enables you to solve specific problems or perform specific tasks (see Figure A.3). Microsoft PowerPoint, for example, can help you create slides for

Figure A.3

PhotoShop and Excel Are Application Software Tools

With Excel you can manipulate numeric and label information. You can also create various types of charts and graphs with the numerical values.

a presentation, so it's application software. Microsoft FrontPage is an example of application software because it helps you create and publish a Web page or Web site. A business would use payroll software, collaborative software such as videoconferencing, and inventory management software.

System software handles tasks specific to technology management and coordinates the interaction of all technology devices. System software includes both operating system software and utility software. *Operating system software* is system software that controls your application software and manages how your hardware devices work together. Popular personal operating system software includes Microsoft Windows, Mac OS (for Apple computers), and Linux (an open-source operating system). There are also operating systems for networks (Microsoft Windows Server is an example), operating systems for personal digital assistants (Windows Mobile is an example), and operating systems for just about every other type of technology configuration, even for refrigerators.

Utility software is software that provides additional functionality to your operating system software. Utility software includes anti-virus software, screen savers, spam blocker software, uninstaller software (for properly removing unwanted software), and a host of other types. Some types of utility software are nice to have, like screen savers, while others are essential. For example, anti-virus software protects you from computer viruses that can be deadly for your computer. You definitely need anti-virus software.

This ends our quick tour of technology. In the remainder of this module we'll explore categories of computers by size, software in more detail, and hardware in more detail.

Categories of Computers by Size

Computers come in different shapes, sizes, and colors. Some are small enough that you can carry them around with you, while others are the size of a family refrigerator. Size is usually related to power and speed, and thus price (see Figure A.4).

PERSONAL DIGITAL ASSISTANTS (PDAS)

A *personal digital assistant (PDA)* is a small handheld computer that helps you surf the Web and perform simple tasks such as note taking, calendaring, appointment scheduling, and maintaining an address book. Most PDA screens are touch sensitive, allowing you to write directly on the screen, with the screen capturing what you're writing. PDAs offer a variety of operating system software; some use Windows CE (which stands for Compact Edition) or Palm OS (specifically for Palm devices). PDAs today cost between $100 and $500, depending on capabilities and features.

TABLET PCS

A *tablet PC* is a pen-based computer that provides the screen capabilities of a PDA with the functional capabilities of a notebook or desktop computer. Similar to PDAs, tablet PCs allow you to use a writing pen or stylus to write notes on the screen and touch the screen to perform functions such as clicking on a link while visiting a Web site. Tablet PCs come in two designs—convertibles and slates. Convertible tablet PCs look like notebook computers, including a screen that you lift up and set in position with a full keyboard and touch pad underneath. Using a convertible PC, you can swivel the screen and lay it flat on the keyboard, converting it into a notebook with no top that closes.

Slate tablet PCs come with no integrated physical keyboard, making the tablet the entire computer. You can buy a docking station for a slate tablet PC, giving you the ability to connect a keyboard and mouse.

Notebooks are fully functional portable personal computers.

PDAs are small handheld computers.

Tablet PCs have screens that swivel and lie flat on top of the system unit.

Some desktops are built especially for gaming.

Figure A.4

PDAs, Tablet PCs, Notebooks, and Desktops

NOTEBOOK COMPUTERS

A *notebook computer* is a small, portable, fully functional, battery-powered computer. Notebooks come equipped with all the technology you need to meet your personal needs and weigh as little as 3 pounds. If you need a fully functional computer in a variety of places—home, work, school, and/or on the road—then a notebook computer may be just the answer. Notebook computers range in price from about $600 to several thousand dollars depending on the selected configuration.

DESKTOP COMPUTERS

A *desktop computer* is the most popular choice for personal computing needs. You can choose a desktop computer with a horizontal system box (the box is where the CPU, RAM, and storage devices are held) or choose a desktop computer with a vertical system box (called a tower) that you usually place on the floor near your work area. Desktop computers range in price from a little less than $500 to several thousand dollars. Dollar for dollar with comparable characteristics, a desktop computer is faster and more powerful than a notebook computer.

Which one you need—PDA, tablet PC, notebook, or desktop computer—is a function of your unique individual needs. PDAs offer great portability and allow you to keep a calendar, send and receive e-mail, take short notes, and even access the Web. But they're not designed to help you write a term paper, build a Web site, or create a complex graph with statistical software. For these and more complex tasks, you would need a notebook, tablet PC, or a desktop computer.

So, the next question is, should you buy a notebook or a tablet PC? Most likely, you need a computer that supports full word processing, spreadsheet, presentation, Web site development, and some other capabilities. You need to decide where you'll need your computer. If you need to use your computer both at home and at school (or perhaps at work), then you should buy one of these because they are, in fact, portable. So, if you'd like to be able to surf the Web and get e-mail in your hotel room while on a business or vacation trip, a notebook computer or a tablet PC may be what you need.

In the future, we believe the capabilities of PDAs will improve so that you can in fact perform "complex" tasks such as creating an elaborate spreadsheet or graph and even integrating speech recognition. To learn more about some of today's best PDAs, connect to the Web site that supports this text at www.mhhe.com/haag.

MINICOMPUTERS, MAINFRAME COMPUTERS, AND SUPERCOMPUTERS

PDAs, notebooks, and desktop computers are designed to meet your personal information-processing needs. In business, however, many people often need to access and use the same computer simultaneously. In this case, businesses need computing technologies that multiple people (perhaps hundreds or even thousands) can access and use at the same time. Computers of this type include minicomputers, mainframe computers, and supercomputers (see Figure A.5).

A *minicomputer* (sometimes called a *mid-range computer*) is designed to meet the computing needs of several people simultaneously in a small to medium-size business environment. Minicomputers are more powerful than desktop computers but also cost

Figure A.5

Minicomputers, Mainframes, and Supercomputers

Minicomputers are well suited for small to medium-size businesses.

Mainframe computers support the information-processing tasks of large businesses.

Supercomputers are very expensive and fast number-crunching machines. They are usually scalable, meaning that you get as many units as you need and they work together on your processing tasks.

more, ranging in price from $5,000 to several hundred thousand dollars. Businesses often use minicomputers as servers, either for hosting a Web site or as an internal computer on which shared information and software is placed. For this reason, minicomputers are well suited for business environments in which people need to share common information, processing power, and/or certain peripheral devices such as high-quality, fast laser printers.

A *mainframe computer* (sometimes just called a *mainframe*) is a computer designed to meet the computing needs of hundreds of people in a large business environment. So mainframe computers are a step up in size, power, capability, and cost from minicomputers. Mainframes can easily cost in excess of $1 million. With processing speeds greater than 1 trillion instructions per second (compared to a typical desktop that can process approximately three billion instructions per second), mainframes can easily handle the processing requests of hundreds (or thousands) of people simultaneously.

A *supercomputer* is the fastest, most powerful, and most expensive type of computer. Organizations such as NASA and the National Weather Service that are heavily involved in research and "number crunching" employ supercomputers because of the speed with which they can process information. Very large, customer-oriented businesses such as General Motors and AT&T also employ supercomputers just to handle customer information and transaction processing. Their business needs require the high level of support and the powerful processing power provided by supercomputers.

How much do you really need to know about the technical specifics (CPU speed, storage disk capacity, and so on), prices, and capabilities of minicomputers, mainframe computers, and supercomputers? Probably not much, unless you plan to major in information technology. What you should concentrate on is the technical specifics, prices, and capabilities of PDAs, tablet PCs, notebooks, and desktop computers. These tools will be your companions for your entire business career. Learn about them and know them well—on an ongoing basis.

Software: Your Intellectual Interface

The most important tool in your technology tool set is software. Software contains the instructions that your hardware executes to perform an information-processing task for you. So, software is really your *intellectual interface,* designed to automate processing tasks. Without software, your computer is little more than a very expensive doorstop. As we've stated, there are two categories of software: application software and system software.

APPLICATION SOFTWARE

Application software is the software you use to meet your specific information-processing needs, including payroll, customer relationship management, project management, training, word processing, and many, many others. Application software can be categorized as either personal productivity software or vertical and horizontal market software.

PERSONAL PRODUCTIVITY SOFTWARE

Personal productivity software helps you perform personal tasks—such as writing a memo, creating a graph, and creating a slide presentation—that you can usually do even if you don't own a computer. You're probably already familiar with some personal productivity software tools including Microsoft Word, Microsoft Excel, Netscape Communicator, Mozilla Firefox, and Quicken (personal finance software).

Category	Examples*
Word processing—Helps you create papers, letters, memos, and other basic documents	• Microsoft Word • Corel WordPerfect
Spreadsheet—Helps you work primarily with numbers, including performing calculations and creating graphs	• Microsoft Excel • Corel Quattro Pro
Presentation—Helps you create and edit information that will appear in electronic slides	• Microsoft PowerPoint • Corel Presentations
Desktop publishing—Extends word processing software by including design and formatting techniques to enhance the layout and appearance of a document	• Microsoft Publisher • Quark QuarkXPress
Personal information management (PIM)—Helps you create and maintain (1) to-do lists, (2) appointments and calendars, and (3) points of contact	• Microsoft Outlook • Corel Central
Personal finance—Helps you maintain your checkbook, prepare a budget, track investments, monitor your credit card balances, and pay bills electronically	• Quicken Quicken • Microsoft Money
Web authoring—Helps you design and develop Web sites and pages that you publish on the Web	• Microsoft FrontPage • Macromedia Dreamweaver
Graphics—Helps you create and edit photos and art	• Microsoft PhotoDraw • Adobe PhotoShop
Communications—Helps you communicate with other people	• Microsoft Outlook • Internet Explorer
Database management system (DBMS)—Helps you specify the logical organization for a database and access and use the information within a database	• Microsoft Access • FileMaker FileMaker Pro

* Publisher name given first.

Figure A.6

Categories of Personal
Productivity Software

Three modules in this text help you learn how to use two of these tools—*Extended Learning Module D* (for Microsoft Excel, spreadsheet software), *Extended Learning Module J* (for Microsoft Access, database management system software), and *Extended Learning Module L* (for Microsoft FrontPage, Web authoring software). Figure A.6 describes the 10 major categories of personal productivity software and some of the more popular packages within each category.

VERTICAL AND HORIZONTAL MARKET SOFTWARE

While performing organizational processes in your career, you'll also frequently use two other categories of application software: vertical market software and horizontal market software.

Vertical market software is application software that is unique to a particular industry. For example, the health care industry has a variety of application software unique to that market segment, including radiology software, patient-scheduling software, nursing allocation software, and pharmaceutical software. Vertical market software is written specifically for an industry. Health care industry patient-scheduling software wouldn't work well for scheduling hair styling and manicure appointments in a beauty salon.

BUYING PERSONAL PRODUCTIVITY SOFTWARE SUITES

When you buy personal productivity software, we recommend that you do so in the form of a software suite. A *software suite* is bundled software (such as word processing, spreadsheet, and a DBMS) that comes from the same publisher and costs less than buying all the software pieces individually.

In this project, your team has two tasks. First, research the most popular personal productivity software suites. These include Microsoft Office, Corel WordPerfect Office, and LotusIBM SmartSuite. For each, identify which specific software pieces fall into the 10 cate-

gories of personal productivity software listed in Figure A.6. Then, try to find some information that describes the market share of each personal productivity software suite.

Second, choose one specific personal productivity software suite. Determine the individual price for each piece of software included in it. Now, perform a price comparison. How much cheaper is the entire suite? Can you think of a situation in which someone would buy the individual pieces as opposed to the entire suite? If so, please describe it.

Horizontal market software, on the other hand, is application software that is general enough to be suitable for use in a variety of industries. Examples of horizontal market software include

- Inventory management
- Payroll
- Accounts receivable
- Billing
- Invoice processing
- Human resource management

The preceding functions (and many others) are very similar, if not identical, across many different industries, enabling software publishers to develop one particular piece of software (e.g., accounts receivable) that can be used by many different industries.

Personal productivity software is actually a type of horizontal market software in that it is general enough to be suitable for use in a variety of industries. No matter what industry you work in, you need basic word processing software for creating memos, business plans, and other basic documents.

There are, however, some key differences between personal productivity software and horizontal (and vertical) market software. First is the issue of price. You can buy a full suite of personal productivity software for less than $400. In contrast, some individual horizontal and vertical market software packages may cost $500,000 or more. Second is the issue of customizability. When you purchase personal productivity software, you cannot change the way it works. That is, you're buying the right to use it but not to change how it operates. With horizontal and vertical market software you may be able to purchase the right to change the way the software works. So, if you find a payroll software package that fits most of your organizational needs, you can buy the software and the right to change the operation of the software so that it meets your needs precisely. This is a very common business practice when purchasing and using horizontal and vertical market software.

In Chapter 6 (Systems Development), we discuss how organizations go about the process of developing software for their particular needs, including how organizations can and do purchase vertical and horizontal market software and then customize that software.

SYSTEM SOFTWARE

System software supports your application software. System software controls how your various technology tools work together as you use your application software to perform specific information-processing tasks. System software includes two basic categories: operating system software and utility software.

OPERATING SYSTEM SOFTWARE

Operating system software is system software that controls your application software and manages how your hardware devices work together. For example, using Excel to create a graph, if you choose to print the graph, your operating system software takes over, ensures that you have a printer attached and that the printer has paper (and tells you if it doesn't), and sends your graph to the printer along with instructions on how to print it.

Your operating system software supports a variety of useful features, one of which is multitasking. *Multitasking* allows you to work with more than one piece of software at a time. Suppose you wanted to create a graph in Excel and insert it into a word processing document (see Figure A.7). With multitasking, you can have both pieces of application software open at the same time, and even see both on the screen. So, when you complete the creation of your graph, you can easily copy and paste it into your word processing document without having to exit the spreadsheet software and then start your word processing software.

There are different types of operating system software for personal environments and for organizational environments that support many users simultaneously. The latter, called *network operating systems* or *NOSs*, we explore in *Extended Learning Module E: Network Basics*. Popular *personal* operating systems include

- *Microsoft Windows XP Home*—Microsoft's latest personal computer operating system designed specifically for home users.
- *Microsoft Windows XP Professional (Windows XP Pro)*—Microsoft's latest personal computer operating system with enhanced features to support home users and business users.
- *Mac OS*—Apple's operating system.
- *Linux*—An open-source operating system that provides a rich operating environment for high-end workstations and network servers.

Figure A.7

Operating Systems
Support Multitasking

The task bar area tells
you what software you're
currently working with.

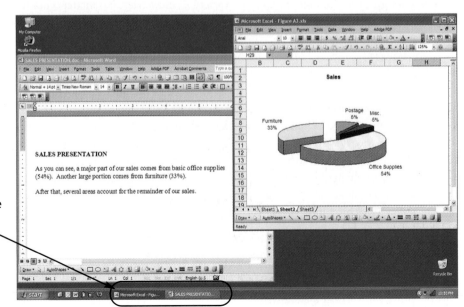

EVALUATING UTILITY SOFTWARE SUITES

Just as you can purchase personal productivity software suites that contain many pieces of software, you can also purchase utility software suites. In the table below, we've included the three most popular utility software suites: McAfee Office Pro, Norton SystemWorks, and Ontrack SystemSuite.

As a team, do some research and determine what major pieces of software are included in each. As you do, fill in the table.

Now, pick a particular utility suite and visit its Web site. What is the process for updating your software? Is it free? How often does the site recommend that you update your utility software?

Utility software piece	McAfee Office Pro	Norton SystemWorks	Ontrack SystemSuite

Open-source software is software for which the source code (how the software was actually written) is publicly available and free of charge. Unlike commercial software, open-source software is created and maintained by a distributed network of engineers, software developers, and users, each making contributions to the open-source software.

The advantages of open-source software are numerous. Because the source code is available, users of the software may modify the software to suit their needs and take comfort in the fact that changes they wish to make to the software are fully under their control. You can compare this with commercial, or closed-source, software, for which the customer must go to the vendor and pay for changes to be made and wait until the vendor has made those changes.

There are many examples of open-source software, including

- The Apache Web server
- Linux operating system
- MySQL, an open-source DBMS with commercial support

If you're considering purchasing a notebook computer that you'll use extensively at school connected to a network there, we recommend that you contact your school's technology support department to determine which operating system is best for you.

UTILITY SOFTWARE

Utility software adds functionality to your operating system software. Sometimes it is crucial. A simple example is screen saver software (which is probably also a part of your operating system). The most important utility software is anti-virus software. *Anti-virus software* is utility software that detects and removes or quarantines computer viruses. Viruses are everywhere today, with 200 to 300 new ones surfacing each month. Some viruses are benign: They do something annoying like causing your screen to go blank but do not corrupt your information. Other viruses are deadly, perhaps reformatting your hard disk or altering the contents of your files. You definitely need anti-virus software to protect your computer. We talk much more about this vitally important topic and guarding against possible attacks that can be launched against your computer from cyberspace in Chapter 8 and *Extended Learning Module H*.

Other types of utility software include

- *Crash-proof software*—Utility software that helps you save information if your system crashes and you're forced to turn it off and then back on again.
- *Uninstaller software*—Utility software that you can use to remove software from your hard disk that you no longer want.
- *Disk optimization software*—Utility software that organizes your information on your hard disk in the most efficient way.
- *Spam blocker software*—Utility software that filters unwanted e-mail from your inbox. Spam is roughly equivalent to unsolicited telephone marketing calls. The term spam is said to derive from a famous Monty Python sketch ("Well, we have Spam, tomato and Spam, egg and Spam, egg, bacon and Spam . . .") that was current when spam first began arriving on the Internet.
- *Anti-spyware software*—Utility software that detects and removes spyware and other unwanted software that can track every electronic move you make.

You definitely need utility software. Don't think of utility software as "optional" software just because it "adds" functionality to your computer. The above examples are just a few of the many types of utility software you'll find in a utility software suite. If you think about the above examples of utility software and what it does for you, especially anti-virus software, you can see how various and helpful it is.

Hardware: Your Physical Interface

To properly understand the significant role of your hardware (the physical components of your computer), it helps to know something about how your computer works. You work with information in the form of characters (A–Z, a–z, and special ones such as an asterisk, a question mark, etc.) and numbers (0–9). Computers, on the other hand, work only with 1s and 0s in terms of what we call bits and bytes. Computers, that is, use electricity to function, and electrical pulses have two states: on and off, which are assigned the values of 0 and 1, respectively.

What are bits and bytes? A **binary digit (bit)** is the smallest unit of information that your computer can process. A bit can either be a 1 (on) or a 0 (off). The technical challenge is to be able to represent all our natural language characters, special symbols, and numbers in binary form. ASCII is one agreed-upon standard to do this. **ASCII (American Standard Code for Information Interchange)** is the coding system that most personal computers use to represent, process, and store information. In ASCII, a group of eight bits represents one natural language character and is called a **byte.**

For example, if you were to type the word *cool* on the keyboard, your keyboard (a hardware device) would change it into four bytes—one byte for each character—that would look like the following to be used by your computer (see Figure A.8):

01100011	01001111	01001111	01001100
c	o	o	l

This grouping of 1s and 0s would be used for "cool" as it moves around or is stored on your computer—as it travels from one device to another, is stored on a storage device, and is processed by your CPU.

There are three important conclusions that you should draw from this discussion so far. First, your hardware works with information in a different form (although with the same meaning) than you do. You work with characters, special symbols, and the numbers 0–9. Your computer, on the other hand, represents all these in a binary form, a unique collection of 1s and 0s. Second, the term *byte* is the bridge between people and a computer. A computer can store one character, special symbol, or number in a byte. One byte is essentially one character. So, a DVD with a storage capacity of 4.7 gigabytes can hold approximately 4.7 billion characters of information.

Third, the primary role of your input and output devices is to convert information from one form to another. Input devices convert information from human-readable form

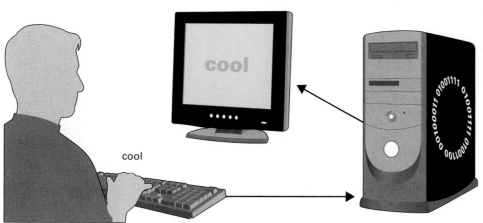

Figure A.8

Information as It Moves from You through Your Computer

into bits and bytes, while output devices convert the 1s and 0s to something people can recognize. All other hardware works internally with information in the form of bits and bytes.

COMMON INPUT DEVICES

An **input device** is a tool you use to enter information and commands (see Figure A.9). You can use a keyboard to type in information, for example, and use a mouse to point and click on buttons and icons. As you saw in the previous section, input devices are responsible for converting information in human-readable form to the binary code that computers use. Below are the principal types of input devices being used today (see Figure A.10 on the opposite page).

- **Keyboards** are the most often used input devices for desktop and notebook computers, while styluses are the most frequently used input devices for PDAs and tablet PCs. A **stylus** is a penlike device used to write or draw on a PDA or tablet PC. Keyboards and styluses allow you to input both information and commands and both are used in business and personal settings.
- **Pointing devices** are devices that are used to navigate and select objects on a display screen.
  - **Mouse**—a pointing device that you use to click on icons or buttons. The three types are mechanical (using a ball), optical (using red light), and wireless (using waves).

Figure A.9

Common Input Devices

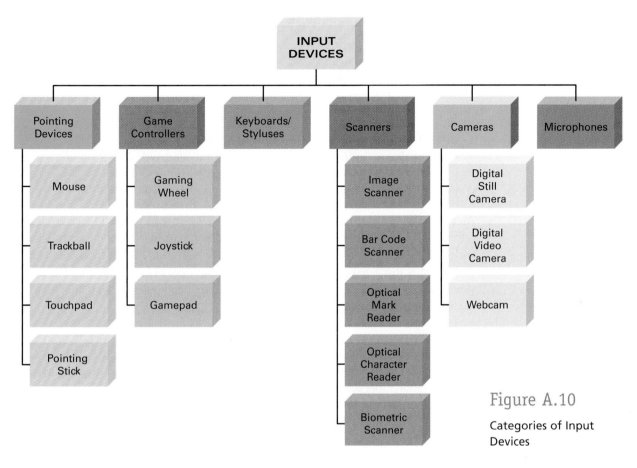

Figure A.10

Categories of Input Devices

- *Trackball*—is similar to a mechanical mouse, but it has the ball on the top.
- *Touchpad*—is the little dark rectangle that you use to move the cursor with your finger, often found on notebook computers.
- *Pointing stick*—is a little rod (like a pencil-top eraser) used almost exclusively on notebook computers.
- *Game controllers* are used for gaming to better control screen action.
  - *Gaming wheel*—is a steering wheel and foot pedals for virtual driving.
  - *Joystick*—is a vertical handle with programmable buttons that control action.
  - *Gamepad*—is a multifunctional input device with programmable buttons, thumb sticks, and a directional pad.
- *Scanners* are used to convert information that exists in visible form into electronic form.
  - *Image scanner*—captures images, photos, text, and artwork that already exist on paper.
  - *Bar code scanner*—reads information that is in the form of vertical bars, where their width and spacing represent digits (often used in point-of-sale [POS] systems in retail environments).
  - *Optical mark reader*—detects the presence or absence of a mark in a predetermined spot on the page (often used for true/false and multiple choice exam answers).
  - *Optical character reader*—reads characters that appear on a page or sales tag (often used in point-of-sale [POS] systems in retail environments).

- *Biometric scanner*—scans some human physical attribute like your fingerprint or iris for security purposes.
- *Digital cameras* capture still images or video as a series of 1s and 0s. Some will capture only stills, others do both.
  - *Digital still camera*—digitally captures still images in varying resolutions.
  - *Digital video camera*—captures video digitally.
  - *Webcam*—captures digital video to upload to the Web.
- *Microphones* capture audio for conversion into electronic form.

COMMON OUTPUT DEVICES

An *output device* is a tool you use to see, hear, or otherwise recognize the results of your information-processing requests. The most common output devices for both business and personal computing environments are monitors and printers, but speakers and plotters (printers that generate drawings) are also output devices (see Figure A.11). Any device that converts the digital form of information in a computer to something that you can see, read, or hear is an output device.

MONITORS

Monitors come in two varieties: CRT or flat-panel displays (see Figure A.12). *CRTs* are the monitors that look like traditional television sets, while *flat-panel displays* are thin, lightweight monitors that take up much less space than CRTs. Flat-panel displays are either liquid crystal display or gas plasma display. *Liquid crystal display (LCD) monitors* make the screen image by sending electricity through crystallized liquid trapped between two layers of glass or plastic. *Gas plasma displays* send electricity through gas trapped between two layers of glass or plastic to create a screen image. A gas plasma dis-

Figure A.11

Categories of Output Devices

play usually provides a better image, but is more expensive than a comparably sized LCD monitor.

When selecting a monitor, the important features to consider, besides its price and physical size, are the monitor's (1) viewable image size, (2) resolution, and (3) dot pitch.

Figure A.12

Monitors Are Common Output Devices

1. The *viewable image size (VIS)* is the size of the image. The quoted size (17", 19", etc.) is measured diagonally from corner to corner. In a flat-panel display, this size is the same as the distance from corner to opposite corner of the monitor's frame, while in a CRT it's slightly less since the image doesn't completely fill the screen area on a CRT. The physical size of a CRT, for a comparable image size, is usually larger since it's much deeper than the flat-panel displays.

2. The *resolution of a screen* is the number of pixels it has. *Pixels (picture elements)* are the dots that make up the image on your screen. For example, a monitor with a resolution of 1,280 × 1,024 has 1,280 pixels across and 1,024 pixels down the screen. The higher the resolution the better the image.

3. *Dot pitch* is the distance between the centers of a pair of like-colored pixels. So, a monitor with .24 mm dot pitch is better than one with .28 mm dot pitch because the dots are smaller and closer together, giving you a better quality image.

PRINTERS

Printers are another common type of output device (see Figure A.13). The sharpness and clarity of a printer's output depend on the printer's resolution. The *resolution of a printer* is the number of dots per inch (dpi) it produces. This is the same principle as the resolution in monitors. As is the case with monitors, the more dots per inch, the better the image, and consequently, the more costly the printer. High-end personal printers

Figure A.13

Printers Are Also Common Output Devices

usually have a resolution of $1,600 \times 1,600$ or better. Multiplying these numbers together gives you 2,560,000 dots per square inch. Some printers, especially those that advertise high-quality photo output, achieve resolutions of $5,760 \times 1,440$ by making multiple passes across the image to produce the clarity needed.

- *Inkjet printers* make images by forcing ink droplets through nozzles. Standard inkjet printers use four colors: black, cyan (blue), magenta (purplish pink), and yellow. Some inkjet printers produce high-quality images and are often advertised as photo printers. These have two shades each of magenta and cyan for a total of six colors.

- *Laser printer*s form images using the same sort of electrostatic process that photocopiers use. Laser printers are usually more expensive than inkjets, but they have become dramatically cheaper lately. They usually provide better quality images than inkjets. They come in black and white and in color versions.

- *Multifunction printers* scan, copy, and fax, as well as print. These devices are very popular in homes and small offices since they offer so many features all in one unit. Multifunction printers can be either inkjet or laser.

- *Plotters* form their output by moving a pen across the surface of a piece of paper. Plotters were the first type of printer that could print with color and render graphics and full-size engineering drawings. As a rule, plotters are much more expensive than printers. They are most frequently used for CAE (computer-aided engineering) applications, such as CAD (computer-aided design) and CAM (computer-aided manufacturing).

COMMON STORAGE DEVICES

As opposed to RAM, which is temporary memory, storage media don't lose their contents when you turn off your computer. The main issues to consider when choosing a storage medium are (1) whether you want portability, (2) how much storage space you need, and (3) whether you need to change the information on the medium.

Some storage devices, such as hard disks, offer you easy update capabilities and high storage capacity, but may not be portable. Others, like flash memory devices, while they are portable and updateable, have less storage space. Still others like DVD-ROMs are portable with high capacity, but the information that comes on them can't be changed (see Figure A.14 on the opposite page).

Capacities of storage media are measured in megabytes, gigabytes, and terabytes. A *megabyte (MB or M or Meg)* is roughly 1 million bytes; a *gigabyte (GB or Gig)* is roughly 1 billion bytes; and a *terabyte (TB)* is roughly 1 trillion bytes. A consumer hard disk would have a capacity of between 1 and 250 gigabytes while a hard disk for a large organization (also called a *hard disk pack*) can hold in excess of 100 TB of information. Common storage devices include

- Magnetic storage media:
  - *Hard disk*—magnetic storage device with one or more thin metal platters or disks that store information sealed inside the disk drive. You usually get one installed in your system unit (the computer box) when you buy a computer. If you need more hard disk space or want portability, you can get an external unit that you can plug into the USB ports. (We'll discuss USB ports in a later section.) A hard disk offers ease of updating and large storage capacity.
  - *Optical storage media* are plastic discs on which information is stored, deleted, and/or changed using laser light (see Figure A.15) and include CDs and DVDs, of which there are several types:

Categories of Storage
Media

- **CD-ROM (compact disc — read-only memory)**—an optical or laser disc whose information cannot be changed. A CD stores up to 800 Meg of information.
- **CD-R (compact disc — recordable)**—an optical or laser disc that you can write to one time only.
- **CD-RW (compact disc — rewritable)**—an optical or laser disc on which you can save, change, and delete files as often as you like.
- **DVD-ROM**—a high-capacity optical or laser disc whose information cannot be changed. The capacity of a DVD, unlike that of a CD, varies according to type.

Figure A.15

Optical Storage Media

- **DVD-R** or **DVD+R (DVD — recordable)**—a high-capacity optical or laser disc to which you can write one time only.
- **DVD-RW** or **DVD+RW** (depending on the manufacturer)—a high-capacity optical or laser disc on which you can save, change, and delete files.

- Flash memory comes in two varieties: flash memory device and flash memory cards (see Figure A.16). A **flash memory device** (also called a jump drive or thumb drive) is a flash memory storage device that is small enough to fit on a key ring and plugs directly into the USB port on your computer. A flash memory card, on the other hand, has to be inserted into a reader, which in turn plugs into the USB port. **Flash memory cards** have high-capacity storage units laminated inside a small piece of plastic. There are several different types.

    - **xD-Picture (xD) cards**—flash memory card that looks like a rectangular piece of plastic smaller than a penny and about as thick, with one edge slightly curved. xD cards have capacities ranging from 32 to 512 megabytes.
    - **Secure Digital (SD) cards** and **MultiMediaCards (MMC)**—flash memory cards that look identical to each other (but SD cards have copy protection built-in), are a little larger than a quarter, and are slightly thicker than a credit card.
    - **CompactFlash (CF) cards**—flash memory cards slightly larger than a half-dollar, with capacities up to 6 gigabyte.
    - **SmartMedia (SM) cards**—flash memory cards that are a little longer than a CF card and about as thick as a credit card with capacities of up to 512 megabytes.
    - **Memory Stick Media cards**—elongated flash memory cards about the width of a penny developed by Sony with capacities up to 1 gigabyte.

Figure A.16

Common Types of Flash Memory

CPU AND RAM

Together, your CPU and RAM make up the real brains of your computer (see Figure A.17). Your CPU largely determines the power (and also the price) of your computer. The **central processing unit (CPU)** is the hardware that interprets and executes the system and application software instructions and coordinates the operation of all other hardware. **Random access memory (RAM)** is a temporary holding area for the information you're working with as well as the system and application software instructions that the CPU currently needs.

You'll often hear the CPU referred to as a microprocessor or a CPU chip. The dominant manufacturers of CPUs include Intel (with its Celeron, Pentium, and Xeon series for personal computers) and AMD (with its Athlon and Opteron series). As a consumer, you'll probably find the most useful information about CPUs is their relative speeds.

Today's CPU speed is usually quoted in gigahertz. **Gigahertz (GHz)** is the number of billions of CPU cycles per second that the CPU can handle. The more cycles per second, the faster the processing and the more powerful the computer. Gigahertz refers to how fast the CPU can carry out the steps it takes to execute software instructions—a process sometimes called the CPU cycle or machine cycle. A **CPU cycle (machine cycle)** consists of retrieving, decoding, and executing the instruction, then returning the result to RAM, if necessary (see Figure A.18). When you load (or open) a program, you're telling your computer to send a copy of the program from the storage device (hard disk or CD) into RAM. In carrying out the software instructions, the CPU repeatedly performs machine cycles as follows:

1. *Retrieve an instruction:* The **control unit,** which is the component of the CPU that directs what happens in your computer, sends to RAM for instructions and the information it needs. If the instruction says to add 4 and 6, for example, the two numbers travel as information with the *add* instruction. The instruction

travels from RAM on the system bus. The ***system bus*** consists of electrical pathways that move information between basic components of the motherboard, including between RAM and the CPU. When the instruction reaches the CPU it waits temporarily in ***CPU cache,*** which is a type of memory on the CPU where instructions called up by the CPU wait until the CPU is ready to use them. It takes much less time to get the instruction from CPU cache to the control unit than from RAM, so CPU cache speeds up processing.

2. *Decode the instruction:* The CPU gets the instruction out of cache and examines it to see what needs to be done, in this case, add 4 and 6.

3. *Execute the instruction:* The CPU then does what the instruction says to do. In our example, it sends the two numbers to the arithmetic logic unit to be added. The ***arithmetic logic unit (ALU)*** is a component of the CPU that performs arithmetic, as well as comparison and logic operations.

4. *Store the result in RAM:* The CPU then sends the result of the addition, 10, to RAM. There's not always a result to send back to RAM. Sometimes the CPU does intermediate calculations that don't get saved.

You'll sometimes hear the CPU speed referred to as the "clock speed." This refers to the CPU clock. Every CPU has its own ***CPU clock,*** which is simply a sliver of quartz that beats at regular intervals in response to an electrical charge. The beat of the CPU clock is like the drummer in a marching band. Just as the drummer keeps everyone marching in time, the CPU clock keeps all your computer's operations synchronized. Each beat or tick of the CPU clock is called a clock cycle and is equivalent to a CPU cycle (machine cycle). The CPU uses the CPU clock to keep instructions and information marching through your CPU at a fixed rate.

RAM is a sort of whiteboard that your CPU uses while it processes information and software instructions. When you turn off your computer, everything in RAM disappears—that's why we call it "temporary." When you first start your computer, system instructions that are necessary to keep your computer running get written into RAM. Then, as you open applications, like Microsoft Word or Excel, the instructions to make those programs run join the operating system in RAM. As you type in your document or enter information into your workbook, that too is stored in RAM. When you've finished your work and save it, a copy is transferred from RAM to your disk or CD.

The most important thing you need to know about RAM is its capacity for storing instructions and information. RAM capacity is expressed in megabytes or gigabytes. You'll remember that a megabyte is roughly 1 million bytes. A byte is equivalent to a character. So RAM with a capacity of 256 megabytes can hold 256 million characters—that includes operating system instructions as well as the applications and information that you're currently using.

NOTEBOOK COMPUTER CPUS AND RAM

A notebook computer is to a desktop computer as a recreational vehicle is to a traditional home—everything is smaller, and power to run devices is limited since you have to carry the power sources with you. A ***mobile CPU*** is a special type of CPU for a notebook computer that changes speed, and therefore power consumption, in response to fluctuation in use. A desktop CPU, running at 1 GHz, uses between 75 and 1,090 watts of power whereas a mobile CPU might run at a much smaller 34 watts. RAM modules for notebook computers are smaller than those for desktop computers.

CONNECTING THE HARDWARE OUTSIDE TO THE HARDWARE INSIDE

Since the CPU controls all computer hardware, all hardware devices must be connected to the CPU, just as your limbs are connected to your brain through your spinal cord.

The CPU, along with RAM, is located on the large circuit board (called the *motherboard*) inside your system unit. The connector (or plug) on the end of the cable coming out of your printer connects it to the motherboard which then carries information between the CPU and the printer.

WIRED CONNECTIONS

All devices that are not wireless have connectors on the ends of cables that plug into ports on the computer. A *port* is the place on your system unit, monitor, or keyboard through which information and instructions flow to and from your computer system. For wired connections it's the opening or socket where you insert the connector, and for wireless devices a port is where the wave information goes in and out.

The ports are accessible on the outside of the system unit and that means that you don't have to open up the system unit to plug in your scanner. There are various types of connectors/ports (see Figure A.19) including:

- *USB (universal serial bus) port*—fit small flat plug-and-play, hot-swap USB connectors, and, using USB hubs, you can connect up to 127 devices to a single USB port on your computer. *Hot swap* is an operating system feature that allows you—while your computer is running—to unplug a device and plug in a new one (without first shutting down your computer). *Plug and play* is an operating feature that finds and installs the device driver for a device that you plug into your computer. USB connectors/ports come in two speeds: USB 1.1 and USB 2.0 (which is faster), and in two physical shapes called Type A and Type B, respectively.

Figure A.19

Categories of Connectors and Ports

Serial connector

Firewire connector

Parallel connector

Ethernet connector

USB connector

Figure A.20

Ports and Connectors to
Connect Devices to the
CPU on the Motherboard

Type A USB connectors/ports are all the same size and shape (see Figure A.20),
but Type B USB connectors are smaller, squarer, and come in several different
sizes. Type B connectors are usually on the end of the cable that plugs into the
device (like a digital camera).

- **Firewire ports**—(also called **IEEE 1394** or **I-Link**) fit hot-swap, plug-and-play
  Firewire connectors, and you can connect up to 63 Firewire devices to a single
  Firewire port by daisy-chaining the devices together (see Figure A.20).

- **PS/2 ports**—fit PS/2 connectors, which you often find on keyboards and mice
  (see Figure A.20). PS/2 is a special type of serial connector/port. Serial
  connectors/ports are gradually being replaced by USB and Firewire.

- **Parallel ports**—fit parallel connectors, which are large flat connectors found
  almost exclusively on printer cables, but which are losing popularity in favor of
  USB (see Figure A.20).

WIRELESS CONNECTIONS

Wireless devices transfer and receive information in the form of waves, either infrared or radio waves. Different types of waves have different frequencies. The three types most frequently used in personal and business computer environments are infrared, Bluetooth, and WiFi.

- ***Infrared***—also called ***IR*** or ***IrDA (infrared data association)*** uses red light to send and receive information. Infrared light has a frequency that's below what the eye can see. It's used for TV remotes and other devices that operate over short distances (the effective distance is about one mile) that are free of obstacles.
- ***Bluetooth***—is a standard for transmitting information in the form of short-range radio waves over distances of up to 30 feet and is used for purposes such as wirelessly connecting a cell phone or a PDA to a computer.
- ***WiFi (wireless fidelity)***—is a standard for transmitting information in the form of radio waves over distances up to about several miles. WiFi has several forms. For example, WiFi is also called ***IEEE 802.11a, b,*** or ***g,*** each of which is a unique type. WiFi is usually the type of wireless communication used in a network environment.

EXPANSION CARDS AND SLOTS

Whether wired or wireless, ports are sometimes directly on the motherboard and sometimes on expansion cards. An ***expansion card*** (or ***board***) is a circuit board that you insert into the expansion slot on the motherboard and to which you connect a peripheral device. An ***expansion slot*** is a long skinny socket on the motherboard into which you insert an expansion card. Information coming from and going to expansion slots and ports moves along wires (called a "bus") to the CPU. The ***expansion bus*** is the set of pathways along which information moves between devices outside the motherboard and the CPU (see Figure A.21). We have already discussed the system bus that moves information between basic motherboard components, including RAM and the CPU.

Figure A.21

The Expansion Bus, Expansion Slots, and Expansion Cards

Figure A.22

PC Cards Connect
External Devices to Your
Notebook Computer

To add devices to your notebook computer, you slide a PC Card into the PC Card slot on the notebook, and connect the device to the PC Card. A **PC Card** (which is an updated version of the traditional PCMCIA card) is the expansion card you use to add devices to your notebook computer. PC Cards look like thick credit cards. **PC Card slots** are the openings, one on top of the other, on the side or front of a notebook, where you connect external devices with a PC Card (see Figure A.22). For example, if you wanted to add a CD-ROM drive, you'd slide a PC Card into the slot and then connect the CD-ROM drive to the connector on the PC Card. One of the great things about PC Cards is that you can hot-swap devices.

Summary: Student Learning Outcomes Revisited

1. **Define information technology (IT) and its two basic categories: hardware and software.** *Information technology (IT)* is any computer-based tool that people use to work with information and support the information and information-processing needs of an organization. For example, IT includes cell phones, PDAs, software such as spreadsheet software, and output devices such as printers. *Hardware* consists of the physical devices that make up a computer (often referred to as a computer system). *Software* is the set of instructions that your hardware executes to carry out a specific task for you.

2. **Describe the categories of computers based on size.** Categories of computers by size include personal digital assistants, tablet PCs, notebook computers, desktop computers, minicomputers, mainframe computers, and supercomputers. A *personal digital assistant (PDA)* is a small handheld computer that helps you surf the Web and perform simple tasks such as note taking, calendaring, appointment scheduling, and maintaining an address book. A *tablet PC* is a pen-based computer that provides the screen capabilities of a PDA with the functional capabilities of a notebook or desktop computer. A *notebook computer* is a small, portable, fully functional battery-powered computer designed

for you to carry around with you. A *desktop computer* is the most popular choice for personal computing needs. These four are all computers designed for use by one person. A *minicomputer (mid-range computer)* is designed to meet the computing needs of several people simultaneously in a small to medium-size business environment. A *mainframe computer (mainframe)* is a computer designed to meet the computing needs of hundreds of people in a large business environment. A *supercomputer* is the fastest, most powerful, and most expensive type of computer. In the order given, PDAs are the smallest, least powerful, and least expensive while supercomputers are the largest, most powerful, and most expensive.

3. **Compare the roles of personal productivity, vertical market, and horizontal market software.** *Application software* executes your specific programs and tasks. *Personal productivity software* helps you perform personal tasks—such as writing a memo, creating a graph, and creating a slide presentation—that you can usually do even if you don't own a computer. *Vertical market software* is application software that is unique to a particular industry. *Horizontal market software* is application software that is general enough to be suitable for use in a variety of industries. Personal

productivity software is very inexpensive when compared to both vertical market and horizontal market software. With personal productivity software, you do not obtain the right to change the way the software works. If you buy vertical market or horizontal market software, you can often buy the right to change the way the software works.

4. **Describe the roles of operating system software and utility software as components of system software.** *System software* handles technology management tasks and coordinates the interaction of all your technology devices. *Operating system software* controls your application software and manages how your hardware devices work together. So, operating system software really enables you to run application software. *Utility software* adds additional functionality to your operating system, including such utilities as anti-virus software, screen savers, crash-proof software, uninstaller software, disk optimization, spam blocking, and anti-spyware software. Although these "add" functionality, you definitely need utility software, especially anti-virus software.

5. **Define the purpose of each of the six major categories of hardware.** The six major categories of hardware are
   - *Input devices*—Convert information and commands from a form that you understand into a form your computer can understand.
   - *Output devices*—Help you see, hear, or otherwise accept the results of your information-processing requests, that is, convert information from a form your computer understands into a form you can understand.
   - *CPU and RAM*—The real brains of your computer that execute software instructions (CPU) and hold the information, application software, and operating system software you're working with (RAM).
   - *Storage devices*—Store information for use at a later time.
   - *Telecommunications devices*—Send information to and from persons and locations.
   - Connecting devices—Connect all your hardware devices to each other.

Key Terms and Concepts

Anti-spyware software, 50
Anti-virus software, 50
Application software, 41
Arithmetic logic unit (ALU), 60
ASCII (American Standard Code for Information Interchange), 51
Bar code scanner, 53
Binary digit (bit), 51
Biometric scanner, 54
Bluetooth, 63
Byte, 51
CD-R (compact disc—recordable), 57
CD-ROM (compact disc—read-only memory), 57
CD-RW (compact disc—rewritable), 57
Central processing unit (CPU), 41
Communications software, 46
CompactFlash (CF) card, 58
Control unit, 59
CPU cache, 60
CPU clock, 60
CPU (machine) cycle, 59

Crash-proof software, 50
CRT, 54
Database management system (DBMS), 46
Desktop computer, 43
Desktop publishing software, 46
Digital camera, 54
Digital still camera, 54
Digital video camera, 54
Disk optimization software, 50
Dot pitch, 55
DVD-R or DVD+R (DVD—recordable), 58
DVD-ROM, 57
DVD-RW or DVD+RW, 58
Expansion bus, 63
Expansion card (board), 63
Expansion slot, 63
Firewire (IEEE 1394 or I-Link), 62
Flash memory card, 58
Flash memory device, 58
Flat-panel display, 54
Game controller, 53

Gamepad, 53
Gaming wheel, 53
Gas plasma display, 54
Gigabyte (GB or Gig), 56
Gigahertz (GHz), 59
Graphics software, 46
Hard disk, 56
Hardware, 40
Horizontal market software, 47
Hot swap, 61
Image scanner, 53
Information technology (IT), 39
Infrared, IR, or IrDA (infrared data association), 63
Inkjet printer, 56
Input device, 41
Joystick, 53
Keyboard, 52
Laser printer, 56
Linux, 48
Liquid crystal display (LCD) monitor, 54
Mac OS, 48
Mainframe computer (mainframe), 45
Megabyte (MB or M or Meg), 56
Memory Stick Media card, 58
Microphone, 54
Microsoft Windows XP Home, 48
Microsoft Windows XP Professional (Windows XP
    Pro), 48
Minicomputer (mid-range computer), 44
Mobile CPU, 60
Mouse, 52
Multifunction printer, 56
MultiMediaCard (MMC), 58
Multitasking, 48
Notebook computer, 43
Open-source software, 50
Operating system software, 42
Optical character reader, 53
Optical mark reader, 53
Optical storage media, 56
Output device, 41
Parallel port, 62
PC Card, 64

PC Card slot, 64
Personal digital assistant (PDA), 42
Personal finance software, 46
Personal information management software (PIM), 46
Personal productivity software, 45
Pixels (picture elements), 55
Plotter, 56
Plug and play, 61
Pointing device, 52
Pointing stick, 53
Port, 61
Presentation software, 46
PS/2 port, 62
Random access memory (RAM), 41
Resolution of a printer, 55
Resolution of a screen, 55
Scanner, 53
Secure Digital (SD) card, 58
SmartMedia (SM) card, 58
Software, 40
Software suite, 47
Spam blocker software, 50
Spreadsheet software, 46
Storage device, 41
Stylus, 52
Supercomputer, 45
System bus, 60
System software, 42
Tablet PC, 42
Telecommunications device, 41
Terabyte (TB), 56
Touchpad, 53
Trackball, 53
Uninstaller software, 50
USB (universal serial bus) port, 61
Utility software, 42
Vertical market software, 46
Viewable image size (VIS), 55
Web authoring software, 46
Webcam, 54
WiFi (wireless fidelity, or IEEE 802.11a, b, or g), 63
Word processing software, 46
xD-Picture (xD) card, 58

Short-Answer Questions

1. What are the two categories of information technology (IT)?
2. What are the six categories of hardware?
3. What is the difference between application software and system software?
4. Dollar for dollar with comparable characteristics, which is faster and more powerful—a desktop computer or a notebook computer?
5. What are the major categories of personal productivity software?
6. What is the difference between vertical and horizontal market software?
7. Why is anti-virus software so important?
8. What do the terms *bit* and *byte* mean?
9. What is the difference between a tablet PC and a PDA?
10. What are two types of pointing devices?
11. What is a gaming wheel and how does it differ from a gamepad?
12. What purpose does a biometric scanner serve?
13. What does a microphone do?
14. What is the difference between a CRT and a flat-panel display?
15. How would you measure the size of a screen?
16. How is the resolution of a printer comparable to the resolution of a screen?
17. What does dot pitch tell you?
18. What are the two main types of printers for personal computers?
19. How does a CD differ from a floppy disk?
20. What are three types of flash memory cards?
21. What is a mobile CPU?
22. What is the expansion bus?
23. Which wireless standard is used by networks?
24. What is an expansion slot?
25. What is a PC Card?

Assignments and Exercises

1. **COMPARING DIFFERENT TYPES OF COMPUTER SYSTEMS** Computers come in varying sizes and levels of power and performance. Use the Web to find out about computer system configurations. Do some comparison shopping for three types of computers: desktops, notebooks, and tablet PCs. Choose three Web sites that sell computer systems. From each of these sites, choose the most expensive and least expensive computer systems you can find for each of the three types of computers. Create a table for each of the three types of computers and compare them based on the following criteria:
   - Type and speed of CPU
   - Type and speed of RAM
   - Amount of CPU cache
   - System bus speed
   - Hard disk capacity and speed (revolutions per minute or rpm)
   - Number and type of ports
2. **CUSTOMIZING A COMPUTER PURCHASE** One of the great things about the Web is the number of e-tailers that are now online offering you a variety of products and services. One such e-tailer is Dell, which allows you to customize and buy a computer. Connect to Dell's site at www.dell.com. Go to the portion of Dell's site that allows you to customize either a notebook or desktop computer. First, choose an already-prepared system and note its price and capability in terms of CPU speed, RAM size, monitor quality, and storage capacity. Now, customize that system to increase CPU speed, add more RAM, increase monitor size and quality, and add more storage capacity. What's the difference in price between the two? Which system is more in your price range? Which system has the speed and capacity you need?
3. **UNDERSTANDING THE COMPLEXITY OF SOFTWARE** Software instructions on how to open Microsoft Word or send information to a printer must be provided to a computer in great detail and with excruciating accuracy. Writing code to make the computer execute these instructions properly and in the

right order is not a simple task. To understand how detailed you must be, pick a partner for this project and envision that you are standing in a kitchen. The task for one of you is to write down all the instructions that are necessary to make a peanut butter and jelly sandwich. When the instructions are complete, have the other person follow those instructions exactly. How successful was the second person in making the sandwich? Did your instructions include every single step? What did you leave out?

4. **WEB-ENABLED CELL PHONES AND WEB COMPUTERS** When categorizing computers by size for personal needs, we focused on PDAs, tablet PCs, notebook computers, and desktop computers. There are several other variations including Web-enabled cell phones that include instant text messaging and Web computers. For this project, you'll need a group of four people, split into two groups of two. Have the first group research Web-enabled cell phones, their capabilities, and their costs. Have that group make a purchase recommendation based on price and capability. Have the second group do the same for Web computers. What's your vision of the future? Will we ever get rid of clunky notebooks and desktops in favor of more portable and cheaper devices such as Web-enabled cell phones and Web computers? Why or why not?

5. **ADDING MEDIA TO A PRESENTATION** We certainly live in a "multimedia" society, in which it's often easy to present and receive information using a variety (multi) of media. Presentation tools such as Microsoft's PowerPoint can help you easily build presentations that include audio, animation, and video. And this may help you get a better grade in school. Using your preferred presentation software, document the steps necessary to add a short audio or video clip to a presentation. How does the representation of the clip appear on a slide? How can you initiate it? Does your presentation software include any clips that you can insert or do you have to record your own? Now, try recording a short audio clip. What steps must you perform?

6. **OPERATING SYSTEM SOFTWARE FOR PDAS** The personal digital assistant (PDA) market is a ferocious, dynamic, and uncertain one. One of the uncertainties is what operating system for PDAs will become the dominant one. For notebooks and desktops right now, you're pretty well limited to the Microsoft family unless you buy an Apple computer (in which case your operating system is Mac OS) or want to venture into using Linux (which we wouldn't recommend for most people). Do some research on the more popular PDAs available today. What are the different operating systems? What different functionality do they offer? Are they compatible with each other? Take a guess—which one will come out on top?

7. **TYPES OF MONITORS AND THEIR QUALITY** The monitor you buy will greatly affect your productivity. If you get a high-resolution, large screen monitor, you'll see the screen content better than if you get a low-resolution, small screen monitor. One factor in this is the monitor type. The various levels of monitor resolution are called QXGA, SVGA, SXGA, UXGA, VGA, and XGA. Do a little research on these resolution levels. Rank them from best monitor to worst (the higher the resolution, the better the quality and clarity of the picture). Also, determine a price for each.

CHAPTER TWO OUTLINE

STUDENT LEARNING OUTCOMES

1. Describe how to use Porter's Five Forces Model to evaluate the relative attractiveness of an industry.

2. Describe the role of value chains in identifying value-added and value-reducing processes.

3. Define supply chain management (SCM) systems and describe their strategic and competitive opportunities and IT support.

4. Define customer relationship management (CRM) systems and describe their strategic and competitive opportunities and IT support.

5. Define business intelligence (BI) systems and describe their strategic and competitive opportunities and IT support.

6. Define integrated collaboration environments (ICEs) and describe their strategic and competitive opportunities and IT support.

INDUSTRY PERSPECTIVES

74 Eliminating Switching Costs in the Cell Phone Arena

83 Implementing Customer Relationship Management with Behaviorally Targeted Online Ads

87 Business Intelligence— Louisville Slugger Bats, Golfer Bionic Gloves, and Hockey Goalie Xceed Leg Pads?

93 When CRM Technology May Become Too Invasive

FEATURES

75 Team Work
Using Porter to Evaluate the Movie Rental Industry

80 Global Perspective
Fulfilling Floral Orders on Valentine's Day

81 On Your Own
Understanding Supply Chain Management in Your Business Strategy

84 On Your Own
Understanding Customer Relationship Management in Your Business Strategy

89 Global Perspective
GlaxoSmithKline Creates "Quality of Life" with Groove Workspace

91 Team Work
Do You Want Spoke Poking Around?

100 Electronic Commerce
Ordering Products and Services on the Internet

WEB SUPPORT

www.mhhe.com/haag

- Books and music
- Clothing and accessories
- Auction houses
- Automobiles

CHAPTER TWO

Major Business Initiatives
Gaining Competitive Advantage with IT

OPENING CASE STUDY:
BUSINESS INTELLIGENCE IS KEY TO THE
SUCCESS OF THE MIAMI DOLPHINS

Make no mistake about it, professional sports is big business. Because sports is a business, not only must teams find the great players and coaches with true leadership capabilities, they must also run their business by monitoring and integrating information on ticket sales, merchandise sales, concession sales, and revenues from stadium and event management.

The Miami Dolphins turned to Hyperion Solutions and its business intelligence (BI) software to manage all its financial operations. Prior to doing so, the organization had gathered information from TicketMaster, which handled the majority of its ticket sales. Individual reports came from each TicketMaster outlet and had to be rekeyed into spreadsheet reports for decision makers to tackle the task of adjusting ticket prices to ensure that all the eight home games sold out. This process was so slow that the reports were created only once or twice per week, not nearly often enough to effectively monitor ticket sales. Creating new or different types of reports usually required several extra weeks of work.

With Hyperion's business intelligence software, ticket sales information is now loaded in real time and reports are generated on a daily basis and e-mailed to each Miami Dolphins decision maker. Ticket sales information is also automatically fed into Hyperion software that supports marketing activities. If a bloc of seats is available for a home game, for example, the marketing department can quickly use ticket purchase history information to create a list of fan clubs and past season ticket holders who might be interested in purchasing the available

seats. Then an automated e-mail system can notify this list of people on a moment's notice.

Hyperion's business intelligence software also supports customer relationship management (CRM) strategies and efforts. Specific buying patterns of customers can be identified and communications tailored to people who might want to purchase various and sundry Miami Dolphins merchandise, for instance.

The Miami Dolphins created another sort of BI system, a data mart (a logical collection of information) on player statistics and activities that is used by the team's recruiting and drafting personnel. Information concerning all eligible college players is stored in this data mart and updated on a weekly basis—a valuable tool for personnel identifying top draft choices by projecting potential player performance on the basis of historical game data.

Business intelligence systems and customer relationship management systems are just two of the many IT applications that organizations employ today for competitive advantage. Moreover, organizations understand the imperative to integrate all their IT applications. An organization can't very well determine how many products to place on a retail shelf (supply chain management and inventory management), for instance, if it has no customer relationship management system in place telling the organization what its customers want and when.

This chapter will tell you about the most important IT applications for major business initiatives—supply chain management, customer relationship management, business intelligence, and integrated collaboration environment systems. It will help you understand how to use those information technologies to support your organization's goals and strategies.[1]

Introduction

Recent studies have shown that as competition intensifies in almost every industry, companies must develop innovative products and business processes to survive and thrive and that information technology (IT) is a powerful tool to help them do so.[2] In this chapter, we focus on some of the most important IT applications businesses are using today:

- Supply chain management (SCM)
- Customer relationship management (CRM)
- Business intelligence (BI)
- Integrated collaboration environments (ICE)

As we have said, what is of first importance is for you to find the proper place for these technologies in the context of your organization's goals and strategies. In Chapter 1, in the section on creating the business vision for information technology, we introduced two very useful concepts: the top-line versus bottom-line approach; and the Run-Grow-Transform (RGT) framework. That is, in the RGT framework you determine the correct percentage allocation of IT dollars depending on your initiatives that focus on running your organization (similar to the bottom-line approach), growing your organization (similar to the top-line approach), and transforming your organization to perform business in entirely new ways.

Two other useful and vitally important tools for creating the business vision for information technology are *Porter's Five Forces Model* and *value chains*. Each will help you determine the most appropriate use of technology given your organization's goals and strategies. We discuss these now.

Porter's Five Forces Model

Michael Porter's framework—called the Five Forces Model—has long been accepted as a useful tool for business people to use when thinking about business strategy and the impact of IT. The **Five Forces Model** helps business people understand the relative attractiveness of an industry in terms of the following five forces (see Figure 2.1):

1. Buyer power
2. Supplier power

Figure 2.1

Michael Porter's Five Forces Model

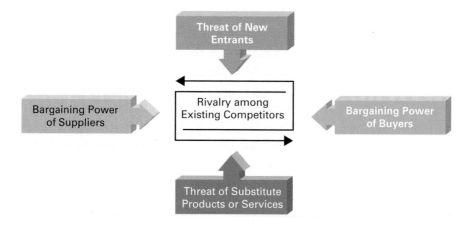

3. Threat of substitute products or services

4. Threat of new entrants

5. Rivalry among existing competitors

You can use Porter's Five Forces Model to decide to (1) enter a particular industry or (2) expand your operations if you are already competing in it. Most important, the strategies you develop should then be supported by enabling technologies.

BUYER POWER

Buyer power in the Five Forces Model is high when buyers have many choices from whom to buy, and low when their choices are few. As a provider of products and services, your organization wishes to reduce buyer power. You create a competitive advantage by making it more attractive for customers to buy from you than from your competition. One of the best IT-based examples of reducing buyer power is the loyalty programs that many organizations offer. *Loyalty programs* reward customers based on the amount of business they do with a particular organization. Such programs are made possible only by the ability to keep track of the activities and accounts of many, perhaps millions, of customers. This would hardly be practical—or even feasible—without large-scale IT systems. Thus, loyalty programs use IT to reduce buyer power. They are very common in the travel industry. Because of the rewards (e.g., free airline tickets, upgrades, and hotel stays) travelers receive, they are more likely to give most of their business to a single organization.

SUPPLIER POWER

Supplier power in the Five Forces Model is high when buyers have few choices from whom to buy, and low when their choices are many. Supplier power is the converse of buyer power: As a supplier organization in a market, you want buyer power to be low and your supplier power to be high.

In a typical supply chain, as we discussed in Chapter 1 (see Figure 2.2), your organization will probably be both a supplier (to customer organizations) and a customer (of other supplier organizations). As a customer of other supplier organizations, you want to increase your buyer power. You can create a competitive advantage by locating alternative supply sources for your organization. IT-enabled B2B e-marketplaces can help you. B2B e-marketplaces are Internet-based services which bring together many buyers and sellers. (This is similar in concept to eBay's popular consumer-centric Web model of bringing together buyers and sellers in an online auction format.) We'll talk about implementations of e-marketplaces in Chapter 5.

Figure 2.2

Evaluating Buyer and Supplier Power for Your Organization

ELIMINATING SWITCHING COSTS IN THE CELL PHONE ARENA

In terms of Porter's Five Forces Model, switching costs reduce the threat of substitute products or services. Cell phone providers want to keep you as a long-term customer. To receive a free phone or unlimited minutes, you may have to sign a one- or two-year contract. That creates a switching cost for you because if you change providers before the end of the contract, you have to pay a penalty in real dollars.

But that hasn't been the greatest switching cost working in favor of cell phone providers. Until 2003, if you switched cell phone providers, you couldn't take your number with you. This stopped many customers from switching.

That switching cost went away in late 2003 with the implementation of *Local Number Portability (LNP)* or the ability to "port" your number from one cell phone provider to another.

In the context of Porter's Five Forces Model, eliminating this switching cost has created a greater threat of substitute products or services. A barrier to entry has been eliminated and thus another of the forces—the threat of new entrants—is higher. So, you can now expect to see more new cell phone providers cropping up over the next several years. That is, new cell phone providers previously had a difficult time attracting competitors' customers because of the lack of LNP. That entry barrier into the fiercely competitive cell phone provider business no longer exists.

When new technology (such as LNP) reduces or eliminates switching costs and entry barriers, you—as a consumer—win because you have more options.

THREAT OF SUBSTITUTE PRODUCTS OR SERVICES

The ***threat of substitute products or services*** in the Five Forces Model is high when there are many alternatives to a product or service, and low when there are few alternatives from which to choose. Ideally, your organization would like to be a supplier organization in a market in which there are few substitutes for the products and services you offer. Of course, that's seldom possible in any market today, but you can still create a competitive advantage by increasing switching costs. ***Switching costs*** are costs that make customers reluctant to switch to another product or service supplier. What you need to realize is that a switching cost does not necessarily have to be an actual monetary cost.

As you buy products at Amazon.com over time, for example, Amazon.com develops a unique profile of your shopping and purchasing habits through such techniques as collaborative filtering. When you visit Amazon.com, products are offered to you that have been tailored to your profile. If you choose to do your shopping elsewhere, there is a switching cost because the new site you visit will not have a profile of you or a record of your past purchases. So, Amazon.com has reduced the threat of substitute products or services, in a market in which there are many substitutes, by tailoring offerings to you, by creating a "cost" to you to switch to another online retailer.

Switching costs can be real monetary costs too. You've probably been introduced to a switching cost when you signed up for the services of a cell phone provider. All the options and plans sound really great. But there is a serious switching cost in that most cell phone providers require you to sign a long-term contract (as long as two years) in order to receive a free phone or unlimited night and weekend calling minutes. These sorts of switching costs, unfortunately, are sometimes hidden in the fine print.

USING PORTER TO EVALUATE THE MOVIE RENTAL INDUSTRY

One hotly contested and highly competitive industry is the movie rental business. You can rent videos from local video rental stores (usually for a specified number of days), you can order pay-per-view from the comfort of your own home (usually to watch as many times as you want in a given 24-hour period), and you can rent videos from the Web at such sites as Netflix (www.netflix.com) and keep the videos as long as you want. Even Blockbuster is going online with its rental business and many people expect Amazon.com to follow.

Using Porter's Five Forces Model, evaluate the relative attractiveness of entering the movie rental business. Specifically, answer the following questions and perform the following tasks (and provide the appropriate justification/description for each of your outputs):

1. Is buyer power low or high?
2. Is supplier power low or high?
3. Which substitute products and services are perceived as threats?
4. What is the level of threat of new entrants? That is, are the barriers to entry high or low? What are the barriers to entry?
5. What is the level of rivalry among existing competitors? Create a list of the top five competitors in the business.

Finally, what is your overall view of the movie rental business? Is it a good or bad industry to enter? How would you use Porter's Five Forces Model to enter this industry?

THREAT OF NEW ENTRANTS

The **_threat of new entrants_** in the Five Forces Model is high when it is easy for new competitors to enter a market, and low when there are significant entry barriers to entering a market. An **_entry barrier_** is a product or service feature that customers have come to expect from organizations in a particular industry and that must be offered by an entering organization to compete and survive. Such barriers are erected, and overcome, and then new ones are created again.

For example, if you're thinking of starting a bank, you must nowadays offer your customers an array of IT-enabled services, including ATM use, online bill paying and account monitoring, and the like. These are significant IT-based entry barriers to entering the banking market because you must offer them for free (or for a very small fee). The first bank to offer such services gained a first-mover advantage and established entry barriers, an advantage nullified as other banking competitors developed similar IT-enabled systems and overcame the barriers to entering or expanding in the industry.

RIVALRY AMONG EXISTING COMPETITORS

The **_rivalry among existing competitors_** in the Five Forces Model is high when competition is fierce in a market, and low when competition is more complacent. Simply put, competition is more intense in some industries than in others, although the overall trend is toward increased competition in just about every industry.

The retail grocery industry is intensely competitive. While Kroger, Safeway, and Albertson's in the United States compete in many different ways, essentially they try to beat or match the competition on price. For example, most of them have loyalty programs that give shoppers special discounts. Customers get lower prices while the store gathers valuable business intelligence on buying habits to craft pricing and advertising strategies. In the future, you can expect to see grocery stores using wireless technologies to track customer movement throughout the store and match it to products purchased to determine purchasing sequences.

Since margins are quite low in the grocery retail market, grocers build efficiencies into their supply chains, connecting with their suppliers in IT-enabled information partnerships. Communicating with suppliers over telecommunications networks rather than using paper-based systems makes the procurement process faster, cheaper, and more accurate. That equates to lower prices for customers—and increased rivalry among existing competitors. We'll discuss supply chain management in more detail later in this chapter.

As you can see, Porter's Five Forces Model is extremely useful in evaluating the relative attractiveness of any industry. When using it, you should have two goals. The first is obvious: Is the industry an attractive one to enter or to expand your operations in? Second, you should look toward how IT can help. As a supplier, can IT help reduce buyer power? Can IT help eliminate entry barriers so your organization can more easily and successfully enter a new market? Can IT help increase switching costs (monetary or otherwise) so your customers are less inclined to leave your organization for another? As a buyer in an industry, can the use of IT give your organization more supplier options, thus reducing supplier power? These are all important questions that you need to answer concerning your use of IT. Be mindful—while you're asking and answering these questions, your competition is performing a similar analysis.

The Value Chain

The **value chain** views your organization as a chain—or series—of processes, each of which adds value to your products or services for your customers. A **business process** is a standardized set of activities that accomplishes a specific task, such as processing a customer's order. The value chain approach is an important graphical tool that helps you identify important business processes within the entire value chain.

Figure 2.3 depicts the components of a value chain. The chain of primary value processes along the bottom half takes the raw materials and makes, delivers, markets and sells, and services your organization's products or services. Processes along the top half of the chain, such as management, accounting, finance, legal, human resources, research and development, and purchasing, support the primary value processes. Your organization requires these support value processes to ensure the smooth operation of the primary value processes.

Figure 2.3

The Components of a Value Chain

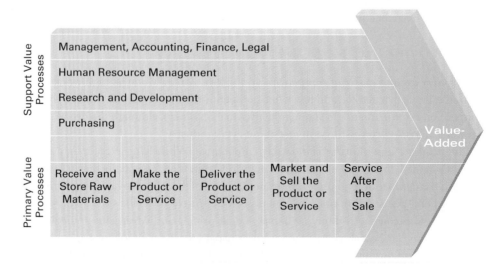

All value processes process an individual value. These processes combined, however, have a total value greater than the sum of their individual values. We call this additional value "value-added," and it's depicted on the far right of the value chain. The larger the value-added, the more value customers place on your organization's product or service. To your organization, this can mean a competitive advantage and often greater profits.

If you've ever purchased a necktie, you may have heard of the Robert Talbott company of Carmel Valley, California.[3] Talbott is the premier necktie manufacturer in the United States. Talbott has always shunned technology; all of its tie orders, historically, were written on paper forms.

That used to work fine, because Talbott has always ensured value-added by utilizing high-quality workmanship, unique designs, and fabrics. Customer "wants" drive their demands, however, and those demands are always changing. Today customers want constantly updated styles and more of them. Talbott now creates four neckwear lines for Nordstrom each year with up to 300 designs per line. How might the value chain help Talbott plan for a better way of meeting new customer demands? Well, it would begin by identifying both value-added and value-reducing processes. Let's look at the identification of value-added processes first.

IDENTIFYING PROCESSES THAT ADD VALUE

Talbott should begin by looking at the firm's business processes and identifying, with help from customers, those processes that add the most value, including above all manufacturing high-quality ties and purchasing quality materials. Talbott should graphically depict customer responses—their opinion of what adds value—on a value chain. Figure 2.4 depicts one possible customer survey result. Notice how the processes in the figure are sized to depict the value that customers attribute to those processes. The largest value-added source is the high-quality manufacturing process. Still, a close second is the purchasing process that provides access to high-quality silks and other fabrics. As these processes are the ones that are most visible to the customers, they will quickly add even more value when supported by new IT systems. Therefore, Talbott has created a computer-aided design system to reduce the time it takes to create and manufacture new ties.

IDENTIFYING PROCESSES THAT REDUCE VALUE

After identifying value-added processes, it's important to identify those processes that reduce value for the customer. Again gathering this information from the customers, Talbott should create a value-reducing value chain. Talbott identified the sales process as

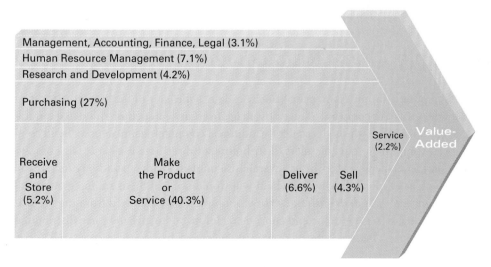

Figure 2.4

The Value-Added View of a Necktie Manufacturer

Figure 2.5

The Value-Reduced View of a Necktie Manufacturer

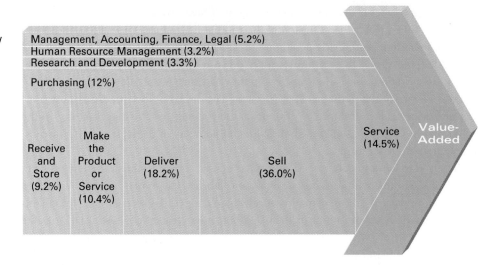

the process that reduced value the most, as shown in Figure 2.5. It found sales were lost because salespeople were promising neckties that were out of stock. Customers were beginning to lose faith in Talbott's ability to deliver high-quality ties. They saw this process failure as one that reduced Talbott's value to them as customers.

To correct its sales process deficiencies, Talbott implemented a new IT system to get timely product information to the sales force. Using laptop computers, the sales force now carries product-line custom CD-ROMs on the road with them. They place orders over their computers from their hotel rooms and receive inventory updates at the same time. As a result, customers have new faith in an old friend who now adds more value than ever.

Evaluating value chains is particularly effective because it forces your organization to gather and analyze quantifiable information. It eliminates much of the need to "fly by the seat of your pants" in making decisions. And as you begin to quantify this type of information, you can build a better return-on-investment case for the acquisition, development, and use of IT to further increase the effectiveness of your processes that add value and further decrease the ineffectiveness of your processes that reduce value.

Again, the goal of introducing you to such tools as Porter's Five Forces Model and value chains is so that you can effectively determine where and how to use technology to support your major business initiatives. With that in mind, let's explore supply chain management, customer relationship management, business intelligence, and integrated collaboration environments.

Supply Chain Management

Dell Computer's supply chain management system is the envy of the industry. Its direct sell model gives the company a huge advantage over any competitor still using a traditional model of selling through retailers. Traditional computer manufacturers build computers and ship them to wholesalers, distributors, or directly to retailers. The computers sit on the retailers' shelves or in a warehouse until you come in and buy one. If you took a look at a typical distribution chain you would see that there are too many computers in inventory. A *distribution chain* is simply the path followed from the originator of a product or service to the end consumer. Holding onto inventory in a distribution chain costs money, because whoever owns the inventory has to pay for it as well as pay

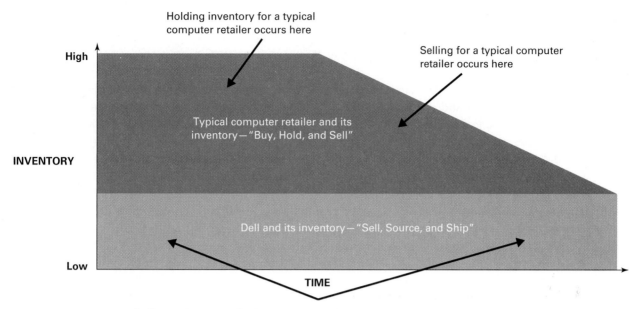

Holding inventory for a typical computer retailer occurs here

Selling for a typical computer retailer occurs here

Typical computer retailer and its inventory—"Buy, Hold, and Sell"

Dell and its inventory—"Sell, Source, and Ship"

Selling and sourcing for Dell occur throughout time, keeping inventory low

Figure 2.6

Buy-Hold-Sell versus Sell-Source-Ship

for the operation of the warehouses or stores while waiting for someone to buy it. In the retailing of computers, not only does excess inventory cost money to hold, but the computers themselves can become obsolete, requiring retailers to slash prices in an effort to sell older models before the newer ones arrive.

Dell's model is different. It sells computers directly from its Web site so there is no inventory in its distribution chain. Dell has enhanced its supply chain as well. It uses i2 supply chain management software to send orders for parts to suppliers every two hours, enabling it to manufacture and deliver exactly what its customers want with little or no inventory in its supply chain.[4] The differences between Dell's "sell, source, and ship" model and the traditional "buy, hold, and sell" model are illustrated in Figure 2.6.

For a company the size of General Motors, with operations all over the world and tens of thousands of suppliers, supply chain management and IT-based supply chain management systems are critical necessities to ensure the smooth flow of parts to GM factories. As we discussed in Chapter 1, ***supply chain management (SCM)*** tracks inventory and information among business processes and across companies. A ***supply chain management (SCM) system*** is an IT system that supports supply chain management activities by automating the tracking of inventory and information among business processes and across companies.

Most large manufacturing companies use just-in-time manufacturing processes, which ensure that the right parts are available as products in process move down the assembly line. ***Just-in-time (JIT)*** is an approach that produces or delivers a product or service just at the time the customer wants it. For retailers, like Target, this means that products customers want to buy are on the shelves when customers walk by. Supply chain management systems also focus on making sure that the right number of parts or products are available, not too many and not too few. Too many products on hand means that too much money is tied up in inventory and also increases the risk of obsolescence. Too few products on hand is not a good thing either, because it could force an assembly line to shut down or, in the case of retailers, lose sales because an item is not in stock when a customer is ready to buy.

Companies with suppliers around the globe often employ inter-modal transportation. ***Inter-modal transportation*** is the use of multiple channels of transportation—railway,

FULFILLING FLORAL ORDERS ON VALENTINE'S DAY

UrbanFlorist (www.urbanflorist.com), a Canadian floral retailer serving all of Canada and the United States, went online several years ago and realized a 1,000 percent annual revenue growth rate over three years. While a tenfold increase in sales is good, to say the least, it also created a number of problems.

In the past, the florist handled all orders manually, which required each and every order to pass through the hands of at least 11 people. According to Alif Somani, CEO of UrbanFlorist, "We used to have a very heavy paper trail and our staff handled almost 10,000 printed pages per day." The manual processes also led to a 6 percent error rate in handling the orders.

The florist then turned to technology, specifically CommercialWare Inc.'s OrderMotion order-management software. OrderMotion helped UrbanFlorist cut error rates in half to 3 percent and realize a 15 percent in-

crease in sales per representative. OrderMotion integrates all the florist's back-office operations including order capture, fulfillment, inventory management, and payment processing. It is also capable of integrating orders across all customer touch points—mail, phone, fax, and the Internet.

Alif sums it up best in these statements: "We invested in a technology that supports our customer-service department so that they can do their jobs more effectively. . . . With OrderMotion we have been able to automate all our order information, customer information, [customer relationship management], and support mechanisms. After all, our concern is not putting out orders but taking care of customers' needs, and having the right technology in place is essential to do that."[5]

truck, boat, and so on—to move products from origin to destination. This further complicates the logistics in SCM because companies are required to monitor and track parts and supplies as they move among different modes of transportation. Consider that a given train may be carrying 50 or more truck trailers that will each eventually be connected to different trucks. Even purely domestic supply chains often employ inter-modal transportation such as railway lines and carrier trucks.

STRATEGIC AND COMPETITIVE OPPORTUNITIES WITH SCM

A well-designed supply chain management system helps your organization by optimizing the following:

- *Fulfillment*—Ensuring the right quantity of parts for production or products for sale arrive at the right time.
- *Logistics*—Keeping the cost of transporting materials as low as possible consistent with safe and reliable delivery.
- *Production*—Ensuring production lines function smoothly because high quality parts are available when needed.
- *Revenue and profit*—Ensuring no sales are lost because shelves are empty.
- *Costs and price*—Keeping the cost of purchased parts and prices of products at acceptable levels.

Cooperation among supply chain partners for mutual success is another hallmark of modern supply chain management systems. For example, many manufacturing companies share product concepts with suppliers early in the product development process. This lets suppliers contribute their ideas about how to make high quality parts at a lower cost.

UNDERSTANDING SUPPLY CHAIN MANAGEMENT IN YOUR BUSINESS STRATEGY

It's now time for you to consider supply chain management (SCM) and SCM systems in the context of business strategy. Prior to answering the following questions, pick any organization you wish and prepare a one-page summary of what it is, its primary customers, and how it attempts to differentiate itself in the market. You are free to choose any organization that provides products to its customers. That is, stay away from organizations that primarily provide services such as financial service firms, insurance firms, and the like. Good candidate organizations may include Microsoft, Coca-Cola, Nordstrom, Wal-Mart, and the like.

1. **Top-line versus bottom-line:** In what ways could your organization use its supply chain management system to support top-line initiatives? In what ways could your organization use its supply chain management system to support bottom-line initiatives?

2. **Porter's Five Forces Model:** In what ways could your organization use its supply chain management system to (1) reduce buyer power as a supplier, (2) reduce supplier power as a buyer, (3) reduce the threat of substitute products or services, and (4) reduce the threat of new entrants?

3. **Value Chain:** Within your organization, would supply chain management be seen as a support value process or a primary value process? Please justify your answer.

IT SUPPORT FOR SUPPLY CHAIN MANAGEMENT

While the SCM software market was pioneered by specialist companies such as i2 and Manugistics, it is now dominated by enterprise software providers such as SAP, Oracle, and PeopleSoft.[6] If your career choice takes you into industries that focus on the manufacturing of products and/or the distribution and use of those products (such as hospitality, resort, and tourism management), you will have a great deal to do with SCM software. To learn more about this area, we encourage you to visit the following resources:

- Supply Chain Knowledge Base—http://supplychain.ittoolbox.com
- Supply Chain Management Review—www.manufacturing.net/scm
- i2 Technologies—www.i2.com
- *CIO Magazine* Enterprise SCM—www.cio.com/enterprise/scm/index.html
- Logistics/Supply Chain—http://logistics.about.com

Customer Relationship Management

Wells Fargo Bank's customer relationship management system tracks and analyzes every transaction made by its 10 million retail customers at its branches, its ATMs, and through its Web-based online banking systems. It has become so good at predicting customer behavior that it knows what customers need even before many of them realize they need it. Wells Fargo's CRM system collects every customer transaction and combines it with personal information provided by the customer. The system is able to predict tailored offerings that will appeal to individual customers (a money-saving second mortgage, for example), at just the right time. As a result, Wells Fargo sells four more banking products or services to its customers than the industry average of 2.2.[7]

Acquiring and retaining customers are the basic objectives of any organization, and thus, customer relationship management systems have become one of the hottest IT systems in business today. A ***customer relationship management (CRM) system*** uses information about customers to gain insights into their needs, wants, and behaviors in order to serve them better. Customers interact with companies in many ways, and each interaction should be easy, enjoyable, and error free. Have you ever had an experience with a company that made you so angry you changed companies or returned the product? It's not uncommon for a customer to change companies after having a negative experience. The goal of CRM is to limit such negative interactions and provide customers with positive experiences.

CRM systems typically include such functions as:

- Sales force automation
- Customer service and support
- Marketing campaign management and analysis

It's important to note that CRM is not just software. It is a total business objective which encompasses many different aspects of a business including software, hardware, services, support, and strategic business goals. The CRM system you adopt should support all these functions and should also be designed to provide the organization with detailed customer information. In many cases, companies begin with a sales force automation application and then progress to the other two functions. ***Sales force automation (SFA) systems*** automatically track all the steps in the sales process. The sales process contains many steps, including contact management, sales lead tracking, sales forecasting and order management, and product knowledge.

Some basic SFA systems perform sales lead tracking, or listing potential customers for the sales team to contact. They also perform contact management, which tracks all the times a salesperson contacts a potential customer, what they discussed, and the next steps. More sophisticated SFA systems perform detailed analysis of the market and customers and can even offer product configuration tools enabling customers to configure their own products. Some of the more robust CRM systems and methodologies, such as General Motors' (see Figure 2.7), focus on creating repeat customers.

Figure 2.7

General Motors' Purchase Funnel[8]

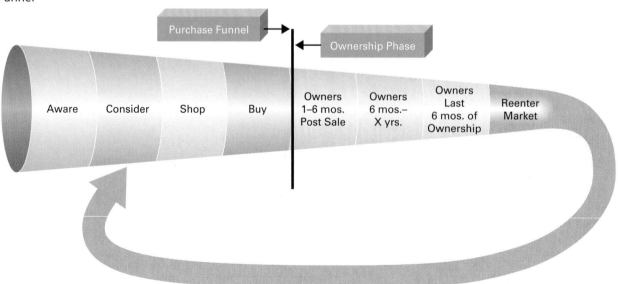

IMPLEMENTING CUSTOMER RELATIONSHIP MANAGEMENT WITH BEHAVIORALLY TARGETED ONLINE ADS

For many Web surfers, the online world is full of advertisements that don't make sense. Teenagers receive e-mails and see banner ads for Viagra. People who rent apartments and condominiums receive e-mails and see banner ads for companies offering to reduce their home mortgage interest rates. Often, this inundation of useless and untargeted ads causes people to ignore them completely.

Quite the contrary, in customer relationship management (CRM), a key goal is to get to know your customers so well that you can target advertisements precisely to them. This is the coveted CRM goal whether in the online business world or the traditional business world. Behaviorally targeted online ads target people based on where they surf and visit on the Web. And they're very successful.

AOL Advertising.com recently completed a study using its LeadBack behavioral marketing technology to identify anonymous Web surfer behavior on its advertiser Web sites. It then developed two sets of advertisements for the study: (1) a generic ad for everyone (called a nontargeted ad) and (2) a series of behaviorally targeted ads for specific groups of people based on their surfing activities.

In the end, both of these sets of advertisements were evaluated on one advertiser Web site according to effective cost-per-thousand (CPM). CPM essentially measures sales dollars per dollar of advertising. For the nontargeted ads, the CPM was $1.49, which means that the advertiser received $1.49 in sales for every advertising dollar spent. For the behaviorally targeted ads, the advertiser received $3.98 in sales for every advertising dollar spent. In this case (as in many others), the results of CRM could be quantifiably measured—almost a $2.50 increase for behaviorally targeted ads.[9]

STRATEGIC AND COMPETITIVE OPPORTUNITIES WITH CRM

One of the rewards of CRM is competitive advantage through superior performance in CRM functions, in particular:

- Devising more effective marketing campaigns based on more precise knowledge of customer needs and wants.
- Assuring that the sales process is efficiently managed.
- Providing superior after-sale service and support, for example, through well-run call centers.

All the classic goals of CRM—treating customers better, understanding their needs and wants, tailoring offerings in response—are likely to result in buyers choosing your product or service instead of the competition's. Predicting the amount or degree to which the CRM-enabled organization will gain market share, however, can be difficult. Certainly, it is something that can be measured after the fact, thus allowing your organization to understand the true results of better CRM on customers' buying decisions. But predicting the degree of gain in market share and then forecasting a net result in terms of incremental revenues is difficult. One way to measure the benefits of CRM systems, according to one expert, is to divide the benefits into two principal categories, revenue enhancers and cost cutters.[10] CRM systems thus support top-line and bottom-line initiatives, although they tend to be more about top-line revenue-enhancing initiatives. In the context of the Run-Grow-Transform framework, CRM systems help in both the running and growing of your organization, but especially the latter.

UNDERSTANDING CUSTOMER RELATIONSHIP MANAGEMENT IN YOUR BUSINESS STRATEGY

As you did for SCM in the previous On Your Own project in this chapter, let's now use business strategy to evaluate another major business initiative, customer relationship management. For this project, suppose that you are a family with your spouse and two children. You have a home mortgage, two car loans, you're building up a retirement account, and you're putting away money for the college education of both your children, all with the same bank.

The bank tracks information about you with a CRM system. First, list every piece of information that you think the bank probably tracks about you, including when you withdraw money from an ATM, the ages of your family members, when you bought your home, your and your spouse's annual salaries, and so on—basically anything and everything you think the bank would know about you and your family.

For the following scenarios, write a short description of any responses of the bank and actions the bank

might take using the information it has acquired in its CRM system. How might it put its CRM information about you to use if

1. You and your spouse decide to have another child.
2. You lose your job.
3. One of your parents is stricken with a severe and long-term illness and has no medical insurance, leaving you to pay the bill.
4. You consistently incur transaction fees for using an ATM not in your bank's ATM network.
5. Your identity is stolen.
6. You decide to build an addition on your home.

As you envision what your bank might do, ask yourself if you would consider any of those actions an invasion of your privacy.

IT SUPPORT FOR CUSTOMER RELATIONSHIP MANAGEMENT

Figure 2.8 is an example of a sample CRM infrastructure. The *front office systems* are the primary interface to customers and sales channels; they send all the customer information they collect to the database. The *back office systems* are used to fulfill and support customer orders and they also send all their customer information to the database. The CRM system analyzes and distributes the customer information and provides the organization with a complete view of each customer's experience with the business. There are many systems available today that a company can purchase that offer CRM functionality. Some of the big providers of these packages are Clarify, Oracle, SAP, and Siebel Systems. Clarify and Siebel are also two of the most prominent SFA software providers; others are Salesforce.com and Vantive. Salesforce.com was the first company to offer CRM using an ASP (application service provider, which hosts its software on a Web server and allows customer organizations to use the software via the Internet) model and others have since followed suit. For additional CRM resources, we encourage you to visit the following:

- Siebel Systems—www.siebel.com
- Salesforce.com—www.salesforce.com
- *CIO Magazine* Enterprise CRM—www.cio.com/enterprise/crm/index.html
- The Customer Management Community by insightexec—www.insightexec.com/
- CRM Today—www.crm2day.com/

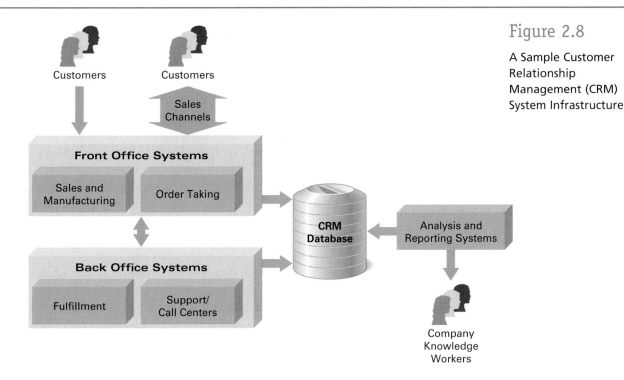

Business Intelligence

FiberMark North America, a manufacturer of specialty packaging and paper, could not easily retrieve business intelligence from its expensive transaction processing systems. "We were desperate to get good information quickly," says Joel Taylor, director of IS. Taylor spent less than $75,000 on QlikView—BI software from QlikTech (www. qliktech.com)—which grabs FiberMark's information from its transaction processing systems and stores it in a readily accessible database.

Now, instead of printing 1,000-page monthly sales reports for each of FiberMark's 29 salespeople, the salespeople can access business intelligence from the corporate intranet. "With a very short training cycle (15 minutes), they're up and flying. They print four pages, not 1,000," says Taylor, who adds that the system paid for itself in nine months in saved paper and related costs alone. More important, though, salespeople and executives can get the specific, up-to-date business intelligence they want anytime they want it.[11]

Business intelligence sounds like a great term, but what exactly is it? ***Business intelligence (BI)*** is knowledge—knowledge about your customers, your competitors, your business partners, your competitive environment, and your own internal operations—that gives you the ability to make effective, important, and often strategic business decisions. ***Business intelligence (BI) systems*** are the IT applications and tools that support the business intelligence function within an organization. The objective of BI is to improve the timeliness and quality of the input for decision making by helping knowledge workers to understand the

- Capabilities available in the firm.
- State of the art, trends, and future directions in the markets.
- Technological, demographic, economic, political, social, and regulatory environments in which the firm competes.
- Actions of competitors and the implications of these actions.[12]

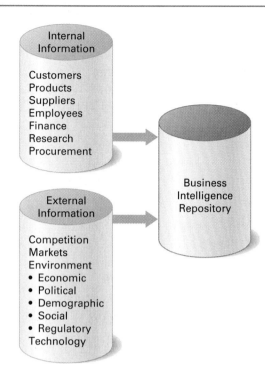

Figure 2.9

Building Business
Intelligence

As illustrated in Figure 2.9, business intelligence encompasses both internal and external information. Some business people treat competitive intelligence as a specialized branch of business intelligence. **Competitive intelligence (CI)** is business intelligence focused on the external competitive environment. There is even an organization for people who specialize in competitive intelligence called the Society for Competitive Intelligence Professionals (SCIP). Visit its Web site at www.scip.org to find out more about its activities, programs, and publications.

Business intelligence has information at its foundation, all kinds of information collected from various sources within an organization and from external sources. As described in Chapter 1, information is collected from transaction processing systems, for instance, and stored in various databases. A company may have databases for different applications, separate databases for customers, products, suppliers, and employees, among many others. Such databases are necessary to support the processing of day-to-day transactions. On the other hand, they contain more detailed information than managers need to make decisions.

To deal with this decision-making need, most organizations summarize information from their various databases into a data repository called a data warehouse. A **data warehouse** is a logical collection of information—gathered from many different operational databases—used to create business intelligence that supports business analysis activities and decision-making tasks. Often, a data warehouse is subdivided into smaller repositories called data marts for use by a single department within an organization. A **data mart** is a subset of a data warehouse in which only a focused portion of the data warehouse information is kept. For example, if an organization has a separate group that focuses on competitive intelligence, it may find it more effective to use its own data mart rather than the organization's data warehouse. We cover data warehouses and data marts in detail in Chapter 3.

STRATEGIC AND COMPETITIVE OPPORTUNITIES WITH BI

Business managers face many kinds of decisions ranging from routine decisions (such as whether to order additional stock) to decisions with long-range strategic implications (such as whether to expand into international markets). A survey by the Gartner Group of the strategic uses of business intelligence found that such uses were ranked by firms in the following order of importance:

1. Corporate performance management.
2. Optimizing customer relations, monitoring business activity, and traditional decision support.
3. Packaged stand-alone BI applications for specific operations or strategies.
4. Management reporting of business intelligence.[13]

Earlier, we mentioned that one of the primary purposes of BI is to improve the timeliness and quality of input to the decision process. Companies with well-designed BI systems available to their managers find that their managers make better decisions on a variety of business issues. Higher quality managerial decision making lets companies gain an advantage over their competitors who operate without the benefit of BI systems for their managers to use. BI systems provide managers with actionable information and knowledge:

BUSINESS INTELLIGENCE—LOUISVILLE SLUGGER BASEBALL BATS, GOLFER BIONIC GLOVES, AND HOCKEY GOALIE XCEED LEG PADS?

Every business in every industry needs business intelligence, even companies making baseball bats, golfing gloves, and hockey leg pads. One such prominent company is Hillerich & Bradsby (H&B). Although you may have never heard the company name, you may have used its products such as Louisville Slugger baseball bats, Bionic golf gloves, and Xceed hockey leg pads.

H&B's challenge was to integrate its reporting of key financial information from offices both domestic and international. As you might well guess, sports like baseball, golf, and hockey are played worldwide and H&B has a strong international presence. All of H&B's offices run SAP, a large enterprise software suite. But according to Scott Robinson, assistant controller at H&B, "The SAP computer system was very good, but its reporting was just not as robust as we needed."

So, H&B turned to WebFocus, business intelligence software by Information Builders (www.information-builders.com/). WebFocus is BI software that is completely interoperable with SAP. The information within SAP is ported over to WebFocus in real time and then employees of H&B use WebFocus to generate the needed BI reports much faster than they could with SAP.

According to Scott, "Running the income statement [through WebFocus] will save me days alone." When previously using SAP to generate reports about inventory, gross margin, and production, he had to generate the information and download it into Excel to create useful business intelligence. Scott now believes he can save 8 to 12 hours per month on that process alone using WebFocus.

Whether you're hitting a home run, making a hole-in-one, or stopping slap shots from the corner, H&B is using its BI software to ensure you have the right products in hand.[14]

1. at the right time,
2. in the right location,
3. in the right form[15]

Despite the fact that the benefits of BI systems are self-evident, many companies today do not yet have them. One of the reasons for this is that knowledge of their value as a competitive tool is not widely understood by business managers. Another reason is that, in some cases, they have been installed in companies but not used effectively.

IT SUPPORT FOR BUSINESS INTELLIGENCE

While the World Wide Web is used to support BI systems in many firms, specialized software is at the heart of BI. In the past, a large number of companies built their own systems. Now the trend is toward buying packages. Gartner Research found that the number of firms that plan to manage their BI integration internally dropped from 49 percent in 2001 to 37 percent in 2002. The reason for this change is that the traditional custom-design, build, and integrate model for BI systems takes too long (at least six months) and costs too much ($2 to $3 million). Implemented quickly, specialized BI software packages can deliver immediate benefits and a quick return on a company's investment.[16]

A large number of firms are involved in aspects of the BI business. Several companies identified as companies to watch in the BI field are Aydatum, Brio Software Decisions, Cognos, Crystal Decisions, E-Intelligence, Hyperion, MicroStrategy, ProClarity, Siebel,

Figure 2.10

Sample Digital
Dashboard

and Spotfire.[17] One interesting feature of many BI software packages is a digital dashboard. A *digital dashboard* displays key information gathered from several sources on a computer screen in a format tailored to the needs and wants of an individual knowledge worker (see Figure 2.10). To learn more about business intelligence and IT support, we encourage you to visit the following resources:

- Business Intelligence Knowledge Base—
  http://businessintelligence.ittoolbox.com
- Business Intelligence.com—www.businessintelligence.com
- Microstrategy—www.microstrategy.com
- Business Intelligence Evaluation Center—www.bievaluation.com
- *Intelligent Enterprise Magazine*—www.intelligententerprise.com/channels/bi/

Integrated Collaboration Environments

Siemens AG, based in Munich, Germany, is a 150-year-old electrical engineering and electronics company with 440,000 employees in 190 countries. Much of its work is done in teams, whose members work in integrated collaborative environments supported by a state-of the-art collaborative software suite, SiteScape's Forum (www.sitescape.com). A top Siemens executive describes his experience with the software this way: "A perfect example of the value Forum brings to Siemens is when I had to institute a cross-functional team of 18–20 people spread across the United States and Germany. We needed a communication channel that would be up 24 × 7. Because of the six-hour time difference, we set 9 A.M. and 3 P.M. as the push time. People were able to discuss ideas and share Web-enabled documents." He also hopes to use Forum in an extranet capacity, streamlining the supply chain management process and exploring Business to Business functions with the tool.

GLAXOSMITHKLINE CREATES "QUALITY OF LIFE" WITH GROOVE WORKSPACE

GlaxoSmithKline's (GSK) mission is to improve the quality of human life by enabling people to do more, feel better, and live longer. GSK is considered to be one of the leaders in the pharmaceutical industry, operating in 39 countries with over 7 percent of the worldwide market, 42,000 employees, and 99 manufacturing sites.

GSK's challenge is to create an effective and highly efficient collaboration environment for all its employees, especially those in research and development (R&D). Equally important, the collaboration environment must be secure and completely safe from outside intruders.

GSK turned to Groove Workspace (www.groove.net) for its "Team & Task" IT collaboration tool. GSK successfully uses Groove Workspace for its internal teams but also for collaboration with industry partners, suppliers, and even research-oriented universities. According to Bob Sutterly, senior business consultant with GSK, "In eight months of using Groove Workspace to collaborate with external partners, we have avoided expenses of $400,000 for several of our alliance projects, no longer incurring the administrative and access costs associated with VPNs, leased lines, and extranet file shares."

Most important, Groove Workspace provides GSK with a collaboration environment in which all employees can share sensitive information in a timely manner, reducing product development times significantly. Employees can create their own collaboration rooms in just a few minutes and have people all over the world working together shortly thereafter.

In any health care business, saving time is not only about saving money, it's also about saving lives.[18]

"I'm really happy with Forum," the executive says. "It helps productivity to have a Web-based collaboration solution which allows each team member to contribute freely to discussions and documents from anywhere, at any time."[19]

Almost everything you do in your organization will be performed in a team environment. So, improving team collaboration greatly increases your organization's productivity and competitive advantage. An *integrated collaboration environment (ICE)* is the environment in which virtual teams do their work. *Virtual teams* are teams whose members are located in varied geographic locations and whose work is supported by specialized ICE software or by more basic collaboration systems. A collaboration system is software that is designed specifically to improve the performance of teams by supporting the sharing and flow of information. More and more, virtual teams are composed of people from your company's alliance partners as well. An alliance partner is a company your company does business with on a regular basis in a collaborative fashion, usually facilitated by IT systems.

Many companies first use e-mail and then move on to collaboration systems incorporating more advanced features such as giving employees access to each other's calendars, group scheduling, imaging, workflow systems, and document management systems. *Workflow* defines all of the steps or business rules, from beginning to end, required for a business process. For example, in order for a bank to process a loan application correctly, there are a specified series of business processes that must be performed by different knowledge workers. *Workflow systems* facilitate the automation and management of business processes. For example, all the steps to process that loan application could be performed by a workflow system with the necessary documents updated and passed from knowledge worker to knowledge worker as electronic documents. Large companies produce millions of documents each month and they need to be organized and managed. A document management system manages a document through all the stages of its

Figure 2.11

An Integrated
Collaboration
Environment

processing. It is similar to a workflow system except that the focus is more on document storage and retrieval. Banks, for example, retain copies of your checks in electronic form and can produce a copy for you should you ever need one. As you can see, workflow systems are important IT-enablers of the value chain concept.

Companies will soon migrate to more sophisticated collaboration systems that use tele-, video-, and Web-conferencing in real time and that incorporate project management and work flow automation. To say the least, the ICE environment is rich with technology tools and support (see Figure 2.11).

Knowledge management systems are a variant of ICE. A **knowledge management (KM) system** is an IT system that supports the capturing, organization, and dissemination of knowledge (i.e., know-how) throughout an organization. The objective of knowledge management systems is to be sure that a company's knowledge of facts, sources of information, and solutions are available to all of its employees whenever needed.

Social network systems are another, newer form of ICE. **Social network systems** are IT systems that link you to people you know and, from there, to people your contacts know. For example, if a salesperson at your company wants an introduction to an influential executive at another company, a social network system could find out if someone in your company has good enough connections to arrange an introduction. This is exactly the kind of question that could get a quick reply from the right kind of social network system.

STRATEGIC AND COMPETITIVE OPPORTUNITIES WITH ICES

The payoffs from collaboration can be huge. For example, while oil and gas exploration companies usually form joint ventures on large projects, they often do not collaborate on purchases of high-dollar-value commodities for the project. A recent survey estimated that the industry could realize up to $7 billion in annual savings by using collaborative technologies and seeking more collaborative preferred provider relationships.[20]

There are many examples of knowledge management systems successfully adding value. For example, in making the case for a knowledge system at Hewlett-Packard (HP), John Doyle, the former head of HP Labs, is credited with saying, "If only HP knew what HP knows."[21] What he meant by this was that there was a huge amount of valuable knowledge in the brains and files (both paper and computer) of HP employees. If HP knew what knowledge was there, and it was shared and accessible to others, it could be useful in solving critical problems, or could lead to ideas for new products and services.

IT SUPPORT FOR INTEGRATED COLLABORATION ENVIRONMENTS

A comparison of ICE software is shown in Figure 2.12. Three ICE vendors dominate the market—IBM/Lotus, Microsoft, and Novell. Each incorporates "presence awareness" in the latest releases of their collaboration products. **Presence awareness** is a software function that determines whether a user is immediately reachable or is in a less-available status. Based on Instant Messaging (IM) technology, presence awareness is built into or will soon be included in all sorts of applications, from e-mail and CRM to knowledge management and social networking.

DO YOU WANT SPOKE POKING AROUND?

Assume that you and your teammates work in the accounting department at a large software company that sells CRM packages. Your company is in a highly competitive business and sometimes people wonder whether or not the company will survive. It has to compete against such big-name players as Seibel Systems and Salesforce.com, as well as scores of other companies.

Your company's management recently purchased a copy of Spoke (www.spoke.com), which we briefly discuss on the next page. Management announced to employees in every department of the company, including yours, that it needed help in getting new sales leads and that Spoke would help in the effort. You know that Spoke's application software searches the names and company affiliations stored in your e-mail contact list on your office computer's hard drive. It looks for companies the sales department is trying to reach, and if it finds a contact at one, refers the contact to someone in the sales department.

Let's say that Spoke finds a few likely contacts/companies in your contact list, or the contact list of one of your teammates, and someone from the sales department gives you a call and asks you to arrange an introduction. Would you be willing to make an introduction or do you feel it would be inappropriate? How do you feel about the Spoke software examining your contact lists whether you like it or not? Do you think a better way for employees to help the company get the additional sales leads it needs would be for employees to submit names of good prospects to the sales department rather than putting you in a position where you might feel pressure to cooperate?

Prepare a team position statement on this issue for class discussion. You may find that your team cannot agree on a single position. In this case, team members may divide into two or more camps, each with a different opinion. In either event, be prepared to justify your position(s) for the class discussion.

Groove and NextPage are both examples of a special kind of information-sharing software called peer-to-peer. **Peer-to-peer collaboration software** permits users to communicate in real time and share files without going through a central server. The peer-to-peer file-sharing feature in the collaboration software is combined with the ability to create and edit documents collaboratively and to send and receive text and voice messages.

While there are literally scores of knowledge management software packages available, social network software is relatively new. Still, there are several social network packages currently available, and more are becoming available each month. Some of them,

Figure 2.12

A Comparison of ICE Software

Type	Basic Functions	Example	Web site
Collaboration	Real-time collaboration and conferencing	LiveMeeting	www.microsoft.com
Workflow	Business process management	Metastorm	www.metastorm.com
Document Management	Enterprise content management	FileNet	www.filenet.com
Peer to Peer	Desktop and mobile collaboration	Groove	www.groove.net
Knowledge Management	Knowledge capture, organization, location, and reuse	IBM Knowledge Discovery	www-306.ibm.com/software/lotus/knowledge/
Social Network	Leveraging your personal and professional network	Linkedin	www.linkedin.com

like Friendster.com and Tickle, focus on dating. Others, like Tribe.net and Linkedin, focus on professional contacts. One of the more interesting and controversial social network packages is Spoke, which allows companies to mine their employees' computerized contact databases. Spoke searches employees' computer contact lists for contacts at other companies that can be used (with the employees' permission, of course) to arrange introductions for salespeople and thereby avoid cold calling.[22]

Back to the Beginning

As we've noted, to determine the most effective and appropriate use of technology you must clearly understand its role in the context of your business goals and strategies. So, let's review the conceptual models and frameworks we've discussed in this chapter and in Chapter 1 that help you do this:

- **Top-line versus bottom-line**—Top-line initiatives or activities focus on increasing revenues—reaching new customer segments, offering new products, cross-selling related services, and offering complementary products, to name just a few. Bottom-line initiatives or activities focus on minimizing the costs you incur in offering your products and services—by optimizing manufacturing processes, decreasing transportation costs, reducing the costs of human capital, and minimizing errors in a process, again, to name just a few. It will help you to be effective if you understand whether in your organization customer relationship management is a top-line initiative or a bottom-line initiative, or more one than the other, and just how. Does supply chain management focus on increasing revenues or cutting costs (perhaps some of both)? What types of business intelligence will help increase revenues and what types of business intelligence will help reduce costs? What is the role of ICEs in helping you increase revenues and/or reduce costs?

- **Run-Grow-Transform framework**—The RGT framework is helpful in decisions about allocating percentages of your IT dollars to the various activities involved in running your existing business and processes, in growing your business, and/or in transforming your business in entirely new ways of operation. Again, you have many questions to answer. Can your organization use a CRM system to find a new market segment of customers? If so, the CRM system enhances the "grow" aspect of the framework. How can your organization use an SCM system to create a tight supply chain, thus driving out costs and supporting the "run" aspect of the framework? How can your organization bring together teams of people (supported by ICEs) and equip them with the necessary business intelligence to determine how to *transform* your organization?

- **Porter's Five Forces Model**—Porter's model helps you analyze your industry. How can your organization use a CRM system to decrease the power of your buyers? How can your organization use an SCM system to reduce the power of your suppliers? What role will ICEs play in helping your organization enter a market or sell substitute and/or complementary products and services in your market? What business intelligence does your organization need to better understand the competitive landscape of a given industry? Porter's model suggests such questions you need to ask—and answer.

- **Value chains**—The value chain approach suggests quantifiable metrics concerning the value-added your organization provides to its customers. But from where will you gather that information about your customers' perceptions?

WHEN CRM TECHNOLOGY MAY BECOME TOO INVASIVE

On the surface, customer relationship management sounds like a good idea for every organization. And it is, except when it goes too far.

Consider this hypothetical—but not too unrealistic—situation. You walk into a retail store, say an electronics store. Upon entering the store, a computer captures your heat signature, which is a graphical map of the heat different parts of your body radiate or emit. Now, the computer can track you wherever you go in the store. It can track how long you spend looking at a computer (and which computer). It can track you as you move into the section of the store with music CDs and movie DVDs. It can track how long it takes before a salesperson talks to you and how long the salesperson spends with you. It tracks how long you stand in line to make your purchase.

Of course, when make your purchase, you use a credit card and then instantly the computer system has your personal information to which it can attach every move you made in the store. Later that week, you receive a phone call from the store offering you a special discount on the computer you were considering. You even start to receive e-mails from the store concerning new music CDs that are available. (They will, of course, be in the genre of music you reviewed while in the store.) What are your feelings about this? Is this an invasion of your privacy? Are retail stores required to inform you in advance that you will be monitored?

You may have seen movies like *Enemy of the State* and *Behind Enemy Lines* in which people are tracked via their heat signature like this. It really is quite possible. Heat signatures cannot uniquely identify who you are, but if you ultimately make a purchase using a personally identifiable device such as a credit card, your shopping profile can then be attached to your records. Such a tactic can be viewed narrowly as customer relationship management. What are your thoughts? Is this CRM gone awry?

Which IT tools, such as ICEs, will your organization use to analyze that information? If raw materials are a value-reducing component of your value chain, for instance, how can your organization use its supply chain management system to change this?

Again, we stress that technology is not a panacea. Business intelligence, for example, without purpose is useless. ICEs may not be particularly useful if the employees using them don't understand your business goals and strategies. Whatever you do in the business world, always drive your use of technology with your business strategies. Business tools such as top-line versus bottom-line, RGT framework, Porter's Five Forces Model, and value chains can help you better understand the role of technology and its usefulness.

Summary: Student Learning Outcomes Revisited

1. **Describe how to use Porter's Five Forces Model to evaluate the relative attractiveness of an industry.** Porter's *Five Forces Model* helps business people understand the relative attractiveness of an industry. Using it, you can determine whether to enter an industry or expand your operations if you already compete in it. The five forces are:

- *Buyer power*—high when buyers have many choices from whom to buy, and low when their choices are few

- *Supplier power*—high when buyers have few choices from whom to buy, and low when their choices are many
- *Threat of substitute products or services*—high when there are many alternatives to a product or service, and low when there are few alternatives from which to choose
- *Threat of new entrants*—high when it is easy for new competitors to enter a market, and low when there are significant entry barriers to entering a market
- *Rivalry among existing competitors*—high when competition is fierce in a market, and low when competition is more complacent

2. **Describe the role of value chains in identifying value-added and value-reducing processes.** The *value chain* concept views your organization as a chain—or series—of processes, each of which adds value to your product or service for your customers. To create a value chain picture of your organization, you must gather and analyze quantifiable information, usually from your customers. This information is then used to identify those processes that add the most value (value-added processes) and those processes that add the least (or even take away) value (value-reducing processes). You can then focus your IT efforts on (1) further adding value by augmenting your best processes and/or (2) eliminating or reducing your value-reducing processes.

3. **Define supply chain management (SCM) systems and describe their strategic and competitive opportunities and IT support.** A *supply chain management (SCM) system* is an IT system that supports supply chain management activities by automating the tracking of inventory and information among business processes and across companies. Strategic and competitive opportunities of SCM systems include optimizing fulfillment (ensuring the right quantity at the right time), logistics (keeping the cost of transporting materials as low as possible), production (ensuring production lines function smoothly), revenue and profit (ensuring no sales are lost because shelves are empty), and costs and prices (keeping the costs of parts and the prices of products at acceptable levels). IT support for SCM systems is now dominated by enterprise software providers such as SAP, Oracle, and PeopleSoft.

4. **Define customer relationship management (CRM) systems and describe their strategic and competitive opportunities and IT support.** A *customer relationship management (CRM) system* uses information about customers to gain insights into their needs, wants, and behaviors in order to serve them better. The strategic and competitive opportunities of a CRM system include treating customers better, understanding their needs and wants, tailoring offerings in response, devising more effective marketing campaigns, assuring that the sales process is efficiently managed, and providing superior after-sale service and support, for example, through well-run call centers. IT support for CRM systems includes Clarify, Oracle, SAP, Siebel Systems, and Salesforce.com.

5. **Define business intelligence (BI) systems and describe their strategic and competitive opportunities and IT support.** *Business intelligence (BI) systems* are the IT applications and tools that support the business intelligence function within an organization. The strategic and competitive opportunities of BI systems include corporate performance management, optimizing customer relations, monitoring business activity, traditional decision support, management reporting, and providing managers with actionable information and knowledge at the right time, in the right location, and in the right form. IT support for BI systems includes Aydatum, Brio Software Decisions, Cognos, Crystal Decisions, E-Intelligence, Hyperion, MicroStrategy, ProClarity, Siebel, and Spotfire.

6. **Define integrated collaboration environments (ICEs) and describe their strategic and competitive opportunities and IT support.** An *integrated collaboration environment (ICE)* is the environment in which virtual teams do their work. Strategic and competitive opportunities of ICEs include automating workflow, enabling geographically dispersed team members to work together, and document management, just to name a few. IT support for ICEs includes workflow systems, knowledge management (KM) systems, social network systems, presence awareness, and peer-to-peer collaboration software. Providers of IT support include Friendstar.com, Tickle, Tribe.net, Linkedin, and Spoke.

CLOSING CASE STUDY ONE

IF WE DON'T HAVE IT, YOU GET IT FOR FREE

You've heard the hype—delivery in 30 minutes or it's free . . . guaranteed freshness . . . and "I guarantee it" (The Men's Wearhouse slogan). Many of today's retailers are attempting to gain customer loyalty (an important component of effective customer relationship management) by making such guarantees. That means that their supply chain management systems must work effectively enough to avoid stock-outs. That means their delivery systems must be integrated with product-ordering systems. Here are a couple of interesting examples of making guarantees.

CASUAL MALE RETAIL GROUP

Casual Male makes a simple guarantee: If it's not in stock, it will be delivered to your doorstep within five business days or it's free. That's a tall order for Casual Male's nearly 500 Big and Tall stores spread across 44 states. And it's certainly contrary to the retail industry as a whole. According to a recent survey of over 300 retailers, only 33 percent stated that regularly priced items were in stock 91 percent of the time. The remaining two-thirds of the retailers stated that stock-outs occurred much more frequently. If you think 91 percent of the time is acceptable, think again. That means 1 out of every 10 customers will not find what he or she wants and opt to go to the competition.

To avoid stock-outs (and thus give away merchandise for free or, at the very least, have to deliver it to customers' homes), Casual Male implemented a new warehouse management system (by Manhattan Associates Inc.) and a new inventory replenishment system (by JDA Software Group Inc.). These systems were then integrated with POS systems in the retail stores. When items are shipped out of the distribution center and received by the stores, the location of the inventory is automatically updated in the replenishment system. Nightly, the POS systems at the retail stores send updated inventory information back to the replenishment system which forecasts needs. If inventory levels at the stores ever fall below the forecasts, Casual Male immediately communicates needed items to its suppliers via electronic data interchange (EDI).

According to Alexi Sarnevitz, research director of retail at AMR Research, "This is advanced retail planning. Having these merchandising systems in place allows [Casual Male] to more accurately match consumer demand with the inventory." This is an excellent way of saying that CRM systems and SCM systems must work together, must be integrated to feed each other information.

According to Casual Male, the systems could cut costs in its distribution center by up to 70 percent, saving the retailer as much as $20 to $25 million annually.

STAPLES INC.

If you were running a highly successful retail operation, would you guarantee the availability of your fastest moving inventory or be safe and only guarantee the availability of your slowest moving inventory that is seldom purchased? If you choose the latter, you're like many retailers playing it safe but you would be beaten by some of the competition such as Staples. Staples makes an in-stock guarantee for its fast-selling lines of ink-jet and toner cartridges, both of which Staples relies on heavily for revenue. If you find a cartridge is not in stock, Staples will ship it to your home with no delivery fee the next business day. It will also include a $10 coupon you can use the next time you purchase the same toner cartridge. Now that's an ambitious guarantee. While Casual Male will deliver an out-of-stock item within five days, Staples will deliver an out-of-stock item the next business day and give you $10 off your next purchase of the same item.

Staples' computer systems are linked with those of shipping companies such as UPS. If an item is out of stock, the Staples systems find the item at another store and immediately send UPS a request for package pickup and delivery. That's the way Staples can guarantee next-day delivery.[23]

Questions

1. In the context of Porter's Five Forces Model, how does making guarantees increase the rivalry among existing competitors? Other than making the same guarantee, how could other men's clothing retailers compete with the Casual Male guarantee? Other than making the same guarantee, how could other office supply retailers compete with the Staples guarantee?

2. How does making guarantees create entry barriers into an industry and thus reduce the threat of new entrants?

3. In the context of the value chain concept, would inventory replenishment be a support value process or a primary value process for Casual Male and Staples? In what ways could Casual Male and Staples gather the necessary information to determine if inventory replenishment was a value-added process or a value-reducing process?

4. Consider the chicken and egg dilemma for this case. You need an effective CRM system to determine the wants and needs of your customers. You need an effective SCM system to have items available for sale so you can start to gather information about customer wants and needs. The dilemma then is: Which system should you implement first—a CRM system or an SCM system? Justify your answer.

CLOSING CASE STUDY TWO

THE RESTAURANT INDUSTRY EATS UP BUSINESS INTELLIGENCE

On November 15, 2004, CKE Restaurants, the company that owns and operates Hardee's, went against every health-kick fad and began selling the Monster Thickburger. With two-thirds of a pound of Angus beef, three slices of cheese, four strips of bacon, and mayonnaise on a buttery sesame seed bun, the Monster Thickburger contains 1,420 calories and 107 grams of fat. From a pure health point of view, the burger is so bad for you that one nutrition advocacy group referred to it as "the fast food equivalent of a snuff film." Even Jay Leno made jokes about it on *The Tonight Show*.

But none of that stopped CKE from rolling out the huge burger in 2004. And since then, nothing has stopped the sale of the burger. In December of 2004, sales were up 5.8 percent for Hardee's stores that had been open for at least a year. According to Brad Haley, Hardee's executive vice president of marketing, ". . . the Monster Thickburger was directly responsible for a good deal of that increase." So, why did CKE take a huge risk of offering a huge burger that had such huge health risks? It relied on business intelligence.

CKE's business intelligence system is called CPR (there has to be some irony there), which stands for CKE Performance Reporting. In test markets, CKE used its BI system to determine if the Monster Thickburger was actually contributing to sales or simply cannibalizing sales of less desirable burgers. The CPR system was also used to evaluate a number of other factors includ-

ing menu mix, production cost of the Monster Thickburger, gross profits and total sales for each store, unit volume comparisons for the Monster Thickburger and other burgers, and finally the contribution margin made by each menu item. In the end, the business intelligence foretold of the nationwide success of the Monster Thickburger. And it wasn't wrong.

Many other restaurants are also using business intelligence systems to make important business decisions (and make money).

In June 2003, on the basis of its business intelligence, Wendy's made the decision to begin accepting credit cards. Typically, orders at fast-food restaurants like Wendy's are for less than $10. Each credit-card transaction carries with it a processing fee and that fee cuts deeply into the profit margin on orders that are less than $10. Wendy's business intelligence, however, pointed out that people paying with a credit card were more likely to spend more money than those paying with cash. It turned out to be true. Customers who use a credit card to pay for an order spend (on the average) 35 percent more than people paying with cash. Interestingly enough, there are still fast-food restaurants that won't accept credit cards.

Carlson Restaurant Worldwide, the company that owns and operates T.G.I. Friday's and Pick Up Stix restaurants, used its business intelligence system to help reduce costs. Carlson's BI system is a sort of best-of-breed collection of tools including analytical tools from Cognos (www.cognos.com) and Hyperion (www.hyperion.com), a data warehouse from Oracle (www.oracle.com), and reporting tools from Microsoft (www.microsoft.com). With this collection of tools, key decision makers at Carlson were able to identify that there were problems in its supply chain. It seems that there was a discrepancy between contract prices and the prices actually charged to the restaurants by suppliers. Carlson renegotiated its contracts, which saved the company $200,000 in just one year.

Nick Ibrahim, CIO of Ruby Tuesday, used a business intelligence system to evaluate underperforming restaurants. At one particular restaurant the business intelligence pointed out that table turnover was 55 to 60 minutes, compared to the average of about 45 minutes. Upon closer inspection, Nick was able to reengineer the kitchen so that orders could be prepared faster, thus enabling customers to get their meals quicker and leave the restaurant sooner. It wasn't that there was insufficient demand to support the restaurant. It was simply that the restaurant could not efficiently respond to the demand that was there.[24]

Questions

1. Consider Carlson and its use of a business intelligence system. Was the focus of the system a top-line initiative or a bottom-line initiative? Justify your answer.

2. Carlson's BI solution is to use a best-of-breed approach and select technologies from multiple vendors. What are the potential downsides to such an approach?

3. Think for a moment about the business intelligence used by CKE to determine to launch the successful Monster Thickburger. Create a list of 20 probable information elements of that business intelligence. For each, identify whether it is internal information or external information.

4. Ruby Tuesday used business intelligence to shorten table turnover time. Which of Porter's Five Forces does this affect? You should be able to identify more than one. For each, provide a short discussion.

5. Wendy's approach to using business intelligence foretold a better yield on the purchases of its credit card–paying customers. Is this a top-line initiative or a bottom-line initiative? What if the costs of accepting credit cards for payments outweigh the incremental revenues gained? Should Wendy's still do it? What if all the competition is accepting credit card payments? How does Wendy's accepting credit card payments relate to the rivalry among existing competitors in Porter's Five Forces Model?

Key Terms and Concepts

Back office system, 84
Business intelligence (BI), 85
Business intelligence (BI) system, 85
Business process, 76
Buyer power, 73
Competitive intelligence (CI), 86
Customer relationship management (CRM) system, 82
Data mart, 86
Data warehouse, 86
Digital dashboard, 88
Distribution chain, 78
Entry barrier, 75
Five Forces Model, 72
Front office system, 84
Integrated collaboration environment (ICE), 89
Inter-modal transportation, 79
Just-in-time (JIT), 79

Knowledge management (KM) system, 90
Loyalty program, 73
Peer-to-peer collaboration software, 91
Presence awareness, 90
Rivalry among existing competitors, 75
Sales force automation (SFA) system, 82
Social network system, 90
Supplier power, 73
Supply chain management (SCM), 79
Supply chain management (SCM) system, 79
Switching cost, 74
Threat of new entrants, 75
Threat of substitute products or services, 74
Value chain, 76
Virtual team, 89
Workflow, 89
Workflow system, 89

Short-Answer Questions

1. Why is it important to consider IT applications in the context of your organization's goals and strategies?
2. What is the role of Porter's Five Forces Model? What are the five forces in that model?
3. How are buyer power and supplier power the converse of each other?
4. How can loyalty programs help reduce buyer power?
5. How can switching costs reduce the threat of substitute products or services?
6. What is an entry barrier? How can the presence of an entry barrier reduce the threat of new entrants?
7. What is a value chain? How can using a value chain help an organization better understand the value each process provides?
8. What is a distribution chain?
9. What is the role of a supply chain management (SCM) system?
10. What are the strategic and competitive opportunities of SCM systems?
11. Who are the leading providers of SCM software?
12. What is the role of a customer relationship management (CRM) system?
13. What are the strategic and competitive opportunities of CRM systems?
14. What is the difference between front office and back office systems?
15. What is business intelligence (BI)? Why is it important?
16. What is the difference between a data warehouse and a data mart?
17. What is a digital dashboard?
18. Why do virtual teams need integrated collaboration environments?
19. What are social network systems?
20. How does presence awareness work?

Assignments and Exercises

1. **COLLABORATION WORK** In a group of three or more students, collaborate on a project to make a list of 100 music CDs or video DVDs. Classify them into groups. For example, if you choose DVDs, your categories might be adventure, comedy, drama, classic, horror, musicals, or others. All communication about the project must be electronic (but not by phone). You can use e-mail, set up a Web site, use a chat room, use instant messaging, or use a collaboration e-room, if your school has that facility. Print out a copy of all correspondence on the project and put the correspondence together in a folder in chronological order. Was this task very different from collaborating face to face with your partners? In which ways was it better, in which ways worse? What additional problems or advantages would you expect if the people you were working with were in a different hemisphere?
2. **REAL WORLD APPLICATIONS** In the chapter we mentioned that many CRM installations have been less than successful. On the other hand, there are many satisfied users of CRM applications. Log on to the Internet and find at least three examples of companies that are getting real business benefits from their CRM systems. Prepare a report on the results they are getting and the way they achieved them. One place to start your search is at www.searchcrm.com. Another good source is the Web sites of CRM application software vendors Siebel and Salesforce.com (www.siebel.com and www.salesforce.com). At least one of your examples must be from a site other than the three mentioned.
3. **UNUSUAL APPLICATIONS OF GROOVE** Groove is one of the best known peer-to-peer collaboration software companies. It has a Web log (or "blog") on its Web site which is full of current information on the benefits of peer-to-peer collaboration software and the experiences of people who use Groove on team collaboration projects. Log on to the Groove Web site at www.groove.net and navigate your way to its blog. Find two examples of unusual ways that people are using Groove and be prepared to summarize your findings in a class discussion. The more unusual the application the better.
4. **WAL-MART'S SCM SYSTEM** Wal-Mart is famous for its low prices, and you may have experienced its low prices first-hand. At least, you have probably seen its motto, "Always Low Prices—Always." One of the biggest reasons Wal-Mart is able to sell at prices lower than almost everyone else is that it has a

superefficient supply chain. Its IT-enabled supply chain management system is the envy of the industry because it drives excess time and unnecessary costs out of the supply chain. So, because Wal-Mart can buy low, it sells low. As a matter of fact, if your company wants to sell items to Wal-Mart for it to sell in its stores, you will have to do business with it electronically. If your company can't do that, Wal-Mart won't buy anything from you. Log on to Wal-Mart's Web site (www.walmart.com), search for supplier information, and find out what Wal-Mart's requirements are for its suppliers to do business with it electronically. Prepare a brief summary of its requirements for presentation in class.

5. **YOUR SCHOOL'S VALUE CHAIN** Develop a value chain for your school. You don't have to gather information to construct the value chain, but you do have to determine which processes are support value processes and which processes are primary value processes. Draw your value chain according to Figure 2.3 on page 76. Finally, list the three most important processes to you as a student and provide a short explanation of why they are the most important to you.

6. **PORTER AND CELL PHONES** In a group of three or four students, select a cell provider that one of your group uses. Now, within the context of Porter's Five Forces Model, define how that cell phone provider (1) reduces buyer power, (2) increases supplier power, (3) reduces the threat of substitute products or services, and (4) reduces the threat of new entrants. Finally, describe the competitive environment of cell phone providers.

Discussion Questions

1. Do you think that your school would benefit from installing a customer relationship management (CRM) system? How might it benefit you as a student? How could it benefit your school?

2. If you were a member of a virtual team using collaboration software, would you want the presence awareness feature as part of the software? Why or why not?

3. As discussed in the chapter, Spoke software examines employees' e-mail contact lists searching for people at potential customer sites who may be known to employees. Do you think a company has an ethical obligation to notify employees it is going to use Spoke, or (because it will search only computer files on company-owned computers) is it none of the employees' business?

4. Think about the difference between top-line initiatives and bottom-line initiatives. Now classify the four major IT applications discussed in this chapter—supply chain management systems, customer relationship management systems, business intelligence systems, and integrated collaboration environments— according to top line versus bottom line. Which focus mainly on the top line? Which focus mainly on the bottom line? Which focus on either depending entirely on the business situation at hand?

5. In the Run-Grow-Transform (RGT) framework, the third component is that of transformation, or enabling your organization to operate in entirely new ways. Of the four major business IT applications we discussed in this chapter, which one(s) do you believe most support organizational transformation? Justify your answer.

6. In a group of three to four students, consider eBay in the context of Porter's Five Forces Model. How does eBay reduce the threat of new entrants? If necessary, you may want to explore eBay's site (www.ebay.com) and determine the role of buyer and seller ratings, its integration with PayPal, and how it helps buyers and sellers resolve disputes.

7. In this chapter, we discussed the use of loyalty programs in the travel industry as a mechanism for reducing buyer power. What is another industry that also uses loyalty programs to reduce buyer power? How does that industry use loyalty programs to do so?

8. In most industries, the rivalry among existing competitors is intense. Name a few industries in which this is not true and describe the uniqueness of those industries that are characterized by a "low" competitive environment.

Ordering Products and Services on the Internet

For most people, electronic commerce is all about business-to-consumer (B2C). On the Internet, you (as an individual consumer) can purchase groceries, clothes, computers, automobiles, music, antiques, books, and much more. If you want to buy it, there's probably an Internet site selling it. Even more, there are probably hundreds of Internet sites selling what it is you want, giving you the opportunity to shop for the best buy.

You can indeed find almost anything you want to buy on the Internet. However, you should carefully consider the person or organization from whom you're making the purchase. You want to be sure you are doing business with someone you can trust. This is especially true if you have to provide a credit card number to make the purchase.

BOOKS AND MUSIC

Books and music make up one category of products you can readily find to purchase on the Internet. One of the most widely known and acclaimed Internet sites engaged in electronic commerce is Amazon.com at www.amazon.com. Amazon offers several million book and music titles for sale.

Of course, as with all products you buy on the Internet, you need to consider price and the amount you'll save on the Internet compared to purchasing books and music from local stores. Sometimes prices are higher on the Internet, and you can certainly expect to pay some sort of shipping and handling charges. We know that there are several sites that let you buy individual songs and download them to your computer in MP3 format, but for right now let's just focus on buying traditional CDs.

Make a list of books and music CDs that you're interested in purchasing. Find their prices at a local store. Next, visit three Web sites selling books and music and answer the following questions.

- **A.** What are the books, CDs, or cassettes you're interested in?
- **B.** What are their prices at a local store?
- **C.** Can you find them at each Internet site?
- **D.** Are the local prices higher or lower than the Internet prices?
- **E.** How do you order and pay for your products?
- **F.** How long is the shipping delay?
- **G.** What is the shipping charge?
- **H.** Overall, how would you rate your Internet shopping experience compared to your local store shopping experience?

CLOTHING AND ACCESSORIES

It might seem odd, but many people purchase all types of clothing on the Internet from shoes to pants to all kinds of accessories (including perfume). The disadvantage in shopping for clothes on the Internet is that you can't actually try them on and stand in front of the mirror. But if you know exactly what you want (by size and color), you can probably find and buy it on the Internet.

Connect to several clothing and accessory sites and experience cyber–clothes shopping. As you do, consider the following.

    A. How do you order and pay for merchandise?

    B. What sort of description is provided about the clothing? Text, photos, perhaps 3D views?

    C. What is the return policy for merchandise that you don't like or that doesn't fit?

    D. Finally, is shopping for clothes on the Internet as much fun as going to the Mall? Why or why not?

AUCTION HOUSES

Auction houses act as clearing stations at which you can sell your products or purchase products from other people in an auction format (essentially, consumer-to-consumer or C2C electronic commerce). eBay (www.ebay.com), the most popular auction house, boasts millions of items for sale.

It works quite simply. First, you register as a user at a particular auction house. Once you do, you'll have a unique user ID and password that allow you to post products for sale or bid on other products. When the auction is complete for a particular product (auction houses set time limits that last typically from 1 to 10 days), the auction house will notify the seller and the winning bidder. Then, it's up to you and the other person to exchange money and merchandise.

So, think of a product you'd like to buy or sell—perhaps a rare coin, a computer, a hard-to-find Beanie Baby, or a car. Connect to a couple of different Internet auction houses and answer the following questions for each.

    A. What is the registration process to become a user?

    B. Do you have to pay a fee to become a user?

    C. Is your product of interest listed?

    D. How do you bid on a product?

    E. What does the auction house charge you to sell a product?

    F. What is the duration of a typical auction?

    G. Can you set a minimum acceptable bid for a product you want to sell?

    H. How does the auction house help you evaluate the credibility of other people buying and selling products?

AUTOMOBILES

A product category that you might not expect to find on the Internet is automobiles—but on the Internet you can find literally any automobile you'd be interested in purchasing. Muscle cars, Jaguars, Rolls Royces, Hondas, and thousands more are for sale on the Internet.

Try connecting to a few automobile sites and browse for an automobile you'd like to own. As you do, think about these issues: What variety can you find (color, engine size, interior, etc.)? Are financing options available? How do you "test drive" a car for sale on the Internet? What happens if you buy a car and then don't like it? What about used cars? Can you trust people selling a used car on the Internet? How do you pay for a car, typically a relatively large purchase?

You can find a variety of sites that provide competitive pricing information concerning cars. Many of these sites are for all cars in general, not just those for sale on the Internet. One of the best sites is AutoSite at www.autosite.com. If you're ever shopping for a new or used car, you should definitely check out that site.

EXTENDED LEARNING MODULE B

THE WORLD WIDE WEB AND THE INTERNET

Student Learning Outcomes

1. DEFINE THE RELATIONSHIPS AMONG WEB SITE, WEB SITE ADDRESS, DOMAIN NAME, WEB PAGE, AND UNIFORM RESOURCE LOCATOR (URL).

2. EXPLAIN HOW TO INTERPRET THE PARTS OF AN ADDRESS ON THE WEB.

3. IDENTIFY THE MAJOR COMPONENTS AND FEATURES OF WEB BROWSER SOFTWARE.

4. DESCRIBE THE DIFFERENCES BETWEEN DIRECTORY AND TRUE SEARCH ENGINES.

5. DESCRIBE THE VARIOUS TECHNOLOGIES THAT MAKE UP THE INTERNET.

6. IDENTIFY KEY CONSIDERATIONS IN CHOOSING AN INTERNET SERVICE PROVIDER (ISP).

7. DESCRIBE THE COMMUNICATIONS SOFTWARE AND TELECOMMUNICATIONS HARDWARE YOU NEED TO CONNECT TO THE INTERNET.

Introduction

The most visible and explosive information technology tool is the Internet, and with it the World Wide Web (Web). No matter where you look or what you read, someone always seems to be referring to one of the two. On television commercials, you find Web site addresses displayed (such as www.ibm.com for an IBM commercial or www.toyota.com for a Toyota commercial). In almost every magazine, you find articles about the Internet because of its growing significance in our society. Most major business publications, such as *Fortune, Forbes,* and *BusinessWeek,* devote entire issues each year to the Internet and how to use it for electronic commerce. Of course, many such publications have been carrying articles detailing how and why so many dot-coms failed in recent years (now affectionately referred to as *dot-bombs*).

The Internet really is everywhere—and it's here to stay. What's really great about the Internet is that it takes only a couple of hours to learn. Once you've read the text for this module, you should try your hand at the Internet scavenger hunts on pages 120–121. You'll be surprised to learn how easy it is to find information on the Internet.

World Wide Web

The **World Wide Web,** or **Web** as you probably know it, is a multimedia-based collection of information, services, and Web sites supported by the Internet. The **Internet** is a vast network of computers that connects millions of people all over the world. Schools, businesses, government agencies, and many others have all connected their internal networks to the Internet. The Internet and all its technological infrastructure are what make the Web possible. People tend to consider the Web and the Internet to be the same. (Although they are not.)

WEB SITES, ADDRESSES, AND PAGES

As you use the Web, you'll most often be accessing Web sites. A **Web site** is a specific location on the Web where you visit, gather information, and perhaps even order products. Each Web site has a specific Web site address. A **Web site address** is a unique name that identifies a specific site on the Web. Technically, this address is called a domain name. A **domain name** identifies a specific computer on the Web and the main page of the entire site. Most people use the term *Web site address* instead of the technical term *domain name.* For example, the Web site address for *USA Today* is www.usatoday.com (see Figure B.1).

Most Web sites include several and perhaps hundreds of Web pages. A **Web page** is a specific portion of a Web site that deals with a certain topic. The address for a specific Web page is called a URL. A **URL (uniform resource locator)** is an address for a specific Web page or document within a Web site. Most people opt for the common term of *Web page address* when referring to a URL. As you can see in Figure B.1, you can click on the link for **Sports** on the main page for *USA Today.* By clicking on that link, you will

Figure B.1

The *USA Today* Web Site and Sports Web Page

Web site address or domain name

Links

then be taken to a specific Web page within the *USA Today* Web site. The URL or Web page address for that page is www.usatoday.com/sports/front.htm. Links are important on the Web. A **link** (the technical name is **hyperlink**) is clickable text or an image that takes you to another site or page on the Web.

UNDERSTANDING ADDRESSES

When you access a certain Web site or page, you do so with its unique address, such as www.usatoday.com (for our *USA Today* example). Addresses, because they are unique, tell you some important information about the site or page. Let's consider two different examples (see Figure B.2): Yahoo! (www.yahoo.com) and the University of Technology in Sydney, Australia (www.uts.edu.au).

Most addresses start with http://www, which stands for *hypertext transfer protocol* (http) and *World Wide Web* (www). The http:// part is so common now that you don't even have to use it in most cases. The remaining portion of the address is unique for each site or page. If you consider www.yahoo.com, you know that it's the address for Yahoo!. You can also tell it's a commercial organization by the last three letters: com. This extension can take on many forms and is referred to as the **top-level domain.** Top-level domains include

- **com**—Commercial or for-profit business
- **coop**—Cooperative
- **edu**—Educational institution
- **gov**—U.S. government agency
- **mil**—U.S. military organization
- **net**—Internet administrative organization
- **org**—Professional or nonprofit organization
- **int**—International treaties organization

- **info**—General information
- **biz**—Business
- **museum**—Accredited museum
- **name**—Personal
- **pro**—Accountant, doctor, lawyer, etc.

The top-level domain ".com" identifies Yahoo! as a commercial or for-profit organization.

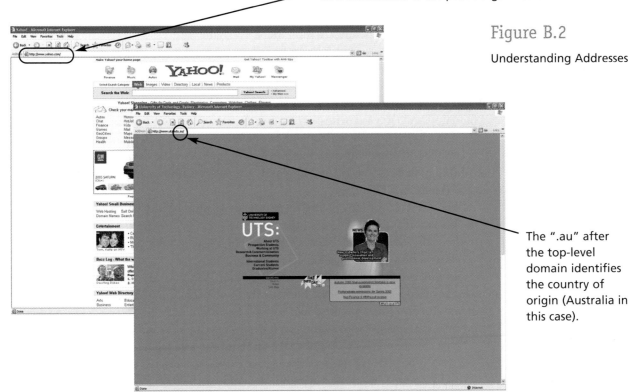

Figure B.2

Understanding Addresses

The ".au" after the top-level domain identifies the country of origin (Australia in this case).

Some addresses have a two-character extension that follows the top-level domain. In this case, it's to identify the country location of the site. For example, the site address for the University of Technology in Sydney, Australia, is www.uts.edu.au. From that address, you can tell it's for an educational institution (edu) located in Australia (au).

USING WEB BROWSER SOFTWARE

Web browser software enables you to surf the Web. When we viewed the sites for *USA Today*, Yahoo!, and University of Technology in Sydney, Australia, we were using Web browser software. The most popular Web browsers today are Internet Explorer (by Microsoft), Netscape 7.2 (Netscape uses only the version number to reference its Web browser product), and Firefox 1.0.2 (by Mozilla). Internet Explorer comes standard on most computers; all are free for you to use and you can download them at the following sites:

- Internet Explorer—www.microsoft.com/downloads
- Netscape 7.2—http://browser.netscape.com/nsb/download/default.jsp (At the time we wrote this text, Netscape had already released the beta version of Netscape 8.0. You can probably download the newer version from the same site.)
- Firefox 1.0.2—www.mozilla.org/

To demonstrate how you use Web browser software, let's take a quick tour of Internet Explorer, Netscape 7.2, and Firefox 1.0.2. In Figure B.3, you can see we have used all three Web browsers to access eBay (www.ebay.com). For each Web browser, the menu bar appears across the top and includes such functions as **File, Edit, View, Tools,** and **Help.** Each also has a few unique menu options, but all the menu bars support the same basic functions. For example, if you click on **File** (using any of the three Web browsers), you'll see a pull-down menu that allows you to initiate other actions such as printing the Web site and sending the Web site via e-mail to someone else.

Below the menu bar, you'll find a button bar on all three Web browsers that supports more functions. We won't go into any of those in detail here; you can play with them at your leisure. Next is the **Address** field. On Internet Explorer, it's located below the button bar; on both Netscape 7.2 and Firefox 1.0.2, the **Address** field is located next to the button bar. If you know the address for where you want to go, click in the **Address** field, type in the address, and then hit **Enter.**

One of the most important features of any Web browser is that you can create, edit, and maintain a list of your most commonly visited addresses on the Web. In Internet Explorer, it's called a **Favorites list,** and in Netscape 7.2 and Firefox 1.0.2 it's called a **Bookmarks list.** So, if you frequently visit eBay, you can save the address in one of these lists while you're viewing it. In Internet Explorer, click on the **Favorites** button and then **Add.** In both Netscape 7.2 and Firefox 1.0.2, click on **Bookmarks** in the menu bar and then **Bookmark This Page.**

Web browser software is the easiest personal productivity software to learn. Most people find that they need very little instruction and seldom need a book. Just connect to the Web, start the Web browser of your choice, play around for an hour or so, and you'll soon be a Web surfing expert.

It really is quite simple. When you start your Web browser software, you'll first see what is called a *home page*—the Web site that your Web browser automatically connects to and displays when you first start surfing. Once you're there, you can click on any of the links that interest you, or you can type in a new address and go to any other site.

If you're not precisely sure of a Web site address, you begin to search for it in one of two ways. The first is to use a search engine, which we'll discuss in the next section. The second is to type in a logical name in the **Address** field. For example, if you want to download tax forms from the IRS Web site but don't know the address of the IRS, you

Figure B.3

Internet Explorer, Netscape 7.2, and Firefox 1.0.2

can simply type in "IRS" or "internal revenue service" in the **Address** field. Your Web browser will automatically begin a search for Web sites related to those terms and hopefully will find the right site for you. (In the instance of searching for the IRS, all three Web browsers do take you to the site you need.)

Search Engines

There will be occasions when you want to find information and services on the Web, but you don't know exactly which site to visit. In this case, you can type in a logical name as we just demonstrated, or you can use a search engine. A *search engine* is a facility on the Web that helps you find sites with the information and/or services you want. There are many types of search engines on the Web, the two most common being directory search engines and true search engines.

A *directory search engine* organizes listings of Web sites into hierarchical lists. Yahoo! is the most popular and well known of these. If you want to find information using a directory search engine, start by selecting a specific category and continually choose subcategories until you arrive at a list of Web sites with the information you want. Because you continually narrow down your selection by choosing subcategories, directory search engines are hierarchical.

A *true search engine* uses software agent technologies to search the Internet for key words and then places them into indexes. In doing so, true search engines allow you to ask questions or type in key terms as opposed to continually choosing subcategories to arrive at a list of Web sites. Google is the most popular and well-known true search engine.

As an illustration of a search, let's consider the task of finding out who won the Academy Awards in 2004. We'll see how directory and true search engines differ.

USING A DIRECTORY SEARCH ENGINE

As we stated, Yahoo! is the most popular and well-known directory search engine. Figure B.4 shows the sequence of pages (categories) you would traverse using Yahoo! to determine who won the Academy Awards in 2004. The sequence of categories includes

- **Arts**
- **Awards**
- **Movies and Film@**
- **Academy Awards**
- **76th Annual Academy Awards (2004)**

In the final screen you can see a list of Web sites from which you can choose.

There are some definite advantages to performing a search in this way. If you look at the next-to-last screen, for example, **Academy Awards,** it also includes subcategories for the Academy Awards in each of the last eight years (1996–2003). So, you can easily find related information using a directory search engine.

You can also use directory search engines in a different fashion. For example, in the first screen, we could have entered **academy +awards +2004** in the field immediately to the left of the **Yahoo! Search** button and then clicked on that button. This particular search would yield a list of Web sites that is very similar to the list we received by choosing subcategories.

You might notice that we included the plus sign (+) in a couple of different places in our key terms list. By doing so, we limited the search to finding just sites that included all three words. Likewise, if you want to limit a search so that it won't show Web sites that contain certain key words, you would use a minus sign (−). For example, if you wanted to find

Figure B.4

Using a Directory Search Engine

Web sites that contain information about the Miami Dolphins NFL team, you could enter **Miami +Dolphins.** That would probably yield a list of suitable sites, but it might also include sites that include information about watching dolphins (the aquatic version) in Miami. You can further refine your search by entering something like **Miami +Dolphins −aquatic −mammal.** That search will yield a list of Web sites that have the terms *Miami* and *Dolphins* but will eliminate any sites that have the terms *aquatic* and *mammal.*

When you use a directory search engine and type in specific terms instead of traversing through subcategories, we definitely recommend that you make use of the plus sign and/or minus sign. For example, if you want to find sites about wind tunnels, using **wind tunnel** will return a list of sites related to wind tunnels but also the wind (weather sites) and tunnels in general. On the other hand, **wind +tunnel** will yield a more refined list of sites. We recommend that you complete the Team Work project (Finding and Using Search Engines) on page 111. As you do, you'll find that some search engines support advanced and unique capabilities that can help you further refine your search criteria.

USING A TRUE SEARCH ENGINE

Google is the most popular and well-known true search engine. Using Google (www.google.com), you simply ask a question or type in some key terms. For finding out who won the Academy Awards in 2004, we would simply enter **Who won the Academy Awards in 2004** and hit the **Google Search** button. As you can see in Figure B.5, Google returned a list of possible Web sites.

Both types of search engines are very easy to use. Which you choose is really a function of how you think. Some people think in terms of hierarchical lists while others think in terms of questions. What you'll undoubtedly find is that directory search engines are better in some cases while true search engines are better in others.

Figure B.5

Using a True Search Engine

Our question

Possible Web sites with answers

FINDING AND USING SEARCH ENGINES

Search engines are easy to find on the Web and even easier to use. In fact, there are about 100 search engines that you can use to find almost any information you need.

Your group's tasks include (1) creating a list of the 5 most popular search engines on the Web and (2) per-forming a search on each for the same information. As you complete the second task, evaluate how easy or difficult it was to use each search engine. Also, evaluate the quality of the Web site list you received from each search engine.

Internet Technologies

To best take advantage of everything the Web has to offer, it often helps to understand what's going on behind the Web, that is, the Internet. The Internet is really the enabling structure that makes the Web possible. Without the Web, the Internet still exists and you can still use it. But the reverse is not true. The Internet is the set of underlying technologies that makes the Web possible. The Web is somewhat of a graphical user interface (GUI) that sets on top of the Internet. The Web allows you to click on links to go to other sites, and it allows you to view information in multiple forms of media.

THE INTERNET BACKBONE

The *Internet backbone* is the major set of connections for computers on the Internet (see Figure B.6). A *network access point (NAP)* is a point on the Internet where several connections converge. At each NAP is at least one computer that simply routes Internet traffic from one place to another (much like an airport where you switch planes to your final destination). These NAPs are owned and maintained by network service providers. A *network service provider (NSP),* such as MCI or AT&T, owns and maintains routing computers at NAPs and even the lines that connect the NAPs to each other. In Figure B.6, you can see that Dallas is a NAP, with lines converging from Atlanta, Phoenix, Kansas City, and Austin.

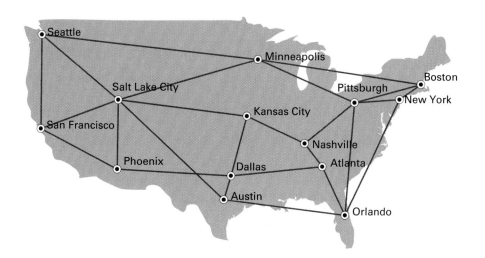

Figure B.6

The Internet Backbone in the United States

At any given NAP, an Internet service provider may connect its computer or computers to the Internet. An *Internet service provider (ISP)* is a company that provides individuals, organizations, and businesses access to the Internet. ISPs include AOL, Juno, and perhaps even your school. In turn, you "dial up" or connect your computer to an ISP computer. So, your ISP provides you access to the Internet (and thus the Web) by allowing you to connect your computer to its computer (which is already connected to the Internet).

If you live in the San Francisco area and send an e-mail to someone living near Boston, your e-mail message might travel from San Francisco to Salt Lake City, then to Minneapolis, and finally to Boston. Of course, your e-mail message may very well travel the route of San Francisco, Phoenix, Dallas, Atlanta, Nashville, Pittsburgh, Orlando, New York, and then Boston. But, no matter—your message will get there. Can you imagine the route that your e-mail message would travel if you were in San Francisco sending it to someone in Venice, Italy? One time, it might go west around the world through Australia. The next time, it might go east around the world through New York and then on to London.

INTERNET SERVERS

There are many types of computers on the Internet, namely, router (which we've already discussed), client, and server computers (see Figure B.7). The computer that you use to access the Internet and surf the Web is called a *client computer*. Your client computer can

Figure B.7

Servers on the Internet

USING A WEB PORTAL

Most Web browser software is already configured to take you to a certain Web site when you start surfing. For example, Internet Explorer usually starts at the Microsoft Network site (MSN at www.msn.com). Sites such as MSN, Yahoo!, and The Go Network (www.go.com) are often referred to as Web portals. A **Web portal** is a site that provides a wide range of services, including search engines, free e-mail, chat rooms, discussion boards, and links to hundreds of different sites.

The nice thing about Web portals is that they often let you customize the first page you see. So, you can request a ticker of your favorite stocks, the weather forecast for your area over the next three days, and a list of sites you commonly visit.

In this project, you are to create a customized and personal Web portal at two different places on the Web. We recommend that you do so at one of these sites (although there are many others):

- www.msn.com
- www.go.com
- www.excite.com
- www.yahoo.com

As you build each personalized Web portal, answer the following questions.

1. What is the registration process required to build a Web portal?
2. Can you receive a free e-mail account? If so, must you establish it?
3. Can you create categories of your most commonly visited sites?
4. Can you request customized local information for your area? If so, what type of information?
5. How do you adjust your Web browser's settings so that it automatically takes you to your Web portal page?

---

be a traditional desktop or notebook computer, a Web or Internet appliance, a PDA, or perhaps even a cell phone.

Internet server computers are computers that provide information and services on the Internet. There are four main types of server computers on the Internet: Web, mail, ftp, and IRC servers. A **Web server** provides information and services to Web surfers. So, when you access www.ebay.com, you're accessing a Web server (for eBay) with your client computer. Most often, you'll be accessing and using the services of a Web server.

A **mail server** provides e-mail services and accounts. Many times, mail servers are presented to you as a part of a Web server. For example, Hotmail is a free e-mail server and service provided by MSN. An **ftp (file transfer protocol) server** maintains a collection of files that you can download. These files can include software, screen savers, music files (many in MP3 format), and games. An **IRC (Internet Relay Chat) server** supports your use of discussion groups and chat rooms. IRC servers are popular hosting computers for sites such as www.epinions.com. There, you can share your opinions about various products and services, and you can also read the reviews written by other people.

COMMUNICATIONS PROTOCOLS

As information moves around the Internet, bouncing among network access points until it finally reaches you, it does so according to various communications protocols. A **communications protocol (protocol)** is a set of rules that every computer follows to transfer information. The most widely used protocols on the Internet include TCP/IP, http, and ftp (and a few others such as PPP, Point-to-Point Protocol, and POP, Post Office Protocol).

TCP/IP, or *transport control protocol/Internet protocol,* is the primary protocol for transmitting information over the Internet. Whenever any type of information moves over the Internet, it does so according to TCP/IP. *Hypertext transfer protocol (http)* is the communications protocol that supports the movement of information over the Web, essentially from a Web server to you. That's why Web site addresses start with "http://." Most Web browser software today assumes that you want to access a Web site on the Internet. So you don't even have to type in the "http://" if you don't want to.

File transfer protocol (ftp) is the communications protocol that allows you to transfer files of information from one computer to another. When you download a file from an ftp server (using ftp), you're using both TCP/IP (the primary protocol for the Internet) and ftp (the protocol that allows you to download the file). Likewise, when you access a Web site, you're using both TCP/IP and http (because the information you want is Web based).

Connecting to the Internet

To access the Web (via the Internet), you need an Internet service provider (ISP), as we discussed earlier. ISPs can include your school, your place of work, commercial ISPs such as AOL, and free ISPs such as NetZero. Which you choose is a function of many things.

One of the nice benefits of going to school or being employed is that you often get free Web access through school or your work. All you have to do is connect your home computer to your school's or work's computer (we'll talk about this process in a moment) and you're ready to surf. However, some schools and places of business may restrict where you can go on the Web. And they may even monitor your surfing.

Commercial ISPs charge you a monthly fee, just as your telephone company charges you a monthly fee for phone service. This fee usually ranges from a few dollars a month to about $20. Popular worldwide commercial ISPs include Microsoft (MSN), AOL, CompuServe, and AT&T WorldNet, just to name a few.

Free ISPs are absolutely free, as their names suggest—you don't pay a setup fee, you don't pay a monthly fee, and some offer unlimited access to the Web. But there are some catches. Many free ISPs do not offer you Web space, as opposed to most commercial ISPs which do. *Web space* is a storage area where you keep your Web site. So, if you want to create and maintain a Web site, you may have to choose a commercial ISP over a free ISP (your school probably also offers you Web space). Also when using a free ISP, you will often see banner ads that you can't get rid of. You can move them around and from side to side, but you can't remove them completely from your screen. Technical support is often limited with a free ISP. Some offer only e-mail support, while others do offer phone support but no toll-free number.

In spite of those drawbacks, many people do choose free ISPs over commercial ISPs, mainly because of cost (remember, $20 per month equals $240 per year). Popular free ISPs include Myfreei (www.access-4-free.com) and NetZero (www.netzero.net, see Figure B.8). To decide which type of ISP is best for you, ask these questions:

- *Do you need Web space?* If yes, a free ISP may not be the right choice.
- *Is great technical support important?* If yes, then a commercial ISP may be the right choice.
- *Is money a serious consideration?* If yes, then a commercial ISP may not be the right choice.
- *Is privacy important to you?* If yes, then your school or work may not be the right choice.

NetZero, in addition to offering free Internet access, also offers a subscription service with more features.

COMMUNICATIONS SOFTWARE

To access and use the Web, you need communications software, namely,

- *Connectivity software*—Enables you to use your computer to dial up or connect to another computer.
- *Web browser software*—Enables you to surf the Web.
- *E-mail software* (short for *electronic mail software*)—Enables you to electronically communicate with other people by sending and receiving e-mail.

Connectivity software is the first and most important. With connectivity software, while using a standard telephone modem, you essentially use your computer (and a phone line) to call up and connect to the server computer of your ISP. Connectivity software is standard on most personal computers today. To use connectivity software, you really only need to know the number to call. Then it's a relatively easy process: Within Microsoft Windows, click on **Start, All Programs, Accessories, Communications, Network Connections,** and then select **Create a new connection** (your exact sequence may vary slightly according to which version of Windows you're using).

Alternatively, if you're using connectivity software in conjunction with a high-speed modem connection such as a cable, DSL, or satellite modem (we'll discuss these further in a moment), you don't really "make a call" to connect to your ISP. Instead, you probably have an "always-on" high-speed Internet connection. So, when you turn on your computer, it goes through the process of connecting you to your ISP.

Web browser software and e-mail software are also standard software today. If your school or work is your ISP, then you'll most often be using commercially available Web browser software such as Internet Explorer, Netscape 7.2, or Firefox 1.0.2, and the

EVALUATING ISP OPTIONS

Choosing an Internet service provider (ISP) is an important, but not too terribly complicated, task. In this project, your group is to evaluate three different ISPs: a well-recognized commercial ISP such as AOL or AT&T WorldNet, a free ISP such as NetZero (there are many others), and a local or regional ISP in your area (you may need to look in your phone book to find one of these).

As you evaluate these three different ISPs, do so in terms of (1) price per month, (2) amount of Web space provided, (3) monthly limit of hours you can be connected without paying an additional fee, (4) customer support, and (5) the ability to have e-mail.

Of the three, which would you choose and why?

e-mail software you use will vary according to your school's or work's preference. If you're using a commercial or free ISP, then your choice of Web browser software and e-mail software will depend on that particular organization.

Regardless of your choice of ISP, the unique Web browser software and e-mail software provided work in similar fashion. So, if you're used to using Internet Explorer and then choose AOL as your ISP, you will see that AOL has its own Web browser software. It will look different on the screen, but it supports the same functionality (favorites list, moving forward and backward through your list of visited Web sites, and so on). All you have to do is get used to a new interface. Different e-mail software will also look different but support the same functionality.

TELECOMMUNICATIONS HARDWARE

In addition to communications software, you also need some telecommunications hardware to access the Web (again, via the Internet). If you're at school or work, you'll probably be able to connect your computer directly to a network that is then connected to the Internet. This often amounts to simply plugging a network line into your computer and starting your preferred Web browser or e-mail software. We discuss this type of connection to the Internet in more detail in *Extended Learning Module E*.

If you're connecting from home, you'll need some sort of modem. There are many types of modems, including

- A *telephone modem (modem)*—A device that connects your computer to your phone line so that you can access another computer or network.
- *Digital Subscriber Line (DSL)*—A high-speed Internet connection using phone lines, which allows you to use your phone line for voice communication at the same time.
- A *cable modem*—A device that uses your TV cable to deliver an Internet connection.
- A *satellite modem*—A modem that allows you to get Internet access from your satellite dish.

Figure B.9

DSL Modem Connection

DSL, cable, and satellite modems are among the newest, most expensive, and fastest. They also don't tie up your phone line. If, for example, you're using a basic telephone modem, you can't use your telephone line for voice communications at the same time. A DSL modem on the other hand, for example, basically splits your telephone line so that you can use it simultaneously for voice communications and for connecting to the Internet (see Figure B.9). Even more so, DSL, cable, and satellite modems offer you an "always-on" Internet connection.

With these high-speed Internet connection options, you may also have the ability to connect wirelessly to the modem using a router or other piece of equipment. As you can see in Figure B.9, the DSL modem is wired directly to one computer and wirelessly connected to another computer. This gives you the ability to connect multiple computers to the DSL modem. Again, we'll cover both wired and wireless connections to the Internet in *Extended Learning Module E.*

The biggest factor in determining your choice of telecommunications hardware (beyond price) may be that of availability. In many areas of the country, phone companies and cable TV service providers do not yet support the use of DSL, cable, and satellite modems. So, you may be limited to just using a basic telephone modem. If some of the other options are available to you, we definitely recommend that you research them.

To learn more about the Web, e-mail, and connectivity hardware and software, visit your MISource CD and choose topics such as Web Browsers, Using E-Mail, and Searching for Information on the Internet.

Summary: Student Learning Outcomes Revisited

1. **Define the relationships among Web site, Web site address, domain name, Web page, and uniform resource locator (URL).** A *Web site* (such as www.usatoday.com for *USA Today*) is a specific location on the Web where you visit, gather information, order products and so on. A *Web site address* (www.usatoday.com) is a unique name that identifies a specific site on the Web. Technically, a Web site address is called a *domain name.* A *Web page* is a specific portion of a Web site that deals with a certain topic. Technically, the address for a specific Web page is called a *URL (uniform resource locator).*

2. **Explain how to interpret the parts of an address on the Web.** Most Web site addresses start with http://www. Beyond that, the address is unique. The first part (using www.uts.edu.au as an example) provides the name of the organization or Web site (UTS or University of Technology in Sydney). The next part tells the type of organization and is called the *top-level domain.* For UTS, it is "edu," describing it as an educational institution. If something follows after that, it usually provides a country of origin ("au" for UTS, which identifies its country of origin as Australia).

3. **Identify the major components and features of Web browser software.** The three most popular Web browsers are Internet Explorer, Netscape 7.2, and Firefox 1.0.2. Each includes a menu bar (with functions such as **File, Edit,** and **View**), a button bar (for commonly performed tasks such as printing), and an address or location field into which you can type a Web site address. Web browsers also include capabilities for maintaining a list of commonly visited sites. In Internet Explorer, this is called a **Favorites list,** while Netscape 7.2 and Firefox 1.0.2 call this a **Bookmarks list.**

4. **Describe the differences between directory and true search engines.** *Search engines* are facilities on the Web that help you find sites with the information and/or services you want. A *directory search engine* organizes listings of Web sites into hierarchical lists. Using a directory search engine, you start by selecting a specific category and continually refine your search by choosing subsequent subcategories. A *true search engine* uses software agent technologies to search the Internet for key words and then places them into indexes. You use a true search engine by asking a question or providing key terms.

5. **Describe the various technologies that make up the Internet.** At the heart of the Internet is the *Internet backbone,* the major set of connections for computers on the Internet. A *network access point (NAP)* is a point on the Internet where several connections converge. *Network service providers (NSPs),* such as MCI or AT&T, own and maintain routing computers at NAPs and even the lines that connect the NAPs to each other. Besides your computer (called a client computer) which you use to access the Internet, there are also four types of *Internet server computers* that provide information and services on the Internet. These include *Web servers* (providing information and services to Web surfers), *mail servers* (providing e-mail services and accounts), *ftp servers* (maintaining a collection of files that you can download), and *IRC servers* (supporting your use of discussion groups and chat rooms). As information travels from these servers to you, it follows a set of *communications protocols*—sets of rules that every computer follows to transfer information. The most common protocols include *TCP/IP* (the primary protocol for transmitting information), *http* (for supporting the movement of information over the Web), and *ftp* (for allowing you to transfer files of information from one computer to another).

6. **Identify key considerations in choosing an Internet service provider (ISP).** When choosing an ISP—whether it is a commercial ISP, a free ISP, your school, or your work—you need to consider the following:

- Web space—If you want to publish a Web site, then your ISP must provide you with Web space
- Technical support—Which can be in the form of e-mail, 24-hour toll-free assistance, or perhaps none at all
- Money—Commercial ISPs are the most expensive, while free ISPs, your school, and your work are free
- Privacy—Your school or work may monitor your surfing activities

7. **Describe the communications software and telecommunications hardware you need to connect to the Internet.** Communications software for connecting to the Internet includes *connectivity software* (for dialing up another computer), *Web browser software* (for actually surfing the Web), and *e-mail software* (for electronically communicating with other people). Telecommunications hardware includes the device that you use to physically connect your computer to a network, which may connect through a phone line or cable line. These devices are called modems and include *telephone modem, DSL, cable modem,* and *satellite modem.*

Key Terms and Concepts

Cable modem, 116
Communications protocol (protocol), 113
Connectivity software, 115
Digital Subscriber Line (DSL), 116
Directory search engine, 108
Domain name, 104
E-mail (electronic mail) software, 115
File transfer protocol (ftp), 114
Ftp (file transfer protocol) server, 113
Hypertext transfer protocol (http), 114
Internet, 104
Internet backbone, 111
Internet server computer, 113
Internet service provider (ISP), 112
IRC (Internet Relay Chat) server, 113
Link (hyperlink), 105
Mail server, 113
Network access point (NAP), 111

Network service provider (NSP), 111
Satellite modem, 116
Search engine, 108
TCP/IP (transport control protocol/Internet protocol), 114
Telephone modem (modem), 116
Top-level domain, 105
True search engine, 108
Uniform resource locator (URL), 104
Web browser software, 106
Web page, 104
Web portal, 113
Web server, 113
Web site, 104
Web site address, 104
Web space, 114
World Wide Web (Web), 104

Short-Answer Questions

1. How do the Web and Internet differ?
2. What is the relationship between a Web site and a Web page?
3. What is the difference between a directory search engine and a true search engine?
4. How can you use plus signs (+) and minus signs (−) to refine a search?
5. What is the relationship between the Internet backbone, a network access point, and a network service provider?
6. What is the role of an ISP?
7. What are the four major types of servers on the Internet?
8. What are the advantages and disadvantages of choosing a commercial ISP?
9. What communications software do you need to use the Web?
10. What are the four main types of modems you can use to access the Internet while at home?

Assignments and Exercises

For each of the following Internet scavenger hunts, find the answer on the Web. When you do, write down the answer as well as the address where you found it. One restriction: You are not allowed to use encyclopedia sites such as *Encyclopedia Britannica*.

1. What is the weight of the moon?

Answer: _____

Address: _____

2. Who was the first U.S billionaire?

Answer: _____

Address: _____

3. Who is Olive Oyl's brother?

Answer: _____

Address: _____

4. Who wrote "It was the worst of times . . ."?

Answer: _____

Address: _____

5. What does the Seine River empty into?

Answer: _____

Address: _____

6. What is a lacrosse ball made of?

Answer: _____

Address: _____

7. Who lives at 39 Stone Canyon Drive?

Answer: _____

Address: _____

8. What is the color of Mr. Spock's blood?

Answer: _____

Address: _____

9. At what number did the Nasdaq stock market close yesterday?

Answer: _____

Address: _____

10. Which is the most frequently broken bone in the human body?

Answer: _____

Address: _____

11. What is a pregnant goldfish called?

Answer: _____

Address: _____

12. Who was the first pope to visit Africa?

Answer: _____

Address: _____

13. How many tusks does an Indian rhinoceros have?

Answer: _____

Address: _____

14. What does a pluviometer measure?

Answer: _____

Address: _____

15. What is the fear of the number 13 called?

Answer: _____

Address: _____

16. Which ear can most people hear best with?

Answer: _____

Address: _____

17. Who is the patron saint of England?

Answer: _____

Address: _____

18. Which boxer's life story was told in the movie *Raging Bull*?

Answer: _____

Address: _____

19. Which was the first domesticated bird?

Answer: _____

Address: _____

20. What is the population of the United States right now?

Answer: _____

Address: _____

21. What is the capital of Bermuda?

Answer: _____

Address: _____

22. Who Wrote *The Ugly Duckling*?

Answer: _____

Address: _____

23. Which Hollywood actress was nicknamed *The Legs*?

Answer: _____

Address: _____

24. What, translated literally, is the ninth month?

Answer: _____

Address: _____

25. What is the national airline of Australia?

Answer: _____

Address: _____

26. Who was Napoleon's first wife?

Answer: _____

Address: _____

27. What is another name for the Aurora Australis?

Answer: _____

Address: _____

28. How many pieces does each player start with in a game of checkers?

Answer: _____

Address: _____

29. Which writer was nicknamed "Papa"?

Answer: _____

Address: _____

30. What term does the computer word *bit* derive from?

Answer: _____

Address: _____

31. Which island was the jungle home of King Kong in the 1933 film?

Answer: _____

Address: _____

32. Which planet travels around the sun every 248 years?

Answer: _____

Address: _____

33. Who was the founder of Islam?

Answer: _____

Address: _____

34. How many sides does a nonagon have?

Answer: _____

Address: _____

35. What was Elvis Presley's middle name?

Answer: _____

Address: _____

36. What's the U.S. southern dish made from pigs' small intestines?

Answer: _____

Address: _____

37. Which French impressionist is famed for his paintings of ballet dancers?

Answer: _____

Address: _____

38. What did Clarence Birdseye perfect in 1924?

Answer: _____

Address: _____

39. What's a young female racehorse called?

Answer: _____

Address: _____

40. What is inside popcorn that makes it pop?

Answer: _____

Address: _____

CHAPTER THREE OUTLINE

STUDENT LEARNING OUTCOMES

1. Describe business intelligence and its role in an organization.

2. Differentiate between databases and data warehouses with respect to their focus on online transaction processing and online analytical processing.

3. List and describe the key characteristics of a relational database.

4. Define the five software components of a database management system.

5. List and describe the key characteristics of a data warehouse.

6. Define the four major types of data-mining tools in a data warehouse environment.

7. List key considerations in information ownership in an organization.

INDUSTRY PERSPECTIVES

132 **Serving Citizens and Government Agencies with a GIS Database**

139 **Delivering Quality Patient Care with Wireless Access to Database Information**

144 **Land O'Lakes Is More than Just Butter**

147 **A Key to Success: IT Strategy and Business Strategy Alignment**

FEATURES

129 **Team Work**
Primary Keys, Foreign Keys, and Integrity Constraints

137 **Global Perspective**
Britannia Airways Flys High with a Content Management Database

138 **On Your Own**
Researching Personal DBMSs

142 **Global Perspective**
Credit Scoring with SAS at Canada's Laurentian Bank

145 **Team Work**
How Up-to-Date Should Data Warehouse Information Be?

148 **On Your Own**
CRUD: Defining Information Ownership

157 **Electronic Commerce**
Searching Online Databases and Information Repositories

WEB SUPPORT

www.mhhe.com/haag

- Financial aid resources
- Libraries
- Consumer information
- Demographics
- Real estate
- Data warehouses and data-mining tools

CHAPTER THREE

Databases and Data Warehouses
Building Business Intelligence

OPENING CASE STUDY:
KRISPY KREME—SEVEN DOUGHNUTS
FOR EVERY MAN, WOMAN, AND CHILD
IN THE UNITED STATES EVERY YEAR

Krispy Kreme Doughnuts is the most well-known name in the doughnut industry. Headquartered in Winston-Salem, North Carolina, Krispy Kreme has 218 company-owned and -franchised stores in 33 states. Those 218 stores sell almost 5 million doughnuts on a daily basis and 2 billion annually, or seven doughnuts for every man, woman, and child in the United States every year.

Both the centralization and decentralization of information are equally important to the organization. At the home office, strategic managers needs access to organizationwide information, including sales, marketing, and supplier data from all 218 stores. At the store level, managers and owners need easy access to their individual store information while still being able to compare their operations to the operations of other stores.

At the store level, Krispy Kreme created a customized Web portal called MyKrispyKreme. Once store managers or owners log into their own MyKrispyKreme portal page, they can access all their own information as well as organizationwide information and organizationwide applications designed to help them run their stores better. Managers and owners can analyze store performance, access point-of-sale (POS) data, review customer and drive-through counts, and get a comprehensive view of cash balances and weekly profit and loss statements.

At the corporate level, strategic managers can view any kind of summary and comparison of any kind of information. They can select certain types of information by certain areas of the country and by specific time frames to analyze the company's overall performance. Other corporate-level processes are also supported by the IT system. Financial analysts can view and massage stock information. Supply chain managers can predict the impact of forecasted weather patterns on a supplier's ability to meet inventory needs. Marketing specialists can determine the effect of a national television campaign on each individual store's performance. Operations managers can even drill so far into the information that they can determine which employees exhibit the greatest productivity in the making of doughnuts.

Like all organizations, Krispy Kreme relies on a variety of technologies to manage and store information and to analyze that information. At the heart of every organization are databases that store vast amounts of transaction information. For Krispy Kreme, that transaction information includes each single POS transaction, including when, where, amount, type of doughnut(s), payment type, and so on. To analyze the information, many organizations turn to a data warehouse and data-mining tools. A data warehouse is a special type of database that stores summaries of information. Krispy Kreme's data warehouse is organizationwide and contains summaries of information by store. Information here includes sales, marketing, supply, inventory, financial, and other types of information as determined by the needs of decision makers.

This chapter focuses on databases and data warehouses as IT tools for managing and storing information. It also focuses on database management systems and data-mining tools as IT tools for working with and analyzing the information stored in databases and data warehouses.[1]

Introduction

As we've discussed in the first two chapters, you and your organization need more than just data and information. You need **business intelligence (BI)**—knowledge about your customers, your competitors, your business partners, your competitive environment, and your own internal operations—that gives you the ability to make effective, important, and often strategic business decisions. Business intelligence enables your organization to extract the true meaning of information so that you can take creative and powerful steps to ensure a competitive advantage. Many such actions by your organization support some or all the initiatives we discussed in Chapter 2—customer relationship management, supply chain management, and collaboration, to name just a few.

Of course, to create business intelligence you need both data and *information* (we'll commonly refer to both as *information* in this chapter). So, business intelligence doesn't just magically appear. You must first gather and organize all your information. Then, you have to have the right IT tools to define and analyze various relationships within the information. In short, knowledge workers such as you use IT tools to create business intelligence from information. The technology, by itself, won't do it for you. However, technology such as databases, database management systems, data warehouses, and data-mining tools can definitely help you build and use business intelligence.

As you begin working with these IT tools (which we'll discuss in great detail throughout this chapter), you'll be performing the two types of information processing we alluded to in Chapter 1: online transaction processing and online analytical processing. **Online transaction processing (OLTP)** is the gathering of input information, processing that information, and updating existing information to reflect the gathered and processed information. Databases and DBMSs are the technology tools that directly support OLTP. Databases that support OLTP are most often referred to as **operational databases.** Inside these operational databases is valuable information that forms the basis for business intelligence.

As you can see in Figure 3.1, you can also query operational databases to gather basic forms of business intelligence, such as how many products individually sold over $10,000 last month and how much money was spent last month on radio advertising. While the results of these queries may be helpful, you really need to combine product and advertising information (with several other types of information including customer demographics) to perform online analytical processing.

Online analytical processing (OLAP) is the manipulation of information to support decision making. At Australian P&C Direct, OLAP within a data warehouse is a must. P&C has created a data warehouse that supports its customer relationship management activities, cross-selling strategies, and marketing campaigns. By creating a data warehouse with customer information (including census data and lifestyle codes), its wide array of insurance and financial products, and its marketing campaign information, P&C agents can view all the products a given customer has purchased and more accurately determine cross-selling opportunities and what marketing campaigns a given customer is likely to respond to.[2]

A data warehouse is, in fact, a special form of a database that contains information gathered from operational databases for the purpose of supporting decision-making tasks. When you build a data warehouse and use data-mining tools to manipulate the data warehouse's information, your single goal is to create *business intelligence.* So, data warehouses support only OLAP; they do not at all support OLTP. As you can see in Figure 3.1, you can perform more in-depth queries to gather business intelligence from a

INFORMATION | **BUSINESS INTELLIGENCE**

Change a product price

How many products individually sold over $10,000 last month?

PRODUCT DATABASE

Change advertising time table

How much money was spent on radio advertising last month?

ADVERTISING DATABASE

Increase customer credit limit

Who is delinquent in paying their bills?

CUSTOMER DATABASE

Information Used in Decision Making

DATA WAREHOUSE

If inventory levels are reduced by 10%, what is the new total cost of inventory carried?

What new advertising strategies need to be undertaken to reach our customers who can afford a high-priced product?

ONLINE TRANSACTION PROCESSING (OLTP) | **ONLINE ANALYTICAL PROCESSING (OLAP)**

Figure 3.1

Building Business Intelligence

data warehouse than you can with a single database. For example, "What new advertising strategies need to be undertaken to reach our customers who can afford a high-priced product?" is a query that would require information from multiple databases. Data warehouses better support creating that type of business intelligence than do databases.

As this chapter unfolds, we'll look specifically at (1) databases and database management systems and (2) data warehouses and data-mining tools. Databases today are the foundation for organizing and managing information, and database management systems provide the tools you use to work with a database. Data warehouses are relatively new technologies that help you organize and manage business intelligence, and data-mining tools help you extract that vitally important business intelligence. Data warehouses and data-mining tools are a subset of the business intelligence software that we discussed in Chapter 2.

As we first look at databases and database management systems in this chapter, we'll be exploring their use by Solomon Enterprises in support of customer relationship management and order processing. Solomon Enterprises specializes in providing concrete to commercial builders and individual homeowners in the greater Chicago area. Solomon tracks detailed information on its concrete types, customers, raw materials, raw materials' suppliers, trucks, and employees. It uses a database to organize and manage all this information. As we discuss Solomon Enterprises and its use of a database, we'll focus mostly on CRM and ordering processing. In *Extended Learning Module C*, which follows this chapter, we'll look at how to design the supply chain management side of Solomon's database.

The Relational Database Model

For organizing and storing basic and transaction-oriented information (that is eventually used to create business intelligence), businesses today use databases. There are actually four primary models for creating a database. The object-oriented database model is the newest and holds great promise; we'll talk more about the entire object-oriented genre in *Extended Learning Module G.* Right now, let's focus on the most popular database model: the relational database model.

As a generic definition, we would say that any *database* is a collection of information that you organize and access according to the logical structure of that information. In reference to a *relational database,* we say that it uses a series of logically related two-dimensional tables or files to store information in the form of a database. The term *relation* often describes each two-dimensional table or file in the relational model (hence its name *relational* database model). A relational database is actually composed of two distinct parts: (1) the information itself, stored in a series of two-dimensional tables, files, or relations (people use these three terms interchangeably) and (2) the logical structure of that information. Let's look at a portion of Solomon's database to further explore the characteristics of the relational database model.

COLLECTIONS OF INFORMATION

In Figure 3.2, we've created a view of a portion of Solomon's database. Notice that it contains five files (also, again, called tables or relations): *Order, Customer, Concrete Type, Employee,* and *Truck.* (It will contain many more as we develop it completely in *Extended Learning Module C.*) These files are all related for numerous reasons—customers make orders, employees drive trucks, an order has a concrete type, and so on. And you need all these files to manage your customer relationships and process orders.

Within each file, you can see specific pieces of information (or *attributes*). For example, the *Order* file contains *Order Number, Order Date, Customer Number, Delivery Address, Concrete Type, Amount* (this is given in cubic yards), *Truck Number,* and *Driver ID.* In the *Customer* file, you can see specific information including *Customer Number, Customer Name, Customer Phone,* and *Customer Primary Contact.* These are all important pieces of information that Solomon's database should contain. Moreover, Solomon needs all this information (and probably much more) to effectively process orders and manage customer relationships.

CREATED WITH LOGICAL STRUCTURES

Using the relational database model, you organize and access information according to its logical structure, not its physical position. So, you don't really care in which row of the *Employee* file Allison Smithson appears. You really need to know only that Allison's *Employee ID* is 984568756 or, for that matter, that her name is Allison Smithson. In the relational database model, a *data dictionary* contains the logical structure for the information in a database. When you create a database, you first create its data dictionary. The data dictionary contains important information (or logical properties) about your information. For example, the data dictionary for *Customer Phone* in the *Customer* file would require 10 digits. The data dictionary for *Date of Hire* in the *Employee* file would require a month, day, and year, as well.

This is quite different from other ways of organizing information. For example, if you want to access information in a certain cell in most spreadsheet applications, you must know its physical location—row number and column character. With a relational

ORDER FILE

Order Number	Order Date	Customer Number	Delivery Address	Concrete Type	Amount	Truck Number	Driver ID
100000	9/1/2004	1234	55 Smith Lane	1	8	111	123456789
100001	9/1/2004	3456	2122 E. Biscayne	1	3	222	785934444
100002	9/2/2004	1234	55 Smith Lane	5	6	222	435296657
100003	9/3/2004	4567	1333 Burr Ridge	2	4	333	435296657
100004	9/4/2004	4567	1333 Burr Ridge	2	8	222	785934444
100005	9/4/2004	5678	1222 Westminster	1	4	222	785934444
100006	9/5/2004	1234	222 East Hampton	1	4	111	123456789
100007	9/6/2004	2345	9 W. Palm Beach	2	5	333	785934444
100008	9/6/2004	6789	4532 Lane Circle	1	8	222	785934444
100009	9/7/2004	1234	987 Furlong	3	8	111	123456789
100010	9/9/2004	6789	4532 Lance Circle	2	7	222	435296657
100011	9/9/2004	4567	3500 Tomahawk	5	6	222	785934444

CUSTOMER FILE

Customer Number	Customer Name	Customer Phone	Customer Primary Contact
1234	Smelding Homes	3333333333	Bill Johnson
2345	Home Builders Superior	3334444444	Marcus Connolly
3456	Mark Akey	3335555555	Mark Akey
4567	Triple A Homes	3336666666	Janielle Smith
5678	Sheryl Williamson	3337777777	Sheryl Williamson
6789	Home Makers	3338888888	John Yu

CONCRETE TYPE FILE

Concrete Type	Type Description
1	Home foundation and walkways
2	Commercial foundation and infrastructure
3	Premier speckled (concrete with pea-size smooth gravel aggregate)
4	Premier marble (concrete with crushed marble aggregate)
5	Premier shell (concrete with shell aggregate)

EMPLOYEE FILE

Employee ID	Employee Last Name	Employee First Name	Date of Hire
123456789	Johnson	Emilio	2/1/1985
435296657	Evaraz	Antonio	3/3/1992
785934444	Robertson	John	6/1/1999
984568756	Smithson	Allison	4/1/1997

TRUCK FILE

Truck Number	Truck Type	Date of Purchase
111	Ford	6/17/1999
222	Ford	12/24/2001
333	Chevy	1/1/2002

Figure 3.2

A Portion of Solomon Enterprises' Database for Customer Relationship Management and Ordering Processing database, however, you need only know the field name of the column of information (for example, *Amount*) and its logical row, not its physical row. As a result, in Solomon's database example, you could easily change the amount for an order, without having to know where that information is physically stored (by row or column).

And with spreadsheet software, you can immediately begin typing in information, creating column headings, and providing formatting. You can't do that with a database. Using a database, you must clearly define the characteristics of each field by creating a data dictionary. So, you must carefully plan the design of your database before you can start adding information.

WITH LOGICAL TIES WITHIN THE INFORMATION

In a relational database, you must create ties or relationships in the information that show how the files relate to each other. Before you can create these relationships among files, you must first specify the primary key of each file. A ***primary key*** is a field (or group of fields in some cases) that uniquely describes each record. In Solomon's database, *Order Number* is the primary key for the *Order* file and *Customer Number* is the primary key for the *Customer* file. That is to say, every order in the *Order* file must have a unique *Order Number* and every customer in the *Customer* file must have a unique *Customer Number*.

When you define that a specific field in a file is the primary key, you're also stating as well that the field cannot be blank. That is, you cannot enter the information for a new employee in the *Employee* file and leave the *Employee ID* field blank. If that were possible, you could potentially have two employees with identical primary keys (blank), which is not possible in a database environment.

Again, this is quite different from working with spreadsheets. Using a spreadsheet, it would be almost impossible to ensure that each field in a given column is unique. This reinforces the notion that, while spreadsheets work with information according to physical location, databases work with information logically.

If you look back at Figure 3.2, you can see that *Customer Number* appears in both the *Customer* and *Order* files. This creates a logical relationship between the two files and is an example of a foreign key. A ***foreign key*** is a primary key of one file that appears in another file. Now look at Figure 3.3. In it, we've provided the logical relationships among all five files. Notice, for example, that *Truck Number* is the primary key for the *Truck* file. It also appears in the *Order* file. This enables Solomon to track which trucks were used to deliver the various orders. So, *Truck Number* is the primary key in the *Truck* file and is also a foreign key that appears in the *Order* file. There are other examples of foreign keys as well in Figure 3.3.

Figure 3.3

Creating Logical Ties with Primary and Foreign Keys

PRIMARY KEYS, FOREIGN KEYS, AND INTEGRITY CONSTRAINTS

Let's consider the information that your school tracks for a class. In this instance, a class is a scheduled course. For example, your school may have FINA 2100—Introduction to International Financial Markets as a course. If the school offers it in the fall, then it becomes a class. Below, we've provided many pieces of information that your school probably tracks about the class. First, which is the primary key (place an X in the second column)? Second, for each piece of information, identify if it's a

foreign key (a primary key of another file). If it is, write down the filename in the third column. Finally, in the fourth column for each piece of information, write down any integrity constraints you can think of. For example, can it be blank or must it contain something? Can it be duplicated across multiple records (classes)? If it's a number, does it have a specific range in which it must fall? There are many others.

Information	Primary Key?	Foreign Key?	Integrity Constraints
Department designation (e.g., FINA)			
Course number (e.g., 2100)			
Course name			
Course description			
Prerequisite			
Number of credit hours			
Lab fee			
Instructor name			
Room number			
Time of day			
Day of week			

Foreign keys are essential in the relational database model. Without them, you have no way of creating logical ties among the various files. As you might guess, we use these relationships extensively to create business intelligence because they enable us to track the logical relationships within many types of information.

WITH BUILT-IN INTEGRITY CONSTRAINTS

By defining the logical structure of information in a relational database, you're also developing *integrity constraints*—rules that help ensure the quality of the information. For example, by stating that *Customer Number* is the primary key of the *Customer* file and a foreign key in the *Order* file, you're saying (1) that no two customers can have the same *Customer Number* and (2) that a *Customer Number* that is entered into the *Order* file must have a matching *Customer Number* in the *Customer* file. So, as Solomon creates a new order and enters a *Customer Number* in the *Order* file, the database management system must find a corresponding and identical *Customer Number* in the *Customer* file. This makes perfect sense. You cannot create an order for a customer who does not exist.

Consumer Reports magazine has rated the Ritz-Carlton first among luxury hotels.[3] Why? It's simple: Ritz-Carlton has created a powerful guest preference database to provide customized, personal, and high-level service to guests of any of its hotels. For example, if you leave a message at a Ritz-Carlton front desk that you want the bed turned down at 9 P.M., prefer no chocolate mints on your pillow, and want to participate in the 7 A.M. aerobics class, that information is passed along to the floor maid (and others) and is also stored in the guest preference database. By assigning to you a unique customer ID that creates logical ties to your various preferences, the Ritz-Carlton transfers your information to all of its other hotels. The next time you stay in a Ritz-Carlton hotel, in Palm Beach for example, your information is already there, and the hotel staff immediately knows of your preferences.

For the management at Ritz-Carlton, achieving customer loyalty starts first with knowing each customer individually (the concept of customer relationship management). That includes your exercise habits, what you most commonly consume from the snack bar in your room, how many towels you use daily, and whether you like a chocolate on your pillow. To store and organize all this information, Ritz-Carlton uses a relational database, and employees use it to meet your needs (or whims).

Database Management System Tools

When working with word processing software, you create and edit a document. When working with spreadsheet software, you create and edit a workbook. The same is true in a database environment. A database is equivalent to a document or a workbook because they all contain information. And while word processing and spreadsheet are the software tools you use to work with documents and workbooks, you use database management system software to work with databases. A *database management system (DBMS)* helps you specify the logical organization for a database and access and use the information within a database. A DBMS contains five important software components (see Figure 3.4):

1. DBMS engine
2. Data definition subsystem
3. Data manipulation subsystem
4. Application generation subsystem
5. Data administration subsystem

The DBMS engine is perhaps the most important, yet seldom recognized, component of a DBMS. The *DBMS engine* accepts logical requests from the various other DBMS subsystems, converts them into their physical equivalent, and actually accesses the database and data dictionary as they exist on a storage device. Again, the distinction between logical and physical is important in a database environment. The *physical view* of information deals with how information is physically arranged, stored, and accessed on some type of storage device such as a hard disk. The *logical view* of information, on the other hand, focuses on how you as a knowledge worker need to arrange and access information to meet your particular business needs.

Databases and DBMSs provide two really great advantages in separating the logical from the physical view of information. First, the DBMS engine handles the physical tasks. So you, as a database user, can concentrate solely on your logical information needs. Second, although there is only one physical view of information, there may be numerous knowledge workers who have different logical views of the information in a

Figure 3.4

Software Subsystems of a
Database Management
System

database. That is, according to what business tasks they need to perform, different knowledge workers logically view information in different ways. The DBMS engine can process virtually any logical information view or request into its physical equivalent.

DATA DEFINITION SUBSYSTEM

The ***data definition subsystem*** of a DBMS helps you create and maintain the data dictionary and define the structure of the files in a database.

When you create a database, you must first use the data definition subsystem to create the data dictionary and define the structure of the files. This is very different from using something like spreadsheet software. When you create a workbook, you can immediately begin typing in information and creating formulas and functions. You can't do that with a database. You must define its logical structure before you can begin typing in any information. Typing in the information is the easy part: Defining the logical structure is more difficult. In *Extended Learning Module C* that follows this chapter, we take you through the process of defining the logical structure for the supply chain management (SCM) side of Solomon Enterprises' database. We definitely recommend that you read that module—knowing how to define the correct structure of a database can be a substantial career opportunity for you.

If you ever find that a certain file needs another piece of information, you have to use the data definition subsystem to add a new field in the data dictionary. Likewise, if you want to delete a given field for all the records in a file, you must use the data definition subsystem to do so.

SERVING CITIZENS AND GOVERNMENT AGENCIES WITH A GIS DATABASE

Databases on the Web typically serve a variety of users. In the case of Pierce County, Washington, its Web-based geographic information system database serves both its citizenry and county agencies. In a geographic information system (GIS) format, users of all types can query information according to geographical location. The county expects to save almost $3 million in maintenance costs by implementing its new Web-based GIS database.

The county citizens will use the database, via a simple Web interface, to query such information as neighborhood crime statistics, property-tax information, property-survey reports, and voting information like polling information and locations. The GIS database serves the citizens of Pierce County by providing easy access to these types of vitally important information.

Government agencies such as law enforcement, natural resource management, land development, and utilities will also have access to the GIS information. They will use the database to access and analyze such information as crime patterns, maps of public facilities, and information on terrains and contours. Law-enforcement and emergency-services personnel can even use wireless handheld devices to access the GIS database while in the field.

All told, Pierce County's databases will serve its citizenry and government agencies with almost 10 terabytes of GIS information.[4]

As you create the data dictionary, you're essentially defining the logical properties of the information that the database will contain. Logical structures of information include the following:

Logical Properties	Examples
Field name	*Customer Number, Order Date*
Type	Alphabetic, numeric, date, time, etc.
Form	Is an area code required for a phone number?
Default value	If no *Order Date* is entered, the default is today's date.
Validation rule	Can *Amount* exceed 8?
Is an entry required?	Must you enter *Delivery Address* for an order or can it be blank?
Can there be duplicates?	Primary keys cannot be duplicates; but what about amounts?

These are all important logical properties to a lesser or greater extent depending on the type of information you're describing. For example, a typical concrete delivery truck can hold at most eight cubic yards of concrete. Further, Solomon may not accept orders for less than four cubic yards of concrete. Therefore, an important validation rule for *Amount* in the *Order* file is "must be greater than or equal to 4 and cannot be greater than 8."

DATA MANIPULATION SUBSYSTEM

The **data manipulation subsystem** of a DBMS helps you add, change, and delete information in a database and query it for valuable information. Software tools within the data manipulation subsystem are most often the primary interface between you as a user and the information contained in a database. So, while the DBMS engine handles your information requests from a physical point of view, it is the data manipulation tools within a DBMS that allow you to specify your logical information requirements. Those logical information requirements are then used by the DBMS engine to access the information you need from a physical point of view.

In most DBMSs, you'll find a variety of data manipulation tools, including views, report generators, query-by-example tools, and structured query language.

VIEWS   A *view* allows you to see the contents of a database file, make whatever changes you want, perform simple sorting, and query to find the location of specific information. Views essentially provide each file in the form of a spreadsheet workbook. The screen in Figure 3.5 shows a view in Microsoft Access for the *Order* file in Solomon's database. At this point, you can click on any specific field and change its contents. You could also point at an entire record and click on the Cut icon (the scissors) to remove a record. If you want to add a record, simply click in the *Order Number* field of the first blank record and begin typing.

Note: we've sorted the file in ascending order by *Concrete Type.* You can easily achieve this by clicking on the A→Z Sort button in the view window. If you want to sort in descending order by *Concrete Type,* simply point to any *Concrete Type* field and click on the Z→A Sort button. You can also perform searches within views. For example, if you want to find all orders for *Customer Number* 3456, simply point anywhere in that column, click on the Find Text button (the binoculars), and enter 3456. Access will respond by highlighting each *Customer Number* field where 3456 appears.

As with most other types of personal productivity software, DBMSs support such functions and tasks as cutting and pasting, formatting (for example, bolding a field), spell checking, hiding columns (just as you would do using spreadsheet software), filtering, and even adding links to Web sites.

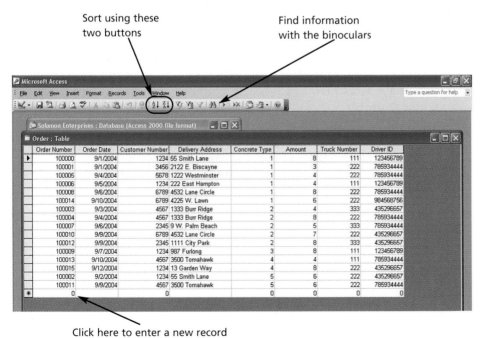

Sort using these two buttons

Find information with the binoculars

Click here to enter a new record

Figure 3.5

A View in Microsoft Access

REPORT GENERATORS   *Report generators* help you quickly define formats of reports and what information you want to see in a report. Once you define a report, you can view it on the screen or print it. Figure 3.6 shows two intermediate screens in Microsoft Access. The first allows you to specify which fields of information are to appear in a report. We have chosen to include *Order Number, Order Date, Customer Number,* and *Amount* from the *Order* file. The second allows you to choose from a set of predefined report formats. Following a simple and easy-to-use set of screens (including the two in Figure 3.6), we went on to specify that sorting should take place by *Customer Number* and that the name of the report should be "Customer and Amount Report." The completed report is also shown in Figure 3.6. Notice that it displays only those fields we requested, that it's sorted by *Customer Number,* and that the title is "Customer and Amount Report."

A nice feature about report generators is that you can save a report format that you use frequently. For example, if you think you'll use the report in Figure 3.6 often, you can save it by giving it a unique name. Later, you can request that report and your DBMS will generate it, using the most up-to-date information in the database. You can also choose from a variety of report formats (we chose a simple one for our illustration). And you can choose report formats that create intermediate subtotals and grand totals, which can include counts, sums, averages, and the like.

Figure 3.6

Using a Report
Generator

Selected fields from
the *Order* file

Report formats

CUSTOMER AND AMOUNT REPORT

Customer Number	Order Number	Order Date	Amount
1234	100000	9/1/2004	8
1234	100002	9/2/2004	6
1234	100006	9/5/2004	4
1234	100009	9/7/2004	8
1234	100015	9/12/2004	8
2345	100007	9/6/2004	5
2345	100012	9/9/2004	8
3456	100001	9/1/2004	3
4567	100003	9/3/2004	4
4567	100004	9/4/2004	8
4567	100011	9/9/2004	6
4567	100013	9/10/2004	4
5678	100005	9/4/2004	4
6789	100008	9/6/2004	8
6789	100010	9/9/2004	7
6789	100014	9/10/2004	6

QUERY-BY-EXAMPLE TOOLS   *Query-by-example (QBE) tools* help you graphically design the answer to a question. Suppose for example that Janielle Smith from Triple A Homes (*Customer Number* 4567) has called and ordered a delivery of concrete. Although she can't remember the name of the driver, she would like to have the driver that comes out the most often to deliver concrete to Triple A Homes. Solomon's task, from a customer relationship management point of view, is to go through all the orders and determine which employee most often delivers concrete to Triple A Homes. The task may seem simple considering that Solomon currently has very few orders in its database. However, can you imagine trying to answer that question if there were thousands of orders in Solomon's database? It would not be fun.

Fortunately, QBE tools can help you answer this question and perform many other queries in a matter of seconds. In Figure 3.7, you can see a QBE screen that formulates the answer to the question. When you perform a QBE, you (1) identify the files in which the needed information is located, (2) drag any necessary fields from the identified files to the QBE grid, and (3) specify selection criteria.

For the names of employees who have delivered concrete to Triple A Homes, we identified the two files of *Order* and *Employee*. Second, we dragged *Customer Number* from the *Order* file to the QBE grid and dragged *Employee Last Name* and *Employee First Name* from the *Employee* file to the QBE grid. Finally, we specified in the Criteria box that we wanted to view only the orders for *Customer Number* 4567 (Triple A Homes). Access did the rest and provided the information in Figure 3.7.

QBEs rely heavily on the logical relationships within a database to find information. For example, *Order Number* 100004 has the *Customer Number* of 4567 (Triple A Homes). So, the QBE tool took the *Driver ID* from the *Order* file for that order and found a match in the *Employee* file. When it found a match, it presented the *Employee Last Name* and *Employee First Name* (John Robertson). Without the logical relationships being correctly defined, this QBE query would not have worked properly.

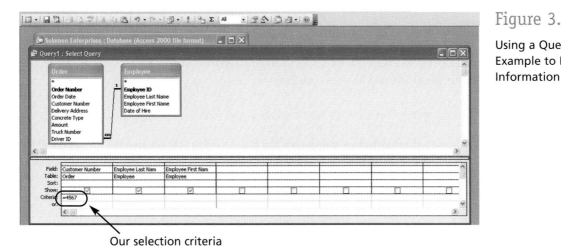

Our selection criteria

Customer Number	Employee Last Name	Employee First Name
4567	Evaraz	Antonio
4567	Robertson	John
4567	Robertson	John
4567	Robertson	John

Figure 3.7

Using a Query-by-Example to Find Information

STRUCTURED QUERY LANGUAGE   *Structured query language (SQL)* is a standardized fourth-generation query language found in most DBMSs. SQL performs the same function as QBE, except that you perform the query by creating a statement instead of pointing, clicking, and dragging. The basic form of an SQL statement is

SELECT . . . FROM . . . WHERE . . .

After the SELECT, you list the fields of information you want; after the FROM, you specify what logical relationships to use; and after the WHERE, you specify any selection criteria. If you consider our QBE above of Who most often delivers concrete to *Customer Number* 4567? the SQL statement would look like the following:

SELECT Order.[Customer Number], Employee.[Employee Last
        Name], Employee.[Employee First Name]
FROM   Employee INNER JOIN [Order] ON Employee.[Employee ID]
        = Order.[Driver ID]
WHERE   (((Order.[Customer Number])=4567));

Thoroughly introducing you to the syntax of building SQL statements is outside the scope of this text and would easily require almost 100 pages of material. But you should be aware that SQL does exist. If you're majoring in IT or MIS, you'll undoubtedly take a course in SQL.

APPLICATION GENERATION SUBSYSTEM

The *application generation subsystem* of a DBMS contains facilities to help you develop transaction-intensive applications. These types of applications usually require that you perform a detailed series of tasks to process a transaction. Application generation subsystem facilities include tools for creating visually appealing and easy-to-use data entry screens, programming languages specific to a particular DBMS, and interfaces to commonly used programming languages that are independent of any DBMS.

As with SQL, application generation facilities are most often used by IT specialists. As a knowledge worker, we recommend that you leave application generation to IT specialists as much as you can. You need to focus on views, report generators, and QBE tools. These will help you find information in a database and perform queries so you can start to build and use business intelligence.

DATA ADMINISTRATION SUBSYSTEM

The *data administration subsystem* of a DBMS helps you manage the overall database environment by providing facilities for backup and recovery, security management, query optimization, concurrency control, and change management. The data administration subsystem is most often used by a data administrator or database administrator—someone responsible for assuring that the database (and data warehouse) environment meets the entire information needs of an organization.

Backup and recovery facilities provide a way for you to (1) periodically back up information contained in a database and (2) restart or recover a database and its information in case of a failure. These are important functions you cannot ignore in today's information-based environment. Organizations that understand the importance of their information take precautions to preserve it, often by running backup databases, a DBMS, and storage facilities parallel to the primary database environment. In Chapters 7 and 8, we talk specifically about how to develop plans and strategies in the event of some sort of failure. We call this contingency planning or disaster recovery planning.

BRITANNIA AIRWAYS FLYS HIGH WITH A CONTENT MANAGEMENT DATABASE

Britannia Airways is a member of the "World of TUI" group of organizations that covers over 90 percent of the European tourism market. To be a vitally important member of this organization, keep its planes running on time, and provide crew members timely access to information, Britannia Airways implemented Livelink, a content management database solution provided by Open Text Corporation (www.opentext.com).

To create a competitive advantage in the highly competitive and fierce international travel market, Britannia Airways needed a system to provide such information as

- Departure and destination times and locations to flight crews and passengers
- Capacity utilization information for flight crews and baggage handlers
- Customer relationship management information to flight attendants

Prior to implementing Livelink, Britannia Airways' employees simply had to manually process too many forms for each flight. According to John Gough, Britannia Airways' E-Business Program Manager, "Britannia had over 120 forms related to the flight. We urgently needed to rationalize the amount of paperwork we were generating and the efficiency of our business processes around that paperwork."

The new system goes far beyond being just an operational database that manages and organizes transaction information. It provides each crew member with a single log-in and point of access through a Web portal. The new system provides automated workflow capabilities to ensure that the right employees receive and process the necessary information in the least amount of time. It even provides forums in which all Britannia employees can record and discuss ideas for making flights better and more comfortable for passengers. So, the new system supports both bottom-line efforts (i.e., optimizing information processing to reduce costs) and top-line initiatives (such as customer relationship management), giving Britannia the ability to grow and nurture relationships with its most frequent flyers.

The system's implementation was very easy. Within three months of acquisition and on budget, Britannia had the new system up and running. According to Gough, "The Livelink implementation at Britannia was a great example of how, despite the complexities of numerous, concurrent IT projects, Open Text was able to help us deliver a project on time . . ."[5]

Security management facilities allow you to control who has access to what information and what type of access those people have. In many database environments, for example, some people may need only view access to database information, but not change privileges. Still others may need the ability to add, change, and/or delete information in a database. Through a system of passwords and access privileges, the data administration subsystem allows you to define which users can perform which tasks and what information they can see. At car dealership JM Family Enterprises (JMFE), security management facilities are an absolute must because its technology is highly decentralized and includes users of mobile technologies.[6] JMFE's system supports encryption and passwords to protect databases, files, and many hardware resources. The system even supports automatic log-offs after a certain amount of time if users accidentally leave their systems running.

Query optimization facilities often take queries from users (in the form of SQL statements or QBEs) and restructure them to minimize response times. In SQL, for example, you can build a query statement that might involve working with as many as 10 different files. As you might well guess, when working with 10 different files, there may be several different solutions for combining them to get the information you need. Fortunately, you

RESEARCHING PERSONAL DBMSs

We believe the ability to use a personal DBMS is becoming more essential every day in finding a good job. All businesses want you to possess expertise in word processing, spreadsheet, and presentation software.

Many more are now beginning to place a high priority on your ability to use a personal DBMS. To the left below are seven well-known personal DBMSs. For each, find the information for the topics to the right.

- Alpha Five
- askSam Professional
- FileMaker Pro
- Microsoft Access
- MyDatabase
- Paradox
- QuickBase

1. Latest version number

2. Security features

3. Support for SQL

4. Export information to HTML format

5. Support for mail merge

6. Support for creating relationships among tables

7. Report wizard support

8. Form wizard support

don't have to worry about structuring the SQL statement in the most optimized fashion. The query optimization facilities will do that for you and provide you with the information you need in the fastest possible way.

Reorganization facilities continually maintain statistics concerning how the DBMS engine physically accesses information. In maintaining those statistics, reorganization facilities can optimize the physical structure of a database to further increase speed and performance. For example, if you frequently access a certain file by a specific order, the reorganization facilities may maintain the file in that presorted order by creating an index that maintains the sorted order in that file. What's really nice is that you don't have to be aware of the changes to your database with respect to physical locations—the DBMS engine will take care of it for you.

Concurrency control facilities ensure the validity of database updates when multiple users attempt to access and change the same information. This is crucial in today's networked business environment. Consider your school's online registration system. What if you and another student try to register for a class with only one seat remaining at exactly the same time? Who gets enrolled in the class? What happens to the person who does not get his or her desired class schedule? These are important questions that must be answered according to your business rules and, once answered, defined in the database environment using concurrency control facilities.

DELIVERING QUALITY PATIENT CARE WITH WIRELESS ACCESS TO DATABASE INFORMATION

The entire business world is rapidly moving to support wireless access to information, which enables employees to access the information they need no matter where they are or what type of IT device they may be using. The flipside to productivity gains in mobile information access, however, is the issue of privacy. Such has been the case at Columbus Regional Healthcare System.

Starting about 2002, Columbus began migrating its paper-based information storage to a database that its over 1,000 employees can access wirelessly. The stored information includes sensitive patient information such as medical reports, test results, x-rays, and pharmacy prescriptions. Employees can now access the information they need while in patients' rooms, doctor lounges, cancer conference centers, and other offices. According to Stephen Lewack, director of technical services and communications at Columbus, "People can access the information they need wherever they happen to be. . . . It makes it easier to deliver care right on the spot."

Concerns about information privacy escalate in a wireless environment, especially in the health care field. Physical constraints that ensure information integrity disappear when employees can use PDAs, note-book computers, Web-enabled cell phones, and tablet PCs to access private and confidential patient information, as they now can at Columbus. One of Lewack's tasks is to ensure that only authorized devices are granted information access. So, each Columbus employee must have his or her wireless device registered with technical services.

Further, Columbus has implemented a wireless gateway system called AirFortress provided by Fortress Technologies (www.fortresstech.com) to ensure its compliance with the U.S. government's FIPS (Federal Information Processing Standards) security-validation program and the Health Insurance Portability and Accountability Act (HIPAA). AirFortress authenticates each user and device using passwords and uses encryption methods to ensure the privacy and security of the wireless transmissions. The system also uses intrusion-detection software to stop unauthorized "information snoopers" and hacker attacks.

Access to the right information at the right time by the right people is essential to competitive survival in today's business world. When providing wireless access to information to provide the best quality medical care, you must also consider the privacy and security of patient information.[7]

Change management facilities allow you to assess the impact of proposed structural changes to a database environment. For example, if you decide to add a character identifier to a numeric truck number, you can use the change management facilities to see how many files will be affected. Recall that *Truck Number* would be the primary key for a Truck file and that it would also be a foreign key in many other files. Sometimes, structural changes may not have much effect on the database (adding a four-digit zip code extension), but others can cause widespread changes that you must assess carefully before implementing.

All these—backup and recovery, security management, query optimization, reorganization, concurrency control, and change management—are vitally important facilities in any DBMS and thus any database environment. As a user and knowledge worker, you probably won't deal with these facilities specifically as far as setting them up and maintaining them is concerned. But how they're set up and maintained will affect what you can do. So knowing that they do exist and understanding their purposes are important.

Data Warehouses and Data Mining

Suppose as a manager at Victoria's Secret, you wanted to know the total revenues generated from the sale of shoes last month. That's a simple query, which you could easily implement using either SQL or a QBE tool. But what if you wanted to know, "By actual versus budgeted, how many size 8 shoes in black did we sell last month in the southeast and southwest regions, compared with the same month over the last five years?" That task seems almost impossible, even with the aid of technology. If you were actually able to build a QBE query for it, you would probably bring the organization's operational database environment to its knees.

This example illustrates the two primary reasons so many organizations are opting to build data warehouses. First, while operational databases may have the needed information, the information is not organized in a way that lends itself to building business intelligence within the database or using various data manipulation tools. Second, if you could build such a query, your operational databases, which are probably already supporting the processing of hundreds of transactions per second, would seriously suffer in performance when you hit the Start button to perform the query.

To support such intriguing, necessary, and complex queries to create business intelligence, many organizations are building data warehouses and providing data-mining tools. A data warehouse is simply the next step (beyond databases) in the progression of building business intelligence. And data-mining tools are the tools you use to mine a data warehouse and extrapolate the business intelligence you need to make a decision, solve a problem, or capitalize on an opportunity to create a competitive advantage.

Figure 3.8

A Multidimensional Data Warehouse with Information from Multiple Operational Databases

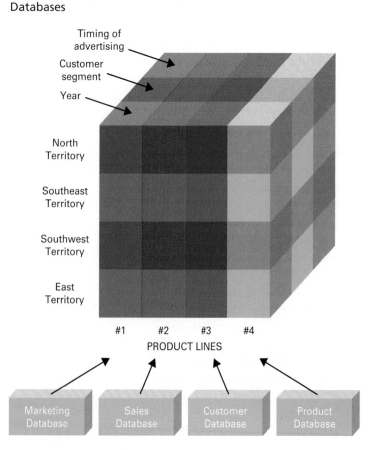

Timing of advertising

Customer segment

Year

North Territory

Southeast Territory

Southwest Territory

East Territory

#1   #2   #3   #4
PRODUCT LINES

Marketing Database   Sales Database   Customer Database   Product Database

WHAT IS A DATA WAREHOUSE?

A **data warehouse** is a logical collection of information—gathered from many different operational databases—used to create business intelligence that supports business analysis activities and decision-making tasks (see Figure 3.8). Sounds simple enough on the surface, but data warehouses represent a fundamentally different way of thinking about organizing and managing information in an organization. Consider these key features of a data warehouse, detailed in the sections that follow.

DATA WAREHOUSES ARE MULTIDIMENSIONAL   In the relational database model, information is represented in a series of two-dimensional files or tables. Not so in a data warehouse—most data warehouses are multidimensional, meaning that they contain layers of columns and rows. For this reason, most data warehouses are really *multidimensional databases*. The layers in a data warehouse represent information according to different dimensions. This multidimensional representation of information is referred to as a *hypercube*.

In Figure 3.8, you can see a hypercube that represents product information by product line and region (columns and rows), by year (the first layer), by customer segment (the second layer), and by the timing of advertising media (the third layer). Using this hypercube, you can easily ask, According to customer segment A, what percentage of total sales for product line 1 in the southwest territory occurred immediately after a radio advertising blitz? The information you would receive from that query constitutes business intelligence.

Any specific subcube within the larger hypercube can contain a variety of summarized information gathered from the various operational databases. For example, the forwardmost and top-left subcube contains information for the North territory, by year, for product line 1. So, it could contain totals, average, counts, and distributions summarizing in some way that information. Of course, what it contains is really up to you and your needs.

DATA WAREHOUSES SUPPORT DECISION MAKING, NOT TRANSACTION PROCESSING   In an organization, most databases are transaction-oriented. That is, most databases support online transaction processing (OLTP) and, therefore, are operational databases. Data warehouses are not transaction-oriented: They exist to support decision-making tasks in your organization. Therefore, data warehouses support only online analytical processing (OLAP).

As we just stated, the subcubes within a data warehouse contain summarized information. So, while a data warehouse may contain the total sales for a year by product line, it does not contain a list of each individual sale to each individual customer for a given product line. Therefore, you simply cannot process transactions with a data warehouse. Instead, you process transactions with your operational databases and then use the information contained within the operational databases to build the summary information in a data warehouse.

WHAT ARE DATA-MINING TOOLS?

Data-mining tools are the software tools you use to query information in a data warehouse. These data-mining tools support the concept of OLAP—the manipulation of information to support decision-making tasks. Data-mining tools include query-and-reporting tools, intelligent agents, multidimensional analysis tools, and statistical tools (see Figure 3.9). Essentially, data-mining tools are to data warehouse users what data manipulation subsystem tools are to database users.

Figure 3.9

The Data Miner's Tool Set

As in a DBMS, a data warehouse system has an engine responsible for converting your logical requests into their physical equivalent.

CREDIT SCORING WITH SAS AT CANADA'S LAURENTIAN BANK

Data mining has an untold number of applications that can help all types of businesses make better decisions. In the financial services industry, Canada's Laurentian Bank has turned to SAS (www.sas.com), the leading provider of statistical tools, to create a credit scoring model to approve loans for snowmobiles, ATVs, boats, RVs, and motorcycles.

According to Sylvain Fortier, senior manager for Retail Risk Management at Laurentian Bank, "Our objective was to improve our use of the technological tools available for data exploitation and analysis that we needed to develop a scorecard internally. We wanted to develop a flexible system that would help us learn about our customers and business through the loan process." The system, called SAS Credit Scoring, develops a credit risk scorecard for each loan applicant based on a variety of information including socioeconomic data and determines the risk level of the applicant in the form of a score.

In just a few shorts months, the bank realized a 33 percent return on investment and expects to reduce losses on automotive loans by 8 percent.[8]

QUERY-AND-REPORTING TOOLS   *Query-and-reporting tools* are similar to QBE tools, SQL, and report generators in the typical database environment. In fact, most data warehousing environments support simple and easy-to-use data manipulation subsystem tools such as QBE, SQL, and report generators. Most often, data warehouse users use these types of tools to generate simple queries and reports.

INTELLIGENT AGENTS   Intelligent agents utilize various artificial intelligence tools such as neural networks and fuzzy logic to form the basis of "information discovery" and building business intelligence in OLAP. For example, Wall Street analyst Murray Riggiero uses OLAP software called Data/Logic, which incorporates neural networks to generate rules for his highly successful stock and bond trading system.[9] Other OLAP tools, such as Data Engine, incorporate fuzzy logic to analyze real-time technical processes.

Intelligent agents represent the growing convergence of various IT tools for working with information. Previously, intelligent agents were considered only within the context of artificial intelligence and were seldom thought to be a part of the data organizing and managing functions in an organization. Today, you can find intelligent agents being used not only for OLAP in a data warehouse environment but also for searching for information on the Web. In Chapter 4, we'll explore artificial intelligence techniques such as intelligent agents.

MULTIDIMENSIONAL ANALYSIS TOOLS   *Multidimensional analysis (MDA) tools* are slice-and-dice techniques that allow you to view multidimensional information from different perspectives. For example, if you completed any of the recommended group projects for Chapter 1, you were using spreadsheet software to literally slice and dice the provided information. Within the context of a data warehouse, we refer to this process as "turning the cube." That is, you're essentially turning the cube to view information from different perspectives.

This turning of the cube allows you to quickly see information in different subcubes. If you refer back to the data warehouse in Figure 3.8 on page 140, you'll notice that information by customer segment and timing of advertising is actually hidden. Using MDA tools, you can easily bring this to the front of the data warehouse for viewing. What you've essentially done is to slice the cube vertically by layer and bring some of the background layers to the front. As you do this, the values of the information are not affected.

STATISTICAL TOOLS   Statistical tools help you apply various mathematical models to the information stored in a data warehouse to discover new information. For example, you can perform a time-series analysis to project future trends. You can also perform a regression analysis to determine the effect of one variable on another.

Sega of America, one of the largest publishers of video games, uses a data warehouse and statistical tools to effectively distribute its advertising budget of more than $50 million a year.[10,11] With its data warehouse, product line specialists and marketing strategists "drill" into trends of each retail store chain. Their goal is to find buying trends that will help them better determine which advertising strategies are working best (and at what time of the year) and how to reallocate advertising resources by media, territory, and time. Sega definitely benefits from its data warehouse, and so do retailers such as Toys "Я" Us, Wal-Mart, and Sears—all good examples of customer relationship management through technology.

To learn more about today's best data warehousing and data-mining tools, visit the Web site that supports this text at www.mhhe.com/haag.

DATA MARTS: SMALLER DATA WAREHOUSES

Data warehouses are often perceived as organizationwide, containing summaries of all the information that an organization tracks. However, some people need access to only a portion of that data warehouse information as opposed to all of it. In this case, an organization can create one or more data marts. A **_data mart_** is a subset of a data warehouse in which only a focused portion of the data warehouse information is kept (see Figure 3.10).

Lands' End first created an organizationwide data warehouse for everyone to use, but soon found out that there can be "too much of a good thing."[12] In fact, many Lands' End employees wouldn't use the data warehouse because it was simply too big, too complicated, and included information they didn't need access to. So, Lands' End created several smaller data marts. For example, Lands' End created a data mart just for the merchandising department. That data mart contains only merchandising-specific information and not any information, for instance, that would be unique to the finance department.

Figure 3.10

Data Marts Are Subsets of Data Warehouses

Merchandising

Marketing

Advertising

Production

Distribution

Service

Sales

Organizationwide Data Warehouse

Accounts Receivable

LAND O'LAKES IS MORE THAN JUST BUTTER

In 2001, Land O'Lakes acquired Purina Mills, making it the nation's largest animal feeding company. (It already owned Land O'Lakes Feed and Farmland Feed.) That presented a real challenge. Sales and marketing managers needed easy access to information across all three feeding operations to properly analyze the sales of more than 40,000 feed products.

To address the challenge (and succeed), Land O'Lakes implemented a series of data-mining tools from Informatica—Informatica PowerCenter, Informatica PowerConnect, and Informatica Analytic Business Components. Land O'Lakes was indeed successful and was rewarded as follows.

- New effective trending and forecasting analyses have resulted in improved sales and manufacturing efficiency.
- Informatica's integrated suite of data-mining tools has resulted in needing to write fewer business intelligence applications from scratch, saving the company valuable development resources.
- The software has enabled Land O'Lakes to reduce development cycles for new products and product revisions.
- The software has enabled Land O'Lakes to easily integrate the business operations of Purina Mills into its other operations.[13,14]

Because of the smaller, more manageable data marts, knowledge workers at Lands' End are making better use of information. If some of your employees don't need access to organizationwide data warehouse information, consider building a smaller data mart for their particular needs.

If you do choose to build smaller data marts for your employees, the data-mining tools are the same. That is, data marts support the use of query-and-reporting tools, intelligent agents, multidimensional analysis tools, and statistical tools. This yields efficiency in an organization with respect to training. Once you've trained your employees to use any or all data-mining tools, they can apply them to an organizationwide data warehouse or smaller data marts.

DATA MINING AS A CAREER OPPORTUNITY

Data mining represents a substantial career opportunity for you, no matter what your career choice. In the business world, you'll face numerous situations in which you need business intelligence to make the right and most effective decisions.

Fortunately, you don't have to be an IT expert to perform data mining. As you'll learn in *Extended Learning Module D (Decision Analysis with Spreadsheet Software)*, you can actually use a spreadsheet tool such as Microsoft Excel to build a three-dimensional cube similar to the one in Figure 3.8. You can then use Excel's other decision support features to build a graph, perform a regression analysis, and "turn the cube" by bringing new layers of information forward. You can do the same with Microsoft Access, by building a three-dimensional cube (i.e., data warehouse) of information stored in a database. We definitely recommend that you learn to use these tools and then note your proficiency in your e-portfolio under "Technology Skills."

Beyond personal productivity tools, you should consider learning how to use some data-mining tools specific to the data warehouse environment. Some of the more popular ones include:

HOW UP-TO-DATE SHOULD DATA WAREHOUSE INFORMATION BE?

Information timeliness is a must in a data warehouse—old and obsolete information leads to poor decision making. Below is a list of decision-making processes that people go through for different business environments. For each, specify whether the information in the data warehouse should be updated monthly, weekly, daily, or by the minute. Be prepared to justify your decision.

1. To adjust class sizes in a university registration environment
2. To alert people to changes in weather conditions
3. To predict scores for professional football games
4. To adjust radio advertisements in light of demographic changes
5. To monitor the success of a new product line in the clothing retail industry
6. To adjust production levels of foods in a cafeteria
7. To switch jobs to various printers in a network
8. To adjust CD rates in a bank
9. To adjust forecasted demands of tires in an auto parts store

- Query and Analysis and Enterprise Analytic tools in Business Objects (www.businessobjects.com)
- Business Intelligence and Information Access tools in SAS (www.sas.com)
- ReportNet, PowerPlay, Visualizer, NoticeCast, and DecisionStream tools in Cognos (www.cognos.com)
- PowerAnalyzer tools in Informatica (www.informatica.com)

There are many, many others. You should have a look at your school's catalog of courses in data mining—you may find them offered in the technology department, statistics department, and other departments. We recommend that at the very least you become acquainted with the following: SAS (the leading vendor in statistical software), Cognos (the leading vendor in data warehousing and data-mining tools), and Informatica (the second-leading vendor in data warehousing and data-mining tools).

IMPORTANT CONSIDERATIONS IN USING A DATA WAREHOUSE

As is true with all types of technology, you can't simply implement a data warehouse and use data-mining tools just because they're a "hot" set of technologies and expect automatically to increase your efficiency and effectiveness. Always let your business needs drive your technology decisions. You have to need the technology and the technology has to fit your needs. With respect to data warehouse and data-mining tools, consider your answers to the following questions.

1. **Do you need a data warehouse?** Although great IT tools, they are not necessarily the best technologies for all businesses because (1) they are expensive, (2) they may not be necessary since some businesses can easily extract all the business intelligence they need from databases, and (3) they require extensive and often expensive support.

2. **Do all your employees need an entire data warehouse?** If not, consider building data marts.

3. **How up-to-date must the information be?** To create a data warehouse, you take "snapshots" of database information and load it into a data warehouse. If crucial information changes every second, this may not be possible.

4. **What data-mining tools do you need?** User needs should always drive the answer to this question. Whichever you choose, training will be key. If your users can fully exploit all the features of their chosen data-mining tools, your entire organization will reap the benefits.

Information Ownership

When you enter today's fast-paced, exciting, and information-based business world, you must be prepared to help your organization manage and organize its information. After all, you will be a knowledge worker—a person who works primarily with information. Your organization will be successful, in part, because of your ability to organize and manage information in a way that best moves the organization toward its goals. As we close this chapter, let's look at the notion of *information ownership* and what it means.

STRATEGIC MANAGEMENT SUPPORT

Organizations have chief executive officers (CEOs), chief operating officers (COOs), and chief financial officers (CFOs), among others. You can also find several other such strategic positions nowadays relating to information ownership, including:

- *Chief privacy officer (CPO)*—responsible for ensuring that information is used in an ethical way and that only the right people have access to certain types of information such as financial records and payroll.
- *Chief security officer (CSO)*—responsible for the technical aspects of ensuring the security of information such as the development and use of firewalls, intranets, extranets, and anti-virus software.
- *Chief information officer (CIO)*—responsible for overseeing every aspect of an organization's information resource. Often, the CPO and CSO functions report to the CIO.

A CIO's responsibilities may range from approving new development activities for data warehouses and data marts to monitoring the quality and use of information within those data warehouses and data marts (and databases).

Two important functions associated with overseeing an organization's information resource are data administration and database administration. **Data administration** is the function in an organization that plans for, oversees the development of, and monitors the information resource. It must be completely in tune with the strategic direction of the organization to assure that all information requirements can be and are being met.

Database administration is the function in an organization that is responsible for the more technical and operational aspects of managing the information contained in organizational information repositories (databases, data warehouses, and data marts). Database administration functions include defining and organizing database structures and contents, developing security procedures (in concert with the CSO), developing database and DBMS documentation, approving and monitoring the development of databases and database applications, reporting/rectifying intrusions or operational anomalies, and maintaining overall system integrity.

In large organizations, both administrative functions are usually handled by steering committees rather than by a single individual. These steering committees are responsi-

A KEY TO SUCCESS: IT STRATEGY AND BUSINESS STRATEGY ALIGNMENT

While the C-level is now littered with IT positions such as chief information officer, chief privacy officer, and chief security officer, most businesses have yet to properly align their IT strategies with their business strategies. Thus, according to the sixth annual Technology Issues for Financial Executives survey, only 10 percent of the surveyed companies achieved a high rate of IT project return on investment. But among those companies that stated that their IT strategies were aligned with their business strategies, that percentage more than doubled to 24 percent.

According to the survey conducted by Computer Sciences Corporation (CSC) and Financial Executives International (FEI), businesses that do align their IT strategies with their business strategies are "significantly more likely to achieve a high return on IT investment." Unfortunately, 60 percent of the companies surveyed stated that they lacked any such formal plan to align IT and business strategies.

Any organization can have C-level executives in charge of IT and IT deployment. Those executives must work in concert with others to ensure that IT strategies are developed in conjunction with and employed to support business strategies. That is the key to success through information technology.[15]

ble for their respective functions and for reporting to the CIO. It's definitely a team effort to manage most organizational resources—information is no different from other assets in that it needs careful oversight and management.

In certain ways information is different from many "typical" organizational resources, however. For example, information is intangible, so it becomes extremely difficult to measure its worth. What dollar value would you attach to a customer record? Realistically, it is impossible to set a precise dollar value on information. So, how can you know how much you should spend on information technology tools? It is a difficult question to answer, yet information administrators have to answer it.

Since information is intangible, it can be shared by numerous people and not actually be "consumed." Money, for instance, is different. If you have money in your department budget and spend it on travel, you can't very well use that same money for employee education expenses. In this way, then, the intangibility of information is good because many people can use it without "consuming" it. But as we've alluded to many times, this is also why information officers have to take special precautions regarding the security of information. That is, the more information available to the appropriate knowledge workers the better, but the indications for security and often privacy are obvious. No other organizational resource, even money, requires this kind of oversight. The more people who have access to information, the greater the responsibility for securing it.

THE SHARING OF INFORMATION WITH RESPONSIBILITY

Information sharing in your organization means that anyone—regardless of title or department—can access and use whatever information he or she needs. But information sharing brings to light an important question: Does anyone in your organization *own* the information? In other words, if everyone shares the information, who is ultimately responsible for providing the information and assuring the quality of the information? Information ownership is a key consideration in today's information-based business environment. Someone must accept full responsibility for providing specific pieces of

CRUD: DEFINING INFORMATION OWNERSHIP

One easy way to determine information ownership is to think of **CRUD**—**c**reate, **r**ead, **u**pdate, and **d**elete. If you can not only read but create, update, and/or delete information, then in some way you own that information because you are responsible for its quality.

Here again, let's consider your school as an example and focus on your personal and transcript information. That information includes your student ID, name, address, phone number, GPA, declared major, declared minor (if you have one), and courses completed (this is your transcript).

For each piece of information, first identify who has create, update, and delete privileges. There may be many individuals or departments that have these sorts of information privileges. If so, who is ultimately responsible for your personal and transcript information? Second, identify all the groups of people at your school who can only view (read) your information.

information and ensuring the quality of that information. If you find that the wrong information is stored in the organization's data warehouse, you must be able to determine the source of the problem and whose responsibility it is.

The issue of information ownership is similar to other management functions. If you manage a department, you're responsible for the work in that department as well as its expenses and people. The same is true for information. If information originates in your department, you essentially own that information because you're providing it to those who need it and you are ensuring its quality.

INFORMATION CLEANLINESS

Information "cleanliness" (an aspect of information ownership) is an important topic today and will be for many years. Have you ever received the same piece of advertising mail (snail mail, that is) multiple times from the same company on the same day? Many people have, and it's an example of "unclean" information. In this instance, your name may appear twice in a database, once without your middle initial and once with your middle initial. Likewise, your name may appear twice in a database with two different spellings of your last name.

In all popular business-oriented DBMSs, such as Oracle, you can find utilities to help you "clean" your information. In the example of having your information twice in a database (with different spellings of your last name), the utility would probably determine that the two records actually belong to the same person (you) because of the identical nature of other associated information such as your address and phone number.

In a data warehouse environment, recall that information comes from multiple databases. It becomes even more important then to consolidate and "clean" the information so no duplicate or erroneous information exists in the data warehouse. To accomplish this, you go through extraction, transformation, and loading. *Extraction, transformation, and loading (ETL)* is a process in which you specify what information you want from each database, how that information is to be associated, and what rules to follow in consolidating the information to ensure its cleanliness in a data warehouse. You certainly don't want duplicate information weakening the foundation of your business intelligence.

Summary: Student Learning Outcomes Revisited

1. **Describe business intelligence and its role in an organization.** *Business intelligence* is knowledge—knowledge about your customers, your competitors, your partners, your competitive environment, and your own internal operations—that gives you the ability to make effective, important, and often strategic business decisions. Business intelligence is much more than just a list of your products or to whom you've sold them. It might combine your product information with your advertising strategy information and customer demographics, for instance, to help you determine the effectiveness of various advertising media on demographic groups segmented by location.

2. **Differentiate between databases and data warehouses with respect to their focus on online transaction processing and online analytical processing.** A *database* is a collection of information that you organize and access according to the logical structure of that information. Databases support both online transaction processing (OLTP) and online analytical processing (OLAP). Databases that support OLTP are often referred to as *operational databases.* These databases contain detailed information about transactions that have taken place. And using various data manipulation tools, you can query a database to extract meaningful information. A *data warehouse* is a collection of information—gathered from many different operational databases—used to create business intelligence that supports business analysis activities and decision-making tasks. So, data warehouses support only OLAP, not OLTP.

3. **List and describe the key characteristics of a relational database.** The *relational database* model uses a series of logically related two-dimensional tables or files to store information in the form of a database. Key characteristics include

   - A collection of information—Composed of many files or tables of information that are related to each other
   - Contain logical structures—You care only about the logical information and not about how it's physically stored or where it's physically located
   - Have logical ties among the information—All the files in a database are related in that some primary keys of certain files appear as foreign keys in others
   - Possess built-in integrity constraints—When creating the data dictionary for a database, you can specify rules by which the information must be entered (e.g., not blank, etc.)

4. **Define the five software components of a database management system.** The five software components of a database management system include

   - *DBMS engine*—Accepts logical requests from the various other DBMS subsystems, converts them into their physical equivalent, and actually accesses the database and data dictionary as they exist on a storage device
   - *Data definition subsystem*—Helps you create and maintain the data dictionary and define the structure of the files in a database
   - *Data manipulation subsystem*—Helps you add, change, and delete information in a database and query it for valuable information
   - *Application generation subsystem*—Contains facilities to help you develop transaction-intensive applications
   - *Data administration subsystem*—Helps you manage the overall database environment by providing facilities for backup and recovery, security management, query optimization, concurrency control, and change management

5. **List and describe the key characteristics of a data warehouse.** The key characteristics of a data warehouse include

   - Multidimensional—While databases store information in two-dimensional tables, data warehouses include layers to represent information according to different dimensions
   - Support decision making—Data warehouses, because they contain summarized information, support business activities and decision-making tasks, not transaction processing

6. **Define the four major types of data-mining tools in a data warehouse environment.** The four major types of data-mining tools in a data warehouse environment include

- *Query-and-reporting tools*—Similar to QBE tools, SQL, and report generators in the typical database environment
- **Intelligent agents**—Utilize various artificial intelligence tools such as neural networks and fuzzy logic to form the basis of "information discovery" and building business intelligence in OLAP
- *Multidimensional analysis (MDA) tools*—Slice-and-dice techniques that allow you to

view multidimensional information from different perspectives

- **Statistical tools**—Help you apply various mathematical models to the information stored in a data warehouse to discover new information

7. **List key considerations in information ownership in an organization.** Key considerations in information ownership in an organization include:

- Strategic management support
- The sharing of information with responsibility
- Information cleanliness

CLOSING CASE STUDY ONE

BEN & JERRY'S, BIGELOW TEAS, AND BUSINESS INTELLIGENCE

Organizations want information. Organizations need information. However, information must be in an organized format that supports the creation of business intelligence. Otherwise, according to Rebecca Wettemann, vice president of Research at Nucleus Research, "It's like having a bank account with millions of dollars in it but no ATM card. If you can't get it [business intelligence] and can't make it work for you, then it is not really useful."

In support of creating and using business intelligence, companies have focused much of their spending efforts on business intelligence software and data-mining tools. According to a Merrill Lynch survey in 2003, business intelligence software and data-mining tools were at the top of the technology spending list of CIOs. And according to A. G. Edwards, the market for that type of software is expected to grow from $4.7 billion in 2003 to $7.5 billion in 2006.

Consider two companies—Ben & Jerry's and Bigelow Teas—and their approach to creating and using business intelligence.

BEN & JERRY'S

Ben & Jerry's, located in Waterbury, Vermont, produces 190,000 pints of ice cream and frozen yogurt daily and ships to over 50,000 grocery stores in the United States

and 12 other countries. Every single pint is meticulously tracked, first by being entered into an Oracle database. With that information carefully organized, Ben & Jerry's uses a sophisticated data-mining tool set from a company called Business Objects.

For example, the sales people can easily monitor sales to determine how much ground Cherry Garcia Frozen Yogurt is gaining on Cherry Garcia Ice Cream, its number one selling product. The consumer affairs staff can even correlate each of the several hundred calls and e-mails received each week to the exact pint of ice cream. If complaints are consistent concerning a specific batch, the consumer affairs staff can drill down to the supplier who provided the ingredients such as milk or eggs.

In one particular instance, Ben & Jerry's received a large number of complaints that its Cherry Garcia Ice Cream didn't have enough cherries. The complaints were coming in from all over the country, so it wasn't a regional problem. Employees continued drilling through business intelligence with Business Objects and determined that the manufacturing process (from the supplies of raw materials to the mixing) was satisfactory and had no anomalies. Eventually the problem was determined to be that the ice cream box for Cherry Garcia Ice Cream had on it a photo of frozen yogurt, a product with more cherries than the ice cream. Simply changing the photo on the box solved the problem.

BIGELOW TEAS

Bigelow Teas provides over 50 varieties of flavored, traditional, iced, decaffeinated, and herbal teas. Over the past 50 years, Bigelow Teas has relied on business intelligence to determine the success of each individual tea, and today is no different.

Although it may not seem like it, bringing a new tea to the market is a risky endeavor. It could fail in every way or it could simply cannibalize the sales of an existing tea, neither of which makes business sense. Employees at Bigelow Teas pore over consumer, sales, marketing, and finance business intelligence to ensure that they are making the right decisions in all aspects of the business.

To help facilitate the creation and use of business intelligence, Bigelow Teas turned to the Andrews Consulting Group and BusinessObjects. Prior to using BusinessObjects, Bigelow employees had a difficult time finding and using the right information. As Melanie Dower, project leader at Bigelow Teas, describes it, "Our existing end-user reporting tool wasn't user-friendly, so users simply weren't using it. Most users were unable to create their own reports, so we looked for a solution that offered self-serve business intelligence (BI) to free up IT resources." BusinessObjects is both easy to learn and easy to use because it looks like Microsoft Excel. Explains Dower, "Enterprise 6 [of BusinessObjects] looks and feels like Microsoft Excel, which speeds up the learning curve for our end users."

With BusinessObjects, Bigelow employees can access and view business intelligence in real time, more accurately predict sales forecasts based on shipment levels, identify where to increase sales efforts before it's too late, and even compare current consumer, sales, and marketing information with similar types of information up to five years old.

Gourmet coffees exploded onto the consumer market about seven years ago and gourmet teas quickly followed. Bigelow Teas is riding this wave of success with success of its own because of its use of business intelligence.[16,17,18]

Questions

1. Ben & Jerry's tracks a wealth of information on each pint of ice cream and frozen yogurt. If you were to design Ben & Jerry's data warehouse, what dimensions of information would you include? As you develop your list of dimensions, consider every facet of Ben & Jerry's business operations, from supply chain management to retail store monitoring.

2. Databases are the underlying technology that allows Ben & Jerry's to track ice cream and frozen yogurt information. Based on your knowledge of databases, what sort of tables or files of information would Ben & Jerry's need in its database? What would be the primary keys for each of those? What would be the foreign keys among those to create the necessary relationships?

3. According to the discussion of Bigelow Teas, part of the success of BusinessObjects comes from its look and feel being similar to Microsoft Excel. Why do you believe this is true? When introducing employees to enterprisewide BI tools such as BusinessObjects, why is it an advantage to have the BI tool look like and work like personal productivity software tools? Why was a similar look and feel to spreadsheet software more important than word processing or presentation software?

4. How could Bigelow Teas open up its business intelligence information to its suppliers and resellers? What benefits would Bigelow Teas gain by keeping its suppliers and resellers more informed with business intelligence? What types of business intelligence would Bigelow Teas want to exclude its suppliers and resellers from seeing? Why?

5. Neil Hastie, CIO at TruServe Corporation, once described most decision making in all types of businesses as "a lot of by-guess and by-golly, a lot of by-gut, and a whole lot of paper reports." That statement is not kind to managers in general or to IT specialists charged with providing the right people with the right technology to make the right decisions. What's the key to turning Neil's statement into a positive one? Is it training? It is providing timely information access? Is it providing everyone with a wide assortment of data-mining tools? Other solutions? Perhaps it's a combination of several answers?

MINING DINING DATA

As you read in one of the closing case studies in Chapter 2, restaurants and fast-food chains rely heavily on business intelligence to make important decisions. Casinos do as well. Some of the leading restaurants, fast-food chains, and casinos using data warehouses include AFC Enterprises (operator and franchiser of more than 3,300 Church's Chicken, Popeye's Chicken and Biscuits, Seattle Coffee Company, Cinnabon, and Torrefazione outlets worldwide); Red Robin International (a 170-unit casual-dining chain); Harrah's Entertainment (owner of 26 U.U. casinos); Pizzeria Uno; and Einstein/Noah Bagel (operator of 428 Einstein's and 111 Noah's New York Bagel stores).

AFC ENTERPRISES

AFC Enterprises cultivates a loyal clientele by slicing and dicing its data warehouse to strategically configure promotions and tailor menus to suit local preferences. AFC's data warehouse helps it better understand its core customers and maximize its overall profitability. AFC tracks customer-specific information from name and address to order history and frequency of visits. This enables AFC to determine exactly which customers are likely to respond to a given promotion on a given day of the week.

AFC also uses its data warehouse to anticipate and manipulate customer behavior. For example, AFC can use its data warehouse to determine that coffee is added to the tab 65 percent of the time when a particular dessert is ordered and 85 percent of the time when that dessert is offered as a promotional item. Knowing that, AFC can run more promotions for certain desserts figuring that customers will respond by ordering more desserts and especially more coffee (coffee is a high-margin item in the restaurant business).

RED ROBIN INTERNATIONAL

Red Robin's terabyte-size data warehouse tracks hundreds of thousands of point-of-sale (POS) transactions, involving millions of menu items and more than 1.5 million invoices. As Howard Jenkins, Red Robin's vice president of Information Systems, explains it, "With data mining in place, we can ask ourselves, 'If we put the items with high margins in the middle of the menu, do we sell more versus putting it at the top or bottom, [and if so], to whom and where?' We can also tell if something cannibalizes the sale of other items and can give the marketing department an almost instant picture of how promotions are being sold and used."

The placement of items on a menu is strategic business, just as the placement of promotional items in a grocery store can mean increased sales for one item and reduced sales for another. The job of finding the right mix is definitely suited to mining a data warehouse.

Using Cognos Business Intelligence, Red Robin now has measurable results of promotion and menu changes, makes better and more timely decisions, and has realized seven-figure savings in operational costs.

HARRAH'S ENTERTAINMENT

Harrah's Entertainment uses its data warehouse to make decisions for its highly successful Total Gold customer recognition program. Depending on their spending records, Total Gold members can receive free vouchers for dining, entertainment, and sleeping accommodations. Knowing which rewards to give to which customers is key.

John Boushy, senior vice president of Entertainment and Technology for Harrah's, says, "We can determine what adds value to each customer and provide that value at the right time." Dining vouchers or free tickets for shows are awarded to day visitors, not sleeping accommodations. Customers who consistently visit a particular restaurant and order higher-end foods receive free dinners and cocktails, not vouchers for free (and cheaper) breakfasts.

PIZZERIA UNO

Pizzeria Uno uses its data warehouse to apply the 80/20 rule. That is, it can determine which 20 percent of its customers contribute to 80 percent of its sales and adjust menus and promotions to suit top patron preferences. These changes can often lead to converting some of the other 80 percent of Pizzeria Uno's customers to the more profitable 20 percent.

EINSTEIN/NOAH BAGEL

Einstein/Noah Bagel uses its data warehouse in real time to maximize cross-selling opportunities. For example, if data warehouse information reveals that a manager in a given store might be missing a cross-selling opportunity on a particular day, an e-mail is automatically sent out to alert managers to the opportunity. Salespeople can then respond by offering the cross-selling opportunity ("How about a cup of hot chocolate with that bagel since it's so cold outside?") to the next customer.[19,20,21,22]

QUESTIONS

1. Consider the issue of timely information with respect to the businesses discussed in the case. Which of the businesses must have the most up-to-date information in its data warehouse? Which business can have the most out-of-date information in its data warehouse and still be effective? Rank the five businesses discussed with a 1 for the one that needs the most up-to-date information and a 5 for the one that is least sensitive to timeliness of information. Be prepared to justify your rankings.

2. Harrah's Entertainment tracks a wealth of information concerning customer spending habits. If you were to design Harrah's Entertainment's data warehouse, what dimensions of information would you include? As you develop your list of dimensions, consider every facet of Harrah's business operations, including hotels, restaurants, and gaming casinos.

3. AFC Enterprises includes information in its data warehouse such as customer name and address. Where does it (or could it) gather such information? Think carefully about this, because customers seldom provide their names and addresses when ordering fast food at a Church's or Popeye's. Is AFC gathering information in an ethical fashion? Why or why not?

4. Visit a local grocery store and walk down the breakfast cereal aisle. You should notice something very specific about the positioning of the various breakfast cereals. What is it? On the basis of what information do you think grocery stores determine cereal placement? Could they have determined that information from a data warehouse or from some other source? If another source, what might that source be?

5. Suppose you're opening a pizza parlor in the town where you live. It will be a "take and bake" pizza parlor in which you make pizzas for customers but do not cook them. Customers buy the pizzas uncooked and take them home for baking. You will have no predefined pizza types but will make each pizza to the customer's specifications. What sort of data warehouse would you need to predict the use of toppings by time of day and by day of the week? What would your dimensions of information be? If you wanted to increase the requests for a new topping (such as mandarin oranges), what information would you hope to find in your data warehouse that would enable you to do so?

Key Terms and Concepts

Application generation subsystem, 136
Business intelligence (BI), 124
Chief information officer (CIO), 146
Chief privacy officer (CPO), 146
Chief security officer (CSO), 146
Data administration, 146
Data administration subsystem, 136
Database, 126
Database administration, 146
Database management system (DBMS), 130

Data definition subsystem, 131
Data dictionary, 126
Data manipulation subsystem, 132
Data mart, 143
Data-mining tool, 141
Data warehouse, 140
DBMS engine, 130
Extraction, transformation, and loading (ETL), 148
Foreign key, 128
Integrity constraint, 129

Logical view, 130
Multidimensional analysis (MDA) tool, 142
Online analytical processing (OLAP), 124
Online transaction processing (OLTP), 124
Operational database, 124
Physical view, 130
Primary key, 128

Query-and-reporting tool, 142
Query-by-example (QBE) tool, 135
Relation, 126
Relational database, 126
Report generator, 134
Structured query language (SQL), 136
View, 133

Short-Answer Questions

1. What is business intelligence? Why is it more than just information?
2. What is online transaction processing (OLTP)?
3. What is online analytical processing (OLAP)?
4. What is the most popular database model?
5. How are primary and foreign keys different?
6. What are the five important software components of a database management system?
7. How are QBE tools and SQL similar? How are they different?

8. What is a data warehouse? How does it differ from a database?
9. What are the four major types of data-mining tools?
10. What is a data mart? How is it similar to a data warehouse?
11. What is the role of a chief information officer (CIO)?

Assignments and Exercises

1. **FINDING "HACKED" DATABASES**   *The Happy Hacker* (www.happyhacker.org/news/newsfeed.shtml) is a Web site devoted to "hacking"—breaking into computer systems. When people hack into a system, they often go after information in databases. There, they can find credit card information and other private and sensitive information. Sometimes, they can even find designs of yet-to-be-released products and other strategic information about a company. Connect to *The Happy Hacker* Web site and find an article that discusses a database that was hacked. Prepare a short report for your class detailing the incident.
2. **DEFINING QUERIES FOR A VIDEO RENTAL STORE**   Consider your local video rental store. It certainly has an operational database to support its online transaction processing (OLTP). The operational database supports such things as adding new customers, renting videos (obviously), ordering videos, and a host of other activities. Now, assume that the video rental store also uses that same database for online analytical processing (OLAP) in the form of creating queries to extract meaningful information. If you were the manager of the video rental store, what kinds of queries would you build? What answers are you hoping to find?
3. **CREATING A QUERY**   On the Web site that supports this text (www.mhhe.com/haag, choose Chapter 3 and then Solomon Enterprises), we've provided the database (in Microsoft Access) we illustrated in this chapter. Connect to the text's Web site and download that database. Now, create three queries using the QBE tool. The first one should extract information from only one file (your choice). The second one should extract information found in at least two files. The third should include some sort of selection criteria. How easy or difficult was it to perform these three queries? Would you say that a DBMS is just as easy to use as something like word processing or spreadsheet software? Why or why not? (By the way, *Extended Learning Module J* takes you through the step-by-step process of creating a query in Access.)
4. **CAREER OPPORTUNITIES IN YOUR MAJOR**   Knowledge workers throughout the business world are building their own desktop databases (often called end-user databases or knowledge worker databases).

To do so, they must understand both how to design a database and how to use a desktop DBMS such as Microsoft Access or FileMaker (made by FileMaker). The ability to design a database and use a desktop DBMS offers you a great career advantage. Research your chosen major by looking at job postings (the Web is the best place to start). How many of those jobs want you to have some database knowledge? Do they list a specific DBMS package? What's your take—should you expand your education and learn more about databases and DBMSs? Why or why not?

5. **SALARIES FOR DATABASE ADMINISTRATORS**   Database administrators (DBAs) are among the highest paid professionals in the information technology field. Many people work for 10 to 20 years to get a promotion to DBA. Connect to Monster.com (www.monster.com) or another job database of your choice and search for DBA job openings. As you do, select all locations and job categories and then use "dba" as the keyword search criteria. How many DBA job postings did you find? In what industries were some of the DBA job openings? Read through a couple of the job postings. What was the listed salary range (if any)? What sort of qualifications were listed?

6. Throughout this chapter, we compared the power of databases to spreadsheet software. In many instances, databases provide greater support for enforcing integrity constraints. However, you can achieve some level of enforcing integrity constraints with spreadsheet software. For example, you can specify that entries into a cell or cells must be in a date format. You can also specify a range of values for a numeric field. Start your preferred spreadsheet software and explore some of the features that enable you to enforce integrity constraints. If you're using Excel, click on **Data** and then **Validation.** What integrity constraint features did you find? How would you use them in building a spreadsheet application? What is the role of an **Input Message** and an **Error Alert**?

Discussion Questions

1. Databases and data warehouses clearly make it easier for people to access all kinds of information. This will lead to great debates in the area of privacy. Should organizations be left to police themselves with respect to providing access to information or should the government impose privacy legislation? Answer this question with respect to (1) customer information shared by organizations, (2) employee information shared within a specific organization, and (3) business information available to customers.

2. Business intelligence sounds like a fancy term with a lot of competitive advantage potentially rolled into it. What sort of business intelligence does your school need? Specifically, what business intelligence would it need to predict enrollments in the coming years? What business intelligence would it need to determine what curriculums to offer? Do you think your school gathers and uses this kind of business intelligence? Why or why not?

3. Consider your school's registration database that enforces the following integrity constraint: to enroll in a given class, the student must have completed or currently be enrolled in the listed prerequisite (if any). Your school, in fact, probably does have that integrity constraint in place. How can you get around that integrity constraint and enroll in a class for which you are not taking nor have completed the prerequisite? Is this an instance of when you should be able to override an integrity constraint? What are the downsides to being able to do so?

4. In this chapter, we listed the five important software components of a DBMS: the DBMS engine, the data definition, data manipulation, application generation, and data administration subsystems. Which of those are most and least important to users of a database? Which of those are most and least important to technology specialists who develop data applications? Which of those are most and least important to the chief information officer (CIO)? For each of your responses, provide justification.

5. Some people used to believe that data warehouses would quickly replace databases for both online transaction processing (OLTP)

and online analytical processing (OLAP). Of course, they were wrong. Why can data warehouses not replace databases and become "operational data warehouses"? How radically would data warehouses (and their data-mining tools) have to change to become a viable replacement for databases? Would they then essentially become databases that simply supported OLAP? Why or why not?

6. Consider that you work in the human resources management department of a local business and that many of your friends work there. Although you don't personally generate payroll checks, you still have the ability to look up anyone's pay. Would you check on your friends to see if they're earning more money than you? For that matter, would you look up their pay just out of simple curiosity, knowing that you would never do anything with the information or share it with anyone else? Why or why not? People working at the Internal Revenue Service (IRS) were caught just curiously looking up the reported incomes of movie stars and other high-profile public figures. Is this acceptable? Why or why not?

7. In spite of the need for "clean" information, many organizations have databases with duplicate records for you. You've probably experienced the consequences of this by receiving two identical pieces of junk mail from the same company. One record in the database may have your middle initial while the other doesn't, or there is some other type of minor discrepancy. Why would some organizations intentionally *not* go through a process of cleaning their database information?

Searching Online Databases and Information Repositories

As you find sites on the Internet that provide information, many of them will do so in the form of a database—a searchable grouping of information that allows you to find specific information by entering key words and key phrases. These words and phrases are, in fact, some sort of keys (similar to primary and foreign keys we discussed in this chapter) that are used as matching criteria in a field of the database.

In this section, you'll explore a variety of information topics that you can find on the Internet. To help you, we've included a number of Web sites related to searching online database and information repositories. On the Web site that supports this text (www.mhhe.com/haag), we've provided direct links to all these Web sites as well as many, many more. These are a great starting point for completing this Electronic Commerce section.

FINANCIAL AID RESOURCES

On the Internet, you can find valuable databases that give you access to financial aid resources as you attend school. These resources can be in the form of scholarships—money you don't have to pay back—and standard student loans. And there are a variety of financial aid lenders, ranging from traditional banks, the government, and private parties wanting to give something back to society. Find at least three Web sites that provide a financial aid database and answer the following questions for each.

- **A.** Do you have to register as a user to access information?
- **B.** Do you have to pay a fee to access information?
- **C.** Can you build a profile of yourself and use it as you search?
- **D.** Can you apply for aid while at the site or must you request paper applications that you need to complete and return?
- **E.** By what sort of categories of aid can you search?

LIBRARIES

LEXIS-NEXIS is now completely on the Internet. Many libraries and other such sites even offer full books online for you to read. You may never have to go to a physical library again. Think for a moment about a term paper you're currently writing or may have to write soon. What is the major topic? Now connect to a couple of different library sites and try to find some of the information you'll need. As you do, answer the following questions for each site.

- **A.** What organization supports the site? Is the organization reputable?
- **B.** Do you have to pay a subscription fee to access the information provided?
- **C.** How good are the search capabilities?
- **D.** How can you obtain printed versions of information you find?
- **E.** Is finding information in libraries on the Internet easier or more difficult than finding information in a traditional library?

CONSUMER INFORMATION

Many consumer organizations also provide databases of information on the Internet. At those sites you can read about the latest product reviews, search for new pharmaceuticals that cure diseases (or alleviate symptoms of them), and access safety information for products such as automobiles and children's toys.

Connect to several consumer organization sites and do some digging around. As you do, think about a product you're considering buying or perhaps have just bought. Is the information helpful? Is the information opinion only, completely factual, or a combination of the two? How important will this type of consumer information become as electronic commerce becomes more widespread on the Internet?

DEMOGRAPHICS

For organizations focusing on meeting wants or desires of end consumers, the demographic makeup of the target audience is key. It's simple: The more you know about your target audience, the better equipped you are to develop and market products.

And you can find all sorts of demographic information on the Internet. Connect to a couple of different demographic-related Web sites and see what they have to offer. As you do, answer the following questions for each.

A. Who is the target audience of the site?

B. Who is the provider of the site?

C. Is the provider a private (for-profit) organization or a not-for-profit organization?

D. How often is the demographic information updated?

E. Does the site require that you pay a subscription fee to access its demographic information?

F. How helpful would the information be if you wanted to start a new business or sell various types of products?

REAL ESTATE

You can't actually live on the Internet, although some people may seem as though they want to try. But you can find real estate for sale and rent. You can find sites that take you through a step-by-step process for buying your first home, that provide mortgage and interest rate calculators, that offer financing for your home, and that even offer crime reports by neighborhood. Connect to several real estate–related sites and see what they have to offer. As you do, answer the following questions for each.

A. What is the focus of the site (residential, commercial, rental, and so forth)?

B. Does the site require you to register as a user to access its services?

C. Can you request that e-mail be sent to you when properties in which you are interested become available?

D. How can you search for information (by state, by zip code, by price range, by feature such as swimming pool)?

E. Does the site offer related information such as loans and mortgage calculators?

EXTENDED LEARNING MODULE C

DESIGNING DATABASES AND ENTITY-RELATIONSHIP DIAGRAMMING

Student Learning Outcomes

1. IDENTIFY HOW DATABASES AND SPREADSHEETS ARE BOTH SIMILAR AND DIFFERENT.

2. LIST AND DESCRIBE THE FOUR STEPS IN DESIGNING AND BUILDING A RELATIONAL DATABASE.

3. DEFINE THE CONCEPTS OF ENTITY CLASS, INSTANCE, PRIMARY KEY, AND FOREIGN KEY.

4. GIVEN A SMALL OPERATING ENVIRONMENT, BUILD AN ENTITY-RELATIONSHIP (E-R) DIAGRAM.

5. LIST AND DESCRIBE THE STEPS IN NORMALIZATION.

6. DESCRIBE THE PROCESS OF CREATING AN INTERSECTION RELATION TO REMOVE A MANY-TO-MANY RELATIONSHIP.

Introduction

As you learned in Chapter 3, databases are quite powerful and can aid your organization in both transaction and analytical processing. But you must carefully design and build a database for it to be effective. Relational databases are similar to spreadsheets in that you maintain information in two-dimensional files. In a spreadsheet, you place information in a cell (the intersection of a row and column). To use the information in a cell, you must know its row number and column character. For example, cell C4 is in column C and row 4.

Databases are similar and different. You still create rows and columns of information. However, you don't need to know the physical location of the information you want to see or use. For example, if cell C4 in your spreadsheet contained sales for Able Electronics (one of your customers), to use that information in a formula or function, you would reference its physical location (C4). In a database, you simply need to know you want *sales* for *Able Electronics*. Its physical location is irrelevant. That's why we say that a **database** is a collection of information that you organize and access according to the logical structure of that information.

So, you do need to design your databases carefully for effective use. In this module, we'll take you through the process of designing and building a relational database, the most popular of all database types. A **relational database** uses a series of logically related two-dimensional tables or files to store information in the form of a database. There are well-defined rules to follow, and you need to be aware of them.

As far as implementation is concerned, you then just choose the DBMS package of your choice, define the tables or files, determine the relationships among them, and start entering information. We won't deal with the actual implementation in this module. However, we do show you how to implement a database using Microsoft Access in *Extended Learning Module J*.

Once you've implemented your database, you can then change the information as you wish, add rows of information (and delete others), add new tables, and use simple but powerful reporting and querying tools to extract the exact information you need.

Designing and Building a Relational Database

Using a database amounts to more than just using various DBMS tools. You must also know *how* to actually design and build a database. So, let's take a look at how you would go about designing a database. The four primary steps include

1. Defining entity classes and primary keys.
2. Defining relationships among entity classes.
3. Defining information (fields) for each relation (the term *relation* is often used to refer to a file while designing a database).
4. Using a data definition language to create your database.

Let's continue with the example database we introduced you to in Chapter 3, that of Solomon Enterprises. Solomon Enterprises specializes in providing concrete to commercial builders and individual home owners in the greater Chicago area. On page 128 (Figure 3.3) in Chapter 3, we provided a graphical depiction of some of the tables in

Solomon's database, including *Customer, Concrete Type, Order, Truck,* and *Employee.* As you recall, an order is created when a customer calls in for the delivery of a certain concrete type. Once the concrete is mixed, Solomon has an employee drive the truck to the customer's location. That illustrates how you can use a database in support of your customer relationship management initiative and order-processing function.

In this module, we want to design and model the supply chain management side for Solomon Enterprises. Figure C.1 contains a supply chain management report that Solomon frequently generates. Let's make some observations.

Figure C.1

A Supply Chain Management Report for Solomon Enterprises

SOLOMON ENTERPRISES

Supply Report Ending October 14, 2005

CONCRETE		RAW MATERIAL				SUPPLIER	
Type	Name	ID	Name	Unit	QOH	ID	Name
1	Home	B	Cement paste	1	400	412	Wesley Enterprises
		C	Sand	2	1200	444	Juniper Sand & Gravel
		A	Water	1.5	9999	999	N/A
			TOTAL:	4.5			
2	Comm	B	Cement paste	1	400	412	Wesley Enterprises
		C	Sand	2	1200	444	Juniper Sand & Gravel
		A	Water	1	9999	999	N/A
			TOTAL:	4			
3	Speckled	B	Cement paste	1	400	412	Wesley Enterprises
		C	Sand	2	1200	444	Juniper Sand & Gravel
		A	Water	1.5	9999	999	N/A
		D	Gravel	3	200	444	Juniper Sand & Gravel
			TOTAL:	7.5			
4	Marble	B	Cement paste	1	400	412	Wesley Enterprises
		C	Sand	2	1200	444	Juniper Sand & Gravel
		A	Water	1.5	9999	999	N/A
		E	Marble	2	100	499	A&J Brothers
			TOTAL:	6.5			
5	Shell	B	Cement paste	1	400	412	Wesley Enterprises
		C	Sand	2	1200	444	Juniper Sand & Gravel
		A	Water	1.5	9999	999	N/A
		F	Shell	2.5	25	499	A&J Brothers
			TOTAL:	7			

- Solomon provides five concrete types: 1—home foundation and walkways; 2—commercial foundation and infrastructure; 3—premier speckled (with gravel); 4—premier marble; 5—premier shell.

- Solomon uses six raw materials: A—water; B—cement paste; C—sand; D—gravel; E—marble; F—shell.

- Mixing instructions are for a cubic yard. For example, one cubic yard of commercial concrete requires 1 part cement paste, 2 parts sand, and 1 part water. The terms "part" and "unit" are synonymous.

- Some raw materials are used in several concrete types. Any given concrete type requires several raw materials.

- QOH (quantity on hand) denotes the amount of inventory for a given raw material.

- Suppliers provide raw materials. For a given raw material, Solomon uses only one supplier. A given supplier can provide many different raw materials.

- QOH and supplier information are not tracked for water (for obvious reasons). However, Solomon places the value 9999 in the QOH for water and uses 999 for the ID of the supplier.

When you begin to think about designing a database application, you first need to capture your business rules. Business rules are statements concerning the information you need to work with and the relationships within the information. These business rules will help you define the correct structure of your database. From the report in Figure C.1 and the observations above, we derived the following business rules.

1. A given concrete type will have many raw materials in it.
2. A given raw material may appear in many types of concrete.
3. Each raw material has one and only one supplier.
4. A supplier may provide many raw materials. Although not displayed in Figure C.1, Solomon may have a supplier in its database that doesn't currently provide any raw materials.

Before you begin the process of designing a database, it's important that you first capture and understand the business rules. These business rules will help you define the correct structure of your database.

STEP 1: DEFINING ENTITY CLASSES AND PRIMARY KEYS

The first step in designing a relational database is to define the various entity classes and the primary keys that uniquely define each record or instance within each entity class. An *entity class* is a concept—typically people, places, or things—about which you wish to store information and that you can identify with a unique key (called a primary key). A *primary key* is a field (or group of fields in some cases) that uniquely describes each record. Within the context of database design, we often refer to a record as an instance. An *instance* is an occurrence of an entity class that can be uniquely described with a primary key.

From the supply chain management report in Figure C.1, you can easily identify the entity classes of *Concrete Type, Raw Material,* and *Supplier.* Now, you have to identify their primary keys. For most entity classes, you cannot use names as primary keys because duplicate names can exist. For example, your school provides you with a unique student ID and uses that ID as your primary key instead of your name (because other students may have the same name as you).

DEFINING ENTITY CLASSES AND PRIMARY KEYS

Learning how to design a relational database really requires that you roll up your sleeves and practice, practice, practice. To help with this, you'll be designing a relational database that might be used at your school while we go carefully through the process of designing the relational database for Solomon Enterprises' supply chain management function. Following is a description of the requirements for a hypothetical relational database that might be used at your school:

In conjunction with taking an introductory computer concepts course, your school has decided to test the idea of offering weekend seminars to cover the basics of the Internet and the Web. Initially, your school will offer two such seminars: Web101—The Basics of the Web and Internet; and Web205—Building a Web Site. Web101 will have five different sections, and Web205 will have four different sections.

Although they are not required to, students can enroll in one or both seminars. The seminars are held for eight hours on a single day. There is no cost associated with taking the seminars. One teacher, from a pool of qualified teachers, will be assigned to each section of each seminar. Some teachers will obviously not be assigned to teach any sections, and some teachers may be assigned to several different sections.

Finally, the system should track the final grades assigned to each student. One more thing. Your school is simply testing this idea in this particular term. So, don't worry about the term (e.g., Fall, Winter, Spring, or Summer) or the year.

For this particular scenario, you are to create a simple two-column table that lists all the entity classes in the left column and their associated primary keys in the right column. Finally, record as many business rules as you can find provided in the description.

From the report, you can see that the entity class *Concrete Type* includes two pieces of information—*Concrete Type* and a name or *Type Description*. Although *Type Description* is unique, the logical choice for the primary key is *Concrete Type* (e.g., 1 for home, 2 for commercial, and so on). Notice that the primary key name is the same as the entity class name. This is perfectly acceptable; if it is a potential point of confusion for you, change the primary key name to something like *Concrete Type ID* or *Concrete Type Identifier*. For our purposes, we'll use *Concrete Type* as the primary key name.

If you consider *Raw Material* as an entity class, you'll find several pieces of information including *Raw Material ID*, *Raw Material Name*, and *QOH*. The logical choice for a primary key here is *Raw Material ID* (e.g., A for water, B for cement paste, and so on). Although *Raw Material Name* is unique, we still suggest that you not use names.

Likewise, if you consider *Supplier* as an entity class, you'll find two pieces of information: *Supplier ID* and *Supplier Name*. Again, we recommend that you use *Supplier ID* as the primary key.

STEP 2: DEFINING RELATIONSHIPS AMONG THE ENTITY CLASSES

The next step in designing a relational database is to define the relationships among the entity classes. To help you do this, we'll use an entity-relationship diagram. An ***entity-relationship (E-R) diagram*** is a graphic method of representing entity classes and their relationships. An E-R diagram includes five basic symbols:

1. A rectangle to denote an entity class
2. A dotted line connecting entity classes to denote a relationship

Figure C.2

An Entity-Relationship
(E-R) Diagram

ENTITY-RELATIONSHIP DIAGRAM SYMBOLS

	Entity class		---- A relationship
	Single relationship	◯ Zero or optional relationship
	Multiple relationship	

3. A | to denote a single relationship

4. A 0 to denote a zero or optional relationship

5. A crow's foot (shown as <) to denote a multiple relationship

To use these symbols, you must first decide among which entity classes relationships exist. If you determine that two particular entity classes have a relationship, you simply draw a dotted line to connect them and then write some sort of verb that describes the relationship.

In Figure C.2 above, you can see the E-R diagram for the supply chain management side of Solomon's database. To determine where the relationships exist, simply ask some questions and review your business rules. For example, is there a relationship between concrete type and raw material? The answer is yes because raw materials are used in mixing the various concrete types. Likewise, the raw materials are provided by suppliers (another relationship). However, there is no logical relationship between concrete type and supplier. So, we drew dotted lines between *Concrete Type* and *Raw Material* and between *Raw Material* and *Supplier*. We then added some verbs to describe the relationships. For example, a *Concrete Type* is composed of *Raw Material,* and a *Supplier* provides a *Raw Material.*

It should also make sense (both business and logical) when you read the relationships in reverse. To do this, simply flip the location of the nouns in the sentence and change the verb accordingly. For example,

- *Concrete Type–Raw Material:* A *Concrete Type* is composed of *Raw Material.*
- *Raw Material–Concrete Type:* A *Raw Material* is used to create a *Concrete Type.*
- *Supplier–Raw Material:* A *Supplier* provides a *Raw Material.*
- *Raw Material–Supplier:* A *Raw Material* is provided by a *Supplier.*

Each of the preceding statements makes logical sense, follows the relationships we identify in Figure C.2, and reflects the business rules listed on page 163. Again, we stress the importance of using business rules. Technology (databases, in this instance) is a set of tools that you use to process information. So, your implementations of technology should match the way your business works. If you always start by defining business rules and using those rules as guides, your technology implementations will most likely mirror how your business works. And that's the way it should be.

DEFINING RELATIONSHIPS AMONG ENTITY CLASSES

Let's continue exploring how to design a relational database for your school and its offering of weekend seminars. If your group correctly completed the tasks in the Team Work on page 164, you know that there are four entity classes. They include (along with their primary keys):

Entity Class	Primary Key
Seminar	Seminar 3-character identifier and number (e.g., Web101 and Web205)
Seminar Section	Seminar 3-character identifier, number, and section number (e.g., Web101-1 through Web101-5 and Web205-1 through Web205-4)
Student	Student ID (whatever your school happens to use)
Qualified Teacher	Teacher ID (your school may use social security number)

Now your task is to define among which of those entity classes relationships exist and then write some verbs that describe each relationship just as we did in Figure C.2. We've drawn rectangles for each of the four entity classes. Connect the rectangles with dotted lines where relationships exist and write the appropriate verbs to describe the relationships.

Seminar

Seminar Section

Qualified Teacher

Student

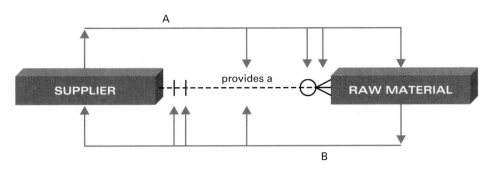

Figure C.3

Reading an Entity-Relationship (E-R) Diagram

Once you determine that a relationship does exist, you must then determine the numerical nature of the relationship, what we refer to as "minimum and maximum cardinality." To describe this, you use a | to denote a single relationship, a 0 to denote a zero or optional relationship, and/or a crow's foot (<) to denote a multiple relationship. By way of illustration, let's consider the portion of your E-R diagram in Figure C.3 above. To help you read the symbols and diagram, we've added blue lines and arrows. Following the line marked A, you would read the E-R diagram as:

"A *Supplier* may not provide any *Raw Material* (denoted with the 0) but may provide more than one *Raw Material* (denoted with the crow's foot)."

So, that part of the E-R diagram states that the logical relationship between *Supplier* and *Raw Material* is that a *Supplier* may provide no *Raw Material* currently in inventory but may provide more than one *Raw Material* currently in inventory. This is exactly what business rule 4 (on page 163) states.

Following the blue line marked B, you would read the E-R diagram as:

"A *Raw Material* must be provided by one *Supplier* (denoted with the first |) and can only be provided by one *Supplier* (denoted with the second |)."

That statement again reinforces business rule 4.

Similarly, you can also develop statements that describe the numerical relationships between *Concrete Type* and *Raw Material* based on that part of the E-R diagram in Figure C.2. Those numerical relationships would be as follows:

- A *Concrete Type* is composed of more than one *Raw Material* and must be composed of at least one *Raw Material*.
- A *Raw Material* can be used to create more than one *Concrete Type* but is not required to be used to create any *Concrete Type*.

Again, these statements reinforce business rules 1 and 2 on page 163.

To properly develop the numerical relationships (cardinality) among entity classes, you must clearly understand the business situation at hand. That's why it's so important to write down all the business rules.

DEFINING THE CARDINALITY AMONG ENTITY CLASSES

As we continue with the design of the relational database at your school, it's time to define the cardinality among the entity classes. If you correctly completed the Team Work project on page 166, the relationships among the entity classes are as follows.

Your task is to create the numerical relationships by adding the symbols of |, O, and crow's foot in the appropriate places. Once you do, complete the table that follows by providing a narrative description of each numerical relationship.

Relationship	Narrative Description
Seminar–Seminar Section	
Seminar Section–Seminar	
Qualified Teacher–Seminar Section	
Seminar Section–Qualified Teacher	
Student–Seminar Section	
Seminar Section–Student	

Figure C.4

Creating an Intersection Relation to Remove a Many-to-Many Relationship

After developing the initial E-R diagram, it's time to begin the process of normalization. *Normalization* is a process of assuring that a relational database structure can be implemented as a series of two-dimensional relations (remember: relations are the same as files or tables). The complete normalization process is extensive and quite necessary for developing organizationwide databases. For our purposes, we will focus on the following three rules of normalization:

1. Eliminate repeating groups or many-to-many relationships.
2. Assure that each field in a relation depends only on the primary key for that relation.
3. Remove all derived fields from the relations.

The first rule of normalization states that no repeating groups or many-to-many relationships can exist among the entity classes. You can find these many-to-many relationships by simply looking at your E-R diagram and note any relationships that have a crow's foot on each end. If you look back at Figure C.2 on page 165, you'll see that a crow's foot is on each end of the relationship between *Concrete Type* and *Raw Material*. Let's look at how to eliminate it.

In Figure C.4 above, we've developed the appropriate relationships between *Concrete Type* and *Raw Material* by removing the many-to-many relationship. Notice that we started with the original portion of the E-R diagram and created a new relation between *Concrete Type* and *Raw Material* called *Bill of Material*, which is an intersection relation. An *intersection relation* (sometimes called a *composite relation*) is a relation you create to eliminate a many-to-many relationship. It's called an intersection relation because it represents an intersection of the primary keys between the first two relations. That is, an intersection relation will have a *composite primary key* that consists of the primary key fields from the two intersecting relations. The primary key fields from the two original relations now become foreign keys in the intersection relation. A *foreign key* is a primary key of one file (relation) that appears in another file (relation). When combined, these two foreign keys make up the composite primary key for the intersection relation.

Figure C.5

The Completed E-R
Diagram for the Supply
Chain Management Side
of Solomon's Database

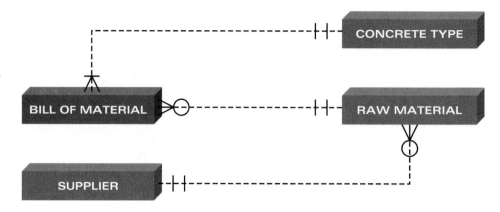

For Solomon's supply chain management portion of its database, the intersection relation *Bill of Material* represents the combination of raw materials that go into each concrete type. Listed below is how you would read the relationships between *Concrete Type*
and *Bill of Material* and *Raw Material* and *Bill of Material* (see Figure C.5).

- *Concrete Type–Bill of Material*

  From left to right: A *Concrete Type* can have multiple listings of *Raw Material* in
  Bill of Material and must have a listing of *Raw Material* in *Bill of Material*.

  From right to left: A *Concrete Type* found in *Bill of Material* must be found and
  can be found only one time in *Concrete Type*.

- *Raw Material–Bill of Material*

  From left to right: A *Raw Material* can be found in many *Bill of Material* listings
  but may not be found in any *Bill of Material* listing.

  From right to left: A *Raw Material* found in *Bill of Material* must be found and
  can be found only one time in *Raw Material*.

If you compare the E-R diagram in Figure C.5 to the E-R diagram in Figure C.2,
you'll notice that they are very similar. The only difference is that the E-R diagram in Figure C.5 contains an intersection relation to eliminate the many-to-many relationship between *Concrete Type* and *Raw Material*.

Removing many-to-many relationships is the most difficult aspect when designing the
appropriate structure of a relational database. If you do find a many-to-many relationship, here are some guidelines for creating an intersection relation:

1. Just as we did in Figure C.4, start by drawing the part of the E-R diagram that
   contains a many-to-many relationship at the top of a piece of paper.
2. Underneath each relation for which the many-to-many relationship exists, write
   down some of the primary keys.
3. Create a new E-R diagram (showing no cardinality) with the original two
   relations on each end and a new one (the intersection relation) in the middle.
4. Underneath the intersection relation, write down some of the composite primary
   keys (these will be composed of the primary keys from the other two relations).
5. Create a meaningful name (e.g., *Bill of Material*) for the intersection relation.
6. Move the minimum cardinality appearing next to the left relation just to the right
   of the intersection relation.
7. Move the minimum cardinality appearing next to the right relation just to the left
   of the intersection relation.

TEAM WORK

CREATING AN INTERSECTION RELATION

Back to work on the project for your school. If you completed the Team Work project on page 168, you are now able to identify a many-to-many relationship between *Student* and *Seminar Section*. That is, a given *Seminar Section* may have many *Students,* and a given *Student* can enroll in many different *Seminar Sections* (two, to be exact). So, that portion of your E-R diagram looks like what follows.

Your task is to eliminate the above many-to-many relationship by creating an intersection relation. As you do, we would encourage you to follow the guidelines given on this page and the previous. What did you name the intersection relation? What does the completed E-R diagram look like?

8. The maximum cardinality on both sides of the intersection relations will always be "many" (the crow's foot).

9. As a general rule, the new minimum and maximum cardinalities for the two original relations will be one and one.

We would stress again that removing many-to-many relationships is the most difficult aspect when designing the appropriate structure of a relational database.

The business world is full of many-to-many relationships that must be eliminated before an organization can correctly implement a relational database. Let's talk through another example of a many-to-many relationship to help you better understand how to eliminate them. Consider that Solomon sometimes has to use more than one truck to make a delivery of concrete to a customer. That is, what if—given that a truck can carry at most 8 cubic yards of concrete—Triple A Homes asks for 12 cubic yards of premier marble for a given delivery. In that case, Solomon would have two choices for modeling and storing multiple trucks for the order. First, it could create two separate orders, one for 8 cubic yards of premier marble concrete and the other for 4 cubic yards of premier marble concrete. That option doesn't make business sense—when a customer places an order, then the entire order should be contained in only *one* order, not two.

The second choice—which is the correct one—is to have the ability to specify multiple trucks on a single order. In that case, Solomon would have a many-to-many relationship between *Order* and *Truck.* That is, the revised business rule would be that an *Order* can have multiple *Trucks* assigned to make the delivery and a *Truck* can be assigned to make a delivery on multiple *Orders.*

But it doesn't stop there. Solomon may wish to sometimes send two employees in one truck to deliver one order of concrete. Then, Solomon would need the ability to specify more than one employee per delivery truck.

As you can see, the business world is complex and full of many-to-many relationships. If you can master the art and science of eliminating many-to-many relationships in a database environment, you have created a substantial career opportunity for yourself.

STEP 3: DEFINING INFORMATION (FIELDS) FOR EACH RELATION

Once you've completed steps 1 and 2, you must define the various pieces of information that each relation will contain. Your goal in this step is to make sure that the information in each relation is indeed in the correct relation and that the information cannot be derived from other information—the second and third rules of normalization.

In Figure C.6 on the opposite page, we've developed a view of the relational database for Solomon based on the new E-R diagram with the intersection relation. To make sure that each piece of information is in the correct relation, look at each and ask, "Does this piece of information depend only on the primary key for this relation?" If the answer is yes, the information is in the correct relation. If the answer is no, the information is in the wrong relation.

Let's consider the *Raw Material* relation. The primary key is *Raw Material ID,* so each piece of information must depend only on *Raw Material ID.* Does *Raw Material Name* depend on *Raw Material ID?* Yes, because the name of a raw material depends on that particular raw material (as does *QOH* or quantity on hand). Does *Supplier ID* depend only on *Raw Material ID?* Yes, because the particular supplier providing a raw material depends on which raw material you're describing. In fact, *Supplier ID* in the *Raw Material* relation is a foreign key. That is, it is a primary key of one relation (*Supplier*) that appears in another relation (*Raw Material*).

What about *Supplier Name* in the *Raw Material* relation? Does it depend only on *Raw Material ID?* The answer here is no. *Supplier Name* depends only on *Supplier ID.* So, now the question becomes, "In which relation should *Supplier Name* appear?" The answer is in the *Supplier* relation, because *Supplier Name* depends on the primary key (*Supplier ID*) for that relation. Therefore, *Supplier Name* should appear in the *Supplier* relation (as it does) and not in the *Raw Material* relation.

Now, take a look at the intersection relation *Bill of Material.* Notice that it includes the field called *Unit. Unit* is located in this relation because it depends on two things: the concrete type you're describing and the raw material in it. So, *Unit* does depend completely on the composite primary key of *Concrete Type + Raw Material ID* in the *Bill of Material* relation.

If you follow this line of questioning for each relation, you'll find that all other fields are in their correct relations. Now you have to look at each field to see whether you can derive it from other information. If you can, the derived information should not be stored in your database. When we speak of "derived" in this instance, we're referring to information that you can mathematically derive: counts, totals, averages, and the like. Currently, you are storing the raw material total (*Raw Material Total*) in the *Concrete Type* relation. Can you derive that information from other information? The answer is yes—all you have to do is sum the *Units* in the *Bill of Material* relation for a given *Concrete Type.* So, you should not store *Raw Material Total* in your database (anywhere).

CONCRETE TYPE RELATION

Concrete Type	Type Description	Raw Material Total
1	Home foundation and walkways	4.5
2	Commercial foundation and infrastructure	4
3	Premier speckled (with smooth gravel aggregate)	7.5
4	Premier marble (with crushed marble aggregate)	6.5
5	Premier shell (with shell aggregate)	7

RAW MATERIAL RELATION

Raw Material ID	Raw Material Name	QOH	Supplier ID	Supplier Name
A	Water	9999	999	N/A
B	Cement paste	400	412	Wesley Enterprises
C	Sand	1200	499	A&J Brothers
D	Gravel	200	499	A&J Brothers
E	Marble	100	444	Juniper Sand & Gravel
F	Shell	25	444	Juniper Sand & Gravel

SUPPLIER RELATION

Supplier ID	Supplier Name
412	Wesley Enterprises
499	A&J Brothers
444	Juniper Sand & Gravel
999	N/A

BILL OF MATERIAL RELATION

Concrete Type	Raw Material ID	Unit
1	B	1
1	C	2
1	A	1.5
2	B	1
2	C	2
2	A	1
3	B	1
3	C	2
3	A	1.5
3	D	3
4	B	1
4	C	2
4	A	1.5
4	E	2
5	B	1
5	C	2
5	A	1.5
5	F	2.5

Unit belongs in this relation because it depends on a combination of how much of a given raw material *(Raw Material ID)* goes into each type of concrete type *(Concrete Type).*

Figure C.6

A First Look at the Relations for the Supply Chain Management Side of Solomon's Database

CONCRETE TYPE RELATION

Concrete Type	Type Description
1	Home foundation and walkways
2	Commercial foundation and infrastructure
3	Premier speckled (with smooth gravel aggregate)
4	Premier marble (with crushed marble aggregate)
5	Premier shell (with shell aggregate)

RAW MATERIAL RELATION

Raw Material ID	Raw Material Name	QOH	Supplier ID
A	Water	9999	999
B	Cement paste	400	412
C	Sand	1200	444
D	Gravel	200	444
E	Marble	100	499
F	Shell	25	499

SUPPLIER RELATION

Supplier ID	Supplier Name
412	Wesley Enterprises
499	A&J Brothers
444	Juniper Sand & Gravel
999	N/A

BILL OF MATERIAL RELATION

Concrete Type	Raw Material ID	Unit
1	B	1
1	C	2
1	A	1.5
2	B	1
2	C	2
2	A	1
3	B	1
3	C	2
3	A	1.5
3	D	3
4	B	1
4	C	2
4	A	1.5
4	E	2
5	B	1
5	C	2
5	A	1.5
5	F	2.5

Figure C.7

The Correct Structure of the Supply Chain Management Side of Solomon's Database

Once you've completed step 3, you've completely and correctly defined the structure of your database and identified the information each relation should contain. Figure C.7 shows your database and the information in each relation. Notice that we have removed *Supplier Name* from the *Raw Material* relation and that we have removed *Raw Material Total* from the *Concrete Type* relation.

CREATING THE FINAL STRUCTURE FOR YOUR SCHOOL

Now it's time for you to fly solo and try a task by yourself. If your group successfully completed the Team Work project on page 171, you should have a relational database model with five relations: *Seminar, Seminar Section, Student, Qualified Teacher,* and *Seminar Section Class Roll.* The first four you identified early on. The last one is the result of eliminating the many-to-many relationship between *Seminar Section* and *Student.* We named this intersection relation *Seminar Section Class Roll.* We did so because it represents a list of students enrolling in all of the sections. If you group those students by section, then you get class rolls.

Your task is to complete a table for each relation. We've provided a sample table below. That is, you must first fill in the column headings by identifying what information belongs in each relation. Be sure to follow steps 2 and 3 of normalization. Then, we encourage you to add in some actual data entries.

A word of caution. You could easily identify hundreds of pieces of information that need to be present in this database. For *Qualified Teacher,* for example, you could include birth date, rank, office hours, phone number, e-mail address, office location, employment starting date, and many more. Here, simply identify no more than five key pieces of information for each relation. And, by all means, identify the primary and foreign keys for each relation.

Seminar Relation

STEP 4: USING A DATA DEFINITION LANGUAGE TO CREATE YOUR DATABASE

The final step in developing a relational database is to take the structure you created in steps 1 through 3 and use a data definition language to actually create the relations. Data definition languages are found within a database management system. A ***database management system (DBMS)*** helps you specify the logical organization for a database and access and use the information within the database. To use a data definition language, you need the data dictionary for your complete database. Recall from Chapter 3 that the ***data dictionary*** contains the logical structure for the information in a database. Throughout this module and in the first part of Chapter 3, we provided you with the overall structure of Solomon's complete database including the relations of *Order, Truck, Customer, Employee, Concrete Type, Raw Material, Supplier,* and *Bill of Material.*

This is the point at which we'll end this extended learning module. But you shouldn't stop learning. We've written *Extended Learning Module J* to take you through the process of using a data definition language in Access to create the database for Solomon Enterprises.

Summary: Student Learning Outcomes Revisited

1. **Identify how databases and spreadsheets are both similar and different.** Databases and spreadsheets are similar in that they both store information in two-dimensional files. They are different in one key aspect: physical versus logical. Spreadsheets require that you know the physical location of information, by row number and column character. Databases, on the other hand, require that you know logically what information you want. For example, in a database environment you could easily request total sales for Able Electronics, and you would receive that information. In a spreadsheet, you would have to know the physical location—by row number and column character—of that information.

2. **List and describe the four steps in designing and building a relational database.** The four steps in designing and building a relational database include
   1. Defining entity classes and primary keys
   2. Defining relationships among entity classes
   3. Defining information (fields) for each relation
   4. Using a data definition language to create your database

3. **Define the concepts of entity class, instance, primary key, and foreign key.** An *entity class* is a concept—typically people, places, or things—about which you wish to store information and that you can identify with a unique key (called a primary key). A *primary key* is a field (or group of fields in some cases) that uniquely describes each record. Within the context of database design, we often refer to a record as an instance. An *instance* is an occurrence of an entity class that can be uniquely described. To provide logical relationships among various entity classes, you use *foreign keys*—primary keys of one file (relation) that also appear in another file (relation).

4. **Given a small operating environment, build an entity-relationship (E-R) diagram.** Building an entity-relationship (E-R) diagram starts with knowing and understanding the business rules that govern the situation. These rules will help you identify entity classes, primary keys, and relationships. You then follow the process of normalization, eliminating many-to-many relationships, assuring that each field is in the correct relation, and removing any derived fields.

5. **List and describe the steps in normalization.** *Normalization* is the process of assuring that a relational database structure can be implemented as a series of two-dimensional tables. The normalization steps include
   1. Eliminate repeating groups or many-to-many relationships
   2. Assure that each field in a relation depends only on the primary key for that relation
   3. Remove all derived fields from the relations

6. **Describe the process of creating an intersection relation to remove a many-to-many relationship.** To create an intersection relation to remove a many-to-many relationship, follow these steps:
   1. Draw the part of the E-R diagram that contains a many-to-many relationship
   2. Create a new E-R diagram with the original two relations on each end and a new one (the intersection relation) in the middle
   3. Create a meaningful name for the intersection relation
   4. Move the minimum cardinality appearing next to the left relation just to the right of the intersection relation
   5. Move the minimum cardinality appearing next to the right relation just to the left of the intersection relation
   6. The maximum cardinality on both sides of the intersection relation will always be "many"
   7. As a general rule, the new minimum and maximum cardinalities for the two original relations will be one and one

Key Terms and Concepts

Composite primary key, 169
Database, 161
Database management system (DBMS), 175
Data dictionary, 175
Entity class, 163
Entity-relationship (E-R) diagram, 164

Foreign key, 169
Instance, 163
Intersection relation (composite relation), 169
Normalization, 169
Primary key, 163
Relational database, 161

Short-Answer Questions

1. How are relational databases and spreadsheets both similar and different?
2. What is a database?
3. What are the four steps in designing and building a relational database?
4. What are some examples of entity classes at your school?
5. What is the role of a primary key?
6. What is an entity-relationship (E-R) diagram?
7. How do business rules help you define minimum and maximum cardinality?
8. What is normalization?
9. What are the three major rules of normalization?
10. What is an intersection relation? Why is it important in designing a relational database?
11. Why must you remove derived information from a database?
12. What is a database management system (DBMS)?

Assignments and Exercises

1. **DEFINING ENTITY CLASSES FOR THE MUSIC INDUSTRY** The music industry tracks and uses all sorts of information related to numerous entity classes. Find a music CD and carefully review the entire contents of the jacket. List as many entity classes as you can find (for just that CD). Now, go to a music store and pick out a CD for a completely different music genre and read its jacket. Did you find any new entity classes? If so, what are they?

2. **DEFINING BUSINESS RULES FOR A VIDEO RENTAL STORE** Think about how your local video rental store works. There are many customers, renting many videos, and many videos sit on the shelves unrented. Customers can rent many videos at one time. And some videos are so popular that the video rental store keeps many copies. Write down all the various business rules that define how a video rental store works with respect to entity classes and their relationships.

3. **CREATING AN E-R DIAGRAM FOR A VIDEO RENTAL STORE** After completing assignment 2 above, draw the initial E-R diagram based on the rules you defined. Don't worry about going through the process of normalization at this point. Simply identify the appropriate relationships among the entity classes and define the minimum and maximum cardinality of each relationship. By the way, how many many-to-many relationships did you define?

4. **ELIMINATING A MANY-TO-MANY RELATIONSHIP** Consider the following situation. At a small auto parts store, customers can buy many parts. And the same part can be bought by many different customers. That's an example of a many-to-many relationship. How would you eliminate it? What would you call the intersection relation? This one is particularly tough: You'll have to actually create two intersection relations to model this correctly.

5. **DEFINING THE CARDINALITY AMONG TWO ENTITY CLASSES** Consider the two entity classes of *Student* and *Advisor* at your school. How would you build an E-R diagram to show the relationship between these two entity classes? What is the minimum and maximum cardinality of the relationship?

CHAPTER FOUR OUTLINE

STUDENT LEARNING OUTCOMES

1. Define decision support system, list its components, and identify the type of applications it's suited to.

2. Define geographic information systems and state how they differ from other decision support tools.

3. Define artificial intelligence and list the different types that are used in business.

4. Define expert systems and describe the types of problems to which they are applicable.

5. Define neural networks and fuzzy logic and the uses of these AI tools.

6. Define genetic algorithms and list the concepts on which they are based and the types of problems they solve.

7. Define intelligent agents, list the four types, and identify the types of problems they solve.

8. Define agent-based modeling and swarm intelligence.

INDUSTRY PERSPECTIVES

183 **Using a DSS to Keep the Cost of Gas Down**

191 **What Medical Procedure Would Suit You?**

195 **Neural Networks to Save Energy**

201 **Intelligent Agents Run Experiments aboard Spacecraft**

208 **Automated Truck-Painting Booths Schedule Themselves**

FEATURES

187 **Global Perspective**
Got Milk? They Do in British Columbia

193 **On Your Own**
Traffic Lights Revisited

194 **Team Work**
How Would You Classify People?

199 **Team Work**
Be a Genetic Algorithm and Put Nails in Boxes

203 **On Your Own**
Go Bargain Hunting Online

216 **Electronic Commerce**
Finding Investment Opportunities on the Internet

WEB SUPPORT

www.mhhe.com/haag

- Learning about investing
- Researching the company behind the stock
- Retrieving stock quotes
- Computer-aided decision support

CHAPTER FOUR

Decision Support and Artificial Intelligence
Brainpower for Your Business

OPENING CASE STUDY:
DECISION SUPPORT SYSTEM—THE
RESIDENT SECOND OPINION

Doctors in the near future will not dream of going into an examination room without automated decision support. So says Dr. C. Martin Harris, CIO at the Cleveland Clinic, who believes that IT will soon become as central to patient care as the stethoscope. Giving this trend a nudge in the right direction, the Cleveland Clinic and the Mayo Clinic have each begun work on data warehouses (see Chapter 3) that will help health care professionals make analyses crucial to providing better patient care.

At the Cleveland Clinic, the first part of this ambitious project is to improve the treatment and survival rate among patients with abdominal aortic aneurysms that are usually spotted only when they are about to erupt, at which time more than half of patients die. An aneurysm is a weak spot in a blood vessel that causes big problems when it ruptures. Predicting which patients are at risk for this medical condition will help doctors to provide treatment to the patient early enough to avert disaster.

The Cleveland Clinic system ties together all the databases in the hospital, including patient histories, genetic makeup records, and countless lab results, among others. This will allow doctors to quickly compare a sick patient with thousands of others to find variables and correlations that would be highly impractical to find manually.

At the Mayo Clinic, using a similar system that has information on 4 million patients, doctors have already made some very useful discoveries. For instance, a new drug was being tested for lung cancer but was producing mixed results until a researcher discovered that a subset of the lung-cancer patients—those with a specific gene makeup—responded very well. This is the type of medical business intelligence that is vital in treating serious illnesses.

The type of computer-aided decision support systems that the Mayo Clinic and the Cleveland Clinic are using incorporate data-mining techniques and neural networks (an artificial intelligence system that identifies patterns and categorizes individual entities into categories), among other tools. With so much information available, treatment can be tailored to each individual's case, taking into account as much information about the patient as possible including the patient's demographic information.

The type of IT system we are discussing here is one type of computer-aided decision-making tool. Computer-aided decision support includes any IT system that allows you to analyze information to reach a decision or that provides the decision or answer for you. These tools for decision making are the focus of this chapter.[1]

Introduction

The objective of decision support systems is to help you analyze information to find business intelligence, which, as you learned in Chapters 2 and 3, is the extraction of the true meaning of information so that you can take creative and powerful steps to gain a competitive advantage. In the opening case study, you saw how decision support systems are starting to be used in the medical profession. Clinics and doctors use the "business intelligence" in their databases to make faster and better diagnoses.

In this chapter we'll investigate the tools that IT can provide to help you to transform business information into business intelligence and make good decisions. According to *Management Review,* the big winners in tomorrow's business race will be those organizations that are "big of brain and small of mass."[2]

For many years, computers have been crunching numbers faster and more accurately than people can. A computer can unerringly calculate a payroll for 1,000 people in the time it takes a pencil to fall from your desk to the floor. Because of IT, knowledge workers have been freed from much of the drudgery of manually handling day-to-day transactions. And now, IT power is augmenting brainpower and thought processes in ways previously seen only in science fiction. In some cases, IT power is actually *replacing* human brainpower to a limited degree.

Businesses, like individuals, use brainpower to make decisions, some big, some small, some relatively simple, and some very complex. As an effective knowledge worker, you'll have to make decisions on issues such as whether to expand the workforce, extend business hours, use different raw materials, or start a new product line. IT can help you in most, if not all, of these decisions. The extended brainpower that IT offers you as a decision maker comes in the form of decision support systems and artificial intelligence.

Whether to use a decision support system or some form of artificial intelligence depends on the type of decision you have to make and how you plan to go about making it. So let's first look at different types of decisions and the process you go through to make a decision. Then we'll discuss decision support systems and artificial intelligence—IT brainpower (see Figure 4.1). To learn even more about decision support systems and artificial intelligence, visit the Web site that supports this text at www.mhhe.com/haag.

Figure 4.1

The Two Categories of Computer-Aided Decision Support

Decision Support

- Decision support systems
- Geographic information systems

Artificial Intelligence

- Expert systems
- Neural networks
- Genetic algorithms
- Intelligent agents

Decisions, Decisions, Decisions

You make many decisions every day from simple to complex. Contrast a decision about which mozzarella cheese to buy based on cost with a decision about which job offer to take. Choosing the right job is definitely a more complex decision because it has multiple decision criteria, not all of which are quantifiable (unlike the price of cheese). Therefore, it's much more difficult to select among job offers.

Decision making is crucial to business. Organizations devote vast resources of time and money to decision-making processes. In this section, we'll consider the phases of decision making and different decision types to help you better understand how IT can benefit the decision-making process.

HOW YOU MAKE A DECISION

In business, decision making has four distinct phases (see Figure 4.2).[3] These four phases are:

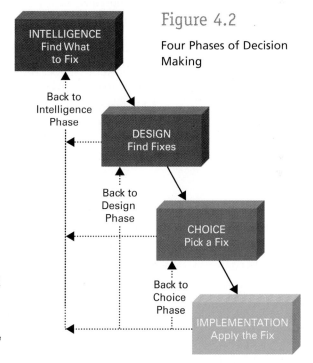

Figure 4.2

Four Phases of Decision Making

1. **Intelligence** (find what to fix): Find or recognize a problem, need, or opportunity (also called the diagnostic phase of decision making). The intelligence phase involves detecting and interpreting signs that indicate a situation which needs your attention. These "signs" come in many forms: consistent customer requests for new-product features, the threat of new competition, declining sales, rising costs, an offer from a company to handle your distribution needs, and so on.

2. **Design** (find fixes): Consider possible ways of solving the problem, filling the need, or taking advantage of the opportunity. In this phase, you develop all the possible solutions you can.

3. **Choice** (pick a fix): Examine and weigh the merits of each solution, estimate the consequences of each, and choose the best one (which may be to do nothing at all). The "best" solution may depend on such factors as cost, ease of implementation, staffing requirements, and timing. This is the prescriptive phase of decision making—it's the stage at which a course of action is prescribed.

4. **Implementation** (apply the fix): Carry out the chosen solution, monitor the results, and make adjustments as necessary. Simply implementing a solution is seldom enough. Your chosen solution will always need fine-tuning, especially for complex problems or changing environments.

This four-phase process is not necessarily linear: You'll often find it useful or necessary to cycle back to an earlier phase. When choosing an alternative in the choice phase, for example, you might become aware of another possible solution. Then you would go back to the design phase, include the newly found solution, return to the choice phase, and compare the new solution to the others you generated.

TYPES OF DECISIONS YOU FACE

It's pretty clear that deciding which cheese to buy when you want the cheapest is a decision with a simple comparison that leads to a correct answer. Thus, it is an example of a *structured decision*, whereas choosing the right job is an example of a decision with nonstructured and structured elements. That is, some parts are quantifiable and some are not.

A *structured decision* involves processing a certain kind of information in a specified way so that you will always get the right answer. No "feel" or intuition is necessary. These are the kinds of decisions that you can program—if you use a certain set of inputs and process them in a precise way, you'll arrive at the correct result. Calculating gross pay for hourly workers is an example. You can easily automate these types of structured decisions with IT.

A *nonstructured decision* is one for which there may be several "right" answers, and there is no precise way to get a right answer. No rules or criteria exist that guarantee you a good solution. Deciding whether to introduce a new product line, employ a new marketing campaign, or change the corporate image are all examples of decisions with nonstructured elements.

In reality, most decisions fall somewhere between structured and nonstructured. The job choice decision is an example (see Figure 4.3). In choosing the right job, the salary part of the decision is structured, whereas the other criteria involve nonstructured aspects (for example, your perception of which job has the best advancement opportunity). Stock market investment analysis is another example of "somewhere in between" because you can calculate financial ratios and use past performance indicators. However, you still have to consider nonstructured aspects of the companies, such as projected prime interest rate, unemployment rates, and competition.

Another way to view decisions is by the frequency with which the decision has to be made. The decision as to which job to take is the sort of decision you don't make on a regular basis; this is a nonrecurring, or ad hoc, decision. On the other hand, determining pay for hourly employees is a routine decision that businesses face periodically. Therefore, determining gross pay for hourly employees is a recurring decision.

A *recurring decision* is one that happens repeatedly, and often periodically, whether weekly, monthly, quarterly, or yearly. You'll usually use the same set of rules each time. When you calculate pay for hourly employees, the calculation is always the same regardless of the employee or time period. A *nonrecurring, or ad hoc, decision* is one that you make infrequently (perhaps only once), and you may even have different criteria for determining the best solution each time. A company merger is an example. These don't happen often, although they are becoming more frequent. And if the managers of a company need to make the merger decision more than once, they will most likely have to evaluate a different set of criteria each time. The criteria depend on the needs of the companies considering the merger, the comparability of their products and services, their debt structure, and so on.

Figure 4.3

Viewing Structured versus Nonstructured Decision Making as a Continuum

USING A DSS TO KEEP THE COST OF GAS DOWN

Think you spend a lot on gas for your car every year? J. B. Hunt Transportation Inc. spends a lot more. J. B. Hunt moves freight around the country on its 10,000 trucks and 48,000 trailers. The company spent $250 million in 2004 on fuel. That figure was up by 40 percent over the previous year. Diesel fuel is the company's second-largest expense (drivers' wages is the largest), and the freight hauler wanted to find a way to reduce that. Part of the answer lay, as it often does, in IT.

In 2000, J. B. Hunt installed a decision support system that provides drivers with help in deciding which gas station to stop at for refueling. Using satellite communications, the system beams diesel-fuel prices from all over the country straight into the cabs of the trucks. The software accesses a database with local taxes for each area of the country and then calculates for the drivers how much refueling will actually cost.

J. B. Hunt doesn't require drivers to use this system, but provides incentives for those who do. The company estimates that the system saves about $1 million annually.[4]

Decision Support Systems

In Chapter 3, you saw how data mining can help you make business decisions by giving you the ability to slice and dice your way through massive amounts of information. Actually, a data warehouse with data-mining tools is a form of decision support. The term *decision support system,* used broadly, means any computerized system that helps you make decisions. There's also a more restrictive definition, however. It's rather like the term *medicine.* Medicine can mean the whole health care industry or it can mean cough syrup, depending on the context.

Narrowly defined, a *decision support system (DSS)* is a highly flexible and interactive IT system that is designed to support decision making when the problem is not structured. A DSS is an alliance between you, the decision maker, and specialized support provided by IT (see Figure 4.4). IT brings speed, vast amounts of information, and

What You Bring	Advantages of a DSS	What IT Brings
Experience	Increased productivity	Speed
Intuition	Increased understanding	Information
Judgment	Increased speed	Processing capabilities
Knowledge	Increased flexibility	
	Reduced problem complexity	
	Reduced cost	

Figure 4.4

The Alliance between You and a Decision Support System

sophisticated processing capabilities to help you create information useful in making a decision. You bring know-how in the form of your experience, intuition, judgment, and knowledge of the relevant factors. IT provides great power, but you—as the decision maker—must know what kinds of questions to ask of the information and how to process the information to get those questions answered. In fact, the primary objective of a DSS is to improve your effectiveness as a decision maker by providing you with assistance that will complement your insights. This union of your know-how and IT power helps you generate business intelligence so that you can quickly respond to changes in the marketplace and manage resources in the most effective and efficient ways possible. Following are some examples of the varied applications of DSSs:

- A national insurance company uses a DSS to analyze its risk exposure when insuring drivers with histories of driving under the influence. The DSS revealed that married male homeowners in their forties with one DUI conviction were rarely repeat offenders. By lowering its rates to this group the company increased it market share without increasing its risk exposure.[5]

- Burlington Northern and Santa Fe (BNSF) railroad regularly tests the rails its trains ride on to prevent accidents. Worn out or defective rails result in hundreds of derailments every year, so it's important to address the problem. Using a decision support system to schedule rail testing, BNSF decreased its rail-caused derailments by 33 percent in 2000, while the other three large railroad companies had a 16 percent rise in such accidents.[6]

- Customer relationship management (CRM), as you saw in Chapter 2, is an important part of any successful company's strategy. Decision support is an important part of CRM. On Wall Street, retail brokerage companies analyze customers' behaviors and goals with decision support, which highlights opportunities and alerts brokers to beginning problems.[7]

COMPONENTS OF A DECISION SUPPORT SYSTEM

DSSs vary greatly in application and complexity, but they all share specific features. A typical DSS has three components (see below and Figure 4.5): model management, data management, and user interface management.

Before we look at these three components individually, let's get a quick overview of how they work together. When you begin your analysis, you tell the DSS, using the user interface management component, which model (in the model management component) to use on what information (in the data management component). The model requests the information from the data management component, analyzes that information, and sends the result to the user interface management component, which in turn passes the results back to you (see Figure 4.5). Here's an example of a decision support system at Lands' End clothing business.

- *Model management:* The DSS at Lands' End has to have models to analyze information. The models create new information that decision makers need to plan product lines and inventory levels. For example, Lands' End uses a statistical model called regression analysis to determine trends in customer buying patterns and forecasting models to predict sales levels.

- *Data management:* The DSS's data management component stores Lands' End's customer and product information. In addition to this organizational information, the company also needs external information, such as demographic information and industry and style trend information.

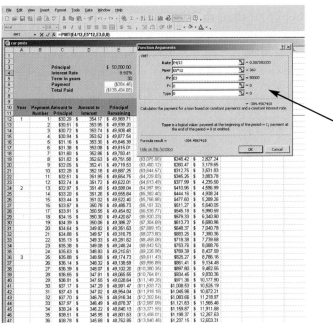

The PMT function calculates the monthly payment on the mortgage. The Rate (interest rate) is usually quoted as an annual rate so you have to divide by 12 to get the monthly rate. Similarly, the NPER (number of periods) is in years so you have to multiply by 12 for monthly payments.

Figure 4.5

Components of a
Decision Support System

- *User interface management:* A user interface enables Lands' End decision makers to access information and specify the models they want to use to create the information they need.

Now we'll examine the three DSS components in more general terms.

MODEL MANAGEMENT COMPONENT   The *model management* component consists of both the DSS models and the DSS model management system. A model is a representation of some event, fact, or situation. Businesses use models to represent variables and their relationships. For example, you would use a statistical model called analysis of variance to determine whether newspaper, television, and billboard advertising are equally effective in increasing sales. DSSs help in various decision-making situations by using models that allow you to analyze information in many different ways. The models you use in a DSS depend on the decision you're making and, consequently, the kind of analysis you require. For example, you would use what-if analysis to see what effect the change of one or more variables will have on other variables, or optimization to find the most profitable solution given operating restrictions and limited resources. You can use spreadsheet software such as Excel to create a simple DSS for what-if analysis. Look again at Figure 4.5 for an example of a spreadsheet DSS you might build to compare how much you'd pay for a house at different interest rates and payback periods.

The model management system stores and maintains the DSS's models. Its function of managing models is similar to that of a database management system. The model management component can't select the best model for you to use for a particular problem—that requires your expertise—but it can help you create and manipulate models quickly and easily.

DATA MANAGEMENT COMPONENT   The *data management* component performs the function of storing and maintaining the information that you want your DSS to use. The data management component, therefore, consists of both the DSS information and the DSS database management system. The information you use in your DSS comes from one or more of three sources:

1. *Organizational information:* You may want to use virtually any information available in the organization for your DSS. You can design your DSS to access this information directly from your company's databases and data warehouses.

2. *External information:* Some decisions require input from external sources of information. Various branches of the federal government, Dow Jones, and the Internet, to mention just a few, can provide additional information for use with a DSS.

3. *Personal information:* You can incorporate your own insights and experience—your personal information—into your DSS.

USER INTERFACE MANAGEMENT COMPONENT   The *user interface management* component allows you to communicate with the DSS. It consists of the user interface and the user interface management system. This is the component that allows you to combine your know-how with the storage and processing capabilities of the computer. The user interface is the part of the system you see; through it you enter information, commands, and models. If you have a DSS with a poorly designed user interface—if it's too rigid or too cumbersome to use—you simply won't use it no matter what its capabilities. The best user interface uses your terminology and methods and is flexible, consistent, simple, and adaptable.

GOT MILK? THEY DO IN BRITISH COLUMBIA

The British Columbia Milk Marketing Board has the responsibility of collecting raw milk from farmers and transporting it to the processing plants. The Marketing Board transfers payments from the processors to the farmers—to the tune of $17 million every two weeks. Milk is picked up from 350 farms per day by a fleet of 70 trucks, so that all 700 farms in the system see collection every other day. The milk goes to 26 processors across the vast province.

The paper-based system of record keeping was collapsing under its own weight. Upon pumping a farmer's milk into his truck, a driver recorded the number of liters collected on a four-part paper form and gave the farmer one copy. To fill a two-trailer truck, a driver collected milk from five farms and kept track, on paper, of how much milk came from each one. When the trailers were full of milk, the driver headed for the processing plant where a receipt for the quantity of milk was filled out. The truck then proceeded to the next farm and repeated the process.

Each day's work generated 350 producer slips from the farms and about 70 truck slips used to keep track of payments to the truck companies. To enter and process all this information, even using a computer, took many hours each day, especially with the problems of slips that truck drivers lost or forgot to turn over and mistakes made entering data onto forms that had to be investigated. The cost of the paper system was about $100,000 per year. The basic accounting of incoming milk and outgoing payments took so much time that there wasn't much left for the in-depth analysis necessary for the type of decision making that would have led to more effective use of resources.

The new decision support system handles data entry in real time. Each driver uses a handheld wireless scanning unit to send information to the central system. Each farm and processing plant has a unique bar code that the driver just has to scan. All that's left is to enter the volume of milk and add any comments like the temperature of the milk and so on. A wireless printer in the truck's cab can produce a printed copy of the transaction for the farmer or processing plant. The data is then sent over the cellular data network to the Marketing Board's Internet access point, and from there to the main computer for processing.

Quite apart from collecting data faster and more accurately, enabling more efficient decision making, the IT system allows the British Columbia Milk Marketing Board to quickly identify any farm that was the source of a substandard shipment so that corrective action can be taken immediately. And it's not just management that benefits from the decision support aspect of the new system. IT also supplies drivers with useful information, such as how much space is left in each trailer and how a load should be divided between trailers. The new decision support system not only brings costs down; it increases profits too.[8]

Geographic Information Systems

In 1992, Hurricane Andrew attacked the east coast of the United States leaving devastation throughout several states in its wake. One of the places hardest hit was Miami, Florida, where the hurricane came on land smashing businesses and private buildings and causing billions of dollars in damage. Reporters at the *Miami Herald* believed that not all the damage was due to Andrew. They hypothesized that at least some of the harm was a result of shoddy construction of homes built after 1980.

Four months after Hurricane Andrew, the paper ran a series of reports and used geographic information system maps to make its point. A *geographic information system (GIS)* is a decision support system designed specifically to analyze spatial information. Spatial information is any information that can be shown in map form, such as roads, the distribution of the bald eagle population, sewer systems, or the path of a hurricane.

Figure 4.6

San Diego Shown in ArcExplorer 2, GIS Software from ESRI[9]

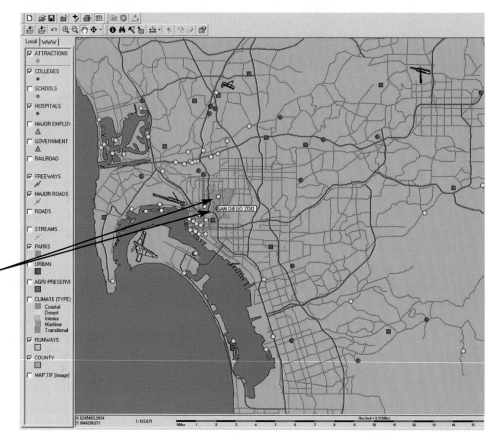

The ArcExplorer software allows you to choose which features you want to view. The Active Theme, which in this case is ATTRACTIONS, allows you to see the name of attraction by placing the cursor on the symbol.

The *Miami Herald* plotted the arrival point of the hurricane where winds were strongest and charted the progress of Andrew inland, where it lost some of its initial punch. Then the reporters plotted the damaged houses with one dot representing 10 homes. These dots were color-coded to show level of damage—blue showed 10 repairable homes and orange dots represented 10 destroyed homes. When the two maps were laid over each other, it was clear that the wind strength did not match up with damage as it should have. That is, the reporters showed that Hurricane Andrew alone was not responsible for all the devastation. The net result was that building codes in Dade County were tightened so that contractors had to use more nails and install stronger windows, doors, and shutters on homes. The *Miami Herald* received the Pulitzer Prize for its investigative work.

Businesses use GIS software too to analyze information, generate business intelligence, and make decisions. GIS is a powerful combination of database and graphics technology. There is virtually no limit to the sort of information you can plot with a GIS, including the placement of roads, the course of rivers, income levels, health conditions, areas of high or low crime, and so on. Of course, you can do this with paper maps too. The strength of an electronic GIS is in the ability you get to layer information with a mouse click.

Figure 4.6 is a map of San Diego shown in ESRI's ArcExplorer 2 GIS software. On the left-hand side you can see the layers (or type of information) that can be shown on the map. In our figure we have shown the *Attractions, Colleges, Hospitals, Freeways, Major Roads, Parks,* and *Runways.* Each type of information has its own symbol and is called a *theme.* When a theme is active, as *Attractions* is in our example, and you move the cursor over the little yellow circle, you can see the name of the attraction—in our case, the San Diego Zoo.

This is an example of the feature of GIS software that represents information thematically (i.e., in map or theme form). With themes, you can show the layers in combination as we did in our example and as the *Miami Herald* reporters did for Hurricane Andrew. You can represent either statistical information, such as the average salary of homeowners, or point information, such as the location of a bank's customers.

When businesses use GIS software to generate maps showing information of interest to them, we call it *business geography*. You can find a wealth of information to incorporate into your GIS from various sources. For example, the U.S. Census Bureau has a vast database of demographic information and the Bureau of Labor Statistics has employment information. Both of these would be statistical information. In the private sector, many research companies would be happy to sell you consumer habit information.

Studies show that how information is presented significantly impacts the effectiveness and efficiency of the decision-making process.[10] Here are other examples of GISs in use (see also this chapter's Closing Case Study One for more examples):

- Clean Harbor is the company that hauled away potentially anthrax-tainted debris from the offices of the NCB during the anthrax scare of 2001. Since hazardous waste removal is such a dangerous job, the company had to keep track of the shipment every minute. Clean Harbor used software that incorporated a GIS map and GPS information to monitor the trucks along their journey.[11]

- Branson, Missouri, is a small town in the Ozark Mountains that boasts more than two dozen theaters offering 75 performances per day to the 5 to 7 million visitors the town hosts every year. The town's motto is "the show must go on." But the show can't go on without electricity. The White River Valley Electric Cooperative (WRVEC) that supplies power to the area has a Web-based GIS where employees can access all the information they need, such as the precise location of poles, meters, transformers, capacitors, and underground facilities.[12]

Artificial Intelligence

DSSs and GISs are IT systems that augment business brainpower. IT can further expand business brainpower by means of artificial intelligence—the techniques and software that enable computers to mimic human behavior in various ways. Financial analysts use a variety of artificial intelligence systems to manage assets, invest in the stock market, and perform other financial operations.[13] Hospitals use artificial intelligence in many capacities, from scheduling staff, to assigning beds to patients, to diagnosing and treating illness. Many government agencies use artificial intelligence, including the IRS and the armed forces. Credit card companies use artificial intelligence to detect credit card fraud, and insurance companies use artificial intelligence to spot fraudulent claims.[14] Artificial intelligence lends itself to tasks as diverse as airline ticket pricing, food preparation, oil exploration, and child protection. It is widely used in the insurance, meteorology, engineering, and aerospace industries and by the military. It was artificial intelligence that guided cruise missiles during the Gulf War in 1991.[15]

Artificial intelligence (AI) is the science of making machines imitate human thinking and behavior. For example, an expert system is an artificial intelligence system that makes computers capable of reasoning through a problem to reach a conclusion. We use the process of reasoning to find out, from what we already know, something that we don't know.

Today computers can see, hear, smell, and, important for business, think (in a manner of speaking). Robots are a well-known form of AI. A *robot* is a mechanical device equipped with simulated human senses and the capability of taking action on its own (in contrast to a mechanical device such as an automobile, which requires direction from the driver for its every action). Robots are in use in many industries. For example, Piedmont Hospital's Pharmacy Dosage Dispenser is a robotic prescription-filling system. Using bar code technology, this pharmaceutical robot receives medication orders online, retrieves prepackaged doses of drugs, and sends them to hospital patients.[16] One of the most exciting new areas of research in robotics is the development of microrobots that can be introduced into human veins and arteries to perform surgery.

A recent U.S. Commerce Department survey reported that 70 percent of the top 500 companies use artificial intelligence as part of decision support, and the sale of artificial intelligence software is rapidly approaching the $1 billion mark. The AI systems that businesses use most can be classified into the following major categories:

- *Expert systems,* which reason through problems and offer advice in the form of a conclusion or recommendation.
- *Neural networks,* which can be "trained" to recognize patterns, and *fuzzy logic,* which is a way of representing ambiguous or subjective information in computerized analysis.
- *Genetic algorithms,* which can generate increasingly better solutions to problems by generating many, many solutions, choosing the best ones, and using those to generate even better solutions.
- *Intelligent agents,* which are adaptive systems that work independently, carrying out specific, repetitive, or predictable tasks.

Expert Systems

Suppose you own a real estate business and generate more than 40 percent of your revenue appraising commercial real estate. Suppose only one person in your firm is capable of performing these appraisals. What if that person quits? How do you replace her or his expertise? How fast can you find someone else? How much business will you lose if it takes you a month to find a suitable replacement?

In business, people are valuable because they perform important business tasks. Many business tasks require expertise, and people often carry this expertise in their heads—often that's the only place it can be found in the organization. AI can provide you with an expert system that can capture expertise, thus making it available to those who are not experts so that they can use it, either to solve a problem or to learn how to solve a problem.

An **expert system,** also called a **knowledge-based system,** is an artificial intelligence system that applies reasoning capabilities to reach a conclusion. Expert systems are excellent for diagnostic and prescriptive problems. Diagnostic problems are those requiring an answer to the question, "What's wrong?" and correspond to the intelligence phase of decision making. Prescriptive problems are those that require an answer to the question, "What to do?" and correspond to the choice phase of decision making.

An expert system is usually built for a specific application area called a *domain.* You can find expert systems in the following domains, among others:

- *Accounting*—for auditing, tax planning, management consulting, and training.
- *Medicine*—to prescribe antibiotics where many considerations must be taken into account (such as the patient's medical history, the source of the infection, and the price of available drugs).

- *Process control*—to control offset lithographic printing, for example.
- *Human resource management*—to help personnel managers determine whether they are in compliance with an array of federal employment laws.
- *Financial management*—to identify delinquency-prone accounts in the loan departments of banks.
- *Production*—to guide the manufacture of all sorts of products, such as aircraft parts.
- *Forestry management*—to help with harvesting timber on forest lands.

A DSS sometimes incorporates expert systems, but an expert system is fundamentally different from a DSS. To use a DSS, you must have considerable knowledge or expertise about the situation with which you're dealing. As you saw earlier in this chapter, a DSS *assists* you in making decisions. That means that you must know how to reason through the problem. You must know which questions to ask, how to get the answers, and how to proceed to the next step. When you use an expert system, however, the know-how is in the system—you need only provide the expert system with the facts and symptoms of the problem for which you need an answer. The know-how, or expertise, that actually solves the problem came from someone else—an expert in the field. What does it mean to have expertise? When someone has expertise in a given subject, that person not only knows a lot of facts about the topic but also can apply that knowledge to analyze and make judgments about related topics. It's this human expertise that an expert system captures.

Rule	Symptom or Fact	Yes	No	Explanation
1	Is the light green?	Go through the intersection.	Go to Rule 2.	Should be safe if light is green. If not, need more information.
2	Is the light red?	Go to Rule 4.	Go to Rule 3.	Should stop, may not be able to.
3	Is the light likely to change to red before you get through the intersection?	Go to Rule 4.	Go through the intersection.	Will only reach this point if light is yellow, then you'll have two choices.
4	Can you stop before entering the intersection?	Stop.	Go to Rule 5.	Should stop, but there may be a problem if you can't.
5	Is traffic approaching from either side?	Prepare to crash.	Go through the intersection.	Unless the intersection is clear of traffic, you're likely to crash.

Figure 4.7

Traffic Light Expert System Rules

> Is the light green (Yes/No)?   No.
>
> Is the light red (Yes/No)?   No.
>
> Is the light likely to change to red before you get through the intersection (Yes/No)?   Why?
>
> Will only reach this point if light is yellow, and then you'll have two choices.
>
> Is the light likely to change to red before you get through the intersection (Yes/No)?   No.
>
> **Conclusion: Go through the intersection.**

Let's look at a very simple expert system that would tell a driver what to do when approaching a traffic light. Dealing with traffic lights is an example of the type of problem to which an expert system is well-suited. It is a recurring problem, and to solve it you follow a well-defined set of steps. You've probably gone through the following mental question-and-answer session hundreds of times without even realizing it (see Figure 4.7).

When you approach a green traffic light, you proceed on through. If the light is red, you need to stop. If you're unable to stop, and if traffic is approaching from either side, you'll surely be in trouble. Similarly, if the light is yellow, you may be able to make it through the intersection before the light turns red. If not, you will again be faced with the problem of approaching traffic.

WHAT EXPERT SYSTEMS CAN AND CAN'T DO

An expert system uses IT to capture and apply human expertise. For problems with clear rules and procedures, expert systems work very well and can provide your company with great advantages. An expert system can

- Handle massive amounts of information
- Reduce errors
- Aggregate information from various sources
- Improve customer service

Create a table similar to Figure 4.7 to extend the traffic light expert system. Include the following situations in the table:

1. There is a wreck in the middle of the intersection.
2. You are turning left at the intersection.
3. You are turning right at the intersection.
4. A pedestrian is crossing in front of you.
5. A dog has wandered into the intersection.
6. A ball belonging to children playing near the intersection has rolled into the street.
7. The car in front of you has stalled.

- Provide consistency in decision making
- Provide new information
- Decrease personnel time spent on tasks
- Reduce cost

You can run into trouble, however, in building and using an expert system. Difficulties can include the following:

1. Transferring domain expertise to the expert system is sometimes difficult because domain experts cannot always explain how they know what they know. Often experts are not aware of their complete reasoning processes. Experience has given them a feel for the problem, and they just "know."

2. Even if the domain expert can explain the whole reasoning process, automating that process may be impossible. The process may be too complex, requiring an excessive number of rules, or it may be too vague or imprecise. In using an expert system, keep in mind that it can solve only the problems for which it was designed. It cannot deal with inconsistency or a newly encountered problem situation. An expert system can't learn from previous experience and can't apply previously acquired expertise to new problems the way humans can.

3. An expert system has no common sense or judgment. One of the early expert systems built into an F-16 fighter plane allowed the pilot to retract the landing gear while the plane was still on the ground and to jettison bombs while the plane was flying upside down.

Neural Networks and Fuzzy Logic

Suppose you see a breed of dog you've never encountered before. Would you know it's a dog? For that matter, would you know it's an animal? Probably so. You know, because you've learned by example. You've seen lots of living things, have learned to classify them, and so can recognize a dog when you see one. A neural network simulates this human ability to classify things without taking prescribed steps leading to the solution. A *neural network* (often called an *artificial neural network* or *ANN*) is an artificial intelligence system that is capable of finding and differentiating patterns. Your brain has learned to consider many factors in combination to recognize and differentiate objects. This is also the case with a neural network. A neural network can learn by example and can adapt to new concepts and knowledge. Neural networks are widely used for visual

HOW WOULD YOU CLASSIFY PEOPLE?

Some people have suggested that neural networks could be applied to people to indicate how likely they are to develop disease or even become criminals. The idea is to input a child's personal characteristics, demographics, and genealogy into a neural network, and the neural network will classify that youngster as being at risk for a disease or for aberrant behavior.

Choose either susceptibility to disease or to criminal behavior, discuss it with your group, and make the following lists, explaining why you chose each one.

1. What personal characteristics would be useful?
2. What demographic factors would strongly influence a person's future?
3. What, if any, inherited characteristics can predict a child's future?

Would such classification on a large scale be legal? Would it be ethical? Would it be effective? Why or why not (to all three questions)?

---

pattern and speech recognition systems. If you've used a PDA that deciphered your handwriting, it was probably a neural network that analyzed the characters you wrote.[18]

Neural networks are useful in a variety of situations. For example, bomb detection systems in U.S. airports use neural networks that sense trace elements in the air that may indicate the presence of explosives. The Chicago Police Department uses neural networks to identify corruption within its ranks.[19] In medicine, neural networks check 50 million electrocardiograms per year, check for drug interactions, and detect anomalies in tissue samples that may signify the onset of cancer and other diseases. Neural networks can detect heart attacks and even differentiate between the subtly different symptoms of heart attacks in men and women.[20,21,22] In business, neural networks are very popular for securities trading, fraud detection, real estate appraisal, evaluating loan applications, and target marketing, to mention a few. Neural networks are used to control machinery, adjust temperature settings, and identify malfunctioning machinery.

Neural networks are most useful for identification, classification, and prediction when a vast amount of information is available. By examining hundreds, or even thousands of examples, a neural network detects important relationships and patterns in the information. For example, if you provide a neural network with the details of numerous credit card transactions and tell it which ones are fraudulent, eventually it will learn to identify suspicious transaction patterns.

Here are some examples of the uses of neural networks:

- Many banks and financial institutions use neural networks. Citibank uses neural networks to find opportunities in financial markets.[23] By carefully examining historical stock market data with neural network software, Citibank financial managers learn of interesting coincidences or small anomalies (called market inefficiencies). For example, it could be that whenever IBM stock goes up, so does Unisys stock. Or it might be that a U.S. Treasury note is selling for 1 cent less in Japan than it is in the United States. These snippets of information can make a big difference to Citibank's bottom line in a very competitive financial market.

- In Westminster, California, a community of 87,000 people, police use neural network software to fight crime. With crime reports as input, the system detects and maps local crime patterns. Police say that with this system they can better predict crime trends, improve patrol assignments, and develop better crime-prevention programs.[24]

NEURAL NETWORKS TO SAVE ENERGY

After the energy crisis that began in California in 1999, many companies, including the Bank of America, started to look for energy management systems. The bank installed a neural network–based system to control energy consumption in its 78 California office buildings. The neural network allows managers to float heating and air conditioning controls so that temperatures remain comfortable for the office occupants without being hotter or colder than necessary.

The Bank hoped to save 5 percent on energy cost but surpassed that figure and paid for the system within a year. Not only is the organization able to save energy, it now has a better understanding of its energy consumption.

The California Department of General Services also uses neural network software to save energy. The software was installed in 65 state-owned offices in 2001 and the agency found that it could save up to 20 percent annually on its energy costs.[25,26]

- Fingerhut, the mail order company based in Minnesota, has 6 million people on its customer list. To determine which customers were and were not likely to order from its catalog, Fingerhut recently switched to neural network software. The company finds that the new software is more effective and expects to generate millions of dollars by fine-tuning its mailing lists.[27]

- Fraud detection is one of the areas in which neural networks are used the most. Visa, MasterCard, and many other credit card companies use a neural network to spot peculiarities in individual accounts. MasterCard estimates neural networks save them $50 million annually.[28]

- Many insurance companies (Cigna, AIG, Travelers, Liberty Mutual, Hartford) along with state compensation funds and other carriers use neural network software to identify fraud. The system searches for patterns in billing charges, laboratory tests, and frequency of office visits. A claim for which the diagnosis was a sprained ankle and which included an electrocardiogram would be flagged for the account manager.[29]

- FleetBoston Financial Corporation uses a neural network to watch transactions with customers. The neural network can detect patterns that may indicate a customer's growing dissatisfaction with the company. The neural network looks for signs like decreases in the number of transactions or in the account balance of one of Fleet's high-value customers.[30]

All of the above situations have pattern recognition in common. They all require identification and/or classification, which may then be used to predict a finding or outcome. Neural networks are often called predictive systems since they can see patterns in huge volumes of information.

INSIDE A NEURAL NETWORK

Neural networks are so called because they attempt to mimic the structure and functioning of the human brain. Conceptually, neural networks consist of three layers of virtual nerve cells, or neurons. There's an input layer and an output layer and between them is a hidden layer, although there may be more than one hidden layer. The input and output layers are connected to the middle layer(s) by connections called weights of various

Figure 4.8

The Layers of a Neural Network

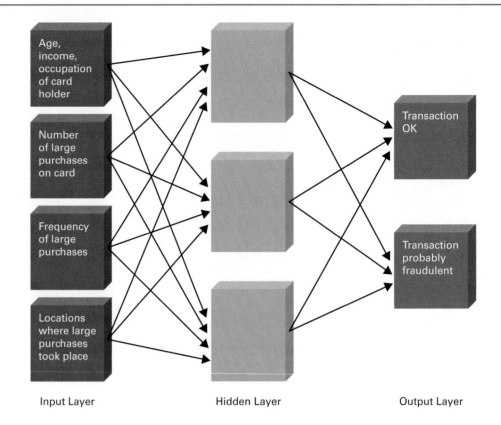

Input Layer   Hidden Layer   Output Layer

strengths (see Figure 4.8). If you were to train a neural network to recognize a "good" stock portfolio, you would input many, many examples of good and bad portfolios, telling the neural network which was which. As the neural network is learning to differentiate between good and bad, the weights change. The flow of information to the output layer also changes. After you have fed the system enough examples, the weights stabilize, and the neural network then consistently classifies portfolios correctly.

So, you may be asking, how is a neural network different from an expert system, since both can take input and produce an answer as to which group the input belongs? An expert system, as we saw, can also classify; that is, it asks questions and, based on the answers, can diagnose or prescribe. The difference is that an expert system does not adjust by itself and is rigid in its application of the rules. For example, if a credit card fraud detection expert system had a rule that said to flag a purchase over a certain amount on certain types of accounts, the expert system would flag a transaction that was even one penny over. A neural network, on the other hand, would learn the spending behavior of cardholders and would be better able to evaluate whether deviations were large enough to be queried or not. A neural network can even adjust to situations not explicitly used in training. For example, if when the neural network was learning, mortgage rates were between 6 percent and 10 percent, the system could interpolate if the rate were to drop to 5 percent.

Neural networks have many advantages. For example, neural networks can

- Learn and adjust to new circumstances on their own.
- Lend themselves to massive parallel processing.
- Function without complete or well-structured information.
- Cope with huge volumes of information with many dependent variables.
- Analyze nonlinear relationships in information (they've been called fancy regression analysis systems).

The biggest problem with neural networks to date has been the fact that the hidden layers are "hidden." That is, you can't see how the neural network is learning and how the neurons are interacting. Newer neural networks no longer hide the middle layers. With these systems you can manually adjust the weights or connections giving you more flexibility and control.

FUZZY LOGIC

Fuzzy logic is a way of reaching conclusions based on ambiguous or vague information. Humans tend to make decisions based on approximate information, since not every type of information can be separated into mutually exclusive categories. For example, you might consider 20 degrees Fahrenheit to be very cold, 40 degrees to be cold, 60 degrees to be warm, 90 degrees to be hot, and 105 to be very hot, but you can't really specify exact degree values that would separate these categories of warmth (or lack of it). Compounding the problem is the fact that somebody else might experience it differently; subjectively, a temperature some people consider warm others would judge to be hot—or cool. Thus, you need a way to translate an approximate or vague judgment into something that a computer, requiring a precise assignment of numbers to all events, can handle. This is the type of situation in which fuzzy logic is very effective.

Fuzzy logic is a mathematical method of handling imprecise or subjective information. The basic approach is to assign values between 0 and 1 to vague or ambiguous information. The higher the value, the closer it is to 1. For example, you might assign the value of 0.8 to the value "hot." Then you would construct rules and processes, called *algorithms,* to describe the interdependence among variables. A fuzzy logic algorithm is a set of steps that relate variables representing inexact information or personal perceptions.

Fuzzy logic and neural networks are often combined to express complicated and subjective concepts in a form that makes it possible to simplify the problem and to apply rules. The rules are executed with a level of certainty. This is similar to, but not the same as, confidence levels in statistics. In statistics, probability is used to estimate the likelihood of an outcome, whereas fuzzy logic describes the data point itself while incorporating subjective perception.

In the business world, fuzzy logic has been applied to financial analysis, the pharmaceutical industry, the wood processing and metal cutting industries, the manufacture of antilock brakes, and washing machines that determine by themselves how much water to use or how long to wash. (They wash until the water is "clean.") In accounting and finance, for example, fuzzy logic allows you to analyze information with subjective financial values (say, on an important intangible resource like goodwill) that are very important considerations in economic analyses.

Fuzzy logic is used by Google to find answers to your search terms, which makes sense, since your perception of a topic often influences how you phrase your query, hence determining the relevance of the Web pages that Google delivers.

Genetic Algorithms

Have you ever wondered how chefs around the world create recipes for great-tasting foods? For example, how did the Chinese discover that cashew nuts and chicken taste good when combined? How did Mexican chefs arrive at combining tomatoes, onions, cilantro, and other spices to create pica de gallo? All those great recipes came about through *evolutionary processes.* Someone decided to put together a few ingredients and taste the result. Undoubtedly, many of those combinations resulted in unpalatable concoctions that were quickly discarded. Others were tasty enough to warrant further experimentation of combinations.

Today significant research in AI is devoted to creating software capable of following a similar trial-and-error process, leading to the evolution of a good result. Such a software system is called a genetic algorithm. A ***genetic algorithm*** is an artificial intelligence system that mimics the evolutionary, survival-of-the-fittest process to generate increasingly better solutions to a problem. In other words, a genetic algorithm is an optimizing system: It finds the combination of inputs that give the best outputs.

Here's an example. Suppose you were trying to decide what to put into your stock portfolio. You have countless stocks to choose from but a limited amount of money to invest. You might decide that you'd like to start with 20 stocks and you want a portfolio growth rate of 7.5 percent.

Probably you'd start by examining historic information on the stocks. You would take some number of stocks and combine them, 20 at a time, to see what happens with each grouping. If you wanted to choose from a pool of 30 stocks, you would have to examine 30,045,015 different combinations. For a 40-stock pool, the number of combinations rises to 137,846,500,000. It would be an impossibly time-consuming, not to mention numbingly tedious, task to look at this many combinations and evaluate your overall return for each one. This is just the sort of repetitive number-crunching task at which computers excel, however.

So, instead of a pencil, paper, and calculator, you might use a genetic algorithm. You could input the appropriate information on the stocks, including the number of years the company has been in business, the performance of the stock over the last five years, price to earnings ratios, and other information.

You would also have to tell the genetic algorithm your exact "success" criteria. For example, you might use a growth rate in the company over the last year of at least 10 percent, a presence in the marketplace going back at least three years, a connection to the computer industry, and so forth. The genetic algorithm would simply combine and recombine stocks eliminating any combinations that don't fit your criteria and continuing to the next iteration with the acceptable combinations—those that give an aggregate growth rate of at least 7.5 percent while aiming for as high a growth rate as possible.

Genetic algorithms use three concepts of evolution:

1. ***Selection***—or survival of the fittest. The key to selection is to give preference to better outcomes.
2. ***Crossover***—or combining portions of good outcomes in the hope of creating an even better outcome.
3. ***Mutation***—or randomly trying combinations and evaluating the success (or failure) of the outcome.

Genetic algorithms are best suited to decision-making environments in which thousands, or perhaps millions, of solutions are possible. Genetic algorithms can find and evaluate solutions intelligently and can get through many more possibilities more thoroughly and faster than a human can. As you might imagine, businesses face decision-making environments for all sorts of problems like engineering design, computer graphics, strategies for game playing, anything, in fact, that requires optimization techniques. Here are some other examples.

- Genetic algorithms are used by business executives to help them decide which combination of projects a firm should invest in, taking complicated tax considerations into account.[31]

- They're used by investment companies to help in trading choices and decisions.[32]

BE A GENETIC ALGORITHM AND PUT NAILS IN BOXES

This project involves packaging nails so that you make the most profit possible (this is a profit maximizing problem). Say you have six types of nails and can make as many as you need of each. These are 4-inch, 3.5-inch, 3-inch, 2.5-inch, 2-inch, and 1.5-inch nails. The cost of making each type of nail depends on how big a nail it is. Those cost and selling prices are listed in the table below along with the weights. The nails will be sold in boxes of up to 30 nails. There must be no more than 10,

but no less than 5, of each of three types of nails in each box. The nails in each box should weigh no more than 20 ounces. You're looking for the combination with the highest profit using a trial-and-error method.

A spreadsheet would be helpful for completing this project. You'll most likely find that you identify some promising paths to follow right away and will concentrate on those to reach the best one.

Nail	Weight	Cost	Selling price
4 inch	1 oz	4 cents	8 cents
3.5 inch	0.85 oz	3.5 cents	6 cents
3 inch	0.7 oz	3 cents	5 cents
2.5 inch	0.5 oz	2.5 cents	4 cents
2 inch	0.25 oz	2 cents	3 cents
1.5 inch	0.1 oz	1.5 cents	2 cents

- In any garment that you buy, the fabric alone accounts for between 35 percent and 40 percent of the selling price. So, when cutting out the fabric to make the garment, it's important that there be as little waste as possible. Genetic algorithms are used to solve this problem of laying out the pieces of the garment and cutting fabric in a way that leaves as little waste as possible.[33]

- US West uses a genetic algorithm to determine the optimal configuration of fiber-optic cable in a network that may include as many as 100,000 connection points. By using selection, crossover, and mutation, the genetic algorithm can generate and evaluate millions of cable configurations and select the one that uses the least amount of cable. At US West, this process used to take an experienced design engineer almost two months. US West's genetic algorithm can solve the problem in two days and saves the company $1 million to $10 million each time it's used.[34]

Genetic algorithms are good for these types of problems because they use selection, crossover, and mutation as methods of exploring countless solutions and the respective worth of each.

You have to tell the genetic algorithm what constitutes a "good" solution. That could be low cost, high return, among other factors, since many potential solutions are useless or absurd. If you created a genetic algorithm to make bread, for example, it might try to boil flour to create moistness. That obviously won't work, so the genetic algorithm would simply throw away that solution and try something else. Other solutions would eventually be good, and some of them would even be wonderful. According to David Goldbert, a genetic algorithm pioneer at the University of Illinois at Urbana–Champaign, evolution is the oldest and most powerful algorithm there is, and "three billion years of evolution can't be wrong!"[35]

Intelligent Agents

Do you have a favorite restaurant? Is there someone there who knows you and remembers that you like Italian dressing, but not croutons, on your salad; and ice cream and a slice of cheddar cheese with your apple pie? Does this person familiar with your tastes put a glass of diet cola on your favorite table when you come in the door? If so, he or she has the qualities that artificial intelligence scientists are working on incorporating into intelligent agents. An *intelligent agent* is software that assists you, or acts on your behalf, in performing repetitive computer-related tasks. Future intelligent agents will most likely be autonomous, acting independently, and will learn and adapt to changing circumstances.

You may not realize it, but you're probably already familiar with a primitive type of intelligent agent—the shifty-eyed paper clip that pops up in some versions of Word. For example, if your document looks as if it is going to be a business letter—that is, you type in a date, name, and address—the animated paper clip will offer helpful suggestions on how to proceed.

You can find hundreds of intelligent agents, or bots, for a wide variety of tasks. The BotSpot and SmartBot Web sites at www.botspot.com and www.smartbots.com are good places to get an idea of the many different types of agents that are available.

Essentially there are four types of intelligent agents:

- Information agents (including buyer agents or shopping bots)
- Monitoring-and-surveillance agents
- Data-mining agents
- User or personal agents

INFORMATION AGENTS

Information agents are intelligent agents that search for information of some kind and bring it back. The best known information agents are buyer agents. A *buyer agent,* also known as a *shopping bot,* is an intelligent agent on a Web site that helps you, the customer, find products and services that you need. They work very efficiently for commodity products such as CDs, books, electronic components, and other one-size-fits-all products. Amazon.com uses intelligent technology to show you a list of books or other products that you might like. The Web site classifies you into a category of people with similar tastes and, based on that category, presents you with a list of products that Amazon hopes you will find appealing enough to buy.

Shopping bots make money by selling advertising space, from special promotions in cooperation with merchants, or by charging click-through fees, which are payments to the site that provided the link to the merchant site. Some shopping bots give preference to certain sites for a financial consideration. The people who run shopping bot sites have two, sometimes competing, objectives. They want to present as many listings as possible to the consumer in the most useful way, but they also want to make money doing it.

MySimon.com is the most successful shopping bot to date with more than a million visitors a month according to Nielsen/NetRatings. MySimon searches for millions of products on thousands of Web sites.[36]

Both the Google and Ask Jeeves Web sites use information agents to find information—and not just when you request it. The URL server at Google sends thousands of

INTELLIGENT AGENTS RUN EXPERIMENTS ABOARD SPACECRAFT

We all know that NASA sends various types of craft into space for a variety of purposes. We've heard of the Hubble telescope that has been sending back terrific pictures for years. A lesser known but similarly spectacular observation craft—although in this case its mission is to observe the earth—is the Earth Observing-1 (or simply EO1) satellite.

During 2004, NASA uploaded intelligent agent software to EO1 to run experiments and even the spacecraft itself. One of EO1's tasks was to avoid wasting fuel without disrupting the onboard experiments or otherwise compromising the mission. This was a job that used to be handled by ground control, but now the people at mission headquarters are free to concentrate on tasks other than routine maintenance while the agents do the job in space.

EO1 was launched in 2001 on a one-year mission to observe the earth from space. It was part of NASA's New Millennium Program mission and was originally intended as a pilot project to test new space technolo-

gies. Now, four years later it's still going strong collecting and sending back to us valuable information about our earth with about 20 times more detail than any previous Earth-observing satellites. The information that EO1 sends back encompasses all manner of happenings on earth, like the spread of forest and bush fires, the impact of cattle grazing in South America, the state of the rain forest, and the spread of harmful plant species.

The beauty of incorporating intelligent agents into the spacecraft is that they can learn and adapt to changing and unexpected conditions. NASA's software engineers have designed these agents to achieve certain goals rather than to react to prespecified situations, making them able to handle complex interactions. Since the software can "learn" and function autonomously, it can react to unexpected situations, allowing scientists to conduct more complex and interesting research on board.[37]

Googlebots out to surf the Web sites of all the sites in Google's index. They copy individual pages, at the rate of more than 100 per second, to Google's repository, where the Google software indexes them. This means that when you perform a Google search, the search engine builds a list of all the pages that have the keywords you specify and presents them to you in PageRank order. Google's PageRanking process sorts the pages in order of links pointing to each page. That is, the more links on the Web that point to a Web site, the higher that Web site will be in the list.[38]

Government sites have information agents you can use to get the information you need. FERRET (Federal Electronic Research and Review Extraction Tool) was developed jointly by the Census Bureau and the Bureau of Labor Statistics. With FERRET you can find information on employment, health care, education, race and ethnicity, health insurance, housing, income and poverty, aging, and marriage and family. Other types of information agents include intelligent agents that scan Web pages and highlight relevant text for you, and still others can assemble customized news reports. There are several versions of these. A CNN Custom News bot will gather news from CNN on the topics you want to read about—and only those.

MONITORING-AND-SURVEILLANCE AGENTS

Monitoring-and-surveillance agents (also called *predictive agents*) are intelligent agents that constantly observe and report on some entity of interest, a network, or manufacturing equipment, for example. NASA's Jet Propulsion Laboratory has an agent that monitors inventory, planning, and the ordering of scheduled equipment to keep costs down.[39] Other monitoring-and-surveillance agents work on the manufacturing shop floor, finding equipment problems and locating other machinery that can perform the same job.

Monitoring-and-surveillance agents are often used to monitor complex computer networks. Allstate Insurance has a network with 2,000 computers. The company uses a network monitoring agent from Computer Associates International called Neugent that watches its huge networks 24 hours a day. Every five seconds, the agent measures 1,200 data points and can predict a system crash 45 minutes before it happens. Neugent combines intelligent agent technology with neural network technology to look for patterns of activity or problems. The neural network part can learn what conditions predict a downturn in network efficiency or a slowing in network traffic. Neugent also watches for electronic attacks and can detect them early so that they can be stopped.

Another type of monitoring-and-surveillance agent is one that works on computer networks keeping track of the configuration of each computer connected to the network. It tracks and updates the central configuration database when anything on any computer changes, like the number or type of disk drives. An important task in managing networks is prioritizing traffic and shaping bandwidth. That means sending enough network capacity or bandwidth to the most important tasks versus those that are secondary. At a university, for example, processing end-of-semester grades might take precedence.

Some other types of monitoring-and-surveillance agents include

- Agents that watch your competition and bring back price changes and special offer information.
- Agents that monitor Internet sites, discussion groups, mailing lists, and so on, for stock manipulation, insider training, and rumors that might affect stock prices.
- Agents that monitor sites for updated information on the topic of your choice.
- Agents that watch particular products and bring back price or terms changes.
- Agents that monitor auction sites for products or prices that you want.

DATA-MINING AGENTS

A *data-mining agent* operates in a data warehouse discovering information. A data warehouse brings together information from lots of different sources. Data mining is the process of looking through the data warehouse to find information that you can use to take action—like ways to increase sales or to keep customers who are considering defecting. Data mining is so called because you have to sift through a lot of information for the gold nuggets that will affect the bottom line (or top line). This sort of nugget spotting is similar to what the FBI and CIA do when they bring together little bits of information from diverse sources and use the overall pattern to spot trouble brewing.

As you learned in Chapter 3, database queries answer questions like "How much did we spend on transportation in March of this year?" Multidimensional analysis is the next step in complexity and answers questions like "How much did we spend on transportation in the southeast during March of the last five years?" Data mining goes deeper and may suggest questions you may not even have thought to ask like the retail manager we mentioned in Chapter 1 who thought "What else do young men buy on Friday afternoons when they come in to buy diapers?" (Remember from Chapter 1 the answer to that one, suggested by data-mining tools, was beer.)[40]

One of the most common types of data mining is classification, which finds patterns in information and categorizes items into those classes. You may remember that this is just what neural networks do best. So, not surprisingly, neural networks are part of many data-mining tools. And data-mining agents are another integral part, since these intelligent agents search for information in a data warehouse.

A data-mining agent may detect a major shift in a trend or a key indicator. It can also detect the presence of new information and alert you. Volkswagen uses an intelligent agent system that acts as an early-warning system about market conditions. If conditions become such that the assumptions underlying the company's strategy are no longer true, the intelligent agent alerts managers.[41] For example, the intelligent agent might see a problem in some part of the country that is about to or will shortly cause payments to slow down. Having that information early lets managers formulate a plan to protect themselves.

USER AGENTS

User agents (sometimes called *personal agents*) are intelligent agents that take action on your behalf. In this category belong those intelligent agents that already perform, or will shortly perform, the following tasks:

- Check your e-mail, sort it according to priority (your priority), and alert you when good stuff comes through—like college acceptance letters.
- Play computer games as your opponent or patrol game areas for you.
- Fill out forms on the Web automatically for you. They even store your information for future reference.
- "Discuss" topics with you from your deepest fears to your favorite sports.

One expanding application of intelligent agent technology is in automating business functions. For example, Mission Hockey, a company that manufacturers and distributes in-line and ice hockey skates and other gear, uses software from Sweden called Movex that has a user-agent component. Movex will search the Internet or a company intranet or extranet to negotiate and make deals with suppliers and distributors. In this case, the intelligent agent is incorporated into an enterprise resource planning system. Enterprise resource planning (or ERP) is a very important concept in today's business world. The term refers to a method of getting and keeping an overview on every part of the business (a bird's-eye view, so to speak), so that production, development, selling, and servicing of goods and services will all be coordinated to contribute to the company's goals and objectives. You'll learn more about the concept of ERP in Chapter 7.

Multi-Agent Systems and Agent-Based Modeling

What do cargo transport systems, book distribution centers, the video game market, a flu epidemic, and an ant colony have in common? They are all complex adaptive systems and thus share some common characteristics. By observing parts of the ecosystem, like ant or bee colonies, artificial intelligence scientists can use hardware and software models that incorporate insect characteristics and behavior to (1) learn how people-based systems behave; (2) predict how they will behave under a given set of circumstances; and (3) improve human systems to make them more efficient and effective. This concept of learning from ecosystems and adapting their characteristics to human and organizational situations is called *biomimicry.*

Complex organizations, those of humans and ants alike, are made up of separate groups of individuals. The groups have different roles, follow their own specific sets of rules, and react to changing conditions; what's more, not every individual in a group acts in precisely the same way.

Let's examine a simplified version of the retail video game market for instance. One group of people designs and writes the code for the games (and within that group are smaller subsets of people), a second group manufactures the CDs or DVDs and distributes them to the retail outlets (the third group), then the last group (consumers) choose to buy, or not to buy, the games to play on their gaming devices. What each group does influences the others.

The traditional approach to studying a system such as this was to examine each group of people and model that group according to its habits and behavior. However, this type of research has serious limitations because the interaction of one group with one or more of the others must be ignored, or studied separately. The difficulty of studying the system as a whole is that it's very complex, making it extremely difficult to keep track of all the variables and their interactions. The traditional model becomes unmanageable very quickly.

In the last few years, AI research has made much progress in modeling complex organizations as a whole with the help of multi-agent systems. In a *multi-agent system* groups of intelligent agents have the ability to work independently and to interact with each other. The simulation of a human organization using a multi-agent system is called agent-based modeling. *Agent-based modeling* is a way of simulating human organizations using multiple intelligent agents, each of which follows a set of simple rules and can adapt to changing conditions.

Agent-based modeling systems are being used to model stock market fluctuations, predict the escape routes that people seek in a burning building, estimate the effects of interest rates on consumers with different types of debt, and anticipate how changes in conditions will affect the supply chain, to name just a few. See Figure 4.9 for examples of companies that have used agent-based modeling to their advantage.

ANT COLONIES AND SWARM INTELLIGENCE

The ant ecosystem is one of the most widely used types of simulations in business problems. If you've ever tried to remove ants from your home, you know how determined and effective ant colonies are. Individual ants are autonomous, acting and reacting independently. (If you drop a crumb into the middle of a group of ants, they'll all scatter in different directions.) However, ants are unusual insects in that they are social. (Less than 2 percent of insects are social, with termites being the only other entirely social species,

- Southwest Airlines—to optimize cargo routing.

- Procter & Gamble—to overhaul its handling of what the company calls its "supply network" of 5 billion consumers in 140 countries.

- Air Liquide America—to reduce production and distribution costs of liquefied industrial gases.

- Merck & Co.—to find more efficient ways of distributing anti-AIDS drugs in Africa.

- Ford Motor Co.—to build a model of consumer preferences and find the best balance between production costs and customers' demands.

- Edison Chouest Offshore LLC—to find the best way to deploy its service and supply vessels in the Gulf of Mexico.

Figure 4.9

Companies That Use Agent-Based Modeling[42]

although some types of bees and wasps are, too.) The term "social" implies that all the members of a colony work together to establish and maintain a global system that's efficient and stable. So, even though the ants are autonomous, each ant contributes to the system as a whole. Ants have been on Earth for 40 million years, compared to the relatively short human occupation of 100 thousand years, and their extraordinary evolutionary success is the result of ants' collective behavior, known as swarm intelligence.

Swarm (collective) intelligence is the collective behavior of groups of simple agents that are capable of devising solutions to problems as they arise, eventually leading to coherent global patterns.[43] That is to say, complex collective behavior can result from the individuals in the system consistently following a small number of simple rules. Swarm intelligence allows the creation and maintenance of systems that have the following four characteristics:

1. *Flexibility,* so that the system can respond to changes, both large and small, in the environment around it. In an ant colony, for example, if you move the food, the ants will find it again very quickly.

2. *Robustness,* so that even if some individual members of the system don't succeed, the work gets done. For example, if you remove some of the ants, others will step in and continue the work.

3. *Decentralization,* in that each individual has a relatively simple job to do and performs that job without supervision. In the ant colony there are forager ants, soldier ants who protect the nest, queens who produce the new generations, ants who take care of and feed the cocoons, and so on.

4. *Self-organization,* in that the methods of problem solving are not prescribed from a central authority, but rather are developed as problem-solving strategies by the individuals in the group who are responsible for the completion of the work. For example, if an ant finds a food morsel that's too large for one ant to carry, others come to help and they run around changing positions until they have the morsel balanced well enough that they can carry it off. See the Web site at www.scottcamazine.com/personal/research/index.htm for other examples of self-organization in nature.[44]

So, how are the workings of ant colonies related to information technology in modern business? Swarm intelligence gives us a way to examine collective systems where groups of individuals have certain goals, solve problems, and make decisions without centralized control or a common plan. Think of our video game market. No one directs the whole system dictating that buyers buy specific games or that manufacturers sell a certain number of games or sell only in a certain region. The four groups of participants act in ways that they believe will further their own goals, and the result of their interaction is a system with its own features that finds its own level of balance between supply and demand.

A comparison of the activities of forager ants and those of the cargo-handling arm of Southwest Airlines affords a striking example of the similarities between ecosystems and human organizations, which we will consider shortly. There are some uncanny parallels that surprised Southwest's management. First, though, let's ponder the ants.

Forager ants have the sole responsibility of providing food to the colony. They don't form committees and discuss strategies or look to a central authority for direction; they just find food and bring it back to the nest, and in doing so follow a simple procedure (see Figure 4.10).

Say two ants leave the same point to search for food. Figure 4.10, panel 1, shows that Ant A finds the food first because of the shorter path. Having found a food source, Ant A returns to the nest (see Figure 4.10, panel 2), leaving behind a trail of pheromones (a biological breadcrumb trail) so that Ant A and the other ants will know what path to take. The first ant that returns "lays the trail" first so that's the one that other ants take. Then the other ants strengthen the pheromone trail on their return journey by leaving their own pheromone tracks (see Figure 4.10, panel 3).

Meanwhile, Ant B arrives back at the nest after the shorter path has already been established. The other ants that are already on the move don't change their route. Additionally, the pheromone trail on the unused path evaporates after a certain length of time so that it's effectively deleted from the system as a desirable route to food. The approach is straightforward but effective, and can be expressed as the following rules:

- Rule 1: Follow the trail if one exists, otherwise create one.
- Rule 2: Find food.
- Rule 3: Return to the nest, making a pheromone trail.

If changes occur (say, for example, that the food source is removed), the ants cease returning to the place where the food used to be, and the trail disappears. Then the process begins again, and proceeds relentlessly, with forager ants finding a new food source and creating pheromone corridors that lead the way.

The problem that the ants have just solved is one of the oldest problems that humans (as well as ants) have faced. It's known as "the shortest path problem" or the "traveling salesman problem." Anyone who schedules drop-off and pick-up routes for delivery trucks, or schedules jobs on the factory floor, or even colors maps, making sure that no two adjacent components have the same color, has had to find a solution to the same type of problem.

Taking their cue from nature, AI researchers built sets of small robots and incorporated software that allowed the robots to follow rules and interact with each other in the same basic ways as the ants. They also dispensed with the physical forms altogether, creating virtual ants in the form of small autonomous blocks of code that we call intelligent agents. And each code block could follow certain rules, interact, and adapt. These virtual ants were then arranged into multi-agent systems that were further refined into agent-based models. Enter Southwest Airlines as a case in point.

Even though cargo is a small part of Southwest's business, it was causing management headaches and bottlenecks at busy airports. Southwest consulted with swarm intelligence experts, who used a virtual model of foraging ants to simulate the cargo-handling process. And that was how Southwest managers discovered, to their surprise, that there were actually better ways to handle cargo than to put it on the first plane flying in the right direction. Surprisingly, the computer's swarm intelligence model showed that it might actually be better to leave cargo on a plane heading in the wrong direction. For example, cargo headed from Chicago to Boston would be better left on a plane going from

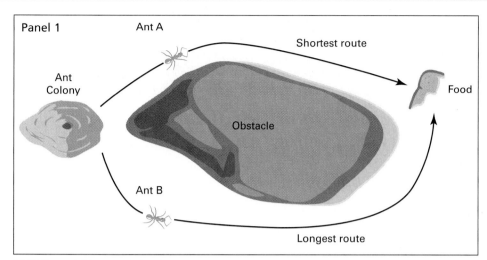

Figure 4.10

Ants Finding Food

Panel 1

Ant A

Shortest route

Ant Colony

Food

Obstacle

Ant B

Longest route

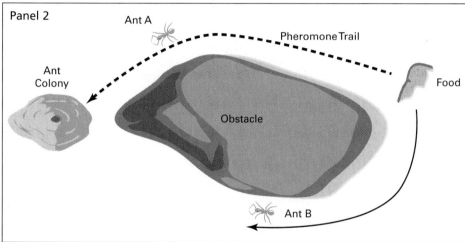

Panel 2

Ant A

Pheromone Trail

Ant Colony

Food

Obstacle

Ant B

Panel 3

Pheromone Trail

Ant Colony

Food

Obstacle

Chicago to Atlanta and then reloaded onto a flight to Boston, requiring less unloading and reloading. Following the ant model, Southwest decreased its cargo transfer rates by 80 percent, reduced the workload of cargo employees by 20 percent, and also found that there was spare cargo space on flights that were previously full, enabling the company to accept more business. The overall gain to Southwest was in excess of $10 million per year.[45] For more examples of business lessons taken from nature, see the Industry Perspective entitled "Automated Truck-Painting Booths Schedule Themselves."

The future will see many more uses of intelligent agents. It's a pretty safe bet that these applications will include swarm intelligence and agent-based modeling. Already,

AUTOMATED TRUCK-PAINTING BOOTHS SCHEDULE THEMSELVES

Honeybees have a very flexible work allocation system. For example, when food is scarce, bees normally assigned other tasks like nursing the young will switch roles to help to find food. The same principle can be applied to painting new trucks. In the factory, as a truck comes off the assembly line, one of the paint booths applies paint. Booths can change the color they're using, but it's a costly process to make the changeover, mainly because of the extraordinary expense of cleaning the lines, spray nozzles, etc. So, using the honeybee principle, each booth is programmed to paint the truck a standard color unless a pressing need arises. Rather than following some centralized schedule generated by the central scheduling system, each booth determines its own workload. The result is very effective. If a large batch of trucks all need to be painted red, the booths that usually paint in blue and black change to red to accommodate the trucks that are waiting. Also, when a booth breaks down, the others take over the load.

Another work allocation system comes from seed-harvester ants whose job it is to carry food back to their nest. They do this in relay-race fashion with each ant handing off the food to the next one. There the analogy ends, however, as there are no predetermined hand-off points; each ant carries the food until it meets the next ant, then hands over the food, and turns back to meet the new load from the ant before it and on up the line. Only the location of the food source and the nest are fixed. This process is known as the "bucket brigade," and is used in fast-food restaurants and book distribution centers.

Say, for example, when a book order came in, the first person put in all the geography books, the next one put in the IT books, and so on. This is called the zone approach and it pretty much guarantees that there will always be some workers waiting around for others to finish their tasks. The solution, taken from the ants, is to reorganize the workflow so that an employee fills his/her own order—stacks a certain number of books—until the person next in line takes over, and then the first employee goes back up the line to help someone else. Using this model, workers became 30 percent more productive than they had been when using the zone approach. Many distribution companies, including McGraw-Hill and Blockbuster Music, have used variations on the bucket brigade approach with great success.[46]

swarm intelligence is being implemented widely for scheduling, resource allocation, and routing. Other applications in the early stages include networks that have self-organizing components and robots that assemble themselves. There must be many, many more that have not yet been dreamt of.[47] Some people believe that intelligent agents will replace many of the other types of simulations in the future since swarm intelligence supports individuality, flexibility, and entities that can adapt quickly and effectively in a fast-changing business environment.

Summary: Student Learning Outcomes Revisited

1. **Define decision support system, list its components, and identify the type of applications it's suited to.** A *decision support system (DSS)* is a highly flexible and interactive IT system that is designed to support decision making when the problem is not structured. A DSS has three components: model management, data management, and user interface management. It's primarily an analysis tool to support your decision making, but you make the final decision.

2. **Define geographic information systems and state how they differ from other decision support tools.** A *geographic information system (GIS)* is a decision support system designed specifically to work with spatial information. It's used for the analysis of information in map form. Information is stored in layers which can be overlaid as appropriate. It's the layering and presentation that separates a GIS from other decision support tools.

3. **Define artificial intelligence and list the different types that are used in business.** *Artificial intelligence* is the science of making machines imitate human thinking and behavior. The types used in business include expert systems, neural networks, genetic algorithms, and intelligent agents.

4. **Define expert systems and describe the types of problems to which they are applicable.** An *expert system* (or *knowledge-based system*) is an artificial intelligence system that applies reasoning capabilities to reach a conclusion. A rule-based expert system asks the user questions and, based on the answers, asks other questions until it has enough information to make a decision or a recommendation. Expert systems are good for diagnostic (what's wrong) and prescriptive problems (what to do). For example, you could use an expert system to diagnose illness or to figure out why a machine is malfunctioning. And you could use an expert system to determine what to do about the problem.

5. **Define neural networks and fuzzy logic and the uses of these AI tools.** A *neural network* (also called an *artificial neural network* or *ANN*) is an artificial intelligence system that is capable of finding and differentiating patterns. Neural networks are good for finding commonalities in situations that have many variables. *Fuzzy logic* is a mathematical method of handling imprecise or subjective information. It is used to represent

relative terms such as "hot" and "cold" so that a computer can use them in processing.

6. **Define genetic algorithms and list the concepts on which they are based and the types of problems they solve.** A *genetic algorithm* is an artificial intelligence system that mimics the evolutionary, survival-of-the-fittest process to generate increasingly better solutions to a problem. Genetic algorithms use the principles of *selection, crossover,* and *mutation* from evolution theory. These systems are best suited to problems where hundreds or thousands of solutions are possible and you need an optimum solution.

7. **Define intelligent agents, list the four types, and identify the types of problems they solve.** An *intelligent agent* is software that assists you, or acts on your behalf, in performing repetitive computer-related tasks. The four types are

   - *Information agents*—the most common are *buyer agents* (or *shopping bots*) that search the Web for products and services
   - *Monitoring-and-surveillance agents* (or *predictive agents*) track conditions, perhaps on a network, and signal changes or troublesome conditions
   - *Data-mining agents* search data warehouses to discover information
   - *User agents* (or *personal agents*) take action for you, particularly in repetitive tasks like sorting e-mail

8. **Define agent-based modeling and swarm intelligence.** *Agent-based modeling* is a way of simulating human organizations and behaviors using multiple intelligent agents, each of which follows a set of simple rules and can adapt to changing conditions. *Swarm (collective) intelligence* is the collective behavior of groups of simple agents that are capable of devising solutions to problems as they arise, eventually leading to coherent global patterns.

CLOSING CASE STUDY ONE

SHUTTLE DEBRIS, TREES, AND SNIPER ATTACKS

What do shuttle debris, trees, and possible locations of sniper attacks have in common? They can all be mapped and managed using a geographic information system (GIS). A GIS, as you learned in this chapter, allows you to see information spatially. Being able to visualize the physical location of objects and their proximity to each other greatly aids the decision-making process. Following are some examples that will give you an idea of how diverse the applications of GIS are.

THE ILL-FATED SPACESHIP COLUMBIA

On January 31, 2003, after 16 days of intensive research conducted while orbiting the earth, the seven-member crew of the space shuttle *Columbia* shut down all experiments, packed up their stuff, and ran tests of the systems they would need to land the next day. On February 1, the shuttle headed for home, but something went terribly wrong and the shuttle exploded over East Texas and arrived on earth in small pieces. To figure out what had happened, it was necessary to gather the pieces and try to reconstruct the sequence of events that led to the disaster. So, within hours of the terrible tragedy, while many of us were still too stunned to think, researchers and students at Stephen F. Austin State University in Nacogdoches, Texas, collected their GPS (global positioning system) gear and headed out looking for the debris. The field crews wanted to pinpoint exactly where all the debris fell—they didn't move or even touch anything they found. Within days there were 60 to 70 teams with up to 200 people collecting the information.

The GPS system they used is accurate to 100 feet, but with further processing the accuracy can be increased to within 3 feet. Using ArchInfo from ESRI, the teams were able to plot all the data points on a digital map that showed topological features, as well as roads and other man-made structures. In all, the volunteers collected 70 megabytes of information that they turned over to the federal agencies that had set up a central command post in Lufkin, Texas.

TREES IN CHATTANOOGA

In Chattanooga, people take the natural beauty and environmental benefits of their trees seriously. The city

has created a GIS that maps the location of the 6,000 trees located in and around the business district. Along with this basic information, the GIS also has details on each tree that include its species, tree-pit dimensions, irrigation status, and trunk diameter. This information is very helpful when working out a maintenance plan to keep the trees healthy. For example, the size of a tree determines how many pruning hours it will need. Having an accurate map of where trees are allows the city to plan for future foliage. The city doesn't want to have more than 10 percent of any one species in such a small area since any insect infestation or disease that takes hold on one tree could spread more easily and potentially eliminate the whole tree population.

With the GIS system, which cost about $7,000 in labor to develop, the city can make more accurate estimates of the cost of materials and labor that are necessary to maintain the trees. This keeps the city from wasting resources or getting nasty surprises at the end of the fiscal reporting period.

RICHMOND MAPS BUS STOPS AND TRACKS BUSES

When GRTC Transit, the public transportation agency serving the City of Richmond and Chesterfield County, in Virginia, created a GIS of its bus routes and stops, it was not part of the plan to use it to protect its ridership from snipers. The idea was to improve its planning process designed to serve its rapidly expanding customer base.

GRTC's first step was to map its 2,500 bus stops. The agency wanted to know the details about each one, such as curb length, type and condition of the signs, benches, shelters, ramps, and trashcans at each stop. Within months of collecting this information, GRTC was using the GIS to analyze its bus routes and to consider requests from customers for changes and additions to the routes and also for amenities at the stops. With the ease of viewing lots of information in context that the GIS provides, the agency has implemented many improvements to its service.

In November 2001, the northern and central parts of Virginia were beset by sniper attacks, and no one knew where they were coming from, why they were occurring, or how to stop them. GRTC Transit was able to use its GIS to quickly provide the police with information on bus stops where passengers' lives could have been at risk from sniper attacks because of on/off highway ramps close by.[48,49,50,51]

Questions

1. You saw examples in this case of a city that used a GIS to keep track of trees and one that mapped its bus stops to better serve its residents. Cities provide many other benefits, for example, firefighting and ambulance services. What sort of city features would a city incorporate into a GIS so that emergency dispatchers could more efficiently send out ambulances and fire trucks?

2. How would NASA use the information that students and other volunteers collected on the widely dispersed bits of the space shuttle *Columbia*? Why is it so important for NASA and

for the Federal Aviation Authority (FAA) to map the location of, collect, and reassemble, as far as possible, this debris?

3. How might a business such as a bank use a GIS to determine where to put a new branch? What sort of information would the bank want to have about the area surrounding the proposed site?

4. Thematic GIS maps show a statistical value for certain locations and link those locations to an underlying geographic feature, such as the distribution of population within a county, or the areas in a nature reserve where birds and animals congregate. A point map shows the location of specific data items, like where your customers live or where fire hydrants are located. For each of the three examples in this case, specify whether each one uses thematic or point maps, or some combination.

CLOSING CASE STUDY TWO

USING NEURAL NETWORKS TO CATEGORIZE PEOPLE

Would your banker give you an A, B, or C? What about your supermarket? You know you're being graded in your classes, but did you know that you're also being graded by businesses?

Special treatment for certain customers is not new. Airline customers who fly first class have always received preferential treatment, even when flights were cancelled or delayed. You won't find them napping on a stone floor with their backpacks as pillows. This makes business sense to the airlines, since these are the customers who are most profitable.

Although companies have always offered preferential treatment to their more profitable customers, the speed and capacity of computers today are making the segmenting of customers possible to a degree unheard of just a few years ago. Part of the reason for this is neural networks. Using neural network software, businesses now have the ability to look for patterns in their customer information and classify customers according

to how they affect the company's bottom line and thus to gauge whether it's worth the trouble of making them happy.

BANKS

The First Union Bank uses software that categorizes people into red, green, and yellow classes depending on the customer's history and value to the bank. Customers who are green might get better credit card rates than customers who are red and are judged to add less to the bank's bottom line.

Say you called the bank that issued you your credit card and said that you didn't want to pay the annual fee anymore. The bank could look at your credit card activity and decide whether it's more profitable to the bank to waive your fee rather than risk your not using the credit card anymore.

CREDIT CARD COMPANIES

Visa has saved millions of dollars using neural network software to spot fraud and to determine which of their customers might default or go bankrupt. Neural networks are good at spotting patterns, and if your profile looks like that of people who have defaulted, you'll be tossed into that category.

SUPPLIERS

Neural network classifying software can be applied to finding the best suppliers, too. Weyerhaueser Corporation's door factory executives have software to rank suppliers and distributors based on price, speed of delivery, and innovation. Using this information, Weyerhaueser doubled its sales and increased its return on net assets from 2 percent to 24 percent.

SUPERMARKETS

Catalina Supermarkets keeps track of which customers buy which products, how frequently, and what price they pay. Using neural network software, the supermarket chain can identify high-value customers and work at retaining them with offers of services such as free home delivery.

MOVIES

Even the movie business is getting in on the act. Twentieth Century Fox slices and dices its information in its databases to determine the most popular movies, actors, and plots in certain theaters, cities, and areas of the country. The aim is to show movies in those areas that will add the most to the bottom line. The result may be that people in certain areas will not get the chance to see certain movies.

There was a time when certain neighborhoods or geographic regions were redlined. That meant that banks and other businesses wouldn't deal with anyone who lived there. Some people think that this sort of market segmentation is a new form of redlining. Do you? Following are some questions for you to answer regarding this practice.[52,53]

Questions

1. A neural network learns to recognize patterns based on past information. Is this fair or reliable when applied to people? How accurate is it for a business to predict the future behavior of customers on the basis of historic information? Don't people change? Have you ever changed your behavior in the course of your life?

2. Customers are not likely ever to see the information that companies are using to pigeonhole them. Even the company executives may not know what criteria the neural network uses. How important are the assumptions underlying the software (i.e., the facts that the neural network is given about customers)? Even the IT specialists who design neural networks can't always vouch for their accuracy or specify exactly how the neural network reaches its conclusions. Is this safe for businesses? What are the possible business consequences of using neural networks without assurances of their reliability?

3. Businesses can use segmenting to suggest products and services to you, or if you request it, prevent your getting junk mail you don't want. Is that good? Would receiving wanted information or avoiding junk mail be worth the price of being categorized?

4. Say you run a business that supplies medical equipment (not prescription drugs)—wheelchairs, hospital beds, heating packs. You're trying to determine which customers you should give preferential treatment to. What assumptions or variables would you use (for example, age, income, and so on) to segment your customer population?

5. Do you think that this segmentation practice is fair? First, consider the business's stockholders, then consider the customers. Does it matter whether it's fair or not? Why or why not? Should there be laws against it, or laws controlling it, or none at all? Explain and justify your answer.

6. Does this differentiating practice make business sense? If you owned stock in a company, how would you feel about this practice? Do you think you should get better treatment if you're a better customer? Do you think people who are not such good customers should get the same deal that you get? Would it make any difference whether the company collected the information and did the neural network analysis itself, or bought the information or the whole package from a third party?

7. Is this practice of classifying the same as "redlining," or is it okay because it looks at behavior to classify people rather than assuming characteristics based on membership in a particular group?

Key Terms and Concepts

Agent-based modeling, 204
Artificial intelligence (AI), 189
Biomimicry, 204
Buyer agent (shopping bot), 200
Choice, 181
Crossover, 198
Data management, 186
Data-mining agent, 202
Decision support system (DSS), 183
Design, 181
Expert system (knowledge-based system), 190
Fuzzy logic, 197
Genetic algorithm, 198
Geographic information system (GIS), 187
Implementation, 181
Information agent, 200
Intelligence, 181

Intelligent agent, 200
Model management, 186
Monitoring-and-surveillance agent (predictive agent), 201
Multi-agent system, 204
Mutation, 198
Neural network (artificial neural network, ANN), 193
Nonrecurring (ad hoc) decision, 182
Nonstructured decision, 182
Recurring decision, 182
Robot, 189
Selection, 198
Structured decision, 182
Swarm (collective) intelligence, 205
User agent (personal agent), 203
User interface management, 186

Short-Answer Questions

1. What are the four types of decisions discussed in this chapter? Give an example of each.
2. What are the four steps in making a decision?
3. What is a DSS? Describe its components.
4. What is a geographic information system used for?
5. How is information represented in a geographic information system?
6. What is artificial intelligence? Name the artificial intelligence systems used widely in business.
7. What are the advantages of an expert system?
8. What sort of problems is an expert system used for?
9. How does a neural network work?
10. What three concepts of evolution are used by the genetic algorithm?
11. What are intelligent agents? What tasks can they perform?
12. What is a multi-agent system?
13. What do monitoring-and-surveillance agents do?

Assignments and Exercises

1. **MAKE A GIS** Make a GIS-type map using transparencies. Draw a map of your campus on one plastic transparency sheet. You can use software or felt-tip pens to do the actual drawing of the map. Next, use a second sheet as an overlay and mark on it what classes you have taken in what buildings. Take a third sheet and enter the type of classroom you had the course in (i.e., auditorium, lab, small, medium, large room). Make a fourth layer with special facilities, like a computer lab or a biology lab, and so on. What problems did you encounter while designing your GIS? What other information would you like to see in a real GIS of this type? Would this handmade GIS be helpful for new students? What layers would you keep for general use? What layers would you keep for sentimental value when your college days are over?

2. **CHOOSE A FINANCING OPTION** Using a spreadsheet (like Excel, for example) evaluate your options for a $12,000 car. Compare the payments (use the =pmt function in Excel), the total amount of interest, and the total you'll pay for the car under the following four options:

   a. 3 years at 0 percent interest

   b. 2 years at 1.99 percent annual percent rate (APR)

   c. 4 years at 5 percent APR

   d. 6 years at 6 percent APR

What other considerations would you take into account if you were going to buy a new car? Are there considerations other than the interest rate and the other parts that can be calculated? What are they? How is a car different from other purchases, such as CDs or TV sets or computers?

3. **WHICH SOFTWARE WOULD YOU USE?** Which type or types of computer-aided decision support software would you use for each of the situations in the table below? Note why you think each of your choices is appropriate. The decision support alternatives are

- Decision support system
- Geographic information system
- Expert system
- Neural network
- Genetic algorithm
- Intelligent agent

Problem	Type of Decision Support
You and another marketing executive on a different continent want to develop a new pricing structure for products	
You want to predict when customers are about to take their business elsewhere	
You want to fill out a short tax form	
You want to determine the fastest route for package delivery to 23 different addresses in a city	
You want to decide where to spend advertising dollars (TV, radio, newspaper, direct mail, e-mail)	
You want to keep track of competitors' prices for comparable goods and services	

4. **WHAT SHOULD THE MUSIC STORE OWNER DO?** A music store owner wants to have enough of the hottest CDs in stock so that people who come in to buy a particular CD won't be disappointed—and the store won't lose the profit. CDs that are not sold within a certain length of time go onto the sale table where they may have to be sold at cost, if they sell at all.

   The owner wants to design a decision support system to predict how many copies she should purchase and what information she will need. List some of the considerations that would go into such a system. Here are a couple to start you off: (1) the population of the target market; (2) sales for particular types of music in similar markets.

Discussion Questions

1. Some experts claim that if a business gets 52 percent of its decisions right, it will be successful. Would using a decision support system guarantee better results? Why or why not? What does the quality of any decision depend on? Do you think it matters what type of decisions are included in this 52 percent? For example, would getting the right type of paper clips be as influential a decision as deciding where to locate the business? Can you think of a situation where the type of paper clip matters a great deal?

2. Consider the topic of data warehouses in Chapter 3. In the future, AI systems will be increasingly applied to data warehouse processing. Which AI systems do you think might be helpful? For which tasks, or situations, might they best be applied? Do you think that AI systems will someday play a greater role in the design of databases and data warehouses? Why or why not?

3. Consider the differences and similarities among the four AI techniques discussed in this chapter. Name some problems that might be amenable to more than one type of AI system. Say you sell baseballs from your Web site. What types of AI systems could you use to generate information that would be useful to you in deciding what direction to take your company in the future? If you were pretty successful at selling baseballs, would you expect to have the amount of information on customers that, say, Wal-Mart has? Why or why not?

4. AI systems are relatively new approaches to solving business problems. What are the difficulties with new IT approaches in general? For each of the systems we discussed, identify some advantages and disadvantages of AI systems over traditional business processes. Say you were selling specialty teas and had both brick and click stores. Would you use the same type of AI systems for each part of your business? In what way would you use them or

why would you not? Is there a place for decision support and artificial intelligence techniques in small specialty businesses? In what way would decision support add value? Can you think of how a DSS or an AI system would be value reducing (in terms of the value chain concept we discussed in Chapter 2)? What do you see as the major differences between running a mammoth concern and a small specialty business?

5. Neural networks recognize and categorize patterns. If someone were to have a neural network that could scan information on all aspects of your life, where would that neural network potentially be able to find information about you? Consider confidential (doctor's office) as well as publicly available (department of motor vehicles) information.

6. What type of AI systems could your school use to help with registration? Intelligent agents find vast amounts of information very quickly. Neural networks can classify patterns instantaneously. What sorts of information might your school administration be able to generate using these (or other AI systems) with all of its student data?

7. For which activities that are part of college life could you use agent-based modeling to simulate what happens? Describe three such scenarios.

Finding Investment Opportunities on the Internet

When you buy stock in a company, you're betting on its success. Sometimes that bet is a good one, and sometimes it's not. Finding a company that's a good bet involves lots of research. To further complicate matters, some people prefer investing in large, safe companies, whereas others prefer the higher return of a small, more risky firm. So how do you make sense of all the options? Well, now you have access to financial information that professional investors use to evaluate stocks. The Internet brings together information-hungry investors with companies that have been anxiously looking to reach out to investors online. More than 900 companies now offer investment information on the World Wide Web, and the number is increasing rapidly. Remember, though, you must proceed with caution. Do your best to verify the source of any information.

You'll find many links on the Web site that supports this textbook (www.mhhe.com/haag, and select "Electronic Commerce Projects").

LEARNING ABOUT INVESTING

Investing can be as simple as finding a company that performs well financially and buying some of their stock. Or, if you want to spread your investment over a number of stocks and you don't want to select each stock personally, you can invest in a mutual fund. Of course, there are thousands of mutual funds with all types of investment objectives. So, any way you go you must pick your investment wisely. To help you get up to speed quickly, you'll find many helpful Web sites on the Internet.

For starters, you might explore the National Association of Securities Dealers (NASD) at www.nasdr.com. Check out their Investor Resources with its Education and Tools. You might also want to retrieve more general information from the online versions of traditional print media such as *The Wall Street Journal* or *Money* magazine.

Find three investment reference sites and explore what information is available. Then answer the following questions.

A. Is the site designed for first-time investors or those that are more experienced?

B. Can you search for a specific topic?

C. Are specific stocks or mutual funds reviewed or evaluated?

D. Does the site provide direct links to brokerage or stock quoting sites?

E. Is a forum for submitting questions available? If so, are frequently asked questions (FAQs) posted?

F. Who sponsors the site? Does it seem as if the sponsor is using the site to advertise its own products or services?

G. Can you download reference documents to read later?

RESEARCHING THE COMPANY BEHIND THE STOCK

One excellent way to pick a stock investment is to research the company behind that stock. Focusing on items such as sales revenues and profits to pick a stock is called *fundamental research*. So you might choose to invest in Hughes stock because you've discovered their sales revenues have been climbing steadily for the last three years. Or you might initially consider buying some Disney stock but change your mind when you find that EuroDisney revenues have been below expectations.

Now that you're ready to research a stock investment, connect to four different company sites. You can find your own or go to the Web site that supports this text where you will find a list of many other company sites. As you connect to the four sites, look up each company's financials and answer the questions that follow. You'll probably want to include at least two companies with which you are familiar and two that are new to you. In addition to reviewing company financials, look around each company site and see to what degree the site is investor oriented.

    A. Do all the company sites offer financial information?

    B. Is the information targeted at investors? How can you tell?

    C. Can you download financial information to your computer and use it in a spreadsheet?

    D. Can you download the company's annual report? Is it a full-color version?

    E. Does the site provide direct links to e-mail addresses for requesting additional information?

    F. Do the companies provide comparisons to others in their industry?

    G. Does the site provide stock quotes as well as financials?

    H. Can you search the site for financial-related information such as press releases?

    I. Was there a charge for retrieving the financial information?

RETRIEVING STOCK QUOTES

Once you find the right stock to buy, you'll then be asking yourself, How much will this stock cost me? Stocks and mutual funds are both offered by the share and so you can easily buy as much or as little of the stock or mutual fund as you like. Still, some individual shares are priced in the hundreds or thousands of dollars, and that alone might make the purchase undesirable to you.

In addition to pricing individual shares to assess the affordability of an investment, you'll probably want to see how the price has varied over time. Even though most financial advisors will tell you that historical price variations provide no indication of future performance, most everyone uses price history to get a feel for whether the investment is trading at all-time highs or lows. So finding a chart of a stock price online might be helpful when deciding to make your purchase.

And even after you've made your purchase, you'll probably want to follow how your investment is doing. The thrill of realizing a "paper profit" is enough to keep many investors checking their investments daily. Of course, realizing a "paper loss" can be equally disappointing. And even if daily tracking isn't for you, you'll certainly want to check on your investments regularly, and doing so online can be quick and painless.

Pick three stock quoting services, examine what it takes to retrieve a stock or mutual fund quote, and answer the following questions.

    A. Are the quotes provided free of charge or for a fee?

    B. Does the site require a ticker symbol (the abbreviation used by experienced investors) or can you type in a company name?

    C. Are the quotes in real time or are they delayed (15 to 20 minutes old)?

    D. Does the site require registration?

    E. Are historical prices available?

    F. Are price charts available? Can you customize the chart display?

    G. Can you create and save a personal portfolio of stocks?

EXTENDED LEARNING MODULE D

DECISION ANALYSIS WITH SPREADSHEET SOFTWARE

Student Learning Outcomes

1. DEFINE A LIST AND LIST DEFINITION TABLE WITHIN THE CONTEXT OF SPREADSHEET SOFTWARE AND DESCRIBE THE IMPORTANCE OF EACH.

2. COMPARE AND CONTRAST THE AUTOFILTER FUNCTION AND CUSTOM AUTOFILTER FUNCTION IN SPREADSHEET SOFTWARE.

3. DESCRIBE THE PURPOSE OF USING CONDITIONAL FORMATTING.

4. DEFINE A PIVOT TABLE AND DESCRIBE HOW YOU CAN USE IT TO VIEW SUMMARIZED INFORMATION BY DIMENSION.

Introduction

As you just read in Chapter 4, technology can and does play a vitally important role in both supporting decision making and, in some instances, actually making decisions or recommendations. In this module, we'll focus on decision-making support, by exploring many of the advanced and productive features of Microsoft Excel.

Microsoft Excel is spreadsheet software that allows you to work with any kind of information, with each individual piece of information located in a cell. A cell is the intersection of a row and column and is uniquely identified by its column character and row number. In Figure D.1 you can see two workbooks. The first (the one in the background) shows all the detailed information for a group of customers. The second shows the number of customers by region (North, South, East, and West) and by rent versus own.

There are a total of 487 customers (cell D9), of which 262 own a home (cell B9) and 225 rent (cell C9). Within this workbook, you can easily see some interesting information. For example, there are 148 customers in the East region while only 98 live in the South region. By region and ownership status, 82 own a home in the East region while only 47 rent in the South region.

Figure D.1

Number of Customers by Region and by Rent versus Own

Customers by region

Customers by rent versus own

Total number of customers

Of course, now the question becomes, How is that information helpful? Well, it depends on the nature of your decision-making task. If you believe that home owners spend more money than those who rent and want to target advertising to the largest region, the information in Figure D.1 might be helpful. Then again, it might not be. It could very well be that home owners actually spend less than customers who rent. And, perhaps you generate more sales in regions with a lower number of customers.

Let's see how spreadsheet software can help you make better decisions. As we do, we'll introduce you to some spreadsheet features including AutoFilter, conditional formatting, and pivot tables. Our goal here is not to provide in great detail how each of these work, but rather what's most important about each one of them in supporting your decision-making tasks. After completing this module, you'll definitely be able to use all features in their basic forms. We recommend that you continue to explore them in detail.

Lists

What we showed in Figure D.1 was a pivot table. A pivot table is a spreadsheet function that summarizes information by category. In our case, it summarized information by region and rent versus own. To create a pivot table (and use many of the other features we'll discuss in this module), you have to first build a list. You should work along with us on this. Connect to the Web site that supports this text (www.mhhe.com/haag and select XLM/D). There, you can download the file called **XLMD_Customer.xls.**

A *list* is a collection of information arranged in columns and rows in which each column displays one particular type of information. In spreadsheet software, a list possesses the following characteristics:

1. Each column has only one type of information.
2. The first row in the list contains the labels or column headings.
3. The list does not contain any blank rows.
4. The list is bordered on all four sides by blank rows and blank columns (it may not have a blank line above it, if it starts in the first row).

Figure D.2

The Complete List of Customers

Labels or column headings

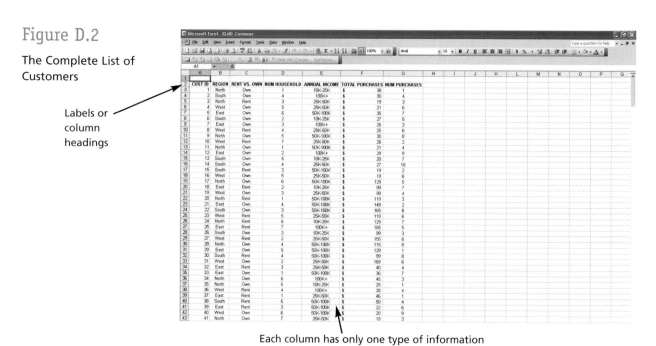

Each column has only one type of information

Take a look at the workbook in Figure D.2. It contains detailed information about our customers. In fact, we used this very list to generate the pivot table in Figure D.1.

First, notice that each column contains only one type of information: column A contains *CUST ID*, column B contains *REGION*, and so on. Second, notice that the first row (row 1) contains the labels or column headings. Third, if you scroll down completely through the list, you'll notice that there are 487 customers and there are no blank rows. Finally, notice that the list is bordered on all sides (except the top) by blank rows and columns. So, this is a list according to the four characteristics we listed.

We're going to be working extensively with this list throughout this module, so let's take a little time to explore the information in it. The columns of information include

A. *CUST ID*—A unique ID for each customer

B. *REGION*—The region in which the customer lives (North, South, East, or West)

C. *RENT VS. OWN*—Whether the customer rents or owns a home

D. *NUM HOUSEHOLD*—Number of family members in the household

E. *ANNUAL INCOME*—Total combined annual income of all family members

F. *TOTAL PURCHASES*—Dollar total of all purchases made by the customer within the last six months

G. *NUM PURCHASES*—Count of all purchases made by the customer within the last six months

What we listed above is called a **list definition table,** a description of a list by column. List definition tables are important. If you can create one just as we did, then you can create a list in a workbook with the appropriate characteristics. If you can't, then you may not be able to use many of the features we're about to show you.

With the good solid list in place, you're now ready to start exploring many of the decision support features in Excel. Let's assume that you work for our hypothetical retail company and have been asked to perform the following tasks to aid in various decisions:

1. Show all information for only customers who live in the North region.

2. Show all information for only customers who (a) live in the North region, (b) own their homes, and (c) have only one household member.

3. Show all information for customers who have at least 4 household members.

4. Show all information for customers who (a) have spent less than $20 or (b) more than $100.

5. Show all information for all customers highlighting those customers who have spent more than $100.

6. Provide a two-dimensional table that counts the number of customers by the categories of *REGION* and *RENT VS. OWN*.

7. Provide a two-dimensional table that both (a) counts the number of customers and (b) sums the *TOTAL PURCHASES* of customers by the categories of *REGION* and *RENT VS. OWN*.

8. Provide a three-dimensional table that counts the number of customers by the categories of *REGION*, *RENT VS. OWN*, and *NUM HOUSEHOLD*.

Basic AutoFilter

Working with small lists that can be displayed in their entirety on a screen is seldom a problem. With a small list you can see the entire domain of information without scrolling up or down. But our list is much larger, containing 487 customers. So, you have to scroll through it to see all the information. If you were looking for specific information, such as all the customers in the North region (your first task in the list on the previous page), you could sort using the *REGION* column but you still get all the information (not to mention that customers in the North would come after the customers in the East region, alphabetically).

To quickly create smaller lists out of a much larger list, you can use the AutoFilter function. The ***AutoFilter function*** filters a list and allows you to hide all the rows in a list except those that match criteria you specify. To filter a list with the AutoFilter function, perform the following steps (see Figure D.3):

1. Click in any cell within the list
2. From the menu bar, click on **Data,** point at **Filter,** and click on **AutoFilter**

Once you complete those two steps, Excel will place list box arrows next to each label or column heading. Now, all you have to do is click on the appropriate list box arrow and select the type of filtering you want. In Figure D.3, you can see that we clicked on the *REGION* list arrow box and chose North. Excel then presented us with a filtered list of only those customers in the North region. Our list is still quite long, but it does show only customers in the North. To turn off the AutoFilter function, from the menu bar, click on **Data,** point at **Filter,** and click on **AutoFilter.**

When using the AutoFilter function, you're not limited to working with just one column. In Figure D.3, we filtered using the *REGION* column. Now, what if you want a filtered list of those customers in the North who own a home and have only one household

Figure D.3

Using AutoFilter to See Customers in the North Region

Shows only customers in the North *REGION*

LISTS, LIST DEFINITION TABLES, AND USING AUTOFILTER

Now it's your turn to practice using the basic AutoFilter function on a list. Go to the Web site that supports this text (www.mhhe.com/haag), select XLM/D, and download the file called **XLMD_Customer2.xls**. Take a moment and review the information in that workbook.

First, in the table below, create the list definition for it just as we did on page 221.

Now perform the following AutoFilter exercises:

1. Show only those customers in the state of California.

2. Show only those customers whose type of business is nonprofit.

3. Show only those customers in the retail business sector.

4. Show only those customers in Texas whose type of business is government.

5. Show only those customers in the manufacturing business sector.

Column Name	Description

member (your second task in the list on page 221)? That's easy. Click in the *RENT VS. OWN* list arrow box and choose **Own.** Then, click in the *NUM HOUSEHOLD* list arrow box and choose **1.** That will show you the complete list (4 to be exact) of customers in the North who own a home and have only one household family member (see Figure D.4).

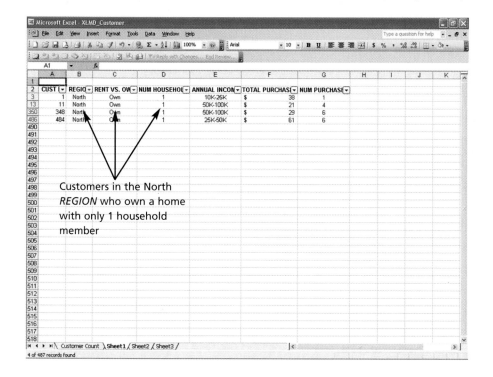

Customers in the North *REGION* who own a home with only 1 household member

Figure D.4

A List Generated with Three Filters

Custom AutoFilter

The basic AutoFilter function allows you to create sublists using exact match criteria: *REGION* must be North, *NUM HOUSEHOLD* must be 1, and so forth. But what if you want to know all those customers who have at least four people in their households (your third task in the list on page 221)? In that case, you can't use the basic AutoFilter function—you need to use the Custom AutoFilter function. The ***Custom AutoFilter function*** allows you to hide all the rows in a list except those that match criteria, besides "is equal to," you specify. Let's see how to use the Custom AutoFilter function.

Figure D.5

Using a Custom AutoFilter

Only customers with more than four people in their households

Given that you want to see a list of all customers who have at least four people in their households, perform the following steps:

1. Make sure you can see the entire list with the AutoFilter function turned on
2. Click on the *NUM HOUSEHOLD* list arrow box
3. Select **(Custom . . .)**

What you'll then see is a Custom AutoFilter box (the top-right box in Figure D.5 on the previous page). For the top-left entry field, click on its pull-down arrow and select **is greater than.** For the top-right entry box, click on its pull-down arrow and select **3** (or type the number **3** directly into the box). Then, all you have to do is click on **OK.** Excel does the rest and shows you the appropriate list of customers with at least four people in their households.

You should notice in Figure D.5 that the Custom AutoFilter box allows you to enter two criteria for creating a filtered list. So, you can easily create a Custom AutoFilter that answers the following question: What customers have spent less than $20 or more than $100 in the past six months (your fourth task in the list on page 221)? In Figure D.6, we've shown you how to do that along with the result.

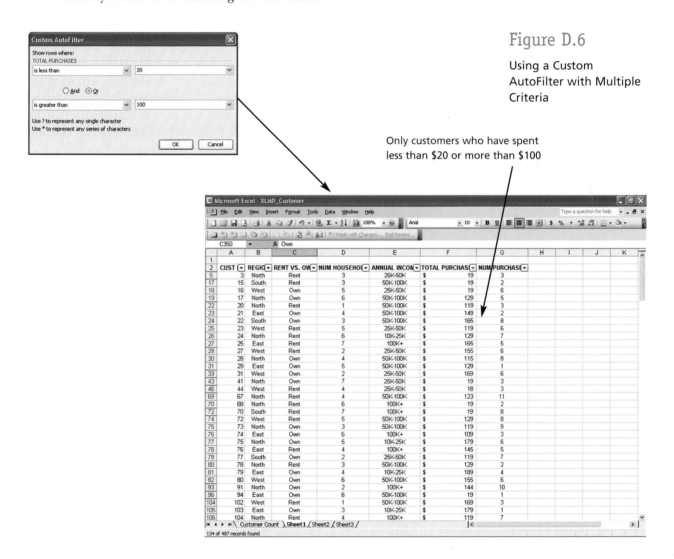

Figure D.6

Using a Custom AutoFilter with Multiple Criteria

Only customers who have spent less than $20 or more than $100

USING CUSTOM AUTOFILTERS

Now it's your turn to practice using the Custom Auto-Filter function on a list. Go to the Web site that supports this text (www.mhhe.com/haag), select XLM/D, and download the file called **XLMD_Customer2.xls** (the same one you used previously for the On Your Own project). Now perform the following Custom AutoFilter exercises:

1. Show only those customers who have more than 100 employees.

2. Show only those customers who have fewer than 100 employees.

3. Show only those customers who have at least 50 employees but no more than 100 employees.

4. Show only those customers in Tennessee who have fewer than 10 employees.

Conditional Formatting

When you use AutoFilter (either basic or custom), in a way you're highlighting information you want to see by basically hiding the other information you don't. As an alternative, you might want to highlight certain information while still being able to see all the other information. If so, you can use conditional formatting. *Conditional formatting* highlights the information in a cell that meets some criteria you specify.

For example, what if you still wanted to be able to scroll through the entire list of customers but also wanted to have all *TOTAL PURCHASES* greater than $100 highlighted (your fifth task in the list on page 221). This is a simple process in Excel. To do that, perform the following steps (see Figure D.7):

1. Select the entire *TOTAL PURCHASES* column (move the pointer over the F column identifier and click once)

2. From the menu bar, click on **Format** and then click on **Conditional Formatting**

You will then see a Conditional Formatting box as shown in the middle-left of Figure D.7.

Now, click on the pull-down arrow for the field second from the left and click on **greater than.** In the field on the right, enter **100.** Finally, you need to select the conditional formatting for the information. To do so, click on the **Format** button. You will then see a Format Cells box. Across the top, you'll see tabs for Font, Border, and Patterns.

In our example, we clicked on the Patterns tab, chose the color red, and clicked on **OK.** Excel returned us to the Conditional Formatting box at which time we clicked on the **OK** button. As you can see in Figure D.8, Excel left the list intact and highlighted all cells in the *TOTAL PURCHASES* column in which the value exceeded $100.

To remove conditional formatting, first highlight the entire column again. Second, from the menu bar, click on **Format** and click on **Conditional Formatting.** Third, click on the **Delete** button in the Conditional Formatting box. Fourth, select **Condition 1** in the Delete Conditional Format box. Finally, click on **OK** in the Delete Conditional Format box, and click on **OK** in the Conditional Format box.

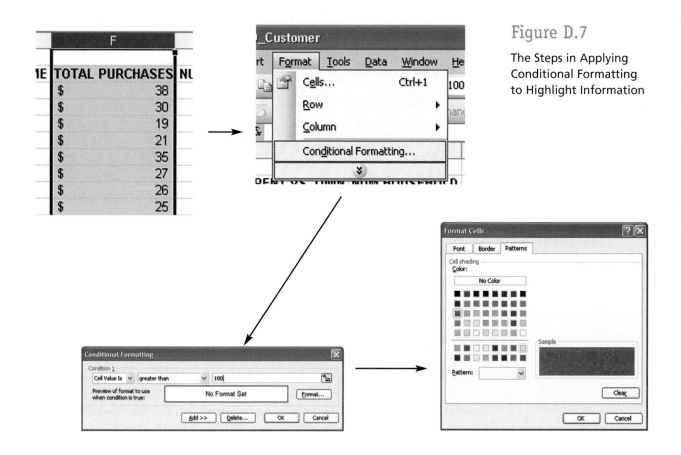

Figure D.7

The Steps in Applying Conditional Formatting to Highlight Information

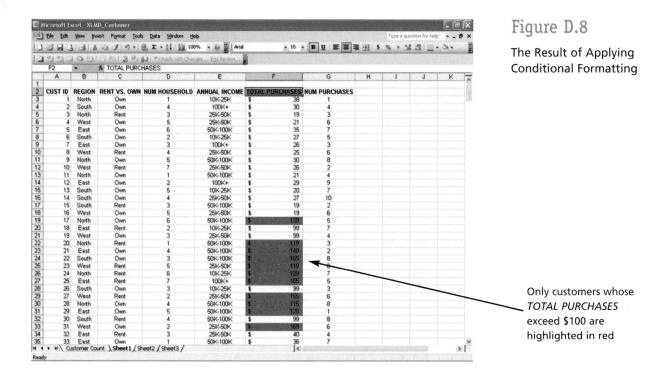

Figure D.8

The Result of Applying Conditional Formatting

Only customers whose *TOTAL PURCHASES* exceed $100 are highlighted in red

CONDITIONAL FORMATTING

On the Web site that supports this text (www.mhhe.com/haag and select XLMD), we've provided a workbook titled **XLMD_Production.xls.** It contains information concerning batches of products produced. Each batch is produced using only one machine by one employee. For each batch, a batch size is provided as well as the number of defective products produced in the batch.

Highlight the following by applying conditional formatting:

1. All batches made by Employee 1111.
2. All batches for which the number of defective products is greater than 10.
3. All batches for which the batch size is greater than 1,000.
4. All batches for Product 10.

Pivot Tables

Now, let's return to our original pivot table in Figure D.1 on page 219. Formally defined, a **pivot table** enables you to group and summarize information. That's just what we did in Figure D.1. We created a two-dimensional pivot table that displayed a count of customers by *REGION* and by *RENT VS. OWN* (your sixth task in the list on page 221). Of all the Excel decision-support features we demonstrate in this module, pivot tables take the most steps to create, but they also tend to yield highly valuable information.

To create a two-dimensional pivot table, first ensure that your list has no conditional formatting and that you do not have the AutoFilter function turned on. To create any two-dimensional pivot table, follow the four steps at the top of the next page (and see Figure D.9).

Figure D.9

The First Steps in Creating a Two-Dimensional Pivot Table

1. From the menu bar, click on **Data** and **PivotTable and PivotChart Report**
2. In the Step 1 of 3 box, click on **Next**
3. In the Step 2 of 3 box, click on **Next**
4. In the Step 3 of 3 box, click on **Finish**

What you will then see is the skeletal structure of a pivot table as shown in Figure D.10.

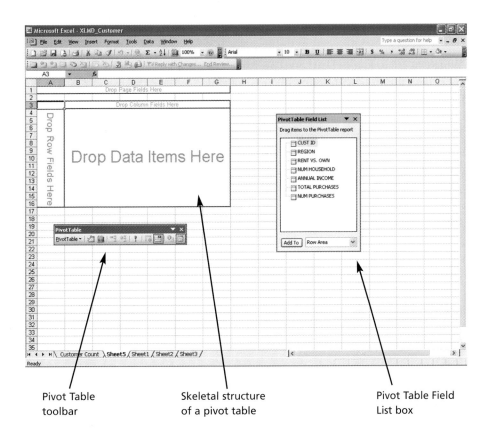

Pivot Table
toolbar

Skeletal structure
of a pivot table

Pivot Table Field
List box

Figure D.10

The Skeletal Structure of
a Pivot Table and the
Pivot Table Toolbar

BUTTON NAME	PURPOSE
PivotTable	Drop-down that displays shortcut menu of pivot table commands
Format Report	Displays a list of pivot table report styles
Chart Wizard	Creates a chart sheet from a pivot table
MapPoint	Creates map from PivotTable data
Hide Detail	Hides detail lines of a pivot table field
Show Detail	Reveals detail lines of a pivot table field
Refresh Data	Updates a pivot table
Include Hidden Items in Total	Items you have hidden are still counted in the PivotTable totals
Always Display Items	Controls when Excel goes to an external data source to determine a pivot table value
Field Settings	Opens the PivotTable field dialog box containing options you can apply to the selected pivot table field
Hide/Show Field Test	Toggles between hiding and displaying the field list

To provide a brief explanation of what we've done so far, let's examine the three dialog boxes in Figure D.9 on page 228. The first box allows you to choose the location of the information from which you want to build a pivot table. We wanted to use an Excel list so we accepted the default. The first box also gives you the ability to choose between creating a pivot table or a pivot table chart. We wanted a pivot table so we accepted the default.

The second box allows you to choose a range of information from which to build a pivot table. The default is the entire list, which we accepted. Finally, the third box allows you to specify a location for the pivot table. The default is a new worksheet, which we accepted. At some point in time, you should explore the various other options.

What you see in Figure D.10 on page 229 takes some more explaining. In the upper left portion is the skeletal structure of the pivot table. To the right, you can see the Pivot Table Field List box. It includes a list of all the labels or column headings we have in the list.

Near the bottom left, you can see the Pivot Table toolbar. It includes numerous buttons for different functions. The primary one of interest to us now is the **Field Settings** button, the second button from the right in the toolbar. Figure D.10 lists and explains all the buttons in the Pivot Table toolbar.

What you do now is to drag and drop the appropriate labels or columns headings from the Pivot Table Field List box into the appropriate areas of the pivot table itself.

Recall that we are attempting to build a two-dimensional pivot table that looks like the one in Figure D.1 on page 219. So, you know that the row information is by *REGION*. To achieve this, drag the *REGION* label from the Pivot Table Field List box to the pivot table and drop it into the area marked "Drop Row Fields Here" (see Figure D.11). You also know that the column information is by *RENT VS. OWN*. So, drag that label from the Pivot Table Field List box and drop it into the area marked "Drop Column Fields Here."

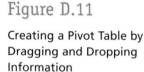

Figure D.11

Creating a Pivot Table by Dragging and Dropping Information

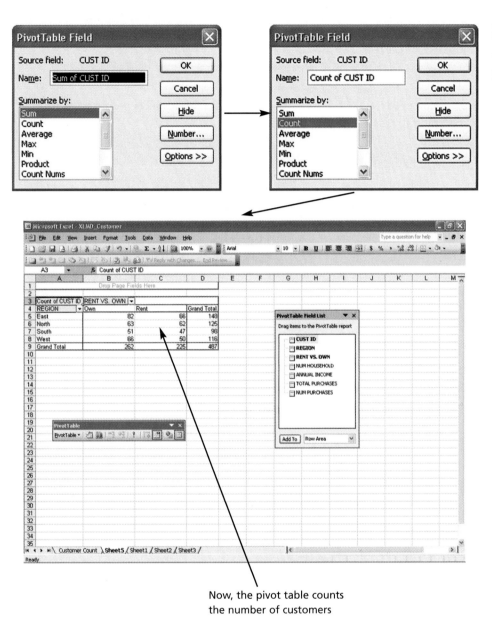

Now, the pivot table counts
the number of customers

Finally, you need to place something in the main area of the pivot table that will en-able you to count customers by region and rent versus own. The simplest way to achieve this is to drag *CUST ID* from the Pivot Table Field List box and drop it into the area marked "Drop Data Items Here." What you will then have is a pivot table that looks like the screen in Figure D.11, on page 230, which is not at all what we want. Why?

When you drop information into the main area of a pivot table, the default aggrega-tion or summarization is by summation. You don't want to sum customer IDs—that doesn't make any sense. What you want to do is count them. To change this, perform the following steps (see Figure D.12):

1. Click on the **Field Settings** button in the Pivot Table toolbar
2. In the PivotTable Field box, click on **Count** in the **Summarize by** list
3. Click on **OK**

The final screen in Figure D.12 shows the correct information.

CREATING A TWO-DIMENSIONAL PIVOT TABLE

Let's return to our workbook containing production information (**XLMD_Production.xls**). Using it, create separate pivot tables that show

- The number of different machines used to produce each product

- The number of defective products produced by employee by product

- The total number of products produced by each employee

- The total number of products produced by each employee as well as the total number of defective products produced by each employee

We now have a pivot table that shows a count of customers by *REGION* and *RENT VS. OWN.* But depending on what decision you're trying to make, that may not be enough information. What else might be helpful? Again, depending on the decision, it might be helpful to also know the total of all purchases by *REGION* and *RENT VS. OWN* (your seventh task in the list on page 221). If so, you don't need to create another pivot table. You can simply add the field *TOTAL PURCHASES* to the main area of the pivot table. To do so, drag that label from the Pivot Table Field List box and drop it into the main area of the pivot table. Figure D.13 shows the result.

Figure D.13

An Added Field of Information to a Pivot Table

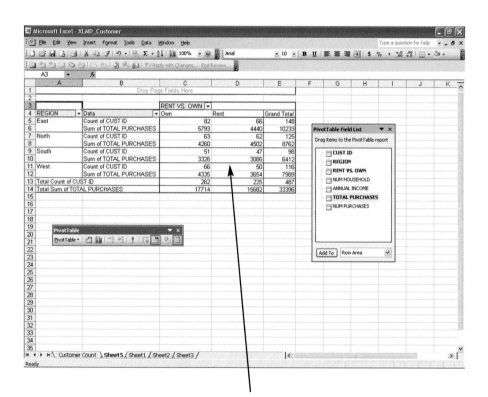

Drag and drop *TOTAL PURCHASES* here to obtain a summary of another dimension of information

Is the information helpful? Again, it depends on the decision you're trying to make. But adding another piece of information to the main area of a pivot table is easy, and it does illustrate the true productivity of spreadsheet software.

Your final task in the list on page 221 is to create a three-dimensional pivot table that counts the number of customers by the categories of *REGION, RENT VS. OWN,* and *NUM HOUSEHOLD.* The result will look similar to the two-dimensional pivot table in Figure D.13 with two exceptions. First, you will not include the sum of *TOTAL PURCHASES* in the main area of the pivot table. Second, you will add depth to the pivot table, making it a three-dimensional pivot table. In short, you do this by dragging the *NUM HOUSEHOLD* label from the Pivot Table Field List box to the pivot table and dropping it into the area marked "Drop Page Fields Here."

In Figure D.14, you can see in the upper left screen that we created a two-dimensional pivot table showing a count of customers by *REGION* and *RENT VS. OWN.* This is the same two-dimensional pivot table we created in Figure D.12 on page 231. To add depth to the pivot table, we dragged the *NUM HOUSEHOLD* label from the Pivot Table Field List box to the pivot table and dropped it into the area marked "Drop Page Fields Here." Notice that the new pivot table (the lower right screen in Figure D.14) still looks like a two-dimensional pivot table and provides the same information in the main area of the pivot table. That's because the default display for a three-dimensional pivot table is to show all summarized information for the depth. You can tell this because to the right of *NUM HOUSEHOLD* in cell A1 is the word "All."

Figure D.14

Creating a Three-Dimensional Pivot Table

The current depth dimension is for "all" customers, regardless of how many members are in a household.

Figure D.15

Viewing Different Depths in a Three-Dimensional Pivot Table

Click on the *NUM HOUSEHOLD* pull-down arrow to see your depth options.

By selecting 4 in the *NUM HOUSEHOLD* depth dimension, you see a summary of customers for only that criteria.

To view the count of your customers by specific values for *NUM HOUSEHOLD*, simply click on the list box arrow immediately to the right of the word "All" as we did in the top screen in Figure D.15. You then click on the value you want in *NUM HOUSEHOLD* for displaying the count of customers for that value by *REGION* and *RENT VS. OWN*. We clicked on 4 and then **OK**. The bottom screen in Figure D.15 shows the result. It shows some interesting information that might help you make a decision. For example, in the West region there are 20 customers who own their homes and only 11 who rent their homes. Furthermore, across all regions there are 66 customers who own their homes and only 40 who rent. Again, is this helpful information? That depends on the decision you're trying to make.

The three-dimensional pivot table feature in Excel is a powerful one. If you recall our discussions of data warehouses in Chapter 3, you can actually build a data warehouse with rows, columns, and layers by simply creating a three-dimensional pivot table in Excel. By selecting different values for the page (depth) field, you are actually bringing layers of information to the front.

Back to Decision Support

Let's take a break from the computer for a moment and discuss what we've just demonstrated within the context of decision support. After all, you don't need to learn the various tools of spreadsheet software just because "they are there." You should learn them because they will be beneficial to you.

In general, the spreadsheet features we've just shown you give you the ability to look at vast amounts of information quickly. Indeed, our customer workbook contained information on 487 customers. Can you imagine trying to summarize or aggregate information on 48,700 customers without the use of spreadsheet software? Even creating simple totals and subtotals would be a daunting task.

AUTOFILTER

The AutoFilter function (either basic or custom) helps you quickly create a view of a partial list of information. The basic AutoFilter function creates a partial list based on exact match criteria, while the custom AutoFilter function allows you to specify ranges (e.g., greater than, less than, and so on).

The purpose of the AutoFilter function is really to help you quickly focus on only the information that's important to you by "hiding" the information that isn't. It's rather like having a very good search engine that gives you only a list of useful articles to help you write a term paper.

CONDITIONAL FORMATTING

Conditional formatting maintains the view of the entire list of information but highlights key pieces of information that you may be looking for. This gives you the ability to see the entire list of information but quickly draws your attention to specific information.

PIVOT TABLE

A pivot table (either two- or three-dimensional) helps you quickly aggregate or summarize information by *dimension*. This gives you a nice overview of the information without bogging you down in any of the details.

Further, a pivot table can help you see relationships among the information. If you look back at the pivot table in Figure D.13 on page 232, you can see the relationship between the number of customers and their total purchases within *REGION* and *RENT VS. OWN*. These types of relationships can certainly be insightful.

Can any of these tools or functions make a decision for you? Definitely not. But they can help you make that decision. That's why spreadsheet software is often called *decision support* software.

Summary: Student Learning Outcomes Revisited

1. **Define a list and list definition table within the context of spreadsheet software and describe the importance of each.** A *list* is a collection of information arranged in columns and rows in which each column displays one particular type of information. A *list definition table* is a description of a list by column. Lists are important within the context of spreadsheet software because they enable you to use such spreadsheet features as AutoFilter, conditional formatting, and pivot tables. Creating a list definition table is important because it requires you to adhere to the necessary rules for creating a list.

2. **Compare and contrast the AutoFilter function and Custom AutoFilter function in spreadsheet software.** The *AutoFilter function* filters a list and allows you to hide all the rows in a list except those that match specific criteria you specify. The *Custom AutoFilter function* allows you to hide all the rows in a list except those that match

criteria, besides "is equal to," you specify. So, the basic AutoFilter function makes use of "is equal to" as the criteria, while the Custom AutoFilter function allows you to use other criteria such as greater than, less than, and so on.

3. **Describe the purpose of using conditional formatting.** *Conditional formatting* highlights the information in a cell that meets some criteria you specify. So, conditional formatting allows you to view the entire list while having certain information called to your attention.

4. **Define a pivot table and describe how you can use it to view summarized information by dimension.** A *pivot table* enables you to group and summarize information. When creating a pivot table, you create dimensions of information by specifying how information is to be summarized by dimension. You define the dimensions by dragging and dropping information labels or column headings into the row, column, and page areas of a pivot table.

Key Terms and Concepts

AutoFilter function, 222
Conditional formatting, 226
Custom AutoFilter function, 224

List, 220
List definition table, 221
Pivot table, 228

Assignments and Exercises

1. **WHAT PRODUCTION PROBLEMS DO YOU HAVE?** Throughout this module, you've been practicing some spreadsheet features using **XLMD_Production.xls.** Its list definition table is as follows:
   A. *BATCH*—A unique number that identifies each batch or group of products produced
   B. *PRODUCT*—A unique number that identifies each product
   C. *MACHINE*—A unique number that identifies each machine on which products are produced
   D. *EMPLOYEE*—A unique number that identifies each employee producing products
   E. *BATCH SIZE*—The number of products produced in a given batch
   F. *NUM DEFECTIVE*—The number of defective products produced in a given batch
   It seems you have some real problems. There are an unacceptable number of defective products being produced. Your task is to use some combination of AutoFilter, conditional formatting, and pivot tables to illustrate where the problems seem to be concentrated, perhaps by product, by employee, by machine, or even by batch size. Based on your analysis, recommend how to correct the problems.

2. **EVALUATING TOTAL PURCHASES AND ANNUAL INCOME** Using **XLMD_Customer.xls,** create a pivot table that illustrates the relationship between *TOTAL PURCHASES* and *ANNUAL INCOME.* What trends do you see in the information? Suppose your task is to concentrate marketing efforts and resources. On which annual income level would you concentrate? Why? If you were the marketing manager, what additional information would be helpful as you make your decision? Where would you be able to obtain such information?

3. **FINDING OUT INFORMATION ABOUT YOUR EMPLOYEES** Suppose you own a small business and have a workbook with the following list:

A. *ID*—Unique employee's identification number

B. *First Name*—Employee's first name

C. *Last Name*—Employee's last name

D. *Department*—Employee's department

E. *Title*—Employee's job title

F. *Salary*—Employee's annual salary

G. *Hire Date*—Date employee was hired

H. *Birth Date*—Employee's birthday

I. *Gender*—Female (F) or male (M)

J. *Clearance*—N (none), C (confidential), S (secret), or TS (top secret)

You can obtain this workbook from the Web site that supports this text (www.mhhe.com/haag and select XLM/D). Its filename is **XLMD_Employee.xls.** Perform the following tasks:

a. Create a pivot table that shows average salary by gender within department.

b. Create a pivot table that shows the number of employees by clearance.

c. Use conditional formatting to highlight those employees in the Engineering department.

d. Use conditional formatting to highlight those employees who have no clearance (none).

e. Use basic AutoFilter to show only those employees who have top secret clearance (TS).

f. Use Custom AutoFilter to show only those employees who earn more than $50,000.

4. **EXPLORING INFORMATION AT B&B TRAVEL** Benjamin Travis and Brady Austin are co-owners of B&B Travel Consultants, a medium-size business in Seattle with several branch offices. B&B specializes in selling cruise packages. Ben and Brady maintain a workbook that contains the following list for each cruise package sale:

A. *LOCATION #*—A unique number that identifies which office location recorded the sale

B. *TRAVEL AGENT #*—A unique number that identifies which travel consultant recorded the sale

C. *CRUISE LINE*—The name of the cruise line for which the package was sold

D. *TOTAL PACKAGE PRICE*—The price charged to the customer for the package

E. *COMMISSION*—The amount of money B&B made from the sale of the package

Ben and Brady have decided to scale back their operations. So, they're looking to you for help. The workbook name is **XLMD_Travel.xls** and you can find it on the Web site that supports this text at www.mhhe.com/haag (select XLM/D). Using AutoFilter, conditional formatting, and pivot tables, prepare a short report that answers each of the following questions and illustrates the justification for your answers.

a. Which, if any, location should be closed?

b. Which, if any, travel consultants should be downsized?

c. On which cruise lines should B&B focus its sales efforts?

5. **CREATE A LIST FOR A BOOKSTORE** Suppose that you're the manager for your school's bookstore. Your task is to create a list in a workbook that contains information about the textbooks it sells. In addition to tracking price, first author name, and publisher, identify five other pieces of information for each textbook. For this list, first provide a list definition table. Second, enter some information for 20 textbooks. Third, illustrate the use of the basic AutoFilter function, the Custom AutoFilter function, conditional formatting, and pivot tables. Finally, address how your bookstore might be able to use this information to support its decision-making tasks.

CHAPTER FIVE OUTLINE

STUDENT LEARNING OUTCOMES

1. Define and describe the two major e-commerce business models (Business to Business and Business to Consumer).

2. Describe the emerging role of e-marketplaces in B2B e-commerce.

3. Identify the differences and similarities among customers and their perceived value of products and services in the B2B and B2C e-commerce business models.

4. Compare and contrast the development of a marketing mix for customers in the B2B and B2C e-commerce business models.

5. Summarize the various ways of moving money in the world of e-commerce and related issues.

6. Define and describe the major e-commerce government models.

INDUSTRY PERSPECTIVES

243 **Gathering Consumers at Epinions.com**

249 **Small Companies Can Benefit from Integrated B2B E-Commerce and Supply Chain Management**

256 **Spoofing eBay Customers to Get Credit Card Information**

264 **Buying Electronic Savings Bonds at TreasuryDirect**

FEATURES

246 **On Your Own**
Your Perception of Product and Service Value

247 **Global Perspective**
The World beyond United States' Borders Is Where the E-Money Is

252 **Global Perspective**
A Global Partnership to Create Global Partnering Opportunities

253 **On Your Own**
Developing a Marketing Mix Strategy for Monster.com

260 **Team Work**
Defining Your Business to Consumer E-Commerce Business

265 **Team Work**
Exploring the World of E-Government

274 **Electronic Commerce**
Getting Your Business on the Internet

WEB SUPPORT

www.mhhe.com/haag

- Competitive intelligence
- Storefront software
- Hosting services
- Marketing your site

CHAPTER FIVE

Electronic Commerce
Strategies for the New Economy

OPENING CASE STUDY:
IS AMERICA ONLINE (AOL) INCHING TOWARD BECOMING AN INTERNET BANK?

In March 2004, America Online (AOL) launched a streamlined new service for online bill payment. No—it doesn't yet provide the capability to pay online bills directly through AOL, but it does seem to be a step by AOL toward making that a reality.

The service—called *AOL Bill Pay*—is free to all AOL members and is provided through an alliance with Yodlee.com, Inc. (www.yodlee.com), a company that provides a variety of online personal financial services. After AOL members sign up for the service, they will receive summaries of their online bills via AOL e-mail messages. The messages will include links directly to the business e-commerce Web sites where members can make their payments.

A nice feature of AOL Bill Pay is that it creates a single portal (the AOL account) with only one user ID and one password. Once inside his or her AOL account, an AOL member does not have to enter a new ID and password at any of the e-commerce Web sites.

AOL members can configure AOL Bill Pay to provide alerts in several different forms: e-mail, instant messaging, or a text-based message to a cell phone. The system can also trigger an alert that is more of a warning message when, for example, an AOL member's bank account balance drops below a certain limit or a credit card transaction exceeds a prespecified amount. It is AOL's hope that its members will see these types of alerts and warnings as value-added services.

AOL Bill Pay connects directly to over 2,500 Web sites that offer bill paying over the Internet. If a certain AOL member makes payments to a Web site not on AOL Bill Pay's list, AOL can easily add the Web site to the list.

Even so, some users may be wary of using such a service. According to Patrick Mahoney, an analyst with The Yankee Group, "Some people may prefer going to individual Web sites instead of having the one password access to everything." But Patrick does think this is a good business model for AOL. He explains, "Although some companies provide this type of service, the market isn't overcrowded and existing offerings haven't been highly publicized. It's not like AOL is coming into a market with a lot of competition."

Just like in the traditional brick-and-mortar business environment, in the world of e-commerce you must constantly strive to stay ahead of the competition. You have to determine innovative ways in which to offer products and services that your customers will perceive add value. You must constantly evaluate industry segments and competitive spaces to determine if there is a lack of competition where you might enter.

In this chapter you'll explore the world of e-commerce, and we'll introduce you to many "special" considerations that you must take into account to be successful. Commerce will always be commerce—the buying and selling of products and services. But the "e" in e-commerce presents new challenges and opportunities.[1,2]

Introduction

You've probably heard the ancient Chinese curse, "May you live in interesting times." It's a curse because it is often easier to live in times that are not so interesting, when things move along pretty much as expected, as they always have. The past 10 years of the new economy introduced by the World Wide Web have certainly been interesting. There has been an entrepreneurial frenzy unlike anything the world has ever seen. Fortunes have been made and lost. Dot-com millionaires and billionaires were literally created overnight—many became dot-bomb paupers in about the same amount of time.

What fueled this frenzy and is still doing so today? It's electronic commerce enabled by information technology. ***Electronic commerce (e-commerce)*** is commerce, but it is commerce accelerated and enhanced by IT, in particular the Internet. E-commerce enables customers, consumers, and companies to form powerful new relationships that would not be possible without the enabling technologies. E-commerce breaks down business barriers such as time, geography, language, currency, and culture. In a few short hours, you can set up shop on the Internet and be instantly accessible to millions of consumers worldwide. The Internet facilitates commerce because of its awesome ability to move digital information at low cost.

Is there a catch? The answer is both no and yes. It's "no" because it doesn't take much effort to create your own e-commerce Web site. It's "yes" because you still have to follow sound business fundamentals and principles to be successful. Let's not forget that fundamentally it's still all about commerce, businesses and people buying and selling products and services. E-commerce is no "silver bullet," as some entrepreneurs have found out to their chagrin. You must know your competition; you must have insight into your customers' demographics and buying habits; you must offer your products and services at a superior price or at a superior level of service to beat the competition; you must make a profit.

As illustrated in Figure 5.1, there are four main perspectives for e-commerce in the private sector: Business to Business (B2B), Business to Consumer (B2C), Consumer to Business (C2B), and Consumer to Consumer (C2C). We'll focus on B2C and B2B in this chapter as they represent the greatest percentage of revenue dollars in e-commerce. Another emerging and important player is governments—we'll look at the explosion of e-government at the end of this chapter.

To succeed in the e-commerce environment, you must develop a strategic position and execute your business operations well. After introducing you to the basics of the B2B and B2C e-commerce perspectives, we'll cover three e-commerce critical success

Figure 5.1

Four Perspectives of Private-Sector E-Commerce

Web Usage by Number of Homes in Top 9 Countries[3]

Country	November 2004	February 2005	% Change
United States	137,996,052	137,827,206	−1.57 %
Germany	29,500,717	29,864,949	1.23
United Kingdom	22,281,069	24,800,954	11.31
France	15,582,952	15,837,988	1.64
Brazil	11,444,102	11,032,316	−3.60
Australia	8,918,141	9,194,242	3.10
Spain	8,353,284	8,824,941	5.65
Switzerland	3,339,753	3,349,881	0.30
Hong Kong	2,539,657	2,602,738	2.48
Total	244,582,851	245,827,225	0.51

Browser Ranking and Market Share[4]

Browser	January 2005		April 2005		% Change
	Rank	% Share	Rank	% Share	
Internet Explorer	1	84.85 %	1	83.07 %	−1.78 %
Mozilla	2	4.48	2	3.81	−0.66
Firefox	3	4.23	3	10.28	6.05
Netscape	4	3.03	4	0.92	−2.11
AOL	5	2.20	5	0.85	−1.35
MSN	6	0.58	6	0.67	0.09
Opera	7	0.34	7	0.41	0.07

Top Search Engines by Queries in January 2005[5]

Search Engine	Search (in thousands)	% Share
Google Search	1,923,153	47%
Yahoo! Search	868,174	21%
MSN Search	523,188	13%

Cell Phone Text Messaging Users by Age[7]

Age	Designation	% Cell Phone Owners Using Text Messaging
18–27	Generation X	63 %
28–39	Generation X	31
40–49	Baby Boomer	18
50–59	Baby Boomer	13
60+	N/A	7

Top 10 Online Retailers Based on Conversion Rate, February 2005[6]

e-Commerce Site	Conversion Rate (%)
QVC	16.3 %
Land's End	14.8
sportsmansguide.com	13.5
FTD.com	13.4
llbean.com	13.4
Amazon	12.8
Coldwater Creek	12.7
eBay	12.3
Yahoo! Shopping	12.1
proflowers.com	11.8

Top 10 Internet Advertisers in April 2005[8]

Position	Advertiser	Expenditures ($000)	Sector
1	Tickle by Emode	$23,770	Dating
2	Vonage	21,829	Technology
3	South Beach Diet	18,607	Health
4	LowerMyBills.com	14,124	Finance
5	HP VAR Computers	13,874	Technology
6	Netflix.com	12,508	Entertainment
7	Classmates.com	10,137	Miscellaneous
8	Verizon ISP	8,506	Technology
9	University of Phoenix Online	8,867	Education
10	TitanTV.com	6,553	Entertainment

Figure 5.2

What's Happening in the World of E-Commerce?

factors: (1) Understand your business and your customers; (2) find and establish relationships with customers; (3) move money easily and securely. There are many other success factors, but these three in particular will help you execute your business operations well. We then turn our attention to e-commerce in the government arena.

E-Commerce Business Models

Of all the variations of e-commerce business models to be found operating in the real world today, Business to Business (B2B) is the most lucrative area. Business to Consumer (B2C) e-commerce, on the other hand, is the most well-known in everyday life.

- *Business to Business (B2B) e-commerce* occurs when a business sells products and services to customers who are primarily other businesses.
- *Business to Consumer (B2C) e-commerce* occurs when a business sells products and services to customers who are primarily individuals.

So, for example, when Gates Rubber Company sells belts, hoses, and other rubber and synthetic products to General Motors or any other manufacturer that needs those parts, this is B2B e-commerce. B2C e-commerce, on the other hand, is all about the commerce between a business and an individual end consumer—you, for example, when you buy a music CD from Circuit City online at www.circuitcity.com.

B2B e-commerce is where all the money is right now, accounting for approximately 97 percent of all e-commerce revenues. Business organizations have realized that there are tremendous efficiencies and potential savings from innovations in doing business electronically. Businesses can shorten cycle times and reduce costs in the supply chain. They can more effectively reach a wider audience of potential customers (other businesses, in this case). Via the Web they can reduce traditional barriers such as time, location, language, and currency. But probably, like most people, you are more familiar with B2C e-commerce. Have you ever bought something on the Internet? B2C e-commerce is typically what you hear about on television or read about in such periodicals as *PC Magazine* and *Wired*.

It's important for you to understand in which environment your organization operates—either in B2B or in B2C (or perhaps a combination of the two), as there are significant differences. Businesses in one area or the other employ different tactics, electronically speaking. For example, as you can see in Figure 5.3, businesses participating in B2B e-commerce are taking advantage of electronic marketplaces, or e-marketplaces. B2B e-marketplaces are virtual marketplaces in which businesses buy and sell products, share information, and perform other important activities. B2B e-marketplaces include many variations such as vertical e-marketplaces, horizontal e-marketplaces, value-added network providers, and many others.

B2B e-marketplaces represent one of the fastest growing trends in the B2B e-commerce model. Businesses are increasingly aware that they must create supply chain management systems, drive out costs, create information partnerships with other businesses, and even collaborate with other businesses on new product and service offerings. B2B e-marketplaces offer tremendous efficiencies to businesses for performing all of these tasks.

Consumers, on the other hand, in the B2C e-commerce business model tend to deal directly with a chosen business on the Internet (see Figure 5.3). That is, consumers usually surf the Web evaluating products and services at numerous separate e-commerce Web sites until they eventually choose one site from which to make a purchase. That is not to say that consumers don't have access to or use e-marketplaces. eBay is a good example of an e-marketplace for consumers, where you can buy and sell just about any-

GATHERING CONSUMERS AT EPINIONS.COM

Epinions.com (www.epinions.com) "helps people make informed buying decisions." It bills itself as "the Web's premier consumer reviews platform and the most reliable source for valuable consumer insight, unbiased advice, in-depth product evaluations and personalized recommendations." In short, it is a special sort of Business to Consumer (B2C) e-marketplace where consumers gather to read each other's opinions.

Epinions.com actively solicits product reviews from its customer base. It doesn't edit the reviews in any way (unless the comments are slanderous or vulgar). That way, you get unbiased and unedited reviews of products you're considering for purchase. On the basis of those reviews, Epinions.com provides a rating of each product anywhere from one to five stars.

Epinions.com will help you find other consumers with tastes and needs similar to your own. You can learn what they purchased and why. This information can help you decide what to buy because you learn what other people have bought who have needs like yours.

Suppose you have determined a particular product to

buy, and have heard of a Web site that sells it. Epinions.com provides you with comparative shopping information in an easy-to-read table that includes such information as the e-commerce Web site name and a link to it, the address of the e-commerce Web site, the Web site's rating, the product price, tax and shipping, total price, and any other product notes such as "in stock" or "currently on backorder."

After you have made your purchase, Epinions.com encourages you to visit its site again and provide your own product review. That information then becomes additional information the next consumer will use.

Epinions.com, and many other B2C e-marketplaces, represent a growing new trend supporting e-gathering places for consumers on the Web. How do these sites make money? It's simple. If you link to an e-commerce Web site from Epinions.com to make a purchase, that e-commerce Web site gives Epinions.com a commission from the sale. It's an interesting and effective "e-referral" business model.[9]

thing you want. As an e-marketplace, eBay brings together many buyers and sellers, offering chat rooms, discussion boards, and a variety of other consumer-centric services. Although eBay is the most well-known of these types of sites, there are other gathering places for individual end consumers such as Epinions.com (www.epinions.com), which you can read about in the accompanying Industry Perspective.

Figure 5.3

Business to Business and Business to Consumer E-Commerce Business Models

Business to Business E-Commerce Model with an Electronic Marketplace

Business to Consumer E-Commerce Model

The distinction presented in Figure 5.3 is a very important one. If your organization has customers who are primarily other businesses, then you need to find the appropriate e-marketplace or e-marketplaces in which to participate. If your organization has customers who are primarily individual end consumers, then you need to create a marketing mix that will allow as many potential individual consumers as possible to find your organization while they surf and search the Web.

To be effective in e-commerce, you must:

1. Understand your business, products, services, and customers.
2. Find customers and establish relationships.
3. Move money easily and securely.

Understand Your Business, Products, Services, and Customers

To gain a competitive advantage and be successful in any business, you must clearly define the nature of your products and services, know who your target customers are, and understand how your customers perceive the use of your products and services in their business activities (for the B2B model) or in their personal lives (for the B2C model). To create sound business strategies you have to understand the value that your customers place on your products and services.

There are many worthwhile business activities. But as important as writing a mission statement and producing glitzy marketing brochures may be, what must come first is an objective, very down-to-earth understanding of what your business does. The reality is you can't be all things to all customers. You must answer two questions: (1) Who are your target customers? and (2) What is the value of your products and services as perceived by your customers? Let's look at each in turn.

WHO ARE YOUR CUSTOMERS?

Just as in a brick-and-mortar business, in the e-commerce world you focus your efforts on selling to other businesses, to individual end consumers, or to some combination of the two. If you were in a business like Gates Rubber Company, which produces mostly rubber and synthetic products primarily for sale to the automotive industry and manufacturers of such products as boats and bicycles, you would focus almost exclusively on the B2B e-commerce model, with other businesses as your target customers. If, however, you were selling résumé writing and job placement services to individuals looking for careers, your customers would be B2C individual end consumers. Finally, you might be like Monster.com (www.monster.com), which provides an electronic marketplace catering to both individuals looking for careers and businesses looking for employees. If you were in a business like Monster's, your customer mix would include both end consumers and businesses and you'd need to carefully consider both groups of customers, their needs, and the value to them of the products and services you sell.

Many businesses in the travel industry, American Express for example, cater to both businesses and end consumers. As an individual consumer, you might work with American Express to plan and pay for a vacation. At the same time, many businesses use the services of American Express to handle all their business travel needs.

Whatever the nature of your business, you must know who your customers are. In the world of e-commerce, that means clearly distinguishing between end consumers (B2C) and other businesses (B2B), even if you target both. As you will see throughout this

Business to Consumer (B2C)	Business to Business (B2B)
• **Convenience**—low-priced but something needed on a frequent basis • **Specialty**—higher-priced, ordered on a less frequent basis, and often requiring customization • **Commoditylike**—the same no matter where you buy it • **Digital**—the best of all because of low cost of inventory and shipping	• **Maintenance, repair, and operations (MRO) materials**— necessary items that do not relate directly to the company's primary business activities • **Direct materials**—materials used in production in a manufacturing company or placed on the shelf for sale in a retail environment

Figure 5.4

B2C and B2B Products and Services

chapter, individual end consumers and other businesses have dramatically different needs. For some categories of products and services needed in the B2C and B2B spheres, see Figure 5.4, and the discussion that follows.

WHAT IS THE VALUE OF YOUR PRODUCTS AND SERVICES AS PERCEIVED BY YOUR CUSTOMERS?

If a customer orders a product or service from your organization, it is because that customer perceives some value in what you provide—the customer either *wants* or *needs* your product or service. When we examine wants and needs, the distinctions between end consumers and businesses as customers become increasingly important and clearly evident. Let's look at product/service categories needed by each customer group in turn.

B2C: CONVENIENCE VERSUS SPECIALTY   In many respects, you can differentiate between convenience and specialty merchandise (or services) on the basis of price and consumers' frequency of purchase. To end consumers, *convenience* merchandise is typically lower priced but something they often need, usually frequently. Nonperishable food items such as breakfast cereals are a good example. From organizations such as Peapod (www.peapod.com), you can easily order food items and have them delivered to your home within 24 hours of making the order or at predetermined time intervals such as weekly. Consumers might pay more for these low-priced items in order to have them "conveniently."

Specialty merchandise might be such things as home stereo systems, computers, name-brand clothing, furniture, and the like. For consumers, these are higher-priced (than convenience merchandise) items, are typically ordered on a less-frequent basis, and often require some sort of customization or feature specification. For specialty merchandise, consumers will spend more time "shopping around," not only to find the best deal in terms of price but also because value for these items is perceived in terms of customization, warranty, service, and other after-sales features.

B2C: COMMODITYLIKE AND DIGITAL   In B2C e-commerce, as a general rule, the best merchandise to sell is either commoditylike, digital, or a combination of the two. This enables you to minimize your internal costs, but requires that you be innovative in how you offer your merchandise and attract consumers to your site.

Commoditylike merchandise, to your customers, is the same regardless of where they purchase it, and it is similar to convenience items in that respect. Books are a good

YOUR PERCEPTION OF PRODUCT AND SERVICE VALUE

In the Business to Consumer e-commerce model all consumers are not the same. They have different tastes and needs and different perceptions of product and service value. Your task is to evaluate the products and services in the table below according to your own personal preferences and perceptions of value and to specify (1) whether for you each is a convenience or specialty item and (2) whether you require some level of customization for each. Place an X in the appropriate column for each.

Product/Service	Convenience	Specialty	Customization
Fiction book			
Textbook			
Cell phone			
Internet access			
Job search			
Computer			
Checking account			
Living space (e.g., apartment)			
Music			
Car stereo			
Home stereo			

example. No matter where you buy a particular book, it is the same. As a business, you compete in a commoditylike environment on the basis of:

- Price
- Ease and speed of delivery
- Ease of ordering
- Your return policy

Of course, commoditylike business environments are typically easy to enter (i.e., they have low barriers to entry) and thus buyer power is high (from Porter's Five Forces Model in Chapter 2). Your organization's goals in this type of environment would have to include (1) minimizing price to the end consumer and (2) minimizing your internal costs by creating a tight supply chain management system. You also want to create a "sticky" Web site that not only attracts consumers but also encourages them to return to your site again and again.

Digital merchandise offerings are also important in the B2C e-commerce model. The goal here is to eliminate shipping costs by delivering the digital product over the Internet once a consumer has made a purchase. Music is a good example. Apple's iTunes Web site (www.apple.com/itunes/store/) allows you to select the exact song you want, pay for it, and then download it from the Internet. Apple can offer each song for just 99 cents because it has no physical delivery costs and no physical inventory. As this example illustrates, digital products are also advantageous (to the business and to the consumer) because they are customizable. That is, customers don't have to purchase an entire music CD—they can pick only the song or songs they want.

THE WORLD BEYOND UNITED STATES' BORDERS IS WHERE THE E-MONEY IS

From 2003 to 2004, the top 50 global companies (those companies with operations in multiple countries) exhibited an average international revenue growth of 26 percent, from $11.6 billion in 2003 to $14.6 billion in 2004. Information technology is a key to their success. According to Roger Leeds, research professor of international finance at the Johns Hopkins University School of Advanced International Studies, "Technology in all its manifestations makes it much easier to operate internationally, whether it's moving money, goods, or information of all sorts."

Symantec Corp., a leading provider of information-security software and among the top 50 global companies, has offices in more than 35 countries worldwide. For Symantec information technology is not only a product but a key enabler of growth and success. Lead-

ership positions on the information side are seen as ever more crucial to the company's growth and success. According to Mark Egan, CIO of Symantec, "The CIO is accountable in terms of providing leadership, resource allocation, resolving conflicts, and overseeing the inspection process." When Symantec develops products for the global market, the IT function and regional employees work together to bring those products to market faster.

Going global is no different in the B2C and B2B realms. From 2003 to 2004, Yahoo! increased its global growth in revenue by 241 percent, with global revenues now accounting for 26 percent of Yahoo!'s revenues. During the same period, eBay increased its global growth in revenue by 82 percent, with global revenues now accounting for 42 percent of eBay's revenues.[10]

B2C: MASS CUSTOMIZATION End consumers are often interested in customizing their purchases. In the B2C e-commerce model this need gives rise to the concept of *mass customization*—the ability of an organization to give its customers the opportunity to tailor its product or service to the customer's specifications. Customization can be appropriate and is a key competitive advantage regardless of other customer value perceptions. For example, Dell Computer (www.dell.com) is well regarded in its market especially for being the best at allowing consumers to customize a computer purchase. Music sites, such as Apple, now allow you to pick the songs you want instead of an entire CD. Clothing sites allow you to select from among various styles, colors, and sizes of clothing to fit your needs.

In a B2C environment, you're potentially dealing with millions of different consumers, each with unique tastes and needs. You must support the concept of mass customization.

B2B: MRO VERSUS DIRECT *Maintenance, repair, and operations (MRO) materials* (also called *indirect materials*) are materials that are necessary for running a modern corporation, but do not relate to the company's primary business activities. MRO materials include everything from ballpoint pens to three-ring binders, repair parts for equipment, and lubricating oils. Thus, B2B MRO materials are similar to convenience and commoditylike items in the B2C e-commerce model.

In their purchases of these materials, however, business customers (B2B) are very different from end consumers (B2C) in many ways. For example, a business because of its volume of MRO materials purchases can bargain with suppliers for a discount (end consumers in the B2C e-commerce model usually don't have this ability). Many businesses may band together to create even more volume and thus demand an even higher discount from a supplier. This practice is known as *demand aggregation*—the combining of purchase requests from multiple buyers into a single large order, which justifies a discount from the business. If your organization is a supplier of MRO materials in the B2B e-commerce model, you will compete mostly on price (including discounts), delivery, and ease of ordering.

Direct materials are materials that are used in production in a manufacturing company or are placed on the shelf for sale in a retail environment. So, as opposed to MRO materials, direct materials relate to a company's primary business activities. It is critically important that the customer business receives exactly what is needed in terms of quality, quantity, and the timing of delivery of direct materials.

For direct materials acquisition, some businesses participate in a reverse auction (through an electronic marketplace). A *reverse auction* is the process in which a buyer posts its interest in buying a certain quantity of items with notations concerning quality, specification, and delivery timing, and sellers compete for the business by submitting successively lower bids until there is only one seller left. Reverse auctions create tremendous "power" for the buyer because multiple sellers are competing for the same business.

B2B: HORIZONTAL VERSUS VERTICAL As a supplier to other businesses, you also need to understand whether you are selling in a horizontal or vertical e-marketplace (see Figure 5.5). An *electronic marketplace (e-marketplace)* is an interactive business providing a central market space where multiple buyers and suppliers can engage in e-commerce and/or other e-commerce business activities. E-marketplaces feature a variety of implementations including value-added network providers (which we'll discuss later in the chapter), horizontal e-marketplaces, and vertical e-marketplaces. A *horizontal e-marketplace* is an electronic marketplace that connects buyers and sellers across many industries, primarily for MRO materials commerce. Again, MRO materials include a broad of range of both products and services including office supplies, travel, shipping, and some financial services. Because horizontal e-marketplaces support MRO materials commerce, much of our previous discussion on B2B e-commerce for MRO materials holds true here.

Figure 5.5

Horizontal and Vertical B2B Electronic Marketplace

SMALL COMPANIES CAN BENEFIT FROM INTEGRATED B2B E-COMMERCE AND SUPPLY CHAIN MANAGEMENT

Star Sales and Services is an automotive parts distributor serving mainly auto repair shops and auto dealerships. With almost 30,000 parts valued at approximately $2 million worth of inventory, Star found its inventory management and customer order processing systems too costly and too ineffective.

So, Star turned to an integrated software suite which included supply chain management within a B2B e-commerce environment. According to John Krieger, CEO and president of Star Sales and Service, the new system has a number of benefits, including:

- Reducing customer inquiry calls to the call center
- Improving inventory management
- Improving inventory turnaround time by 95 percent
- Improving forecasting of inventory demand from trend analysis

"We've identified $500,000 in wasted inventory," Krieger stated. That is a significant amount of money remembering that Star's total inventory value is approximately $2 million.

For Star's customers, the new Web-based system is much more effective than the previous one. Often, customers had to call twice—first check on the availability of a part and second to actually order the part. The new system handled 1,300 orders in April 2005, the equivalent of the 2,600 calls using the previous system. According to Krieger, "This is a much more effective way to do business."[11]

A *vertical e-marketplace* is an electronic marketplace that connects buyers and sellers in a given industry (e.g., oil and gas, textiles, and retail). Covisint (www.covisint.com) is a good example. Covisint provides a B2B e-marketplace in the automotive industry where buyers and sellers specific to that industry conduct commerce in products and services, share mission-critical information for the development of products and parts, collaborate on new ideas, and deploy infrastructure applications that enable the seamless communication of each other's proprietary IT systems.

To summarize, we have offered you some ideas to think about regarding the following aspects of e-commerce that will help you in understanding the nature of your business, products, services, and customers.

- **Business to Consumer**
  - Greatly varying customer demographics, lifestyles, wants, and needs
  - Distinctions of products and services by convenience versus specialty
  - E-commerce works best for commoditylike and digital products and services
  - Mass customization adds value in some instances
- **Business to Business**
  - Distinctions of products and services by maintenance, repair, and operations (MRO) materials versus direct materials
  - Demand aggregation and negotiation capabilities enhanced for businesses as customers (buyer power)
  - E-marketplaces connect buyers and sellers—horizontal e-marketplaces (primarily for MRO materials) and vertical e-marketplaces (specific to a given industry)

Find Customers and Establish Relationships

You can't make a sale until you find and reach customers and establish a relationship with them. This is *marketing*. There are special features of and technical considerations about marketing and creating customer relationships in e-commerce to keep in mind that can create a competitive advantage for you.

BUSINESS TO CONSUMER

With almost 1 billion people on the Internet, you'd think it would be easy to find and attract customers to your B2C e-commerce site. But that's not necessarily true because all your competition is trying to do the same thing—drive customers to their Web site and encourage them to make a purchase.

First, you need to determine your appropriate ***marketing mix***—the set of marketing tools that your organization will use to pursue its marketing objectives in reaching and attracting potential customers. In B2C e-commerce, your marketing mix will probably include some or all of the following: registering with search engines, online ads, viral marketing, and affiliate programs.

Many Web surfers use *search engines* to find information and products and services. While some search engines will include your site for free (FreeSearch.com at www. freesearch.com is an example), almost all the popular search engines such as Yahoo! and Google require you to pay a fee. Most of these sites will guarantee that your site appears in the top portion of a search list for an additional fee.

Online ads (often called ***banner ads***) are small advertisements that appear on other sites (see Figure 5.6). Variations of online ads include pop-up and pop-under ads. A ***pop-up ad*** is a small Web page containing an advertisement that appears on your screen

Figure 5.6

An Online Ad at Cnet.com

Banner ad for TiVo

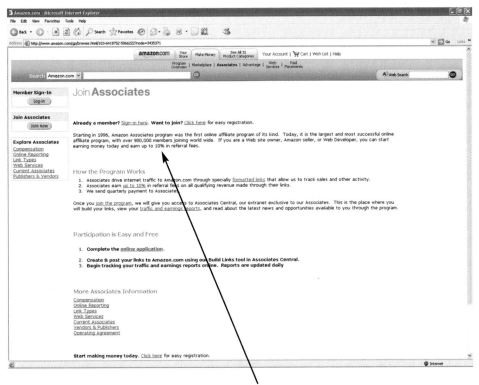

Figure 5.7

Amazon.com's Affiliate Program Is Called *Associates*

As an Amazon Associate, you can earn up to 10% for referrals.

outside the current Web site loaded into your browser. A ***pop-under ad*** is a form of a pop-up ad that you do not see until you close your current browser window. A word of caution here: Most people don't mind banner ads because they appear as a part of the site they're visiting. However, most people consider pop-up and pop-under ads to be very annoying.

Viral marketing encourages users of a product or service supplied by a B2C e-commerce business to encourage friends to join in as well. Blue Mountain Arts (www. bluemountain.com) is a good example. When you use Blue Mountain to send an e-birthday card (or some other type of card), the intended recipient will receive an e-mail directing him or her to Blue Mountain's site. Once the recipient views the card, Blue Mountain provides a link so that person can send you a card in return. Of course, Blue Mountain charges for each card sent, so it makes money both ways.

An ***affiliate program*** is an arrangement made between two e-commerce sites that directs viewers from one site to the other. Amazon.com is the most well-known creator of an affiliate program. If you become an Amazon associate, your e-commerce Web site directs viewers to Amazon's site for certain purchases. If a sale results, Amazon pays you a fee, which is usually a percentage of the sale (see Figure 5.7). Likewise, you can pay another site to direct traffic to yours, which may be through an online ad. In some instances, affiliate programs create relationships such that a payment is made for each click-through. A ***click-through*** is a count of the number of people who visit one site, click on an ad, and are taken to the site of the advertiser.

In general, you want your marketing mix to drive as many potential customers as possible to have a look at your B2C e-commerce offerings. From there, however, you need to focus on your conversion rate. A ***conversion rate*** is the percentage of potential customers who visit your site who actually buy something. So, while total views or "hits" to your e-commerce Web site is important, obviously even more so is your conversion rate.

A GLOBAL PARTNERSHIP TO CREATE GLOBAL PARTNERING OPPORTUNITIES

In March 2004, Business Commerce Limited, the Hong Kong subsidiary of Global eXchange Services (GXS), and ChinaECNet announced a new business partnership to establish a B2B electronic marketplace named "e-Hub." E-Hub connects China-based electronics manufacturers with other China-based manufacturers and international customers and suppliers as well.

ChinaECNet is China's leading digital media and e-commerce network, focused mainly on the electronic manufacturing industry. It represents a joint venture between the China Centre for Industry Information Development, Avnet Inc., and Global Techmart.

Global eXchange Services provides one of the largest B2B e-commerce business networks in the world, supporting over 1 billion transactions annually among over 100,000 trading partners.

E-Hub provides buyers and sellers with a standards-based transaction environment that supports more efficient and effective sourcing, purchasing, and tracking of inventory. According to Gou Zhongwen, vice minister of China's Ministry of Information Industry,

"Strengthening the electronics supply chain and material information management is an important step toward utilizing advanced information technology to reform and improve the manufacturing supply and distribution of electronics enterprises." As Wayne Chao, chairman and CEO of ChinaECNET, further explains, "We anticipate that the e-Hub will be China's premier procurement and logistic data exchange platform to connect Chinese electronics OEMs with other Chinese manufacturers of all sizes, and as importantly, with international customers and suppliers. This will greatly help the Chinese OEM market improve material management efficiency and overcome the challenges caused by the rapid globalization of the Chinese electronics industry."

Sometimes, you build partnerships with other businesses specifically so you can support e-commerce activities among other businesses that also want to build partnerships. In the case of Global eXchange Services and ChinaECNET, their partnership will enable other businesses to create partnerships.[12,13]

BUSINESS TO BUSINESS

Finding and attracting customers to your B2B e-commerce site is much different. Businesses—customers in the B2B model—don't usually find products and services by surfing the Web or using search engines. Instead, business customers prefer to actively participate in e-marketplaces to find suppliers. Within an e-marketplace, an organization can participate in a reverse auction to find a supplier, as we discussed earlier.

Moreover, an organization can search an e-marketplace for suitable suppliers and then enter into negotiations outside the e-marketplace. This happens for organizations needing to purchase millions of dollars in inventory, parts, or raw materials, and it occurs for organizations wanting to establish a long-term relationship with just one supplier.

Relationships among businesses in B2B are very important. These relationships, characterized by trust and continuity, extend into the IT realm. In the B2B e-commerce business model, you must provide a level of integration of your IT systems with those of your business partners. Once a formal business relationship has been established, the goal is to use IT to streamline the ordering and procurement processes to create tight supply chain management systems and drive out cost, so your IT systems have to work closely together.

DEVELOPING A MARKETING MIX STRATEGY FOR MONSTER.COM

Monster.com (www.monster.com) is a premier service provider in the job placement industry. It exhibits both a B2B e-commerce business model because it provides services for organizations seeking employees and a B2C e-commerce business model because it provides services to individuals hoping to find jobs.

You've been hired by Monster.com to create a marketing mix strategy. Your tasks are many. Complete the table below by filling in the appropriate information. If you feel that it is not in the best interest of Monster.com to advertise in a certain media, leave that part of the table blank.

	B2B	B2C
Television Advertising		
• What type of TV station(s)?		
• What type of shows?		
• What time of day?		
Newspaper Advertising		
• What day of the week?		
• What section of the newspaper?		
Internet Advertising		
• What sites for online ads?		
• What sites for affiliate programs?		
• What types of viral marketing?		
Other Advertising		
• Anything not listed in the above three categories		

To summarize, some ideas about marketing, or finding customers and creating relationships with them, in e-commerce are:

- **Business to Consumer**
  - Design marketing mix to drive potential customers to a Web site
  - Register with a search engine; use online ads, viral marketing, and affiliate programs
  - Conversion rates measure success
- **Business to Business**
  - Businesses participate in e-marketplaces—business customers don't surf the Web, so e-marketplaces need your attention, not a broad and generic marketing mix
  - Formal establishment of business relationships based on trust and continuity required
  - Some level of IT system integration between you and your customer required
  - Online negotiations for pricing, quality, specifications, and delivery timing

Move Money Easily and Securely

In the world of e-commerce, you must create IT systems that enable your customers (other businesses or end consumers) to pay electronically, easily, and securely for their purchases. Of course, you can still accept credit cards as the form of payment just like in the brick-and-mortar world, but credit card payments are really an electronic form of payment.

BUSINESS TO CONSUMER PAYMENT SYSTEMS

Your customers in the Business to Consumer e-commerce model will most often pay for products and services using credit cards, financial cybermediaries, electronic checks, Electronic Bill Presentment and Payment (EBPP), or smart cards.

- *Financial cybermediary*—an Internet-based company that makes it easy for one person to pay another person or organization over the Internet. PayPal (www.paypal.com) is the best-known example of a financial cybermediary (see Figure 5.8). You create a PayPal account by logging on to the PayPal Web site and providing it with personal, credit card, and banking information. When you want to send money, you go to the PayPal site and enter the amount of money you want to send and provide information for either the person or organization you want to send the money to. You can also accumulate money in your personal PayPal account by accepting money from other people. You can transfer the money to one of your banking accounts, use it for other purposes, send the funds to someone else, or just leave it there for awhile.
- *Electronic check*—a mechanism for sending money from your checking or savings account to another person or organization. There are many implementations of electronic checks, with the most prominent being online banking.
- *Electronic Bill Presentment and Payment (EBPP)*—a system that sends bills (usually to end consumers) over the Internet and provides an easy-to-use mechanism (such as clicking on a button) to pay for them if the amount looks correct. EBPP systems are available through local banks or online services such

Figure 5.8

PayPal Is the Most
Well-Known Financial
Cybermediary

In some instances, PayPal is free to use.

as Checkfree (www.checkfree.com) and Quicken (www.quicken.com/banking_and_credit/).

- **Smart card**—plastic card the size of a credit card that contains an embedded chip on which digital information can be stored and updated. The chip, in this case, can contain information about how much money you have. When you swipe your card to pay for a purchase, the swiping device deducts the purchase amount from the amount you have stored on the chip. Some debit cards are implementations of the smart card concept.

The entire payment process encompasses more than accepting a form of payment. It also includes determining the shipping address for your customer. You can create a competitive advantage by having a way of asking each customer only once for his or her delivery information and storing it, thus creating a switching cost because when your customer makes another purchase, you can simply ask him or her to verify the delivery information and not have to provide it all over again. One implementation of this is called a digital wallet. A **digital wallet** is both software and information—the software provides security for the transaction and the information includes payment information (for example, the credit card number and expiration date) and delivery information. Digital wallets can be stored either on the client side or the server side. A *client-side digital wallet* is one that you create and keep on your computer; you can then use it at a variety of e-commerce Web sites. Most browsers such as Internet Explorer support your ability to create this type of digital wallet. A *server-side digital wallet* (sometimes referred to as a *thin wallet*) is one that an organization creates for and about you and maintains on its server. Many credit card issuers use this type of digital wallet to verify your credit card transactions.

SPOOFING eBAY CUSTOMERS TO GET CREDIT CARD INFORMATION

When you register as a user at eBay, you set up a personal account that includes your shipping information and important financial information such as your credit card number. At any time, you can log in with eBay and change your personal and financial information. These are necessary aspects of creating the world's largest online auction e-marketplace.

But there is a drawback. Now thieves are trying to steal your credit card information, not by looking through your trash for a credit card statement or by monitoring your electronic communications but rather by pretending to be eBay.

It's called *spoofing*—the forging of the return address on an e-mail so that the e-mail message appears to come from someone other than the actual sender. The thief will send you an e-mail that looks like one coming from eBay. The message will instruct you to do something in order to keep your eBay account active, like clicking on a link that will take you to a page so you can update your credit card information.

In reality, you'll be taken to a site that looks very much like eBay but isn't eBay at all. When you type in your credit card information, things will go bad in a big way and in a big hurry. The thief now has your credit card information and can use it online.

Sometimes, thieves simply ask you to enter your eBay user ID and password on a fictitious site. Then, they have that information and can log into your eBay account and take your information that way.

It's up to you to protect your most personal and confidential information.

All of this is significant because your customers in the B2C e-commerce model exhibit some common characteristics when paying for your products and services.

- They tend to make numerous purchases for small amounts.
- They pay for each transaction individually.
- You must validate each transaction.

BUSINESS TO BUSINESS PAYMENT SYSTEMS

Payments for products and services in the Business to Business e-commerce model are usually much different from those in the Business to Consumer e-commerce model. In B2B e-commerce, your customers tend to make very large purchases and will not pay using a credit card or a financial cybermediary such as PayPal. Instead, other businesses will want to pay (1) through financial EDI and (2) often in large, aggregated amounts encompassing many purchases.

ELECTRONIC DATA INTERCHANGE   In the B2B model, another business wants to order products and services from your organization via electronic data interchange. *Electronic data interchange (EDI)* is the direct computer-to-computer transfer of transaction information contained in standard business documents, such as invoices and purchase orders, in a standard format. Your organization can implement EDI-facilitated transactions in many ways; one of the more prominent is a B2B e-marketplace that supports EDI through a value-added network. Global eXchange Services (GXS at www.gsx.com) is one such B2B e-marketplace. (We introduced you to GXS in the Global Perspective on page 252.)

GXS, formerly known as General Electric (GE) Information Services, supports one of the largest B2B e-marketplaces in the world with more than 100,000 trading busi-

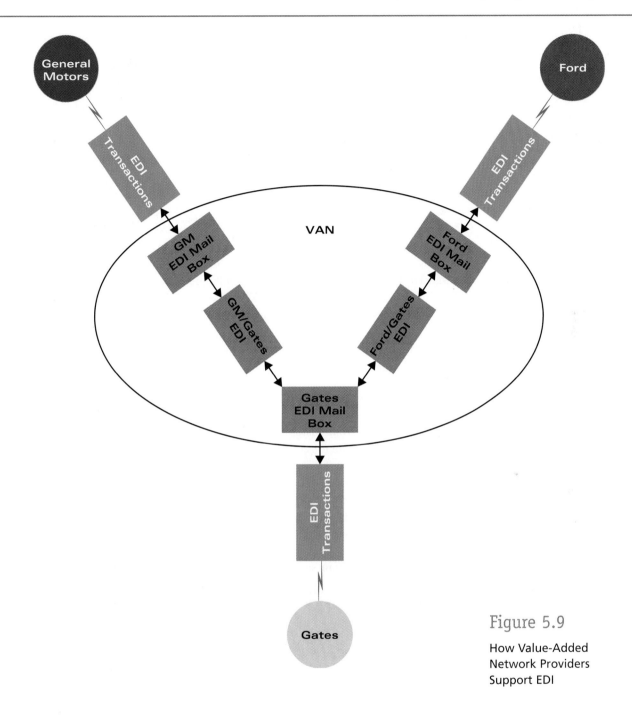

Figure 5.9

How Value-Added
Network Providers
Support EDI

nesses processing 1 billion transactions annually and accounting for over $1 trillion in products and services. GXS focuses on providing value-added network capabilities primarily to supply chain management activities. Figure 5.9 illustrates how General Motors, Ford, and Gates Rubber Company might use GXS's services to support electronic data interchange. In this case, General Motors and Ford would submit orders to Gates through GXS's value-added network (VAN). The VAN supports electronic catalogs (from which orders are placed), EDI-based transactions (the actual orders), security measures such as encryption (which we'll discuss in a moment), and EDI mail boxes (similar to your personal e-mail box). When GM sends an order, for example, to Gates, the order waits in Gates's EDI mail box for processing. Once the order is processed, Gates sends an order confirmation back through the VAN to GM's mail box.

FINANCIAL ELECTRONIC DATA INTERCHANGE   Thereafter, at some predetermined time, Gates would create an invoice totaling many of the orders and purchases from GM. That invoice would be sent through the VAN much like the orders themselves. When the invoice was accepted and approved by GM, GM would make a financial EDI payment to Gates. ***Financial EDI (financial electronic data interchange)*** is an electronic process used primarily within the Business to Business e-commerce model for the payment of purchases. The actual reconciliation of the funds may occur through a bank or an automated clearing house (ACH) support site such as National Cash Management System (www.ach-eft-ncms.com/index.asp).

As you can see, B2B transactions among businesses are much more involved and complex than B2C transactions between a business and an end consumer such as yourself. Most notably, Business to Business transactions require a level of system integration between the businesses. Considering our previous example in Figure 5.9, Gates's order fulfillment and processing systems would have to be integrated with similar systems at GM and Ford. That is to say, Gates's order fulfillment and processing systems would have to be able to accept and process EDI-based and standardized electronic order records. GM and Ford would have to have similar systems to create EDI-based and standardized electronic order records. In doing so, costs for order processing among all businesses are minimized as the orders can be handled electronically, without paper and without much human intervention.

SECURITY: THE PERVADING CONCERN

Regardless of whether your customers are other businesses or end consumers, they are all greatly concerned about the security of their transactions. This includes all aspects of electronic information, but focuses mainly on the information associated with payments (e.g., a credit card number) and the payments themselves, that is, the "electronic money." Here, you need to consider such issues as encryption, Secure Sockets Layers, and Secure Electronic Transactions. This is by no means an exhaustive list but rather representative of the broad field of security relating to electronic commerce.

ENCRYPTION   ***Encryption*** scrambles the contents of a file so that you can't read it without having the right decryption key. Encryption can be achieved in many ways: by scrambling letters in a known way, replacing letters with other letters or perhaps numbers, and other ways.

Some encryption technologies use multiple keys. In this instance, you would be using ***public key encryption (PKE)***—an encryption system that uses two keys: a public key that everyone can have and a private key for only the recipient (see Figure 5.10).

Figure 5.10

Public Key Encryption
(PKE) System

Figure 5.11

Secure Sockets Layer
(SSL) on a Web Site

The "s" in http://s and the lock icon denote a
Secure Sockets Layer (SSL).

When implementing security using multiple keys, your organization provides the public key to all its customers (end consumers and other businesses). The customers use the public key to encrypt their information and send it along the Internet. When it arrives at its destination, your organization would use the private key to unscramble the encrypted information.

SECURE SOCKETS LAYERS   A *Secure Sockets Layer (SSL)* (1) creates a secure and private connection between a Web client computer and a Web server computer, (2) encrypts the information, and (3) then sends the information over the Internet. SSLs do provide good security for transferring information and are used widely by B2C e-commerce Web sites. As an end consumer, you can tell your information is being transferred via SSL if you see either (1) the Web site address starts with https:// (notice the inclusion of the "s") as opposed to just http:// or (2) the presence of a lock icon in the bottom portion of your Web browser window (see Figure 5.11).

SECURE ELECTRONIC TRANSACTIONS   A *Secure Electronic Transaction (SET)* is a transmission security method that ensures transactions are *legitimate* as well as secure. Much like an SSL, an SET encrypts information before sending it over the Internet. Taking it one step further, an SET enables you, as a merchant, to verify a customer's identity by securely transmitting credit card information to the business that issued the credit card for verification. SETs are endorsed by major e-commerce players including MasterCard, American Express, Visa, Netscape, and Microsoft.

To summarize, we offer the comments on page 261 about moving money easily and securely.

DEFINING YOUR BUSINESS TO CONSUMER
E-COMMERCE BUSINESS

It's now time for you to gather everything you've learned in this chapter and use it to create the overall strategy for a B2C e-commerce business. First, as a group, think of and define a B2C e-commerce business you wish to operate. It can be anything from selling tutoring services to offering music on the Web. Then, you need to clearly define your customers according to their demographics and lifestyles. Next, define your products/services according to your customers' perception of their value. Define the best marketing mix to reach your customers. Finally, evaluate your new e-commerce business in light of Porter's Five Forces Model (refer back to Chapter 2). Complete the table below with all this information.

Your B2C e-commerce business (provide a one-paragraph description):	_____ _____ _____ _____ _____ _____
Your customers (provide their demographics and lifestyles):	_____ _____ _____ _____ _____
Your customers' perception of value (discussion of convenience versus specialty, commoditylike, digital, and extent of needed customization):	_____ _____ _____ _____ _____ _____
Your marketing mix (where you will advertise, when, etc.):	_____ _____ _____ _____
Porter's Five Forces Model (look again at Chapter 2—describe your competitive space according to each of Porter's five forces):	_____ _____ _____ _____ _____ _____

- **Business to Consumer**
  - Methods include credit cards, financial cybermediaries, electronic checks, Electronic Bill Presentment and Payment (EBPP), smart cards, and digital wallets.
  - Consumers make numerous individual purchases for small amounts that must each be validated.
- **Business to Business**
  - The use of electronic data interchange (EDI) facilitates the ordering process.
  - Value-added network providers used for EDI and financial EDI.
  - Financial EDI used for payment of purchases.
- **Both Business to Consumer and Business to Business**
  - Security is an overriding concern.
  - Security is provided by the use of encryption, Secure Sockets Layers (SSLs), and Secure Electronic Transactions (SETs).

The Broadening of E-Government

As we discussed at the beginning of this chapter, the four main perspectives of e-commerce in the private sector include interactions between and among businesses (B) and consumers (C). The relatively new, but very large, player to enter the e-commerce market is governments (G). This movement has been led by the United States. In summer 2001, the president of the United States, George W. Bush, released the President's Management Agenda (PMA). This document, in many ways, served to "light the fire" of the federal government to move into the electronic world of the Internet. Subsequently, all levels of government in the United States—state, local, tribal, etc.—have followed suit.

The PMA focuses on improving the management and performance of the federal government in five key areas:

1. Strategies management of human capital
2. Competitive sourcing
3. Improved financial performance
4. Expanded electronic government
5. Budget and performance integration[14]

Electronic government (e-government) is defined as the use of digital technologies to transform government operations in order to improve efficiency, effectiveness, and service delivery. Expanded electronic government, according to the PMA, outlines ways in which the federal government is to make the government into a click-and-mortar enterprise. ***Click-and-mortar*** refers to those organizations that have a presence in the physical world, that is, buildings you can visit and representatives you can talk to, and also a presence in the virtual world of the Internet.

Within the e-government arena, there are four primary focuses:

1. Government to Government (G2G, also called intra-G2G)
2. Government to Business (G2B)
3. Government to Consumer (G2C)
4. International Government to Government (inter-G2G)

Figure 5.12

Government to
Government (G2G,
intra-G2G)

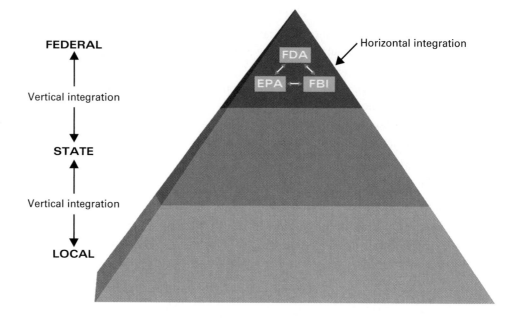

GOVERNMENT TO GOVERNMENT (G2G, INTRA-G2G)

Government to Government (G2G, intra-G2G) refers to the electronic commerce activities performed within a single nation's government. Here, the focus can be on vertical integration, horizontal integration, or—most commonly—a combination of the two (see Figure 5.12).

Vertical government integration refers to the electronic integration of agencies, activities, and processes up and down federal, state, and local government levels. For example, if a manufacturing operation will be creating landfills of waste and pumping sanitized fluids into rivers and streams, it must meet EPA (Environmental Protection Agency) guidelines at the local, state, and federal levels, and guidelines among those levels may differ. While the federal level may have one set of sanitization standards for fluids that go into rivers and streams, state and local government environmental agencies can impose more stringent requirements. Thus, the goal of vertical integration is to automate the electronic movement of information among those various agencies. Another example here falls in the education arena. At all levels of government, there must be information sharing concerning K-12 education standards, test results, and the like.

Horizontal government integration refers to the electronic integration of agencies, activities, and processes across a specific level of government. For example, at the federal level, the EPA may work with the FDA (Food and Drug Administration) to develop standards for food processing plants that emit gases into the atmosphere as a result of their operations. The EPA and FDA share this information horizontally to ensure that each food processing plant is meeting both sets of guidelines (i.e., EPA guidelines and FDA guidelines). Another good example here is that of the armed forces and the Department of Veterans Affairs (VA). As a member of the armed forces moves from active service to the VA (through retirement, injury, etc.), a large amount of information must be communicated to the VA including vitally important medical information.

GOVERNMENT TO BUSINESS (G2B)

Government to Business (G2B) refers to the electronic commerce activities performed between a government and businesses for such purposes as purchasing direct and MRO materials, soliciting bids for work, licensing applications, meeting equal employment opportunity regulations, and so on. Here, the focus is twofold. First, G2B e-government

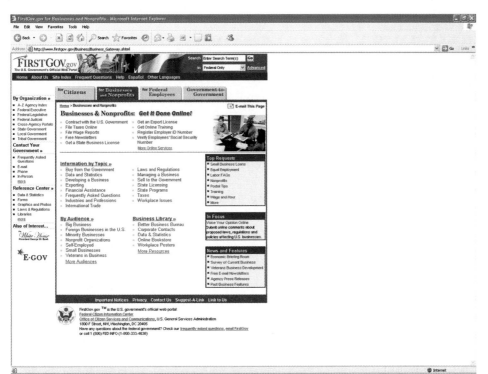

Figure 5.13

Business and Nonprofit Gateway in the FirstGov Portal

seeks to provide an effective electronic platform for communication, information sharing, and processing activities between a government and its business partners. This is very similar to the notion of B2B (Business to Business), except that the first "B" is now "G." Second, G2B e-government seeks to provide an effective platform for all businesses as they attempt to find and meet government guidelines for operational matters such as applying for SBA (Small Business Administration) loans, meeting equal employment opportunity guidelines, filing tax information for employees, and the like.

To help support all aspects of e-government, the U.S. federal government has created a single portal Web site, called FirstGov (www.firstgov.gov), where everyone (including citizens, businesses, and other governments) begin their interactions with the federal government. The U.S. federal government boasts over 20 million Web pages, and it makes no sense to specify the URL for each. So, you—as a citizen or a business—can start at FirstGov and find whatever you need. Figure 5.13 shows the screen that acts as the gateway for businesses and nonprofits in the FirstGov site.

GOVERNMENT TO CONSUMER (G2C)

Government to Consumer (G2C) refers to the electronic commerce activities performed between a government and its citizens or consumers including paying taxes, registering vehicles, and providing information and services, and so on. This is the aspect of e-government that will have the greatest impact on your personal life. The U.S. government is moving aggressively toward providing communication, information delivery, transaction processing, and service delivery via the Web to its citizens.

In many instances, you can expect that the government will do this to such an extent that it is no longer a click-and-mortar enterprise but rather a click-and-order enterprise. ***Click-and-order*** (also known as ***pure play***) refers to an organization that has a presence in the virtual world but no presence in the physical world. One such example is that of buying, holding, and redeeming savings bonds. As you'll read in the accompanying Industry Perspective, the government is already at the click-and-mortar level and it plans to move to the click-and-order level in the not-too-distant future.

BUYING ELECTRONIC SAVINGS BONDS AT TREASURYDIRECT

Savings bonds, specifically Series EE and I, have long been a safe and solid investment. Parents buy them for their children. Many people purchase them as gifts. Workers enroll in payroll-deduction programs with the money going toward the purchase of savings bonds.

That will all remain the same; however, the Treasury Department now wants you to purchase your savings bonds online. Not only that; you will no longer receive the paper bonds in the mail. Instead, you'll have an account in which the bonds reside. It's called Treasury-Direct (www.treasurydirect.gov). When you first visit the site, you create a personal account and provide such information as your checking or savings account number and other personal information. You can then buy savings bonds in any denomination offered. (You can also enroll in a payroll deduction program.) You pay with a credit card. Then, at any time, you can visit your account and the system will tell you exactly what your savings bonds are worth should you redeem them

on that day. If you choose to do so, you instruct the system into which bank account to transfer the money. Your money will arrive within two working days.

Parents can set up accounts for their children. They can create different accounts for their children such as "College Tuition," "First Car," or "Happy 16th Birthday." Once the accounts are created, anyone can log into the system and buy bonds for the child. So, friends, grandparents, and other relatives can buy bonds for a child and place them in the appropriate account. When any of your bonds mature, TreasuryDirect will send an e-mail notifying you that the bonds are mature and will accrue no more interest.

The ultimate goal is to completely eliminate the use of paper bonds and your need to interact in any way with your bank. This is an instance of expanded e-government moving from click-and-mortar to click-and-order.

INTERNATIONAL GOVERNMENT TO GOVERNMENT (INTER-G2G)

International Government to Government (inter-G2G) refers to the electronic commerce activities performed between two or more nations' governments including providing foreign aid. As an example, the U.S. government interacts extensively with the governments of Canada and Mexico regarding the movement of livestock and produce across borders. The U.S. government also interacts in this way with all other countries regarding all types of imports and exports.

GOVERNMENT SPENDING ON INFORMATION TECHNOLOGY

Consider that the U.S. federal government is the single largest acquirer and user of information technology and related services (see Figure 5.14). The numbers presented in the figure are for the fiscal year 2002 but are still representative (in percentage terms) of how the U.S. government spends its money on technology and who within the U.S. government spends it. In 2002, the U.S. federal government spent just over $46 billion on IT and related services. Almost 25 percent of that $46 billion went to internal staffing, which is essentially IT personnel. So, there are substantial career opportunities in e-government. Even if you don't want to work directly for the federal government but perhaps as an IT consultant to the federal government, notice in Figure 5.14 that over 25 percent of federal government IT dollars went to professional services ($7.8 billion) and outsourcing ($6.4 billion). Current estimates within the U.S. federal government have IT spending increasing at a rate of 10 percent annually for the next several years.

EXPLORING THE WORLD OF E-GOVERNMENT

Because expanded e-government is becoming such an important part of society, you should take some time to explore what the U.S. federal government offers at FirstGov. Connect to it at www.firstgov.gov and do some research. Consider and answer the following questions.

1. How has the U.S. federal government tailored its Web site to specific audiences within the G2C arena?

2. In what ways does the U.S. federal government offer support for you during your educational years?

3. What sort of medical and health information is provided?

4. How does the U.S. federal government support you as you plan international travel?

5. What sort of activities concerning which you have had "physical" interaction with the U.S. federal government can you now do on the Internet?

In Figure 5.14 you can also see the allocation of IT dollars across the major spending agencies. Defense and the armed forces are at the top, followed by the Treasury Department (it accepts and distributes all government monies), NASA (heavily involved in research), and then a series of more socially oriented agencies such as Health and Human Services and Agriculture. The table in Figure 5.14, because it includes 2002 data, does not show the positioning of the Homeland Security Department, which had an IT budget of approximately $3 billion for 2005.

We offer you this insight into e-government for three good reasons. First, many e-government applications will have a direct impact on your personal life. In the not-too-distant future, the IRS will no longer accept paper-based income tax returns. That is, you'll be using G2C e-commerce to submit your tax forms electronically. Most state governments now allow you to renew your driver's license online and file your state income tax returns online. Second, many governmental agencies are also using G2B to send out and accept bids for work. Those government agencies simply refuse to work with businesses that cannot perform this electronic commerce activity. If your organization can't, don't rely on getting any government contracts.

Figure 5.14

How the U.S. Federal Government Spends Its IT Dollars[15]

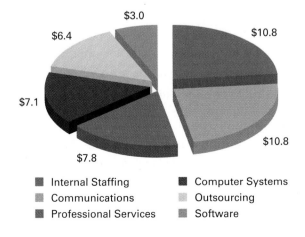

- ■ Internal Staffing
- ■ Communications
- ■ Professional Services
- ■ Computer Systems
- ■ Outsourcing
- ■ Software

$3.0
$6.4
$7.1
$7.8
$10.8
$10.8

Major Agency Spenders (in billions)	
Pentagon	$6.3
Air Force	4.3
Army	3.6
Navy	3.5
Treasury	2.6
NASA	2.1
Transportation	2.1
Justice	1.7
Health/Human Services	1.5
Agriculture	1.2

Finally, you may want to consider employment in government, specifically the e-government arena. Many IT positions in the government exhibit salaries comparable to those of the private industry. With the government's continued push toward expanded electronic government, you can expect to see salaries continue to increase.

Summary: Student Learning Outcomes Revisited

1. **Define and describe the two major e-commerce business models (Business to Business and Business to Consumer).** *Business to Business (B2B) e-commerce* occurs when a business sells products and services to customers who are primarily other businesses. B2B e-commerce is all about the commerce interactions among two or more businesses. *Business to Consumer (B2C) e-commerce* occurs when a business sells products and services to customers who are primarily individuals. B2C e-commerce is all about the commerce interactions among a business and an end consumer.

2. **Describe the emerging role of e-marketplaces in B2B e-commerce.** An *electronic marketplace (e-marketplace)* is an interactive business providing a central market space where multiple buyers and suppliers can engage in e-commerce and/or other e-commerce business activities, such as sharing mission-critical information for the development of products and parts, collaborating on new ideas, and deploying infrastructure applications. Two variations of B2B e-marketplaces include horizontal and vertical e-marketplaces. A *horizontal e-marketplace* is an electronic marketplace that connects buyers and sellers across many industries, primarily for MRO materials commerce. A *vertical marketplace* is an electronic marketplace that connects buyers and sellers in a given industry (e.g., oil and gas, textiles, and retail).

3. **Identify the differences and similarities among customers and their perceived value of products and services in the B2B and B2C e-commerce business models.** Customers in the B2C e-commerce business model are end consumers. They (1) exhibit greatly varying demographics, lifestyles, wants, and needs,

(2) distinguish products and services by convenience versus specialty, (3) often shop for commoditylike and digital products, and (4) sometimes require a level of *mass customization* to get exactly what they want. Customers in the B2B e-commerce business model are other businesses. They (1) distinguish products and services by *maintenance, repair, and operations (MRO) materials* versus *direct materials,* (2) aggregate demand to create negotiations for volume discounts on large purchases, and (3) most often perform e-commerce activities within an e-marketplace.

4. **Compare and contrast the development of a marketing mix for customers in the B2B and B2C e-commerce business models.** A *marketing mix* is the set of marketing tools that your organization will use to pursue its marketing objectives in reaching and attracting potential customers. In B2B e-commerce, marketing mixes do not usually include broad and generic strategies that reach all potential businesses. Instead, marketing often occurs in the context of an e-marketplace. Once a contact has been made between businesses, the development of the relationship is still formal and often includes negotiations for pricing, quality, specifications, and delivery timing.

   In B2C e-commerce, a marketing mix will include some or all of the following:

   - Registering your site with a search engine.
   - *Online ads* (small advertisements that appear on other sites), including *pop-up ads* (small Web pages containing an advertisement that appear on your screen outside the current Web site loaded into your browser) and *pop-under ads* (a form of a pop-up ad that you do not see until you close your current browser session).

- *Viral marketing*—encourages users of a product or service supplied by a B2C e-commerce business to encourage friends to join in as well.
- *Affiliate program*—arrangement made between two e-commerce sites that directs viewers from one site to the other.

5. **Summarize the various ways of moving money in the world of e-commerce and related issues.** B2C e-commerce payment systems most commonly include credit cards, *financial cybermediaries* (such as PayPal), *electronic checks* (with online banking being an implementation), *Electronic Bill Presentment and Payment (EBPP)*, *smart cards* (credit card with an embedded computer chip on which digital information can be stored and updated), and *digital wallets* (software and instructions for completing a transaction). In the B2B e-commerce business model, financial EDI is the norm. *Financial EDI* is an electronic process used primarily in the Business to Business e-commerce business model for the payment of purchases. Security for the electronic transfer of funds is an overriding concern. Techniques such as *encryption, public key encryption (PKE), Secure Sockets Layers (SSLs),* and *Secure Electronic Transactions (SETs)* all address this issue of security.

6. **Define and describe the major e-commerce government models.** The broadening of e-government will come in four forms:
   - *Government to Government*—the electronic commerce activities performed within a single nation's government focusing on vertical integration (up and down levels such as local-state-federal) and horizontal integration (between agencies at one level).
   - *Government to Business*—the electronic commerce activities performed between a government and businesses for such purposes as purchasing direct and MRO materials, soliciting bids for work, licensing applications, meeting equal employment opportunity regulations, and so on.
   - *Government to Consumer*—the electronic commerce activities performed between a government and its citizens or consumers including paying taxes, registering vehicles, and providing information and services.
   - *International Government to Government*—the electronic commerce activities performed between two or more national governments including providing foreign aid.

CLOSING CASE STUDY ONE

WHEN YOU'RE BIG, YOU CAN BE YOUR OWN B2B E-MARKETPLACE

Business to Business (B2B) e-marketplaces are the growing trend in the B2B e-commerce business model. Businesses from all industries and countries can gather, perform commerce functions, share mission-critical information, and deploy infrastructure applications that allow those organizations to tie their internal systems to each other.

But some companies—the largest ones—don't have to play in the generic B2B e-marketplaces. Instead, they can build their own and literally require that their suppliers participate. Once such company is Volkswagen AG. Its B2B e-marketplace is called VWgroupsupply .com (www.vwgroupsupply.com).

Volkswagen AG offers eight brands of automobiles—Volkswagen (passenger), Volkswagen Commercial Vehicles, Audi, Bentley, Bugatti, Lamborghini, Seat, and Skoda. In 2003, Volkswagen spent almost 60 billion euros, or approximately $77 billion, on components, automotive parts, and MRO materials for its manufacturing operations. When you spend that much money with your suppliers, you can open and run your own B2B e-marketplace.

VWgroupsupply.com handles 90 percent of Volkswagen global purchases. Almost all request for quotes, contract negotiations, catalog updating and buying, purchase-order management, vehicle program management, and payments are handled electronically and online through VWgroupsupply.com.

Gains in efficiency and productivity coupled with material costs reductions have been tremendous. The cost savings alone generated over the last three years were more than 100 million euros, or approximately $127 million.

Volkswagen requires that each of its 5,500 suppliers use VWgroupsupply.com for any interactions. Suppliers place product and pricing catalogs on the system, respond to requests for quotes, and collaborate with Volkswagen engineers on new product designs, all in the safe and secure environment of Volkswagen's proprietary B2B e-marketplace.

By requiring its suppliers to interact with Volkswagen in the e-marketplace, purchasing agents no longer have to spend valuable time searching for information and pricing. Volkswagen has, in essence, created a system that brings the necessary information to the purchasing agents. This new system within VWgroupsupply.com is called iPAD, or Internal Purchasing Agent Desk.

Prior to the implementation of iPAD, purchasing agents entering a purchase order for a vehicle front module had to use numerous separate systems to complete the process. They had to retrieve information from a supplier system and its database, query information in Volkswagen's internal parts information system, obtain information from a request-for-quotes database, enter information into a contract-negotiation transcript system, and interact with several other systems and databases. In all, the purchasing agent had to log into and use seven separate systems. Analysis revealed that Volkswagen purchasing agents were spending 70 percent of their time finding, retrieving, analyzing, validating, and moving information. This took away valuable time from such tasks as negotiating better prices with suppliers.

Using a form of an integrated collaboration environment, or ICE, which we discussed in Chapter 2, purchasing agents now participate in a simple three-step process. First, iPAD captures and sends a business event to the purchasing agent, such as the need to order vehicle front modules. Second, iPAD attaches to that communication other necessary information such as information about potential suppliers, their costs, and other forms of analysis and descriptive information. Finally, iPAD sends the corresponding business processes and work flows to be completed electronically.

It works much like a digital dashboard, which we also introduced you to in Chapter 2. When purchasing agents log onto the iPAD portal in the morning, they receive a customized Web page with announcements, business alerts, analyses, and digital workflows to be completed. The purchasing agents can set out immediately to complete the tasks for the day, without having to spend 70 percent of their time finding, retrieving, and analyzing information. iPAD even customizes the Web page according to the purchasing agent's native language, something very necessary for a global manufacturer of automobiles with more than 2,000 purchasing agents worldwide.[16,17]

Questions

1. Volkswagen operates its own proprietary B2B e-marketplace in which its suppliers participate. What are the disadvantages to Volkswagen of not using a generic B2B e-marketplace with even more suppliers? What are the advantages to Volkswagen of developing and using its own proprietary B2B e-marketplace?

2. When Volkswagen needs a new part design, it uses VWsupplygroup.com to get its suppliers involved in the design process early. This creates a tremendous amount of interorganizational collaboration. What are the advantages to the suppliers and to Volkswagen in doing so?

3. How is Volkswagen's VWgroupsupply.com B2B e-marketplace an example of a vertical e-marketplace implementation? How is it an example of a horizontal e-marketplace implementation? Why is it necessary that Volkswagen combine both of these e-marketplaces into one e-marketplace? What would be the drawbacks to creating two different e-marketplaces—one for suppliers of direct materials and one for suppliers of MRO materials?

4. To make effective purchasing decisions, Volkswagen's purchasing agents need business intelligence. What kind of business intelligence does iPAD provide to purchasing agents for carrying out their tasks? What additional kinds of business intelligence not discussed in this case could Volkswagen's purchasing agents take advantage of to make more effective decisions?

5. IPAD manages the workflow for purchasing agents. Describe how iPAD manages this process including information provided, steps to be executed, and the presentation of information.

CLOSING CASE STUDY TWO

TOTING THE E-COMMERCE LINE WITH EBAGS

For a true e-commerce success story you don't have to look any further than eBags (www.ebags.com). While many pure-play e-commerce Web sites have fallen by the wayside, eBags is not only surviving, it is thriving. It is the world's leading online provider of bags and accessories for all lifestyles. With 180 brands and over 8,000 products, eBags has sold more than 2.5 million bags since its launch in March 1999. It carries a complete line of premium and popular brands, including Samsonite, JanSport, The North Face, Liz Claiborne, and Adidas. You can buy anything from backpacks and carry-ons to computer cases and handbags at extremely competitive prices from its Web site.

eBags has received several awards for excellence in online retailing, among them:

- Circle of Excellence Platinum Award, Bizrate.com
- Web Site of the Year, *Catalog Age Magazine* (for the second year in a row)
- Email Marketer of the Year, ClickZ.MessageMedia
- Marketer of the Year, Colorado AMA
- Rocky Mountain Portal Award
- Gold Peak Catalog, Colorado AMA
- Entrepreneur of the Year—Rocky Mountain Region, Ernst and Young
- E-Commerce Initiative Award of Merit, Colorado Software and Internet Association
- Best of Show, eTravel World Awards
- 50 Essential Web Sites, *Condé* Naste Traveler
- Internet Retailer's Best of the Web

A good part of the reason for eBags's success is its commitment to providing each customer with superior service, 24 hours a day, 365 days a year. eBags provides customers with the ability to contact customer service representatives for personal assistance by telephone or e-mail and also provides convenient, real-time UPS order tracking. According to Jon Nordmark, CEO of eBags.com, "From a customer perspective, we've spent a great deal of time developing pioneering ways to guide our shoppers to the bags and accessories that enhance their lifestyles through function and fashion."

Although you would never know it, this superior customer service is not provided by eBags employees.

For the past several years, eBags has outsourced both the handling of phone orders and customer service calls to Finali Corporation (www.finali.com). "The call center is often the only human contact customers have with our brand," says eBags CEO Jon Nordmark. "By maintaining a call center staff that can think on its feet, Finali delivers real value to our customers and a measurable return on our call center investment."

Typically, the conversion rate of inbound customer calls to sales at the call center has been about 25 percent. But during the 2001 holiday season, special training and incentives for Finali call center reps servicing the eBags Web site helped raise that number to 44 percent. In addition, the average size of orders placed through the call center hit $100, topping the average Web order of just over $75. The increased conversion rates and order size meant that for every dollar eBags spent with Finali, Finali generated $3.79 in sales.

eBags's many online services also distinguish it from the rest of the online marketplace. eBags's Laptop Finder searches for compatible laptop cases based on the brand and model number of your computer. And eBags's Airline Approved Carry-On Finder will show you all the carry-on bags that fit in each airline's overhead bins. eBags has also tightly integrated its systems with those of UPS to provide accurate estimated arrival dates and free returns.

eBags announced profits for the first time in December 2001, posting 5.4 percent earnings before interest, taxes, depreciation, and amortization. "Part of that achievement was due to smart outsourcing like the call center," says eBags CFO Eliot Cobb. As of early 2004, eBags had posted seven consecutive profitable quarters.[18,19]

Questions

1. According to Porter's Five Forces Model how would you characterize the competitive space in which eBags operates according to buyer power, supplier power, threat of substitute products or services, threat of new entrants, and rivalry among existing competitors? (You may wish to reread the section on Porter's Model in Chapter 2.) You may have to do some research on the

Web to determine what other e-commerce Web sites sell similar products. Pick one of Porter's five forces and describe what steps eBags has undertaken to shift that force in a positive way in its direction.

2. In our discussions of customers and their perceptions of value, we noted that customers tend to categorize products and services as either convenience or specialty. How would you characterize what eBags provides—convenience, specialty, or perhaps a combination of the two? Justify your answer.

3. We also noted in this chapter that commoditylike and digital products work extremely well within the B2C e-commerce business model. eBags sells products that are neither. How can it be so successful without selling these types of products?

4. How would you describe the majority of eBags's customers (end consumers)? What sort of demographics would you like to know about eBags's customers if you were an eBags employee?

5. Given that eBags's customers are end consumers, and on the basis of your answer to Question 4, what sort of marketing mix would you recommend for eBags? If you specify creating affiliate programs, identify the types of Web sites with which to enter into an affiliate program.

6. What innovative steps could eBags employ to offer mass customization to its customers? Do you think this would have any measurable positive effect on sales? Why or why not?

7. What sort of payment options does eBags accept? You may have to visit its Web site to determine this. Should eBags consider broadening the payment options it accepts? Why or why not?

Key Terms and Concepts

Affiliate program, 251
Business to Business (B2B) e-commerce, 242
Business to Consumer (B2C) e-commerce, 242
Click-and-mortar, 261
Click-and-order (pure play), 263
Click-through, 251
Conversion rate, 251
Demand aggregation, 247
Digital wallet, 255
Direct materials, 248
Electronic Bill Presentment and Payment (EBPP), 254
Electronic check, 254
Electronic commerce (e-commerce), 240
Electronic data interchange (EDI), 256
Electronic government (e-government), 261
Electronic marketplace (e-marketplace), 248
Encryption, 258
Financial cybermediary, 254
Financial EDI (financial electronic data interchange), 258
Government to Business (G2B), 262

Government to Consumer (G2C), 263
Government to Government (G2G, intra-G2G), 262
Horizontal e-marketplace, 248
International Government to Government (inter-G2G), 264
Maintenance, repair, and operations (MRO) materials (indirect materials), 247
Marketing mix, 250
Mass customization, 247
Online ad (banner ad), 250
Pop-under ad, 251
Pop-up ad, 250
Public key encryption (PKE), 258
Reverse auction, 248
Secure Electronic Transaction (SET), 259
Secure Sockets Layer (SSL), 259
Smart card, 255
Spoofing, 256
Vertical e-marketplace, 249
Viral marketing, 251

Short-Answer Questions

1. What is electronic commerce? What are the four main perspectives for e-commerce?
2. How can you use a B2B e-marketplace to reduce your dependency on a particular supplier?
3. How do convenience and specialty items differ in the B2C e-commerce business model?
4. Why do commoditylike and digital items sell well in the B2C e-commerce business model?
5. What is mass customization?
6. What are maintenance, repair, and operations (MRO) materials?
7. What is demand aggregation?
8. What are direct materials?
9. How does a reverse auction work?
10. How are vertical and horizontal e-marketplaces different?
11. What is spoofing?
12. What can a marketing mix include for a B2C e-commerce business?
13. How do pop-up and pop-under ads differ?
14. What is a conversion rate?
15. What are the major types of B2C e-commerce payment systems?
16. What is the difference between a client-side digital wallet and a server-side digital wallet?
17. What is financial EDI?
18. How does public key encryption work?
19. How are Secure Sockets Layers (SSLs) and Secure Electronic Transactions (SETs) different? How are they the same?
20. How do electronic government and expanded electronic government differ? How are they similar?
21. What are the four primary focuses of e-government?

Assignments and Exercises

1. **YOUR STATE AND LOCAL GOVERNMENT E-COMMERCE ACTIVITIES** Visit the Web sites for your state and local governments. Do some looking around and make a list of what services, information deliveries, and transaction processing they offer that you previously could handle only by visiting a physical building. How are these different from and similar to comparable e-government activities now offered by the U.S. federal government?

2. **DEALING WITH THE GREAT DIGITAL DIVIDE** The "great digital divide" is a term coined to address the concerns of many people that the world is becoming one marked by "have's" and "have not's" with respect to technology—that is, the traditional notion of a "third world" is now also being defined by the extent to which a country has access to and uses technology. Find out what, if anything, the United Nations is doing about this issue and express an opinion on whether or not you believe its efforts will be successful. Determine if there are organizations such as private companies or foundations that have the digital divide high on their agendas. For any such organizations you find, evaluate their efforts and express an opinion as to whether or not they will be successful. Finally, search for a less developed country that is making significant local efforts to deal with the digital divide. If you can't find one, prepare a list of the countries you reviewed and briefly describe the conditions in one of them with respect to technology.

3. **RESEARCHING A BUSINESS TO BUSINESS E-MARKETPLACE** Biz2Biz (www.biz2biz.com/Marketplace/) is a B2B e-marketplace. Connect to its site and do some looking around. What sort of marketing services does it provide through its Biz2BizCommunication program? What sort of services does it provide for creating and maintaining an electronic catalog? If you owned a business and wanted to join, what process would you have to go through? How much does it cost your organization to join Biz2Biz? What buyer tools does Biz2Biz provide its membership?

4. **DEVELOPING M-COMMERCE SCENARIOS FOR GPS CELL PHONES** Soon, cell phones will be equipped with GPS chips that enable users to be located to within a geographical location about the size of a tennis court. The primary purpose for installing GPS chips in phones is to enable emergency services to locate a

cell phone user. For example, if you dial an emergency assistance number (911 in the United States) from your home now, it is possible for a computer system to use your home telephone number to access a database and obtain your address. This could be very useful in situations in which you were unable to give address information to the emergency operator for some reason. The problem with trying to do the same thing with present-day cell phones is that you could be calling from anywhere and that is the problem GPS-enabled cell phones are intended to overcome.

As you might imagine, marketers have been monitoring this development with great interest because GPS-phones will support m-commerce, which we discussed in Chapter 1. When the new cell phones become available, marketers visualize scenarios where they will know who you are (by your telephone number) and where you are (by the GPS chip). One possible way they could use this information, for example, is to give you a call when you are walking past their shop in the mall to let you know of a special sale on items they know you would be interested in buying. Of course, retailers would have to possess IT systems that would permit them to craft such personalized offers, and you would have had to give them permission to call you.

Find out what at least three e-commerce marketers are saying about personalized marketing using GPS-equipped cell phones and prepare an analysis of how the phones will be likely to be used when the technology is widely available.

5. **FINDING THE MOST POPULAR B2C E-COMMERCE SITES** Connect to the Web and do some research to find the most popular B2C e-commerce Web sites in terms of number of hits or views per month. What are the sites? Which of the sites in some way or another support the concept of an e-marketplace where end consumers can gather?

Discussion Questions

1. In what ways can shopping over the Internet be more convenient for consumers? In what ways can it be less convenient? List at least five products you would have no hesitation buying over the Internet, five products you might want to think about a bit before buying, and five products you would never consider buying over the Internet. Justify your reasons in each case.

2. In your opinion, according to Porter's Five Forces Model (refer to Chapter 2), has competition increased or decreased overall as a result of the Internet and e-commerce? Specifically address each of the five forces in Porter's model.

3. Why is the ability to change prices instantaneously considered an advantage for e-commerce Web sites? When might the use of personalized pricing be a disadvantage for an e-commerce Web site?

4. There have been a string of e-commerce Web sites running out of cash, not being able to attract more money from investors, and going out of business as a result. What are some of the main reasons this happened?

5. Under what circumstances would it be appropriate to consider using viral marketing? See if you can think of an organization with an online presence that could benefit from viral marketing but is not currently using it. It could be your school, for example, or it could be an organization you are involved with. How would you suggest the organization go about using viral marketing in order for it to achieve the desired results? What are some of the other marketing techniques available for an e-commerce Web site to use? Why is it important to consider a mix of techniques rather than just relying on a single one?

6. Describe the services provided by value-added networks that make it easier for companies to exchange EDI transactions with each other. What are the pros and cons of using value-added networks for B2B e-commerce? Why don't more companies use the Internet for EDI since it is much cheaper than using a value-added network? Assume that you work for a telecommunications company that operates a value-added network (AT&T or GXS). What

sort of strategies would you encourage your company to explore to deal with the possibility of losing considerable amounts of revenues as your customers leave you in favor of using other Internet-based services?

7. What are the advantages and disadvantages of B2B marketplaces for buyers? For sellers? How could a supplier company play on the relationships that it has with a long-standing customer to avoid getting pulled into a reverse auction in an open B2B marketplace? Why do some observers say that B2B marketplaces can be risky ventures?

8. In this chapter, we've identified differences between end consumers and businesses as customers. Review those differences and then write down the three you consider most significant. Discuss those three. For the differences that you did not choose as the three most important, be prepared to justify your decision.

9. In this chapter, we discussed using such technologies as B2B e-marketplaces to create tighter supply chain managements, thereby driving out costs. If you refer back to Chapter 2, you'll recall that another major business initiative is customer relationship management (CRM). How can B2C e-commerce businesses use the Internet to further enhance their CRM initiatives? How can B2B e-commerce businesses use the Internet to further enhance their CRM initiatives? Does it become easier or harder to maintain relationships with customers as businesses move toward more "electronic" commerce? Why?

Getting Your Business on the Internet

Let's say you've decided it might be fun (and profitable) to establish a retail-oriented Internet-based business. You can use the one your team created in the Team Work project on page 260 if it's appropriate or you can create a new one. You know that many such e-commerce businesses don't make it, but you'd like to be one that is successful. There are a lot of resources on the Internet that can help you with the tasks of selecting the right business in the first place, getting the site up and running, deciding who should host your site, marketing your site, understanding privacy issues, and obtaining the funds you need to pay your expenses until your business begins to show a profit. On the Web site that supports this text (www.mhhe.com/haag, select "Electronic Commerce Projects"), we've provided direct links to many useful Web sites. These are a great starting point for completing this project. We also encourage you to search the Internet for others.

COMPETITIVE INTELLIGENCE

The first thing you need is an idea for the business. What would you like to sell? A product or a service? Make sure you have expertise, or something special to offer. After you've come up with a candidate, it's time to see how much competition is out there and what they're up to. One of the things many new business owners fail to do is to see how many competitors there are before they launch their business. You may find there are too many and that they would be tough competition for you (review Porter's Five Forces Model). Or, you may find that there are few competitors and the ones who are out there aren't doing a terrific job.

Seek out and look at some of the Web sites of businesses in the competitive space you're thinking of entering. As you do, answer the following questions.

A. How many sites did you find that are offering the same product or service you're planning to offer?

B. How many are in your country and how many are in other countries?

C. Did you come across a site from another country that has a unique approach that you did not see on any of the sites in your own country?

STOREFRONT SOFTWARE

If you decide to sell products, there is software that you can use to make it easy to create a Web site. There are many software products for you to choose from. Some will cost you a lot of money, but others are free. FreeMerchant.com, for example, has a Basic Store for $9.95 per month, a Bronze Package for $24.95 per month, a Silver Package for $49.95 per month, and a Gold Package for $99.95 per month. What you get in each of these packages is listed in detail on the FreeMerchant.com Web site (www.freemerchant.com). Since there are many options to choose from, it would be worth your while to do a little research to see if you can find an article that compares current versions of storefront software. A site like ZDNet.com (www.zdnet.com) would be a good place to start your search. Build up a list of features that you will need for your e-commerce site, and then compare your needs with the features offered by the various software packages. They all sound good when you read about them on the vendors' Web sites so be sure you take a "test drive" of the software before you sign up.

Another possibility would be to sign up for a shopping mall. Find your way to Amazon.com's zShops or Yahoo!Store and see what you think of these alternatives. Finally, you'll need a way for your customers to pay you for what they buy. This involves getting a merchant account which permits you to accept credit cards. Most of the storefront sites will explain how merchant accounts work and will help you get a merchant account (see www.bigstep.com, for example).

A. What features have you decided your storefront software must provide?

B. How have you evaluated the pros and cons of using a storefront software package versus the options offered by Amazon.com and Yahoo!?

C. See if you can track down users of software options you are considering. Send them an e-mail and ask them what they like and dislike. You may be surprised at their answers.

HOSTING SERVICES

You've got some options here. You can decide to acquire the necessary computer and communications hardware and software to manage your own technical infrastructure, or you can let a specialist firm do it for you. Unless you're really into the technical side of things, it's probably better to work with a firm that specializes in it. They are called *Web hosting services* and there are plenty of them around. Cost, reliability, security, and customer service are some of the criteria you might use in selecting a hosting service. If you're planning to have your business located in a country with poor telecommunications services, don't forget that you can choose a hosting service located in a country with a more reliable telecommunications infrastructure, anywhere in the world. Some companies provide directories that make it easy for you to find and compare prices and features of Web hosting companies, sort of like shopping malls for Web hosting services. An example of such a company is FindYourHosting.com (www.findyourhosting.com). Take a look at its site to see some of the options available. As you consider Web hosting services, answer the following questions.

A. Compare the costs of the various hosting services. Were you able to find one that seems to be within your budget?

B. How can you evaluate the reliability of the various Web hosting services?

C. How can you evaluate the quality of a Web hosting company's customer service? What do you have a right to expect in the way of customer service and also security?

MARKETING YOUR SITE

In this chapter, we discussed several options for marketing a Web site: registering with search engines, online ads, viral marketing, and affiliate programs. Deciding on the marketing mix that will be most effective and still permit you to stay within a reasonable budget will be critical to the success of your venture. You may want to consider employing an Internet marketing consultant to help you lay out a marketing plan. One, AdDesigner.com (www.addesigner. com), even offers some free services. Also, you may want to see what marketing services your storefront software or Web hosting service may offer. As you consider how to market your site, answer the following questions.

A. How have you defined your target market? Who are the people that will be most interested in your product or service?

B. Which of the available marketing techniques have you selected as being most appropriate to market your site? Why have you selected this particular marketing mix?

C. What have you decided about using the services of a marketing consultant? How did you justify your decision?

EXTENDED LEARNING MODULE E

NETWORK BASICS

Student Learning Outcomes

1. IDENTIFY AND DESCRIBE THE FOUR BASIC CONCEPTS ON WHICH NETWORKS ARE BUILT AND DESCRIBE WHAT IS NEEDED TO SET UP A SMALL PEER-TO-PEER NETWORK AT HOME.

2. DESCRIBE THE COMPONENTS USED TO BUILD LARGE BUSINESS NETWORKS AND DEFINE AND COMPARE LOCAL AREA NETWORKS (LANS), WIDE AREA NETWORKS (WANS), AND METROPOLITAN AREA NETWORKS (MANS).

3. COMPARE AND CONTRAST THE VARIOUS INTERNET CONNECTION POSSIBILITIES.

4. COMPARE AND CONTRAST THE TYPES OF COMMUNICATIONS MEDIA.

5. STATE THE FOUR PRINCIPLES OF COMPUTER SECURITY AND DESCRIBE HOW DIFFERENT NETWORK SECURITY DEVICES REFLECT THOSE PRINCIPLES.

6. DESCRIBE CLIENT/SERVER BUSINESS NETWORKS FROM A BUSINESS AND PHYSICAL POINT OF VIEW.

Taking Advantage of the CD

When you're surfing the Web, accessing software on your school's server, sending e-mail, or letting your roommate use his/her computer to access the files on your computer, your computer is part of a network. A **computer network** (which we simply refer to as a network) is two or more computers connected so that they can communicate with each other and share information, software, peripheral devices, and/or processing power. Many networks have dozens, hundreds, or even thousands of computers.

Networks come in all sizes from two computers connected to share a printer, to the Internet, which is the largest network on the planet, joining millions of computers of all kinds all over the world. In between are business networks, which vary in size from a dozen or fewer computers to many thousands.

Some networks are extremely complex with perhaps thousands of computers connected together. These networks require highly skilled professionals to keep them up and running. However, regardless of their size, some basic principles apply to all networks.

1. Each computer on a network must have a network interface (either as an expansion card or integrated into the motherboard or through software for a modem) that provides the entrance or doorway for information traffic to and from other computers.

2. A network usually has at least one connecting device (like a hub or a router) that ties the computers on the network together and acts as a switchboard for passing information.

3. There must be communications media like cables or radio waves connecting network hardware devices. The communications media transport information around the network between computers and the connecting device(s).

4. Each computer must have software that supports the movement of information in and out of it. This could be modem software and/or a network operating system.

We definitely believe that it's worth your time and energy to pop in the CD and read this module. This module is the same as the modules in your text—it includes Team Work and On Your Own projects and great end-of-module Assignments and Exercises. In it, you'll learn many things including

- How to share an Internet connection among multiple computers in your home with a broadband or home router and a DSL or cable modem
- Five ways to connect to the Internet
  - Phone line and dial-up modem
  - Phone line and Digital Subscriber Line (DSL) modem
  - Cable TV line and cable modem
  - Satellite dish and satellite modem
  - T1 and DS3 lines
- How to add wireless access to a network
- Client/server networks from a business point of view
- Client/server networks from a physical point of view
- What differentiates LANs, MANs, WLANs, and WANs
- The types of telecommunications media that networks use
- Network security issues

CHAPTER SIX OUTLINE

STUDENT LEARNING OUTCOMES

1. List the seven steps in the systems development life cycle (SDLC) and associated activities for each step.

2. Describe the four systems development methodologies.

3. Define the role of outsourcing.

4. List and describe the three different forms of outsourcing.

5. Describe business process outsourcing (BPO).

6. Describe prototyping and profile an example of a prototype.

7. Describe the advantages of prototyping.

INDUSTRY PERSPECTIVE

284 **The Life Cycle of Boise Office Solutions**

287 **Making Your Software Work**

298 **Do Your Homework!**

302 **St. Jude Children's Research Hospital Cures**

FEATURES

283 **On Your Own**
Analyzing Business Requirements

285 **Team Work**
Writing Test Conditions

295 **Global Perspective**
Outsourcing Help Desks Offshore

296 **Team Work**
How Many Are There?

299 **Global Perspective**
lastminute.com

304 **On Your Own**
Build vs. Buy

311 **Electronic Commerce**
Finding Freeware and Shareware on the Internet

WEB SUPPORT

www.mhhe.com/haag

- Using your computer for more than work
- Protecting your computer investment
- Searching for freeware and shareware

CHAPTER SIX

Systems Development
Phases, Tools, and Techniques

OPENING CASE STUDY
MERCEDES-BENZ ONLINE
BUILT-TO-ORDER TRUCKS

"Which driver's cabs and radios are available for a 24-ton rig?" In the past, such a question would have cost Mercedes-Benz dealers a lot of time leafing through big manuals. Today, the Mercedes-Benz Web site offers orientation in the multitude of equipment variations with the Mercedes-Benz customer advisory system, developed by CAS Software AG.

The online program, called Truck Online Configurator (TOC), required much more development time than was required to simply display the finished online system internally for the automobile and transporter divisions. The TOC was given a completely new user guide for Web site visitors that orients itself on the different demands of the site visitors in three ways: through technical features, trade solution, and transport task. Interested customers are able to compile their own vehicle preference by entering the required technical details, like the type of drive, wheelbase, or engine performance needed. Or the interested customer can select by trade solution (where he or she simply tells the TOC that a truck is required for the transportation of frozen foods, for example) and a list of suitable models is offered. These can then be viewed in video sequences or as a 360° view. The third alternative for visitors to the site is to let the interested customer find the desired commercial vehicle by entering the transport task, that is, by feeding the TOC with the necessary approximate power per mile per year or the distance profile. On every single page, numerous information windows or buttons are opened containing explanatory text and graphics.

CAS had only five months in which to produce this complex and extensive application, from the definition of the specialist requirements, to the technical specifications, right up to the development, testing, and installation of the software. This tight deadline required a risk-driven project management, which meant that individual phases of the project would overlap. While a few developers, together with the project managers of Mercedes-Benz, were clarifying the technical requirements of the individual functions, other parts of the TOC were already being implemented, providing feedback for the developers. This approach to system development is called rapid application development (RAD).

The CAS solution was virtually tailor-made for this project. The finished programs run in an extremely fast and stable manner. These were the central, technical requirements of Mercedes-Benz for the TOC: The company wanted an application which boasted a maximum availability but with minimum response times.

Thanks to using the rapid application development (RAD) process, CAS was able to create a very fast high-quality application.[1]

Introduction

Have you ever wondered why businesses develop information systems (IT systems) in the first place, or how a business knows when it's time to replace an old information system? Almost any position you take in a company today will require you to work with information systems because they are by now one of the most important elements of any business. Information systems supply the support structure for meeting companies' strategies and goals. Typically, new systems are created because employees request the systems to help them perform their work. For example, a marketing manager might request a system to provide product information and track customer sales information (CRM activities) or a human resource manager might request a new system to track employee vacation and sick days.

Billions of dollars are spent each year on the acquisition, design, development, implementation, and maintenance of information systems. The ongoing need for safe, secure, and reliable system solutions is the consequence of companies' increasing dependence on information technology to provide services and develop products, administer daily activities, and perform short- and long-term management functions.

Systems developers must ensure all the business's needs and requirements are met when developing information systems, establish uniform privacy and security practices for system users, and develop acceptable implementation strategies for the new systems. This chapter focuses on the many factors that must come together to develop a successful information system.

The Systems Development Life Cycle

The *systems development life cycle (SDLC)* is a structured step-by-step approach for developing information systems. There are literally hundreds of different activities associated with each phase in the SDLC. Typical activities include determining budgets, gathering business requirements, designing models, and writing detailed user documentation. The activities you perform during each systems development project will vary depending on the type of system you're building and the tools you use to build it. Since we can't possibly cover them all in this brief introduction, we have chosen a few of the more important SDLC activities that you might perform on a systems development project. Figure 6.1 displays the seven phases in the SDLC along with the associated activities discussed in this chapter.

As we introduce you to the SDLC in this section, we'll focus on how the overall process works (see Figure 6.2), key activities within each phase, roles you may play in a project, and opportunities you can capitalize on to ensure that your systems development effort is a success.

PHASE 1: PLANNING

In the *planning phase* of the systems development life cycle you create a solid plan for developing your information system. The following are the three primary activities you'll perform during the planning phase:

1. *Define the system to be developed:* You must identify and select the system for development or determine which system is required to support the strategic goals of your organization. Organizations typically track all the proposed systems

SDLC Phase	Activities
1. Planning	• Define the system to be developed • Set the project scope • Develop the project plan including tasks, resources, and timeframes
2. Analysis	• Gather the business requirements for the system
3. Design	• Design the technical architecture required to support the system • Design system models
4. Development	• Build the technical architecture • Build the database and programs
5. Testing	• Write the test conditions • Perform the testing of the system
6. Implementation	• Write detailed user documentation • Provide training for the system users
7. Maintenance	• Build a help desk to support the system users • Provide an environment to support system changes

Figure 6.1

The Systems Development Life Cycle (SDLC) and Associated Activities

and prioritize them based on business impact or critical success factors. A **critical success factor (CSF)** is a factor critical to your organization's success. This allows the business to strategically decide which systems to build.

2. *Set the project scope:* You must define the project's scope and create a project scope document for your systems development effort. The **project scope** clearly defines the high-level system requirements. Scope is often referred to as the 10,000-foot view of the system or the most basic definition of the system. Setting the project scope is important for many reasons; most important it helps you avoid scope creep and feature creep. **Scope creep** occurs when the scope of the project increases beyond its original intentions. **Feature creep** occurs when developers add extra features that were not part of the initial requirements. A **project scope document** is a written definition of the project scope and is usually no longer than a paragraph.

3. *Develop the project plan:* You must develop a detailed project plan for your entire systems development effort. The **project plan** defines the what, when, and who questions of systems development including all activities to be performed, the individuals, or resources, who will perform the activities, and the time required to complete each activity. The detailed project plan is the guiding force behind ensuring the on-time delivery of a complete and successful information system.

Figure 6.2

The Systems Development Life Cycle (SDLC)

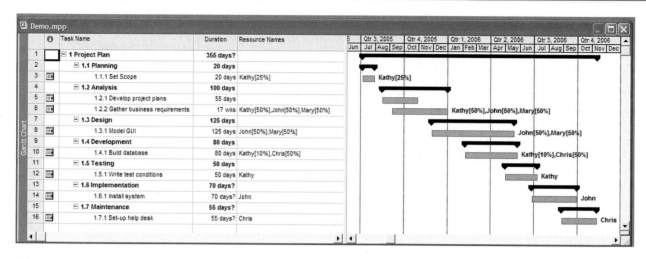

Figure 6.3

A Sample Project Plan

Figure 6.3 displays a sample project plan. A ***project manager*** is an individual who is an expert in project planning and management, defines and develops the project plan, and tracks the plan to ensure all key project milestones are completed on time. ***Project milestones*** represent key dates by which you need a certain group of activities performed. For example, completing the planning phase might be a project milestone. If all your project milestones are being completed on time, this is a good indication that your project is on schedule and will be successful.

To learn more about project planning and management, visit the Web site that supports this text at www.mhhe.com/haag.

PHASE 2: ANALYSIS

Once your organization has decided which system to develop, you can move into the analysis phase. The ***analysis phase*** of the systems development life cycle involves end-users and IT specialists working together to gather, understand, and document the business requirements for the proposed system. The following are the two primary activities you'll perform during the analysis phase:

1. *Gathering the business requirements: **Business requirements*** are the detailed set of employee requests that the system must meet to be successful. The business requirements drive the entire system. A sample business requirement might state, "The CRM system must track all customer sales by product, region, and sales representative." The business requirement states what the system must do from the business perspective. Gathering business requirements is similar to performing an investigation. You must talk to everyone who has a claim in using the new system to find out what is required. An extremely useful way to gather business requirements is to perform a joint application development session. During a ***joint application development (JAD)*** session users and IT specialists meet, sometimes for several days, to define and review the business requirements for the system.

2. *Prioritize the requirements:* Once you define all the business requirements, you prioritize them in order of business importance and place them in a formal comprehensive document, the ***requirements definition document.*** The users receive the requirements definition document for their sign-off. ***Sign-off*** is the

ANALYZING BUSINESS REQUIREMENTS

You have been hired to build an employee tracking system for a new coffee shop. Review the following business requirements and highlight any potential issues.

- All employees must have a unique employee ID.
- The system must track employee hours worked based on employee last name.
- Employees must be scheduled to work a minimum of 8 hours per day.
- Employee payroll is calculated by multiplying the employee's hours worked by $7.25.

- Managers must be scheduled to work morning shifts.
- Employees cannot be scheduled to work over 8 hours per day.
- Servers cannot be scheduled to work morning, afternoon, or evening shifts.
- The system must allow managers to change and delete employees from the system.

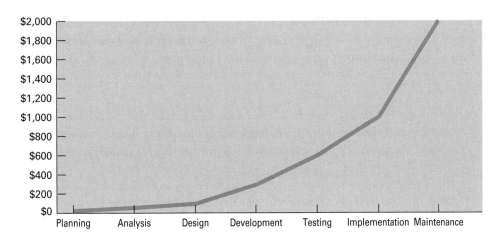

Figure 6.4

The Cost of Finding Errors

users' actual signatures indicating they approve all the business requirements. Typically, one of the first major milestones in the project plan is the users' sign-off on business requirements.

One of the key things to think about when you are reviewing business requirements is the cost to the company of fixing errors if the business requirements are unclear or inaccurate. An error found during the analysis phase is relatively inexpensive to fix; all you typically have to do is change a Word document. An error found during later phases, however, is incredibly expensive to fix because you have to change the actual system. Figure 6.4 displays how the cost to fix an error grows exponentially the later the error is found in the SDLC.

PHASE 3: DESIGN

The primary goal of the ***design phase*** of the systems development life cycle is to build a technical blueprint of how the proposed system will work. During the analysis phase, end users and IT specialists work together to develop the business requirements for the proposed system from a logical point of view. That is, during analysis you document business requirements without respect to technology or the technical infrastructure that

THE LIFE CYCLE OF BOISE OFFICE SOLUTIONS

Boise Office Solutions is a premier multinational distributor of office and technology products, office furniture, and paper, with annual sales totaling $3.5 billion. The company, headquartered in Itasca, Illinois, has customers ranging in size from small organizations to multinational corporations. Boise Office Solutions has operations throughout the United States, Australia, New Zealand, Canada, and Mexico, and also serves customers in Europe.

Boise already had its own unique system life cycle process, but it lacked many of the traditional systems development life cycle (SDLC) capabilities. The company began looking at the SDLC to help facilitate designs and incorporate them into its own life cycle process. The main interest was in creating diagrams, as well as generating code and creating good design. By standardizing an SDLC, any member of the development team can walk over to another developer's desk, jump right in, and they can work together on a project. Everyone uses the same process, with the same look and feel.[2]

will support the system. As you move into design, the project team turns its attention to the system from a physical or technical point of view. You take the business requirements generated during the analysis phase and define the supporting technical architecture in the design phase. The following are the primary activities you'll perform during the design phase:

1. *Design the technical architecture:* The **technical architecture** defines the hardware, software, and telecommunications equipment required to run the system. Most systems run on a computer network with each employee having a workstation and the application software running on a server. The telecommunications requirements encompass access to the Internet and the ability for end users to connect remotely to the server. You typically explore several different technical architectures before choosing the final technical architecture.

2. *Design the system model:* **Modeling** is the activity of drawing a graphical representation of a design. You model everything you build including screens, reports, software, and databases (with E-R diagrams as we described in *Extended Learning Module C*). There are many different types of modeling activities performed during the design phase including a graphical user interface screen design. The **graphical user interface (GUI)** is the interface to an information system. **GUI screen design** is the ability to model the information system screens for an entire system. You must decide many things when modeling a GUI, including the placement of items on the screen and the number of items contained in a drop-down list. You base your decisions as to how and where to display menu items on whatever is easiest for the users to use. If the menu items are placed incorrectly on the GUI, users could waste a significant amount of time just searching the GUI to find the correct item.

PHASE 4: DEVELOPMENT

During the **development phase** of the systems development life cycle, you take all your detailed design documents from the design phase and transform them into an actual system. This phase marks the point at which you go from physical design to physical im-

WRITING TEST CONDITIONS

Your manager has asked you to test the cut and paste functionality for a word processing application. Write 10 detailed test conditions using the template below. Be sure to think about cutting and pasting such things as different fonts, varying font sizes, bold and italic fonts, graphics, etc. We have provided a sample for you. Once you have completed your test conditions, estimate how many test conditions would be required to completely test the cut and paste functionality for Microsoft Word.

Test Condition Number	Date	Tester Name	Test Condition	Expected Result	Actual Result	Pass/Fail
1	5/27/2005	McLeod	Highlight text	Highlighted text	Highlighted text	Pass

plementation. The following are the two main activities you'll perform during the development phase:

1. *Build the technical architecture:* For you to build your system, you must first build the platform on which the system is going to operate. In the development phase, you purchase and implement equipment necessary to support the technical architecture you designed during the design phase.

2. *Build the database and programs:* Once the technical architecture is built, you initiate and complete the creation of supporting databases and writing the software required for the system. These tasks are usually undertaken by IT specialists, and it may take months or even years to design and create the databases and write all the software.

PHASE 5: TESTING

The ***testing phase*** of the systems development life cycle verifies that the system works and meets all the business requirements defined in the analysis phase. Testing is critical. The following are the primary activities you'll perform during the testing phase:

1. *Write the test conditions:* You must have detailed test conditions to perform an exhaustive test. ***Test conditions*** are the detailed steps the system must perform along with the expected results of each step. The tester will execute each test condition and compare the expected results with the actual results to verify that the system functions correctly. Each time the actual result is different from the expected result, a "bug" is generated, and the system goes back to development for a "bug fix." A typical systems development effort has hundreds or thousands of test conditions. You must execute and verify all of these test conditions to ensure the entire system functions correctly.

2. *Perform the testing of the system:* You must perform many different types of tests when you begin testing your new system. A few of the more common tests include:
   - *Unit testing*—tests individual units or pieces of code for a system.
   - *System testing*—verifies that the units or pieces of code written for a system function correctly when integrated into the total system.
   - *Integration testing*—verifies that separate systems can work together.
   - *User acceptance testing (UAT)*—determines if the system satisfies the business requirements and enables users to perform their jobs correctly.

PHASE 6: IMPLEMENTATION

During the *implementation phase* of the systems development life cycle you distribute the system to all the users and they begin using the system to perform their everyday jobs. The following are the two primary activities you'll perform during the implementation phase:

1. *Write detailed user documentation:* When you install the system, you must also provide employees with **user documentation** that highlights how to use the system. Users find it extremely frustrating to have a new system without documentation.

2. *Provide training for the system users:* You must also provide training for the users who are going to use the new system. You can provide several different types of training, and two of the most popular are online training and workshop training. **Online training** runs over the Internet or off a CD or DVD. Employees perform the training at any time, on their own computers, at their own pace. This type of training is convenient because they can set their own schedule to undergo the training. **Workshop training** is held in a classroom environment and is led by an instructor. Workshop training is most suitable for difficult systems for which employees need one-on-one time with an individual instructor.

You also need to choose the implementation method that best suits your organization, project, and employees to ensure a successful implementation. When you implement the new system, you have four implementation methods you can choose from:

1. *Parallel implementation* uses both the old and new systems until you're sure that the new system performs correctly.

2. *Plunge implementation* discards the old system completely and immediately uses the new system.

3. *Pilot implementation* has only a small group of people using the new system until you know it works correctly and then the remaining people are added to the system.

4. *Phased implementation* installs the new system in phases (e.g., accounts receivable, then accounts payable) until you're sure it works correctly and then the remaining phases of the new system are implemented.

PHASE 7: MAINTENANCE

Maintaining the system is the final phase of any systems development effort. During the **maintenance phase** of the systems development life cycle, you monitor and support the new system to ensure it continues to meet the business goals. Once a system is in place, it must change as your business changes. Constantly monitoring and supporting the new system involves making minor changes (for example, new reports or information retrieval) and reviewing the system to be sure that it continues to move your organization toward its strategic goals. The following are the two primary activities you'll perform during the maintenance phase:

1. *Build a help desk to support the system users:* One of the best ways to support users is to create a help desk. A **help desk** is a group of people who respond to users' questions. Typically, users have a phone number for the help desk they call whenever they have issues or questions about the system. Providing a help desk that answers user questions is a terrific way to provide comprehensive support for users using new systems.

2. *Provide an environment to support system changes:* As changes arise in the business environment, you must react to those changes by assessing their impact on the system. It might well be that the system needs to be adapted or updated to meet the ever-changing needs of the business environment. If so, you must modify the system to support the new business environment.

Systems Development Methodologies

Most systems development is a chaotic activity, often characterized by the phrase "code and fix." The software is written without much of an underlying plan, and the design of the system is cobbled together from many short-term decisions. This actually works pretty well if your system is small, but as your system grows it becomes increasingly difficult to add new features to the system. Furthermore, bugs become increasingly prevalent and difficult to fix.

Today, systems are so large and complex that teams of architects, analysts, developers, testers, and users must work together to create the millions of lines of custom-written code that drive these systems. For this reason, developers have come up with a number of different systems development life cycle methodologies to organize and make sense of the process—such as, the waterfall, rapid application development (RAD), extreme programming, and agile methodologies.

Figure 6.5

The Waterfall
Methodology

WATERFALL METHODOLOGY

The traditional **waterfall methodology** is a sequential, activity-based process in which one phase in the SDLC is followed by another, from planning through implementation. The waterfall methodology is one of the oldest software development methodologies and has been around for over 30 years (see Figure 6.5). The success rate for software development projects pursuing this approach is only about 1 in 10. The primary reason for such a low success rate for the waterfall methodology is that it does not accommodate the level of uncertainty characteristic of and thus the creativity often required to complete complex software development projects including:

- **The business problem:** Accurately defining and articulating the business problem in terms of what the business users actually require. It may take persistence and more than one stab at the problem to distinguish between what users want and what they really need.
- **The plan:** Managing cost, resource, and time constraints. What happens to the schedule if a programmer quits? How will a schedule delay in a specific phase impact the total cost of the project?
- **The solution:** Defining the appropriate IT infrastructure that is flexible, cost-efficient, scalable, and reliable. Finalizing the optimal IT infrastructure is not likely to happen via a step-by-step approach, when so many factors must converge from all directions.

The problem with the waterfall methodology is that it assumes users can specify all business requirements in advance. Unfortunately, business requirements change as the business changes, which calls for considerable feedback and reiterative consultation for all business requirements as the development process proceeds. You can think of software as "soft" and it must be easily changed and manipulated to meet the changing dynamics of an organization. As business problems evolve over time, so must the software. For this reason, it is counterproductive to define all requirements precisely upfront since, by the time the software goes into production, which can be several months or even years after completing the initial analysis phase, chances are the business problem will have changed as well as the business.

RAPID APPLICATION DEVELOPMENT METHODOLOGY

In response to the fast pace of the economy, rapid application development has become a popular route for accelerating systems development. The **rapid application develop-**

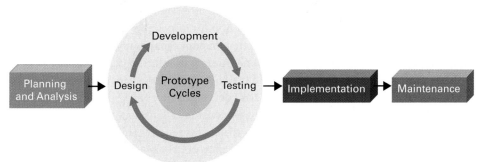

Figure 6.6

The Rapid Application Development Methodology

ment (RAD) (also called *rapid prototyping) methodology* emphasizes extensive user involvement in the rapid and evolutionary construction of working prototypes of a system to accelerate the systems development process (see Figure 6.6). The fundamentals of RAD include:

- Focus initially on creating a prototype (i.e., a working model) that looks and acts like the desired system.
- Actively involve system users in the analysis, design, and development phases.
- Accelerate collecting the business requirements through an interactive and iterative construction approach.

A *prototype* is a smaller-scale representation or working model of the users' requirements or a proposed design for an information system. The prototype is an essential part of the analysis phase when using the RAD methodology.

EXTREME PROGRAMMING METHODOLOGY

The *extreme programming (XP) methodology* breaks a project into tiny phases and developers cannot continue on to the next phase until the current phase is complete. XP is a lot like a jigsaw puzzle; there are many small pieces. Individually, the pieces make no sense, but when they are combined together an organization can gain visibility into the entire system. The primary difference between the waterfall and XP methodologies is that XP divides its phases into iterations. For example, the waterfall approach develops the entire system, whereas XP develops the system in iterations (see Figure 6.7).

Microsoft Corporation developed Internet Explorer and Netscape Communications Corporation developed Communicator using extreme programming. Both companies did a nightly compilation (called a *build*) of the entire project, bringing together all the current components. They established release dates and expended considerable effort

Figure 6.7

The Extreme Programming Methodology

to involve customers in each release. The extreme programming approach allowed both Microsoft and Netscape to manage millions of lines of code as specifications changed and evolved over time. Most important, both companies frequently held user design reviews and strategy sessions to solicit and incorporate user feedback.[4]

XP is a significant departure from traditional software development methodologies, and many organizations in different industries have developed successful software using it. One of the reasons for XP's success is that it stresses customer satisfaction. XP empowers developers to respond to changing customer and business requirements, even late in the systems development life cycle, and emphasizes teamwork. Managers, customers, and developers are all part of a team dedicated to delivering quality software. XP implements a simple, yet effective, way to enable group style development. The XP methodology supports quickly being able to respond to changing requirements and technology.

AGILE METHODOLOGY

The *agile methodology,* a form of XP, aims for customer satisfaction through early and continuous delivery of useful software components. Agile is similar to XP but with less focus on team coding and more on limiting project scope. An agile project sets a minimum number of requirements and turns them into a deliverable product. Agile means what it sounds like: fast and efficient; small and nimble; lower cost; fewer features; shorter projects.

The Agile Alliance, a group of software developers, has made its mission to improve software development processes. Its manifesto includes the following tenets:

- Satisfy the customer through early and continuous delivery of valuable software.
- Welcome changing requirements, even late in development.
- Business people and developers must work together daily throughout the project.
- Build projects around motivated individuals. Give them the environment and support they need, and trust them to get the job done.
- The best architectures, requirements, and designs emerge from self-organizing teams.
- At regular intervals, the team reflects on how to become more effective, then tunes and adjusts its behavior accordingly.[5]

Outsourcing

You have two primary choices as to who will build your IT system. Here we're not talking about personal productivity software you can buy at a local computer store, but large software packages that may cost millions of dollars. First, you can choose *insourcing,* which involves using IT specialists within your organization to develop the system. Second, you can choose *outsourcing,* which is the delegation of specific work to a third party for a specified length of time, at a specified cost, and at a specified level of service.

Outsourcing, as we know it, grew up as the industrial revolution spread and companies specialized. The oldest form of outsourcing is specialized machinery. The original cotton and woolen mills that defined the start of the industrial revolution were self-contained entities. Mechanics made everything on site except the bricks and mortar for the buildings. Over time, people discovered that they could sell equipment to mills by designing and making cheaper and better equipment. They succeeded and gave birth to the outsourcing industry.

You may argue that this is not outsourcing. However, it meets the criteria: An outside party provides a product or service designed to meet the buyer's specification; and the buyer is motivated because the seller is offering specialized expertise and/or a lower price. Manufacturing is by far the biggest user of outsourcing and has done so with great success for many years. Industries such as automobiles, aircraft, and footwear are major outsourcers.

With competitive pressures to cut costs and reduce time-to-market, many organizations are looking to outsource their IT systems development. The Outsourcing Research Council recently completed a study indicating that human resources (HR) is a top outsourcing area for many companies. Fifty percent of the companies surveyed said they were already outsourcing some or all of their payroll processing and another 38 percent said they were considering it.[6]

Energizer, the world's largest manufacturer of batteries and flashlights, outsourced its HR operations to ADP, one of the top HR outsourcing companies. Energizer currently has more than 3,500 employees and 2,000 retired employees who all require multiple HR services. ADP provides Energizer with centralized call centers, transaction processing services, and Web-based employee self-service systems. Energizer's vice president of Human Resources, Peter Conrad, stated, "ADP was clearly the most capable, and offered the kind of one-stop shopping our company was looking for." For several of the systems provided by ADP employee usage topped over 80 percent in the first six months the systems were active.[7]

Another high profile company relying heavily on outsourcing some of its IT functions is Dell. By the end of 2005, Dell plans to increase the number of staff at its Indian call center and software development operations to 10,000. Dell opened its first customer contact center in Bangalore, India, in 2001, initially providing technical support for customers in the United States. It set up another contact center in Hyderabad, India, in 2004, and a third in Mohali, India, during 2005. The company has also set up a product team in Bangalore that develops and tests some of Dell's enterprise server and storage products and a software development center that serves Dell's internal information systems requirements.

According to PricewaterhouseCoopers' survey of CEOs from 452 of the countries' fastest growing companies, "Businesses that outsource are growing faster, larger, and more profitably than those that do not. In addition, most of those involved in outsourcing say they are saving money and are highly satisfied with their outsourcing service providers." Figure 6.8 lists common areas for outsourcing opportunities across some industries.[8]

Industry	Outsourcing Opportunities
Banking and finance	Check and electronic payment processing, credit report issuance, delinquency management, securities and trades processing
Insurance	Claims reporting and investigation, policy administration, check processing, risk assessment
Telecommunications	Invoice and bill production, transaction processing
Health care	Electronic data interchange, database management, accounting
Transportation	Ticket and order processing
Government	Loan processing, Medicaid processing
Retail	Electronic payment processing

Figure 6.8

Outsourcing Opportunities across Industries

The main reasons behind the rapid growth of the outsourcing industry include the following:

- **Globalization:** As markets open worldwide, competition heats up. Companies may engage outsourcing service providers to deliver international services.
- **The Internet:** Barriers to entry, such as lack of capital, are dramatically reduced in the world of e-business. New competitors enter the market daily.
- **Growing economy and low unemployment rate:** Building a competitive workforce is much harder and more expensive.
- **Technology:** Technology is advancing at such an accelerated rate that companies often lack the resources, workforce, or expertise to keep up.
- **Deregulation:** As private industries such as telecommunications and energy deregulate, markets open and competition increases.

The many benefits associated with outsourcing include:

- Increased quality and efficiency of a process, service, or function.
- Reduced operating expenses.
- Outsourcing noncore processes or nonrevenue-producing areas allows businesses to focus resources on their core profit-generating competencies.
- Reduced exposure to risks involved with large capital investments.
- Access to outsourcing service provider's economies of scale.
- Tap into the outsourcing services provider's expertise and best-in-class practices.
- Access to advanced technologies.
- Increased flexibility with the ability to respond quickly to changing market demands.
- Avoid costly outlay of capital funds.
- Reduced headcount and associated overhead expense.
- Reduced frustration and expense related to hiring and retaining employees in an exceptionally tight job market.
- Reduced time to market for products or services.

IT outsourcing today represents a significant opportunity for your organization to capitalize on the intellectual resources of other organizations by having them take over and perform certain business functions in which they have more expertise than the users in your company. Information technology outsourcing enables organizations to keep up with market and technology advances—with less strain on human and financial resources, and more assurance that the IT infrastructure will keep pace with evolving business priorities.

The outsourcing process is both similar to and quite different from the systems development life cycle. It's different in that you turn over much of the design, development, testing, implementation, and maintenance steps to another organization. It's similar in that your organization begins with planning and defining the project scope. It's during one of these phases that your organization may come to understand that it needs a particular system but it cannot be developed through insourcing.

Outsourcing involves telling another organization what you want. What you *want* is essentially the logical requirements for a proposed system, and you convey that information by developing a request for proposal. A ***request for proposal (RFP)*** is a formal document that describes in detail your logical requirements for a proposed system and invites outsourcing organizations (or "vendors") to submit bids for its development. An RFP is the most important document in the outsourcing process. For systems of great size, your organization may create an RFP that's hundreds of pages long and requires months of work to complete.

It's vitally important that you take all the time you need to create a complete and thorough RFP. Eventually, your RFP will become the foundation for a legal and binding contract into which your organization and the vendor will enter. For your organization, the ability to develop a complete and thorough RFP means that you completely understand what you have and what you want. For the vendors, a complete and thorough RFP makes it easier to propose a system that will meet most, if not all, your needs.

OUTSOURCING OPTIONS

IT outsourcing for software development can take one of four forms (see Figure 6.9):

1. Purchasing existing software.
2. Purchasing existing software and paying the publisher to make certain modifications.
3. Purchasing existing software and paying the publisher for the right to make modifications yourself.
4. Outsourcing the development of an entirely new and unique system for which no software exists.

Which option should you choose? Every organization has to track financial information, for example, and there are several different systems they can purchase that help them perform this activity. Building a financial system for your organization would probably be a waste of your time and money since there are several good systems already built that will likely meet your organizational needs. So option 1 would be appropriate, purchasing existing software, such as Oracle Financials, an application suite your organization can buy that tracks all your organizational financial information.

In a geopolitical sense, there are furthermore three types of outsourcing:

1. ***Onshore outsourcing*** is the process of engaging another company in the same country for services. Much of the current jargon relating to outsourcing is based on the United States as the reference point. Thus, "onshore" outsourcing typically means contracting a U.S. company to provide business services.

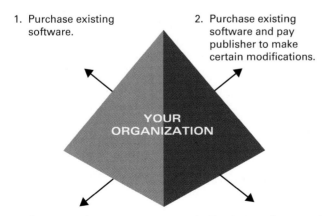

1. Purchase existing software.

2. Purchase existing software and pay publisher to make certain modifications.

YOUR ORGANIZATION

4. Outsource the development of an entirely new and unique system for which no software exists.

3. Purchase software and pay publisher for the right to make changes yourself.

Figure 6.9

Major Forms of Outsourcing Systems Development

2. ***Nearshore outsourcing*** is contracting an outsourcing arrangement with a company in a nearby country. Often this country will share a border with the native country. Again, this term is often used with the United States as the frame of reference. In this case, nearshore outsourcing will take place in either Canada or in Mexico.

3. ***Offshore outsourcing*** is contracting with a company that is geographically far away. For many companies, certain IT services, such as application development, maintenance, and help desk support, fall within the category of functions that are ideal for offshore outsourcing.

In today's high-tech world, the terms "onshore," "nearshore," and "offshore" refer only to the physical location. Thanks to the advancement in technology, terrestrial and satellite links, videoconferencing, online chats, e-mails, and telephones, a delivery system works as a single virtual unit, regardless of where people are actually located.

Although onshore and nearshore outsourcing are important forms in the outsourcing industry, when outsourcing is spoken about nowadays, it is usually offshore outsourcing that is being referenced.

OFFSHORE OUTSOURCING   From a humble beginning as a mere cost-cutting concept, offshore outsourcing has gradually moved ahead and established itself as a successful business model by rendering not only cost-effective but also sophisticated and highly efficient quality services. According to International Data Corporation (IDC), U.S.-based companies tripled their offshore outsourcing spending from $5.5 billion in 2000 to more than $17.6 billion in 2005. The offshore outsourcing trend has overcome all barriers of political turmoil, language problems, and culture differences, and has proved that no matter in which part of the world your outsourcer resides, what really matters is industry-standard, high-quality service together with decisive cost advantage.[9]

Since the mid-1990s, major U.S. companies have been sending significant portions of their software development work offshore—primarily to vendors in India, but also to vendors in China, Eastern Europe (including Russia), Ireland, Israel, and the Philippines. The big selling point for offshore outsourcing to these countries is "good work done cheap." A programmer who earns $63,000 per year in the United States is paid as little as $5,000 per year overseas (see Figure 6.10). Companies can easily realize cost savings of 30 to 50 percent through offshore outsourcing and still get the same, if not better, quality of service.

Figure 6.10

Typical Salary Ranges for Computer Programmers

Country	Salary Range per Year
China	$ 5,000–$ 9,000
India	$ 6,000– 10,000
Philippines	$ 6,500– 11,000
Russia	$ 7,000– 13,000
Ireland	$21,000– 28,000
Canada	$25,000– 50,000
United States	$60,000– 90,000

Stories about U.S. companies outsourcing work offshore to India have been reported for years; however, it is becoming increasingly apparent that Romania, Bulgaria, Russia, China, Ghana, the Philippines, and dozens of other countries are also clamoring for and getting business from the United States. The reality is that offshore outsourcing is a growing trend. According to a recent study from Meta Group, the worldwide offshore outsourcing market will grow 20 percent annually through 2008. Meta also claims that offshoring growth will outpace outsourcing in general and predicts that the average enterprise will offshore 60 percent of application development by 2008 or 2009.[10]

What types of functions or projects make good candidates for offshore outsourcing? Data conversions and system migrations with well-defined requirements and specifications

OUTSOURCING HELP DESKS OFFSHORE

There are two classes of help desk–support customers— high paying and low paying. Today, vendors are tailoring support based on the amount of money customers pay and are transferring the lower-paying customers to offshore support sites. More and more companies, however, are finding that offshore help desks are causing their customers major problems.

Jim Miller, chief technology officer at Creditex Inc., a Wall Street–based credit derivative trading firm, recently requested help with a Microsoft Exchange server that supports users in New York and London. The Microsoft help desk in India answered Jim's call and the technician on the other end of the line merely consulted online Microsoft knowledge-base articles, some-

thing Miller said he could have done himself. The technician told him that the only way to rectify the problem was to rebuild the whole machine and reinstall Exchange, an effort that Miller said would have entailed "a huge investment in time, the loss of significant data and e-mail down for an extended period of time."

Miller took a pass on the advice and asked the technician to place him back in the call queue, only to end up back in India four times. Finally, Creditex "escalated" its request for help to Microsoft support managers and finally received a call from a knowledgeable technician in Dallas who resolved the problem in 15 minutes.[11]

and minimal end-user interaction with the development team are typical projects taken offshore. Naturally, the company must be willing to allow its application code to be located offsite during development. Application development projects are also good offshore candidates. From a SDLC perspective, offshore work is most beneficial in the development and testing phases where end-user interaction is limited, and the task is well defined. For stable applications, most maintenance activities can be performed remotely so application maintenance is also a good candidate for offshore outsourcing. With the right communication infrastructure and a clear understanding of your company's business language requirements, call center or help desk functions can also be moved offshore.

THE ADVANTAGES AND DISADVANTAGES OF OUTSOURCING

Making the decision to outsource may be critical one way or the other to your organization's success. Thus far in our discussion of outsourcing, we've alluded to some advantages and disadvantages of outsourcing. Following is a summary of the major advantages and disadvantages of outsourcing the systems development process, in order to help you make the important outsourcing decision.

ADVANTAGES Your organization may benefit from outsourcing because outsourcing allows you to:

- *Focus on unique core competencies:* By outsourcing systems development efforts that support noncritical business functions, your organization can focus on developing systems that support important, unique core competencies.
- *Exploit the intellect of another organization:* Outsourcing allows your organization to obtain intellectual capital by purchasing it from another organization. Often you won't be able to find individuals with all the expertise required to develop a system. Outsourcing allows you to find those individuals with the expertise you need to get your system developed and implemented.

HOW MANY ARE THERE?

Assume your company is looking to outsource its payroll activities including calculating the payroll and generating the paychecks each month. Search the Internet to find different companies that offer this outsourcing service. Fill in the following table comparing the advantages and disadvantages of the different companies you find. Discuss which one you would choose and why.

Company Name	Advantages	Disadvantages

- *Better predict future costs:* When you outsource a function, whether systems development or some other business function, you know the exact costs.
- *Acquire leading-edge technology:* Outsourcing allows your organization to acquire leading-edge technology without having to acquire technical expertise and bear the inherent risks of choosing the wrong technology.
- *Reduce costs:* Outsourcing is often seen as a money saver for organizations. Reducing costs is one of the important reasons organizations outsource.
- *Improve performance accountability:* Outsourcing involves delegating work to another organization at a specified level of service. Your organization can use this specified level of service to guarantee that it gets exactly what it wants from the vendor.

DISADVANTAGES   Outsourcing may *not* be a beneficial option for you because it:

- *Reduces technical know-how for future innovation:* Outsourcing is a way of exploiting the intellect of another organization, so it can also mean that your organization will no longer possess that expertise internally. If you outsource because you don't have the necessary technical expertise today, you'll probably have to outsource for the same reason tomorrow.
- *Reduces degree of control:* Outsourcing means giving up control. No matter what you choose to outsource, you are in some way giving up control over that function.
- *Increases vulnerability of your strategic information:* Outsourcing systems development involves telling another organization what information you use and

how you use that information. In doing so, you could be giving away strategic information and secrets.

- *Increases dependency on other organizations:* As soon as you start outsourcing, you immediately begin depending on another organization to perform many of your business functions.

BUSINESS PROCESS OUTSOURCING (BPO)

Today's world economy is driving many companies to seek increasingly aggressive ways to meet the demands of shareholders, investors, and employees. In a quest for higher profits and increased competitive advantage, you would be hard-pressed to find an executive or manager not motivated by lower costs and better productivity. Additionally, most companies are focusing on value-added, customer-centric functions and striving to reduce investments in operations that don't directly affect the bottom line. What are major corporations doing to achieve all this? One strategy is business process outsourcing. ***Business process outsourcing (BPO)*** is using a contractual service to completely manage, deliver, and operate one or more (typically IT—or call center–intensive) business processes or functions. Figure 6.11 displays a few of the typical BPO business processes or functions.

IT services have been successfully outsourced for many years as an effective way for companies to lower cost and raise productivity. Business process management uses technology to break down barriers between traditional functional silos, such as those found in finance, order fulfillment, and call centers. The goal is to redesign the process, reduce unnecessary steps, and eliminate redundancies. Outsourcing uses skills and resources of specialized outside service providers to perform many of these critical, yet noncore activities. In short, BPO means examining the processes that make up the business and its functional units and then working with specialized service providers to both reengineer and outsource these processes. Thus, BPO lowers costs and raises productivity at the same time, speeding implementation and ensuring that the intended benefits really hit the bottom line.

Figure 6.11

Business Processes and Functions of Business Process Outsourcing

DO YOUR HOMEWORK!

The complexity of today's IT systems and the technical demands placed on an organization and its IT department are leading many companies down the path of business process outsourcing.

However, achieving success is no simple matter. Not only is it important to know when to outsource, it's also essential to know how to use outsourcing to your full advantage. Here are some questions you should ask before embracing BPO:

- **Does the outsourcing opportunity match the organization's business needs?** If an outsourcing initiative can create a strategic advantage, then it's worth pursuing.

- **Will outsourcing improve performance?** A successful outsourcing initiative translates into service that is better than it would be if an organization handled the tasks internally.

- **Are the financial projections accurate?** Take a critical look at the numbers, particularly those generated by a vendor, and try to spot assumptions, oversimplifications, or just plain misleading figures.

There can also be dramatic savings in technology investments, such as enterprise resource planning (ERP) systems and call centers. Because of the transactional nature of BPO functions, BPO service providers themselves make heavy investments in these technologies, thereby saving their clients the burden of purchasing, implementation, ongoing support, and maintenance of ERP software and call center technology.

Ideal processes for BPO are ones that can be standardized or automated. The financial services industry is particularly suitable for BPO on account of its repetitive and transaction-oriented nature. Financial services is one of the major markets for BPO, particularly its payroll and call center functions. Financial services pioneered BPO, and leads other business sectors in spending in this outsourcing area. Merrill Lynch decided that its IT help desk would be a good candidate for BPO. Merrill Lynch needed a BPO service provider to manage the support function for approximately 11,000 users in the United States and the United Kingdom. The help desk was broken down into a number of components: a help desk for routine troubleshooting; a service to deal with hardware failure; desk-side support for investment managers; and associated procurement processes, asset management, and reporting functions. Merrill Lynch was able to reduce its IT costs by 20 percent using a BPO service provider.[12]

Prototyping

Prototyping is the process of building a model that demonstrates the features of a proposed product, service, or system. A prototype, then, is simply a model of a proposed product, service, or system. If you think about it, people prototype all the time. Automobile manufacturers build prototypes of cars to demonstrate safety features, aerodynamics, and comfort. Building contractors construct models of homes and other structures to show layout and fire exits.

In systems development, prototyping can be a valuable tool for you. Prototyping is an iterative process in which you build a model from basic business requirements, have

LASTMINUTE.COM

Launched in October 1998, lastminute.com, the online provider of last minute travel and leisure solutions, has grown to become one of Europe's most popular and successful e-commerce sites, offering a range of travel, entertainment, and gift services.

In order to allow team members to effectively manage the design, modeling, quality assurance, and deployment aspects of software development projects, lastminute.com needed to select a systems development methodology. After it went through an extensive two-month evaluation period, lastminute.com chose to implement an agile methodology—a stable, well-crafted methodology that really appealed to its developers. The methodology makes no demands on how lastminute.com structures its code; therefore, it was able to begin using it right from the start. The software development teams at lastminute.com are focused on specific business areas such as flights, hotels, and leisure. lastminute.com anticipates that the agile systems development methodology will help it to quickly and effectively deliver further functionality in these key business areas to enhance customer experience and generate increased revenues.[13]

other users review the prototype and suggest changes, and further refine and enhance the prototype to include suggestions. Most notably, prototyping is a dynamic process that allows you to see, work with, and evaluate a model and suggest changes to that model to increase the likelihood of success of the proposed system. Prototyping is a common tool in extreme programming, RAD, and the agile methodology.

You can use prototyping to perform a variety of functions in the systems development process:

- *Gathering requirements:* Prototyping is a great requirements gathering tool. You start by simply prototyping the basic system requirements. Then you allow users to add more requirements (information and processes) as you revise the prototype.

- *Helping determine requirements:* In many systems development projects, users aren't sure what they really want. They simply know that the current system doesn't meet their needs. In this instance, you can use prototyping to help users determine their exact requirements.

- *Proving that a system is technically feasible:* Let's face it, there are some things to which you cannot apply technology, and knowing whether you can or not is often unclear while defining the scope of the proposed system. If you're uncertain about whether something can be done, prototype it first. A prototype you use to prove the technical feasibility of a proposed system is a ***proof-of-concept prototype.***

- *Selling the idea of a proposed system:* Many people resist changes in IT. The current system seems to work fine, and they see no reason to go through the process of developing and learning to use a new system. In this case, you have to convince them that the proposed system will be better than the current one. Because prototyping is relatively fast, you won't have to invest a lot of time to develop a prototype that can convince people of the worth of the proposed system. A prototype you use to convince people of the worth of a proposed system is a ***selling prototype.***

THE PROTOTYPING PROCESS

Prototyping has proved an excellent tool in systems development. The prototyping process involves four steps (see Figure 6.12):

1. *Identify basic requirements:* During the first step, you gather the basic requirements for a proposed system. These basic requirements include input and output information desired and, perhaps, some simple processes. At this point, you're typically unconcerned with editing rules, security issues, or end-of-period processing (for example, producing W-2s for a payroll system at the end of the year).

2. *Develop initial prototype:* Having identified the basic requirements, you then set out to develop an initial prototype. Most often, your initial prototype will include only user interfaces, such as data entry screens and reports.

3. *User review:* Step 3 starts the truly iterative process of prototyping. When users first initiate this step, they evaluate the prototype and suggest changes or additions. In subsequent returns to step 3 (after step 4), they evaluate new versions of the prototype. It's important to involve as many users as possible during this iterative process. This will help resolve any discrepancies in such areas as terminology and operational processes.

4. *Revise and enhance the prototype:* The final sequential step in the prototyping process is to revise and enhance the prototype according to any user suggestions. In this step, you make changes to the current prototype and add any new requirements. Next, you return to step 3 and have the users review the new prototype; then step 4 again, revision, and so on.

Figure 6.12

Prototyping Steps

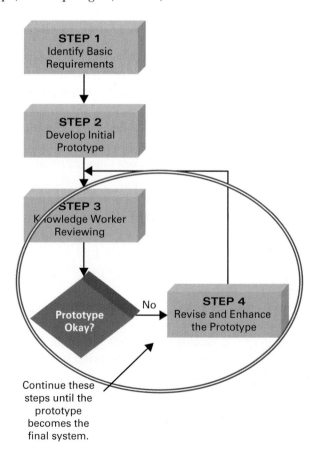

Who uses prototyping and for what purpose determines how the prototyping process occurs. Most often, IT specialists use prototyping in the SDLC only to form a technical system blueprint; on the other hand, if end users develop prototypes to create their own system, they would cycle through steps 3 and 4 until the prototype becomes the final system.

Most often, IT specialists develop prototypes using special prototyping development tools. Many of these tools don't support the creation of a final system—you simply use them to build prototypes. Therefore, the finished prototype becomes a blueprint or technical design for the final system. In the appropriate stages of the SDLC, IT specialists implement the prototypes in another application development environment better suited to the development of whole systems.

THE ADVANTAGES OF PROTOTYPING

- *Encourages active user participation*—First and foremost, prototyping encourages users to actively participate in the development process. As opposed to interviewing and reviewing documentation, prototyping allows users to see and work with working models of the proposed system.

- *Helps resolve discrepancies among users*—During the prototyping process, many users participate in defining the requirements for and reviewing the prototype. The word "many" is key. If at least several users participate in prototyping, you'll find it's much easier to resolve any discrepancies the users may encounter.

- *Gives users a feel for the final system*—Prototyping, especially for user interfaces, provides a feel for how the final system will look and work. When users understand the look and feel of the final system, they are more apt to see its potential for success.

- *Helps determine technical feasibility*—Proof-of-concept prototypes are great for determining the technical feasibility of a proposed system.

- *Helps sell the idea of a proposed system*—Prototypes can help break down resistance barriers and sell the system. Many people don't want new systems because the old one seems to work just fine, and they're afraid the new system won't meet their expectations and won't work properly. If you provide them with a working prototype that proves the new system will be successful, they will be more inclined to buy into it.

THE DISADVANTAGES OF PROTOTYPING

- *Leads people to believe the final system will follow*—When a prototype is complete, many people believe that the final system will follow shortly. After all, they've seen the system at work in the form of a prototype—how long can it take to bring the system into production? Unfortunately, it may take months or years. You need to be sure that people understand that the prototype is only a model, not the final system missing only a few simple bells and whistles.

- *Gives no indication of performance under operational conditions*—Prototypes very seldom take all operational conditions into consideration. This problem surfaced for the Department of Motor Vehicles in a state on the East Coast. During prototyping, the system, which handled motor vehicle and driver registration for the entire state, worked fine for 20 workstations at two locations. When the system was finally installed for all locations (which included more than 1,200 workstations), the system spent all its time just managing communications traffic; it had absolutely no time to complete any transactions. This is potentially the most significant drawback to prototyping. You must prototype operational conditions as well as interfaces and processes.

ST. JUDE CHILDREN'S RESEARCH HOSPITAL CURES

St. Jude Children's Research Hospital (www.stjude.org) works to find cures for children with catastrophic illnesses through research and treatment. Researchers at St. Jude continually conduct clinical trials to study the effects on patients of new combinations, types, and amounts of drugs and other medical therapies.

Before a new clinical trial can begin, each research team must establish a treatment regime—known as a clinical research protocol—and a protocol application/database to collect the unique patient data gathered during the study. Historically, protocol applications/databases were coded from scratch: a labor-intensive, time-consuming process that kept software development costs high while also hindering research efforts. An especially complex application/database could take from several months to a year for full life cycle development. Because of the long development cycles, many

of the protocol applications/databases failed to meet researchers' ongoing needs. Even "standard" industry practices were insufficient for this environment because requirements changed so rapidly that they were out of date before developers could produce a custom application/database.

The St. Jude team now uses the analysis and design features of the systems development life cycle to identify requirements—including baselining those necessary for compliance with the federal Food and Drug Administration (FDA) and Health Insurance Portability and Accountability Act (HIPAA). The new analysis and design methodologies also help improve communications between business analysts and developers by providing a way for analysts to clearly define and track requirements.[14]

- *Leads the project team to forgo proper testing and documentation*—You must thoroughly test and document all new systems. Unfortunately, many people believe they can forgo testing and documentation when using prototyping. After all, they've tested the prototype; why not use the prototype as the documentation for the system? Don't make this mistake.

End-User Development

End-user development (EUD) is the collection of methods for the creation of important software applications by end users. End users are individuals who will use a system, who, although skilled in their own domain, are not IT or computer experts, and yet they know very well what they want from a system and are capable of being involved in prototyping, since they have basic IT skills.

End-user development of applications is an important source of organizational information systems. Applications developed by end users support a wide range of decision-making activities and contribute to business processing in a wide range of tasks. The major tools used for end-user system development have been spreadsheets and database management systems and Web development.

Rapidly gaining in acceptance is that end-user development can be a potent source of stress relief rather than a cause of stress. Rather than combating the trend toward end-user application development, IT staff should leverage it to offload solution building to end users. IT then frees its own scarce resources for complex, visible, infrastructure management tasks. A successful strategy for end-user development relies on two keys: (1) knowing which applications are good candidates and (2) providing end users with the right tools.

WHICH APPLICATIONS FOR IT TO OFFLOAD

The following checklist helps IT staff to determine which applications are in IT's domain and which are good candidates for end-user development. IT delivers maximum value to the enterprise by focusing on high-cost, high-return applications with the following characteristics:

- Infrastructure-related
- Mission-critical including ERP, CRM, business intelligence and e-business
- Support large numbers of concurrent users, for example, call center applications

Other applications may be good candidates for end-user development.

THE RIGHT TOOL FOR THE JOB

Requirements of end-user development tools and enterprise development tools (for IT analysts) are quite different. Ease of use is paramount for end-user development tools. That's because end users are not skilled programmers and might use the developmental tool so infrequently that they can forget commands that aren't intuitive. Therefore, end users must have development tools that:

- *Are easy to use:* This is essential for rapid, low-cost development. For application programs, specific characteristics of ease-of-use include:
  - Simple data entry
  - Error checking for value lists and ranges
  - Easy report generation, for example, by drag and drop
  - Ease of Web publishing
- *Support multiple platforms:* To minimize support requirements, end users should select one or two development tools that run on the range of hardware platforms and operating systems.
- *Offer low cost of ownership:* Cost factors include not only the tool's purchase price, but also training time, speed of application development, and required skill level. When assessing cost of ownership you should ask, "How easy is it to use after not having used it in a month or two?" and "How quickly can someone with subject matter expertise develop a simple application?"
- *Support a wide range of data types:* By its very nature, data is dynamic. Therefore, the toolset should support all the features normally found in database products.

However, not all end-user development is greatly accepted for the following reasons:

- *Version control:* One person creates a spreadsheet and distributes it to five others, each of whom modifies the formulas and passes the spreadsheet to others. Soon, scores of hundreds of people in the enterprise are working with a different version of the document.
- *Low quality:* It is estimated that 30 percent of spreadsheets contain errors, not only entry errors, which occur at the rate of one per each 100 cells, but also serious inaccuracies.
- *Loss of control:* IT groups traditionally struggle to attain a balance between centralized control and rapid response to workgroup needs. End-user development is sometimes seen as a relinquishing of control.

BUILD VS. BUY

When an organization decides it needs a new information system, it has many acquisition/development choices, two of which are (1) purchasing the information system from a vendor and (2) building the system itself. Typically, a cost/benefit analysis forms the basis of this buy versus build decision. You must consider the following during the buy versus build decision:

- Are there any currently available products that fit the organization's needs?

- Are there features that are not available but important enough to warrant the expense of in-house development?

- Can the organization customize or modify an existing application or application suite to fit its needs?

- Is there a justification to purchase or develop based on the cost of acquisition?

Search the Internet to find other criteria not mentioned above that would help an organization with the build versus buy decision.

We need to stress to you that end-user development of applications is an important source of many organizational information systems. End-user development aims to empower users who are not professional programmers to develop or modify software.

Applications developed by end users support a wide range of decision-making activities and contribute to business processing in a wide range of tasks. End users will no longer depend solely on programmers, enabling the production of a wide range of applications in a shorter amount of time as well as the increased number and diversity of people creating applications will promote innovation.

Summary: Student Learning Outcomes Revisited

1. **List the seven steps in the systems development life cycle (SDLC) and associated activities for each step.** The *systems development life cycle (SDLC)* is a structured step-by-step approach for developing information systems. The seven steps and associated activities are as follows:

   1. *Planning:* Define system, set project scope, develop project plan.
   2. *Analysis:* Gather business requirements.
   3. *Design:* Design technical architecture, design system models.
   4. *Development:* Build technical architecture, build database and programs.
   5. *Testing:* Write the test conditions, perform testing.

   6. *Implementation:* Perform user training, write user documentation.
   7. *Maintenance:* Provide a help desk and support system changes.

2. **Describe the four systems development methodologies.** The traditional *waterfall methodology* is a sequential, activity-based process in which each phase in the SDLC is performed sequentially from planning through implementation. *Rapid application development (RAD)* (also called *rapid prototyping*) *methodology* emphasizes extensive user involvement in the rapid and evolutionary construction of working prototypes of a system to accelerate the systems development process. *Extreme programming (XP) methodology*

breaks a project into tiny phases, and developers cannot continue on to the next phase until the first phase is complete. The *agile methodology*, a form of XP, aims for customer satisfaction through early and continuous delivery of useful software components. Agile is similar to XP but with less focus on team coding and more on limiting project scope.

3. **Define the role of outsourcing.** *Outsourcing* is the delegation of specific work to a third party for a specified length of time, at a specified cost, and at a specified level of service.

4. **List and describe the three different forms of outsourcing.** *Onshore outsourcing* is the process of engaging another company within the same country for services. *Nearshore outsourcing* refers to contracting an outsourcing arrangement with a company in a nearby country. *Offshore outsourcing* refers to contracting with a company that is geographically far away. For many companies, certain IT services, such as application development, maintenance, and help desk support, fall within the category of functions that are ideal for offshore outsourcing.

5. **Describe business process outsourcing (BPO).** *Business process outsourcing (BPO)* is using a contractual service to completely manage, deliver, and operate one or more (typically IT—

or call center–intensive) business processes or functions.

6. **Describe prototyping and profile an example of a prototype.** *Prototyping* is the process of building a model that demonstrates the features of a proposed product, service, or system. A prototype, then, is simply a model of a proposed product, service, or system. Automobile manufacturers build prototypes of cars to demonstrate safety features, aerodynamics, and comfort. Building contractors construct models of homes and other structures to show layout and fire exits. And systems developers model, or prototype, a system.

7. **Describe the advantages of prototyping.** Prototyping encourages active knowledge worker participation in the development process. As opposed to interviewing and the reviewing of documentation, prototyping allows knowledge workers to see and work with working models of the proposed system. This gives users a feel for the system. Prototyping also helps resolve discrepancies among the many end users participating in defining the requirements for and reviewing the prototype. Finally, prototypes help determine the technical feasibility of a system, and prototypes can help sell users on a new system.

CLOSING CASE STUDY ONE

GETTING SOFTWARE DEVELOPMENT RIGHT

Effective software development is the backbone of today's most successful businesses. Seeking a competitive edge, organizations are expanding the roles of IT leaders, business leaders, and developers who participate in the strategic software development process. Together, these stakeholders are charged with maximizing the value of corporate information across their enterprises.

Still, market research shows that software development projects have a high risk of failure. Many projects suffer from delays and budget overruns. Others don't fulfill the original project scope and some wind up being canceled entirely. Industry regulations and service level agreements mean there's less margin for

experiment and error. This pressure can result in missed financial opportunities and squandered competitive advantages.

Poor project planning, poor cost estimating, poor measurements, poor milestone tracking, poor change control, and poor quality control are the six most frequent problems that can undermine software projects, according to industry experts. Their impact hits the bottom line—software errors cost the American economy nearly $60 billion a year.

U.S. businesses spent $234 billion in 2004 to buy or build software, and roughly 37 percent of that figure, or about $86 billion, was spent on software built in-house, according to Forrester Research Inc. of Cambridge, Massachusetts. With so much money at stake, organizations can't afford to embark on software projects that are doomed to delay or complete failure. So, it's time to redefine the way that software is conceived, designed, built, and delivered in order to meet quality and user goals on time and on budget.

Historically, programming has largely been an unpredictable art form in many organizations. Now it's time for software development to become a manageable, repeatable business process. Getting software "right" requires a lot of effort incorporating the people, processes, and technology involved in the development process. Working together, business people, IT operations people, and application developers must minimize gaps in communication and comprehension between their specialized roles. These communication gaps have only intensified with globalization (distributed development teams and the rise of offshoring and outsourcing) and the increased complexity of IT.

In a managed business process, the software development team is integrated into the overall fabric of the enterprise, ensuring their participation as an equal partner in shaping business-driven IT initiatives. In fact, software development has the potential to dramatically improve the way business units and IT groups collaborate.[15]

Questions

1. What are some ways that a company can help to minimize the poor project planning, poor cost estimating, poor measurements, poor milestone tracking, poor change control, and poor quality control of software development?

2. One specific problem in any software development project is testing. Describe some ways in which an organization can help ensure proper testing in software development.

3. Evaluate the SDLC phases that seem most important to you and outline specific areas of the software development process that deserve greatest attention.

4. Explain the cost of finding errors later rather than sooner and explain how more time spent in the analysis and the design phases could save money.

CLOSING CASE STUDY TWO

TO OUTSOURCE OR NOT TO OUTSOURCE

At first glance, retailer Sears, Roebuck & Co. and financial services company Huntington National Bank seem to have little in common. Over the past few years, however, the CIOs at both companies faced a similar challenge. To outsource or not to outsource, that was the question.

SEARS, ROEBUCK

CIO Gerald F. Kelly Jr. joined Sears, Roebuck & Co. in order to turn around the company's IT department as Sears focused on ways to compete with Target and Wal-Mart, among others. Kelly was informed in his first few days on the job that the company's aging and unreliable technical infrastructure was a big problem. There were signs that the company had not invested appropriately and had not kept the infrastructure at a level of capability consistent with business objectives. Among the signs were network failures, CPU failures,

extended recovery times and root cause analysis, and lack of redundancy, backup, and recovery.

Kelly knew Sears was a retail company, not a technology company. He also felt that infrastructure was largely a commodity. If he insourced this work, it would mean denying a number of employees access to the best opportunities for career growth (those that support the core mission). So he began to investigate alternatives that would minimize the time issue and maximize the economic potential of transforming the IT infrastructure.

So in the end the decision for Sears to outsource wasn't led by the usual "to outsource or not to outsource" debate. It was led by an analysis of where the company was headed. After nine months of analysis, Sears executives weighed the time and costs involved in insourcing the IT infrastructure versus outsourcing it against the effect outsourcing would have on opportunities for affected employees. It seemed that outsourcing would allow Sears to get the maximum value out of its dispersed infrastructure, achieve the goal of a stable infrastructure faster, save a significant amount of money, avoid having to hire a large number of technical specialists—and free up remaining staff for developing new retail systems. Kelly decided to outsource the infrastructure work.

HUNTINGTON NATIONAL BANK

Huntington National Bank already relied on an outsourcer for deposit and loan systems; the outsourcer was hoping to win some of the financial services BPO market. Joe Gottron, CIO for Huntington National Bank and a 16-year IBM veteran, understood intimately the nature of outsourcing relationships, which led him to some reservations. His main concern was that outsourcing agreements are loss leaders to start, with revenue built into the latter year. Gottron, however, was particularly interested in the possibilities of outsourcing business processes.

Once Gottron could compare internal benchmarks to the BPO and other outsourcing offers, it became clear that the bank's size was a major factor in the BPO decision. With 8,300 employees (500 of them in IT), Joe stated, "We're big enough to afford good talent but small enough to get in a room, figure things out and make things happen." A larger financial services company, more geographically dispersed, with more people or more complexity, probably could have gotten more value out of the BPO proposition, Gottron says, especially in terms of costs. The sourcing decision process took 18 months. Huntington National Bank chose to reject the BPO proposal and keep IT in-house based upon executives' understanding of where IT improvements should be made, business alignment and project management concerns, and the fact that outsourcing would likely save little, if any, money in the long term and could introduce risk to the corporate culture.[16,17]

Questions

1. Summarize the reasons for the outsourcing decisions of Sears, Roebuck & Co and Huntington National Bank.
2. Explain why Sears, Roebuck & Co. did not insource its IT development.
3. Explain why Huntington National Bank did not outsource its IT development.
4. Describe some of the factors that may have "forced" Sears to outsource.
5. Describe some of the factors that may have "forced" Huntington National Bank to insource.

Key Terms and Concepts

Agile methodology, 290
Analysis phase, 282
Business process outsourcing (BPO), 297
Business requirement, 282
Critical success factor (CSF), 281
Design phase, 283
Development phase, 284
End-user development (EUD), 302
Extreme programming (XP) methodology, 289
Feature creep, 281
Graphical user interface (GUI), 284
GUI screen design, 284
Help desk, 287
Implementation phase, 286
Insourcing, 290
Integration testing, 286
Joint application development (JAD), 282

Maintenance phase, 286
Modeling, 284
Nearshore outsourcing, 294
Offshore outsourcing, 294
Online training, 286
Onshore outsourcing, 293
Outsourcing, 290
Parallel implementation, 286
Phased implementation, 286
Pilot implementation, 286
Planning phase, 280
Plunge implementation, 286
Project manager, 282
Project milestone, 282
Project plan, 281
Project scope, 281
Project scope document, 281

Proof-of-concept prototype, 299
Prototype, 289
Prototyping, 298
Rapid application development (RAD) (rapid
    prototyping) methodology, 288
Request for proposal (RFP), 292
Requirements definition document, 282
Scope creep, 281
Selling prototype, 299
Sign-off, 282

Systems development life cycle (SDLC), 280
System testing, 286
Technical architecture, 284
Test condition, 285
Testing phase, 285
Unit testing, 286
User acceptance testing (UAT), 286
User documentation, 286
Waterfall methodology, 288
Workshop training, 286

Short-Answer Questions

1. What is the systems development life cycle (SDLC)?
2. What are the seven steps in the SDLC?
3. What is a critical success factor?
4. What is feature creep?
5. How does a project plan help the project manager do his or her job?
6. In which step in the SDLC do you define business requirements?
7. Why would a company outsource?
8. In which step in the SDLC do you build the technical architecture?
9. Why must you provide sign-off on the business requirements?
10. Will a project be successful if you miss business requirements?
11. What is business process outsourcing?
12. Why would you build a prototype?
13. What is a selling prototype?
14. What is an advantage of end-user development?
15. What is an advantage of prototyping?
16. How do onshore, nearshore, and offshore outsourcing differ?

Assignments and Exercises

1. **SDLC AND THE REAL WORLD** Think of the seven steps in the SDLC and apply them to one of your daily activities—for example, getting dressed in the morning. First, you plan what you are going to wear. This will vary depending on what you are going to do that day which could mean shorts, formal wear, jeans, or other attire. Second, you analyze what you have in your closet compared to what you plan to wear. Third, you design the outfit. Fourth, you get the clothes out of the closet and assemble them on your bed. Fifth, you test the outfit to ensure it matches and fits your day's plans. Sixth, you put on the outfit. Seventh, you wear the outfit throughout the day adjusting it as needed.

2. **HOW CREATIVE ARE YOU?** You've been appointed as the manager of the design team for Sneakers-R-Us. Your first activity is to design the GUI for the main system. The only requirements you are given is that the colors must be bold and the following buttons must appear on the screen.
   • Order Inventory
   • Enter Sales
   • Schedule Employees
   • Tax Reports
   • Sales Reports
   • Employee Vacation and Sick Time
   • Administrative Activities

   Create two different potential GUI screen designs for the main system. Provide a brief explanation of the advantages and disadvantages of each design.

3. **UNDERSTANDING END-USER DEVELOPMENT** The advantages and disadvantages of end-user development and of outsourcing are covered in this chapter. Compile a list of the different advantages and disadvantages of end-user development compared to outsourcing.

4. **MANAGING THE PROJECT PLAN** You are in the middle of an interview for your first job. The manager performing the interview asks you to explain why managing a project plan is critical to a project's success. The manager also wants to know what scope creep and feature creep are and how you would manage them during a project. Please write a one-page document stating how you would answer these questions during the interview.

5. **WHY PROTOTYPE?** You are in the middle of the design phase for a new system. Your manager does not understand why it's important to develop a prototype of a proposed system before building the actual system. In a one-page document, explain what potential problems would arise if you didn't develop a prototype and went straight to developing the system.

6. **BUSINESS REQUIREMENTS** Gathering accurate and complete business requirements is critical to the successful development of any system. Review the following requirements and explain any problems they might have.
   - The GUI must be red.
   - There should be three buttons labeled "Start" and "Stop."
   - Buttons 1 through 8 are required for the calculator function.
   - There should be a text field for the user name and a button for the user password.

7. **CONSTRUCTION AND THE SDLC** The systems development life cycle is often compared to the activities in the construction industry. Fill in the following chart listing some of the activities performed in building a house and how they relate to the different SDLC steps.

SDLC	Activities for Building a Home
Planning	
Analysis	
Design	
Development	
Testing	
Implementation	
Maintenance	

Discussion Questions

1. Why is it important to develop a logical model of a proposed system before generating a technical architecture? What potential problems would arise if you didn't develop a logical model and went straight to developing the technical design?

2. If you view systems development as a question-and-answer session, another question you could ask is, "Why do organizations develop IT systems?" Consider what you believe to be the five most important reasons organizations develop IT systems. How do these reasons relate to topics in the first five chapters of this book?

3. When deciding how to staff a systems development project, what are some of the primary questions you must be able to answer to determine if you will outsource? What are some of the advantages and disadvantages of outsourcing versus insourcing?

4. Your company has just decided to implement a new financial system. Your company's financial

needs are almost the same as those of all the other companies in your industry. Would you recommend that your company purchase an existing system or build a custom system? Would you recommend your company use end-user development or outsource the new system?

5. Why do you think system documentation is important? If you had to write system documentation for a word processing application, what would be a few of the main sections? Do you think it would be useful to test the documentation to ensure it's accurate? What do you think happens if you provide system documentation that is inaccurate? What do you think happens if you implement a new system without documentation?

6. What would happen to an organization that refused to follow the systems development life cycle when building systems? If you worked for such an organization, what would you do to convince your manager to follow the systems development life cycle?

7. There are seven phases in the systems development life cycle. Which one do you think is the hardest? Which one do you think is the easiest? Which one do you think is the most important? Which one do you think is the least important? If you had to skip one of the phases, which one would it be and why?

8. What would happen to a systems development effort that decided to skip the testing phase? If you were working on this project, what would you do to convince your team members to perform the activities in the testing phase?

9. If you were working on a large systems development project, and after reviewing the business requirements you were positive several were missing, would you still sign off on the requirements? If you did, what would happen?

10. You are talking with another student who is complaining about having to learn about the systems development life cycle, because he is not going to work in an IT department. Would you agree with this student? What would you say to him to convince him that learning about the systems development life cycle is important no matter where he works?

11. A company typically has many systems it wants to build, but unfortunately it usually doesn't have the resources to build all the systems. How does a company decide which systems to build?

12. When you start working on a new system, one of your first activities is to define the project scope. Do you think this is an easy activity? Why is the project scope so important? Do you think everyone on the project should know the project's scope? What could happen if people on the project are not familiar with the project scope?

13. People often think that a system is complete once it is implemented. Is this true? What happens after a system is implemented? What can you do to ensure the system continues to meet the knowledge workers' needs?

14. Imagine your friends are about to start their own business and they have asked you for planning and development advice with respect to IT systems. What would you tell them? What if their business idea was completely Internet-based? What if their business idea didn't include using the Internet at all? Would your answers differ? Why or why not?

Finding Freeware and Shareware on the Internet

Even upgrading to the latest version of your existing software can make a real dent in your pocketbook. And after installing new software, you may find it simply doesn't meet your needs. That's when you notice that you can't return opened software; you can only exchange it for a new copy. Therefore, if it doesn't meet your needs you're out of luck with commercial consumer software.

An alternative to commercial software that you might consider is shareware or freeware. Shareware is sometimes called "try before you buy" software because users are permitted to try the software on their own computer system (generally for a limited time) without any cost or obligation. Then you make a payment if you decide you want to keep using the software beyond the evaluation (trial) period. Freeware is software available at no charge to users for as long as they choose to use the software.

USING YOUR COMPUTER FOR MORE THAN WORK

By far the most popular freeware/shareware applications are games. The quality of these software titles is truly amazing for software that is free to download and begin playing immediately whenever you want. Shareware/freeware games are so numerous on the Internet that you'll often find games grouped by categories. Common categories are action/adventure, board, card, casino, educational, role-playing, simulation, sports, strategy and war, and word games.

Connect to the Internet and several sites that offer freeware and shareware games. Pick at least two games and download them. For each, answer the following questions:

  A. Is a description of the game provided?
  B. Are system requirements listed?
  C. Can you tell if the game is freeware or shareware without downloading it?
  D. Are any of the games you selected really commercial software that requires a purchase before you download the game?
  E. If the game is shareware, how long are you permitted to use it until registration is required?
  F. If the game is shareware, does the game cease to function after the free period is over?
  G. How can you tell without waiting that long?
  H. How long does it take to download the game?
  I. Is it worth it?

PROTECTING YOUR COMPUTER INVESTMENT

Have you ever been frantically typing away, desperately trying to make an assignment deadline, when all of a sudden something goes wrong with your computer? If you're lucky, the problem is something easy to identify, so you correct the problem and go on about your work. At other times the solution eludes you. Most of the time these problems have nice logical explanations such as hardware or software conflicts or failures of some kind. In a few rare instances, the problem may have been caused intentionally by a computer virus, a program that someone develops with malicious intent to harm an IT system.

So how does a computer virus get into your system? Anytime you download software, open a file attachment to an e-mail, or read a file off a diskette from another computer, you stand the chance of contracting a computer virus. And access to the Internet increases your opportunity to download files from many different sources. So on every one of its computers virtually every company installs anti-virus protection software that scans new files for known viruses and purges them from the system. The catch is that traditional anti-virus software can find only viruses that it knows about. As new viruses come along, anti-virus software must be updated. The deviant minds that develop viruses seem to find more and better ways to infiltrate your system every day.

Connect to a site that allows you to download anti-virus software, download the software, and answer the following questions:

A. Is the anti-virus software shareware, freeware, or traditional retail software?

B. What viruses does the software detect?

C. Does the software remove the virus as well as detect it?

D. Are updates for the software available to detect new viruses? How often are they available? At what cost?

E. Does the software detect viruses not yet created? How does it do that?

F. Does the software site offer recommendations to reduce your chance of contracting a virus?

G. Does the site tell you what to do if you have already contracted a virus?

SEARCHING FOR SHAREWARE AND FREEWARE

So maybe the shareware/freeware software concept appeals to you. You'd like to be able to try the software before you buy. If you want software such as screen savers or anti-virus software, you're in luck. But what if you want some shareware to help you compose music or keep track of your soccer team's schedule? Well, then you'll have to go searching for that software. You could use a general-purpose search engine such as Yahoo! and type in shareware and music or soccer. If you do this you will find a few shareware software titles to download. But suppose those few titles don't meet your needs.

Finding shareware/freeware titles can be daunting for two reasons. First, currently there are over 1 million shareware and freeware titles available to you. Unless a search engine is designed specifically for this type of software, you'll probably miss many of these titles using a general-purpose search engine. Second, most shareware/freeware developers don't have their own Web sites. As many don't develop their software as a business, they can't justify the cost of supporting their own Web sites. To address both of these challenges, Web sites have been created that maintain databases of thousands of shareware/freeware software titles. Most also include a search engine to help you navigate through these thousands of titles.

Find a site that maintains a database of freeware and shareware software. As you peruse it, answer the following questions:

A. How does the site group the software?

B. Can you search by operating system or platform?

C. Does the site provide descriptions of the software?

D. Can you search by file size?

E. Are screen captures from the software provided?

F. Are reviews and/or ratings of the software provided?

G. When was the last update for the site?

EXTENDED LEARNING MODULE F

BUILDING A WEB PAGE WITH HTML

Student Learning Outcomes

1. DEFINE AN HTML DOCUMENT AND DESCRIBE ITS RELATIONSHIP TO A WEB SITE.

2. DESCRIBE THE PURPOSE OF TAGS IN HYPERTEXT MARKUP LANGUAGE (HTML).

3. IDENTIFY THE TWO MAJOR SECTIONS IN AN HTML DOCUMENT AND DESCRIBE THE CONTENT WITHIN EACH.

4. DESCRIBE THE USE OF BASIC FORMATTING TAGS AND HEADING TAGS.

5. DESCRIBE HOW TO ADJUST TEXT COLOR AND SIZE IN A WEB SITE.

6. DESCRIBE HOW TO CHANGE THE BACKGROUND OF A WEB SITE.

7. LIST THE THREE TYPES OF LINKS IN A WEB SITE AND DESCRIBE THEIR PURPOSES.

8. DESCRIBE HOW TO INSERT AND MANIPULATE IMAGES IN A WEB SITE.

9. DEMONSTRATE HOW TO INSERT LISTS IN A WEB SITE.

Taking Advantage of the CD

You'll find this extended learning module on the CD that accompanies this text. It's just like any other module in this text—it includes Team Work and On Your Own projects and great end-of-module Assignments and Exercises.

Creating a Web site . . . everyone seems to be doing it. Businesses create Web sites to sell products and services, provide support information, and conduct marketing activities. Individuals build Web sites for a variety of reasons. Some want a family Web site. Some want a Web site for their evening sports leagues. Your instructor has probably built a Web site to support your class. And we've created a Web site to support your use of this text.

Whatever the case, building a basic Web site is actually not that difficult. If you want a Web site that supports product ordering capabilities, then you'll need some specific expertise, but putting up a Web site with just content is simple and easy. In this extended learning module, we'll show you how.

Before we begin, let's discuss several important issues. First, be careful what sort of private personal information you include on your Web site. We definitely recommend that you do not include your social security number, your address, or your telephone number. You always need to keep in mind that there are almost 1 billion people on the Internet. Do you really want them to know where you live?

You also need to consider your target audience and their ethics. Having a Web site with profanity and obscene images will offend many people. And, more than likely, your school won't allow you to build a Web site of questionable content. Even more basic than that, you need to consider your target audience and their viewing preferences. For example, if you're building a Web site for school-age children, you'll want to use a lot of bright colors such as red, blue, green, and yellow. If you're targeting college students to advertise concerts and other events, you'll want your Web site to be more edgy and include sharp contrasting colors (including black).

Just remember this: The most elegant solution is almost always the simplest. Consider eBay's Web site. eBay uses a very simple and elegant presentation of information. The background is basic white. You'll see very little if any flashy movement. You'll hear very little sound. eBay is one of the most visited sites on the Web today. And it's making money with a very simple and elegant Web site.

We definitely believe it's worth your time and energy to pop in the CD and read this module. You'll learn many things including

- How to build and view a Web site on your own computer without connecting to the Web
- How to use a simple text editor to create a Web site
- How to size and position images in your Web site
- How to include e-mail links in your Web site
- How to change the background color or insert a textured background for your Web site
- How to change the color and size of text

If you're interested in learning more about what you can do with a Web site, we recommend that you connect to the Web site that supports this text at www.mhhe.com/haag (and select XLM/F). There, we've included more about building a Web site and useful resources on the Web.

CHAPTER SEVEN OUTLINE

STUDENT LEARNING OUTCOMES

1. Define an enterprise system.

2. Describe an enterprise resource planning (ERP) system.

3. List and describe the seven "ilities."

4. List the key traits that an IT infrastructure should exhibit.

5. Describe the differences among the four types of information technology infrastructures.

6. Explain the difference between backup and recovery.

7. State the purpose of a disaster recovery plan.

8. Explain the need for system integration.

INDUSTRY PERSPECTIVE

331 **I Hear You Calling**

336 **World Bank in Real Time**

338 **CBS Sportsline.com**

341 **1,900 Gap Stores Integrated**

FEATURES

324 **Global Perspective**
ERP's Dilemma

328 **Team Work**
Ranking the "ilities"

329 **Global Perspective**
Abercrombie & Fitch's
Online Lifestyle

333 **On Your Own**
The Future of Client/Server

339 **On Your Own**
Do You Have a Backup?

340 **Team Work**
Infrastructure Components

349 **Electronic Commerce**
Living Life on the Internet

WEB SUPPORT

www.mhhe.com/haag

- Online magazines
- Online movie listings and reviews
- Cooking from the Internet
- Highly useful miscellaneous sites

CHAPTER SEVEN

Enterprise Infrastructure and Integration
Building the Dynamic Enterprise

OPENING CASE STUDY:
ONE VIEW FOR DEL MONTE FOODS

From its roots in the California Gold Rush era, San Francisco–headquartered Del Monte Foods has grown to become the nation's largest producer and distributor of premium quality processed fruits, vegetables, and tomato products. With annual sales of over $3 billion, Del Monte is also one of the country's largest producers, distributors, and marketers of private-label food and pet products with a powerful portfolio of brands including Del Monte, StarKist, Nature's Goodness, 9Lives, and Kibbles 'n Bits.

Del Monte's acquisition of certain businesses (such as StarKist, Nature's Goodness, 9Lives, and Kibbles 'n Bits) from the H. J. Heinz Company required an integration between Del Monte's and H. J. Heinz's business processes. Del Monte needed to overhaul its IT infrastructure, migrating from multiple platforms including UNIX and mainframe systems and consolidating applications centrally on a single system. The work required integration of business processes across manufacturing, financial, supply chain, decision support, and transactional reporting areas.

The revamp of Del Monte's architecture stemmed from a strategic decision. Del Monte decided to implement an ERP system to support its entire U.S. operations, headquarters in San Francisco, operations in Pittsburgh, and distribution centers and manufacturing facilities across the country. The company concluded that the only way it could unite its global operations and open its system to its customers, which are mainly large retailers, was through the use of an ERP system. Among other key factors was the need to embrace an e-business strategy. The challenge facing Del Monte was to select an ERP system to merge multiple systems quickly and cost effectively. If financial and customer service targets were to be achieved, Del Monte needed to integrate new businesses that more than doubled the size of the company. Since implementing the ERP system, customers and trading partners are now provided with a single, consistent, and integrated view of the company.

In this chapter, we introduce you to the notion of enterprise infrastructure and integration. In previous chapters and modules, you learned about specific technologies from a somewhat "isolated" point of view. For example, you learned about databases and data warehouses in Chapter 3; in Chapter 4 you learned about decision support and artificial intelligence; and in *Extended Learning Module E* you learned about network technologies.

In the business world, all these technologies need to be integrated to best support your organizational goals and strategies. As you just read with Del Monte, every organization—to be successful and stay competitive—must integrate all technologies throughout the organization. Del Monte achieved this with an ERP system or enterprise resource planning system. In this chapter, we introduce you to ERP systems, along with a myriad of other integrating technologies and important considerations for each.[1,2]

Introduction

The growth of e-business and the Internet is bringing fundamental change to businesses, societies, and economies. Accelerating the pace of change, with the advancement of information technologies, customers, suppliers, and business partners are demanding ever more from businesses.

Businesses are always looking internally for ways to drive growth, increase revenue, and gain competitive advantages through the use of technology. They are incorporating a range of intelligence systems and analytical applications that include data warehouses and data marts, online analytical processing (OLAP), decision support systems (DSSs), and executive information systems (EISs), all of which we have described in previous chapters. As the number of users who need access to these mission-critical tools and analytical applications has risen, companies have had to look for applications that are simple to use with easy Web user interfaces, since most business tools and applications are increasingly Internet-centric. Enterprise systems provide the integration mechanism to make this possible and keep all the stakeholders happy.

So far, we've explored with you the organizational and strategic importance of IT. IT systems are successful when they provide an integrated view of business, extend analytical capabilities to users, and leverage a corporation's information and expertise. In this chapter, we explain enterprise systems, enterprise resource planning (ERP), IT infrastructure, and the need for integration to orchestrate the organization's IT systems and achieve closer collaboration with key internal players and business partners. These are fundamental elements in building the dynamic enterprise.

Enterprise Systems

Around the globe companies are becoming more connected, one business function with another, one business unit with another, one company with another. Businesses are putting information systems in place that will yield better information more quickly than ever before. For the first time, managers will be able to monitor the company in real time, without having to wait for monthly reports that must be cross-referenced with other monthly reports, all of which may be out of date, or just plain wrong, by the time the managers receive them.

With enterprise systems, information will flow seamlessly across diverse business functions, business units, and geographic boundaries. What the Internet is doing for communications between organizations, these enterprise systems are doing within companies. No business transaction, no customer purchase, no supplier invoice, no product produced, will go unnoticed by enterprise systems. Ultimately, every bit of computer-based information used for running a company's operations can be supplied by these systems.

WHAT ARE ENTERPRISE SYSTEMS?

An ***enterprise system (ES)*** is a large software application that companies use to manage their operations and to distribute information of all kinds to their workforce, to their suppliers, and to their customers. From finance to manufacturing, from sales to service, enterprise systems support thousands of business activities (see Figure 7.1). Aside from personal productivity applications such as spreadsheets and word processors on personal computers, highly specialized production systems, and Internet-based systems, an ES may be the only business information system an organization requires.

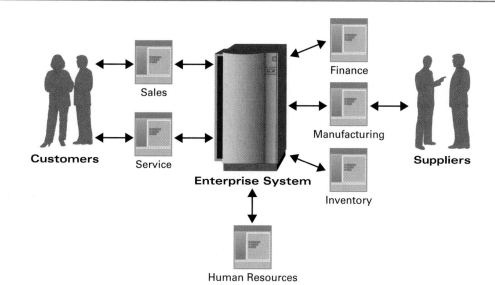

Figure 7.1

Enterprise System

Enterprise applications started out as back-office systems (such as an accounts payable, accounts receivable, and general ledger system), automating the business transactions that customers never saw or cared about. Sure, ledgers needed to be updated, suppliers paid, and employee vacation balances debited, but accuracy and speed in these types of transactions rarely led to any competitive advantage or increased customer satisfaction. On the other hand, poorly functioning back-office systems can lead to dissatisfied customers, suppliers, auditors, or regulators. If a company can't generate an accurate invoice, meet a promised delivery date, find a missing shipment, or properly account for costs and revenues, it can get in trouble quickly. So, such back-office systems have gone unnoticed unless things went wrong. More recently, however, ESs have moved into the front office, supporting supply chain optimization, sales force automation, and customer service. You may recall we discussed these functions in Chapter 2.

The Internet and intranets have largely erased the distinction between front- and back-office operations as the ideal method (or tool) for distributing and providing access to information. Employees, suppliers, and customers can all access the organization's information with just the use of a browser.

Enterprise systems are perfectly suited for information transactions; they're the underlying information "factory" producing the information for internal and external consumption. Using the Internet to give employees and customers access to poor-quality, unintegrated information is like opening more bank branches when the currency is worthless. You have to work on both access and high-quality information simultaneously. The combination of enterprise systems as the primary platform for organizational information and of Internet technology for providing access to it will be the hallmark of leading organizations.

Whether front-office or back-office, by themselves or in combination with other technologies, ESs are distinguished by their information integration. It's great to have the entire business supported by a single type of information system.

Of course, with every benefit there is risk. A few companies have failed at implementing ESs; many more have spent more than they intended or encountered resistance from managers and workers who were unprepared for the changes ESs bring. Companies are willing to take these kinds of risks because of the impact the systems can have on quality, cost reduction, and customer satisfaction and loyalty.

Enterprise systems offer the first great opportunity to achieve true connectivity, a state in which everyone knows what everyone else is doing in the business all over the world at the same time. Because they represent the first great opportunity for connectivity, they pose one of the greatest threats to the status quo that companies have ever faced. Since companies are made up mostly of people, ESs mean you will have to change people and the way they do things at the same time that you change all the computers and the software. That is why ESs may be more rewarding, and more challenging, than any computer system a company has ever tried to install.

ENTERPRISE RESOURCE PLANNING (ERP) SYSTEMS

Enterprise systems (ESs) are also known as enterprise resource planning (ERP) systems. ***Enterprise resource planning (ERP) systems*** are software systems for business management, supporting areas such as planning, manufacturing, sales, marketing, distribution, accounting, finance, human resource management, project management, inventory management, service and maintenance, transportation, and e-business. As you can see in Figure 7.2, the ERP system allows transparent integration of functions, providing flows of information between all areas within the enterprise in a consistently visible manner. ERPs allow companies to implement a single integrated system replacing their legacy information systems. A ***legacy information system (LIS)*** represents a massive, long-term business investment; such systems are often brittle, slow, and nonextensible.

The American Production and Inventory Control Society (APICS) has defined an ERP system as "a method for the effective planning and controlling of all the resources needed to take, make, ship, and account for customer orders in a manufacturing, distribution or service company." ERP systems are commercial software that provides the seamless integration of all the information flowing through the company—financial, accounting, human resources, supply chain, and customer information. ERP systems are configurable information systems packages that integrate information and information-based processes within and across functional areas in an organization. What this really

Figure 7.2

Overview of ERP System

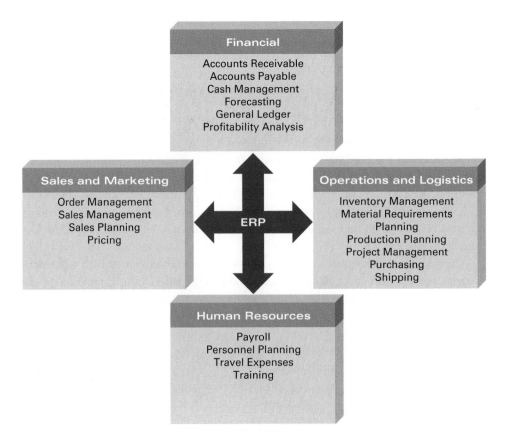

means is one database, one application, and a unified interface across the entire enterprise. An ERP system is required to have the following characteristics:

- Modular design comprising many distinct business functions such as financial, manufacturing, distribution, and the like
- Centralized DBMS
- Integrated functions that provide seamless information flow among the functions
- Flexible, best business practices
- Functions that work in real time
- Internet-enabled[3]

Different ERP vendors provide ERP systems with some degree of specialty but the core functions are almost the same for all of them (see Figure 7.3). Some of the core ERP functions found in the successful ERP systems are the following:

- Accounting management
- Financial management
- Manufacturing management
- Production management
- Transportation management
- Sales and distribution management
- Human resources management
- Supply chain management
- Customer relationship management
- E-business

The functions (as listed in Figure 7.3) of an ERP system can either work as stand-alone units, or several functions can be combined together to form an integrated system.

You need to realize that ERP systems will not improve organizations' functionalities overnight. The high expectation of achieving cost savings and service improvements is very much dependent on how good the chosen ERP system fits the organizational functionalities and how well the tailoring and configuration process of the system

Figure 7.3

ERP Vendors

Vendor/Web Address	ERP Specialties/Characteristics	Target Market
SAP www.sap.com	Customer relationship management, financial management, human resource management, and supply chain management	Large businesses
Oracle/PeopleSoft www.oracle.com	Financial management, human resources management, and supply chain management	Large businesses
SSA Global (Baan) www.ssaglobal.com	Customer relationship management, financial management, human resource management, and supply chain management	Large businesses
Microsoft (Great Plains) www.microsoft.com	Financial management, distribution, manufacturing, project accounting, human resource management, and business analytics	Small-to-medium businesses

matches with the business culture, strategy, and structure of the organization. Overall, an ERP system is expected to improve both back-office and front-office functions simultaneously. Organizations choose and deploy ERP systems for many different benefits and reasons. In many cases the calculation of return on investment (ROI) is weighted against the many benefits. The benefits that an ERP system may bring to organizations are described in Figure 7.4. To reap the benefits of ERP systems, however, organizations need to overcome certain problems and disadvantages, which are also listed in Figure 7.4.

ERP systems are big business. At the top of the IT spending list is the ERP market. For instance, the U.S. federal government will spend $7.7 billion on ERP products and services in fiscal year 2009, up 37 percent from 2004 spending of $5.6 billion. More than 60 percent of the Fortune 1000 companies have installed or are in the process of

Figure 7.4

Advantages and Disadvantages of Enterprise Resource Planning Systems

Advantages of ERP Systems

Advantage	Benefit
Reliable information access	Common DBMS, consistent and accurate data, improved reports
Avoid data and operations redundancy	Modules access same data from the central database, avoid multiple data input, and update operations
Delivery and cycle time reduction	Minimizes retrieving and reporting delays
Cost reduction	Time savings, improved control by enterprisewide analysis of organizational decisions
Easy adaptability	Changes in business processes easy to adapt and restructure
Improved scalability	Structured and modular design with "add-ons"
Improved maintenance	Vendor-supported long-term contract as part of the system procurement
Global outreach	Extended modules such as CRM and SCM
E-business	Internet commerce, collaborative culture

Disadvantages of ERP Systems

Disadvantage	How to Overcome
Time-consuming	Minimize sensitive issues, internal politics, and raise general consensus
Expensive	Cost may vary from thousands of dollars to millions; business process reengineering cost may be extremely high—be cautious
Lack of conformity of the modules	The architecture and components of the selected system should conform to the business processes, culture, and strategic goals of the organization
Vendor dependence	Single vendor vs. multivendor consideration, options for "best of breeds," look for long-term committed support
Too many features, too much complexity	ERP system may have too many features and modules so the user needs to consider carefully and implement the needed only
Questionable scalability and global outreach	Look for vendor investment in R&D, long-term commitment to product and services, consider Internet-enabled systems
Not enough extended ERP capability	Be sure "add-on" facilities and extended modules such as CRM and SCM are available

implementing ERP systems to support their business activities. These packages implemented by the Fortune 1000 companies run well over the IT budgets for most small-to-medium-size enterprises. ERP vendors are targeting this untapped market with scaled-back systems suitable for smaller firms by offering simple, cheaper, preconfigured solutions easy to install within budget and time constraints. For instance, Microsoft now offers an ERP solution (called Microsoft Great Plains) geared toward the small-to-medium-size company.[4,5]

THE EVOLUTION OF ERP SYSTEMS

ERP systems replace "islands of information" with a single, packaged software solution that integrates all the traditional enterprise management functions such as financials, human resources, and manufacturing and logistics. Knowing the history and evolution of ERP is essential to understanding its current application and its future developments. To help give you a better perspective, let's review the evolution of ERP systems (also see Figure 7.5).

The early stage of ERP was carried out in the 1970s through a system called *Materials Requirement Planning (MRP)*. The focus of the MRP software was on internal production planning, calculating time requirements components, procurement, and materials planning. The MRP software did not focus on any type of service orientation, but rather was developed to provide the right materials at the right time.

MRP, or "little MRP," represented a huge step forward in the planning process. For the first time, based on a schedule of what was going to be produced, which was supported by a list of materials that were needed for that finished item, the computer could calculate the total needed and compare it to what was already on hand or committed to arrive. This comparison could suggest an activity—to place an order, cancel orders that were already placed, or simply move the timing of these existing orders. The real significance of MRP was that, for the first time, management was able to answer the question "when?"

The next generation of these systems was introduced by the early 1980s under the name *Manufacturing Resources Planning* or *MRPII*. MRPII does not mean that MRP was done incorrectly the first time; it is rather its significant evolution. MRPII closed the loop with the accounting and financial management systems. MRPII systems crossed the boundaries of the production functionality and started serving as decision support systems (DSS) as well as executive information systems (EIS—in the modern day many people refer to implementations of these as digital dashboards).

For the first time, a company could have an integrated business system that provided visibility for the requirements of material and capacity. Good information leads to good decisions, and therefore these integrated IT systems provided a competitive advantage.

By the time each functional area of a company had developed its own software program, the need for tightly integrating them became obvious. The next major shift during the late 1980s and early 1990s was that "time to market" was becoming increasingly short. Lead times expected by the market continued to shorten and customers were no longer satisfied with the service level that was considered world class only a few years earlier.

Figure 7.5

Evolution of Enterprise Resource Planning Systems

ERP'S DILEMMA

Not all implementations of an ERP system are successful, or at least not at first; for instance:

- U.S. food giant Hershey Foods installed an ERP system in spite of experiencing major problems in a previous ill-fated deployment of a like system. The original $112 million ERP project caused order-processing problems that hampered the company's ability to ship products to retailers at one of the busiest times in its business cycle. The problems caused the company to fall short of its third-quarter sales target by $100 million. However, the new ERP implementation has allowed it to consolidate the processing of more than 95 percent of its revenue and business transactions within a single system. The new system is providing the company with greater consistency, visibility, and real-time access to critical business information.
- After seven years and about $500 million trying to implement a mainframe-based ERP package, Dow

Chemical scrapped the project and started from scratch with a client/server version instead.

- Dell Computer spent two years and $250 million customizing an ERP system, then discovered it wouldn't be flexible enough to meet the rapidly changing business processes of the much touted make-to-order business model that has fueled Dell's success on the Web.[6,7]

Here are some interesting facts about ERP systems:

- Only 7 percent of IT directors report failed ERP initiatives.
- 22 percent of directors never expect payback from ERP.
- Only 11 percent of ERP projects have "mammoth" budgets.
- 64 percent of companies plan to integrate e-business with ERP systems.

The need to develop a tightly integrated system that would use data stored in one common database and would be used enterprisewide became the highest priority for IT professionals. No longer was it tolerable to submit a request to the IT department and wait several months to obtain this critical information. This common-database, companywide integrated system appeared at the beginning of the 1990s and was named *enterprise resource planning (ERP)*.

ERP encompasses all the resource planning for the enterprise including product design, warehousing, material planning, capacity planning, and communication systems. ERP systems help companies become leaner by integrating the basic transaction programs for all departments, allowing quick access to timely information.

ERP systems have evolved into what is now commonly referred to as *ERPII*. During the last few years, the functional perimeter of ERPII systems has begun an expansion into its adjacent markets, such as supply chain management (SCM), customer relationship management (CRM), data warehousing/business intelligence (DWBI), and e-business. The major ERP vendors have been busy developing, acquiring, and/or bundling new functionality so that their packages go beyond the traditional realms of finance, materials planning, and human resources.

ERP VENDORS AND MARKET TRENDS

The dominating ERP software suppliers are SAP, Oracle/PeopleSoft, SSA Global, and Microsoft (refer back to Figure 7.3). Together they control more than 70 percent of the multibillion-dollar global market. Each vendor, for historical reasons, has a specialty in one particular module area such as SAP in logistics, Oracle/PeopleSoft in financials, SSA

Global in manufacturing, and Microsoft in retail management. There are also about 50 established and a few more newly emerging smaller and midsize ERP vendors including third-party developers competing for the very lucrative ERP market. Figure 7.6 displays a list of some other top ERP companies (those beyond what we mentioned in Figure 7.3) with links to their Web sites. There is stiff competition and overlapping products difficult to differentiate. The vendors are continuously updating their products and adding new technology-based features. Long-term vision, commitment to service and support, specialty features, experience and financial strength for research and development are considered the major vendor qualities for product selection and implementation.

The ERP market has been growing at a rate of more than 30 percent per year and most forecasts predict the same. The growth of the ERP market has been boosted by both business and technical factors. With respect to business, the most cited reason is globalization, which has fostered mergers and stimulated the creation of big corporations with high information requirements that the former individual information systems were not able to fulfill. Another factor is general market maturity in developed countries, which has fostered competition among all companies and increased the power of consumers, thus forcing enterprises to upgrade the efficiency of their business processes.

Figure 7.6

Additional ERP Vendors and Their Web Addresses

Invensys	Cincom	Visibility
www.invensys.com	www.cincom.com	www.visibility.com
ABB Automation	Computer Associates	PowerCerv
www.abb.com/automation	www.interbiz.cai.com	www.powercerv.com
i2	GEAC	Clarus Corp
www.i2.com	www.geac.com	www.claruscorp.com
SSA Global Technologies	Sage	Friedman Corp
www.ssagt.com	www.sage.com	www.friedmancorp.com
Intentia International	Navision	ROI Systems
www.intentia.com	www.navision.com	www.roisysinc.com
Epicor	Scala	Ramco
www.epicor.com	www.scala-na.com	www.ramco.com
Lawson Software	Flexi Int'l	Intuitive Manufacturing
www.lawson.com	www.flexi.com	www.mrp9000.com
QAD	Glovia International	Ceecom, Inc.
www.qad.com	www.glovia.com	www.ceecom.com
IFS	AremisSoft Corp.	Technology Group International
www.ifsab.com	www.aremissoft.com	www.techgroupintl.com
Mapics	Syspro Group	Deltek
www.mapics.com	www.sysprousa.com	www.deltek.com
Mincom	ProfitKey International	Fourthshift
www.mincom.com	www.profitkey.com	www.fs.com
American Software	Solomon Software	Lilly Software
www.amsoftware.com	www.solomon.com	www.lillysoftware.com
Ross Systems	Macola	
www.rossinc.com	www.macola.com	
SCT	Made2Manage	
www.sctcorp.com	www.made2manage.com	

Finally, advances in information and communication technologies have made the development of ERP systems possible by allowing the database centralization to integrate with a distributed ERP environment. With respect to technical reasons, the introduction of the European Union (EU) currency, the euro, has stimulated the ERP growth in the EU area in the past few years, since most of the information systems in the EU zone were not able to handle multiple currencies.

Developing Agile IT Systems

Everywhere you look today, change is occurring at warp speed. Nothing is changing faster than the business world. With the rise of the Internet and e-business, change isn't something that you decide to do anymore; it's something that you live with daily.

You hear a lot of talk about business "agility," but what does this mean really? It certainly isn't the ability of the CEO to leap tall buildings in a single bound. *Business agility* means being prepared for change at a moment's notice. The reason organizations need agile IT systems is very simple: More change happens in business than IT or the business can anticipate. To cope with countless (and often unforeseen) changes and competitive demands, businesses must have flexible, adaptive—agile—IT systems.

There are a number of factors or abilities relating to agility that you should consider whenever you are developing an IT system. These factors or abilities to be concerned about are commonly referred to as the "ilities"—as in availability, accessibility, reliability, scalability, flexibility, performance, and capacity planning. (We realize that the last two terms do not end in "ility," but they are still important "ilities" in this discussion.) Your IT system needs these abilities in order to be agile.

AVAILABILITY

It's not uncommon for an employee to arrive at work early, or to stay late, or to work on the weekend to meet a deadline. For this reason, it's crucial that the IT system supports varied schedules.

Availability is determining when an IT system will be available for employees to access. Most companies have IT systems available $24 \times 7 \times 365$, or 24 hours a day, 7 days a week, 365 days a year. One reason why a company might support $24 \times 7 \times 365$ system availability is time zones. For example, Jon Nordmark, president and CEO of eBags.com, an online seller of luggage, handbags, and shoes based in Denver, Colorado, has an office in London, England. When the London eBags.com employees are finishing work, the Colorado eBags.com employees are just starting work. Since eBags.com takes orders on behalf of manufacturers, who then ship the goods directly to customers, Jon needs to have access to information during times when the London employees are not available. The same IT systems are worked on by both sets of employees so they must be available around the clock. Supporting global customers mandates that the eBags.com IT systems be available $24 \times 7 \times 365$ in order to support all of the customers in the different time zones.

ACCESSIBILITY

Accessibility refers to the question of who has the right to access different types of IT systems and information. What would happen if all employees had access to payroll information? Payroll information is considered confidential, and at some companies you can be fired for having knowledge of or sharing this type of information.

Accessibility determines not only who can access the information, but also how they can access or manipulate the information—whether they can create, read, update, and/or delete information. Therefore, it's important that a business define how each employee can access information and build this into the IT system.

RELIABILITY

Reliability means the assurance that your IT systems are functioning correctly and providing accurate information. Inaccurate information exists for many reasons, from the information being entered incorrectly to the information becoming corrupt. Whatever the reason, if employees can't receive reliable information, their jobs or functions become compromised.

Ensuring information is reliable is a critical and difficult task for all organizations. *Data cleansing* (discussed in Chapter 3) is the process of ensuring that all information is accurate. The more an organization can do to build in reliability into its IT systems and to see to it that its IT infrastructure promotes reliable information, the more money it will save by catching errors before they occur.

SCALABILITY

Estimating how much growth an organization is expected to experience over a period of years is an almost impossible task. Many factors in the market, the industry, and the economy can affect organizational growth. If an organization grows faster than anticipated, it may find its IT systems experiencing all types of problems from running out of disk space to slowing transaction performance speed. **Scalability** refers to how well a system can adapt to increased demands. To keep employees working and productive, organizations must try to anticipate growth and make sure the IT infrastructure will be able to adjust to handle it.

FLEXIBILITY

A single system can be designed in a number of different ways to perform exactly the same function. When choosing which design to implement, you must think about the system's *flexibility,* or the system's ability to change quickly. Building an inflexible system will cost a company money because it won't be able to handle market, business, or economic changes.

PERFORMANCE

Performance measures how quickly an IT system performs a certain process. **Benchmarks** are baseline values a system seeks to attain. **Benchmarking** is a process of continuously measuring system results, comparing those results to optimal system performance (benchmark values), and identifying steps and procedures to improve system performance. Many factors affect the performance of an IT system, ranging from the design of the system to the hardware that supports it, and especially its IT infrastructure.

One of the most common performance problems you'll find occurs because of uncontrolled growth. For example, if business is booming and a company doubles the size of its order entry department, it must ensure the system performs at the same speed with twice as many users. If you had 50 order entry specialists and you now have 100 order entry specialists, your IT systems might not function correctly because of the increased number of users.

RANKING THE "ILITIES"

Understanding and ensuring each of the IT system "ilities" is critical to any organization's success. In a group, review the list of IT infrastructure "ilities" below and rank them in order of their impact on an organization's success. Use a rating system of 1 to 7, where 1 indicates the biggest impact and 7 indicates the least impact. As a basis for your ranking, apply the "ilities" to one of the companies discussed in the chapter's Industry Perspective or Global Perspective boxes. Be prepared to justify your rankings.

COMPANY: _____

IT Infrastructure "ilities"	Business Impact
Availability	
Accessibility	
Reliability	
Scalability	
Flexibility	
Performance	
Capacity Planning	

CAPACITY PLANNING

Capacity planning determines your projected future IT infrastructure requirements for new equipment and additional network capacity. It's cheaper for an organization to implement an IT infrastructure that considers capacity growth at the beginning of a system deployment than to try to upgrade equipment and networks after the system has already been implemented. Not having enough capacity leads to performance issues and hinders the ability of employees to perform their jobs. For example, if you have 100 employees using the Internet to perform their jobs and you purchase network hardware that is too slow and the network capacity is too small, your employees will spend a great deal of time just waiting to get information from the Internet.

Information Systems Infrastructure

Information systems infrastructure has a critical impact on many organizations' ability to use IT competitively. When we speak about infrastructure we are referring to more than the physical components. Hardware, software, information, and a network must be combined in a coherent pattern to make a sustainable infrastructure.

Information systems infrastructure can be considered at several levels. The infrastructure may support the enterprise as a whole and alone, or it may also focus on inter-organizational layers, laying a framework for communication with customers, suppliers, and/or other stakeholders.

Because infrastructures are the base on which many information systems are built, changes to the infrastructure are often considered "disruptive." (Remember our discus-

ABERCROMBIE & FITCH'S ONLINE LIFESTYLES

Abercrombie & Fitch uses the Internet to market its distinctive image as fashion trendsetter to one of its largest customer segments, college students. The company created an e-commerce Web site (www.abercrombie.com) that reflects the casual college lifestyle conveyed by Abercrombie & Fitch and parallels the sleek but simple design of A&F Quarterly, the company's flagship magazine.

The highly successful Web site gives customers not only an opportunity to shop online, but also a taste of the Abercrombie & Fitch lifestyle through downloadable MP3s, calendars, and desktop accessories.[8] Young customers tend to be Internet savvy and their purchasing habits vary from shopping for sale items at midnight to knowing exactly what they want immediately. Thus Abercrombie & Fitch's Web architecture design and development, infrastructure planning, implementation, and maintenance had to be accessible, available, reliable, and scalable to meet the demands of its young customers.

sion of disruptive technology in the opening case study in Chapter 1.) *Disruptive technology* is a new product or service that disrupts the way things are done in an industry and that eventually is successful and wins market share.

We need to point out that the two terms *architecture* and *infrastructure* are often used interchangeably; however, they have very different meanings. An IT **architecture** is the blueprint for translating a business strategy into a plan. A blueprint shows how a system, house, vehicle, or product will look and how the parts interrelate. The more complex an item, the more important its architecture, so that the interrelationships among the components are well defined.

Generally, **infrastructure** is a relative term meaning "the structure beneath a structure." This definition implies different layers of structure, which provide support or services. An IT infrastructure is the implementation of an architecture. In a city, the infrastructure includes its streets and street lighting, hospitals and schools, utility lines running above and below the ground, police and fire departments, and so on. We all depend on this public infrastructure. In a corporation, the IT infrastructure includes the hardware, software, enterprise systems, and information that ensure the components work together (see Figure 7.7).

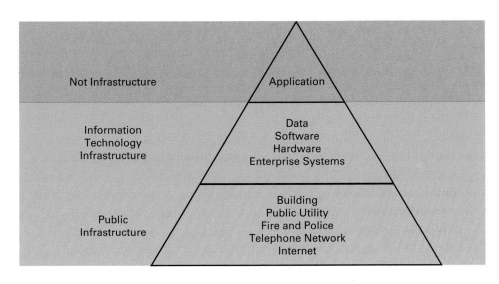

Figure 7.7
Infrastructures

You may be thinking that the huge number of IT choices available, coupled with the incredible speed of technological advances, makes the task of designing an IT infrastructure seem a bit impossible. Sometimes you are right; however, you can better understand this by breaking down the tasks into two major steps: (1) translating a business strategy into an IT architecture, and (2) translating the IT architecture into an IT infrastructure. Before we go into specific technical detail, let's look at the reasons why IT architectures and infrastructures really matter.

WHY ARCHITECTURE MATTERS

The development of an IT architecture involves converting the corporate strategy into a technology plan. The plan—the architecture—defines both the key capabilities required from the technology infrastructure and the places where the technologies, the management responsibility, and the support will be located. The IT architecture identifies what information must be standardized corporatewide and what will be standardized at a regional level. More simply put, this means an IT architecture specifies where and how information will be located and accessed. Similarly, an IT architecture differentiates between processes that must be standardized across locations and processes that must be integrated. (We will talk about integration in more detail later in this chapter.)

The detail of an IT architecture should help companies distinguish between capabilities that are competitive necessities and those that offer strategic advantage. For instance, Wal-Mart, Dell, and Schwab have placed enormous value on their IT architectures to gain a strategic advantage over their competition. As you may have already guessed, these architectures have led to the success of these companies.

WHY INFRASTRUCTURE MATTERS

From the description above, you understand that IT architectures are orderly plans of the capabilities that an IT infrastructure should provide. Although at many businesses key elements of the IT infrastructure have been in place for 20 to 30 years, today IT infrastructures tend to be in a constant state of change. An IT infrastructure should exhibit several key traits, such as:

- **Efficiency**—The ability to provide reusable components that are priced reasonably and can be turned around quickly for application development projects.
- **Effectiveness**—The easy integration of all components in a way that supports their operation.
- **Agility**—Good planning and design processes that allow companies to develop new applications quickly and to repurpose or upgrade their existing infrastructure to support new requirements for existing and/or new applications.

Building a solid IT infrastructure requires your organization to understand the fundamental IT infrastructure components. The task of translating the architecture into an infrastructure entails creating details about certain technologies, specifically:

- **Hardware**—The physical components of the IT infrastructure (e.g., personal computers, servers, network cabling).
- **Software**—The programs that run on hardware (e.g., operating systems, DBMS, spreadsheets).
- **Network**—Software and hardware components, such as switches, hubs, and routers, which create a path for communication and information sharing.

I HEAR YOU CALLING

VoIP, or **Voice over Internet Protocol,** allows you to send voice communications over the Internet and avoid the toll charges that you would normally receive from your long-distance carrier. Originally, Internet telephony had a reputation of poor call quality, lame user interfaces, and low call-completion rates. With new and improved technology and IT infrastructures, VoIP now offers similar quality to traditional telephone.

If you want to make VoIP phone calls over the Internet, you need to find a vendor that offers VoIP services. At first, only a few companies such as Cisco and Lucent offered VoIP services, but the large telecommunications carriers—such as AT&T and Sprint—now offer VoIP. The way that VoIP works is very similar to e-mail.

You simply send your call over the Internet in packets of audio tagged with the same destination. VoIP reassembles the packets once they arrive at their final destination.

Typically, vendors are providing the same VoIP service. For instance, most VoIP vendors provide the features that traditional telephone companies charge extra for when they are added to your service plan, such as caller ID, call waiting, call transfer, repeat dial, return call, and three-way calling.

Its IT infrastructure affects a company's product or service offering. Designing and building the correct IT infrastructure is critical to the success of any business.

- **Information**—Decisions concerning the quantity, quality, and format of information, and how often it must be transferred from one piece of hardware to another or translated from one format to another.

Designing, implementing, and maintaining an IT infrastructure has become one of the most important tasks for corporate IT management (CIOs, CTOs, and the like, which we discussed in Chapter 3), and the intensifying speed of technological change has made these responsibilities both increasingly important and increasingly difficult. Recently, some large companies have made some very large investments in their IT infrastructures. For example:

- Citicorp invested over $750 million in a new global database system.
- Dow Corning and most other Fortune 500 companies invested tens of millions of dollars to purchase and install enterprise resource planning systems.
- Johnson & Johnson broke with tradition by committing corporate funds to help its individual operating companies acquire standard desktop equipment.
- Statoil presented all 15,000 of its employees with a high-end computer for home or office use.[9, 10, 11, 12]

Companies all over the world are investing their time and money to support their IT infrastructures. In the past, many of these companies had, in effect, given their IT units a generous allowance, asking them to spend it wisely. Now they are engaging in intense negotiations over network capabilities, information standards, and IT funding limits. The recognition that global markets are creating enormous demands for increased information sharing within and across companies has led to the realization that a powerful, flexible IT infrastructure has become a prerequisite for doing business.

The capabilities built into an infrastructure can either limit or enhance a company's ability to respond to changing market conditions. New infrastructure technologies are enabling new organizational processes, creating a competitive environment that increasingly demands cost-effectiveness. One example is designing a wireless infrastructure that allows communication from remote locations using a variety of technologies (e.g., cellular, wireless LAN, satellite, infrared, and GPS).

Characteristics	Decentralized	Centralized	Distributed	Client/Server
Cost efficiency	Moderate	Excellent	Moderate	Very reasonable
Data location	Distributed	Centralized	Distributed	Distributed
Ease of management	Simple	Easy	Difficult	Moderate
Network performance	Excellent	Constrained	Varies	Constrained
Processing location	Distributed	Centralized	Distributed	Shared
User control	Full	Very limited	Varies	Varies

Figure 7.8

Type of Infrastructures

Information Technology Infrastructure

By the term *information technology infrastructure* we specify the technological and organizational structures needed for the integration of information resources. There are four types of information technology infrastructures:

1. Decentralized infrastructure
2. Centralized infrastructure
3. Distributed infrastructure
4. Client/server infrastructure

Figure 7.9

Decentralized
Infrastructure

Figure 7.8 identifies several differences among these IT infrastructures and describes the characteristics of each.

DECENTRALIZED INFRASTRUCTURE

A ***decentralized infrastructure*** involves little or no sharing of information systems. Generally, this infrastructure arises from users or departments developing their own systems or applications, without any central control (see Figure 7.9).

The decentralized infrastructure gives users the liberty to develop applications that meet their needs and maintain control over the applications they develop. However, this infrastructure generally prevents users from easily combining processing power or even comparing information between

Finance Department

Marketing Department

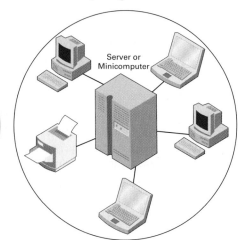

Shipping Department

THE FUTURE OF CLIENT/SERVER

The term client/server was first used in the 1980s in reference to personal computers (PCs) on a network. The actual client/server model started gaining acceptance in the late 1980s. Client/server is a versatile, message-based and modular infrastructure that is intended to improve usability, flexibility, interoperability, and scalability as compared to centralized, mainframe, time-sharing computing.

No technology is right for every situation, and each technology has associated costs (monetary and otherwise). Some examples of the kinds of costs and limitations that a technology may impose are the following: A technology may impose an otherwise unnecessary interface standard; may require investment in other technologies; may require investment of time or money; or may directly conflict with security or real-time requirements.

Search the Internet and determine the following:

- As the client/server infrastructure matures, what is its future?
- Will it remain the application infrastructure of choice or will another infrastructure emerge?
- If we had known of the power of the PC in its early days 15 years ago and the client/server infrastructure 10 years ago, would we have designed and implemented systems differently?

---

various information systems. It also encourages data duplication, frequently leading to inconsistencies. For example, Figure 7.9 illustrates a finance, a marketing, and a shipping department, each technologically isolated from the other. Decentralized infrastructures often arise in companies having a decentralized management approach and typically in companies built through acquisition.

In a decentralized infrastructure, each department within an organization has its own hardware and software to satisfy the specific information needs of that department, without necessarily considering other units. In a fully decentralized infrastructure, the systems of the independent departments are not linked to each other or to the organization's corporate office.

The major disadvantage of a decentralized infrastructure is that with a variety of independent systems, it is difficult to share applications and information. It is also more expensive for an organization to establish maintenance and service contracts with many vendors than with just one or a few.

CENTRALIZED INFRASTRUCTURE

A *centralized infrastructure* involves sharing of information systems in one central area or one central mainframe. For a long time, mainframes were the only computers available for business. By their nature, they dictated that information systems infrastructures be centralized because typically all applications and information were stored on a company's single mainframe. As an example, Figure 7.10 shows a typical layout of a centralized infrastructure. With the introduction of inexpensive desktop computers and reliable data communications technology, almost all organizations have moved away from the centralized infrastructure.

The great advantage of a centralized infrastructure is that it allows a high degree of control, making it easy to (1) maintain standards of hardware, software, procedures, and operations, and (2) control access to information. The main disadvantage of a centralized infrastructure is its inflexibility. A centralized

Figure 7.10

Centralized Infrastructure

333

infrastructure is run so that it can be used by everyone, but that does not mean that the system is optimal for everyone. Different departments and remote sites have different information needs.

DISTRIBUTED INFRASTRUCTURE

A *distributed infrastructure* involves distributing the information and processing power of IT systems via a network. By connecting all the information systems via a distributed infrastructure, all locations can share information and applications (see Figure 7.11). The major benefit of this is that processing activity can be allocated to the location(s) where it can most efficiently be done. To improve performance and reduce network traffic, a distributed architecture will often store the same application and/or information in two or more locations.

Distributed architectures are more complex than centralized architectures for several reasons. First, the distributed architecture must be able to determine the location of specific applications and information. Second, it must be more sophisticated in determining the optimal way to request the application and information. The order in which the system processes a request can make a significant difference in the amount of data transmitted over the network.

CLIENT/SERVER INFRASTRUCTURE

A *client/server infrastructure* (or *client/server network*) has one or more computers that are *servers* which provide services to other computers, called *clients*. The client/server infrastructure is a form of distributed infrastructure. The basic notion, as

Figure 7.11

Distributed Infrastructure

Denver Office

New York Office

Dallas Office

suggested in Figure 7.12, of a client/server infrastructure is that application processing is divided between the client and the server. The functions of an information system are divided among connected computers (or clients) on a network while centralizing processing and storage for all information on a server. For instance, when you are surfing on the Internet, this is an example of a client/server infrastructure. Typical components of this type of infrastructure include an Internet browser, a personal computer (e.g., the client), and a Web server.

The primary advantage of the client/server infrastructure is that it "off-loads" the application programs and information from the server. Because processing occurs at many client locations, and the client and server interact frequently and extensively, information must flow rapidly between server and clients for adequate performance. The client/server infrastructure thereby places a heavy load on the network capacity, which can sometimes be a disadvantage.

Figure 7.12
Client/Server
Infrastructure

OTHER TYPES OF INFRASTRUCTURES

Most enterprise applications are now developed using a tiered infrastructure. In a ***tiered infrastructure*** (sometimes referred to as a ***layer infrastructure***), the IT system is partitioned into tiers (or layers) where each tier (or layer) performs a specific type of functionality. The concept of a tiered infrastructure has evolved from 1-tier to n-tiers. A "tier" can be defined as "one of two or more rows, levels, or ranks arranged one above another." Figure 7.13 illustrates the concept of a tiered infrastructure. A brief overview of each is given on the next page.

Figure 7.13

N-Tier Infrastructure
Model

Tier	Example
1-tier (Presentation Tier)	Web Client
2-tier Application Tier	Web Server
3-tier Data Tier	Database
N-tier Business Logic Tier	Application Server

WORLD BANK IN REAL TIME

World Bank implemented a SAP ERP system, which enabled the bank to replace 65 fragmented administrative systems—a patchwork that had produced inconsistent financial reporting and was costly to maintain. The ERP system also enabled real-time global access to its headquarter-centric system from more than 100 locations via its global network. SAP provides an n-tier architecture with a presentation interface on the desktop, application logic running on multiple application servers, and a database machine primarily for database software.

Seven SAP components—SAP Financials (FI), SAP Fund Management (FM), SAP Controlling (CO), SAP Ma-

terials Management (MM), SAP Project System (PS), SAP Human Resources—Travel Management, and SAP Enterprise Buyer—were put in place to help the World Bank streamline procurement, materials management, project systems, and financial reporting.

Since implementation, the World Bank has realized significant benefits, many of which stem from the ability to integrate people, processes, and data. Information is now transparent, comprehensive, and available from any location, enabling the organization to be more of a development partner, not just a provider of financial aid.

- A *1-tier* infrastructure is the most basic setup because it involves a single tier on a single machine. Think of an application that runs on your PC—everything you need to run the application (data storage, business logic, user interface, and so forth) is wrapped up together. An example of a 1-tiered application is a basic word processor or a desktop file utility program.

- A *2-tier* infrastructure is the basic client/server relationship. In essence, the client handles the display, the server handles the request (e.g., database query), and the application tier is contained on one or both of the two tiers.

- A *3-tier* infrastructure is the most common approach used for Web applications today. A typical example of this model is the Web browser that acts as the client, an application server that handles the business logic, and a separate tier (such as a DBMS) that handles database functions.

- An *n-tier* infrastructure balances the work of the network over several different servers. The letter "n" stands for any number of tiers. Traditionally, an n-tier infrastructure starts with a basic 3-tier model and expands on it to allow for greater performance, scalability, and a host of other benefits.

THE INFRASTRUCTURE INVESTMENT

IT investments are some of the most important decisions made by an organization. By their very nature, IT infrastructure investments are large, long term, and have no (real) value on their own. An infrastructure's value lies in its ability to quickly and economically enable the implementation of new applications, often across business units, which in turn generate even greater business value.

One of the strengths of an infrastructure is the standardization of services, such as an integrated telecommunications network or a unified customer database. This standardization allows easier integration and information access across business units. For example, companies seeking more collaboration between business units have significantly more infrastructure investment and capability. However, this extensive infrastructure capability costs more up front, and these costs, as well as the benefits, are reflected in the relationships to the business value of the company.

You can start to understand that the issues of investing in and managing information technology infrastructure are very similar to those of managing the public infrastructure of roads, bridges, hospitals, and schools.

Investing in information technology infrastructure involves difficult decisions for senior managers. These are large investments with long-term business implications. Infrastructure investments are significant, accounting for more than 58 percent of information technology dollars. Forrester Research Group expects small and medium-size businesses (SMBs) to increase IT spending 6.6 percent during 2005 as companies look to upgrade their infrastructure.[13]

The purpose of building information technology infrastructures is to enable sharing of information and expensive resources, sharing execution of business processes, and connecting to customers and suppliers as part of the extended enterprise. This sharing and connecting can create cross-unit or cross-functional integration that allows the company to benefit from a combination of economies of scale and flexibility. Having separate and incompatible infrastructures limits the company's strategic options.

To put information technology infrastructure in context, let's look at two market leaders who made different infrastructure decisions driven by their distinct strategic contexts. Developing a solid infrastructure over the past few years has helped GM reduce computing complexity by trimming the number of applications in use at the company from 7,000 to 3,000, and has contributed to saving $1 billion annually for the past five years. Wachovia Corporation is the fourth-largest financial services company and the third-largest brokerage firm in the United States, serving more than 14 million households and businesses. Wachovia developed an enterprise content strategy in 2003 that had a total infrastructure investment of $1.4 million. Within a two-year span, Wachovia has saved $2.3 million, a 64 percent return.[14, 15]

SUPPORTING AN IT INFRASTRUCTURE

Now that you have a fundamental understanding of a few of the important issues in IT infrastructure, let's turn our attention to how you can support an IT infrastructure—backup/recovery and a disaster recovery plan.

BACKUP/RECOVERY   Have you ever lost a document on your computer because your computer crashed and you hadn't saved or backed up the document? Have you ever accidentally deleted a file you needed? *Backup* is the process of making a copy of the information stored on a computer. *Recovery* is the process of reinstalling the backup information in the event the information was lost. There are many different types of media your organization can choose to back up information including tapes, disks, CD-ROMs, and storage area network (SAN). A *storage area network (SAN)* is an infrastructure for building special, dedicated networks that allow rapid and reliable access to storage devices by multiple servers.

We cannot stress enough the importance of making backups. How many times do you think employees have lost information because they didn't have a backup? How often do you think employees should back up their files? The answer to these questions varies depending on the organization's goals. For example, if the organization deals with large volumes of critical information, it might require daily backups. If the organization deals with small amounts of noncritical information, it might require only weekly backups. Deciding how often to back up computer information is a critical decision for any organization.

DISASTER RECOVERY PLAN   Unfortunately, disasters—such as power outages, floods, and even harmful hacking—occur all the time. They are also unpredictable. Therefore,

CBS SPORTSLINE.COM

The next time you see someone dialing their cell phone, ask that person to tell you which team just won the big game. Chances are they know the answer. That's because huge numbers of avid sports fans are using small wireless devices, like digital cell phones and alphanumeric pagers, to stay in touch with their favorite teams.

One of the most popular sources for this kind of information is the no-fee SportsLine.com "All-the-Time Wireless" service, which delivers in-progress scoring updates for almost every sport. Fans can customize the SportsLine.com service to send only the information they want, as soon as it happens. Fantasy leagues, late-breaking news and scores, and many more options are available through a personalized Web page and specialized software that enables any wireless device to log in.

Ultimately what SportsLine.com had to do to offer its wireless services was to develop an infrastructure that was portable between devices, so a single application works across multiple device types. The infrastructure also needed to allow applications to be downloaded and installed utilizing wireless technology, while providing a secure interface to a variety of mobile devices.[16]

an organization needs to develop a disaster recovery plan. A ***disaster recovery plan*** is a detailed process for recovering information or an IT system in the event of a catastrophic disaster such as a fire or flood.

A good disaster recovery plan takes into consideration the location of the backup information. Many organizations choose to store backup information in an off-site storage facility, or a place that is located separate from the company and often owned by another company, such as a collocation facility. A ***collocation facility*** is available to a company that rents space and telecommunications equipment from another company. One such company is StorageTek, which specializes in providing off-site data storage and disaster recovery solutions.

A good disaster recovery plan also considers the actual facility where employees will work. A ***hot site*** is a separate and fully equipped facility where the company can move immediately after a disaster and resume business. A ***cold site*** is a separate facility that does not have any computer equipment but is a place where employees can move after the disaster.

A disaster recovery plan should be based on a disaster recovery cost curve (see Figure 7.14). A ***disaster recovery cost curve*** charts (1) the cost to your organization of the unavailability of information and technology and (2) the cost to your organization of recovering from a disaster over time. Where the two curves intersect is, in fact, the best recovery plan in terms of cost and time. Being able to restore information and IT systems quickly in the event of a disaster is obviously a crucial aspect of an IT infrastructure.

Figure 7.14

Deciding How Much to Spend on Disaster Recovery

The best disaster recovery plan in terms of cost and time

The cost to the organization of recovering from a disaster over time

The cost to the organization of the unavailability of information and technology

Dollars

Time from Disaster to Recovery (in hours)

REAL WORLD IT INFRASTRUCTURES

Components of a solid IT infrastructure include everything from documentation to business concepts to software and hardware. In this chapter, we've discussed some IT infrastructure components and integrations. It may seem that we covered a great deal of

DO YOU HAVE A BACKUP?

We are sure that most of you would agree that backing up your computer information is critical. However, how many of you are actually making backups of the information stored on your computer? What would happen if your computer crashed right now and you couldn't recover any of the information? How many papers, projects, and course notes would you lose? If you did decide to perform a backup, would you know what information you need to back up and where to find this information on your computer?

There are numerous ways that you can back up the information on your computer including saving your information to disks, CDs, external hard drives, and remote locations such as www.mydocsonline.com. Search the Internet and determine the following:

- What is the best way for you to back up your computer information?
- How frequently do you need to back up your computer information?
- What is the exact location of the information you need to back up?

territory, but there are actually thousands of additional components that are important in building a solid IT infrastructure. Deciding which components to implement and how to implement them can be a challenge.

New IT components are released daily, and business needs continually change. An IT infrastructure that meets an organization's needs today may not meet those needs tomorrow. Building an IT infrastructure that is available, accessible, and reliable and also scalable and flexible is critical to any organization's success.

Before approving the design of an IT infrastructure, ask yourself the following questions:

- How big is my department going to grow? Will the system be able to handle additional users?
- How are my customers going to grow? How much additional information do I expect to store each year?
- How long will I maintain information in the systems? How much history do I want to keep on each customer?
- When do the people in my department work? What are the hours I need the system to be available?
- How often do I need the information to be backed up?
- What will happen to my system if there is a disaster? What is the disaster recovery plan for my system?
- How easy is it to change the system? How flexible is the system?

Seeing to it that the system design addresses each of these questions will put you on the path toward building an IT infrastructure that supports your organization today and tomorrow.

Integrating the Enterprise

Perhaps the most visible and compelling business trend today is integrating the enterprise. Although we have used the term *integration* throughout this chapter, we need to formally define and describe it in detail. **Integration** allows separate applications to

339

INFRASTRUCTURE COMPONENTS

You are a senior manager at Brewers.com, a start-up online coffee supply company that has two main office locations, one in Chicago, and one in Denver. The company is just beginning to develop its IT infrastructure, which must deploy its primary applications for e-mail, payroll, and e-business. One of your business partners has put together a diagram (see below) showing the IT Infrastructure components that are currently available. In a group, assemble the IT infrastructure that will best support your organization.

Chicago Office Servers

Internet

Denver Office Clients

Chicago Office Clients

Network Connections

Denver Office Servers

communicate directly with each other by automatically exporting data files from one application and importing them into another. In short, building integrations between applications helps an organization maintain better control of its information.

Most applications in an enterprise aren't designed to interact with other applications, much less exchange information meaningfully and work cooperatively with them. Integrated information systems are often achieved using ERP systems. The purpose of implementing an ERP system is to integrate supplier, manufacturing, and customer information throughout the supply chain. Enterprises rely on a variety of different information systems, each providing a different piece of key business functionality. Each system may perform its function well, but performs only the function that it is designed for; integration is necessary to get the enterprisewide "big picture." Integrating different information systems is a challenge though, because systems were often never built with the intention of integration.

WHY INTEGRATION IS NECESSARY

Webster's dictionary defines *integration* as "To make whole or complete by adding or bringing together parts." Information systems integration involves bringing together previously isolated information systems with the goal of providing a more whole or complete information resource for the organization.

1,900 GAP STORES INTEGRATED

Gap Inc. is a leading international specialty retailer offering clothing, accessories, and personal care products for men, women, children, and babies under the Gap, Banana Republic, and Old Navy brand names. Gap brand includes Gap, GapKids, BabyGap, GapBody, and Gap Outlet. The Gap has 1,900 stores around the world, employing more than 13,000 people, and generated $16.3 billion in revenue in 2004. The company's primary goal is to achieve and maintain a 20 percent growth rate each year. To achieve this goal, the Gap needs to keep all employees connected with immediate access to real-time information.

The challenge facing the Gap was to implement an infrastructure that would integrate its different systems allowing programs at different locations developed by different vendors to communicate. The integration would enable information sharing among legacy systems and new applications.

Building an IT infrastructure based in system integration and the use of the Internet has allowed the GAP to exchange real-time sales, inventory, and shipping information among all its information systems and employees. The new infrastructure also allows the Gap to send information to and from any IT system in the world, which has increased employee and company performance.[17]

On the organizational process level, integration requires the simplification and streamlining of organizational processes using techniques such as business process reengineering (BPR) and workflow redesign. **Business process reengineering (BPR)** is the analysis and redesign of workflow within and between enterprises. **Workflow** defines all the steps or business rules, from beginning to end, required for a business process.

Albert Einstein once said, "In the middle of difficulty lies opportunity." Integrating the information systems across a large modern enterprise is by no means an easy task. It is a highly complex undertaking involving factors ranging from high tech to high touch. It is often very expensive, entailing unusually large exposure to financial risk because of its time-consuming and resource-intensive nature.

MOTIVES FOR INTEGRATION

There are many motives for enterprise integration. An organization may choose to integrate because of its concerns about its operations, both internal processes and external relationships. Figure 7.15 illustrates this concept. Enterprise integration may be viewed as a possible solution to a number of problems with internal organizational processes. Many organizations are concerned about controlling costs—in inventory, production, personnel, and almost every other area of the enterprise—and view integration efforts as

Operational Motives	Technical Motives
Poor performance	Disparate systems
High cost structure	Poor quality of information
Responsiveness to customers	Systems not integrated
Complex processes	Obsolete systems
Globalization	Limited growth potential

Figure 7.15

Motives for Integration

one way to reduce their cost structures without sacrificing quality. To many organizations, their existing processes are overly complex and often ineffective and inconsistent. Enterprise integration is perceived as a way to streamline these processes and improve their overall effectiveness. Externally, enterprise systems offer a hope of enhancing competitive performance, increasing responsiveness to customers, and supporting strategic initiatives. As business becomes increasingly global, integrated systems show promise for tying together the geographically dispersed organization.

BENEFITS OF INTEGRATION

The actual benefits that an organization receives from its integration efforts are not necessarily consistent with the factors that motivated such efforts in the first place. Many of the benefits that an organization receives are tangible and can be easily measured in financial terms. Other benefits of integration are intangible, but many are at least as important as the tangible benefits to the overall success of the organization (see Figure 7.16).

Foremost among tangible benefits is cost reduction, and the two areas that show the greatest benefit to the bottom line are the reduction of inventory costs and personnel costs. IT costs are also reduced but to a substantially smaller amount than is typically anticipated by those involved prior to the beginning of an integration effort. On the other hand, productivity gains are usually much larger than anticipated and are ranked among the greatest benefits of enterprise integration. The other major tangible area of benefit is the reduction of cycle times, particularly those associated with the processing and management of orders as well as financial processes such as quarterly reporting.

By far the largest intangible benefit to enterprise integration is the improved availability of information—information about the organization that is widely available throughout the organization. This increased "information visibility" that results from integrated information systems enables managers and senior executives to make informed and timely decisions. Other intangible benefits of integration include the addition of new organizational processes and the improvement of existing ones, an increase in customer responsiveness, the establishment of enterprisewide standards for information resources, and the added flexibility that these standards provide.

INTEGRATION OBSTACLES

Despite the motives for integrating systems that we have described, most organizations face many potential stumbling blocks. The obstacles to integration can be grouped in three broad categories: people, process, and technology obstacles.

Figure 7.16

Integration Tangible/Intangible Benefits

Ranking	Tangible Benefits	Intangible Benefits
1	Inventory reduction	Information visibility
2	Personnel reduction	New/improved process
3	Productivity improvements	Customer responsiveness
4	Order processing improvements	Integration
5	IT cost reduction	Standardization
6	Procurement reduction	Flexibility
7	Revenue/profit increases	Globalization
8	Transportation logistics	Business performance

Of these three kinds of obstacles to enterprise integration, by far the greatest concern is the people issues. Integrating information systems across the organization is an enormous undertaking for people in all but the smallest companies. Adding to their concern about being able to properly manage the change to integrated systems, people are apprehensive over the availability of adequate training resources. The prioritization and allocation of resources to help people in the process is a high concern that is often associated with support from top management.

Process and technology obstacles, though less critical than people obstacles, are still significant and must be overcome to achieve successful integration of the enterprise. Poor management of the overall implementation program, inadequate reengineering of organizational processes, and clumsy or poorly planned transitions from one stage of enterprise system implementation to another are all examples of process-related obstacles. Inadequate functionality in the integrated systems, weaknesses of the applications within the enterprise system, and difficulties with system enhancement or upgrading are examples of some of the major technology-related obstacles to enterprise integration.

Summary: Student Learning Outcomes Revisited

1. **Define an enterprise system.** An *enterprise system (ES)* is a large software application that companies use to manage their operations. These systems have become a key way by which large organizations distribute information of all kinds to their workforce, to their suppliers, and to their customers.

2. **Describe an enterprise resource planning (ERP) system.** *Enterprise resource planning (ERP) systems* are software systems for business management, supporting areas such as planning, manufacturing, sales, marketing, distribution, accounting, financial, human resource management, project management, inventory management, service and maintenance, transportation, and e-business.

3. **List and describe the seven "ilities."**
   1. Availability is determining when your IT system will be available for employees to access.
   2. Accessibility is determining who has the right to access different types of IT systems and information.
   3. Reliability means your IT systems are functioning correctly and providing accurate information.
   4. Scalability refers to how well your system can adapt to increased demands.

   5. Flexibility means the system is designed with the ability to quickly change.
   6. Performance measures how quickly an IT system performs a certain process.
   7. Capacity planning determines your projected IT infrastructure requirements.

4. **List the key traits that an IT infrastructure should exhibit.** *Efficiency* is the ability to provide reusable components that are priced reasonably and can be turned around quickly for application development projects. *Effectiveness* is the easy integration of all components in a way that supports their operation. *Agility* is good planning and design processes that allow companies to develop new applications quickly and to repurpose or upgrade their existing infrastructure to support new requirements for existing or new applications.

5. **Describe the differences among the four types of information system infrastructures.** Decentralized infrastructure has little or no sharing of information systems. Centralized infrastructure shares information systems in one central area or one central mainframe only. Distributed infrastructure distributes the information and processing power of IT systems via a network. Client/server infrastructure has one or more computers that are servers which

provide services to other computers, called clients.

6. **Explain the difference between backup and recovery.** *Backup* is making a copy of the information stored on a computer in case it is lost. *Recovery* is the process of reinstalling the backup information in the event the information was lost.

7. **State the purpose of a disaster recovery plan.** Disasters—such as power outages, floods, fires, and even harmful hacking—occur all the time and are unpredictable. A disaster recovery plan is a detailed process for recovering information or an IT system in the event of such a disaster.

8. **Explain the need for system integration.** Organizations may have a separate IT system for each department, sometimes ending up with hundreds of different systems that do not communicate with each other. System integration brings together previously isolated information systems with the goal of providing a more complete and effective information resource for the whole organization.

CLOSING CASE STUDY ONE

LINUX SUPPORTS AN INFRASTRUCTURE

Linux has proved itself the most revolutionary software undertaking of the past decade, and estimates are that Linux spending will reach $280 million by 2006. Linus Torvalds wrote the core of the Linux operating system at age 21. Torvalds posted the operating system on the Internet and invited other programmers to improve his code and users to download his operating system for free. Since then, tens of thousands of people have been making Linux perhaps the single largest collaborative project in the planet's history.

Today, Linux is everywhere. You can find Linux inside a variety of computers, machines, and devices. Linux is robust enough to run the world's most powerful supercomputers yet sleek and versatile enough to run consumer products like TiVo and cell phones. Even more impressive than Linux's increasing prevalence in living rooms and pockets is its growth in the market for corporate computers. According to a recent poll by CIO.com, 39 percent of IT managers agree that Linux will dominate corporate systems by 2007.

Since its introduction in 1991, no other operating system in history has spread as quickly across such a broad range of systems as Linux, and it has finally achieved critical mass. One of the primary reasons for its popularity is its unique open-source format that allows anyone to update, change, and delete its source code. According to studies by market research firm IDC, Linux is currently the fastest growing server operating system, with shipments expected to grow by over 34 percent per year over the next four years. With its innovative open-source approach, strong security, reliability, and scalability, Linux can help companies achieve the agility they need to respond to changing consumer needs and stay ahead of the game. Gartner Group estimates Linux's server market share will grow seven times faster than Windows.[18]

Questions

1. The Linux operating system is a competitor to Microsoft's operating systems. Search the Internet to find information on the ongoing competition between Linux and Microsoft and discuss the similarities and differences between the two operating systems.

2. An IT infrastructure includes the hardware, software, and telecommunications equipment that, when combined, provide the underlying foundation to support the organization's goals. A good IT infrastructure will support all your organization's business and information needs. An IT infrastructure that ignores your organization's business or information needs will cause certain failure. Describe how you could use the Linux operating system in your IT infrastructure. You might consider using your school's IT infrastructure as an example.

3. Almost anything you do in an organization is performed in a team. Very few tasks and

activities are performed individually in the working world. Improving knowledge workers' ability to collaborate can be a huge benefit for organizations. Linux has a unique open-source format that allows anyone to update, change, and delete its source code. Search the Internet to determine some of the advantages and disadvantages of allowing open-source systems in an organization.

4. Linux is growing rapidly and chances are high that you will encounter it in your career. You'll find Linux articles and advertisements in all kinds of magazines from *BusinessWeek* to *Fortune*. Search the Internet and find out as much information as you can about Linux. Put together a small PowerPoint presentation describing what Linux is and how corporations today are using it.

CLOSING CASE STUDY TWO

NETFLIX—TRANSFORMING THE ENTERTAINMENT INDUSTRY

The online DVD rental pioneer Netflix is transforming the movie rental business with its unique business model, streamlined shipping strategy, and efficient application infrastructure. Netflix is quickly becoming one of Hollywood's most promising new business partners and is experiencing staggering growth with over 2 million subscribers, accounting for 3 to 5 percent of all U.S. home video rentals.

Typically, video rental stores focus on major films and ignore older movies and smaller titles with niche audiences. With over 35,000 DVD titles, Netflix is turning that idea upside down by offering a serious market for every movie, not just blockbusters. How? Netflix attributes its success to its proprietary software, called the Netflix Recommendation System, which constantly suggests movies you might like, based on how you rate any of the 35,000 titles in the company's catalog. Beyond recommendations, Netflix has figured out how to get DVDs from one subscriber to the next with unbelievable efficiency with its corporate application infrastructure.

Netflix operates by allowing its subscribers to rent unlimited videos for less than $20 a month, as long as they have no more than three DVDs rented at a time. Its "no late fees, no due dates" online movie rental model has eliminated the hassle of choosing, renting, and returning movies. Currently there are more than 3 million discs in the hands of its customers at any given time, with an average of 300,000 DVDs shipped out of the company's 20 leased distribution centers daily. Net-flix's unique application infrastructure allows it to track, monitor, and maintain detailed information on each of its discs, customers, and shippers. At any point in time the company can tell you the exact location of each of its discs, a critical component for Netflix's business model.

To handle the rental logistics for its 5.5 million DVD library the company created several proprietary applications. One of its most successful systems is its Web-based supply chain management system. The system works by having operators scan a bar code on each label for every single disc that arrives in its warehouses. The software then retrieves the name and address of the next person on the wait list for that DVD, prints out a label, and the disc is dropped back into the mail. The custom-built systems have allowed Netflix to slow hiring and reduce labor costs by 15 percent, and the vast majority of its DVDs never touch a warehouse shelf. On any given day, 98 percent of the 35,000 titles in Netflix's inventory are in circulation with its customers.[19]

Questions

1. Netflix makes the majority of its sales over the Internet. Having a great Web site and a solid IT infrastructure is critical to Netflix's business model. How can Netflix leverage the wireless industry to gain more market share? What must Netflix do to their current infrastructure to allow communication to wireless devices?

2. The "ilities" are important factors for supporting IT infrastructures. Describe each of the seven "ilities" and their importance to Netflix's IT infrastructure.
3. Netflix has hired you as its IT infrastructure expert. Netflix would like you to explain how a solid IT infrastructure can help the company support its primary goals. Netflix also wants you to explain what a 3-tier infrastructure is and how it can help the organization.
4. Netflix has a massive amount of inventory that it must distribute around the country daily.

Explain why a disaster recovery plan is critical to its business operations. Also, explain what might happen to Netflix if it lost all its customer information.
5. Netflix requires several different departments to make its business work. What types of systems do you think Netflix maintains in its different departments? Can you explain why Netflix would want to integrate the system information among its different departments?

Key Terms and Concepts

1-tier infrastructure, 336
2-tier infrastructure, 336
3-tier infrastructure, 336
Architecture, 329
Backup, 337
Benchmark, 327
Benchmarking, 327
Business process reengineering (BPR), 341
Capacity planning, 328
Centralized infrastructure, 333
Client/server infrastructure, 334
Cold site, 338
Collocation facility, 338
Decentralized infrastructure, 332
Disaster recovery cost curve, 338
Disaster recovery plan, 338

Distributed infrastructure, 334
Enterprise resource planning (ERP) system, 320
Enterprise system (ES), 318
Hot site, 338
Infrastructure, 329
Integration, 339
Legacy information system (LIS), 320
N-tier infrastructure, 336
Performance, 327
Recovery, 337
Scalability, 327
Storage area network (SAN), 337
Tiered infrastructure (layer infrastructure), 335
Voice over Internet Protocol (VoIP), 331
Workflow, 341

Short-Answer Questions

1. What is an enterprise system?
2. What are the core functions of an enterprise resource planning system?
3. Describe the evolution of ERP systems.
4. What is a legacy information system (LIS)?
5. Name three of the "ilities."
6. What is IT architecture?
7. What is IT infrastructure?
8. What are the primary differences among 1-tier, 2-tier, 3-tier, and n-tier infrastructure?
9. Why do you need a backup of information?
10. Why would you need to recover information?
11. Why does a business need a disaster recovery plan?
12. Why would an organization use a collocation facility?
13. What is a SAN?
14. What is the difference between centralized and decentralized architecture?
15. What is the difference between benchmarks and benchmarking?
16. What is the difference between a hot site and a cold site?
17. What is the primary reason for system integration?

Assignments and Exercises

1. **IT INFRASTRUCTURE SPONSOR** To build a solid IT infrastructure you must have executive sponsorship. Your current boss doesn't understand the importance of building a solid IT infrastructure. In fact, your boss doesn't even understand the term IT infrastructure. First, explain to your boss what an IT infrastructure is and why it is critical for any organization. Second, explain three primary components of an IT infrastructure.

2. **IT INFRASTRUCTURE COMPONENTS AND THE REAL WORLD** Throughout this chapter we discussed many IT infrastructure concepts, features, and trends including client/server infrastructure and the concept of integration, among others. Pick two of them and find business examples of how companies are using them in the real world. Search the Internet to see if you can find two additional IT infrastructure concepts, components, or features that were not discussed in this chapter along with business examples of how businesses are using them in the real world.

3. **CREATING THE IDEAL INFRASTRUCTURE** This chapter focused on many different IT infrastructure concepts and components. Choose three of them and explain how you could use them to improve the IT infrastructure at your school. Be sure to think of current requirements as well as future requirements for the IT infrastructure.

4. **INTEGRATING INFORMATION** Imagine you are working for a large cookie manufacturing company. The company is 75 years old and is just starting to implement technology to help improve operations. Your direct manager has asked you to put together a presentation discussing integration. In your presentation you must include the definition of integration along with an example of the problems associated with nonintegrated systems as relating to cookie manufacturing.

5. **CREATING A CAMPUS IT INFRASTRUCTURE** You have been assigned the role of student IT infrastructure manager. Your first assignment is to approve the designs for the new on-campus Internet infrastructure. You're having a meeting at 9:00 A.M. tomorrow morning to review the designs with the student IT employees. To prepare for the meeting, you must understand the student requirements and their current use of the Internet, along with future requirements. The following is a list of questions you must answer before attending the meeting. Provide an answer to each question.
   - Do you need to have a disaster recovery plan? If so what might it include?
   - Does the system require backup equipment?
   - When will the system need to be available to the students?
   - What types of access levels will the students need?
   - How will you ensure the system is reliable?
   - How will you build scalability into the system?
   - How will you build flexibility into the system?
   - What are the minimum performance requirements for the system?
   - How will the system handle future growth?

Discussion Questions

1. IT infrastructures often mimic organizational hierarchies. Describe two different types of organizational hierarchies and how the IT infrastructure would be built in order to support them.

2. IT infrastructure features can include anything from software to strategic functions. After reading this chapter and learning about a few of the primary features of IT infrastructure, explain why a company's IT infrastructure can have so many different features.

3. Organizations spend a great deal of time determining their primary goals, objectives, structures, and strategies. Define your school's goals, and then define your school's objectives, structure, and strategies that support those

goals. Explain how your school's IT infrastructure supports its goals.

4. Your good friend, Murphy Schilling, owns a very large golf supply company. Murphy has just acquired another golf supply company through a recent merger and acquisition. Murphy has come to you for advice on IT infrastructures, especially ERP systems. Murphy has heard of ERP systems, but he is not sure what they are or if he needs them. Explain what an ERP system is to Murphy along with an explanation of how he can use one to gain insight into his business.

5. IT infrastructures should support the creation of flexible and scalable systems that can quickly adapt to support new business requirements. What would be an example of an IT infrastructure that is inflexible and not scalable and a barrier to supporting a changing business? What is an example of an IT infrastructure that is flexible and scalable and supports expanding a business?

6. What type of IT infrastructure does your school have? If it uses a client/server infrastructure how does your school's client/server network increase student productivity? What recommendations, based on the contents of this chapter, could you recommend to the IT people who manage the infrastructure?

Living Life on the Internet

The personal computer is quickly becoming a household necessity as much as a stove or a refrigerator. The primary reason the personal computer has become such an important part of our lives is the Internet. There are literally thousands of ways people use the Internet to perform tasks. Many great Web sites are available, and all of them can help you accomplish things such as finding movie times, cooking a delicious meal, or seeking medical advice.

In this section we'll provide you with a few key Web sites you can use to help you live your life, and you can find many more sites on the Web site that supports this text at www.mhhe.com/haag.

ONLINE MAGAZINES

Each year people spend an incredible amount of money buying magazines. Many of these magazines are received through the mail and are never read. These end up in a giant recycling pile. The following is a list of a few of the many hundreds of magazines available on the Internet:

- *National Geographic*—www.nationalgeographic.com
- *Rolling Stone*—www.rollingstone.com
- *Sports Illustrated*—sportsillustrated.cnn.com
- *Cosmopolitan*—http://magazines.ivillage.com/cosmopolitan
- *Newsweek*—www.newsweek.com
- *PC Magazine*—www.pcmagazine.com
- *TV Guide*—www.tvguide.com
- *Popular Mechanics*—www.popularmechanics.com

Connect to a few of these magazines and answer the following questions.

- **A.** Does the Web site contain the most recent issue of the magazine?
- **B.** Is it easy to view past issues or search for articles on a particular topic?
- **C.** Can you find three additional magazines you enjoy that are not listed above?
- **D.** Are there any additional features in the online version of the magazine that are not available in the paper version?
- **E.** Do you enjoy reading the magazine online better than reading a paper magazine? Why or why not?

ONLINE MOVIE LISTINGS AND REVIEWS

Your time is incredibly valuable and so is your money. Wasting time and money on a bad movie happens to us all, but there is a way to eliminate this problem—the Internet.

The Internet has a wealth of information regarding movies including theater locations, movie times, and movie ratings and reviews. Spending a few minutes on the Internet researching the movie you want to see or browsing movie lists will save you time and money. You can check out detailed movie reviews at the Movie Review Query Engine Web site, www.mrqe.com. If you want a quick overview of a movie from a wide variety of critics, visit Check The Grid, www.checkthegrid.com. If you are interested in what movies are coming out over the next few month, try the Coming Attractions Web site, corona.bc.ca/films/main.html. You can search for movie times at your local theaters by visiting the Moviefone Web site, www.moviefone.com. Lastly, visit the Internet Movie Database, www.imdb.com, for tons of information on any movie ever made.

A. Can you find the movies that are currently playing at a theater near you?

B. Research a classic movie such as *Grease* or *Animal House* to find out the movie's rating and the year it was released.

C. Locate three new movies that are coming out over the next year.

D. Log in to the Internet Movie Database and search for all the movies made by your favorite actor or actress. Were any movies listed that you have not seen?

E. Log in to the Internet Movie Database and research the top 10 movies of all time.

COOKING FROM THE INTERNET

There are hundreds of cooking Web sites that provide recipes, detailed cooking instructions, and nutritional information. The first site you should visit is the Nutrition Analysis Tool (NAT) Web site, www.nat.uiuc.edu. NAT analyzes the foods you eat for various different nutrients and gives you recommendations on the types of food that are missing from your diet. Next, visit www.cooking.com for information on everything from cookbooks and cookware to recipes and cooking tips. For those of you interested in healthy meals try www.cookinglight.com, and those of you interested in gourmet cooking try www.goodcooking.com.

A. Find a recipe for barbequed chicken and mashed potatoes on one of the above Web sites.

B. Log in to the Nutritional Analysis Tool and find out the nutritional value of your last meal.

C. Find a Web site that will help you plan a menu for a dinner party of six people.

D. Log in to the gourmet Web site and see how many different recipes you can find for your favorite food.

E. Log in to the cooking light Web site and find a few tips on how you can decrease cholesterol in your diet.

HIGHLY USEFUL MISCELLANEOUS SITES

There are so many helpful Web sites available that it's impossible to share them all with you.

- Ever need to find out the exact time? Try the official U.S. time site at www.time.gov.
- If you need to find out the weather forecast quickly try weather.yahoo.com.
- You can also find the full text of more than 16,000 books online for free at digital.library.upenn.edu/books/.
- You can visit an online museum in Paris, France, at www.oir.ucf.edu/wm/.
- If you are sick and wondering if you should visit the doctor, try to seek advice at the world-famous mayo clinic, www.mayoclinic.com.
- A great site that can help you purchase or trade in a car is Kelley's Blue Book Web site, www.kbb.com.

A. Log in to the Mayo clinic and research remedies for the common cold.

B. Log in to Kelley's Blue Book Web site and determine the current value of your car or a car you would like to purchase.

C. Log in to the online museum in Paris and view the most current art exhibit.

D. We have listed a few helpful Web sites for living your life on the Internet. Try to find three additional Web sites that you and your classmates will find useful.

EXTENDED LEARNING MODULE G

OBJECT-ORIENTED TECHNOLOGIES

Student Learning Outcomes

1. EXPLAIN THE PRIMARY DIFFERENCE BETWEEN THE TRADITIONAL TECHNOLOGY APPROACH AND THE OBJECT-ORIENTED TECHNOLOGY APPROACH.

2. LIST AND DESCRIBE THE FIVE PRIMARY OBJECT-ORIENTED CONCEPTS.

3. EXPLAIN HOW CLASSES AND OBJECTS ARE RELATED.

4. DISCUSS THE THREE FUNDAMENTAL PRINCIPLES OF OBJECT-ORIENTED TECHNOLOGIES.

5. DESCRIBE TWO TYPES OF OBJECT-ORIENTED TECHNOLOGIES.

Taking Advantage of the CD

Extended Learning Module G is found on the CD that accompanies this text. This module is the same as the modules in your text—it includes Team Work and On Your Own projects and great end-of-module Assignments and Exercises. This module explains object-oriented technologies, concepts, and terms in an easy and understandable way.

The explosion of object-oriented technologies is radically changing the way businesses view information and develop information systems. Object-oriented technologies are everywhere in the business world today. It's difficult to find a business or IT department that isn't using object-oriented concepts and technologies. Every single Fortune 500 company is using some type of object-oriented technology. System developers everywhere are quickly learning how to write software in object-oriented programming languages, create databases using object-oriented database management systems, and design new systems using object-oriented analysis and design techniques. The race to learn and understand object-oriented concepts began many years ago and is still going strong.

One of the goals of this module is to introduce you to the object-oriented approach for developing information systems. By first taking a look at the traditional technology approach for developing systems you'll quickly understand the advantages you can gain by using an object-oriented approach. The ***object-oriented (OO) approach*** combines information and procedures into a single view. This statement probably seems a bit confusing at first but, after reading this module, it will become crystal clear. Just remember the key to understanding the object-oriented approach is to recognize that combining information and procedures is quite different from the traditional technology approach in which information is separated from procedures. In *Extended Learning Module G* we will discuss the following:

- The ***traditional technology approach,*** which has two primary views of any system—information and procedures—and it keeps these two views separate and distinct at all times.
- The five primary concepts of object-oriented technologies:
  1. Information as key characteristics stored within a system.
  2. ***Procedure*** that manipulates or changes information.
  3. ***Class*** that contains information and procedures and acts as a template to create objects (instances of a class).
  4. ***Object*** which is an instance of a class.
  5. ***Messages*** that allow objects to communicate with each other.
- The three fundamental principles of object-oriented technologies—inheritance, encapsulation, and polymorphism.
- Several real-world object-oriented examples.
- A detailed business case example, Ice Blue Snowboards, Inc., in which you can apply your object-oriented knowledge.
- Three types of object-oriented technologies: object-oriented programming languages, object-oriented databases, and object-oriented technologies and client/server environments.

Be sure to take advantage of this module on your CD. You'll be taking a giant leap toward understanding object-oriented concepts. You might already be familiar with a few of the key concepts related to object-oriented technologies—information, procedures, classes, objects, or messages. If you're unfamiliar with these important concepts there's no need to worry, because you'll gain a solid understanding of each of them in this module.

CHAPTER EIGHT OUTLINE

STUDENT LEARNING OUTCOMES

1. Define ethics and describe the two factors that affect how you make a decision concerning an ethical issue.

2. Define and describe intellectual property, copyright, Fair Use Doctrine, and pirated software.

3. Define privacy and describe the ways in which it can be threatened.

4. Describe the ways in which information on your computer or network is vulnerable.

5. Define risk management and risk assessment and describe the seven security measures that companies can take to protect their information.

INDUSTRY PERSPECTIVES

360 **What Price an Idea?**

367 **The Casino Chips Are Watching You**

369 **Protection or Spying Device?**

373 **Catching Killers**

374 **Was It an "Honest" Click or a "Fraudulent" One?**

FEATURES

361 **On Your Own**
Trace the Route of Your Journey to a Web Site

365 **Global Perspective**
Help Desk Employee Helps Himself to 30,000 Stolen Identities

366 **Team Work**
What Would You Do?

378 **Global Perspective**
Online Blackmail

380 **Team Work**
How Protected Are Computers in Your Part of the World?

381 **On Your Own**
Find Firewall Protection

388 **Electronic Commerce**
Making Travel Arrangements on the Internet

WEB SUPPORT

www.mhhe.com/haag

- Air travel
- Rental cars
- One-stop travel sites
- Privacy
- Security

CHAPTER EIGHT

Protecting People and Information
Threats and Safeguards

OPENING CASE STUDY:
THEY KNOW ABOUT 96 PERCENT
OF AMERICAN HOUSEHOLDS

There's a company in Little Rock, Arkansas, called Acxiom, that handles consumer information, mainly for marketing purposes. That is to say that Acxiom stores and analyzes information, both its own and its clients'. Acxiom gets the information it sells from many sources, including the three major credit bureaus (TransUnion, Equifax Inc., and Experian Inc.). Nine of the country's 10 largest credit-card issuers are clients along with many other high profile financial companies in the banking and insurance industries. Forty percent of Acxiom's revenue comes from banking alone.

The company's inventory includes 20 billion records on consumers that include names, addresses, Social Security numbers, and public-record information. In fact, Acxiom has a database with information on about 110 million Americans, or 96 percent of U.S. households. The company categorizes consumers into one of 70 lifestyle clusters that include such groups as "Rolling Stones," "Single City Struggles," and "Timeless Elders." In any given year, about 33 percent of the people in the database move from one cluster to another when they change their lives in some significant way, as when they get married, have children, or retire.

Acxiom was one of the first companies to use grid-based computing ". . . enabling data analysis, modeling and applications at previously unachievable speed—and with a lowered cost," according to Charles Morgan, Chairman and CEO of Acxiom. With so much information belonging to so many clients, it made sense to have a very scalable and flexible system.

To help clients react quickly to changing market conditions, Acxiom offers hundreds of lists.

One of these is a daily updated "pre-movers file" which lists people who are about to change residences. Another list is of people who use credit cards, and the list is sorted in order of frequency of use. A further list is sorted according to the square footage of consumers' homes. This type of information helps companies selling goods and services to target their customers and develop solid marketing strategies.

For example, Capital One Financial Corporation, a financial services company based in Virginia, spent $290 million (about 14 percent of its revenue) on marketing for the last quarter of 2003. The company sends out about 1 billion pieces of mail every year that largely consist of advertising intended to entice consumers to sign up for credit cards. Acxiom's information and analysis help Capital One send credit card solicitations only to those who are likely to want another credit card.

Another service that Acxiom provides is the merging of huge databases. The merger of Bank One and J. P. Morgan is a case in point. Both companies had huge, independent databases, and merging such mountains of information is Acxiom's specialty. First the information must be cleaned (called "data hygiene" in the industry), that is, duplicate records must be identified and combined. Acxiom also adds records from its own database to those of its clients, complementing and completing the clients' customer information.

To support these information services, Acxiom has thousands of servers and storage units. Some clients request that their information be kept separate, and so Acxiom supplies a locked room for that purpose. Another client company wants its information stored underground and far away from Acxiom's main site and, again, Acxiom fills the need.[1,2,3,4]

Introduction

As you've already learned, the three components of an IT system are people, information, and information technology. Most of what you've seen in previous chapters has dealt with IT and how it stores and processes information. In this chapter we're going to concentrate on information—its use, ownership, and protection. The best environment for handling information is one that has stability without stagnation and change without chaos.

To handle information in a responsible way you must understand

- The importance of ethics in the ownership and use of information.
- The importance to people of personal privacy and the ways in which it can be compromised.
- Threats to information and how to protect against them (security).

The most important part of any IT system consists of the people who use it and are affected by it. How people treat each other has always been important, but in this information-based and digital age, with huge computing power at our fingertips, we can affect more people's lives in more ways than ever before. How we act toward each other, and this includes how we view and handle information, is largely determined by our ethics.

You don't have to look far to see examples of computer use that is questionable from an ethical viewpoint. For example,

- People copy, use, and distribute software they have no right to.
- Employees search organizational databases for information on celebrities and friends.
- Organizations collect, buy, and use information and don't check the validity or accuracy of that information.
- People create and spread viruses that cause trouble for those using and maintaining IT systems.
- Information system developers put systems on the market before they're completely tested. A few years ago, the developers of an incubator thermostat control program didn't test it fully, and two infants died as a result.[5]
- People break into computer systems and steal passwords, information, and proprietary information.
- Employees destroy or steal proprietary schematics, sketches, customer lists, and reports from their employers.
- People snoop on each other and read each other's e-mail and other private documents.

Ethics

Ethical people have integrity. They're people who are just as careful of the rights of others as they are of their own rights. They have a strong sense of what's fair and right and what isn't. But even the most ethical people sometimes face difficult choices.

Ethics are the principles and standards that guide our behavior toward other people. Acting ethically means behaving in a principled fashion and treating other people with respect and dignity. It's simple to say, but not so simple to do since some situations are complex or ambiguous. The important role of ethics in our lives has long been recognized. As far back as 44 B.C., Cicero said that ethics are indispensable to anyone who wants to have a good career. Having said that, Cicero, along with some of the greatest minds over the centuries, struggled with what the rules of ethics should be.

Our ethics are rooted in our history, culture, and religion, and may stay the same and yet also shift over time. In this electronic age there's a new dimension in the ethics debate—the amount of personal information that we can collect and store, and the speed with which we can access and process that information.

TWO FACTORS THAT DETERMINE HOW YOU DECIDE ETHICAL ISSUES

How you collect, store, access, and use information depends to a large extent on your sense of ethics—what you perceive as right and wrong. Two factors affect how you make your decision when you're faced with an ethical dilemma. The first is your basic ethical structure, which you developed as you grew up. The second is the set of practical circumstances inevitably involved in the decision that you're trying to make, that is, all the shades of gray in what are rarely black or white decisions.

Your ethical structure and the ethical challenges you'll face exist at several levels (see Figure 8.1).[6] At the outside level are things that most people wouldn't consider bad, such as taking a couple of paper clips or sending an occasional personal e-mail on company time. Do these things really matter? At the middle level are more significant ethical challenges. One example might be accessing personnel records for personal reasons. Could there ever be a personal reason so compelling that you would not feel ethical discomfort doing this? Reading someone else's e-mail might be another middle-level example. At the innermost ethical level are ethical violations that you'd surely consider very serious, such as embezzling funds or selling company records to a competitor. And yet, over time, your ethical structure can change so that even such acts as these could seem more or less acceptable. For example, if everyone around you is accessing confidential records for their own purposes, in time you might come to think such an act is no big deal. And this might spell big trouble for you.

It would be nice if every decision were crystal clear, such as in the innermost circle in Figure 8.1, but ethical decisions are seldom so easy. Ideally, your personal ethics should

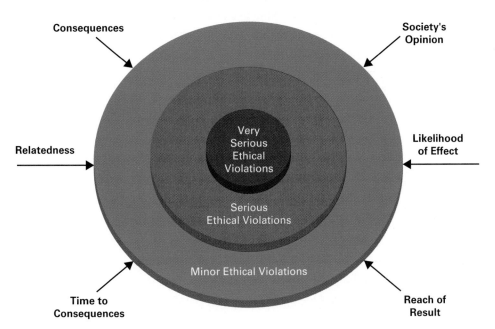

Figure 8.1

Your Ethical Structure

tell you what to do. But the practical circumstances of a decision inevitably also influence you in an ethical dilemma:[7]

1. *Consequences.* How much or how little benefit or harm will come from a particular decision?

2. *Society's opinion.* What is your perception of what society really thinks of your intended action?

3. *Likelihood of effect.* What is the probability of the harm or benefit that will occur if you take the action?

4. *Time to consequences.* How long will it take for the benefit or harm to take effect?

5. *Relatedness.* How much do you identify with the person or persons who will receive the benefit or suffer the harm?

6. *Reach of result.* How many people will be affected by your action?

No matter how strong your sense of ethics is, these practical aspects of the situation may affect you as you make your decision—perhaps unduly, perhaps quite justifiably. Thus, ethical dilemmas usually arise not out of simple situations but from a clash between competing goals, responsibilities, and loyalties. Ethical decisions are complex judgments that balance rewards for yourself and others against responsibilities to yourself and others. Inevitably, your decision process is influenced by uncertainty about the magnitude of the outcome, by your estimate of the importance of the situation, sometimes by your perception of conflicting "right reactions," and more than one socially acceptable "correct" decision.

GUIDELINES FOR ETHICAL COMPUTER SYSTEM USE

It's sometimes difficult to decide what to do in situations where there are few hard and fast rules. Knowing the law doesn't always help because what's legal is not always ethical and vice versa. In Figure 8.2 you see the four quadrants of ethical and legal behavior. You're safe if you can manage to stay in quadrant I, ethical *and* legal.

So, what do you do if you're faced with a choice that is not perfectly ethically clear? If you think you are in an ethical quandary, you probably are. If you find you're giving the situation a whole lot of thought, the situation very likely deserves it. You may wish to talk to a friend, a teacher, a supervisor, or a mentor. Know that we're all faced with such dilemmas, they are real, and they do have consequences. And there is a line that you shouldn't cross, and most of us know where it is. Still, ambiguous cases do arise.

You can certainly ask questions about what you're being asked to do—and you should. Sometimes legitimate actions look unethical, but if you find out more about the situation, you might find that it's perfectly all right. Other times something that seems

Figure 8.2

Acting Ethically and Acting Legally Are Not Necessarily the Same Thing[8]

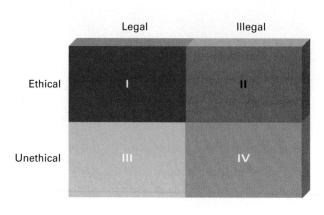

okay starts to nag at you. You must keep digging until you're very sure and comfortable about what you're being asked to do.

If you really believe that what you're expected to do is wrong, you'll have to say so to your boss and be prepared to quit if you have to. But first, explain what you think is so bad and couch it in terms of the company's future and reputation if at all possible.[9] Be sure to think also of your own future and reputation (many former Enron employees wish they had taken a firmer stand when they had the chance).

Your company may well have an office or person (sometimes called an ombudsman) whose job it is to give advice on work-related ethical dilemmas. Failing that, you could look up your company's code of ethics. If you can't find that or don't think it's taken seriously in your place of work, you can check your profession's ethical code. The ACM (Association for Computing Machinery), for example, has a code of ethics for IT employees. Or you can go to the Computer Ethics Institute Web site for its guidelines ("Ten Commandments") at www.cspr.org/program/ethics.htm.

INTELLECTUAL PROPERTY

An ethical issue you will almost certainly encounter is one related to the use or copying of proprietary software. Software is a type of intellectual property. ***Intellectual property*** is intangible creative work that is embodied in physical form.[10] Music, novels, paintings, and sculptures are all examples of intellectual property. So also are your company's product sketches and schematics and other proprietary documents. These documents along with music, novels, and so on are worth much more than the physical form in which they are delivered. For example, a single U2 song is worth far more than the CD on which it's purchased. The song is also an example of intellectual property that is covered by copyright law.

Copyright law protects the authorship of literary and dramatic works, musical and theatrical compositions, and works of art. ***Copyright*** is the legal protection afforded an expression of an idea, such as a song, video game, and some types of proprietary documents. Having a copyright means that no one can use your song or video game without your permission. As a form of intellectual property, software is usually protected by copyright law, although sometimes it falls under patent law, which protects an idea, such as the design of a sewing machine or an industrial pump valve.

Copyright law doesn't forbid the use of intellectual property completely. It has some notable exceptions. For example, a TV program could show a video game you created without your permission. This would be an example of the use of copyrighted material for the creation of new material, i.e., the TV program. And that's legal; it falls under the Fair Use Doctrine. The ***Fair Use Doctrine*** says that you may use copyrighted material in certain situations, for example, in the creation of new work or, within certain limits, for teaching purposes. One of those limits is on the amount of the copyrighted material you may use.

Generally, the determining factor in legal decisions on copyright disputes is whether the copyright holder has been or is likely to be denied income because of the infringement. Courts will consider factors such as how much of the work was used and how, and when and on what basis the decision was made to use it.

Remember that copyright infringement is *illegal*. That means it's against the law, outside of a fair use situation, to simply copy a copyrighted picture, text, or anything else without permission, whether the copyrighted material is on the Internet or not. In particular, it's illegal to copy copyrighted software. But there's one exception to that rule: In the United States, you may always make one copy of copyrighted software to keep for

WHAT PRICE AN IDEA?

A patent protects a form of intellectual property. A patent applies to the implementation of an idea, such as how to construct an ergonomic mouse. IBM, the computer industry's giant, has for nine years filed more patents with the U.S. Patent and Trademark Office than any other company. In 2001, IBM received 3,454 patents. That's almost 10 new patents *every day*. IBM has always been proud of its patent record, and it certainly gives stockholders and the public in general the impression that the company is working hard and is producing future technology. However, good press is not the only reason IBM files so many patent applications. There are many other reasons—1.5 billion of them, in fact. That's the number of dollars that IBM got from licensing income in 2001 alone, money the company put back into research and development. Since it's very hard to tell which new technology will ultimately be successful, IBM patents everything, and then licenses out those ideas that other companies want to use.

IBM isn't the only technology company to take patents seriously. Also busy in the technology-patent-generating race are Hewlett-Packard, Lucent Technologies, NEC, and Microsoft. Many other industries are realizing great return on the licensing of patents, too. For example,

- Bayer AG, a German drug company, clears profits of 78 percent after expenses on its intellectual property licensing fees.

- Du Pont revenues from intellectual property were $100 million in 1996 and grew to $450 million in 2001.

- Eastman Kodak even created a separate company, Eastman Chemical's Global Technology Ventures (GTV), to extract value from the company's intellectual assets. Since 1999, the company has made 20 deals worth more than $50 million with a further $100 million in net present value of future earnings.[11,12]

backup purposes. When you buy copyrighted software, what you're paying for is the right to use it—and that's all.

How many more copies you may make depends on the copyright agreement that comes with the software package. Some software companies state emphatically that you may not even put the software on a second computer, even if they're both yours and no one else uses either one. Other companies are less restrictive, and agree to let you put a copy of software on multiple machines—as long as only one person is using that software package at any given time. In this instance, the company considers software to be like a book in that you can have it in different places and you can loan it out, but only one person at a time may use it.

If you copy copyrighted software and give it to another person or persons, you're pirating the software. ***Pirated software*** is the unauthorized use, duplication, distribution, or sale of copyrighted software.[13] Software piracy costs businesses an estimated $12 billion a year in lost revenue. Microsoft gets more than 25,000 reports of software piracy every year, and the company reportedly follows up on all of them. Countries that experience the greatest losses are (in rank order) the United States, Japan, the United Kingdom, Germany, China, France, Canada, Italy, Brazil, and the Netherlands. One in four business applications in the United States is thought to be pirated.[14] In some parts of the world, more than 90 percent of business software is pirated. The Software and Information Industry Association (SIIA) and the Business Software Alliance (BSA) say that pirated software means lost jobs, wages, and tax revenues, and is a potential barrier to success for software start-ups around the globe.

TRACE THE ROUTE OF YOUR JOURNEY TO A WEB SITE

When you send e-mail or visit a Web site, your request for service goes through lots of computers after your own. First, it goes from your computer to the server that's connecting you to the Internet. It may even move between computers within your school or service provider.

The **tracert** function in DOS (which stands for <u>D</u>isk <u>O</u>perating <u>S</u>ystem, the operating system that we used before Windows) allows you to see that journey. To get to DOS, you have to go to the **Command Prompt** option in Windows.

Click on the **Start** button

Click on **All Programs**

Click on **Accessories**

Click on **Command Prompt**

You'll get a DOS screen window and the first thing you'll see is a note about the version of Windows you're using and a declaration of Microsoft's copyright. Next comes the C:\ prompt with the name of the folder you're currently in. It will look something like this (regular text—not the bold):

Microsoft Windows XP [Version 5.1.2600]

<C> Copyright 1985-2001 Microsoft Corp

C:\Documents and Settings\Maeve>**tracert www.pittstate.edu**

DOS is a command-driven user interface—there's no click-and-point capability—so you have to type in commands. At the last greater-than symbol (>) type in the word **tracert** and the address of a Web site (see the boldface in the example above).

You'll get a listing (up to 30 hops) of the computers that your message went through to get to its destination. You'll see the number of the hop (1,2,3, etc.), the time in milliseconds it took to get there, and the address of each computer it encountered on the way along with the computer's IP address (digits grouped in 4 sets consisting of 1 to 3 digits each—example: 192.168.1.50). When you're finished close the window as always or type **exit** at the C:\ prompt.

Try this for your own school and two other Web site addresses. To print out your results, capture the screen with the **Print Screen** key on your keyboard (usually on the top right-hand side), then paste it into Word or Paint, and print from there.

Privacy

Privacy is the right to be left alone when you want to be, to have control over your own personal possessions, and not to be observed without your consent. It's the right to be free of unwanted intrusion into your private life. Privacy has several dimensions. Psychologically, it's a need for personal space. All of us, to a greater or lesser extent, need to feel in control of our most personal possessions, and personal information belongs on that list. Legally, privacy is necessary for self-protection.[15] If you put the key to your house in a special hiding place in your yard, you want to keep that information private. This information could be abused and cause you grief. In this section, we'll examine some specific areas of privacy: individuals snooping on each other; employers' collection of information about employees; businesses' collection of information about consumers; government collection of personal information; and the issue of privacy in international trade.

Figure 8.3

The E-Mail You Send Is Stored on Many Computers

| Sender's Computer | Sender's Server | Recipient's Server | Recipient's Computer |

PRIVACY AND OTHER INDIVIDUALS

Other individuals, like family members, associates, fellow employees, and hackers, could be electronically invading your privacy. Their motives might be simple curiosity, an attempt to get your password, or to access something they have no right to. Obviously, there are situations in which you're well within your rights, and would be well advised to see what's going on. Examples may be if you suspect that your child is in electronic contact with someone or something undesirable, or if you think that someone is using your computer without permission. Many Web sites are offering programs, collectively referred to as snoopware, to help people monitor what's happening on a computer.

For general snooping you can get key logger software and install it on the computer you want to monitor. ***Key logger,*** or ***key trapper, software,*** is a program that, when installed on a computer, records every keystroke and mouse click. It records all e-mail (whether you're using Eudora or Microsoft Outlook), instant messages, chat room exchanges, Web sites you visit, applications you run, and passwords you type in on that computer.

Also available for monitoring computer use are screen capture programs that periodically record what's on the screen. (They get the information straight from the video card.) These programs don't trap every single screen, just whatever is on the screen when the capturing program activates. But they still give whoever is doing the monitoring a pretty good idea of what the computer user is up to. Other tools for monitoring include packet sniffers (that examine the information passing by) on switches, hubs, or routers (the devices on networks that connect computers to each other), and log analysis tools that keep track of logons, deletions, and so forth.

As you're probably already aware, e-mail is completely insecure. E-mail content might as well be written on a postcard for all the privacy it has. Not only that, but each e-mail you send results in at least three or four copies being stored on different computers (see Figure 8.3). It's stored first in the computer you're using. Second, it's stored by the e-mail server, the computer through which it gets onto the Internet. Third, it's stored on the recipient's computer, and may also be archived on the recipient's e-mail server.

IDENTITY THEFT

About 9 million adults in the United States were victims of identity theft between October 2003 and September 2004, according to a survey released by Javelin Strategy and Research. The Better Business Bureau estimates the average loss to be about $1,000 per person, not to mention the countless hours spent in cleaning up credit reports and filing for new identification documents, such as Social Security numbers and driver's licenses. The Federal Trade Commission says that the cost of identity theft to businesses and consumers is as much as $60 billion per year.

Identity theft is the forging of someone's identity for the purpose of fraud. The fraud is often for financial gain, and the stolen identity is used to apply for and use credit cards in the victim's name or to apply for a loan. But it can also be simply to disguise a real identity, particularly if the thief is hiding from law enforcement or is running some sort of scam. Figure 8.4 shows that more than half of all identity theft victims are between the ages of 18 and 39. Following are some examples of cases of what happened when people became the victims of identity theft.

- An 82-year-old woman in Fort Worth, Texas, discovered that her identity had been stolen when the woman using her name was involved in a four-car collision. For 18 months, she kept getting notices of lawsuits and overdue medical bills that were really meant for someone else. It took seven years for her to get her financial good name restored after the identity thief charged over $100,000 on her 12 fraudulently acquired credit cards.

- A 42-year-old retired Army captain in Rocky Hill, Connecticut, found that an identity thief had spent $260,000 buying goods and services that included two trucks, a Harley-Davidson motorcycle, and a time-share vacation home in South Carolina. The victim discovered his problem only when his retirement pay was garnished to pay the outstanding bills.

- In New York, members of a pickpocket ring forged the driver's licenses of their victims within hours of snatching the women's purses. If you steal someone's purse, your haul usually won't be more than $200, probably much less. On the other hand, if you steal the person's identity, you can net on average between $4,000 and $10,000.

- Another crime gang took out $8 million worth of second mortgages on victims' homes. It turned out the source of all the instances of identity theft came from a car dealership.

- The largest identity-theft scam to date in U.S. history was broken up by police in 2002 when they discovered that three men had downloaded credit reports using stolen passwords and sold them to criminals on the street for $60 each. Many millions of dollars were stolen from people in all 50 states.

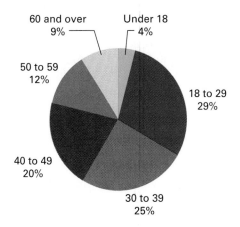

Figure 8.4

Identity Theft Complaints (by Victim Age) Received by the FTC in 2004
The FTC had 234,263 Complaints of Identity Theft in 2004 and 95% of the Complainants Gave Their Ages.

A common way to steal identities online is called phishing. **Phishing** (also called **carding** or **brand spoofing**) is a technique to gain personal information for the purpose of identity theft, usually by means of fraudulent e-mail. One way this is done is to send out e-mail messages that look as though they came from legitimate businesses like AOL, MSN, eBay, PayPal, insurance companies, or online retailers like Amazon.com. The messages look genuine with official-looking formats and logos. These e-mails typically ask for verification of important information like passwords and account numbers. The reason given is often that this personal information is needed for accounting or auditing purposes. Since the e-mails look authentic, up to one in five recipients responds with the information, and subsequently becomes a victim of identity theft and other fraud.

Legitimate businesses hardly ever send out such e-mails. If you get such an e-mail, DON'T provide any information without checking further. For example, you could call the company and ask about it. Another clue is bad grammar and misspellings. More than one typo in an official communication is a warning sign.

A second kind of phishing is to persuade people in an e-mail to click on a Web site included in the message, and provide personal information there. This is what happened on November 17, 2003, to customers of eBay's auction site. On that day, many eBay customers got notice by e-mail that their accounts had been compromised and they were

Figure 8.5

Phishing Facts and What
to Do If You're at Risk

Some Facts on Phishing . . .

- In January 2004 there were 198 phishing sites, but by February 2005 that number had risen to 2,625, according to the Anti-Phishing Working Group.

- The same group says that the number of unique phishing e-mails reached 13,141 in February of 2004.

- Symantec says that its Brightmail spam filters blocked an average of 33 million phishing attempts per week in December 2004, compared to an average of only 9 million during the previous July.

- The Phemon Institute says consumers lost $500 million to phishers in 2004.

- Also from the Phemon Institute: Of 1,335 people surveyed, about 70 percent visited a fake site, and as many as 15 percent said they had provided personal information to the fake site.

. . . And What to Do If You Suspect You're at Risk

The FTC says that if you believe your personal information may have been compromised, you should:

- Close your credit-card accounts (using an ID Theft Affidavit form) and change all your passwords.

- Place a fraud alert on your credit reports with one of the major credit bureaus (Equifax, Experian, and TransUnion).

- Ask government agencies like the Department of Motor Vehicles to flag your file so that no one can get documents in your name.

asked to click on a Web site and reregister by providing their credit card number, ATM number, Social Security number, date of birth, and their mother's maiden name. eBay had not, of course, sent the e-mails.[16]

Usually there's something a bit off about the addresses of these kinds of Web addresses, so look carefully. For example, one from PayPal may arrive as PayPa1 with a "1" (one) instead of the letter "l." The letter "O" and zero can also be interchanged, and the longer the Web site address, the easier it is to fake.[17,18] See Figure 8.5 for some advice from the Federal Trade Commission on how to handle possible theft of your personal information.

PRIVACY AND EMPLOYEES

Companies need information about their employees and customers to be effective in the marketplace. But people often object to having so many details about their lives available to others. If you're applying for a job, you'll most likely fill out a job application, but that's not the only information a potential employer can get about you. For a small fee, employers, or anyone else, can find out about your credit standing, your telephone usage, your insurance coverage, and many other interesting things. An employer can also get information on what you said on the Internet from companies who collect and collate chat room exchanges. And an employer can ask a job applicant to take drug and psychological tests, the results of which are the property of the company.

After you're hired, your employer can monitor where you go, what you do, what you say, and what you write in e-mails—at least during working hours. The American Management Association says that as of March 2005, 60 percent of employers monitored em-

HELP DESK EMPLOYEE HELPS HIMSELF TO 30,000 STOLEN IDENTITIES

In January 2005, Philip Cummings, a Briton, was sentenced in a New York court to 14 years in prison. Over the course of three years, Cummings, 35, stole personal information on more than 30,000 consumers who were customers of the banks that used Teledata Communications software.

Teledata develops software that banks use to request credit reports. Since, as part of his job, Cummings was helping bank employees to use the software, he had access to the passwords and codes of bank employees and so could download the credit reports of banking customers. He got more than 15,000 credit reports using a single password that belonged to Ford Motor Credit, making the source of the scam harder to detect.

He sold the credit reports for about $30 each to an accomplice, who then sold them to others for about $60. The buyers were then able to access the bank accounts of the original bank customers and use their credit cards. Further, they were able to change some personal details of the stolen identities and get new credit and ATM cards. The total estimated cost of the fraud was between $50 and $100 million.[19]

ployee e-mails, both incoming and outgoing. That figure is up from 47 percent in 2001.[20] One reason that companies monitor employees' e-mail is that they can be sued for what their employees send to each other and to people outside the company.

Chevron Corporation and Microsoft settled sexual harassment lawsuits for $2.2 million each because employees sent offensive e-mail to other employees and management didn't intervene. Other companies such as Dow Chemical Company, Xerox, the New York Times Company, and Edward Jones took preemptive action by firing people who sent or stored pornographic or violent e-mail messages.[21]

About 70 percent of Web traffic occurs during work hours, and this is reason enough for companies to monitor what, and for how long, employees are surfing the Web. The FBI reports that 78 percent of surveyed companies indicated that employees had abused Internet privileges by downloading pornography, pirating software, or some other activity that wasn't work related. Also, 60 percent of employees said that they visit Web sites or surf for personal use at work. Again, various software packages are available to keep track of people's Web surfing. Some software actually blocks access to certain sites.

Businesses have good reasons for seeking and storing personal information on employees. They

- Want to hire the best people possible and to avoid being sued for failing to adequately investigate the backgrounds of employees.
- Want to ensure that staff members are conducting themselves appropriately and not wasting or misusing company resources. Financial institutions are even required by law to monitor all communications including e-mail and telephone conversations.
- Can be held liable for the actions of employees.

MONITORING TECHNOLOGY   Numerous vendors sell software products that scan e-mail, both incoming and outgoing. The software can look for specific words or phrases in the subject lines or in the body of the text. An e-mail-scanning program can sneak into your computer in Trojan-horse software. That is, it can hide in an innocent-looking e-mail or some other file or software.

WHAT WOULD YOU DO?

Analyze the following situation. You have access to the sales and customer information in a flower shop. You discover that the boyfriend of a woman you know is sending roses to three other women on a regular basis. The woman you know is on the flower list, but she believes that she's the only woman in his romantic life. You really think you should tell the woman. Your dilemma is that you have a professional responsibility to keep the company's information private. However, you also believe that you have a responsibility to the woman. Do you tell her?

Are there factors that would change your decision? Each team member should individually consider the additional information below. Indicate whether any one or more of these factors would change your decision. Then form a consensus with your team.

Additional Facts	Yes	No	Why?
1. The woman is your sister.			
2. The man is your brother.			
3. The woman is about to give the man her life savings as a down payment on a house in the belief that they will soon be married.			
4. The woman is already married.			

Some companies use an approach less invasive than actually reading employees' e-mail. Their e-mail inspection programs just check for a certain level of e-mail to and from the same address. This indicates that there may be a problem, and the employee is informed of the situation and asked to remedy it. No intrusive supervisory snooping is necessary.[22]

An employer can track your keyboard and mouse activity with the type of key logger software that you read about in the previous section. An alternative that's sometimes harder to detect is a hardware key logger. A **_hardware key logger_** is a hardware device that captures keystrokes on their journey from the keyboard to the motherboard. These devices can be in the form of a connector on the system-unit end of the cable between the keyboard and the system unit. There's another type of hardware key logger that you can install into the keyboard. Both have enough memory to store about a year's worth of typing. These devices can't capture anything that's not typed, but they do capture every keystroke, including backspace, delete, insert, and all the others. To defeat them you'd have to copy the password (or whatever you want kept secret) and paste it into its new location. The key logger keeps a record of the keystrokes you use, if any, in your copy-and-paste operation, but not what you copied and pasted.

There is little sympathy in the legal system for the estimated 27 million employees whom the American Management Association says are under surveillance. Employers have the legal right to monitor the use of their resources and that includes the time they're paying you for. In contrast to your home, you have no expectation of privacy when using the company's resources.

The most recent federal bill that addressed electronic monitoring of employees is the Electronic Communications Privacy Act of 1986. Although, in general, it forbids the interception of wired or electronic communications, it has exceptions for both prior consent and business use.

THE CASINO CHIPS ARE WATCHING YOU

Everyone knows that the casinos in Las Vegas have numerous cameras that track all activity on the floor. But the Hard Rock Hotel and Casino has gone one better by keeping track of individual betting tokens in its high-limit blackjack room where minimum bets are $100. Managers know where each high denomination token is at all times and can better guard against token theft and counterfeiting.

The way the casino does this is to fit the plastic tokens that are about the size of a half-dollar with RFID (radio frequency identification) chips like the ones that Wal-Mart uses to track its products all the way from the factory to the store shelves. It's also the same technology that's used to keep track of health care supplies, aerospace parts, and many other products.

Up until now, casinos have been able to track slot-machine players by means of "frequent player" cards that players insert into the machines. Table games, however, were more difficult since the only objective option was video cameras, and otherwise it was up to dealers and pit bosses to estimate how much money gamblers were wagering. The level of betting by customers determines the type and number of freebies and/or discounts customers are entitled to.

With RFID chips embedded into the gambling tokens, pit bosses can keep track of players, their average bets, the denomination of chips they're using, and a wealth of other information.

It works like this: The gambling chips with RFID are sold to a gambler, and when the chips hit the table, sensors below the surface of the table read the data and send it to the computer system. The pit boss then just has to watch the monitor to keep track of how the players are betting and how much they're winning or losing.[23]

Some state laws have addressed the issue of how far employers can go and what they can do to monitor employees. Connecticut has a law that took effect in 1999 that requires employers in the private sector to notify employees in writing of electronic monitoring. And Pennsylvania, a year earlier, permitted telephone marketers to listen in on calls for quality control purposes as long as at least one of the parties is aware of the action.[24]

PRIVACY AND CONSUMERS

Businesses face a dilemma.

- Customers want businesses to know who they are, but, at the same time, they want them to leave them alone.

- Customers want businesses to provide what they want, but, at the same time, they don't want businesses knowing too much about their habits and preferences.

- Customers want businesses to tell them about products and services they might like to have, but they don't want to be inundated with ads.

Like it or not, massive amounts of personal information are available to businesses from various sources. A relatively large Web site may get about 100 million hits per day, which means that the site gets about 200 bytes of information for each hit. That's about 20 gigabytes of information per day.[25] This level of information load has helped to make electronic customer relationship management (eCRM) systems one of the fastest growing areas of software development. Part of managing customer relationships is personalization. Web sites that greet you by name and Amazon.com's famous recommendations that "People who bought this product also bought . . ." are examples of personalization, which is made possible by the Web site's knowledge about you.[26]

Apart from being able to collect its own information about you, a company can readily access consumer information elsewhere. Credit card companies sell information, as do the Census Bureau and mailing list companies. Web traffic tracking companies such as DoubleClick follow you (and other surfers) around the Web and then sell the information about where you went and for how long. DoubleClick can collect information about you over time and provide its customers with a highly refined profile on you. DoubleClick is also an intermediary for companies that want to advertise to Web surfers. When hired by a company wanting to sell something, DoubleClick identifies people who might be receptive and sends the ad to them as a banner or pop-up ad. Proponents of this practice claim that it's good for the surfers because they get targeted advertising and less unwanted advertising. You can judge for yourself how true this claim is. DoubleClick, at first, undertook to track consumers without attaching their identity to the information. Then, in 1999, DoubleClick changed its policy and announced that it would attach consumer names to personal information and e-mail addresses. However, in response to negative consumer reaction, DoubleClick withdrew its proposed change. Interestingly, DoubleClick didn't state it would never resume the abandoned policy, but agreed only to wait until standards for such activity are in place.[27]

COOKIES   The basic tool of consumer Web monitoring is the cookie. A **cookie** is a small file that contains information about you and your Web activities, which a Web site you visit places on your computer. A cookie has many uses. For example, it's used to keep ID and password information so that you don't have to go through the whole verification process every time you log onto a Web site. It's also used to store the contents of electronic shopping carts, so that the next time you log on, the Web site will be able to see your wish list (which is stored on your computer in a cookie).

A cookie can also be used to track your Web activity. It can monitor and record what sites you visit, how long you stay there, what Web pages you visited, what site you came from and the next site you went to. This type of cookie is called a *unique cookie.* Some cookies are temporary and some stay on your computer indefinitely.

Third-party or *common cookies* are the ones that have many privacy advocates disturbed. These are different from the unique cookies that a Web site you visit puts onto your hard disk. A common cookie is one that started out as a unique cookie, but the original site sold access to it to a third party, like DoubleClick, that can then change the cookie so that the third party can track the surfer's activity across many sites. The third party collects information about surfers without names or other identifiable personal information. They usually collect an IP address, which they then link to a random identifying ID so that the surfer can be identified at other sites. Surveys have shown that the vast majority of people (91 percent) don't like the idea of unknown companies gathering information about them that they have provided to sites with whom they chose to interact.[28]

You have two options if you want to block cookies. First, you can set your browser to accept or reject all cookies. Or you can get it to warn you when a site wants to put a cookie on your computer. Second, you can get cookie management software with additional options that are not available on your browser. For example, CookieCop 2, from *PC Magazine,* will let you accept or reject cookies on a per-site basis. It also allows you to replace banner ads with the image of your choice and to block ads for sites you find offensive. With this or other cookie-stopper software, you can disable pop-up windows, and stipulate that certain cookies can stay on your hard drive for the duration of one session only.

SPAM   *Spam* is unsolicited e-mail (electronic junk mail) from businesses that advertise goods and services. Often spam mass mailings advertise pornography, get-rich-quick schemes, and miracle cures. If you haven't been inundated with spam, you're either very

PROTECTION OR SPYING DEVICE?

It's every teenager's nightmare—parents practically in the car with you every minute you're driving. A whole host of systems are on the market now that can track where you go and how you get there. Such a device records whether you're driving recklessly, wearing seat belts, or going where you said you would. The technology is the same type that truck companies have been using for several years, is usually installed under the dashboard, and can record acceleration and braking and how far you drive.

The type of spying device designed for private vehicles can include interactive features that alert parents about exceeding a speed limit or driving further than is permissible The alerts can be sent via e-mail or phone, or to a Web site where parents can retrieve the information.

Some devices allow parents to send messages to the driver in the form of a flashing light on the dashboard or a honk of the car's horn. Parents can also remotely block the car from being restarted once the engine has been turned off.

Many parents say that the teenagers knowing they're being watched can keep them safe. Some teenagers say that the presence of the device actually helps them if their buddies urge them to speed or otherwise endanger themselves.[29]

lucky or you don't use the Internet much. Spam has become a severe irritant to consumers and a costly matter for businesses, who must sort through hundreds of e-mail messages every day deleting spam and hoping that they don't delete e-mail messages that are actually legitimate customer orders.

You can get spam filters to block out spam, but spammers are clever about including nonprinting characters in their subject lines and addresses that fool the filters into letting them pass. For example, say a spammer wanted to send out a message about a new weight loss drug called *Off*. The spammer would alter the spelling of the word or add invisible HTML tags so that the subject line would be: O*F*F or O<i></i>F<u></u>F. The HTML tags <i> and <u> would normally italicize and underline text, respectively, and the </i> and </u> would undo the italicizing and bolding, but since there's no text in between the tags do nothing except evade the filter.

Experts estimate that up to 70 percent of e-mail traffic in 2004 was spam and in June and July of 2004 spam reached the staggering figure of over 85 percent.[30] An individual spammer can send out 80 million or so spams per day. AOL and Microsoft say that their servers block a billion spam messages every day.[31] Many states have passed laws to regulate spam and the Federal Government passed an anti-spam law in 2003 called the CAN-Spam Act (see Figure 8.7 on page 374), which was widely criticized by anti-spam activists as legitimizing spam, since it set down rules for spamming rather than banning it altogether.

Most experts doubt that the CAN-Spam Act will hurt the spammers who are the source of most of the spam. They say that it will just cost legitimate businesses time and money since they have to maintain do-not-spam lists and follow the legal guidelines when sending out e-mails to customers. Since the bulk of spam comes from spammers who spoof (disguise) the origin of the e-mail, they can usually operate for a long time in defiance of the law. Irate spam trackers, some of whom have become cyber vigilantes, have gone so far as to "out" spammers and publicize information about them on the Web in an effort to stop them.

One trick that spammers use to collect addresses for spamming is to send out e-mail purporting to add you to a general do-not-spam list if you reply. In fact, what it does is add your e-mail address to the list of "live" ones.

369

Figure 8.6

Adware in a Free Version of Eudora, an E-Mail Application from Qualcomm

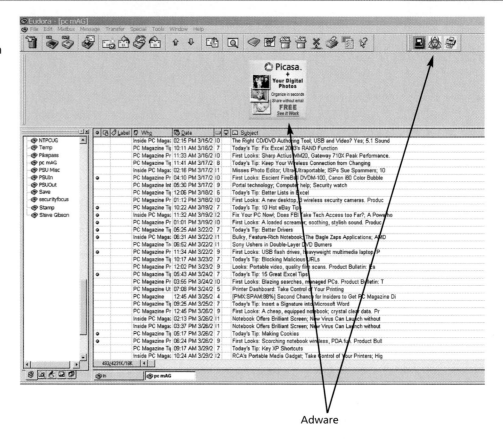

Adware

ADWARE AND SPYWARE   If you've downloaded a game or other software from the Web for free, you may have noticed that it came with banner ads. These ads are collectively known as adware. *Adware* is software to generate ads that installs itself on your computer when you download some other (usually free) program from the Web (see Figure 8.6). Adware is a type of *Trojan horse software,* meaning that it's software you don't want hidden inside software you do want. There's usually a disclaimer, buried somewhere in the multiple "I agree" screens, saying that the software includes this adware. At the bottom of several small-print screens you're asked to agree to the terms. Very few people read the whole agreement, and advertisers count on that. This sort of product is sometimes called *click-wrap* because it's like commercial software that has an agreement that you agree to by breaking the shrink-wrap.

Most people don't get upset about pure adware, since they feel it's worth having to view ads to get software for free. However, there's a more insidious extra that's often bundled with free downloadable software called spyware. *Spyware* (also called *sneakware* or *stealthware*) is malicious software that collects information about you and your computer and reports it to someone without your permission. It usually comes hidden in downloadable software and tracks your online movements and/or mines the information stored on your computer. The first release of RealNetworks' RealJukebox sent information back to the company about what CDs the people who downloaded the software were playing on that computer. This information collection was going on when the customer wasn't even on the Web.[32]

Spyware is fast becoming the hidden cost of free software. Software such as Kazaa Media Desktop and Audiogalaxy, the successors to Napster for sharing music and other files online, include spyware. If you download free software and it has banner ads, it's quite possible that it has spyware, too. There's usually something in the "I agree" screens telling you about spyware, but it can be hard to find. Spyware can stay on your computer long after you've uninstalled the original software.

You can detect various kinds of Trojan horse software with The Cleaner from www.moosoft.com. Also check out www.wilders.org for Trojan First Aid Kit (TFAK). The best-known spyware detection programs, also called stealthware blockers, are Ad-Aware (free from www.lavasoftUSA.com) and PestPatrol. The software scans your whole computer, identifies spyware programs, and offers to delete them. If you want to check out free software for spyware before you download it, go online to www.spychecker.com, a site that will tell you if particular free software includes adware or spyware.

Even without spyware, a Web site can tell a lot about its Web visitors from its Web log.[33] A **Web log** consists of one line of information for every visitor to a Web site and is usually stored on a Web server. At the very least, a Web log can provide a Web site company with a record of your clickstream.

A **clickstream** records information about you during a Web surfing session such as what Web sites you visited, how long you were there, what ads you looked at, and what you bought. If, as a consumer, you want to protect information about your surfing habits, you can use various software packages to do so. Apart from cookie management software you can avail yourself of **anonymous Web browsing (AWB)** services, which, in effect, hide your identity from the Web sites you visit. An example is Anonymizer at www.anonymizer.com. This site, and others like it, sends your Web browsing through its server and removes all identifying information. Some of the ABW services that are available include disabling pop-up promotions, defeating tracking programs, and erasing browsing history files. If you don't want to go through an outside server, you can download software to do the job. SurfSecret is a shareware antitracking package available from www.surfsecret.com.

As a final note on the subject, remember that even if a company promises, and fully intends, to keep its customer information protected, it may not be possible. When faced with a subpoena, the company will have to relinquish customer records. Furthermore, courts have ruled in bankruptcy cases that customer files are assets that may be sold to pay debts.

PRIVACY AND GOVERNMENT AGENCIES

Government agencies have about 2,000 databases containing personal information on individuals.[34] The various branches of government need information to administer entitlement programs, such as social security, welfare, student loans, law enforcement, and so on.

LAW ENFORCEMENT   You've often heard about someone being apprehended for a grievous crime after a routine traffic stop for something like a broken taillight. The arrest most likely ensued because the arresting officer ran a check on the license plate and driver's license. The officer probably checked the National Crime Information Center (NCIC) database and found the outstanding warrant there. Timothy McVeigh and those responsible for the bombing of the Federal building in Oklahoma City were caught in this way.

The NCIC database contains information on the criminal records of more than 20 million people. It also stores information on outstanding warrants, missing children, gang members, juvenile delinquents, stolen guns and cars, and so on. The NCIC has links to other government and private databases, and guardians of the law all over the country can access NCIC information. Sometimes they do so in response to something suspicious, and other times it's just routine. For example, Americans returning from outside the country are routinely checked through the NCIC when they come through customs.

Given the wealth of information and accessibility, it's not surprising that NCIC information has been abused. Several police departments have found that a significant number of employees illegally snooped for criminal records on people they knew or wanted to know.

The Federal Bureau of Investigation (FBI) has caused a stir lately because of its electronic surveillance methods. First there was Carnivore, a rather unfortunate name, which has since been changed to DCS-1000. DCS-1000 connects hardware to an ISP to trap all e-mail sent to or received by the target of the investigation. It takes a court order to use DCS-1000, and, of course, the target is typically unaware of the surveillance. Intercepting communications is not new: The FBI put the first tap on a phone in 1885, just four years after the invention of the telephone.[35] DCS-1000, with a court order, traps all communications involving the individual named in the court order.

Because it can be hard to identify the data packets of one individual's e-mail amongst all the other Internet traffic, it's entirely possible that other people's e-mail might be scooped up in the net. And this is what happened in March 2000 when FBI agents were legally intercepting messages of a suspect, but someone else was caught in the trap. The information on the innocent party was obtained under the Freedom of Information Act. The FBI said the incident was an honest mistake and a result of miscommunication between it and the ISP.[36] But, this is the sort of mistake that scares people. Most people want law enforcement to be able to watch the bad guys—that's necessary for our collective safety. But the prospect of information being collected on law-abiding citizens who are minding their own business worries a lot of people.

In 2001, the FBI acknowledged an enhancement to DCS-1000 called Magic Lantern, which is key logger software. The FBI installs it by sending the target an innocent-looking Trojan-horse e-mail, which contains the key logger software. The hidden software then sends information back to the FBI periodically.[37]

Another federal agency, the National Security Agency (NSA), uses a system called Echelon that uses a global network of satellites and surveillance stations to trap phone, e-mail, and fax transmissions. The system then screens all this information looking for certain keywords and phrases and analyzes the messages that fit the search criteria.

At the local level, the actions of the Tampa Police Department at the 2001 Super Bowl caused an outcry from privacy advocates. Police, with the agreement of the NFL, focused video cameras on the faces of tens of thousands of spectators as they entered the stadium. The images were sent to computers which, using facial recognition software, compared the images to a database of pictures of suspected criminals and terrorists. The police spokesperson said that the action was legal since it's permissible to take pictures of people in public places. That's true in so far as you have no expectation of privacy in a public place. Indeed surveillance of people has been going on for years without much protest in gambling casinos, Wal-Mart stores, and other businesses in the private sector. But the American Civil Liberties Union (ACLU) protested the surveillance of Super Bowl spectators on the grounds that it was surveillance by a government agency without court-ordered authorization. The fact that the state was involved made it unacceptable to the ACLU.

OTHER FEDERAL AGENCIES   The Internal Revenue Service (IRS) gets income information from taxpayers. But the agency has access to other databases, too. For example, the IRS keeps track of vehicle registration information so that it can check up on people buying expensive cars and boats to make sure they're reporting an income level that corresponds to their purchases. The IRS can go to outside government databases as well. Verizon says that it gets 22,000 requests for phone records from the IRS, FBI, and other government agencies per year. It seldom informs the customer of the request. America Online (AOL) has a special fax number reserved just for subpoenas.

The Census Bureau collects information on all the U.S. inhabitants it can find every 10 years. All citizens are requested to fill out a census form, and some people get a very long and detailed form requiring them to disclose a lot of personal information. The in-

CATCHING KILLERS

In 2005, Kansas had two high profile murder cases. One was the infamous BTK (bind, torture, kill) strangler, Dennis Rader, who was accused of killing 10 women over three decades. The other was an English professor, Thomas E. Murray, who was convicted of killing his wife and sentenced to 25 years in prison. Evidence gleaned from computers used by the accused in each of these crimes went a long way in helping the prosecutors make the case.

The BTK strangler had taunted police and the media over many years through letters and packages, some of which contained photos of the victims. But it was the package containing a diskette that he sent to a TV station on February 16, 2005, that finally helped identify him. The TV station turned the diskette over to police, who in turn, called in computer forensic investigators. They found evidence of a deleted file that referenced the Christ Lutheran Church in Wichita. Police asked the church to allow them to examine its computer and found that Rader had used it to print out a church meeting agenda. Then they got a warrant to examine the computer in Rader's home and found evidence that he was, indeed, the BTK strangler.

The case of Thomas Murray, who killed his wife, was strengthened when, during the investigation, police found e-mails he had sent to his wife and friends. The messages showed how upset he was with the fact that his wife was divorcing him and taking their daughter to California. Computer forensic experts found that he had done Yahoo! searches for "how to make a bomb," "murder for hire," "how to hire an assassin," and "how to murder someone and not get caught."

In both these murder cases, the perpetrators hadn't realized that information that has been deleted and terms used in search engines can be recovered. You can find out more about computer forensics in *Module H: Computer Crime and Forensics.*[38,39]

---

formation that the Census Bureau collects is available to other government agencies and even to commercial enterprises. The bureau doesn't link the information to respondents' names but sells summarized information about geographic regions. Some of these regions are relatively small, however, consisting of fewer than 100 city blocks.

It's fairly safe to assume that anytime you have contact with any branch of government, information about you will be subsequently stored somewhere. For example, if you get a government-backed student loan, you provide personal information such as your name, address, income, parents' income, and so on. Some of the information nuggets attached to the loan would be the school you're attending, the bank dispersing the loan, your repayment schedule, and later, your repayment pattern.

LAWS ON PRIVACY

The United States doesn't have a comprehensive or consistent set of laws governing the use of information. However, some laws are in place. Recent legislation includes the Health Insurance Portability and Accountability Act (HIPAA) and the Financial Service Modernization Act. HIPAA, enacted in 1996, requires that the health care industry formulate and implement the first regulations to keep patient information confidential. The act seeks to

- Limit the release and use of your health information without your consent.
- Give you the right to access your medical records and find out who else has accessed them.
- Overhaul the circumstances under which researchers and others can review medical records.

- **Identity Theft and Assumption Deterrence Act,** 1998, strengthened the criminal laws governing identity theft, making it a federal crime to use or transfer identification belonging to another. It also established a central federal service for victims.
- **USA Patriot Act,** 2001 and 2003, allows law enforcement to get access to almost any information, including library records, video rentals, bookstore purchases, and business records when investigating any act of terrorism or hostile intelligence activities. In 2003 Patriot II broadened the original law.
- **Homeland Security Act,** 2002, provided new authority to government agencies to mine data on individuals and groups including e-mails and Web site visits; put limits on the information available under the Freedom of Information Act; and gave new powers to government agencies to declare national heath emergencies.
- **Sarbanes-Oxley Act,** 2002, sought to protect investors by improving the accuracy and reliability of corporate disclosures and requires companies to (1) implement extensive and detailed policies to prevent illegal activity within the company and (2) respond in a timely manner to investigate illegal activity. (You'll find more about the business implications of Sarbanes-Oxley in *Extended Learning Module H: Computer Crime and Forensics.*)
- **Fair and Accurate Credit Transactions Act,** 2003, included provisions for the prevention of identity theft including consumers' right to get a credit report free each year, requiring merchants to leave all but the last five digits of a credit card number off a receipt, and requiring lenders and credit agencies to take action even before a victim knows a crime has occurred when they notice any circumstances that might indicate identity theft.
- **CAN-Spam Act,** 2003, sought to regulate interstate commerce by imposing limitations and penalties on businesses sending unsolicited e-mail to consumers. The law forbids deceptive subject lines, headers, return addresses, etc., as well as harvesting e-mail addresses from Web sites. It requires businesses that send spam to maintain a do-not-spam list and to include a postal mailing address in the message.

Figure 8.7

Recent Information-Related Laws

- Release health information on a need-to-know basis only.
- Allow the disclosure of protected health information for business reasons as long as the recipient undertakes, in writing, to protect the information.

The Financial Services Modernization Act requires that financial institutions protect personal customer information and that they have customer permission before sharing such information with other businesses. However, the act contains a clause that allows the sharing of information for "legitimate business purposes." See Figure 8.7 for recent information-related laws.

Security

So, what can put your important information resource in jeopardy? Well, countless things. Hard disks can crash, computer parts can fail, hackers and crackers can gain access and do mischief, thieves engaged in industrial espionage can steal your information, and disgruntled employees or associates can cause damage. The FBI estimates that computer sabotage costs businesses somewhere close to $10 billion every year. Companies are increasing their spending on Internet security software, a fact that Symantec Corp. can attest to. Symantec is the largest exclusive developer of computer security software and has a market value of $19 billion, making it one of the most valuable software companies in the world.[40]

SECURITY AND EMPLOYEES

Most of the press reports are about outside attacks on computer systems, but actually, companies are in far more danger of losing money from employee misconduct than they are from outsiders. It's estimated that 75 percent of computer crime is perpetrated by in-

WAS IT AN "HONEST" CLICK OR A "FRAUDULENT" ONE?

We all know that Yahoo! and Google make money not by charging surfers who use their search engines, but by charging advertisers. The way it works is that the more click-throughs an advertiser gets, the more that company pays Yahoo! or Google or one of the other search sites. Such fees range from a few cents to several dollars per click.

For example if you use the search term "private jet" on Yahoo!, you'll get a small ad from Blue Star Jets and, if you click on the link in the ad, Blue Star will pay Yahoo! $9.21. However, if you click on ExcelAire's ad, that company will only have to pay Yahoo! $0.18. The range of prices has to do with the placement of the ad in the list and so on. On average, click-through payments are about 50 cents but can go up to $90 or so for sought-after terms such as Vioxx, where massive lawsuit activity is under way.

Believe it or not, people are "fraudulently clicking" as a means of sabotage, perhaps to drive up competitors' advertising costs, for example. Some people estimate that about 20 percent of click-throughs are not from serious customers and are therefore fraudulent. Another feature of search site ads is that companies buying those ads usually have a cap on the amount that they will spend in one day's ads on search sites. When that cap is reached the ad slips down or drops off the list.

One type of guerilla warfare being waged between sites involves a company clicking repeatedly on another's link to use up the competitor's allotted daily advertising budget. This happened to Blue Star Jets when a competitor, Tag Aviation Holding, became annoyed that Blue Star bought ads based on the search string "Tag Aviation." Tag employees were instructed to keep clicking until the Blue Star ads disappeared.

Search sites are very worried about these irregularities, and with good reason. The amount of money involved is huge. Search companies earned about $4 billion in the United States in 2004 from clicks on ads that appeared based on search terms. Both Google and Yahoo! refund fees on click-throughs that they deem to be fraudulent. However, this isn't the only problem. There are many other schemes in operation.

For example, outsourced ads also come under attack. Google and Yahoo! run the same ads, then the search site pays the hosting site according to the number of click-throughs. Some sites are suspected of clicking on the ads to increase their own revenue. Some even use bot programs that will click automatically on the ad links—perhaps thousands of times each day.

The fallout has already started. CharterAuction.com, a charter jet company, for example, has cut its search-ad spending from $20,000 per month down to $1,000 because of a loss of confidence in the medium as a good advertising outlet. An Arkansas retailer has filed suit charging that Google, Yahoo!, and Ask Jeeves knowingly charged for fraudulent clicks. There will undoubtedly be more turbulence in the industry while such problems are slowly being solved.[41]

Figure 8.8

Statistics on White-Collar Crime

- White-collar crime costs an estimated $400 billion per year
- Average nonmanagerial embezzlement is $60,000
- Average managerial embezzlement is $250,000
- Two-thirds of insider fraud is not reported
- Of the known losses, one-quarter cost more than $1 million

siders, although this is not a problem that's restricted to computer misuse. A 300-restaurant chain with 30 employees in each location loses, on average, $218 per employee.

But white-collar crime is where the big bucks are lost (see Figure 8.8). White-collar crime in general, from Fortune 100 firms to video stores to construction companies, accounts for about $400 billion in losses every year—$400 billion is $108 billion more than the whole federal defense budget—and information technology makes it much easier to accomplish and conceal the crime. Of all white collar fraud, the biggest losses are those incurred by management misconduct. Manager theft of various kinds is about four times that of other employees. Take embezzlement, for example. The average cost of a nonmanagerial employee's theft is $60,000, while that for managerial employees is $250,000. The most astonishing aspect of this is that most insider fraud (up to two-thirds) is never reported to the legal authorities, according to the Association of Certified Fraud Examiners (ACFE). A survey by Ernst & Young disclosed that two out of five businesses suffered more than five fraud losses, and fully one-quarter of those resulted in a loss of over $1 million. The reasons most often cited for lack of legal action was fear of damaging the company's reputation or brand name.[42]

Computer-aided fraud includes the old standby crimes like vendor fraud (sending payment to a nonexistent vendor or payment for goods not delivered), writing payroll checks to fictitious employees, claiming expense reimbursements for costs never incurred, and so on. In addition, there are newer crimes such as stealing security codes, credit card numbers, and proprietary files. Intellectual property is one of the favorite targets of theft by insiders. In fact, the companies that make surveillance software say that employers are buying and installing the software not so much to monitor employees as to track how intellectual property, like product design sketches, schematics, and so on, is moving around the network.

Fraud examiners have a rule of thumb that in any group of employees, about 10 percent are completely honest, 10 percent will steal, and, for the remaining 80 percent, it will depend on circumstances. Most theft is committed by people who are strapped for cash, have access to funds that are poorly protected, and perceive a low risk of getting caught.

SECURITY AND OUTSIDE THREATS

An FBI Computer Security Institute survey found that the computer systems of 85 percent of large companies and governmental agencies were broken into during 2001. Of those, 64 percent said they had suffered financial loss, but only 35 percent wanted to put a figure on the loss. Even so, the total of reported losses came to more than $375 million. "There's no Fortune 500 company that hasn't been hacked, I don't care what they tell you," says one hacker.[43] "Hacking" means unauthorized access to computers and computer information. 3Com gets "thousands of attacks a week. From kids to criminals to foreign governments," says David Starr, senior vice president.[44] Even Microsoft's computers have been hacked.

The threats from outside are many and varied. Competitors could try to get your customer lists or the prototype for your new project. Cyber vandals could be joyriding in cyberspace looking for something interesting to see, steal, or destroy. You could become the victim of a generalized attack from a virus or worm, or could suffer a targeted attack like a denial-of-service attack. If you have something worth stealing or manipulating on your system, there could be people after that, too. For example, the online gambling industry is plagued by attacks where hackers have illicitly gained access to the servers that control the gambling, corrupting games to win millions of dollars. Exploiting well-known system weaknesses accounts for 95 percent of hacker damage, while only 5 percent results from breaking into systems in new ways.[45]

The people who break into the computer systems of others are "hackers" (see Figure 8.9). *Hackers* are generally knowledgeable computer users who use their knowledge to invade other people's computers. They have varying motives. Some just do it for the fun of it. Others (called hacktivists) have a philosophical or political message they want to share, and still others (called crackers) are hired guns who illegally break in, usually to steal information, for a fee. The latter can be a very lucrative undertaking. Some highly

Figure 8.9

Hacker Types

- White-hat hackers find vulnerabilities in systems and plug the holes. They work at the request of the owners of the computer systems.
- Black-hat hackers break into other people's computer systems and may just look around, or they may steal credit card numbers or destroy information, or otherwise do damage.
- Hacktivists have philosophical and political reasons for breaking into systems. They often deface a Web site as a protest.
- Script kiddies, or script bunnies, find hacking code on the Internet and click-and-point their way into systems, to cause damage or spread viruses.
- Crackers are hackers for hire and are the hackers who engage in corporate espionage.
- Cyberterrorists are those who seek to cause harm to people or to destroy critical systems or information. They try to use the Internet as a weapon of mass destruction.

skilled crackers charge up to $1 million per job. There are also "good guys," called white-hat hackers, who test the vulnerability of systems so that protective measures may be taken.

TYPES OF CYBER CRIME Cyber crimes range from electronically breaking and entering to cyberstalking and murder. In October 1999, a 21-year-old woman was shot and killed outside the building where she worked. Her killer had been electronically stalking her for two years. He became obsessed with the young lady and had even posted a Web site dedicated to her on which he announced his intention to kill her. He got her Social Security number online, found out where she worked, tracked her down, and shot her, after which he shot himself.

Most cyber crimes are not as bad as murder, but they can be serious nonetheless. Computer viruses and denial-of-service attacks are the two most common types of cyber crime against which companies need to protect themselves.

A *computer virus* (or simply a *virus*) is software that is written with malicious intent to cause annoyance or damage. A virus can be benign or malicious. The benign ones just display a message on the screen or slow the computer down, but don't do any damage. The malicious kind targets a specific application or set of file types and corrupts or destroys them.

Today, worms are the most prevalent type of virus. Worms are viruses that spread themselves; they don't need your help, just your carelessness.

A *worm* is a type of virus that spreads itself, not just from file to file, but from computer to computer via e-mail and other Internet traffic. It finds your e-mail address book and helps itself to the addresses and sends itself to your contacts, using your e-mail address as the return address. The Love Bug worm was one of the early worms that did a lot of damage and got major press coverage. It's estimated that the Love Bug and its variants affected 300,000 Internet host computers and millions of individual PC users causing file damage, lost time, and high-cost emergency repairs costing about $8.7 billion.[46,47] Ford Motor Company, H. J. Heinz, Merrill Lynch, AT&T, Capitol Hill, and the British Parliament all fell victim to the Love Bug worm. Newer versions of worms include Klez, a very rapidly spreading worm, Nimda, and Sircam.

A *denial-of-service attack (DoS)* floods a server or network with so many requests for service that it slows down or crashes. The objective is to prevent legitimate customers from accessing the target site. E*Trade, Yahoo!, and Amazon.com have all been victims of this type of attack. For more information about viruses and DoSs see *Extended Learning Module H.*

ONLINE BLACKMAIL

"You can ignore this email and try to keep your site up, which will cost you tens of thousands of dollars in lost customers, or you can send us $10K bank wire to make sure that your site experiences no problems + we will give you our protection for a year."

Above is the message that the managers of Protx, an online-payment processing firm in London, received by e-mail. The incident was the third time the company had been attacked within the year, and it was the most savage attack. At one point, the Protx network was bombarded by a blitz of traffic, to the tune of 500 megabits per second (that's about five times more traffic per second than a large ISP would handle). This barrage came from thousands of computers whose power had been commandeered by the attackers in what's called a distributed denial-of-service attack, and it knocked the company offline.

As is often the case, the attacks were conducted with bot viruses. A bot virus is a program that attackers plant in someone else's computer that allows the perpetrator to use the resources—the CPU or hard disk, for example—for their own purposes.

In the case of Protx, computer security experts were called in to stop the attacks and prevent the same sort of thing from happening in the future. They found that as soon as they shut down one stream of attacks, another one would start from a different hijacked network. It cost Protx about $500,000 to secure its network against future attacks. Such costs are usually annual expenses and don't include the cost of shutting down the original attacks or the cost of the business lost by the victim company.[48]

As well as knowing what viruses can do, you need to know what they can't do. Computer viruses can't

- Hurt your hardware, such as your monitor, or processor.
- Hurt any files they weren't designed to attack. A virus designed for Microsoft's Outlook, for example, generally doesn't infect Qualcomm's Eudora, or any other e-mail application.
- Infect files on write-protected disks.

SECURITY PRECAUTIONS

It has been said that while in years past, managers had nightmares about takeover bids, they now have nightmares about teenagers with computers and Internet access. Lloyd's of London says that 70 percent of risk managers see the Internet and e-commerce as the biggest emerging risks in this new century.[49] Security spending by U.S. companies is about 5 percent of the total information technology budget. That's approximately $15 billion per year.[50]

The only really safe computer system is one that is never connected to any other computer and is locked away so that almost no one can get to it. In today's business world that's just not practical. Computers are like motor vehicles; they can be used to cause harm both unintentionally and maliciously, and just driving one puts you at risk, especially when you're on the road with other cars. However, we still use motor vehicles, although we build in safety features and take precautions to lessen the risk. So it is with computers. The big difference is that security threats in cyberspace are always changing.

Given the extraordinary importance of information in an organization, it's imperative that companies make their best efforts to protect that information; that is, they should practice risk management. *Risk management* consists of the identification of risks or threats, the implementation of security measures, and the monitoring of those measures for effectiveness. The first step in the process is establishing the extent of the potential threats and identifying the parts of the system that are vulnerable. That process is called risk assessment. *Risk assessment* is the process of evaluating IT assets, their importance to the organization, and their susceptibility to threats, to measure the risk exposure of these assets. In simple terms, risk assessment asks (1) What can go wrong? (2) How likely is it to go wrong? and (3) What are the possible consequences if it does go wrong?[51]

Implementing the correct amount and type of security is not an easy matter. Too much security can hamper employees' ability to do their jobs, resulting in decreased revenue. Too little security leaves your organization vulnerable. You need security strong enough to protect your IT systems but not so much that authorized people can't access the information they need in a timely fashion. Generally, security consists of a combination of measures such as backup procedures, anti-virus software, firewalls, access authentication, encryption, intrusion-detection software, and system auditing.

BACKUPS   As always, an ounce of prevention is worth a pound of cure. The easiest and most basic way to prevent loss of information is to make backups of all your information. *Backup* is the process of making a copy of the information stored on a computer. There's no action you can take that's more rudimentary or essential than making copies of important information methodically and regularly (at least once a week). Employee carelessness and ignorance cause about two-thirds of the financial cost of lost or damaged information.

Make sure you back up *all* information. It's easy to forget about the information that's not stored in the main computer system or network, such as correspondence and customer information kept only by administrative assistants and receptionists, and private information not kept in the main organizational databases or data warehouses. Your backup schedule should include not only your information, but also your software. See Chapter 7 for more on backup and recovery.

ANTI-VIRUS SOFTWARE   Anti-virus software is an absolute must. *Anti-virus software* detects and removes or quarantines computer viruses. New viruses are created every day and each new generation is more deadly (or potentially deadly) than the previous one. When you're looking for virus protection, *PC World* magazine has the following advice. Look for virus protection that finds

- Viruses on removable media like floppies, CDs, and Zip disks, as well as on the hard disk.
- Trojan-horse viruses (viruses hiding inside good software) and backdoor programs (viruses that open a way into the network for future attacks).
- Polymorphic viruses and worms, which are sometimes hard for anti-virus programs to find because they change their form as they propagate.
- Viruses in .zip or compressed files, and even .zip files inside other .zip files.
- Viruses in e-mail attachments.

Two final points: First, your anti-virus software should be able to get rid of the virus without destroying the software or information it came with. Second, you must update your anti-virus software frequently since new viruses come along every day. Some software sites will automatically send updates to your anti-virus software, if you set up the software to accept it.

HOW PROTECTED ARE COMPUTERS IN YOUR PART OF THE WORLD?

The Firewall Guide Web site at www.firewallguide.com has the following advice on protecting your computer.

- First line of defense—Choose an Internet service provider (ISP), an e-mail service, and/or a Web site hosting service that offers online virus, spam, and content filters.

- Second line of defense—Install a hardware *router* with a built-in firewall between your modem and your computer or network.

- Third line of defense—Use personal firewall, anti-virus, anti-Trojan, anti-spyware, anti-spam, and privacy software on your desktop computer.

- Important tips—After installing any security software, immediately check for updates at the vendor's Web site. After installing a firewall, use an online testing service to make sure that it is working correctly.

Do a survey to get an idea of how many people you know implement any of the above safeguards. Each person in your group must ask five people (don't ask anyone who is taking this class with you) which of these protective measures they use. For each person, list the software or hardware they use to protect their computers. Some software has multiple uses; for example, anti-virus software might protect against worms and Trojan horse viruses. See if they really know specifically what their protection software protects against.

FIREWALLS A *firewall* is hardware and/or software that protects a computer or network from intruders. The firewall examines each message as it seeks entrance to the network, like a border guard checking passports. Unless the message has the "right" markings, the firewall blocks the way and prevents it from entering. Any competent network administrator will have at least one firewall on the network to keep out unwelcome guests.

A firewall will also detect your computer communicating with the Internet without your approval, as spyware on your computer may be attempting to do. A very popular software firewall is ZoneAlarm from www.zonealarm.com. ZoneAlarm also offers protection from ads and cookies.

ACCESS AUTHENTICATION While firewalls keep outsiders out, they don't necessarily keep insiders out. In other words, unauthorized employees may try to access computers or files. One of the ways that companies try to protect computer systems is with authentication systems that check who you are before they let you have access.

There are three basic ways of proving your access rights: (1) what you know, like a password; (2) what you have, like an ATM card; (3) what you look like (more specifically what your fingerprint or some other physical characteristic looks like).

Passwords are very popular and have been used since there were computers. You can password-protect the whole network, a single computer, a folder, or a file. But passwords are not by any means a perfect way to protect a computer system. People forget their passwords, so someone has to get them new passwords or find the old one. Banks spend $15 per call to help customers who forget their passwords. Then if a hacker breaks into the system and steals a password list, everyone has to get a new password. One bank had to change 5,000 passwords in the course of a single month at a cost of $12.50 each.[52]

Which brings us to biometrics, or what you look like. *Biometrics* is the use of physiological characteristics—such as your fingerprint, the blood vessels in the iris of your eye, the sound of your voice, or perhaps even your breath—to provide identification.

You can install a router to give your computer or network hardware protection. Alternatively, or in addition, you can install anti-intruder software to alert you when your computer is receiving a communication from the Internet or sending out information to a location on the Internet. The software will ask you each time whether you want to allow the traffic. You can usually set the software to always, or never, admit certain communications.

Do some research and find five anti-intruder software packages and compare the features of the programs you find. Two such software firewalls are ZoneAlarm from Zone Labs and Symantec's Norton Personal Firewall. Compare the packages in terms of what they block, what dangers they alert you to, and what they cost.

Roughly a dozen different types of biometric devices are available at the moment, with fingerprint readers being the most popular. About 44 percent of the biometric systems sold are fingerprint systems. They work just like the law enforcement system where your fingerprint is stored in the database, and when you come along, your finger is scanned, and the scan is compared to the entry in the database. If they match, you're in.

Another promising type of biometric system is facial recognition. Chicago's O'Hare airport, the busiest in the world, has been using biometrics for years to authenticate employees' identity. Many U.S. airport security officials are proposing biometric systems to check that passengers are who they say they are. Most envision the system as a voluntary recording of passengers' biological characteristics, so that frequent flyers could sign up, have their physical characteristic scanned, then in the future bypass the long manual clearing process. See Chapter 9 for more information on biometrics.

ENCRYPTION   If you want to protect your messages and files and hide them from prying eyes, you can encrypt them. ***Encryption*** scrambles the contents of a file so that you can't read it without having the right decryption key. There are various ways of encrypting messages. You can switch the order of the characters, replace characters with other characters, or insert or remove characters. All of these methods alter the look of the message, but used alone, each one is fairly simple to figure out. So most encryption methods use a combination.

Companies that get sensitive information from customers, such as credit card numbers, need some way of allowing all their customers to use encryption to send the information. But they don't want everyone to be able to decrypt the message, so they might use public key encryption. ***Public key encryption (PKE)*** is an encryption system that uses two keys: a public key that everyone can have and a private key for only the recipient. So if you do online banking, the bank will give you the public key to encrypt the information you send them, but only the bank has the key to decrypt your information. It works rather like a wall safe, where anyone can lock it (just shut the door and twirl the knob), but only the person with the right combination can open it again.

INTRUSION-DETECTION AND SECURITY-AUDITING SOFTWARE   Two other types of security software are intrusion-detection and security-auditing software. An ***intrusion-detection system (IDS)*** is software and/or hardware that watches network traffic for intrusion attempts, reports them, and optionally takes action agains them. For example, someone might be trying lots of passwords trying to gain access. "Honey pots" are a type of intrusion-detection software that creates attractive, but nonexistent, targets for hackers. What actually happens is that hackers' keystrokes are recorded instead.

Security-auditing software checks out your computer or network for potential weaknesses. The idea is to find out where hackers could get in and to plug up the hole. Many third parties, such as accounting firms or computer security companies, also provide this service.

Summary: Student Learning Outcomes Revisited

1. **Define ethics and describe the two factors that affect how you make a decision concerning an ethical issue.** *Ethics* are the principles and standards that guide our behavior toward other people. How you decide ethical issues must depend especially on your basic ethical structure but also for better or worse on the practical circumstances. Your basic ethics you probably acquired growing up. The practical circumstances that you might allow to affect you include

   - *Consequences.* How much or how little benefit or harm will come from a particular decision?

   - *Society's opinion.* What do you perceive society thinks of your intended action?

   - *Likelihood of effect.* What is the probability of the harm or benefit if you take the action?

   - *Time to consequences.* How long will it take for the benefit or harm to take effect?

   - *Relatedness.* How much do you identify with the person or persons who will receive the benefit or suffer the harm?

   - *Reach of result.* How many people will be affected by your action?

2. **Define and describe intellectual property, copyright, Fair Use Doctrine, and pirated software.** *Intellectual property* is intangible creative work that is embodied in physical form. *Copyright* is the legal protection afforded an expression of an idea, such as a song or a video game and some types of proprietary documents. The *Fair Use Doctrine* says that you may use copyrighted material in certain situations. *Pirated software* is the unauthorized use, duplication, distribution or sale of copyrighted software.

3. **Define privacy and describe ways in which it can be threatened.** *Privacy* is the right to be left alone when you want to be, to have control over your own personal possessions, and not to be observed without your consent. Your privacy can be compromised by other individuals snooping on you; by employers monitoring your actions; by businesses that collect information on your needs, preferences, and surfing practices; and by the various government agencies that collect information on citizens.

4. **Describe the ways in which information on your computer or network is vulnerable.**

   - Employees can embezzle and perpetrate fraud of other types. Most of the financial losses due to computer fraud that is suffered by companies is caused by employees.

   - You give access to your computer information to collaboration partners who could do damage.

   - Grid computing will mean many computers working together with the potential for information to move between computers when it shouldn't.

   - Hackers and crackers try to break into computers and steal, destroy, or compromise information.

   - Hackers can spread *computer viruses* or launch *denial-of-service attacks (DoS)* that can cost millions in prevention and cleanup.

5. **Define risk management and risk assessment and describe the seven security measures that companies can take to protect their information.** *Risk management* consists of the identification of risks or threats, the implementation of security measures, and the

monitoring of those measures for effectiveness. *Risk assessment* is the process of evaluating IT assets, their importance to the organization, and their susceptibility to threats, to measure the risk exposure of these assets. The seven security measures are as follows

- **Backups.** Make sure there is more than one copy of everything, including files not on the main servers, like correspondence and other information stored on the computers of individual employees.

- **Anti-virus software** detects and removes or quarantines computer viruses. You can set your software to perform this task automatically. However, to be effective it must be updated regularly and often. Antivirus software should check *all* files that are introduced to your computer.

- A **firewall** is hardware and/or software that protects a computer or network from intruders.

- Access authorization makes sure that those who have access to information have the authorization to do so with password or biometrics. **Biometrics** is the use of physiological characteristics—such as your fingerprint, the blood vessels in the iris of your eye, the sound of your voice, or perhaps even your breath—to provide identification.

- **Encryption** scrambles the contents of a file so that you can't read it without having the right decryption key.

- An **intrusion-detection system (IDS)** watches network traffic for intrusion attempts, reports them, and optionally takes action against them.

- **Security-auditing software** checks out your computer or network for possible weaknesses.

CLOSING CASE STUDY ONE

CAUTIONARY TALES OF INDISCREET E-MAIL

Wrongdoing at Computer Associates and at Enron, once giants in their respective industries, was brought to light by forgotten and/or deleted e-mails. The recovered e-mails brought down guilty individuals, but caused some innocents to suffer as well.

COMPUTER ASSOCIATES

In 2000, Charles Wang, chairman of Computer Associates (CA), a business software development giant, was number one on *Forbes*'s list of wealthiest people with earnings of $650 million, $649 million of which was performance-based. However, early in 2002, federal investigators began investigating Computer Associates for improperly booking more than $2 billion in revenue. It had apparently become common practice for executives to keep quarterly reports open so that later deals could be backdated, making the quarterlies look better. By the end of 2002, Wang had been retired to an honorary, uncompensated position, largely because of the accounting discrepancies being investigated.

Computer Associates' Board of Directors, hoping to avoid the sort of disaster that killed Arthur Andersen, hired experienced criminal lawyers to conduct an investigation to get to the truth. After searching hun-

dreds of employee computers, the investigation turned up e-mails, deleted and saved, that provided evidence of fraud. These e-mails were not on the main system, but rather were stored on individual machines.

By April 2004, three former executives of the company had pled guilty to obstruction of justice charges and by September that number had risen to seven who had pled guilty or been indicted. The obstruction of justice charges came from the top executives' misleading the independent lawyers about the facts of their actions, knowing that the falsehoods would be passed on to federal investigators. Attorney–client privilege did not apply since the outside lawyers were hired to do an independent investigation and did not represent individual executives. By the time the main part of the investigation was over, most of the top-level executives of CA had been fired.

ENRON

When the Federal Energy Regulatory Commission (FERC), which was investigating Enron, unearthed and published confiscated e-mails, not only Enron's employees got a nasty shock when their old e-mails turned up on the Web. Everyone who had sent e-mails to Enron e-mail addresses found themselves caught in the federal net. So, people who were never accused of wrongdoing and didn't even work at Enron suddenly found their e-mail messages displayed for all the world to see, even if the message was as innocent as the confirmation of a golfing date.

FERC gathered a boatload of records, paper and electronic, during its investigation of Enron's alleged energy-market manipulations. In March 2003, FERC posted 1.6 million e-mail messages and other documents on the Web in a searchable database. The e-mails are from the period 2000–2003. So anyone can go to the Web site (www.ferc.gov/industries/electric/indus-act/wem/03-26-03-release.asp) and easily view the e-mails and calendars of 176 current and former Enron employees. The e-mails appear in full—including sender and receiver names.

Among the e-mail messages are lots of personal communications like executives discussing employees and vice versa; romantic messages; discussions of breakups (liaisons and marriages); in-law problems; personal photos, and so on.

FERC said that, since Enron owned the messages, it was incumbent on the company to identify personal communications and request their exclusion.

A couple of days after the e-mail database appeared on the Web, FERC agreed to take off the most sensitive documents, like a document that listed the Social Security number of every employee. In early April, on the order of a U.S. Court of Appeals, the database was shut down for 10 days to allow Enron to examine all the documents and make up a list of documents it wanted removed.

About 100 Enron volunteers spent 350 hours going through hundreds of thousands of e-mails looking for specific terms like "Social Security Number," "credit card number," "kids," and "divorce." FERC removed about 8 percent of the database, which amounted to about 141,000 documents.[53,54]

Questions

1. If you were to give advice to someone who had just started using e-mail, or even someone who's been using e-mail for a while, what would you tell that person should be the one guiding principle in all their e-mail communications? Put your advice into one sentence.

2. Now expand on your one guiding principle in question 1, and offer 10 rules for writing e-mails. What should those 10 rules be?

3. Imagine you're a manager in a lawn care business and you have an office staff of five people. Your lawyer suggests that you issue guidelines or rules to your staff about storing e-mail on the company's server and on the computers they use in their work for you. What should those guidelines be? What would the rules be? Be sure to explain your rationale.

4. Do you think there should be federal guidelines governing a business's e-mail traffic just as there are regarding a business's financial records? If so, what should they be? If not, why not?

CLOSING CASE STUDY TWO

THE PROBLEM OF INFORMATION PROTECTION

The theft of consumer information—particularly financial information—is causing huge headaches for financial and data companies. This case looks at three incidents that occurred recently at ChoicePoint, Bank of America, and Polo Ralph Lauren.

CHOICEPOINT

The opening case study in this chapter highlighted the Acxiom Corporation, a company that gathers, packages, and sells information about consumers. A direct competitor to Acxiom is ChoicePoint, a company that is a spin-off of Equifax, which is one of the three major credit bureaus.

ChoicePoint has 19 billion records that include information on almost every adult in the United States. ChoicePoint sells this information to customers, such as potential employers, for purposes of verification.

ChoicePoint found itself in the headlines when personal financial information on 145,000 customers was stolen in a very high-profile identity fraud theft. And this time there was no sophisticated electronic attack or break-in; rather the theft was accomplished through old-fashioned "social engineering." Social engineering is getting information that you have no right to by conning people who have access to it. What the identity thieves did was to pose as fake companies buying information on people in every state and the District of Columbia. So far, 750 confirmed cases of identity theft have surfaced from the ChoicePoint security breach.

The U.S. Attorney's Office in Los Angeles charged that ChoicePoint had been scammed previously in 2002 resulting in fraud to the tune of $1 million.

THE BANK OF AMERICA

The Bank of America was also the victim of information theft accomplished in an old-fashioned way. Personal information recorded on tapes belonging to 1.2 million federal employees, including members of Congress, was on a commercial jet en route to a safe backup facility when the tapes were stolen.

Both the Bank of America and ChoicePoint thefts occurred in February 2005 and were followed very quickly by the introduction of privacy legislation at both the state and federal levels.

POLO RALPH LAUREN

Another example of embarrassment and worse involved Polo Ralph Lauren. It seems that between June 2002 and December 2004, the company was storing credit card information on its point-of-sale system instead of deleting it immediately after transactions had been completed. The realization that this data had been compromised led HSBC North America—the issuer of some of the credit cards whose numbers had been stolen—to notify 180,000 consumers of the possibility of identity theft. MasterCard, Visa U.S.A. and Discover Financial Services customers have all been affected. American Express says it has not seen any activity that has looked suspicious.[55,56]

Questions

1. If you were the manager of a company where it was discovered that credit card information had been stolen, what responsibility would you have to the people whose personal information was compromised? What are the pros and cons of notifying and of not notifying possible victims?

2. E*Trade, a leader in online brokerage services, is the first company to go to a two-factor authentication system optionally available to its customers with accounts of $50,000 or more. The first factor is the ID and password that customers have always needed, and second, they use a security token or, as E*Trade calls it, a *Digital Security ID.* This is a little device that you can carry on your key chain that displays a new random six-digit number every minute. E*Trade's host system must, of course, synchronize with the device.

   When you log in, you have to type in this number after your ID and password. Since the number changes so often it's virtually impossible to hack an account with this two-pronged protection. From a consumer's point of view, do you think this is a good idea? What are the advantages and disadvantages of the system to businesses and customers? With which online transactions would you consider it worthwhile to enforce this level of security? Remember that you might have a lot of these tokens if you use a lot of online services.

3. In this case study you saw how personal information can be stolen from huge databases and data warehouses. What other ways are there that thieves can obtain personal information about you that would allow them to steal your identity and run up debts in your name? To what extent would you be liable for these debts? What would you have to do (what steps would you take) to reestablish your financial identity if you discovered your identity had been stolen?

4. In the case of the Bank of America, the data was being shipped on tapes to a safe location. This is very good backup policy to make sure that in the event of a major disaster like a fire or flood, data can be quickly restored enabling the company to be back in operation as soon as possible. However, this procedure leaves the company vulnerable to old-fashioned theft of the physical tapes containing personal information. What are two ways that this information that travels on trucks and planes could be protected?

Key Terms and Concepts

Adware, 370
Anonymous Web browsing
   (AWB), 371
Anti-virus software, 379
Backup, 379
Biometrics, 380
Clickstream, 371
Computer virus (virus), 377
Cookie, 368
Copyright, 358
Denial-of-service attack (DoS), 377
Encryption, 381

Ethics, 356
Fair Use Doctrine, 359
Firewall, 380
Hacker, 376
Hardware key logger, 366
Identity theft, 362
Intellectual property, 359
Intrusion-detection system (IDS), 381
Key logger software (key trapper
   software), 362
Phishing (carding or brand
   spoofing), 363

Pirated software, 360
Privacy, 361
Public key encryption (PKE), 381
Risk assessment, 379
Risk management, 379
Security-auditing software, 382
Spam, 368
Spyware (sneakware or
   stealthware), 370
Trojan horse software, 370
Web log, 371
Worm, 377

Short-Answer Questions

1. What are ethics, and how do ethics apply to business?
2. What situation would qualify as an exception to the copyright law?
3. What is privacy?
4. What is pirated software?
5. What is identity theft?
6. What does a key logger do?
7. What is spyware?
8. What is a denial-of-service attack?
9. What is risk assessment?
10. What is access authentication?

Assignments and Exercises

1. **HELPING A FRIEND** Suppose you fully intend to spend the evening working on an Excel assignment that's due the next day. Then a friend calls. Your friend is stranded miles from home and desperately needs your help. It will take most of the evening to pick up your friend, bring him home, and return to your studying. Not only that, but you're very tired when you get home and just fall into bed. The next day your friend, who completed his assignment earlier, suggests you just make a copy, put your own name on the cover, and hand it in as your own work. Should you do it? Isn't it only fair that since you helped your friend, the friend should do something about making sure you don't lose points because of your generosity? What if your friend promises not to hand in his or her own work so that you can't be accused of copying? Your friend wrote the assignment and gave it to you, so there's no question of copyright infringement.

2. **FIND OUT WHAT HAPPENED** In December 2001, British Telecom (BT) filed a lawsuit against Prodigy in New York federal court, claiming it owns the hyperlinking process. If BT wins this lawsuit then the company will be able to collect licensing revenue from the 100 billion or so links on the Web. BT has a patent that it says amounts to ownership of the hyperlinking process. Prodigy (and everyone else in the world) stores Web pages with a displayed part, which the browser shows, and a hidden part that the viewer doesn't see, and which contains hidden information including the addresses that are used by the displayed portion. This, BT said, is the essence of its U.S. patent No. 4873662. In reference to this case, answer the following questions:
   A. Has a ruling been handed down on this matter yet? If so, what was the result?
   B. If any kind of hyperlinking is, in fact, the essence of the patent held by BT, what about library card catalogs; are they infringements, too? Why or why not? What else could be?

3. **INVESTIGATE MONITORING SYSTEMS** The text listed several monitoring systems, other systems that defeat them, and an e-mail encryption program. Find two more of the following:
   A. Programs that monitor keyboard activity
   B. Programs that find keyboard monitoring programs
   C. E-mail encryption programs

4. **CHECK OUT THE COMPUTER ETHICS INSTITUTE'S ADVICE** The Computer Ethics Institute's Web site at www.cspr.org/program/ethics.htm offers the "Ten Commandments of Computer Ethics" to guide you in ethical computer use. The first two are
- *Thou shalt not use a computer to harm other people.* This one is the bedrock for all the others.
- *Thou shalt not interfere with other people's computer work.* This one stems from the first and includes small sins like sending frivolous e-mail and crimes like spreading viruses and electronic stalking.

Look up the other eight and give at least two examples of acts that would be in violation of these guidelines.

Discussion Questions

1. When selling antiques, you can usually obtain a higher price for those that have a provenance, which is information detailing the origin and history of the object. For example, property owned by Jacqueline Kennedy Onassis and Princess Diana sold for much more than face value. What kinds of products have value over and above a comparable product because of such information? What kind of information makes products valuable? Consider both tangible (resale value) and intangible value (sentimental appeal).

2. Personal checks that you use to buy merchandise have a standard format. Checks have very few different sizes, and almost no variation in format. Consider what would happen if everyone could create his or her own size, shape, and layout of personal check. What would the costs and benefits be to business and the consumer in terms of buying checks, exchanging them for merchandise, and bank check processing?

3. Consider society as a business that takes steps to protect itself from the harm of illegal acts. Discuss the mechanisms and costs that are involved. Examine ways in which our society would be different if no one ever broke a law. Are there ever benefits to our society when people break the law, for example, when they claim that the law itself is unethical or unjust?

4. Can you access all the IT systems at your college or university? What about payroll or grade information on yourself or others? What kinds of controls has your college or university implemented to prevent the misuse of information?

5. You know that you generally can't use a PC to access the information stored on a Macintosh-formatted disk. What other instances of difficulty in accessing information have you experienced personally or heard of? For example, have you used different versions of MS PowerPoint or MS Access that won't work on all the PCs that you have access to?

6. Have you, or someone you know, experienced computer problems caused by a virus? What did the virus do? Where do you think you got it? How did you fix the problem? What was the cost to you in time, trouble, and stress?

7. What laws do you think the United States should pass to protect personal information? Or none? Why? Should some personal information be more protected than other information? Why or why not?

8. The issue of pirated software is one that the software industry fights on a daily basis. The major centers of software piracy are in places like Russia and China where salaries and disposable income are comparatively low. Given that people in developing and economically depressed countries will fall behind the industrialized world technologically if they can't afford access to new generations of software, is it reasonable to blame someone for using pirated software when it costs two months' salary to buy a legal copy of MS Office? If you answered no, specify at what income level it's okay to make or buy illegal copies of software. What approach could software companies use to combat the problem apart from punitive measures, like pressuring the government to impose sanctions on transgressors?

Making Travel Arrangements on the Internet

It's very likely that in the course of business you'll be expected to travel either within the United States or abroad. You can use the Internet to check out all aspects of your journey, from mode of travel to the shopping opportunities that are available. The Internet can also give you pointers and directions about aspects of the trip you might not even have thought about.

In this section, we've included a number of Web sites related to making travel arrangements on the Internet. On the Web site that supports this text (www.mhhe.com/haag, click on "Electronic Commerce Projects"), we've provided direct links to all these Web sites as well as many, many more. This is a great starting point for completing this section. We would also encourage you to search the Internet for other sites.

AIR TRAVEL

Some people are happy to travel with whatever airline provides the flight that fits into their schedule. Others insist on certain airlines, or won't travel on particular airlines. No matter how you feel, the Internet can help you find a flight. On the Internet, you can even get maps of the airports you'll be using. Many airports have sites on the Internet, such as Dallas/Ft. Worth International Airport at www.dfwairport.com. These sites can help you with provisions at the airport for disabled people, among other available services.

The Federal Aviation Authority site (www.faa.com) has a comprehensive list of airlines in this country and all over the world. Find five appropriate Web sites and answer the following questions.

A. Can you make a flight reservation online at this site?

B. If you can book flights, does the site ask you to type in your departure and destination cities, or can you choose from a menu?

C. Again, if you can book flights at this site, on a scale of 1 to 10, rate how difficult it is to get to the flight schedule. That is, how many questions do you have to answer, how many clicks does it take, how much do you have to type in?

D. Is there information on when the lowest fares apply (for example, three-week advance booking, staying over Saturday night, etc.)?

E. Does the site offer to send you information on special deals via e-mail?

F. Does the site offer information on frequent flier mileage? Can you check your frequent flier account online?

G. Does the site offer you a map of the airports you will be using?

RENTAL CARS

When you arrive at your destination, you may need a car. Some sites such as Rental Car Info's site at www.bnm.com have information on multiple companies, and all the large car rental companies have sites on the Internet. Find six Web sites that rent cars and answer the following questions.

A. Can you reserve a car at the Web site?

B. Can you search by city?

C. Is there a cancellation penalty? If so, how much?

D. Can you get a list of car types? Does this company rent sports utility vehicles?

E. Are there special weekend rates?

F. What does the site say about collision insurance purchased from that company in addition to your own insurance?

G. Can you get maps from the site?

H. Are special corporate rates specified on the site?

ONE-STOP TRAVEL SITES

Some travel sites on the Internet allow you to book your entire trip from start to finish, offering a combination of airline, hotel, and other helpful information. Two of the most widely used are Microsoft's Expedia at expedia.msn.com and Preview at www.previewtravel.com. Choose five Web sites and answer the following questions.

A. How many different booking services are offered from this site (airlines, hotels, rental cars, rail travel, etc.)?

B. If the site offers flight booking, how many flight alternatives does it offer? 3? 10? 20? 30? More than 30?

C. Does the site have information on low-cost specials for airlines, hotels, and/or rental cars?

D. Is there a traveler's assistance section?

E. Will the site answer your specific questions?

F. Can you search by destination or company for flights and lodging?

EXTENDED LEARNING MODULE H

COMPUTER CRIME AND FORENSICS

Student Learning Outcomes

1. DEFINE COMPUTER CRIME AND LIST THREE TYPES OF COMPUTER CRIME THAT CAN BE PERPETRATED FROM INSIDE AND THREE FROM OUTSIDE THE ORGANIZATION.

2. IDENTIFY THE SEVEN TYPES OF HACKERS AND EXPLAIN WHAT MOTIVATES EACH GROUP.

3. DEFINE COMPUTER FORENSICS AND DESCRIBE THE TWO PHASES OF A FORENSIC INVESTIGATION.

4. IDENTIFY AND DESCRIBE FOUR PLACES ON A HARD DISK WHERE YOU CAN FIND USEFUL INFORMATION.

5. IDENTIFY AND DESCRIBE SEVEN WAYS OF HIDING INFORMATION.

6. DESCRIBE TWO WAYS IN WHICH CORPORATIONS USE COMPUTER FORENSICS.

Introduction

Computers play a big part in crime! They're used to commit crime, unfortunately. But they are also used to solve crimes. This should come as no surprise since computers are by now such an integral player in every part of our lives. Computers are involved in two ways in the commission of crime: as targets and as weapons or tools. A computer or network is a target when someone wants to bring it down or make it malfunction, as in a denial-of-service attack or a computer virus infection. Crimes that use a computer as a weapon or tool would include acts such as changing computer records to commit embezzlement, breaking into a computer system to damage information, and stealing customer lists. See Figure H.1 for examples of computer-related offenses in which computers are used as weapons/tools and targets of crime.

Some crimes are clearly what we call computer crimes, like Web defacing, denial-of-service attacks, e-mail scams, and so on. But, as is the case in so many parts of our modern lives, computers are also so integrated into crime that it's hard to separate them out. Here's an example from the case files of Walt Manning, an expert in computer forensic investigation. Would you call this a computer crime?

A member of a crime syndicate was sprayed with drive-by gunfire and was severely wounded. Believing that his services were no longer wanted by his crime gang, he switched sides, agreeing to become a witness for the state. The police secured an isolated intensive care unit room for him and guarded it heavily, allowing access only to medical staff and those on a very short list of visitors. Because the man was so badly wounded, there was a distinct danger of infection, and since he was allergic to penicillin, the doctor prescribed a synthetic alternative.

One evening, a nurse wheeling a medicine cart went through the police cordon and into the man's room. He injected the patient with penicillin, and the patient died shortly thereafter. An investigation started immediately and the nurse was potentially in big trouble. He insisted that when he looked at the patient's chart on the computer, there was an order there for penicillin. Subsequent examination of the computer records showed no such order. Eventually, it occurred to someone that perhaps a computer forensic expert should look at the computer angle more closely. Having retrieved the backup tapes (nightly backups are standard operating procedure in most places), the expert found evidence that exonerated the nurse. The patient chart had been changed in the computer to indicate penicillin and later changed back to its original form. Examination further revealed the point and time of access, and indicated that the medical record was changed by someone outside the hospital. A hacker had electronically slipped into the hospital's network unnoticed, made the change, and slipped out again—twice.

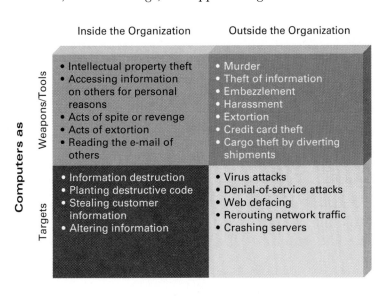

Inside the Organization | Outside the Organization

Computers as Weapons/Tools
- Intellectual property theft
- Accessing information on others for personal reasons
- Acts of spite or revenge
- Acts of extortion
- Reading the e-mail of others

- Murder
- Theft of information
- Embezzlement
- Harassment
- Extortion
- Credit card theft
- Cargo theft by diverting shipments

Computers as Targets
- Information destruction
- Planting destructive code
- Stealing customer information
- Altering information

- Virus attacks
- Denial-of-service attacks
- Web defacing
- Rerouting network traffic
- Crashing servers

Figure H.1

Examples of Computer Crimes That Organizations Need to Defend Against

Most crimes involving a computer are not as lethal as murder, but that doesn't mean they're insignificant. Organizations want to make sure their networks' defenses are strong and can prevent their computers from being used for unlawful or unethical acts. That's why so much time, money, and effort goes into security. We discussed security in Chapter 8.

This module focuses on the sort of threats that computer systems are susceptible to and the examination of electronic evidence. The latter is called *computer forensics*.

Computer Crime

For our purposes, a **computer crime** is a crime in which a computer, or computers, play a significant part. See Figure H.2 for a list of crimes in which computers, although perhaps not essential, usually play a large part.

In this section we'll focus on crime from the organization's viewpoint. First, we'll examine some of the more high-profile types of computer crime committed against organizations that are perpetrated from the outside. Then we'll discuss the varying motivations of people who commit these acts. Lastly, we'll briefly discuss computer crime within the organization.

OUTSIDE THE ORGANIZATION

Businesses are very concerned about the threat of people breaking into their computers and causing trouble. The Computer Security Institute (CSI) together with the FBI's Computer Intrusion Squad conduct studies every year in an effort to assess the extent of the problem nationwide. Their studies suggest that widespread awareness and billions of dollars spent on security software have created a downturn in the hitherto soaring rate of cyber crimes. The percentage of companies that experienced successful attacks on computer systems has been in decline since 2000. In 2000, 70% of the organizations surveyed said they experienced unauthorized use of computer systems compared to only 53% in 2004. The CSI/FBI study also showed that total losses fell in 2004 to $142 million from $202 million in 2003. The greatest financial losses came from viruses and worms and other common threats.[1]

Figure H.2

Crimes in Which Computers Usually Play a Part

- Illegal gambling
- Forgery
- Money laundering
- Child pornography
- Hate message propagation
- Electronic stalking
- Racketeering
- Fencing stolen goods
- Loan sharking
- Drug trafficking
- Union infiltration

Surprisingly, corporations are very reluctant to report computer crime to the authorities and the number is declining. About 20% of companies reported attacks to law enforcement in 2004, compared to 36% in 2001. Most companies are attacked multiple times every day but the vast majority of the attempted intrusions are viruses and are usually successfully repelled. Reporting other, more serious, attacks leaves the organizations in the position of having to admit to inadequate security, and many prefer not to.[2] A large portion of computer and network attacks are caused by *malware,* software designed to harm your computer or computer security.

VIRUSES

Viruses are a type of malware. The term *computer virus* is a generic term for lots of different types of destructive software. A ***computer virus*** (or ***virus***) is software that was written with malicious intent to cause annoyance or damage. Two hundred new ones are developed every day.[3] There are two categories of viruses. The first category comprises benign viruses that display a message or slow down the computer but don't destroy any information.

Malignant viruses belong in the second category. These viruses do damage to your computer system. Some will scramble or delete your files. Others will shut your computer down, or make your Word software malfunction, or damage flash memory in your digital camera so that it won't store pictures anymore until you reformat it. Obviously, these are the viruses that cause IT staff (and everyone else) the most headaches.

The macro virus is one very common type of malignant computer virus. ***Macro viruses*** spread by binding themselves to software such as Word or Excel. When they infect a computer, they make copies of themselves (replicate) and spread from file to file destroying or changing the file in some way.

This type of virus needs human help to move to another computer. If you have a macro virus on your system and you e-mail an infected document as an attachment, the person who gets the e-mail gets the virus as soon as the infected attachment is opened. When you click on the attachment, Word (or the appropriate program) also loads, thereby setting the executable statements in motion.

Worms are the most prevalent type of malignant virus. A ***worm*** is a computer virus that replicates and spreads itself, not only from file to file, but from computer to computer via e-mail and other Internet traffic. Worms don't need your help to spread. They find your e-mail address book and help themselves to the addresses, sending themselves to your contacts. The first worm to attract the attention of the popular press was the Love Bug worm, and permutations of it are still out there.

THE LOVE BUG WORM

Released on an unsuspecting world in 2000, the Love Bug worm caused the Massachusetts state government to shut down its e-mail, affecting 20,000 workers. It also caused problems on Capitol Hill and shut down e-mail in the British Parliament building. Companies as diverse as Ford Motor Company, H. J. Heinz, Merrill Lynch & Company, and AT&T were infected.[4] All in all, the Love Bug and its variants affected 300,000 Internet host computers and millions of individual PC users causing file damage, lost time, and high-cost emergency repairs totaling about $8.7 billion.[5,6]

A closer look at the Love Bug worm will give you a general idea of what worms do. The Love Bug arrives in your e-mail as an attachment to an e-mail message. The subject of the e-mail is "I LOVE YOU"—a very alluring message to be sure. The text says to open the attached love letter, the name of which is, appropriately, LOVE LETTER. However, what's attached is anything but love. It's a mean piece of software that is set loose in your computer system as soon as you open the attachment.

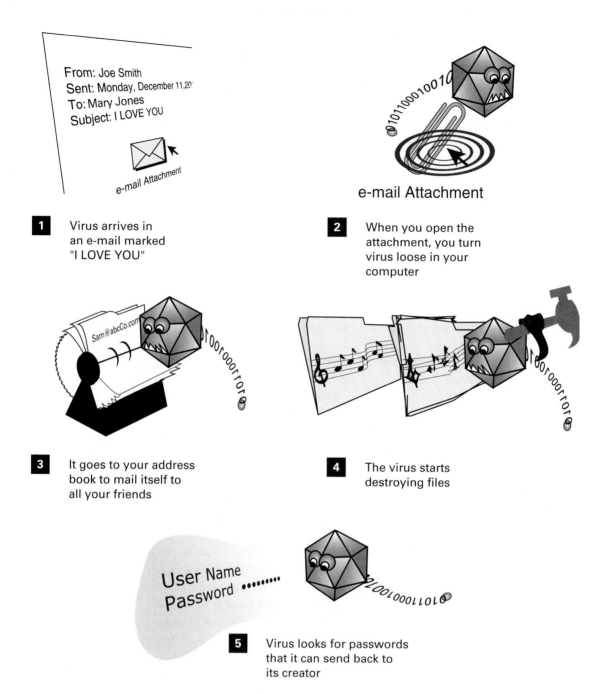

From: Joe Smith
Sent: Monday, December 11,20
To: Mary Jones
Subject: I LOVE YOU

e-mail Attachment

e-mail Attachment

1 Virus arrives in an e-mail marked "I LOVE YOU"

2 When you open the attachment, you turn virus loose in your computer

Sam@abcCo.com

3 It goes to your address book to mail itself to all your friends

4 The virus starts destroying files

User Name Password

5 Virus looks for passwords that it can send back to its creator

Figure H.3

The Love Bug Worm

The Love Bug has three objectives: to spread itself as far and as fast as it can, to destroy your files, and to gather passwords and other information (see Figure H.3). First, it spreads itself by mailing itself to everyone in your Outlook address book. (A previous worm of the same type named Melissa sent itself only to the first 50 people listed in Outlook's address book.) And, as if that weren't enough, it also uses your Internet chat software to spread itself to chat rooms.

Second, the Love Bug locates files on your computer that have certain extensions, .MP3 music files, .jpg picture files, .doc Word files, .xls Excel files, .wav sound files, .html browser files, and many others. Having found these files it wipes them out and puts itself in their place, appending .vbs to the end of the filename. For example, if you had a file called MySong.wav on your hard disk drive, the Love Bug virus would change the name to MySong.wav.vbs after it had done its dirty work.

Before it's done, the Love Bug worm changes your Internet Explorer start page and downloads a program that looks for passwords and network information, sending this information off by e-mail to the virus originator.[7]

There are at least 29 versions of the Love Bug virus. After people were warned not to open the LOVE LETTER attachment, the originators of the virus changed the name of it to something else. For example, one version is MOTHER'S DAY, and the body of the text says that the receiver has been charged hundreds of dollars for a Mother's Day "diamond special." You have to open the attachment to print the invoice, and then the virus goes into action.

The moral of the story is that you should be very careful about opening an attachment if you're not sure what it is and where it came from. That won't necessarily save you from all virus attacks, but it will certainly help a great deal.

SOBIG, SLAMMER, AND BLASTER

The year 2003 was called the "worst year ever" for viruses and worms. Among the biggest, in terms of cost and name recognition, were the SoBig virus and the Slammer and Blaster worms.

There are several variations of mass-mailer viruses, but the SoBig virus is probably the best known. On Tuesday, August 19, 2003, the SoBig virus began spreading through networks generating e-mail traffic at levels never seen before. It arrived as an attachment in the victim's inbox with varying subject lines like "Your details," "Your application," and "Wicked screensaver." When the recipient opened the attachment, the virus searched through hard drives for e-mail addresses in document files, cached Web pages, and Microsoft Outlook Express databases. Then it sent out huge numbers of useless e-mail messages. At its peak, security experts estimate that 1 out of every 17 e-mail messages carried the SoBig virus, even more than the Love Bug's 1 in 20. It was estimated that SoBig sent out a mass mailing from infected computers—there were about 100,000 of those—at the rate of one every 10 minutes.

Postini Inc., an e-mail management and screening company, intercepted 1.9 million SoBig e-mails on their way to the company's customers on the first day of the virus's activation. By the next day the volume had increased to 3.5 million.

Whirlpool, a company with $11 billion a year in sales, says that about 95 percent of its sales come through the Internet and that its fast response to protect its 20,000 computers and 800 servers saved the company from suffering much damage. Others weren't so lucky. Experts say that part of the reason that SoBig was so effective was that it incorporated a line in its header that said "X-Scanner: Found to be clean," fooling a popular anti-virus application that many Internet service providers use into letting the virus through.

SoBig was preprogrammed to stop replicating itself on September 10, 2003. By that time, it had infected more than 5 million e-mails. About eight times as many private computers were infected as corporate systems, since organizations moved faster to apply the patch that blocked the destruction.

Two of the many worms that hit networks in 2003 were the Slammer worm that hit in January and the Blaster worm that arrived in August. A worm looks for some flaw, or way to enter a computer, in software (often a Microsoft network operating system product) and sneaks in to do damage. Slammer kept flooding the victim server until its buffer memory was full, then it could trick that computer into sending out thousands of new copies to other servers that were vulnerable. Slammer sent out 55 million bursts of information per second onto the Internet and at that rate it took only 10 minutes for the worm to find and invade almost all the vulnerable servers. Microsoft had a patch (a way of plugging the entry point) available on its Web site, but if the network administrators didn't download and apply it, their networks remained vulnerable until they did.

The Blaster worm appeared only 26 days after Microsoft publicized the vulnerability that the worm utilized. Blaster spread like wildfire and among the thousands of companies that were affected were CSX, the third largest railroad company in North America, Amtrak, the commuter train company, and Air Canada. Passengers and freight in all three organizations experienced delays as their network traffic ground to a halt. Commuter trains in Washington, D.C., were delayed for two hours while IT experts worked feverishly to clean out the worm's effects while Air Canada's phone-reservation system and some check-in processes were slowed down.[8,9,10,11]

STAND-ALONE VIRUSES

In any given month, between 200 and 300 viruses are traveling from system to system around the world, seeking a way in to spread mayhem.[12] And they're getting more deadly. Whereas the Love Bug worm was a Visual Basic script virus (i.e., it needed Visual Basic to run), the latest worms can stand alone and run on any computer that can run Win32 programs (Windows 98 or later versions). Examples are SirCam, Nimda, and Klez. Nimda adds JavaScript to every home page on the server it infects, then passes it on to visitors to the site. Viruses of this independent type are very numerous.

The Klez virus is actually a family of worms that introduced a new kind of confusion into the virus business. They spoof e-mail addresses. *Spoofing* is the forging of the return address on an e-mail so that the e-mail message appears to come from someone other than the actual sender. Previous worms went to the recipient from the infected sender's computer and contained the infected person's return e-mail address. The worm found recipient addresses in the infected computer's address book.

Klez goes a step further and uses the address book to randomly find a return address as well as recipient addresses. The result is that people who are not infected with the virus get e-mail from the irate recipients and spend time looking for a virus they may not have. Even worse, some of the virus-laden e-mails look as though they came from a technical support person, leading an unsuspecting victim to open them, believing them to be safe.

TROJAN HORSE VIRUSES

A type of virus that doesn't replicate is a Trojan-horse virus. A *Trojan horse virus* hides inside other software, usually an attachment or download. The principle of any Trojan horse software is that there's software you don't want hidden inside software you do want. For example, Trojan horse software can carry the ping-of-death program that hides in a server until the originators are ready to launch a DoS attack to crash a Web site.

Key-logger software is usually available in Trojan horse form, so that you can hide it in e-mail or other Internet traffic. *Key logger,* or *key trapper, software* is a program that, when installed on a computer, records every keystroke and mouse click. Key logger software is used to snoop on people to find out what they're doing on a particular computer. You can find out more in Chapter 8.

MISLEADING E-MAIL

One type of misleading e-mail is a virus hoax. This is e-mail sent intending to frighten people about a virus threat that is, in fact, bogus. People who get such an alert will usually tell others, who react in the same way. The virus is nonexistent, but the hoax causes people to get scared and lose time and productivity. Within companies the losses can be very severe since computer professionals must spend precious time and effort looking for a nonexistent problem.

Following are some general guidelines for identifying a virus hoax.[13]

- Urges you to forward it to everyone you know, immediately.
- Describes the awful consequences of not acting immediately.
- Quotes a well-known authority in the computer industry.

These are signs that the e-mail is not meant to help but to cause harm. If you get such an e-mail, delete it immediately.

Another type of misleading e-mail is designed to get people to actually take action that results in setting a virus loose or to do something that will disrupt the functioning of their own computers. The first step is usually to make people believe that they have inadvertently e-mailed a virus to others. They get a message (maybe it purports to come from Microsoft) that they have sent out a virus and that they need to run an attached program or delete a file to fix the problem. They then do what the e-mail says believing it to be genuine, and furthermore, they e-mail everyone they sent messages to telling them about the problem. The recipients e-mail the people in their address books and so on. Be advised that Microsoft *never* sends out attachments in any official e-mail in a public mass mailing. It's possible that Microsoft may e-mail you warning you of a problem, but it will only indicate where you can download a file to take care of it. Before you delete a file from your computer, which may be an important system file without which your computer can't function, ask someone who knows or check out the various Web sites that keep up with the latest viruses, like www.symantec.com.

DENIAL-OF-SERVICE ATTACKS

Many organizations have been hit with denial-of-service attacks. *Denial-of-service (DoS) attacks* flood a server or network with so many requests for service that it slows down or crashes. The objective is to prevent legitimate customers from getting into the site to do business. There are several types of DoS attacks. A DoS attack can come from a lone computer that tries continuously to access the target computer, or from many, perhaps even thousands, of computers simultaneously. The latter is called a distributed denial-of-service attack and is considerably more devastating.

DISTRIBUTED DENIAL-OF-SERVICE ATTACKS

Distributed denial-of-service (DDos) attacks are attacks from multiple computers that flood a server or network with so many requests for service that it slows down or crashes. A common type is the Ping of Death, in which thousands of computers try to access a Web site at the same time, overloading it and shutting it down. A ping attack can also bring down the firewall server (the computer that protects the network), giving free access to the intruders. E*Trade, Amazon.com, and Yahoo!, among others, have been victims of this nasty little game. The process is actually very simple (see Figure H.4 on the next page).

The plan starts with the hackers planting a program in network servers that aren't protected well enough. Then, on a signal sent to the servers from the attackers, the program activates and each server "pings" every computer. A ping is a standard operation that networks use to check that all computers are functioning properly. It's a sort of roll call for the network computers. The server asks, "Are you there?" and each computer in turn answers, "Yes, I'm here." But the hacker ping is different in that the return address of the are-you-there? message is not the originating server, but the intended victim's server. So on a signal from the hackers, thousands of computers try to access E*Trade or Amazon.com, to say "Yes, I'm here." The flood of calls overloads the online companies' computers and they can't conduct business.

For many companies, a forced shutdown is embarrassing and costly but for others it's much more than that. For an online stockbroker, for example, denial-of-service attacks can be disastrous. It may make a huge difference whether you buy shares of stock today or tomorrow. And since stockbrokers need a high level of trust from customers to do business, the effect of having been seen to be so vulnerable is very bad for business.

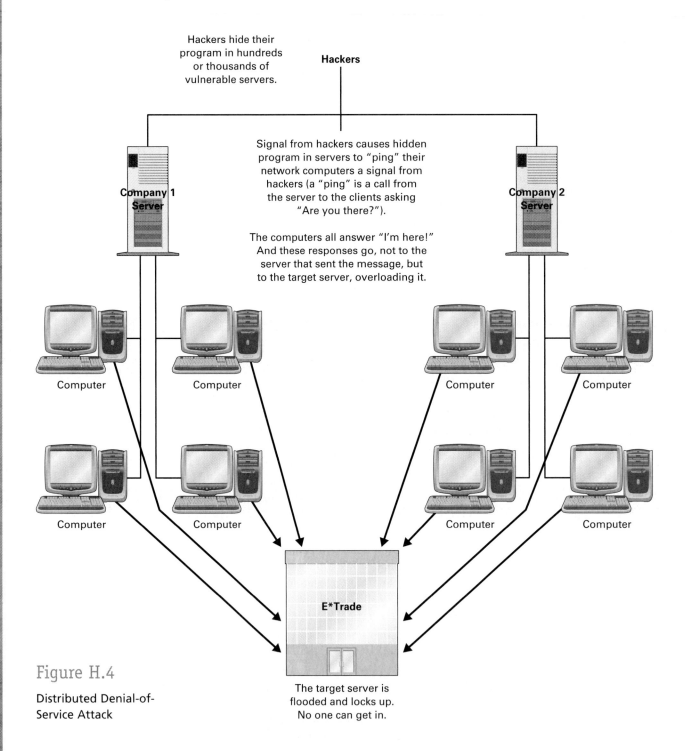

Hackers hide their program in hundreds or thousands of vulnerable servers.

Hackers

Signal from hackers causes hidden program in servers to "ping" their network computers a signal from hackers (a "ping" is a call from the server to the clients asking "Are you there?").

The computers all answer "I'm here!" And these responses go, not to the server that sent the message, but to the target server, overloading it.

Company 1 Server

Company 2 Server

Computer   Computer   Computer   Computer

Computer   Computer   Computer   Computer

E*Trade

The target server is flooded and locks up. No one can get in.

Figure H.4

Distributed Denial-of-Service Attack

COMBINATION WORM/DOS

Code Red, discovered in 2001, was the first virus that combined a worm and DoS attack. Code Red attacked servers running a specific type of system software. It used e-mail address books to send itself to lots of computers, and it was very efficient, with the ability to infect as many as 500,000 new servers per day. Its first action was to deface the Web site it infected. Then it went about finding other servers to infect. The last part of the plan was for all the infected servers to attack the White House Web site and shut it down. Having been warned of the impending attack, the White House changed the IP address of its Web site. Before it was all over, Code Red cost an estimated $2.4 billion in prevention, detection, and cleanup even though it didn't destroy files or otherwise do much damage. However, this type of attack power is potentially very dangerous.

The Blaster worm in 2003 was also of the combination worm/DoS type. Blaster was programmed to launch a DoS against Microsoft's upgrade page on the Internet on August 16. Microsoft changed the address of its page so that the attempt would fail.

MALWARE BOTS

A vital component of the increase in the spread of viruses and denial-of-service attacks is the use of bots. A **bot** is a computer program that runs automatically. Bots (the term comes from robot) can perform all sorts of tasks, both good and evil. In Chapter 4, Decision Support and Artificial Intelligence, you saw how bots take the form of intelligent agents, finding information and automatically performing computer-related tasks. Two examples are bots or intelligent agents that continuously monitor networks to find a problem before it knocks out the network and shopping bots that find products and services on the Internet for you.

However, there's another class of bots—the bad kind. In *Extended Learning Module E, Network Basics,* you learned that bots are a type of malware. This type of bot is designed to distribute illegal copies of movies and music. They can be used to spread worms. Bots can hide in a target computer or network to be activated at a later time as part of a denial-of-service attack to bring down the network or cause some other kind of trouble.

Bots are also used for fraud or sabotage. **Malware bots** are bots that are used for fraud, sabotage, DoS attacks, or some other malicious purpose. For example, to keep clicking on an ad on a Web site, perhaps to distort the number of click-throughs. If you're hosting an ad for Google, Google will pay you for the number of people who click on that ad from your site and if you have a bot that clicks thousands of times, you can fraudulently increase your revenue. You can also use bots to sabotage a competitor's ad on a search site by clicking repeatedly. Since advertisers pay search sites based on the number of click-throughs, constant clicking that doesn't come from possible customers raises the advertiser's rates.

WEB DEFACING

Web defacing is a favorite sport of some of the people who break into computer systems. They replace the site with a substitute that's neither attractive nor complimentary (see Figure H.5 on the next page). Or perhaps they convert the Web site to a mostly blank screen with an abusive or obscene message, or the message may just read "So-and-so was here." In essence, Web site defacing is electronic graffiti, where a computer keyboard and mouse take the place of a paint spray can.

In 2000, during a flare-up in tensions between Israel and the Palestinians, Israelis defaced the Web sites of Hezbollah and Hamas. In retaliation, Palestinians brought down Israeli government sites and then turned their attention to Web sites of pro-Israeli groups in the United States.

Web site defacing is becoming increasingly popular, and sites that are accessed by many people worldwide are particular favorites. The *USA Today* Web site was attacked in July 2002, causing the newspaper to shut down the whole site for three hours to fix the problem. The hackers replaced several news stories on the site with bogus stories that were full of spelling errors. One story said that the Pope had called Christianity "a sham." The phony stories were only on the site for 15 minutes before they were spotted and the site was taken offline.[14]

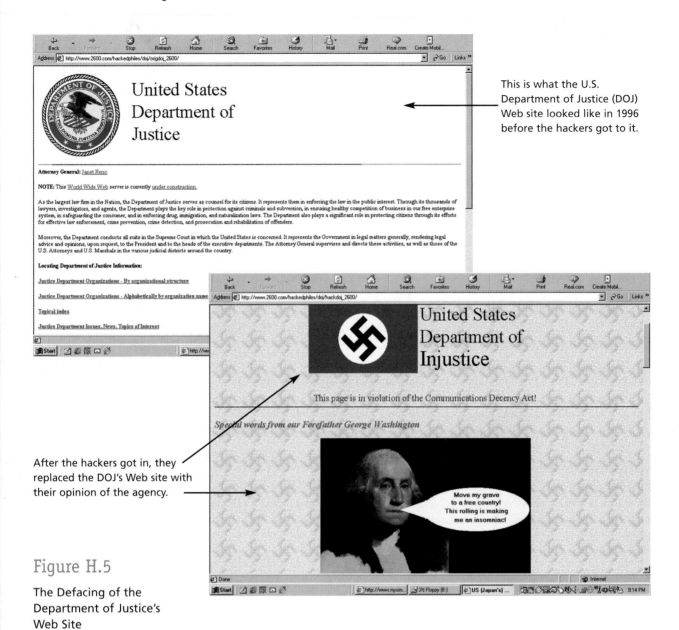

This is what the U.S. Department of Justice (DOJ) Web site looked like in 1996 before the hackers got to it.

After the hackers got in, they replaced the DOJ's Web site with their opinion of the agency.

Figure H.5

The Defacing of the Department of Justice's Web Site

THE PLAYERS

Who's spreading all this havoc? The answer is hackers. This is the popular name for people who break into computer systems. *Hackers* are knowledgeable computer users who use their knowledge to invade other people's computers. There are several categories of hackers, and their labels change over time. The important thing to note in the following discussion is that the motivation and reasons for hacking are as many and varied as the people who engage in it.

THRILL-SEEKER HACKERS

Thrill-seeker hackers break into computer systems for entertainment. Sometimes, they consider themselves to be the "good guys" since they expose vulnerabilities and some even follow a "hackers' code." Although they break into computers they have no right to access, they may report the security leaks to the victims. Their thrill is in being able to get into someone else's computer. Their reward is usually the admiration of their fellow hackers. There's plenty of information on the Web for those who want to know how to hack into a system—about 2,000 sites offer free hacking tools, according to security experts.

WHITE-HAT HACKERS

The thrill-seeker hackers used to be called white-hat hackers. But lately, the term *white-hat* is being increasingly used to describe the hackers who legitimately, with the knowledge of the owners of the IT system, try to break in to find and fix vulnerable areas of the system. These **white-hat hackers,** or **ethical hackers** are computer security professionals who are hired by a company to break into a computer system, so as to find security lapses. These hackers are also called counter hackers, or penetration testers.

BLACK-HAT HACKERS

Black-hat hackers are cyber vandals. They exploit or destroy the information they find, steal passwords, or otherwise cause harm. They deliberately cause trouble for people just for the fun of it. They create viruses, bring down computer systems, and steal or destroy information.

A 16-year-old black-hat hacker was sentenced to detention for six months after he hacked into military and NASA networks. He caused the systems to shut down for three weeks. He intercepted more than 3,000 e-mails and stole the names and passwords of 19 defense agency employees. He also downloaded temperature and humidity control software worth $1.7 billion that helps control the environment in the international space station's living quarters.[15]

CRACKERS

Crackers are hackers for hire and are the people who engage in electronic corporate espionage. This can be a pretty lucrative undertaking, paying up to $1 million per gig. Typically an espionage job will take about three weeks and may involve unpleasant tasks like dumpster diving to find passwords and other useful information and "social engineering." **Social engineering** is conning your way into acquiring information that you have no right to. Social engineering methods include calling someone in a company and pretending to be a technical support person and getting that person to type in a login and password, sweet talking an employee to get information, and for difficult jobs, perhaps even setting up a fake office and identity. Often when crackers have accumulated about $500 million, they retire to some country that doesn't have an extradition agreement with the country they cracked in.[16]

HACKTIVISTS

Hacktivists are politically motivated hackers who use the Internet to send a political message of some kind. The message can be a call to end world hunger, or it can involve an alteration of a political party's Web site so that it touts another party's candidate. It can be a slogan for a particular cause or some sort of diatribe inserted into a Web site to mock a particular religious or national group.

Hacktivism, in the form of Web defacing, is becoming a common response to disagreements between nations. When the U.S. military plane made an emergency landing in China and a dispute arose about the return of the crew and plane, U.S. hackers started to attack Chinese Web sites, and Chinese hackers returned the favor, targeting government-related sites.

CYBERTERRORISTS

Since the September 11, 2001, terrorist attacks on New York and the Pentagon, officials have become increasingly worried about the threat of *cyberterrorists.* This group of hackers, like the hacktivists, is politically motivated, but its agenda is more sinister. A **cyberterrorist** is one who seeks to cause harm to people or destroy critical systems or information. Possible targets of violent attacks would be air traffic control systems and nuclear power plants, and anything else that could harm the infrastructure of a nation.

MAKE UP A GOOD PASSWORD

One way to protect files, folders, entry into stock trading, banking, and other sites is to have a good password. That's the theory anyway. The problem is that most people choose passwords that are easy to remember, and consequently they're easy for others, who perhaps have malevolent intentions, to crack. Others write passwords down, which makes them very accessible to anyone who comes near your desk. Often hackers can get access to a server by way of a legitimate user's ID and password.

Another problem that companies face is that people seem to be unaware of how important it is to keep passwords secret. In a London underground (subway) station, an experiment was conducted in which commuters were offered a cheap pen if they would disclose the password to their company's system. A very large number of people took the deal. Of course, there's no way to know whether they actually gave their real passwords or not, but based on other studies, it's not unlikely that they did.

ZDNet offers some good advice on picking passwords. You should never pick a password that has a word from any dictionary, or one that is a pet's name or a person's. Instead, you should pick a phrase and use the first letter of each word. Then capitalize some letters and substitute punctuations and digits for others.

For example, the saying "just hang loose, just have fun, you only live once" would become JhL?H6+oLo. If you can remember the mnemonic and your substitutions, you'll certainly have a password that will be hard to break.

To find out about breaking passwords, look on the Web for information about "Jack the Ripper," which is a well-known password-cracking program. Find three more password-cracking programs and note whether they're public domain, freeware, shareware, or whether you have to pay for them. At www.elcomsoft.com you'll find all sorts of password crackers for Microsoft and other popular products. The stated purpose of this site is to help you recover lost corporate files. What other "helpful" products do this and what do other similar sites have and what do they do?

At a less lethal level, cyberterrorist acts would include shutting down e-mail or even part of the Internet itself, or destroying government records, say, on social security benefits or criminals.

However, the FBI and other government agencies are very much aware of the threats they face from computer-based attacks, and have taken steps to protect the infrastructure that supports cyberspace. They can enjoy a reasonable expectation of success since a computer system is a lot easier to protect than public structures like buildings and bridges.

SCRIPT KIDDIES

Script kiddies or *script bunnies* are people who would like to be hackers but don't have much technical expertise. They download click-and-point software that automatically does the hacking for them. An example of this was the young man in Holland who found a virus toolkit on the Web and started the Kournikova worm. It was very similar to the Love Bug worm in that it sent itself to all the people in the Outlook address book. Tens of millions of people got the virus after opening the attachment hoping to see a picture of Anna Kournikova.[17]

The concern about script kiddies, according to the experts, apart from the fact that they can unleash viruses and denial-of-service attacks, is that they can be used by more sinister hackers. These people manipulate the script kiddies, egging them on in chat rooms, encouraging and helping them to be more destructive.

DIGITAL SIGNATURES AND CERTIFICATES

Digital signatures are a way of protecting electronic messages, like e-mails, on their journey through cyberspace. They are antitampering devices. The basis of a digital signature is that a set of characters in the message is used in arithmetic operations to generate a unique "key" for that message. When the message arrives, the recipient repeats the operations in the exact order. The result should be the original key. If it's not, then the message has been tampered with.

Digital signatures are often used in conjunction with digital certificates. What are digital certificates? Do some research and write a one-page report on digital certificates and how they're used.

INSIDE THE ORGANIZATION

There are plenty of attacks visited on an organization's computer system from outside the organization but insider fraud and embezzlement are where the big bucks are lost. You can find more information on insider crime in Chapter 8.

Along with the traditional crimes of fraud and other types of theft managers sometimes have to deal with harassment of one employee by another. Chevron Corporation and Microsoft settled sexual harassment lawsuits for $2.2 million each because employees sent offensive e-mail to other employees and management didn't intervene. Other companies such as Dow Chemical Company, Xerox, the New York Times Company, and Edward Jones took preemptive action by firing people who sent or stored pornographic or violent e-mail messages.

But companies have learned to be careful when investigating harassment complaints, as the following example from Walt Manning's case files shows. One company had a complaint from a woman who claimed a male colleague was sending her offensive e-mail. The colleague denied it, but when his computer was checked, the pornographic pictures that the woman claimed she had received from him in e-mails were found. This could have meant his dismissal. But, fortunately for the man, a computer forensics expert was called in. The expert looked beyond the pictures and discovered that the times and dates the e-mails were downloaded and sent corresponded with times the man was out of town. Later, the woman admitted that she had downloaded the pictures and e-mailed them to herself from the man's computer. If the company hadn't been as thorough in its investigation, it could have escaped a harassment lawsuit only to find itself facing a wrongful termination lawsuit. So what exactly did the computer forensics expert do? We'll discuss that in the next two sections.

Computer Forensics

You may remember some of the following recent news stories:

- In November 2004, Scott Peterson was convicted of killing his wife Laci and the couple's unborn son, Connor. Both bodies washed ashore separately in San Francisco Bay during April of 2003. While gathering evidence to solve the crime, police had searched the hard drives of four computers in the Petersons' home. On a notebook computer they found that someone had examined maps, fishing reports, and charts of water currents in the Bay Area just before Laci disappeared. Someone at the couple's home, presumably Scott, had also done searches for keywords—divorce, silencer, and shooter—within a couple of minutes of checking the Petersons' joint e-mail account, at a point in time when prosecutors speculated that Laci was already dead.

- A search that ended on March 5, 2002, found 339 discarded bodies on the grounds of Tri-State Funeral home in Walker County. Ray Brent Marsh was formally charged with multiple counts of abusing a corpse and almost two hundred counts of fraud for allegedly taking money for cremations that were not performed and for giving loved ones fake remains. Photos of the dead bodies arranged in lewd poses appeared on the Internet.

- An engineer left Company A and went to Company B. Company A suspected that he had illegally brought intellectual property in the form of designs to his new employer. On his home computer, investigators found evidence that this was true. The engineer claimed that the clock on his home computer had malfunctioned and that the transfer of the designs occurred during the course of his work for Company A. However, his girlfriend's computer and a letter he wrote about the same time exposed this lie.[18]

- A *USA Today* veteran reporter was discovered to have fabricated many of his stories over the period 1993 to 2003. Furthermore, an examination of his company-owned computer revealed pieces that he had written to mislead investigators. This finding indicated consciousness of guilt.[19]

What all of these news stories have in common is the investigative technique that unearthed information—the process of the finding, examining, and analyzing electronic information saved on computer storage media. This process is called *computer forensics*. Many computer forensic investigations involve intellectual property cases, where a company believes that an employee is secretly copying and perhaps selling proprietary information like schematics, customer lists, financial statements, product designs, or notes on private meetings. Other investigations involve child exploitation, domestic disputes, labor relations, and employee misconduct cases. In all such cases, computer forensics is usually the appropriate response strategy.

Computer forensics is the collection, authentication, preservation, and examination of electronic information for presentation in court. Electronic evidence can be found on any type of computer media, such as hard disks, floppy disks, or CDs and also on digital cameras, PDAs, cell phones, and pagers. Computer forensic experts are trained in finding and interpreting electronic evidence to discover or reconstruct computer-related activities.

There are basically two motivations for engaging in computer forensics. The first is to gather and preserve evidence to present in court. The second is to establish what activities have occurred on a computer, often for the purposes of a dispute settlement. You probably know that if you're going to court, you must meet different evidentiary standards for criminal and civil cases. In criminal cases, the standard is "beyond a reasonable doubt." In civil cases, it's the "preponderance of evidence." If you don't have to, and don't want to, involve the legal system, your standard can be lower, perhaps just enough to release someone from employment while reducing the risk of being caught in a wrongful termination lawsuit.

In a well-conducted computer forensics investigation, there are two major phases: (1) collecting, authenticating, and preserving electronic evidence; and (2) analyzing the findings.

THE COLLECTION PHASE

Step one of the collection phase is to get physical access to the computer and related items. Thus, the computer forensic team collects computers, disks, printouts, post-it notes, and so on and takes them back to the lab. This process is similar to what police do when investigating crime in the physical world, collecting hair, clothing fibers, blood-stained articles, papers, and anything else that they think might be useful. The crime investigators usually take these potential clue carriers with them and secure them under lock and key, where only authorized personnel may have access, and even they must sign in and out.

Computer forensic experts use the same kind of protocol. To conduct a thorough investigation, they first take digital photos of the surrounding environment and start developing extensive documentation. Then they start collecting anything that might store information. The hard disk is an obvious place to look, but computer forensic investigators also collect any other media where information might be stored (see Figure H.6). If they can't take a clue source with them, they secure it and create an exact copy of the contents of the original media.

As well as electronic media, investigators collect any other potentially helpful items, especially passwords, for use in case any of the files they come across are encrypted or are otherwise difficult to access. Apparently, a favorite hiding place for passwords that people write down (which you should *not* do) is under the keyboard, so that's the first place that investigators look. Then they look in desk drawers and anywhere else that passwords might be, perhaps on post-it notes or slips of paper. Other helpful items might be printouts and business cards of associates or contacts of the person being investigated.

Step two of the collection process is to make a forensic image copy of all the information. A ***forensic image copy*** is an exact copy or snapshot of the contents of an electronic medium. It is sometimes referred to as a bit-stream image copy. To get a forensic image copy, specialized forensic software copies every fragment of information, bit-by-bit, on every storage medium—every hard disk (if there's more than one), every floppy disk, every CD, every Zip disk. That's usually a lot of stuff. Remember that a CD holds about a half gigabyte of information, and you can build a hard disk array (several hard disks tied together into one unit) that holds a terabyte (one trillion bytes) or more. It can take

- Floppy disks

- CDs

- DVDs

- Zip disks

- Backup tapes of other media

- USB mass storage devices such as Thumb drives

- Flash memory cards, like an xD-Picture card, CompactFlash card, or similar storage medium for digital cameras and other devices

- Voice mail

- Electronic calendars

- Scanners

- Photocopiers

- Fax machines

Figure H.6

Where You Might Find Electronic Evidence

a long, long time to copy it all. And the investigator must be able to swear in court that he or she supervised the entire copying process, and that no one and nothing interfered with the evidence. This could mean sitting in the lab literally for days just copying files. Also, many experts advise that the investigator make two copies of everything in case there's a problem later with the first copy.

THE AUTHENTICATION AND PRESERVATION PROCESS

To get a forensic image copy of hard disk and other media contents, investigators physically remove the hard disk from the computer. They never turn the suspect computer on, because when the PC is turned on, Windows performs more than 400 changes to files. Access dates change, and so do temporary files, and so on. So, once turned on, the hard drive is no longer exactly the same as it was when it was shut down.[20] Thus, opposing counsel could argue that this is not the same hard disk that the suspect used.

Having removed the hard disk, investigators connect it to a special forensic computer that can read files but can't write or rewrite any medium. (They prefer to remove storage devices, but if that's not possible, they copy the contents in place using cables.) Then they use forensic software like EnCase to extract a forensic image copy of the original medium without changing the files in any way.

How do we know that nothing changed on any disk during the entire investigation, from the time the computer was seized up to the present time? That's the question that opposing counsel will ask the computer forensic expert on the witness stand. So, during the collection phase and later, the analysis phase, the investigators have to make absolutely sure that evidence to be used in a trial could not have been planted, eliminated, contaminated, or altered in any way. This is a basic evidentiary rule for all court proceedings. They have to be able to document a chain of custody and be able to account for the whereabouts and protection of evidence. To help establish a complete chronology of activity, investigators also check the BIOS, which a computer uses to time and date stamp files and actions like deleting, updating, and so on.

In a computer forensic investigation, investigators use an authentication process so that they can show sometime in the future—perhaps even two years later—that nothing changed on the hard drive or other storage medium since seizure. They can do this with an MD5 hash value. An *MD5 hash value* is a mathematically generated string of 32 letters and digits that is unique for an individual storage medium at a specific point in time. The MD5 hash value is based on the contents of that medium. Any change in the content changes the MD5 hash value.

A hash value is a seemingly meaningless set of characters. An example of a hash value would be the sum of the ISBNs and the number of pages in all the books on a bookstore shelf. The result, which would be a mixture of ISBN codes and quantities of pages, would be meaningless for anything except identification. If a book, or even a page, were added to or removed from the shelf, the hash total would change, so the contents of the shelf could be shown not to be the same as they were when the hash value was originally computed. Similarly, adding so much as one space in one tiny Word document on a disk will change the MD5 hash value. See Figure H.7 for an example of an MD5 hash value generated by EnCase forensic software.

MD5 hash values are considered very reliable and have become an industry standard accepted by the FBI, the U.S. Marshall Service, and most other law enforcement authorities, as well as private professional firms, as a way of uniquely authenticating a set of contents on a particular storage medium. This confidence in MD5 hash values is based on the fact that the probability of two hard disks with different contents having the same MD5 hash value is 1 in 10 to the 38th power: that's 1 with 38 zeros behind it. This makes the MD5 hash value a sort of DNA or fingerprint for computer media contents.

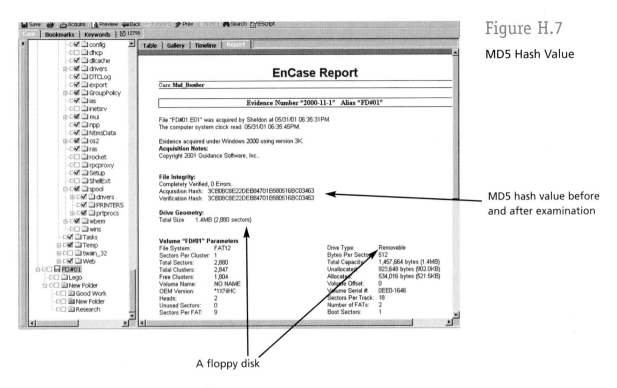

Figure H.7

MD5 Hash Value

MD5 hash value before and after examination

A floppy disk

Actually, it's more reliable than those physiological identifiers, since the probability of two sets of hard disk contents resulting in the same MD5 hash value are less than the odds of two individuals' DNA and fingerprints being identical. As an example of this probability, consider that you would have better odds of winning the Powerball lottery 39 times in your lifetime than you would of finding two hard disks with different contents that have matching MD5 hash values.

FORENSIC HARDWARE AND SOFTWARE TOOLS

As we've already mentioned, computer forensic experts use special hardware and software to conduct investigations. Usually the computer system has more power than the standard computer on a desktop and much more RAM, as well as much more hard disk capacity. This is to speed up the copying and analysis process. Computer forensic experts are also very careful not to let static electricity cause any damage or changes to magnetic media (like hard disks, Zips, and floppies). Therefore they use nonconductive mats under all computer parts, and wear wristbands that connect by wire to the ground of an electrical outlet. And just in case they need a tool, such as a screwdriver, they have a special nonmagnetic set of tools nearby, too.

There are many kinds of software in a computer forensics toolkit, in addition to forensic software, that can help in computer forensic investigations. Quick View Plus, used by many forensic experts, is an example. This is software that will load Word, Excel, image, and many other file formats. If it comes across a file with an .xls extension, which is actually an image and not a spreadsheet file, Quick View will show the file as an image regardless of its extension. That saves the investigator having to try it in multiple programs after loading fails in Excel. Conversions Plus is a package that does the same sort of thing. Other helpful software includes Mailbag Assistant, which reads many e-mail formats, and IrfanView, which is an image viewer that will read most picture files.

For investigations that might be headed toward litigation, computer forensic experts often use EnCase, since it's widely accepted as robust and reliable. EnCase has routinely been judged acceptable by the courts in meeting the legal standard for producing reliable evidence.

THE ANALYSIS PHASE

The second phase of the investigation is the analysis phase when the investigator follows the trail of clues and builds the evidence into a crime story. This is the phase that really tests the skill and experience of the investigators. The analysis phase consists of the recovery and interpretation of the information that's been collected and authenticated. If all the necessary files were there in plain sight with names and extensions indicating their contents, life would be much easier for the forensic investigator, but that's seldom the case. Usually, particularly if those being investigated know that they're doing something wrong, the incriminating files will have been deleted or hidden.

Investigators can recover all of a deleted file pretty easily as long as no new information has been written to the space where the file was. But they can also recover fragments—perhaps rather large fragments—of files in parts of a disk where new files have been written, but have not completely filled the space where the old file was. With the appropriate software they can recover files or fragments of files from virtually any part of any storage medium (see Figure H.8).

Computer forensic programs can pinpoint a file's location on the disk, its creator, the date it was created, the date of last access, and sometimes the date it was deleted, as well as file formatting, and notes embedded or hidden in a document (see Figure H.9).

Also stored on the hard disk is information about where the computer user went on the Web. For example, every graphic image you view on the Internet is copied to your hard disk, usually without your knowledge. In addition, Web servers have information on which computer connected to the Web and when. The same server can also tell you the sites visited by the user of that computer, the date and time of the visits, and the actions of the user at the site. These attributes are useful if the suspect claims to have reached an inappropriate site by accident, since delving deeper into the site implies a deliberate action. And, of course, if a password was required to reach the material in question, you can rest your case.

Figure H.8

Some of the Files Recoverable from Storage Media

E-Mail Files
• E-mail messages
• Deleted e-mail messages
Program Files and Data Files
• Word (.doc) and backup (.wbk) files
• Excel files
• Deleted files of all kinds
• Files hidden in image and music files
• Encrypted files
• Compressed files
Web Activity Files
• Web history
• Cache files
• Cookies
Network Server Files
• Backup e-mail files
• Other backup and archived files
• System history files
• Web log files

History of File Activity

File marked as deleted

Details of where files are located on the disk, whether they've been deleted, overwritten, or archived

Information on whether the contents matches the extension or not

Recovery and Interpretation

As with all evidence, the analysis of the electronic clues and the assembling of the pieces into a credible and likely scenario of what happened are very important. Much of the information may come from recovered deleted files, currently unused disk space, and deliberately hidden information or files. Some people's e-mail that was recovered to their extreme embarrassment (or worse) but arguably to society's benefit is shown in Figure H.10.

Following is a discussion, not necessarily exhaustive, of places from which computer forensic experts can recover information.

PLACES TO LOOK FOR USEFUL INFORMATION

Information is written all over a disk, not only when you save a file, but also when you create folders, print documents, repartition the disk, and so on. System and application software alike continually create temporary files resulting in space and file locations being rearranged. Leftover information stays on the disk until another file writes over it, and is often recoverable with forensic software. Next, we'll examine three places where files or file remnants could be: slack space, unallocated disk space, and unused disk space.

DELETED FILES AND SLACK SPACE

It's actually not very easy to get rid of electronically stored information completely. A surprising number of people think that if they delete a file it's gone. It's not—at least not immediately, and perhaps never. When you delete a file, all you're actually doing is marking it as deleted in the disk's directory. The actual file contents are not affected *at all* by a delete action.

Figure H.10

Recovered E-mail
Messages

" . . . something could get screwed up enough . . . and
then you are in a world of hurt . . . "

and

"I can only hope the folks . . . are listening . . . "

Excerpts of e-mail traffic
that flew back and forth
only two days before the
February 1, 2003,
Columbia shuttle disaster,
in which an engineer
discussed his misgivings
about the possibility of a
disaster

To: David B. Duncan
Cc: Michael C. Odom@ANDERSEN WO: Richard Corgci@ANDERSEN WO
BCC:
Date: 10/16/2001 08:39 PM
From: Nancy A. Temple
Subject: Re: Press Release draft
Attachments: ATT&ICIQ: 3rd qtr press release memo.doc

Dave - Here are a few suggested comments for consideration.

- I recommend deleting reference to consultation with the legal group and deleting my
name on the memo. Reference to the legal group consultation arguably is a waiver of
attorney-client privileged advice and if my name is mentioned it increases the chances
that I might be a witness, which I prefer to avoid.

- I suggested deleting some language that might suggest we have concluded the
release is misleading.

- In light of the "non-recurring" characterization, the lack of any suggestion that this
characterization is not in accordance with GAAP, and the lack of income statements in
accordance with GAAP, I will consult further within the legal group as to whether we
should do anything more to protect ourselves from potential Section 10A issues.

One of the "smoking
gun" e-mails that helped
sink Andersen Consulting
and Enron

From the arresting
officer in the Rodney
King beating

"oops I haven't beaten anyone so bad in a
long time...."

" . . . do we have a clear plan on what we
want Apple to do to undermine Sun . . . ?"

From Bill Gates in an
intraoffice e-mail about
a competitor in the
Microsoft antitrust action

If you delete a file from a hard disk you usually get a message asking you if you want
it in the *Recycle Bin* and then you can recover it simply by using the *Undelete* option. On
a removable medium, like a Zip or floppy disk, it's a little harder, but not much. The message you get asks whether you're sure you want to delete the file because it may not be
recoverable. Actually that message should read "not as easily recoverable as files in the
recycle bin," since you can get it back with utility programs such as Norton Utilities, and
of course, forensic software.

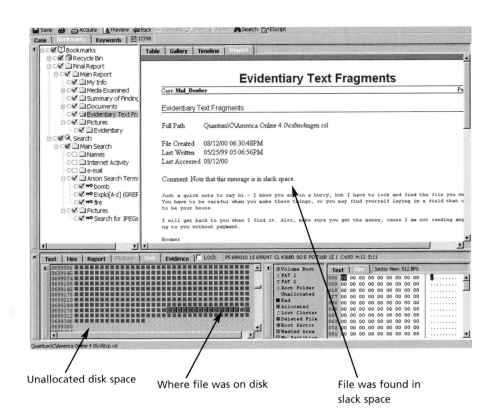

Unallocated disk space

Where file was on disk

File was found in
slack space

When you mark a file as deleted, the space is freed up for use by some other file. So, another file may shortly be written to that space. However, it's not quite that straightforward. The operating system divides storage space into sectors of bytes or characters. The sectors are grouped into clusters. A file is assigned a whole number of clusters for storage, whether it completely fills the last cluster or not. This storage allocation method usually leaves unused portions of clusters. This is analogous to writing a three and one-half page report. You'd have to use the top half of the fourth page and leave the rest of the page blank. So, the fourth page is allocated to the report but not completely used. If the previously stored file (the deleted one) was bigger and used that last part of the space, then the remnants of the deleted file remain and can be recovered using the appropriate software. The space left over from the end of the file to the end of the cluster is called **slack space,** and information left there from previous files can be recovered by forensic software (see Figure H.11).

SYSTEM AND REGISTRY FILES

Operating system files manage the hardware and software of your computer and let your application software access hardware without having to know how all the various types of hardware function. As one of its many functions, the operating system controls virtual memory. Virtual memory is hard disk space that is used when RAM is full. Details of virtual memory activity are stored in system files. For example, if you have several applications running and you're instant messaging someone, that exchange may be stored on the hard disk without your knowing it simply because there wasn't room for it in RAM.

The Registry is the database that Windows uses to store configuration information. Registry files have information such as preferences for users of the system, settings for the hardware, system software, and installed programs. This information can be very valuable. For example, even if you uninstall a program, remnants of the install process remain in the registry file. Registry files also contain the MAC (Media Access Control) address, which is a special ID for a computer on a network. When this MAC address is contained in a file, as it is in a Word document, it links that document file to its "owner" computer.

UNALLOCATED DISK SPACE

If your hard disk gets a lot of use, it's probable that each sector has had information put into it many times. The operating system is always moving files around, and if you changed a Word file and resaved it, the previous version is marked as deleted and the space becomes unallocated. *Unallocated space* is the set of clusters that has been marked as available to store information, but has not yet received a file, or still contains some or all of a file marked as deleted. Until the new information takes up residence, the old information remains. The bigger the hard disk, the longer it usually takes for old space to be used.

UNUSED DISK SPACE

Unused space results from rearranging disk space. For example, when a hard drive is repartitioned, the new partitioning may not use all the space on the hard disk. So, again, those unused portions are not overwritten. The partition table and other operating system information are stored on their own tracks and are not visible under normal circumstances, but may have once stored a Word document. To be able to see the fragments of files tucked away in these tracks the user needs forensic software.

ERASED INFORMATION

By now you may be asking whether it's possible to completely erase information from a storage medium. It is possible, but you need to know what you're doing. You can get disk-wiping programs that erase information from a disk by writing nonsense information over the previous contents. Utilities like Norton have this feature. However, erasing a disk takes a lot of time. A 10-gigabyte hard disk (not very big) would take several hours to clean. Even then you're not necessarily safe, for three reasons:

- A single overwrite may not erase the information completely. The Department of Justice recommends that government agencies write over old information seven times to be sure it's completely gone.
- Some programs keep track of what was deleted by whom, and that record is viewable if you know where to look.
- Disk-wiping programs vary greatly in which parts of the hard disk they clean. For most of them, you have to change the settings to reach certain parts of the disk. Some claim to go through the wipe process up to 35 times, but that still doesn't erase the areas that the software isn't set to erase. Also keep in mind that if you're trying to erase information because of some illicit activity, traces may still be left of the information you're trying to discard, and unless you are very careful, you'll leave traces of your attempt to wipe the disk. At the very least, you'll most likely leave a record in the Registry that you installed the wiping program.

WAYS OF HIDING INFORMATION

There are many ways of deliberately hiding information (other than deleting the file) and some are easy to defeat and others are not so easy. Following is a sampling of methods that people use to try to hide files.

RENAME THE FILE

The simplest, and most easily detected, way of deliberately hiding a file in Windows is to change the extension of the file. Say you had an Excel file that had calculations you didn't want anyone to know about, you could name the file Space Needle.jpg. Then it would appear in Explorer in the list of files as a .jpeg image file, with the name implying that it's just a vacation photo or something else innocuous.

However, if you try to click on that file, Windows will try to load it with the default .jpg viewer. And, of course, it won't load. What computer forensic experts usually do is load the file into a program that accommodates many file formats. This way, you save a lot of time trying to load the renamed file into lots of different types of software. Even more helpful is a forensic tool like EnCase that actually flags files with extensions that don't match the contents and also show files in their true formats.

MAKE THE INFORMATION INVISIBLE

They always say that the best hiding place is in plain sight. A very simple way to hide information inside a file, say a Word document, is to make the information the same color as the background. This works in Excel and other types of files, too. So if you suspect that something interesting is hidden this way, you could check the size of the file to see if it looks consistent with the contents. Also, software like EnCase is not affected by formatting. So, even white-on-white text will be easily searchable and readable by the forensic investigator.

USE WINDOWS TO HIDE FILES

Windows has a utility to hide files of a specific type. You simply open up that drive or folder, choose *View,* then *Options,* and hide the files by indicating what extensions you want hidden. If you go through this process, you'll probably see that there's a list of hidden files already on your computer. These are files that have to do with the correct functioning of your computer and to list them would just clutter up Windows Explorer and risk their being changed or deleted by accident. Again, forensic software takes special note of hidden files and flags them for further investigation.

PROTECT THE FILE WITH A PASSWORD

Word lets you password protect files so that when someone tries to open the file a pop-up window asks for the password. Unless you know the password, you won't be able to read the file. Forensic software can view the contents of many file types without opening the file, eliminating the effectiveness of many types of password protection.

ENCRYPT THE FILE

Encryption scrambles the contents of a file so that you can't read it without the right decryption key. Often investigators can find the decryption key in a password file or on a bit of paper somewhere around the keyboard. There are also password-cracking programs that will find many passwords very easily (alarmingly easily, in fact). They have dictionaries of words from multiple languages, so whole words from any language are not hard to crack. Some people put a digit or two on the front or back of a word. That doesn't fool password-cracking programs at all.

Sometimes investigators can figure out passwords from knowing something about the person. That's why birthdays, anniversaries, children's or pets' names are not good passwords. Also, since you usually need passwords for lots of reasons and it's hard to remember lots of different random ones, many people use just two or three different passwords. So if investigators find one password, they can try that in multiple places. Also, having one password often offers a clue as to what the other passwords might be. For example, if one password an investigator discovers is a fragment of a nursery rhyme, then the others might be, too.

USE STEGANOGRAPHY

Steganography is the hiding of information inside other information. Paper money is a good example of steganography. If you hold a dollar bill up to the light you'll see a watermark. The watermark image is hidden inside the other markings on the bill, but can be viewed if you know what to do to see it.

Figure H.12

Steganography Hides a
File in an Image

You can't see the parts of the picture that were changed to encode the hidden
message. You'll only be able to access the hidden file when you put the right
password into a pop-up window.

You can electronically hide information using this method. For example, if you want
to hide a text file inside an image file, you can use a program called Steganos that does
the work for you. Steganos takes nonessential parts of the image and replaces them with
the hidden file. "Nonessential" means that these are parts of the picture that you can't
see anyway, so changing those to the hidden message makes the message invisible (see
Figure H.12). Steganography is a process similar to file compression, where nonessential information is removed to save space, rather than to hide it.

The FBI and other law enforcement agencies believe that worldwide terrorist networks
communicate using steganography. They set up a Web site and find pictures in which
they can hide messages. When the message is hidden, the innocent-looking picture goes
back up on the Web site. Fellow terrorists can download the picture, and open it with special software. With the correct password, the hidden message appears. Forensic investigators look for clues about steganography by searching for the names of steg programs.

COMPRESS THE FILE

Compressing a file makes it invisible to keyword searches. To find out what's in it you'll
have to decompress it with the right software or use a newer version of EnCase that reads
compressed files. This decompression software may be on the hard disk or on another
disk somewhere around the suspect's desk. That's why investigators take all media for
examination.

Who Needs Computer Forensics Investigators?

Computer forensics is widely used wherever and whenever the investigation of electronically stored files is warranted, such as:

- In the military, both as part of national security intelligence gathering and analysis and for internal investigations of military personnel.
- In law enforcement, when the FBI, state investigatory agencies, and local police departments need to gather electronic evidence for criminal investigations.
- Inside corporations or not-for-profit organizations, when conducting internal audits, for example, or investigating internal incidents.
- In consulting firms that specialize in providing computer forensic services to corporations and law enforcement.

Computer forensics experts work both proactively, educating and warning people about possible problems, and reactively, when they're called in to help in response to an incident. The need for such expertise is growing, especially considering that it is estimated that 93 percent of all information is generated in digital form. Since computing and investigative techniques are improving continuously, computer forensics experts need a forum to exchange ideas and information (see Figure H.13).

PROACTIVE COMPUTER FORENSICS EDUCATION FOR PROBLEM PREVENTION

Companies are increasingly providing proactive education for two reasons: first, to educate employees on what to do and not to do with computer resources and why; and second, to teach employees what to do if they suspect wrongdoing, and how not to make things worse by destroying evidence.

Professional organizations exist that support computer forensic experts in doing their jobs. The organizations below provide interaction between members who share information, experience, and methods. Such organizations also provide ethical guidelines and certification.

- IACIS (International Association of Computer Investigation Specialists) is open to law enforcement personnel and sets standards and guidelines for computer forensic investigations.
- ACFE (Association of Certified Fraud Examiners) focuses on serving those who investigate fraud. Members include people in law enforcement, auditors, accountants, and computer forensic experts.
- The HTCIA (High Technology Crime Investigation Association) is open to law enforcement and corporate investigators alike and facilitates the sharing of resources among its members.

A group called the Sedona Conference Working Group on Electronic Document Production published *The Sedona Principles: Best Practices, Recommendations & Principles for Addressing Electronic Document Production.* The document, the first draft of which emerged in 2003, is a new set of standards pertaining to properly conducting a computer forensic investigation. These principles were developed by lawyers, consultants, academics, and jurists to address the many issues involved in antitrust suits, intellectual property disputes, and other types of complex litigation.

Figure H.13

Professional Organizations and Standards

It's been said that what you don't know can't hurt you. That may be true in some circumstances but not in the cyber world. What you don't know about what happens on your computer can cause you all kinds of trouble. Test your knowledge about what goes on inside your computer. If someone asked you to respond as to the wisdom or foolishness of the following statements, what would you say (include explanations of your answers)?

1. My computer at work is safe, secure, and private.

2. When I delete a file from my hard disk, it's removed from the disk.

3. I'll be safe from any investigators as long as I use a disk-wiping program on my hard disk.

4. Computers store files only when you explicitly save them.

5. As long as I don't save the inappropriate images I view on the Web, no one will ever be the wiser.

6. Sending a joke from my work e-mail will be fine as long as I put a smiley face emoticon after it.

7. As long as I don't open e-mail attachments I don't recognize, I can't possibly get a virus.

People who use computers every day are often not very knowledgeable about what, when, and how information is stored on computers. For example, many corporations have strict policies on how long e-mails will be kept on the system (or in the form of backups). Usually the period of time is about 60 days. You might decide to save your e-mails on your hard disk so that you'll have them indefinitely. This might not be wise since the reason that companies have this policy is that should the company find itself involved in litigation, all electronic information, including e-mail, may be discoverable. That is, the company may have to hand it over to opposing counsel. The more there is, the more it costs to collect, organize, and deliver it.

In Chapter 8 you saw the Industry Perspective box detailing Enron's e-mail situation. Lots of personal information that was not directly related to the legal case became public information and was put on the Internet. See the nearby On Your Own project to see what you know about some basic issues that face employees.

The second reason for providing some education in computer forensics has to do with conducting internal investigations properly. Say a company wants to file a complaint with law enforcement about the suspected illegal activity of an employee. Before law enforcement can look into the situation, however, it needs to have sufficient cause to do so. It can happen that in collecting relevant information the company inadvertently contaminates or destroys the "crime scene." The result may be that law enforcement can't prosecute after all because of lack of evidence.

REACTIVE COMPUTER FORENSICS FOR INCIDENT RESPONSE

Companies need computer forensics, in a reactive mode, to track what employees have been doing with company resources. You saw in Chapter 8 that employees may be using the Internet to such an extent during working hours that their productivity is affected, and the level of personal traffic on the company network may be such that people who are actually working are slowed down. This is just one example of misuse of the company computer system. The evidence of such misappropriation of computer resources can be found on the system itself—on individual client computers and on the servers.

A second reason for reactive computer forensics is changes in laws and government regulations and new laws passed as a consequence of recent corporate crime and misbehavior, probably the most important being the Sarbanes-Oxley Act of 2002, signed into law by President Bush. Known as "Sarbanes-Oxley," the law requires companies to (1) implement extensive and detailed policies to prevent illegal activity within the company and (2) respond in a timely manner to investigate illegal activity.

The act expressly states that executives must certify that their financial statements are accurate. They will be held criminally liable for fraudulent reporting, removing the insulation that executives previously had of being able to say that they didn't know about misstatements. Sarbanes-Oxley also specifically requires publicly traded companies to provide anonymous hotlines so that employees and others can report suspicious activity.

The provision that suspicious activity must be investigated in a timely manner in many instances automatically requires computer forensics. In earlier litigation, courts have determined that computer-stored evidence is crucial to the proper investigation of alleged corporate fraud. Add to that the fact that delay in investigating alleged wrongdoing meets with severe penalties and that courts impose severe sanctions on those judged guilty of destroying evidence including electronic information.

A DAY IN THE LIFE OF A COMPUTER FORENSICS EXPERT

You may be considering computer forensics as a profession. If so, you're contemplating a vocation that's very demanding but very rewarding. You have to know a lot about computers, and you have to keep learning to keep up with the fast pace of the computer world. You have to have infinite patience and be very detail-oriented. You also have to be good at explaining to lawyers, juries, and other nonexperts how computers work. You have to be able to remain very cool under pressure and think fast since some of the situations you face will be quite adversarial. Lanny Morrow has these qualities.

Lanny is a computer forensics expert with the Forensic and Dispute Consulting division of BKD, LLP, one of the largest accounting firms in the United States. All sorts of organizations, both for-profit and not-for-profit, and legal firms needing detective work done inside computers hire BKD's computer forensics services called Data Probe.

Lanny's cases are many and varied, making his life very interesting. Some cases take a long time and others are resolved pretty fast like the divorce case where the wife believed that her husband was hiding assets and that the records were on their home computer. No one (wife, lawyers, friends) could find anything incriminating on the hard drive or on any other storage medium. But the wife was adamant that the records were there. Lanny was called in. His first step as always was to open up the computer and have a look inside to see if anything in there looked unusual. And there it was—a second hard drive that wasn't plugged in, and was just sitting inside the system unit. When the husband wanted to do his secret accounting, he just opened up the box and swapped hard disk connections, reversing the process when he was done.

Sometimes Lanny can save a reputation, rather than prove wrongdoing, as in the case of the popular schoolteacher. As a lark, some of the teacher's female students, who were using his computer, decided to search for .jpg image files. They found some pornography and were very upset. They told their parents who immediately contacted a lawyer who in turn contacted the school. The school's information technology staff confirmed that there were many pornographic pictures on the computer. The local media picked up the story and, as outrage spread across the community, the teacher was suspended. The teacher then hired a lawyer who called Lanny in to get the facts.

When Lanny investigated the computer, he found that things weren't quite as they seemed. Having looked at the dates and origins of the images, he found that these images had come as pop-ups in e-mails that the teacher had opened, but had viewed only for seconds. The teacher had not gone searching for this material and had not perused it when it arrived in his e-mail. The reason he even saw the pictures was that, instead of looking at the subject line of the e-mails (which, in many cases, specified the nature of the contents) and then choosing which ones to open, he had simply pushed the Next button to view his e-mail messages in order of arrival. The teacher was absolved of any wrongdoing and was subsequently reinstated.

A sales representative who changed jobs and was suspected by his former employer of stealing intellectual property didn't fare so well. The suspicious manager viewed all the videotape footage of the former employee coming in and going out of the building without finding anything suspicious. The other possibility was, of course, that the information had been spirited out electronically.

When he started looking into it, Lanny found a trail of where the former employee had been viewing customer lists, product specifications, and other information that he wouldn't have needed in the normal course of doing his job. Interestingly, these files had been accessed during the lunch hour and had left a trail showing that someone had been burning large numbers of files to a CD. The final confirmation was that when the CD copying box had popped up asking the employee whether he wanted to save his CD project to the hard disk, he inadvertently had answered "Yes" so that all the file names were saved to his hard disk in the *My Documents* folder. Having realized his mistake, the salesman deleted all these file names to the recycle bin where they were easily retrievable. The manager remarked that the employee had left with a dolly-load of information, not in the physical sense, of course, but with a more modern dolly in the form of a CD.

Summary: Student Learning Outcomes Revisited

1. **Define computer crime and list three types of computer crime that can be perpetrated from inside and three from outside the organization.** *Computer crime* is a crime in which a computer, or computers, played a significant part in its commission. Crimes perpetrated outside the organization include

   - *Computer viruses*
   - *Denial-of-service (DoS) attacks*
   - *Malware bots*
   - Web defacing
   - *Trojan-horse virus*

   Crimes perpetrated inside the organization include

   - Fraud
   - Embezzlement
   - Harassment

2. **Identify the seven types of hackers and explain what motivates each group.** *Hackers* are knowledgeable computer users who use their knowledge to invade other people's computers. The seven types are

   - *Thrill-seeker hackers,* who are motivated by the entertainment value of breaking into computers
   - *White-hat hackers,* who are hired by a company to find the vulnerabilities in its network
   - *Black-hat hackers,* who are cyber vandals and cause damage for fun
   - *Crackers,* who are hackers for hire and are the people who engage in electronic corporate espionage
   - *Hacktivists,* who are politically motivated hackers who use the Internet to send a political message of some kind
   - *Cyberterrorists,* who seek to cause harm to people or destroy critical systems or information for political reasons
   - *Script kiddies* or *script bunnies,* who would like to be hackers but don't have much technical expertise

3. **Define computer forensics and describe the two phases of a forensic investigation.**

Computer forensics is the collection, authentication, preservation, and examination of electronic information for presentation in court. Electronic evidence can be found on any type of computer storage medium. A computer forensic investigation has two phases: (1) collecting, authenticating, and preserving electronic evidence; and (2) analyzing the findings. The collection phase consists of

- Getting physical access to the computer and any other items that might be helpful
- Creating a *forensic image copy* of all storage media
- Authenticating the forensic image copy by generating an *MD5 hash value,* that, when recalculated at a later date will be the exact same number, as long as nothing at all on the storage medium has changed in any way
- Using forensic hardware that can read storage media but cannot write to them
- Using forensic software that can find deleted, hidden, and otherwise hard-to-access information

The analysis phase consists of

- Finding all the information and figuring out what it means
- Assembling a crime story that fits the information that has been discovered

4. **Identify and describe four places on a hard disk where you can find useful information.** The four places are

- *Slack space* which is the space left over from the end of the file to the end of the cluster
- System and registry files that have lots of information about your hardware, software, and files

- *Unallocated space,* which is the set of clusters that has been marked as available to store information
- Unused space that results from actions like repartitioning a disk

5. **Identify and describe seven ways of hiding information.** The seven ways of hiding information are

- Rename the file to make it look like a different type of file
- Make information invisible by making it the same color as the background
- Use the Windows operating system's hide utility to hide files
- Protect the file with a password, so that the person who wants to see the file must provide the password
- *Encrypt* the file, scrambling the contents of the file so you have to have the key to unscramble and read it
- Use *steganography* to hide a file inside another file
- Compress the file so that a keyword search can't find it

6. **Describe two ways in which corporations use computer forensics.** Corporations use computer forensics for proactive education and for reactive incident response. Education serves to explain to employees what they should and should not do with computer resources and also how to conduct an internal computer forensic investigation. Incident response involves uncovering employee wrongdoing and preserving the evidence so that action can be taken.

Key Terms and Concepts

Black-hat hacker, 401
Bot, 399
Computer crime, 392
Computer forensics, 404
Computer virus (virus), 393
Cracker, 401
Cyberterrorist, 401
Denial-of-service (DoS) attack, 397
Distributed denial-of-service (DDoS) attack, 397

Encryption, 413
Forensic image copy, 405
Hacker, 400
Hacktivist, 401
Key logger (key trapper) software, 396
Macro virus, 393
Malware, 393
Malware bot, 399
MD5 hash value, 406

Script bunny (script kiddie), 402
Slack space, 411
Social engineering, 401
Spoofing, 396
Steganography, 413
Thrill-seeker hacker, 400
Trojan horse virus, 396
Unallocated space, 412
White-hat hacker (ethical hacker), 401
Worm, 393

Short-Answer Questions

1. In what two ways are computers used in the commission of crimes or misdeeds?
2. What constitutes a computer crime?
3. What kind of software is a computer virus?
4. What differentiates a worm from a macro virus?
5. How does a denial-of-service attack work?
6. What is the effect of a virus hoax?
7. What is the difference between the Klez family of viruses and previous worms?
8. What is a white-hat hacker?
9. What do crackers do?
10. Is there a difference between a cyberterrorist and a hacktivist? If so, what is it?
11. What is computer forensics?
12. What are the two phases of a computer forensic investigation?

Assignments and Exercises

1. **FIND COMPUTER FORENSICS SOFTWARE** On the Web there are many sites that offer computer forensics software. Find five such software packages and for each one answer the following questions:
   - What does the software do? List five features it advertises.
   - Is the software free? If not, how much does it cost?
   - Is there any indication of the software's target market? If so, what market is it (law enforcement, home use, or something else)?

2. **WHAT EXACTLY ARE THE SEDONA PRINCIPLES?** Figure H.13 mentioned the *Sedona Principles*. These 14 principles were developed by lawyers, consultants, academics, and jurists to address the many issues involved in antitrust suits, intellectual property disputes, and other types of complex litigation.

   Write a report on the stipulations of the *Sedona Principles.* Do some research and find out exactly what the *Sedona Principles* suggest. Here's the first one to get you started:

   1. Electronic data and documents are potentially discoverable under Fed.R. Civ. P. 34 or its state law equivalents. Organizations must properly preserve electronic data and documents that can reasonably be anticipated to be relevant to litigation.

   Be sure to explain in your paper any legal terms, such as "discoverable," which appears in the 1st principle above, and "spoliation," in the 14th principle.

3. **THE INTERNATIONAL ANTI-CYBERCRIME TREATY** Find out what the provisions of the international anti-cybercrime treaty are and how they will affect the United States. One of the concerns that will have to be addressed is the issue of whether laws of one country should apply to all. For example, if certain sites are illegal in Saudi Arabia, should they be illegal for all surfers? Or if Germany has a law about hate language, should a German or a U.S. citizen be extradited to stand trial for building a neo-Nazi Web site? What do you think?

4. **DOES THE FOURTH AMENDMENT APPLY TO COMPUTER SEARCH AND SEIZURE?** The U.S. Department of Justice's Computer Crime and Intellectual Property Section has an online manual to guide computer forensics experts through the legal requirements of the search and seizure of electronic information. It's available at www.cybercrime.gov/searchmanual.htm and has a section on "Reasonable Expectation of Privacy." There are four subsections: general principles, reasonable expectation of privacy in computers as storage devices, reasonable expectation of privacy and third-party possession, and private searches. Read and summarize these four subsections.

CHAPTER NINE OUTLINE

STUDENT LEARNING OUTCOMES

1. Describe the emerging trends and technologies that will have an impact on the changing Internet.

2. Define the various types of technologies that are emerging as we move toward physiological interaction with technology.

3. Describe technological innovations and trends that will increase portability and mobility.

4. Describe the emerging trends of cell phones and RFID as they relate to the wireless environment.

INDUSTRY PERSPECTIVES

426 **F2b2C: A New E-Commerce Business Model**

429 **Getting Small with Nanotechnologies**

442 **RFID When "Seeing" Is Not an Option**

444 **Virtual Reality Simplifies Patient's World**

FEATURES

428 **On Your Own**
Where Should the Decision Rest?

430 **Team Work**
Finding Applications of Virtual Reality

434 **Global Perspective**
Facial Recognition Software at Airports around the World

439 **Global Perspective**
Buying Soda with a Cell Phone

443 **Team Work**
How Many Computers Do You Rely On in a Week?

445 **On Your Own**
Necessity, Convenience, and Privacy

452 **Electronic Commerce**
Continuing Your Education through the Internet

WEB SUPPORT

www.mhhe.com/haag

- MBA programs
- Specialized MBA programs
- Graduate school information and tips
- Tele-education (distance learning)
- Automatic speech recognition

CHAPTER NINE

Emerging Trends and Technologies
Business, People, and Technology Tomorrow

OPENING CASE STUDY:
THE FUTURE: TECHNOLOGY OUT,
PRINGLES IN

You might hold a future technological innovation in your hand right now if you are eating Pringles. It's true. In 2002, i-sec, a security company in England, built a wireless antenna from a Pringles can, attached it to a computer, and then drove around London's financial district. Because of the particular construction of the can (a long tube with aluminum-type material inside), i-sec employees were able to detect and attach to over two-thirds of the wireless networks in that financial district. More alarming, they were then able to break into the networks because there was no security.

In a rich neighborhood in New York, hackers used a Pringles can antenna and drove around the neighborhood during the late night hours trying to detect home wireless networks. When they found one, they stopped and spray-painted a small dot on the curb in front of the house. On a later date, the hackers drove around (in the middle of the day) in a construction van, stopped at every marked house, and attempted to break into the wireless network. If they were successful (and many times they were), they were able to steal bank account numbers, passwords, and other personal and sensitive information.

Technology of the future will take on many forms, with a can of Pringles being an extreme example. Some of the more plausible and helpful coming technological innovations include:

- Digital cash that you can use on the Internet just like folding cash without a credit card or traditional money transfer.
- Renting personal productivity software from an application service provider for only a few pennies while you use your PDA.
- CAVEs that re-create 3-D likenesses of people so you believe they are in the room with you.
- Biometrics that will use your physiological characteristics (such as your iris scan) to determine your identity and perhaps even tell if you have low blood sugar.
- Biochips that will help blind people regain some of their sight.

The list is really endless. In this chapter, we want to introduce you to several such upcoming technological innovations. The primary focus of the chapter isn't just on the technology, however, but on what future technologies will enable you to do. Equally important, we want you to think about the societal ramifications of these technologies. As we've emphasized throughout this book, technology is important but how you choose to use it is far more important.

By the way, some schools now teach hacking with a Pringles can. One such school is Intense School, which provides CEH (Certified Ethical Hacker) Certification courses. There, you can learn the right way to use an empty can of Pringles.[1,2]

Introduction

Technology is changing every day. But even more important than simply staying up with the changes in technology, you need to think about how those changes will affect your life. It's fun to read and learn about "leading- and bleeding-edge" technologies. It is something we encourage you to do. The consequences of those technology changes, however, may have an impact on all our lives more far reaching than you can imagine.

In this final chapter, we will take a look at several leading- and bleeding-edge technologies, including speech recognition, biometrics, implant chips, and digital cash, among others. These new technologies can and will impact your personal and business life. Technology for the sake of technology (though fun) is never necessarily a good thing, and can even be counterproductive. Using technology appropriately to enhance your personal life and to move your organization toward its strategic initiatives, on the other hand, are always both good things.

This has been both an exciting and a challenging chapter for us to write. The excitement is in the opportunity to talk with you about some emerging technological innovations. The challenge has been to not spotlight the technologies themselves overmuch, so as to help you focus on how those technologies will affect your life.

So, as you read this chapter, have fun but don't get caught up exclusively in the technology advances themselves that are on the horizon. Try to envision how those new technologies will change the things that you do and the way you do them, both from a personal and organizational perspective. As throughout this book, we remind you always to consider how to make new technology relevant and productive for you.

To introduce you to just a few of the many new technologies on the horizon, we've chosen those that we believe will have the greatest impact. We present those emerging technologies within the context of four important trends (see Figure 9.1).

Figure 9.1

Emerging Trends and Technologies

The Changing Internet

Few technologies have grown to widespread use and changed as fast as the Internet. Over the next several years, you will witness many new Internet-based trends and technologies. Among those will be software-as-a-service; push (not pull) technologies and personalization; F2b2C (which also enables personalization—see the nearby Industry Perspective); and Internet telephony (i.e., Voice over Internet Protocol, VoIP).

SOFTWARE-AS-A-SERVICE

Software-as-a-service (SaaS) is a delivery model for software in which you pay for software on a pay-per-use basis instead of buying the software outright. As more technology choices become available to you (smart phones, PDAs, tablet PCs) and your need to be mobile using them also increases, these devices may not have the capacity necessary to store all your software needs. For that matter, you may need a given piece of software—photo and video editing software, for instance—perhaps only a couple of times a year. It makes sense then that renting software would be a good alternative. That is what the SaaS model aims to deliver.

In the SaaS model you pay for software on a pay-per-use basis using a personal application service provider. An *application service provider (ASP)* supplies software applications (and often related services such as maintenance, technical support, information storage, and the like) over the Internet that would otherwise reside on customers' computers. ASP is already very popular among businesses. For example, many businesses use CRM software provided by Salesforce.com, which hosts its CRM software on its Internet servers. Employees of businesses subscribing to Salesforce.com's CRM software access it over the Internet, thus eliminating the need to buy, store, and maintain the software on their own computers.

Let's focus for a moment on your personal use of an ASP (see Figure 9.2). In the future, ASPs will provide personal productivity software for you to use (for a pay-per-use

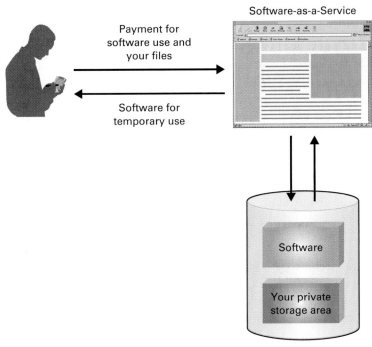

Software-as-a-Service

Payment for
software use and
your files

Software for
temporary use

Software

Your private
storage area

Personal ASP

Figure 9.2

The Software-as-a-Service Model and a Personal Application Service Provider (ASP)

F2B2C: A NEW E-COMMERCE BUSINESS MODEL

In the e-commerce world, business models are identified by the players such as B2B (Business to Business) and G2C (Government to Consumer). We now have the notion of introducing a third player to create an entirely new e-commerce business model. The first of these new business models to surface is *F2b2C (Factory to business to Consumer),* an e-commerce business model in which a consumer communicates through a business on the Internet and directly provides product specifications to a factory that makes the customized and personalized product to the consumer's specifications and then ships it directly to the consumer.

You should notice in F2b2C that the "F" and "C" are capitalized while the "b" (for business) is not. In this model, the business is simply an Internet intermediary that provides a communication conduit between the factory and the consumer. When this happens, a form of disintermediation occurs. Broadly defined, *disintermediation* is the use of the Internet as a delivery vehicle, whereby intermediate players in a distribution channel can be bypassed. The travel agent industry is a good example of where disintermediation has occurred. Now, you can connect directly to an airline and purchase tickets, often receiving bonus mileage if you do. This is an example of how the Internet has disintermediated the need for travel agents.

Think about connecting to a site on the Internet and custom-ordering something like a pair of pants. You would specify your exact size, inseam, waist, hip and thigh measurements, and so on, and other information such as color, style of pockets, how many belt loops (if any) . . . the list could grow quite long. The Web site would immediately pass along your information to a factory that would create a customized and personalized pair of pants for you and ship them to your door.

Is this possible? Well, it already exists to some extent. In the next section, you'll read about how companies are using biometrics to create custom-fitting clothing and shoes.[3]

---

fee or monthly subscription fee using the SaaS model) and storage so you can store your files on their Web servers as opposed to on your own personal devices.

For example, you might be in an airport and need to build a workbook with your PDA, which might not have a complete version of Excel. So, you would use your PDA to connect to the Internet and a personal ASP. With your PDA, you would use the personal ASP's Excel software to create your workbook and save it on the ASP's Web server. When you finally got back to the office, you would use your computer there, connect to the same ASP, and retrieve your workbook and save it on your computer.

There are many issues you'll have to consider when determining whether or not to use a personal ASP, with privacy and reliability definitely being important ones. If all your information is on a Web-based server, it will be easier for someone to gain access to it (for the wrong reasons) than if you stored all your information on your home or office computer. When considering reliability, you need to think about what happens if the personal ASP's Web site goes down. How will you perform your work? In spite of potential drawbacks, we believe personal ASPs and the SaaS model will become a part of your everyday life in the future.

PUSH, NOT PULL, TECHNOLOGIES AND PERSONALIZATION

We live in a *pull* technology environment. That is, you look for, request, and find what you want. On the Internet, for example, you visit a specific site and request information, services, and products. So, you're literally "pulling" what you want. Future emphasis will be on *push* technologies. In a *push technology* environment, businesses and orga-

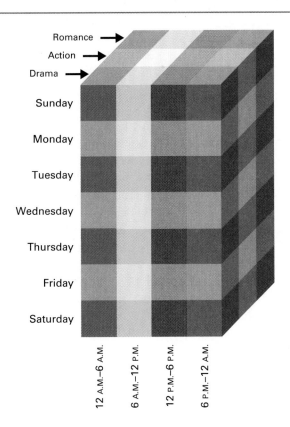

Figure 9.3

Tracking What You Want
and When You Want It
with a Data Warehouse

nizations come to you with information, services, and product offerings based on your profile. This isn't spam or mass e-mailings.

For example, in some parts of the country you can subscribe to a cell service that pushes information to you in the form of video rental information. Whenever you pass near a video store, your cell phone (which is GPS-enabled) triggers a computer within the video store that evaluates your rental history to see if any new videos have arrived that you might be interested in viewing. In this case, the system generates a personal data warehouse of rental history—including dimensions for the day of the week, the time of the day, and video categories—concerning you and then evaluates information in the smaller cubes (see Figure 9.3). The evaluation seeks to affirm that (1) you usually rent videos on that particular day, (2) you usually rent videos during that time of that day, and (3) there is a distinct video category from which you rent videos during that time of the day. If so, the system then checks to see if there are any movies in that category that you haven't rented and that it hasn't previously contacted you about.

If so, the video store computer will call your cell phone with a message concerning a new release. It will also give you street-by-street directions to the video store and hold the video for you. If the video store doesn't have any new releases that might interest you, you won't receive a phone call.

You might also someday receive a personalized pizza delivery message on your television as you start to watch a ball game. The message might say, "We'll deliver your favorite sausage and mushroom pizza to your doorstep before the game begins. On your remote control, press the ORDER NOW button."

Of course, situations such as these rely on IT's ability to store vast amounts of information about you. Technologies such as databases and data warehouses will definitely play an important role in the development of push technologies that do more than just push spam and mass e-mail. In the instance of the pizza delivery message on your television, a local pizza store would have determined that you like sausage and mushroom pizza and that you order it most often while watching a ball game.

WHERE SHOULD THE DECISION REST?

In the future, you can expect to see the movement toward *intellectual computing,* a step beyond artificial intelligence (review Chapter 4) in which computers will learn, become increasingly smarter, and take over many decision-making tasks for you.

The degree to which you allow a computer to take over a decision-making task is often a function of the decision being made. For example, most inventory management systems are very good at determining what quantities of a given product line to reorder. If the system orders too many, no real harm is done because excess inventory just sits on the shelf. If not enough is ordered, the business will simply experience a stock-out for a given period of time.

On the other hand, you should never let a computer system tell you how much dosage of a given medicine to give a patient without first verifying the recommendation somehow. The wrong dosage—either too much or too little—can have catastrophic and detrimental effects on the patient, potentially leading to serious illness and even death.

Your task is to list three decisions in the business world that can largely be left to a computer and three decisions in the business world that should definitely not be left to a computer. Don't use the examples given in this chapter.

VOICE OVER INTERNET PROTOCOL (VOIP)

VoIP, or *Voice over Internet Protocol,* allows you to send voice communications over the Internet and avoid the toll charges that you would normally receive from your long distance carrier. Simply put, VoIP allows you to use your Internet connection (which must be broadband such as DSL or cable) to make phone calls. This is different from today's DSL model which splits your phone line so that you can make phone calls and surf the Web at the same time. In today's model, your telephone calls are still routed through your traditional telephone service provider to whom you must pay charges for long distance phone calls. Using VoIP, your telephone calls are routed through a VoIP provider (which may be your ISP) and you pay only a flat monthly fee—usually in the neighborhood of $20 to $25 per month) to make unlimited long distance calls.

For home use, you can already use the VoIP services offered by the likes of Vonage, Lingo, Quintum, and AT&T. You can keep your existing phone number and you do have access to a number of value-added features such as call-waiting, caller ID, and so on. Most VoIP providers offer you free unlimited long distance calling only within your country; international long distance calls may still incur an additional fee.

This certainly speaks to the growing importance of the Internet. Most of you probably cannot imagine life without the Internet already. That will be even more true once the Internet becomes the technological infrastructure that also supports all your phone calls.

Physiological Interaction

Right now, your primary physical interfaces to your computer include a keyboard, mouse, monitor, and printer (basically, your input and output devices). These are physical devices, not physiological. Physiological interfaces capture and utilize your real body characteristics, such as you breath, your voice, your height and weight, and even the iris in your eye. Physiological innovations include automatic speech recognition, virtual reality, cave automatic virtual environments, and biometrics, along with many others.

GETTING SMALL WITH NANOTECHNOLOGIES

One of the single greatest drawbacks to technological advances is size. The best chip manufacturers can do is to make circuit elements with a width of 130 nanometers. A nanometer is one-hundred-thousandth the width of a human hair. That may seem very, very small, but current manufacturing technologies are beginning to limit the size of computer chips, and thus their speed and capacity.

Nanotechnologies aim to change all that. In nanotechnology, everything is simply atoms. Nanotechnology researchers are attempting to move atoms and encourage them to "self-assemble" into new forms.

Nanotechnology is a bleeding-edge technology worth watching. The changes it will bring about will be unbelievable. Consider these:

Change the molecular structure of the materials used to make computer chips, for instance, and electronics could become as cheap and plentiful as bar codes on packaging. Lightweight vests enmeshed with sensors could measure a person's vital signs. Analysis of a patient's DNA could be done so quickly and precisely that designer drugs would be fabricated on the fly. A computer the size of your library card could store everything you ever saw or read.[4,5]

AUTOMATIC SPEECH RECOGNITION

An *automatic speech recognition (ASR)* system not only captures spoken words but also distinguishes word groupings to form sentences. To perform this, an ASR system follows three steps.

1. *Feature analysis*—The system captures your words as you speak into a microphone, eliminates any background noise, and converts the digital signals of your speech into phonemes (syllables).

2. *Pattern classification*—The system matches your spoken phonemes to a phoneme sequence stored in an acoustic model database. For example, if your phoneme was "dü," the system would match it to the words do and due.

3. *Language processing*—The system attempts to make sense of what you're saying by comparing the word phonemes generated in step 2 with a language model database. For example, if you were asking a question and started with the phoneme "dü," the system would determine that the appropriate word is do and not due.

ASR is certainly now taking its place in computing environments. For example, Microsoft's Office XP and Office 2003 include easy-to-use speech recognition capabilities for both content and commands. The important point is that ASR allows you to speak in a normal voice; thus it supports physiological interaction. Visit the Web site that supports this text (www.mhhe.com/haag) to learn more about ASR systems.

VIRTUAL REALITY

On the horizon (and in some instances here today) is a new technology that will virtually place you in any experience you desire. That new technology is *virtual reality,* a three-dimensional computer simulation in which you actively and physically participate. In a virtual reality system, you make use of special input and output devices that capture your physiological movements and send physiological responses back to you. These devices include a (see the list on the next page)

FINDING APPLICATIONS OF VIRTUAL REALITY

Virtual reality is quickly taking its place in the technology world. In our discussion of it, we listed several well-known applications of virtual reality.

Your task is twofold in this project. First, search the Web for more applications of virtual reality. Find at least three and provide a brief description of each. Only one of these applications can be in the area of entertainment. That is, you cannot use more than one game-oriented application of virtual reality.

Second, identify five potential applications for virtual reality. For each application, describe how virtual reality would be used and why it would be beneficial. Each of these potential applications must relate to the use of virtual reality by an organization. As you describe each of the potential applications, list the type of organization or industry that would use it.

- *Glove*—An input device that captures and records the shape and movement of your hand and fingers and the strength of your hand and finger movements.
- *Headset (head-mounted display)*—A combined input and output device that (1) captures and records the movement of your head and (2) contains a screen that covers your entire field of vision and displays various views of an environment based on your movements.
- *Walker*—An input device that captures and records the movement of your feet as you walk or turn in different directions.

APPLICATIONS OF VIRTUAL REALITY   Virtual reality applications are popping up everywhere, sometimes in odd places. The most common applications are found in the entertainment industry. There are a number of virtual reality games on the market, including downhill Olympic skiing, race-car driving, golf, air combat, and marksmanship. Other applications include

- Matsushita Electric Works—You design your kitchen in virtual reality and then choose the appliances you want and even request color changes.
- Volvo—For demonstrating the safety features of its cars.
- Airlines—To train pilots how to handle adverse weather conditions.
- Motorola—To train assembly-line workers in the steps of manufacturing a new product.[6]
- Health care—To train doctors how to perform surgery using virtual cadavers.[7]

Let's consider the potential ramifications of virtual reality and how you might someday interact with your computer. New virtual reality systems include aroma-producing devices and devices that secrete fluid through a mouthpiece that you have in your mouth. So, you could virtually experience a Hawaiian luau. The aroma-producing device would generate various smells and the mouthpiece would secrete a fluid that tastes like pineapple or roasted pig. If you were using virtual reality to surf big waves, the mouthpiece would secrete a fluid that tastes like salt water.

Such examples are the "fun" uses of virtual reality. But consider beneficial societal uses of VR, such as those that employ haptic interfaces. A **haptic interface** uses technology to add the sense of touch to an environment that previously had only visual and auditory elements. With a haptic interface, sight-challenged people can feel and read text with their fingers while interacting with a computer.

The fact is anyone can use technology to make money. Perhaps the most exciting thing about new technology is the potential benefits for people. Can you envision ways to use technology to help people less fortunate than you?

CAVE AUTOMATIC VIRTUAL ENVIRONMENTS

A ***CAVE (cave automatic virtual environment)*** is a special 3-D virtual reality room that can display images of other people and objects located in other CAVEs all over the world. CAVEs are ***holographic devices,*** that create, capture, and/or display images in true three-dimensional form. If you watch any of the *Star Trek* movies, you'll see an example of a holographic device called the holodeck.

In working form, you would enter a CAVE room. At the same time, someone else would enter another CAVE room in another location (see Figure 9.4). Numerous digital video cameras would capture the likenesses of both participants and re-create and send those images to the other CAVEs. Then, you and the other person could see and carry on a normal conversation with each other, and you would feel as if that other person were in the same room with you.

Current CAVE research is also working on the challenges of having other physical objects in the room. For example, if you sat on a couch in your CAVE, the couch would capture the indentation you made in it and pass it to the couch in the other CAVE. That couch would respond by constricting a mesh of rubber inside it so that your indentation would also appear there. And what about playing catch? Which person would have the virtual ball and which person would have the real ball? The answer is that both would have a virtual ball. When throwing it, the CAVE would capture your arm movement to determine the speed, arc, and direction of the ball. That information would be transmitted to the other CAVE, and it would use that information to make the virtual ball fly through the air accordingly.

Unlike virtual reality, you don't need any special gear in a CAVE. Let your imagination run wild and think about the potential applications of CAVEs. An unhappy customer could call a business to complain. Within seconds, a customer service representative would not answer the phone but rather appear in the room with the unhappy customer. That would be an example of great customer service. Your teacher might

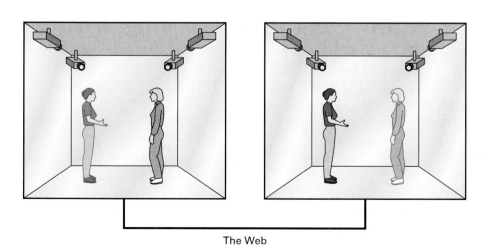

The Web

Figure 9.4

CAVEs (Cave Automatic Virtual Environments)

never attend your class. Instead the teacher would enter a CAVE and have his or her image broadcast into the classroom. You might not really be in class either but rather a holographic likeness of you. Are CAVEs a realistic possibility? The answer is definitely yes. We believe that CAVEs are the successor to virtual reality. So, virtual reality may not be a long-term technological innovation but rather a stepping-stone to the more advanced CAVE. Whatever the case, CAVEs will not only significantly alter how you interact with your computer (can you imagine the thrill of video games in a CAVE?), they will even more significantly alter how you interact with other people. With CAVE technologies, you can visit your friends and relatives on a daily basis no matter where they live. You may even have television shows and movies piped into your home CAVE.

BIOMETRICS

Biometrics is the use of physiological characteristics—such as your fingerprint, the blood vessels in the iris of your eye, the sound of your voice, or perhaps even your breath—to provide identification. That's the strict and narrow definition, but biometrics is beginning to encompass more than just identification. Consider these real-world applications in place today (see Figure 9.5):

- *Internet-enabled toilets*—These toilets use your physiological output to capture readings (e.g., white-cell count, red-cell count, sodium level, sugar level, the presence of certain types of drugs, etc.) and send that information via the Internet to your doctor's computer. Your doctor's computer can then analyze that information to determine if you're getting sick or perhaps using the wrong type of medication. Of course, you have to plug an Internet-enabled toilet into both an electrical outlet and an Internet connection. Internet-enabled toilets are finding their way into assisted-care living facilities in which older people need 24-hour monitoring of their physiological characteristics.
- *Custom shoes*—Several shoe stores, especially those that offer fine Italian leather shoes, no longer carry any inventory. When you select a shoe style you like, you place your bare feet into a box that scans the shape of your feet. That information

Figure 9.5

Custom-Fit Clothes through Biometrics

is then used to make a custom pair of shoes for you. It works extremely well if your feet are slightly different from each other in size or shape (as is the case with most people).

- *Custom wedding gowns*—Following the custom-fit shoe idea, many bridal boutiques now do the same thing for wedding dresses. Once the bride chooses the style she likes, she steps into a small room that scans her entire body. That information is used to create a wedding dress that fits perfectly. Both custom shoes and custom wedding dresses are examples of the future implementation of F2b2C (see the Industry Perspective on page 426).

- *Custom bathrobes*—Some high-end spa resorts now actually have patrons walk through a body-scanning device upon check-in. The scanning device measures the patron's body characteristics and then sends that information to a sewing and fabricating facility that automatically creates a custom-fit bathrobe. Some of these same spa resorts are using the readings from Internet-enabled toilets to design nutritionally optimal meal selections for patrons.

BIOMETRIC SECURITY   The best form of security for personal identification encompasses three aspects:

1. What you know
2. What you have
3. Who you are

The first—*what you know*—is something like a password, something that everyone can create and has. The second—*what you have*—is something like a card such as an ATM card you use at an ATM (in conjunction with your password, what you know). Unfortunately, most personal identification security systems stop there. That is, they do not include *who you are,* which is some form of a biometric.

It's no wonder crimes like identity theft are spiraling out of control. Without much effort, a thief can steal your password (often through social engineering) and steal what you have. For the latter, the thief doesn't actually have to steal your physical card; he or she simply has to copy the information on it. However, stealing a biometric—such as your fingerprint or iris scan—is much more difficult.

Many banks are currently converting ATMs to the use of biometrics, specifically an iris scan, as the third level of personal identification security. When you open an account and request ATM use, the bank will issue you an ATM card (you pick the password). The bank will also scan your iris and create a unique 512-byte representation of the scan. To use an ATM, you must insert your card, type in your password, and allow the machine to scan your iris. The ATM uses all three forms of identification to match you to your account. You can then perform whatever transaction you wish.

Some private schools for young children now require parents and guardians to submit to iris scans. Once the scan is captured and the person is verified as a parent or guardian, the information is entered into a security database. Then, when the parent or guardian comes to the school to pick up a child, his or her iris scan is compared to the one stored in the database. Parents and guardians cannot, under any circumstances, take a child from the school without first going through verification via an iris scan.

INTEGRATING BIOMETRIC PROCESSING AND TRANSACTION PROCESSING
Once society accepts the use of biometrics for security and identification purposes, organizations of all types will be able to add another dimension of business intelligence

FACIAL RECOGNITION SOFTWARE AT AIRPORTS AROUND THE WORLD

Airport security is now a must. And most airports and airlines are no longer relying on government-issued forms of identification for determining who should and who should not be allowed on a plane. Instead, they're relying on facial recognition software such as Facelt, a joint-venture product of ARINC and Visionics Corporation. Facelt creates a digital map of a person's face and compares it to a database that contains the facial images of unwanted fliers and known terrorists.

Facial recognition software plays an important role in the use of biometrics for providing and authenticating identification. Facelt's ARGUS system can handle an unlimited number of video cameras capturing facial images and comparing them to a database that is also unlimited in size. To learn more about Facelt, visit ARINC at www.arinc.com and Visionics at www.visionics.com.

Facial recognition software has made great strides over the past couple of years. Consider these facts:

- Tests conducted in 2002 showed a 50 percent reduction in error rates over those conducted in 2000.
- In determining if a person is who he or she claims to be, the best facial recognition systems yield a 90 percent verification rate, with only a 1 percent false-acceptance rate.
- Males are still easier to identify than females.
- Older people are still easier to identify than younger people.[8,9,10]

to their data warehouses—that dimension will capture and record changes in physiological characteristics (see Figure 9.6).

Consider, as a hypothetical example, a woman using an ATM—equipped with iris scanning capabilities—to withdraw cash. Current research suggests that it might be possible to use an iris scan to determine not only that a woman is pregnant but also the sex of the unborn child. (That is a very true statement.) When the woman has her iris scanned, the bank might be able to tell that she is pregnant and expecting a boy. When the woman receives her cash and receipt, the receipt would have a coupon printed on the back for 10 percent off any purchase at Babies "Я" Us. Furthermore, the ATM would generate another receipt that says "buy blue."

The key here is for you to consider that transaction processing systems (TPSs) of the future will be integrated with biometric processing systems (BPSs). The TPS will capture and process the "events" of the transaction—when, by whom, where, and so on.

Figure 9.6

Integrating Biometric and Transaction Processing to Create Business Intelligence

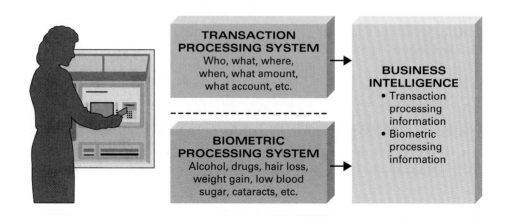

TRANSACTION PROCESSING SYSTEM
Who, what, where, when, what amount, what account, etc.

BIOMETRIC PROCESSING SYSTEM
Alcohol, drugs, hair loss, weight gain, low blood sugar, cataracts, etc.

BUSINESS INTELLIGENCE
- Transaction processing information
- Biometric processing information

The BPS will capture and process the physiological characteristics of the person performing the transaction. Those physiological characteristics may include the presence of alcohol or illegal drugs, hair loss, weight gain, low blood sugar, vitamin deficiencies, cataracts, and yes—even pregnancy.

When businesses start to gather this type of intelligence, you can leave it to your imagination to envision what will happen. For example, because of the noted pregnancy in our previous example of the woman using an ATM, the bank might offer financing for a mini-van, evaluate the size of the family's home and perhaps offer special financing for a second mortgage so another room can be added, or establish a tuition account for the child and place $25 in it. These possibilities will further intensify competition in almost all industries.

OTHER BIOMETRICS AND BIOMETRIC DEVICES   Biometrics is a "hot topic" in research circles right now. Although we haven't the space to discuss them all, you might want to watch for these:

- *Biochip*—a technology chip that can perform a variety of physiological functions when inserted into the human body. Biochips have been proven in some cases to block pain for people who suffer severe spinal injuries, help paralyzed people regain some portion of their motor skills, and help partially blind people see better.
- *Implant chip*—a technology-enabled microchip implanted into the human body that stores important information about you (such as your identification and medical history) and that may be GPS-enabled to offer a method of tracking.
- *Facial recognition software*—software that provides identification by evaluating facial characteristics (see the Global Perspective on the previous page).

Whatever becomes a reality in the field of biometrics promises to forever change your life and how you interact with technology.

Increasing Portability and Mobility

Portability and mobility go hand-in-hand. *Portability,* in this instance, refers to how easy it is for you to carry around your technology. *Mobility* is much broader and encompasses what you have the ability to do with your technology while carrying it around. For example, PDAs are very portable; they weigh less than a pound and easily fit in your pocket or purse. However, your mobility may be limited with a PDA. That is, while you can manage your schedule, take some notes, and even use e-mail with a PDA, you certainly can't generate spreadsheets with elaborate graphs. You want technology that is no more intrusive than your wallet or purse. Ideally, your watch would really be a powerful computer system with speech and holographic capabilities (it may happen someday). If your watch is a powerful computer system, then it maximizes your mobility.

It goes without saying that to achieve maximum portability and mobility we'll need completely wireless communications. This is a vast and dynamically changing field. We won't delve into it here, but we will need it for portability and mobility. You can learn more about wireless communications in *Extended Learning Module E.*

To further advance the portability and mobility of technology, you can expect to find digital cash, wearable computers, multi-state CPUs, and holographic storage devices in the future.

DIGITAL CASH

When the digital economy arrives, so must digital money. Coins and folding cash have little or no value themselves; they are representations of value. They became the standard on which the economy works because it's much easier to pay for products and services with them than it is to use gold and silver or some other precious metal. ***Digital cash*** (also called ***electronic cash*** or ***e-cash***) is an electronic representation of cash.

To use digital cash, you must first purchase it from an electronic bank (see Figure 9.7). You can do this by sending real cash in the mail, using a debit or credit card, or actually opening an account with the electronic bank and requesting that an amount of digital cash be deducted from your balance and sent to you. Whatever the case, the electronic bank will electronically send you your digital cash files. For example, you could request $100 in digital cash in $20 increments. What you would end up with is five digital cash files, each representing $20 on your hard disk.

Now all you have to do is find a product or service on the Internet you want to buy. You would send the merchant the appropriate number of digital cash files to equal the purchase amount. The merchant could then use those digital cash files to buy other merchandise or return it to the electronic bank for real money.

The concept seems quite simple when you think about it. The implementation, however, has turned out to be extremely difficult for many reasons including the following:

- If your system crashes and your digital cash files are wiped clean, you've lost your money. It's rather like losing your wallet. The electronic bank will not replace the files.

- There is no standard for how digital cash should look. So, a digital cash file from one electronic bank may not look like digital cash from another electronic bank. That makes many merchants very hesitant to accept digital cash.

- Digital cash makes money laundering easy. Because none of your personal information travels with the digital cash when you use it to make a purchase, it's

Figure 9.7

How Digital Cash Will Work on the Internet

extremely difficult to tell where it came from. So, illegally obtained cash can be easily exchanged for digital cash.

- Digital cash travels across the vast Internet and is susceptible to being stolen. Digital information (which includes digital cash) is easy to steal and hard to trace. This may be the single biggest obstacle to the widespread use of digital cash.

In spite of the above challenges and many others, digital cash is destined to take its place as a standard technology. The real question is how soon.

WEARABLE COMPUTERS

Focusing on portability now, let's turn our attention to wearable computers. A ***wearable computer*** is a fully equipped computer that you wear as a piece of clothing or attached to a piece of clothing similar to the way you would carry your cell phone on your belt.

In reality, wearable computers are not some far-fetched cutting-edge technology that will take years to arrive. Today, Charmed Technologies and Xybernaut® (just to name a few) are already manufacturing and selling wearable computers (see Figure 9.8). The leader in this area is Xybernaut (www.xybernaut.com) with its many lines of wearable computers designed for manufacturing environments, disaster areas, and even children at school.

For schoolchildren, Xybernaut offers XyberKids, a fully functional computer in the form of a pen-based flat-panel display that can be easily held in hand or set on a desk along with a lightweight backpack for carrying the other computer components such as the system unit and hard disk. At the time we wrote this text, Xybernaut's XyberKids computer included a 500MHz processor; 128MB RAM expandable to 256MB; 1GB Compact Flash card; Compact Flash, USB, and Firewire ports; an 800 × 600 color SVGA flat-panel display with an 8.4-inch viewable screen; and an onscreen keyboard and built-in handwriting recognition. What's really nice is that the technology components in the backpack (i.e., everything but the flat-panel display) weigh less than one pound total.

Again, the focus of wearable computers is portability first and mobility second. Right now, wearable computers are very nonintrusive (portability). But they do have limited

Figure 9.8

Wearable Computers

processing capabilities, so your mobility is limited. You can certainly expect that to change very soon. As technology increases in capability and decreases in price and size, wearable computers will offer you as much processing capability (mobility) as a standard desktop or notebook computer.

Let your imagination run wild again. Think about a military application and camouflage. It might someday be possible to develop computerized clothing for use in a military environment. The clothing material would be encased LCD (liquid crystal display, the same material used for screens on many types of computers). On a person's back would be mounted a wide-angle-lens video camera. The computer would capture the video behind the person and display it on the clothing on the front of the person, rendering them almost invisible. If you've seen the movie *Predator*, then you understand how this might work and look.

MULTI-STATE CPUS AND HOLOGRAPHIC STORAGE DEVICES

To increase portability and mobility, technology will have to become increasingly faster and capable of storing more information in exceedingly smaller spaces. Multi-state CPUs and holographic storage devices are two technological innovations on the horizon that promise to help in those areas.

Right now, CPUs are binary-state, capable of working only with information represented by a 1 or a 0. That greatly slows processing. What we really need to increase speed are CPUs that are multi-state. ***Multi-state CPUs*** work with information represented in more than just two states, probably 10 states with each state representing a digit between 0 and 9. When multi-state CPUs do become a reality, your computer will no longer have to go through many of the processes associated with translating characters into binary and then reversing the translation process later. This will make them much faster. Of course, the true goal is to create multi-state CPUs that can also handle letters and special characters without converting them to their binary equivalents.

Again, right now, storage devices store information on a two-dimensional surface, but research in the holographic realm will change that, and ***holographic storage devices*** will store information on a storage medium that is composed of 3-D crystal-like objects with many sides or faces (see Figure 9.9). This is similar in concept to small cards that you may have seen which change the picture or image as you view the cards from different angles.

If and when holographic storage devices do become a reality, you may be able to store an entire set of encyclopedias on a single crystal that may have as many as several hundred faces. Think how small technology will become then.

Figure 9.9

3-D Crystal-Like Objects in a Holographic Storage Device

BUYING SODA WITH A CELL PHONE

In many countries in Europe, especially in Scandinavian countries, you can't find a slot on a vending machine to insert money into to buy a soda. No, it's not because the sodas are free or because there's an extremely high rate of vandalism. You have to buy the soda with your cell phone.

On the soda machine is a telephone number that you call. When you do, the telephone call automatically triggers the soda machine so you can make a selection. The best part is that the cost of the soda is charged to your cell phone bill. No more trying to find the right change when the "CORRECT CHANGE" message is blinking. No more trying to get the creases out of a dollar bill. You simply charge the cost of the soda to your cell phone. Of course, at the end of every month you still have to pay for it, but it is indeed convenient.

This is an example of how B2C (Business to Consumer) e-commerce is beginning to incorporate nontraditional computing technologies. Within the context of C2C (Consumer to Consumer) e-commerce, this example should help you expand your mind and think of endless wild possibilities for selling products and services to other consumers.

Could you set up some sort of product-selling business that requires consumers to use a cell phone to charge the cost of the product to their cell phone bill? If you answer no, then our next question to you is, Have you actually contacted an ISP and cell phone service provider to determine that you can't do it? How would you answer that question?

C2C e-commerce will require that everyone "think outside the box" or "beyond your ears" as we like to put it. Don't rule out any idea, no matter how strange or far-fetched. Thomas Watson, former CEO and chairman of IBM, in 1943 stated, "I think there is a world market for maybe five computers." He was definitely wrong and narrow-minded in his futuristic views, don't you think? Don't make the same mistake.

The Wireless Arena

Throughout this text, we've discussed the technologies that make wireless communications possible and applications of wireless technologies in which companies have gained a significant competitive advantage. We've discussed such wireless technologies as Bluetooth and WiFi—both of which were designed to activate wireless communication via technology devices such as cell phones, printers, network hubs, and of course computers.

Let's now turn our attention to (1) cell phones and (2) RFID (radio frequency identification). Cell phones are a significant "disruptive technology" now and will be more so in the future. RFID, while still emerging as a technology, will definitely be around for many years and dramatically change your personal life and the way the business world works.

THE NEXT GENERATION OF CELL PHONE TECHNOLOGY

For most people, a cell phone is a necessary part of life. Even today's most basic cell phones support phone calls (that's obvious) and also real-time text messaging, photos (taking, sending, and receiving), games, and many other features. Tomorrow's cell phones may very well become the only technology you need.

Among the many innovations you'll see in cell phones over the next couple of years will be storage (in the form of a hard disk), processor capability, music enhancements, and video support. Already, new cell phones are being demonstrated that have 2 gigabytes of storage and processor speeds up to 500 Mhz. As these capacities and speeds increase, you may be able to wirelessly connect a keyboard, monitor, mouse, and printer to your cell phone. Your cell phone will essentially become your notebook computer.

Tomorrow's cell phones may spell the end for dedicated MP3 players like Apple's iPod. With enough battery life and storage capacity, many people will opt to use their cell phones for music and eliminate the other piece of equipment they have to carry around to listen to music. Video on demand will also become a reality through your cell phone. Many of the major TV network providers are currently creating *mobisodes,* short one-minute video clips of TV shows designed for viewing on a small cell phone screen. You could download each clip, have your cell phone integrate them all into a single show, and then watch it wherever you may happen to be. Some of the newest and most advanced cell phones now support HD (high-definition), the same technology that makes HDTV shows so vivid and real.

But there is a downside. Cell phones are the next great and uncharted space for hackers and viruses. The even worse news is that the development of anti-virus cell phone software is very much in its infancy, far behind the capabilities of the people wanting to hack into your cell phone and unleash deadly cell phone viruses. Think about your ISP. It has anti-virus software (and many more types of "anti" software such as spam blocker software and anti-spyware software) on its servers to stop a lot of malware from making it to your computer via e-mail. But that doesn't stop all malware from getting to you. You still need all types of "anti" software loaded onto and running on your computer at all times.

When was the last time your cell phone service provider contacted you about new types of "anti" software you can download onto your cell phone for added protection? That has probably never happened, and it should raise a red flag for you. Do you download ring tones from the Internet? If so, your cell phone is susceptible to getting a virus. Some cell phone viruses, created in a laboratory environment, can make international calls and run your battery dead and your bill into the thousands of dollars.

As your cell phone becomes increasingly more important to you—and it will—and becomes increasingly more supportive of complex computer tasks, your challenge will continue to be: Be protected.

RFID (RADIO FREQUENCY IDENTIFICATION)

RFID (radio frequency identification) uses a microchip (chip) in a tag or label to store information, and information is transmitted from, or written to, the tag or label when the microchip is exposed to the correct frequency of radio waves. You're probably already familiar with some implementations of RFID. For example, toll roads have lanes through which drivers can move if they have an RFID device that automatically charges to an account as they drive down the road. Exxon/Mobil provides an RFID-enabled key ring (called Speedpass) to its customers. The Speedpass key ring contains customer account information. A customer, when making a purchase, simply waves the key ring at a reader (as opposed to swiping a credit card). The reader communicates with the RFID chip on the key ring, reads the customer's account information, and proceeds with the account charge.

The most common implementation of RFID is the passive RFID chip (see Figure 9.10). A passive RFID chip has no power source itself and sits idle until passed near a reader that emits radio waves. The antenna surrounding the RFID chip picks up the radio waves and the RFID chip stores those waves as a form of energy until it has enough to literally "jolt" itself to life. The RFID chip then sends its information to the reader, which is connected to some sort of computer system containing account information and the like. After sending its information, the RFID chip goes back into passive mode. This is exactly how Exxon/Mobil's Speedpass RFID key ring works.

Figure 9.10

How Passive RFID Works

RFID IN USE TODAY The current applications of RFID technologies are many, including:

- **Anti-theft car keys**—inside the casing of the car key is an RFID chip. When you insert the key into the ignition, the RFID chip must communicate with the reader in your ignition system (and pass the equivalent of a password) for the car to start. So, it does criminals no good to make a copy of your car key. Of course, if you lose your car keys, it often costs in excess of $300 to get them replaced.

- **Library book tracking**—instead of a bar code on which the ISBN is stored, the RFID chip contains that information. Books are much easier to check in and check out. Even the Vatican library now uses RFID chips in its books. The old inventory process took over 30 days. Using wireless handheld RFID readers, the new inventory process takes only a day.

- **Livestock tracking**—livestock of all kinds is now tagged with RFID chips upon entering the country. The system can then track where the livestock has been on its journey throughout the United States. In the case of a biological outbreak, the system can easily identify which livestock were at the location where the outbreak is believed to have occurred.

- **Supply chain**—almost every major participant in the supply chain process is now mandating that the other participants tag merchandise, trays of merchandise, boxes and skids of merchandise, and so on with RFID chips. These major participants include Wal-Mart, the Department of Defense (DOD), the Food and Drug Administration (FDA), Target, Albertson's, TESCO (United Kingdom retailer), and Carrefour (France retailer).

- **Passports**—it is already planned that future U.S. passports (as of about the year 2007) will contain an RFID chip in the cover of the passport. The RFID chip will contain all your passport information and a biometric, your fingerprint.

The above list is just a few of the thousands of implementations of RFID in the business world.

THE FUTURE OF RFID Today, almost every product is identified uniquely by a UPC (universal product code). However, every like product has the same UPC. So, two cans of diet Coke with lime, for example, have identical UPCs. This makes them indistinguishable. With RFID technologies, each individual piece of merchandise will

RFID WHEN "SEEING" IS NOT AN OPTION

Earlier in this chapter, we discussed haptic interfaces, which provide the sense of touch via technology to environments that previously supported only sight and sound. If you extend the haptic interface concept, you can envision technology that will help sight-challenged people to hear what they cannot see.

For example, if all automobiles had RFID chips, those chips could wirelessly communicate with a reader being carried by a sight-challenged person. The reader would emit a long constant tone, for example, when no cars were oncoming. That way the sight-challenged person would know that it was safe to cross the street. Likewise, the reader could emit a constant beeping to alert the person that traffic was oncoming. Based on the strength of the RFID signal, the reader might be able to determine how fast the car was moving and project when it would drive through an intersection.

If you flip forward a couple of pages in this chapter, you'll read another Industry Perspective concerning how virtual reality can help people with autism. In this chapter you'll also read the sections "Closing the Great Digital Divide" and "Technology for the Betterment of Society." As you close your studies of MIS, we hope that you will expand your thinking and remember that although we all have to make a living, technology is not just a tool to make money, but is primarily an enabler of "quality of life." We encourage you to find a way to give back to society in your use and exploration of technology. It will make you feel good! Feeling good about doing something for others is an acceptable ulterior motive, perhaps the only acceptable ulterior motive left in the business world. New technologies offer us a great opportunity to feel good by helping others.

have a unique EPC (electronic product code). The EPC will include the UPC designation but then also provide a unique number for each different can of diet Coke with lime that can be tied to expiration dates, supply chain movements, and just about anything else you can imagine.

Once again, use your imagination here. If every product in a grocery store can wirelessly communicate with the checkout system, there will be no need to go through that process. While you shop, you'll bag your items when placing them in your cart. When you walk out the front door, an RFID system will wirelessly communicate with your credit card in your wallet, wirelessly communicate with every product in your grocery cart, tally up your bill, and charge your credit card account appropriately.

And think about washing clothes. Suppose you load your washer full of "whites" like socks and towels. Accidentally, you throw in a red shirt but don't see it. Fortunately, each piece of clothing will have an RFID chip that will include washing instructions. Your washing machine will wirelessly communicate with each piece of clothing and determine that one piece does not belong. The washing machine will not work and will notify you that you are mixing clothes.

Are these all realities destined for the future? We believe so. What the future holds for RFID is limited only by your imagination.

Most Important Considerations

Throughout this chapter, we've discussed some key emerging trends and technologies. They certainly are exciting and promise that the future will be different and dynamic, to say the least. We have suggested that you anticipate these changes and how they will affect you personally and in your career.

As we close this chapter (and perhaps your studies in this course), let's take a close look at five key topics. Each is a culmination in some way of the material you've learned

HOW MANY COMPUTERS DO YOU RELY ON IN A WEEK?

Technology is certainly a necessity in today's society. If computers and computer systems go down, trains stop running, airline flights are delayed, and stoplights may not work. Your everyday life depends on the use of computers. According to one study, the average American relies on approximately 264 computers every day.

You won't have to think long or hard to come up with a list of computers that you depend on in your everyday life—that's your task for this project. Your team is to develop a list of computers that you rely on in a week's time. Did you recently go to the movies? If so, you relied on the computer that issued your ticket, the cash register computer that totaled your concession bill, and the computer that showed the movie. (No—most movie theaters don't show movies from rolls of film anymore.)

As you create your list, critically evaluate the importance of each computer. Although it might be a nuisance to have the computer go down that's showing you a movie, it's much more critical that other computers in your life be working all the time, without fail.

in this course. Each is inescapable in that it will happen and you must deal with it. Finally, each is vitally important and reaches far beyond the technologies that either necessitate or support it. For you, these last few pages are a chance to reflect on what you've learned and to place that knowledge within the bigger picture.

THE NECESSITY OF TECHNOLOGY

Like it or not, technology is a necessity today. It's hard to imagine a world without it. Just as we need electricity to function on an everyday basis, we need technology as well.

Of course, that doesn't mean you should adopt technology just for the sake of the technology or only because it sounds fun. Rather, you need to carefully evaluate each technology and determine if it will make you more productive, enhance your personal life, enrich your learning, or move your organization in the direction of its strategic goals and initiatives.

Technology is not a panacea. If you throw technology at a business process that doesn't work correctly, the result will be that you'll perform that process incorrectly millions of times faster per second. At the same time, you can ill afford to ignore technology when it really will help you and your organization become more efficient, effective, and innovative.

CLOSING THE GREAT DIGITAL DIVIDE

We must, as a human race, completely eliminate the great digital divide. As we alluded to in Chapter 5, the *great digital divide* refers to the concerns of many people that the world is becoming one marked by "have's" and "have not's" with respect to technology. That is, the traditional notion of a third world economy is now being defined by the extent to which a country has only limited access to and use of technology.

The power of technology needs to be realized on a worldwide scale. We cannot afford to have any technology-challenged nation or culture (within reason). The great digital divide only adds to global instability. If you live and work in a technology-rich country, don't keep it to yourself. When possible, take it to other countries by creating international business partnerships and strategic alliances. Join in a nonprofit program to spread computer literacy and access in a third world country, or in this country. This may afford you great satisfaction, and the world will benefit greatly from your efforts.

VIRTUAL REALITY SIMPLIFIES PATIENT'S WORLD

Imagine a world in which the color blue feels like sandpaper, the only furniture you can sit on must be green, or the sound of a pin dropping on the floor sounds like the cracking of thunder. Fortunately, most of us can't, but unfortunately, that's the real world for a person with autism. Autism is a disease that interferes with the development of the part of the brain that processes sensory perceptions. So, autistic people may feel sandpaper grinding across their skin when they see a color or they may be unable to correlate objects, such as chairs, bar stools, couches, and love seats (all items on which you can sit).

For autistic people, the world is a mishmash of objects that make no sense to them when they have to deal with them all at once. That makes teaching autistic people very difficult. For example, if you place two differently colored chairs in front of an autistic person and tell him or her that they are both chairs, that person may become confused and disoriented.

A simple world is the best world for individuals suffering from autism. Unfortunately, the real world is not so simple. So Dorothy Strickland and many others are researching ways to use virtual reality to teach people with autism. In a virtual reality simulation, researchers can eliminate all forms of background noise, colors, and objects, except those that they want the autistic person to focus on. As the autistic person becomes comfortable with the virtual reality simulation, new objects or colors can be introduced without the usual adverse effects.

Technology is really great—it can help an organization gain a competitive advantage in the marketplace or help you get a job in the future. But the greatest uses of technology may never make anyone rich; instead those uses will help many mentally and physically challenged individuals cope with daily life.[11,12]

TECHNOLOGY FOR THE BETTERMENT OF SOCIETY

Life isn't just about making money. As you approach the development and use of technological innovations (or even standard technologies), think in terms of the betterment of people and society in general. (Making money and helping people often go hand in hand, in fact.)

Medical research is performing marvelous work in the use of technology to treat ailments and cure diseases. But if these efforts are purely profit-driven, we may never wholly realize the fruits of them. For example, therapists are using virtual reality to teach autistic people to cope with increasingly complex situations (see the accompanying Industry Perspective). We know for a fact that this use of technology isn't making anyone a lot of money. But it isn't always about making money. It's about helping people who face daily challenges far greater than ours. You're fortunate to be in an environment of learning. Give back when you have the chance.

EXCHANGING PRIVACY FOR CONVENIENCE

On a personal level, you need to consider how much of your personal privacy you're giving up in exchange for convenience. The extreme example is GPS-enabled implant chips. The convenience is knowing where you are and being able to get directions to your destination. But you're obviously giving up some privacy. Is this okay? Convenience takes on many forms. When you use a discount card at a grocery store to take advantage of sales, that grocery store then tracks your purchasing history in great detail. You can bet that the grocery store will use that information to sell you more tailored products.

It really is a trade-off. In today's technology-based world, you give up privacy when you register for sweepstakes on certain Web sites. You give up privacy just surfing the

NECESSITY, CONVENIENCE, AND PRIVACY

As you consider your own use of technology, it's important that you consider it in the context of necessity, convenience, and your own privacy. You really have two questions to answer. They are

1. *Necessity*—If you truly need technology to perform a personal task, how much of your personal privacy are you willing to forgo?

2. *Convenience*—If you can use technology to make your life more convenient (but your use of it isn't an absolute necessity), how much of your personal privacy are you willing to forgo?

Regarding question 1, provide your answer on a scale of 1 to 5. A 1 represents the fact that you would

relinquish all your privacy to use technology that is a necessity. A 5 represents the fact that you would not relinquish any privacy even if it meant not being able to use a technology that was a necessity.

Regarding question 2, also provide your answer on a scale of 1 to 5. A 1 represents the fact that you would relinquish all your privacy in exchange for using technologies that would make your life more convenient. A 5 represents the fact that you would not relinquish any of your privacy even if it meant not being able to use a technology that made your life more convenient.

Compare your answers with those of several classmates. How do your answers compare to everyone else's?

Web because tracking software monitors your activities. Even when you click on a banner ad, the Web site you go to knows where you came from. Although such trade-offs may seem insignificant, small trade-offs can add up to a big trade-off over time.

Because you are very much a part of this trend, it's often hard to see the big picture and understand that every day you're giving up just a little more privacy in exchange for a little more convenience. Don't ever think that organizations won't use the information they're capturing about you. They're capturing it so they can use it. Of course, much of it will be used to better serve you as a customer, but some of it may not.

ETHICS, ETHICS, ETHICS

As our final note to you, we cannot stress enough again the importance of ethics as they guide your behavior toward other people in your career. We realize that business is business and that businesses need to make money to survive. But the recent scandals involving Enron and others in the corporate world should be a reminder of how important your personal ethical compass is to you. Success shouldn't come to the detriment of other people. It's quite possible to be very ethical and very successful. That's our challenge to you.

Summary: Student Learning Outcomes Revisited

1. **Describe the emerging trends and technologies that will have an impact on the changing Internet.** The Internet is the single most visible aspect of technology and is changing every day.

In the future, you can expect to see a number of emerging trends and technologies including:

- *Software-as-a-service (SaaS)*—delivery model for software which you use on a pay-per-use basis instead of buying the software outright.

- *Push technology*—when businesses and organizations come to you with information, services, and product offerings based on your profile.

- *F2b2C*—e-commerce business model in which a consumer communicates through a business on the Internet that directly provides product specifications to a factory for personalization and customization of the customer's order.

- *VoIP (Voice over Internet Protocol)*—sending voice communications over the Internet and avoiding the toll charges that you would normally receive from your long distance carrier.

2. **Define the various types of technologies that are emerging as we move toward physiological interaction with technology.** Emerging technologies in the area of physiological interaction include

- *Automatic speech recognition (ASR)*—a system that not only captures spoken words but also distinguishes word groupings to form sentences.

- *Virtual reality*—a three-dimensional computer simulation in which you actively and physically participate.

- *Cave automatic virtual environments (CAVEs)*—holographic devices that create, capture, and/or display images in true three-dimensional form.

- *Biometrics*—the use of physiological characteristics—such as your fingerprint, the blood vessels in the iris of your eye, the sound

of your voice, or perhaps even your breath—to provide identification.

3. **Describe technological innovations and trends that will increase portability and mobility.** Technological innovations that will focus on increasing portability and mobility include:

- *Digital cash*—an electronic representation of cash.

- *Wearable computers*—fully equipped computers that you wear as a piece of clothing or attached to a piece of clothing similar to the way you would carry your cell phone on your belt.

- *Multi-state CPUs*—work with information represented in more than just two states, probably 10 states with each state representing a digit between 0 and 9.

- *Holographic storage devices*—devices that store information on a storage medium that is composed of 3-D crystal-like objects with many sides or faces.

4. **Describe the emerging trends of cell phones and RFID as they relate to the wireless environment.** Cell phones and RFID are now and will continue to be disruptive technologies.

- Cell phones—advances in storage, processor capability, music enhancements, and video support—and threats such as viruses and hackers.

- *RFID (radio frequency identification)*—the use of a chip in a tag or label to store information, by which information is transmitted from, or written to, the tag or label when the chip is exposed to the correct frequency of radio waves.

CLOSING CASE STUDY ONE

WILDSEED—A CELL PHONE FOR EVERY FASHION

U.S. manufacturers of cell phones and providers of cell phone service are heavily targeting one select group of customers—teenagers. In the United States, only about 38 percent of all teenagers have cell phones, compared to over 80 percent in most European countries and some Asian countries. Cell phone providers and manufacturers know that there is plenty of room to grow in the teenage market, not only because 62 percent don't currently have cell phones but also because teenagers are very quick to embrace and use new technologies. Those same companies know that teenagers aren't as frugal with money and tend to spend much more time talking on a cell phone than adults.

Of course, cell phones aren't really new technologies, but what you can do with them is. Motorola, for example, manufactures a cell phone with FM radio capability (XM radio may not be far behind). Samsung and many others offer cell phone service that includes AOL Instant Messenger (with audio and limited video). Most cell phone providers offer cell phones with cameras and multimedia messaging.

One of the leaders in this dynamic and changing industry is Wildseed, which regularly holds cell phone focus groups just for teenagers. Wildseed has determined that teenagers have three cell phone concerns:

1. *Visual appeal*—A cell phone should make a fashion statement. Teenagers also believe that cell phones should be a statement about individuality ("I want a cell phone that doesn't look like anyone else's").
2. *Functionality*—A cell phone should do more than just support phone-calling capabilities.
3. *Price*—Long-term calling plans are not the way to go.

VISUAL APPEAL

Wildseed has tested numerous cell phone designs on teenagers. One cell phone holder was designed to be worn like a garter belt, and it flopped in a big way. According to one young man in the focus group, "Is a guy supposed to wear that?" And a young girl in the focus group commented, "It looks like something for a prostitute." But Wildseed did hit upon a good idea. It now manufactures "smart skins," cell phone covers that have an embedded computer chip. According to what the teenager is wearing, he or she can quickly change the design of the cell phone face plate. While skateboarding one day, for example, a young man could change his cell phone face plate to a splashy rendition of hard colors such as red, yellow, and green. Teenagers can also choose from among music-oriented themes according to their favorite artist.

FUNCTIONALITY

Cell phones are certainly no longer devices just for talking. Most cell phones have e-mail capabilities and support surfing the Web. Those are no longer a competitive advantage for any cell phone manufacturer. Wildseed tried a couple of new ideas on teenage focus groups; the first failed and the second met with great success. The first additional functionality was a cell phone that supported Morse code. No one liked that because no one knew how to send and interpret Morse code. Additionally, teenage girls stated they would have a problem sending Morse code because their long

fingernails made it difficult to type. The second function was "airtexting." Using an airtexting-enabled cell phone, you type in a brief message (e.g., "Call me") and then wave your cell phone back and forth in the air. Blinking red lights on the cell phone are synchronized to display the message in the air. That way, someone across the room can receive your message without having to use a cell phone. You may have seen airtexting clocks that have an arm that moves back and forth through the air and seems to suspend the time and day in the air. As one young lady put it, "That's tight."

PRICE

Price is a major drawback for most teenagers, not necessarily the per-minute charge but rather the long-term contract that must be signed. In the United States, as opposed to most other countries, you must typically sign a six-month or one-year contract for cell phone service. That prohibits many teenagers from getting a cell phone because they have to get their parents to co-sign on the contract. Unfortunately, Wildseed is a manufacturer of cell phones and not a cell phone service provider.[13,14]

Questions

1. The role and purpose of cell phones have certainly changed over the past few years. Not too long ago, business professionals were the only ones to use cell phones. Now, over one in three teenagers in the United States have a cell phone and about 99 percent of them don't use them for business. Are cell phones becoming a technology of convenience and not of necessity? If people use them just for the convenience of communicating anywhere at anytime, are they really a necessity? On the other hand, if you use a cell phone as your primary mode of communication, is it no longer just a convenience?

2. Airtexting sounds like a good idea. From across a room, you'll be able to easily send someone a short message without using your minutes or having the other person's cell phone ring. But you are giving up some privacy. If you airtext your message, everyone in the room will be able to see it. Are you willing to give up some amount of privacy to use an airtexting feature? Why or why not? What about while sitting in a classroom? Should you be able to airtext a message in the middle of class? Does your

school have a policy requiring you to turn off your cell phone when entering a classroom? If so, should this policy apply to airtexting? Why or why not?

3. Functionality is very important for cell phones. What types of functionality does your cell phone support beyond making and receiving phone calls? If you could design the "perfect"

cell phone, what additional functionality would you include?

4. Do you foresee a day when cell phones will be the standard phone and we'll simply do away with land-based phone lines? It's probably going to happen. If cell phones do become the standard, how will you access the Internet from home?

CLOSING CASE STUDY TWO

T2C—NOT ANOTHER NEW E-COMMERCE BUSINESS MODEL

Throughout this text, we've introduced you to the various players in e-commerce—B (Business), C (Consumer), G (Government), and F (Factory). What about "T"? What would that stand for? In this particular case study, it stands for toast. It's actually not a real player in the e-commerce world, but it does in some way represent one of the many dramatic ways in which technology has changed our lives.

In 2005, Jennifer Wilbanks ran away the day before her wedding. Later, she called authorities and claimed to have been kidnapped. As it turned out, she simply got "cold feet" and scared. At this point, you're probably wondering where toast comes into the picture. Just a few days after the story of Jennifer broke in the news and the world found out that she wasn't abducted, a man placed an auction on eBay. He burned a piece of toast and used a dull instrument to carve a likeness of Jennifer into the toast. It really wasn't much of a likeness at all, but rather a childlike rendering of the face of a woman with hair flipping up near her shoulders.

What's even more astonishing is that the world seemed to flock to the auction. When it ended, over 200 people had bid on the piece of toast (again, just a piece of toast), and the winner paid over $15,000. As that auction ended, a quick search on eBay for "toast" yielded a list of other pieces of toast as follows:

- Elvis Presley (5 of them)
- Jesus
- Calista Flockhart

- *Desperate Housewives* (the television show)
- Devil
- Mystery cross
- Bill O'Reilly
- Lynndie England
- Yoda or Gremlin (whichever you choose to see in the toast)
- Frankentoast
- Finger (not the good finger)
- Corey Clark and Paula Abdul (from the show *American Idol*)
- Michael Jackson (3 of them—he was in the news at the same time)
- A cat
- Jennifer Wilbanks (20 others attempting to capitalize on the story)

It's hard to believe, but that is a true story.

On the ever-changing Internet, you can find just about anything you want, even a piece of burned toast with a likeness of anyone you would care to name. Even Donald Trump is getting on the Internet. He started Trump University, an online college campus of business courses. He even claims to teach some of the courses, which cost students about $300 each. At the time we wrote this case study, Trump University wasn't offering degrees, but that may be a reality as you now read this.

The point is that technology, in this case specifically the Internet, has dramatically changed everything we do. Prior to the Internet, would anyone have paid over $15,000 for a burned piece of toast with anyone's likeness on it? When cell phones first arrived on the scene, you typically paid about $.15 per minute of call time. Very few people used them unless it was an absolute emergency. Now, students use them to make calls and send text messages while participating in graduation events.

It's now your turn to predict the next 10 years. In the early 1990s, very few people had ever even heard the term "World Wide Web." That wasn't too long ago. There is only one question to this final case study, although it has many parts.

Question

1. What is your prediction of the future and what role technology will play in shaping and molding it? For each of the areas identified below, think about the emerging trends and technologies we've discussed in this chapter (and any others as well). What is the future for each area? Search the Web and see if you can find any supporting evidence. Most important, think outside the box and use your imagination.
   - Movies
   - Music
   - Professional sports
   - Travel
   - Homes
   - Education

Key Terms and Concepts

Application service provider (ASP), 425
Automatic speech recognition (ASR), 429
Biochip, 435
Biometrics, 432
CAVE (cave automatic virtual environment), 431
Digital cash (electronic cash, e-cash), 436
Disintermediation, 426
F2b2C (Factory to business to Consumer), 426
Facial recognition software, 435
Feature analysis, 429
Glove, 430
Haptic interface, 430
Headset (head-mounted display), 430
Holographic device, 431

Holographic storage device, 438
Implant chip, 435
Language processing, 429
Mobisode, 440
Multi-state CPU, 438
Pattern classification, 429
Push technology, 426
RFID (radio frequency identification), 440
Software-as-a-service (SaaS), 425
Virtual reality, 429
VoIP (Voice over Internet Protocol), 428
Walker, 430
Wearable computer, 437

Short-Answer Questions

1. How does software-as-a-service differ from today's traditional notion of purchasing software?
2. What is a push technology environment?
3. How will push technologies support personalization?
4. Why will it be cheaper to use VoIP as opposed to a traditional telephone service provider?
5. What is the role of physiological interfaces?
6. What are the three steps in automatic speech recognition?
7. What is virtual reality?
8. What type of special input and output devices does virtual reality make use of?
9. What are CAVEs?
10. What are some examples of biometric applications?

11. How will biometrics aid in providing security and identification?
12. What is the function of a biochip?
13. What is the role of an implant chip?
14. How will digital cash someday work on the Internet?
15. What is a wearable computer?
16. How do multi-state CPUs differ from today's standard CPUs?

17. Why will holographic storage devices be able to store more information than today's storage devices?
18. How will mobisodes work with a cell phone?
19. What are some applications of RFID?
20. What is the great digital divide?

Assignments and Exercises

1. **SELLING THE IDEA OF IMPLANT CHIPS AT YOUR SCHOOL** Let's assume for a moment that your team is in favor of using implant chips that contain vitally important information such as identification and medical information. Your task is to put together a sales presentation to your school that would require all students to obtain implant chips. In your presentation, include the following:
   A. The school-related information that each implant chip would contain
   B. The nonschool-related information that each implant chip would contain
   C. The processes within your school that would use the information on the implant chips
   D. The benefits your school would realize by requiring implant chips
   E. The benefits students would realize by having implant chips
   Your presentation should be no more than five minutes, so it must be a powerful selling presentation.

2. **RESEARCHING WEARABLE COMPUTERS** One of the leading-edge manufacturers of wearable computers is Xybernaut. Connect to its Web site at www.xybernaut.com and research its various lines of wearable computers. What are the names of the lines of Xybernaut's wearable computers? What are their CPU speeds? How much RAM do they include? What functions can you perform with them? What sort of technology devices (e.g., wireless Internet access) can you add to each line? Is there any line advanced enough and cheap enough that you would consider buying one? Why or why not?

3. **FINDING A GOOD AUTOMATIC SPEECH RECOGNITION SYSTEM** Research the Web for automatic speech recognition (ASR) systems. Make a list of the ones you find. What are the prices of each? Are they speaker-independent or speaker-dependent? Do they support continuous speech recognition or discrete speech recognition? What sort of add-on vocabularies can you purchase? How comfortable would you feel speaking the contents of a term paper as opposed to typing it? Would you have to be more or less organized to use speech recognition as opposed to typing? Why?

4. **UNDERSTANDING THE RELATIONSHIPS BETWEEN TRENDS AND TECHNOLOGICAL INNOVATIONS** In this chapter, we presented you with numerous key technologies and how they relate to six important trends. (See Figure 9.1 on page 424 for the list of technologies and trends.) For each trend, identify all the technologies presented in this chapter that can have an impact. For each technology that you do identify, provide a short discussion of how it might have an impact.

5. **RESEARCHING APPLICATIONS OF RFID** Visit the Web and perform a search on RFID for applications that we didn't discuss in this chapter. Prepare a short PowerPoint presentation highlighting each. Also, search the Web for the leading providers of RFID technologies. What companies did you find? Does one seem to stand out above the rest? If so, which is it?

6. **RESEARCHING INTELLIGENT HOME APPLIANCES** Visit a local appliance store in your area and find three home appliances that contain some sort of intelligence (i.e., an embedded computer chip that takes over some of the functionality and decision making). For each appliance, prepare a short report that includes the following information:
   • A description and price for the intelligent home appliance
   • The "intelligent" features of the appliance
   • How those features make the appliance better than the nonintelligent version

Discussion Questions

1. There is currently much legislation pending in many states that would make it illegal for people to use a cell phone while driving a car. The reason is that society has already noticed a significant increase in the number of traffic accidents in which one of the drivers involved in the accident was using a cell phone. Think beyond that for a moment and include wearable computers. As this new technology becomes more widely available, isn't it possible for someone to be driving a car while using a computer? Should the government enact legislation to prevent it? Why or why not?

2. In a push technology environment, businesses and organizations will come to you with information, services, and product offerings based on your profile. How is a push technology environment different from mass mailings and spam? Is it an invasion of your privacy to have organizations calling you on your cell phone every time you come near a store? Why or why not? Should you be able to "opt in" or "opt out" of these offerings? Is this really any different from someone leaving a flyer at your house or on your car while it's parked in a parking lot?

3. There are three steps in automatic speech recognition (ASR): feature analysis, pattern classification, and language processing. Which of those three steps is the most challenging for a computer to perform? Why? Which of those three steps is the least challenging for a computer to perform? Why? If ASR systems are to become automatic speech understanding systems, which step must undergo the greatest improvement in its capabilities? Why?

4. Much debate surrounds the use of biometrics. Many people like it because biometrics can provide identification and increase security. Other people see it as a tremendous invasion of your privacy. Just as you read in this chapter, a bank—by using biometric identification—may be able to tell if a woman is pregnant. So, the greatest challenge to overcome is not technological but rather societal. What do you think needs to happen for society to accept the use of biometrics? How long do you think it will be before society accepts the use of biometrics? In what year do you believe the U.S. federal government will begin requiring a biometric of every newborn child?

5. Digital cash is destined to greatly impact the use of coins and folding cash. What sort of future do you foresee if we do away completely with traditional forms of currency and just use electronic forms? Will this help eliminate the digital divide or will the digital divide provide a barrier to the widespread use of electronic forms of payment? Justify your answer.

6. What are the ethical dilemmas associated with using facial recognition software? Is the use of this type of software really any different from a store asking to see your driver's license when you use your credit card? Why or why not? Should the government be able to place digital video cameras on every street corner and use facial recognition software to monitor your movements? Why or why not?

7. When (and if) CAVEs become a common reality, you'll be able to visit your family and friends anytime you want no matter where they live. What sort of impact will this have on the travel industry? If you can see your relatives in a CAVE as often as you want, will you be more or less inclined to buy a plane ticket and visit them in person? Why or why not?

Continuing Your Education Through the Internet

To be perfectly honest, it's a dog-eat-dog world out there. The competitive landscape of business is more intense than it ever has been. And that competitiveness spills into your personal life. Many of you are in school right now to get an education to better compete in the job market. But many knowledge workers are finding out that an undergraduate degree is simply not enough to compete in the business world, and so they wish to acquire more education.

Just like businesses, graduate schools (and all schools in general) are using the Internet as a way to communicate information to you. Many of these schools are even offering you online courses through the Internet to further your education.

MBA PROGRAMS

Many of you will undoubtedly choose to continue your education by obtaining an MBA. And you probably should. The market for the best business positions is extremely competitive, with hiring organizations seeking individuals who can speak more than one language, have job experience, and have extended their educational endeavors beyond just getting an undergraduate degree.

Each year, *U.S. News & World Report* ranks the top business schools in the nation. On the Web site that supports this text, you'll find a list of the Web sites for some of the top 50 business schools in the nation.

Choose a couple of different business schools from the list of 50, visit their Web sites, and answer the following questions for each:

A. What business school did you choose?

B. Does that school offer a graduate program in your area of interest?

C. Can you apply online?

D. Does the site list tuition and fee costs?

E. Does the site contain a list of the graduate courses offered in your area of interest?

SPECIALIZED MBA PROGRAMS

In the previous section, you explored a few of the top 50 business schools in the nation. Those schools were ranked irrespective of any specialization, focusing rather on overall academic reputation. *U.S. News & World Report* also compiles an annual list of the best business schools in 10 specializations: accounting, entrepreneurship, finance, health services administration, management information systems, international business, general business, marketing, nonprofit organizations, and production/operations. If you're interested in a specialized MBA, you should consider viewing schools in these lists.

Choose at least three schools that offer a specialization in your area of interest and visit their Web sites. Based on what you find, rank those three schools according to your first, second, and third choices. What factors did you consider? Was cost an overriding concern? Before you began your analysis, did you already have a preconceived notion of the best school? Did you change your mind once you visited the schools' sites?

GRADUATE SCHOOL INFORMATION AND TIPS

Before you begin your decision-making process concerning which graduate school to attend, you should gather a variety of material. For example, obtaining a directory of universities (both domestic and international) would be helpful. Perhaps even more important, you should ask yourself several questions. Are you ready for graduate school? Why are you considering going to graduate school? How do you determine which school is best for you based on such issues as price, location, and area of specialization?

Many of these questions are very personal to you. For example, we can't help you determine if you're really ready for graduate school or answer why you're considering going to graduate school. But what we can do is point you toward some valuable resources on the Internet to help you answer some of your questions and find a wealth of information relating to universities. On the Web site that supports this text, we've included many links to those types of sites.

At your leisure, we recommend that you connect to several of these sites and see what they have to offer. Some simply provide a list of universities, whereas others may be particularly useful as you make that all-important decision.

TELE-EDUCATION (DISTANCE LEARNING)

Throughout this text, you've explored the concept of 24×7 connectivity through information technology. Using IT (part of which is the Internet), organizations today are sending out telecommuting employees, and medical and health facilities are establishing telemedicine practices.

Tele-education, which goes by a number of names including e-education, distance learning, distributed learning, and online learning, enables you to get an education without "going" to school. Quite literally, you can enroll in a school on the East Coast and live in Denver, enjoying great winter skiing. Using various forms of IT (videoconferencing, e-mail, chat rooms, and the Internet), you can take courses from schools all over the world. Some of those schools even offer complete degree programs via IT.

These schools include graduate programs in business. For example, the Massachusetts Institute of Technology and Duke University have graduate programs that combine traditional classroom instruction courses and computer-delivered courses. In 1997, Ohio University (Athens) introduced MBA without Boundaries, an MBA program that is completely online except for a required six-week orientation session.

Connect to at least five of these sites and explore the possibilities of tele-education. As you do, consider the issues below.

A. Can you just take courses or enroll in a complete degree program?

B. What is the cost of tele-education?

C. What process do you go through to enroll in a tele-education program?

D. How would you feel about staying at home instead of going to class?

E. How do tele-education programs foster interactivity between students and teachers?

EXTENDED LEARNING MODULE I

BUILDING AN E-PORTFOLIO

Student Learning Outcomes

1. DESCRIBE THE TYPES OF ELECTRONIC RÉSUMÉS AND SPECIFY WHEN EACH IS APPROPRIATE.

2. DISCUSS NETWORKING STRATEGIES YOU CAN USE DURING A JOB SEARCH.

3. EXPLAIN HOW SELF-ASSESSMENT IS VALUABLE TO RÉSUMÉ WRITING.

4. USE THE INTERNET TO RESEARCH CAREER OPPORTUNITIES AND POTENTIAL EMPLOYERS.

5. DEVELOP POWERFUL JOB SEARCH E-PORTFOLIO CONTENT.

6. DOCUMENT EFFECTIVE WEB SITE STRUCTURE AND DESIGN COMPONENTS.

7. CREATE A JOB SEARCH E-PORTFOLIO WEB SITE AND PLACE IT ON AN INTERNET SERVER.

Introduction

Welcome to the 21st century—the anytime, anywhere job market. In this information age, Internet technology has undoubtedly had an impact on résumé development, job networking, and their effectiveness in uncovering hidden job opportunities. The Internet provides instant access to job-market intelligence, such as: who is hiring, what skills are in demand, and how much those skills are worth—24 hours a day. For the first time ever, individual job seekers have access to the same information once available only to corporate insiders and recruiters.

Although there are many forms of electronic recruitment, this module will concentrate on electronic documents that you as a potential employee need to have prepared to compete in today's electronic job market. The final product will be an electronic portfolio designed to help you successfully promote yourself in the electronic job market.

In this module, we assume that you are familiar with the Internet and research tools and have at least a little knowledge of HTML. For a review of the Internet, see *Extended Learning Module B*. For a review of HTML, refer to *Extended Learning Module F*. To learn to build an electronic portfolio using FrontPage, see *Extended Learning Module L*.

The Electronic Job Market— Extending Your Reach

The online recruiting industry has been developing for several years and is poised for explosive growth. It happens all the time. A new industry forms and simmers for a while, and then someone discovers the last piece of the puzzle, the missing link that explodes the industry out of its infancy, into the limelight, and into the mainstream.

Since the early 1990s the term electronic portfolio (e-portfolio) has been described in a range of ways, with most recognizing the primary role of information and communications technologies in describing the "e." Common to most definitions is the relationship with paper-based portfolios (or résumés) that have traditionally been used as documented evidence of experience and achievement. Formally, an ***electronic portfolio (e-portfolio)*** is a cohesive, powerful, and well-designed collection of electronic documents that demonstrate your skills, education, professional development, and the benefits you offer to a hiring organization.

E-portfolios are much more than innovative résumés or scrapbooks. Neither of those forms can show reflection, evolution of thought, or professional development. In education and training contexts e-portfolios are learner-centered and outcomes-based. They are created when individuals selectively compile evidence of their own electronic activities and output as a means to indicate what they have learned or achieved. In this sense, e-portfolios function as a learning record or transcript. But given their developmental character, e-portfolios function as both an archive and a developmental repository that is used for learning management and self-reflective purposes.

The online recruiting industry, or the ***electronic job market,*** makes use of many Internet technologies to recruit employees. The average cost per hire through online recruiting is $152 compared with $1,383 using traditional methods. Additionally, a much broader worldwide selection of candidates can be screened, significantly increasing the likelihood of finding a good match for the hiring organization. As more and more hiring employers turn to the Internet to recruit employees, it is critical that you learn to capitalize on the technologies that help organizations locate and evaluate potential employees. Although the basic parts of your résumé stay the same and the purpose of your résumé is still to present your skills and qualifications, how you do so must change dramatically in the electronic job market.

HELEN SULLIVAN
1234 Somewhere Drive
Denver CO, 80283
303-123-4878
hsulli@du.edu
Personal Web Site: www.du.edu/~hsulli/home.htm

OBJECTIVE
General Sales Representative with a pharmaceutical house using extensive chemistry background and self-directed personality to manage a marketing territory. Personal Goal: to increase sales and improve customer satisfaction. Willing to relocate.

EMPLOYEMENT HISTORY
A pril 2001 – Present
SPQ Pharmaceuticals Corp., Denver, CO
Currently working as a General Sales Manager responsible for sales and distribution of pharmaceutical supplies to doctor's offices, pharmacies, and clinics in the Midwest Region.
– Volume of two million dollars in annual sales
– Salesperson of the month for the past five months
– Increased SPQ customer base by five percent
– Improved customer understanding of SPQ products and their benefits
– Initiated cost saving sales procedures to reduce the overall expenditures of the sales department by over $30,000 annually
– Developed and implemented technical training for the sales force to improve their understanding of SPQ products and how to effectively market them
– Analyzed sales trends and improved the focus of the sales force

January 1999 – April 2000
How2.com, Inc., Denver, CO
Managed the sales force for a dynamic and evolving web company.

HELEN SULLIVAN

1234 Somewhere Drive   303-123-4878
Denver CO, 80283   hsulli@du.edu
Personal Web Site: www.du.edu/~hsulli/home.htm

OBJECTIVE
General Sales Representative with a pharmaceutical house using extensive chemistry background and self-directed personality to manage a marketing territory. Personal Goal: to increase sales and improve customer satisfaction. Willing to relocate.

EMPLOYMENT HISTORY
SPQ Pharmaceuticals Corp., Denver, CO   April 2000 – Present

Currently working as a General Sales Manager responsible for sales and distribution of pharmaceutical supplies to doctor's offices, pharmacies, and clinics in the Midwest Region. • Volume of two million dollars in annual sales • Salesperson of the month for the past five months • Increased SPQ customer base by five percent • Improved customer understanding of SPQ products and their benefits	• Initiated cost saving sales procedures to reduce the overall expenditures of the sales department by over $30,000 annually • Developed and implemented technical training for the sales force to improve their understanding of SPQ products and how to effectively market them • Analyzed sales trends and improved the focus of the sales force

How2.com, Inc., Denver, CO   January 1999 – April 2000

Managed the sales force for a dynamic and evolving web company. • Sales force of 8.	• Increased overall sales by 28 percent • Improved sales force morale and productivity using team management

STR Systems, Bloomington, IN   August 1996 – December 1998

Managed the sales force for a dynamic and evolving web company. • Sales force of 8.	• Increased overall sales by 28 percent • Improved sales force morale and productivity using team management

EDUCATION
Indiana University, Bloomington   B.S. in Marketing and Chemistry, 1996

Figure I.1

Sample Résumés

The Internet provides $24 \times 7 \times 365$ access to information for both the employer and you as a potential employee. During your electronic job search, your effective use of Internet tools is critical to a successful job hunt. Since meeting the needs of employers is the basis for getting hired, your preresumé tasks must center on gathering information about who is hiring, what skills are in demand, how much those skills are worth, and what you need to do to be considered for the available jobs. With this information in hand, you are prepared to create the electronic documents that will place you in a position to be considered for not just a job, but a career (see Figure I.1).

Résumés are the currency of the recruitment industry. They are the cornerstone of communication between candidates, recruiters, and employers. To put the matter in perspective, ask yourself, "When was the last time you were hired as a professional without submitting a résumé?" If you are like most people, the answer is "never." Technology is automating elements of the recruitment process, but a complete solution requires proper handling of the actual development of all the pieces and parts of not only your e-résumé, but your e-portfolio.

Historically, applicants prospected for jobs by sending out large numbers of unsolicited paper résumés in the hope of uncovering hidden opportunities. Even the best techniques for converting these paper résumés into electronic formats were labor intensive, slow, and prone to inaccuracy.

As all companies large and small expand their operational efficiency with technology, it will be necessary for job seekers to expand their computer competency to online job searching and résumé posting. The Internet also provides job seekers with a way to contact more of the right employers in less time and, therefore, build a larger network of potential job leads.

Convergence of Online Networking and Résumé Development

In the always-available job market created by the Internet, organizations post and remove jobs on a continuous and instantaneous basis. Businesses have many options for where and how to list positions. Most Internet-savvy organizations have recruiting pages on their Web sites. Others use job database Web sites such as www.monster.com that reach a worldwide audience. Some organizations use their intranets to recruit from within.

Even in this all-encompassing electronic job market, some jobs are never posted. Collectively, unposted positions are referred to as the **hidden job market.** It is important to prepare yourself to search for jobs in the traditional (newspaper and magazine), electronic, and hidden job markets to maximize your job opportunities.

Many companies still select candidates to interview by visually reviewing résumés. However, in today's electronic world more and more firms supplement such manual methods with automated résumé tracking systems. Employers use such systems because they drastically reduce the time it takes to manually review, sort, and file large numbers of résumés. Using these systems, employers collect and store text from thousands of résumés in electronic databases. Such databases can then be sorted to find applicant résumés which contain skills, experience or education that match specified job requirements. Selected résumés can then be viewed onscreen or printed in their entirety, or specific information can be extracted from each one.

For job seekers, this new electronic world means that you must have two versions of your résumé: (1) a nicely formatted one for human eyes, which we will refer to as your "visual résumé"; and (2) one designed for computers, which we are calling your "electronic résumé." Later in this module you will learn how to create an electronic résumé by converting your résumé word processing file into "plain text or ASCII format" as well as an HTML format.

To achieve job search success in today's electronic arena, there are two key points to guide you:

1. You want to learn how to create a résumé (which will morph into an e-résumé) that will come to the top when an employer sorts for keywords or areas of experience that he or she needs. You will achieve this by knowing the type of job you want and the skills needed for such a position, and then effectively matching your skills to that position.

2. You want to use Internet job search strategies to find employer Web sites and job postings so that you can apply for them.

START TO NETWORK

If you read the want ads, send out résumés, and wait for employers to discover you, the odds of finding a satisfying job are not very good. According to JobStar (www.jobstar. org), a job board and collection of job search information offered in association with *The Wall Street Journal* (www.CareerJournal.com), "80 percent of all positions are filled without employer advertising. These positions are filled by—or created for—candidates who come to an employer's attention through employee recommendations, referrals from trusted associates, recruiters, or direct contact with the candidate." This means that networking and preparing résumé content targeted to a specific job and industry are critical to your success. Networking involves:

BUILD YOUR 30-SECOND COMMERCIAL

Building a quality 30-second commercial can be tougher than it sounds. The goal is to be able to tell people who you are, what your skills are, and why you are approaching them.

1. Narrow your focus by selecting one job type (a job type can encompass several job titles but the skills are the same) and one industry. Write your job description. For example,

   - Online researcher for a major law firm specializing in corporate contracts and patents.
   - Java and C++ programmer in the Texas oil and gas industry.

2. Start a list of job title synonyms. For example, a Java and C++ programmer could also be called a Web Applet developer or simply a programmer/analyst. This list will help you research and write your résumé.

3. Create a list of words describing your skills and interests. Begin broadly and then narrow your list to skills related to your current job search (see Figure I.2).

4. Put together your script. Include who you are, your top three skills, and what you would like from this contact. For example,

   > Hello my name is _____. I am working on an Information Technology degree at the University of Denver. You are registered as a mentor in the Career Placement Center and your job title is listed as Java Developer. I am very analytical, have enjoyed all of my programming courses, and am particularly interested in Java programming. Can you give me some advice on how to secure a job?

5. Practice your script before attending face-to-face networking functions. Edit your script as appropriate before using it in electronic communications.

6. Create a list of follow-up questions to use when your contact responds. For example,

   - How did you get your first job in this area?
   - Do you know of any open positions that I should apply for?

- **Creating relationships.** Target people who are in a position to further your career search. Make a list of everyone that you call on the phone, e-mail, electronically chat with, or have even had passing conversations with. This list should be quite long. The goal here is to get a list of potential contacts.

- **Developing a 30-second commercial.** This is a short description of who you are, what job you are looking for, and the skills that make you suited for the job. Having a short script makes it easier to contact people and avoids wasting their time.

- **Employing electronic means.** No matter how you are contacting people, use the technology to further your reach, such as e-mail, and learn how to develop an e-portfolio Web site (which is the basis of this learning module).

- **Avoiding sending bulk e-mails.** The personal touch of sending individual e-mail is more likely to obtain results. Set a goal to contact a specific number of people each week, keep track of whom you have contacted and the responses you have received, and finally make sure you send a follow-up message.

- **Joining mailing lists.** *Mailing lists* are discussion groups organized by area of interest. By subscribing to such a list, you can communicate with members via e-mail. Mailing lists allow you to gain industry information and make contacts that would not otherwise be available. On occasion, job announcements are also circulated through these lists. You can find mailing lists by topic at groups.yahoo.com, lists.topica.com, tile.net/lists, and groups.google.com.

PERFORM A SELF-ASSESSMENT

Contrary to popular belief and traditional résumé-writing styles, employers are not really interested in what you have already done; they want to know what you will do for *them* and to have documented evidence of those skills. To effectively communicate your skills and how they will benefit a potential employer, you must know what those skills are and that means spending some time evaluating yourself. While it is nice to be a "people person," that does not tell an employer that you work well under stress, mediate, negotiate contracts, and follow procedures. Being a "people person" will not get you a job, but detailing your skills in that area may.

Remember that the paper and electronic documents you create are your personal marketing tools. Most people want to jump right in and write a résumé, but you must get employer-focused first. Employers typically process résumés looking for things that exclude candidates by sorting applicants into three groups: Definitely, Maybe, and No. Ideally, you would like to be in the Definitely group, but the Maybe group can result in a position if you have done your homework and documented what you offer an employer.

There are many good tools for self-assessment: personality profiles, checklists (see Figure I.2), strength identification, achievement lists, and any number of writing and projection exercises. You can even ask people what your strengths are. Believe it or not, others are often better at articulating your strengths than you may be. Most colleges and universities have an array of assessment tools available to their students, such as the Myers-Briggs Type Indicator test. There are also many organizations offering testing from the Web. Some are free, for example, www.jobstar.org, and others charge a fee, such as www.careermaze.com. Use the methods that are available and that suit your needs, but do not shortchange this step. Time spent here will pay off when you do begin to write.

The goal of performing a self-assessment exercise is to develop a list of evocative words that you can use to describe your objective and experience in a manner that employers can understand. Typically these words are nouns and adjectives called ***skill words*** that stress your capabilities, which you should weave into the text of your résumé.

RESEARCH CAREERS, INDUSTRIES, AND COMPANIES

The Web is an incredible resource for researching topics such as résumé writing, career forecasts, job availability, skills required to be hirable, industry trends, and virtual communities. Although there are other approaches, most Web users find that search tools significantly improve the quality of the material located when browsing. We encourage you to review *Extended Learning Module B* to learn more about how to use electronic search tools.

Many job seekers underestimate the role of research in creating effective documents such as a résumé. A résumé should not be simply a history of your education and work, but should be a document targeted to one position and industry.

Research is the key to creating powerful employer-centered résumé content directed to a specific industry. There is so much information available to help you develop powerful résumé content that the task of sifting through it can be overwhelming.

To make the most of the available information, develop a list of search terms based on your goals and then visit job database Web sites, search engines, government sites, and business Web pages. You should be able to find information on planning your career, the education or training needed to be successful, expected earnings by geographic location, the work environment, attire, normal career path, projected number of openings, and current job postings. Additionally you should find specific organizations, contacts, and communities that will help you fine-tune your target.

Figure I.2

Sample Self-Assessment Tool

Transferable Skills

Transferable skills are those that can be applied to any job or work situation. Everyone has them. Each transferable skill has keywords that can be used to describe your strengths. Select each skill below that applies to you and then write how you effectively exhibit that skill.

General Keywords

___ critical thinking	___ self-discipline	___ general knowledge	___ self-confidence
___ research techniques	___ insight	___ cultural perspective	___ imagination
___ perseverance	___ writing	___ teaching ability	___ leadership

Research Keywords

___ initiating	___ attaining	___ achieving	___ reviewing
___ updating	___ interpreting	___ analyzing	___ synthesizing
___ communicating	___ planning	___ designing	
___ performing	___ estimating	___ implementing	

Teaching Keywords

___ organizing	___ assessing	___ public speaking	___ reporting
___ counseling	___ managing	___ coordinating	___ administering
___ motivating	___ problem solving		

Personality Keywords

___ dynamic	___ sensitive	___ responsible	___ creative
___ imaginative	___ accurate	___ easygoing	___ adept
___ innovative	___ expert	___ successful	___ efficient
___ perceptive	___ astute	___ humanistic	___ honest
___ outstanding	___ calm	___ outgoing	___ self-starting
___ reliable	___ unique	___ experienced	___ talented
___ vigorous	___ versatile	___ diplomatic	

Object Keywords

___ data	___ systems	___ relations	___ theories
___ recommendations	___ programs	___ events	___ outputs
___ facts	___ conclusions	___ goals	___ surveys
___ procedures	___ methods	___ statistics	___ strategy
___ feelings	___ designs	___ tools	___ journals
___ techniques	___ communications	___ charts	___ presentations
___ reports	___ research projects	___ information	___ human resources

START YOUR RESEARCH

Research is time-consuming and the sheer volume of information available on the Web is daunting. Target your research and stay focused. When you come upon items of interest that will not further your current goal, copy and paste their URLs into a word processing document and then proceed with the your research.

In a second word processing document, track career-related data and their sources gathered from your search. Refine your search words as necessary. Remember that you should be gathering as much data as you can about your chosen career, but it may be helpful to search for each type of information separately. For example, salary information may not be available from the sources discussing the projected number of jobs over the next five years or the normal work week in an industry. Use the following list of Web resources as a starting point.

Search Engines

- www.google.com—The largest Web index.
- www.search.com—Search using several search engines at once.
- www.searchengineguide.com—Listing of search engines by topic.
- www.job-search-engine.com—A meta job search engine dedicated to employment.

Media

- www.jobsmarket.com—Online classifieds.
- www.careerpath.com—Online classifieds.
- www.classifieds2000.com—Online classifieds.

Government

- www.bls.gov—Bureau of Labor Statistics. Excellent source for work environment, job forecast, and regional data. Try the kids' pages.

Job Boards

- www.monster.com—Largest job board consistently listed in the top five sites.
- www.hotjobs.com—Job postings by location, industry, or company. International postings and salary wizard.
- www.collegegrad.com—Excellent resource for entry-level job seekers. Offers job search, résumé, and networking strategies.

Other Resources

- www.careers.org—Job search and career resource directory organized by topic and region.

Résumé Building—A Lifelong Process

Electronic résumés, or e-résumés, have moved into the mainstream of today's job market at lightning speed. E-résumés have stepped up the efficiency of job placement to such a point that you could get a call from a recruiter just hours after submitting your e-résumé. With this kind of opportunity, you cannot afford to be left in the dark ages of using only a hardcopy (visual) résumé.

A *résumé* is a summary of your qualifications. It is an organized collection of information that will "sell" your skills to an employer. A résumé and accompanying applications correspondence are likely to be the most important documents you will create. They are advertisements that get you noticed in the crowded, competitive job market.

A generation ago it was common to work for a single company throughout your entire career. This type of job security is no longer possible in today's volatile business climate. Most people will end up making at least a half-dozen major job changes in a lifetime of work.

The average employer looks at a résumé for less than 34 seconds. In some situations, a computer may actually scan in your résumé looking for specific skills and abilities. Your résumé must therefore be professionally written, attractive, and concise, and demonstrate your skills and value to a potential employer.

CONTENT, CONTENT, CONTENT

Through beginning to network, assessing your skills, and researching, you will gain the knowledge critical for creating targeted résumé content. Use the job titles, skills, and jargon from one industry to describe yourself and your experience. If you are job seeking in multiple industries or in a variety of position titles, you may need to develop a separate résumé for each.

When you begin writing, concentrate on creating solid content that is targeted, is grammatically correct, and convincingly outlines your skills. Since we are concentrating on electronic documents, old rules governing the writing style, length, and content of paper résumés do not apply. For example, creating a résumé that will print on one page (or two at most) is not relevant in this arena.

No one wants to be considered conceited or boastful. When it comes to looking for a job, however, you must emphasize your abilities, focus on your strengths, and create a dynamic first impression. A well-written and neatly organized résumé can do all of that. The topics covered in this section will enable you to analyze the components of a good résumé and to design an effective résumé for yourself.

IMPORTANT CONTACT INFORMATION

You should dedicate the first section of your résumé to your name and how you can be contacted. Although this seems obvious, there are a couple of important contact issues to mention. Contact information must be complete, correct, and permanent. Depending on the policies of the company receiving your résumé, it could remain on file for months or even years. If your résumé is pulled for consideration six months from now, the contact information should still be valid.

Since we are focusing on electronic documents, it is important to note that privacy is a concern. While paper documents are typically routed to a person or department within an organization who has the responsibility of protecting your privacy, electronic documents can be generally distributed with no party directly responsible for privacy. Especially for documents posted to the Internet, it may be preferable to omit your address and phone numbers; instead use an e-mail account devoted to job hunting. If you elect to use an e-mail address, be sure to check your e-mail regularly and then provide the remaining contact information to legitimate organizations who contact you.

KEYWORDS

All résumés stored electronically can be sorted by key skills, experience, or education. Such items are referred to as "keywords." For example, an employer looking for an accountant might enter the following keywords or phrases: Staff Accountant, B.A. Degree in Accounting, Full-Cycle Accounting, Financial Statements and Cost Accounting. A computer query of all résumés in the database could be performed and those that contain all or some of these keywords would be identified. An employer could then read them via the computer screen, print the entire résumés, or print abstracted data from some or all of the résumés.

Some automated résumé tracking systems can read and retain an unlimited number of keywords contained in an entire résumé. Other, usually older, systems may be able to retain only 35 to 45 keywords. Either way, you can see why keywords are the "magic door" for generating interviews with employers who use résumé tracking systems. Key-

WRITE YOUR OWN OBJECTIVE STATEMENT

Strong objective statements clearly state the position and industry of interest along with your strongest skills. Do not use "I," "me," or "my." Focus on the benefit to the employer. Here are two examples:

- Pharmaceutical sales representative capitalizing on extensive chemistry background and self-directed personality to manage a marketing territory.

- Researcher in investment and analysis. Interests and skills include securities analysis, financial planning, and portfolio management. Long-range goal: to become a chartered financial analyst. Willing to travel and relocate.

1. Identify the position, industry, skill words, and jargon in the two sample objectives above.

2. Rewrite the following weak objective statement:

    A position in marketing with a progressive firm.

3. Create a strong objective statement for your planned career. Start with "I would like a job where I can use my ability to _____ which will result in _____." Rewrite the statement to be employer centered, contain industry jargon, and use skills keywords.

words are how employers find you in their systems. If you do not supply the right keywords, then your résumé has a limited chance of being found at all.

Whenever possible, use a minimum of 50 percent of the keywords found in an assortment of ads for the type of position you want. If possible, use all of them as long as you have the skills you are listing. Obviously you never want to lie or exaggerate by adding keywords to describe skills you do not possess. Such an unethical strategy could land you an interview, or a call from an employer, but would backfire when employers see you do not have the skills you have marketed.

Use the following steps to compile keywords and keyword phrases for your e-résumé:

1. Underline all keywords and keyword phrases in each ad.

2. Group keywords and keyword phrases into skill categories.

3. Create skill headings using keywords or keyword phrases for each group of skill categories.

4. Prioritize and number the skill categories.

5. Select the top 35 to 45 keywords to create a keyword section for the top of your e-résumé.

6. Write statements using as many keywords as possible for use in the rest of the e-résumé.

POWERFUL OBJECTIVE STATEMENTS

An objective statement specifies your target market. A well-developed objective statement is a potent tool for getting employers to look more deeply into your potential. Although some résumé styles omit this statement, it can be a critical résumé component when it provides an executive summary of your qualifications. Typical objective statements are short—between one and three sentences—and appear below the contact information.

For first-time job seekers or those changing careers, an objective statement should include a job title, an industry, the top three to five skills that qualify you for the job, and the benefit you will bring to the hiring organization. Using a decisive writing style lets employers know that you understand their business and helps them better determine that your skills can benefit their organization. A well-written, strong objective statement

Figure I.3

Weak vs. Strong
Objective Statements

Weak Objective Statements	Strong Objective Statements
Management position which will utilize business administration degree and will provide opportunities for rapid advancement.	An entry-level position in software development designing and implementing operating systems.
A position in social services which will allow me to work with people in a helping capacity.	A mid-level public relations position with opportunities to develop and implement programs, organize people and events, and communicate positive ideas and images.
A position in personnel administration with a progressive firm.	Employment counselor/job development position working with disabled clients.
Sales representative with opportunity for advancement.	Entry position in financial analysis with a major financial institution.

can provide a focus for organizing the content of your résumé. Refer to Figure I.3 for a comparison of weak and strong objective statements.

Experienced job seekers can break this content into two sections: (1) a single-line objective with a job title and (2) industry followed by a summary of qualifications section. The summary of qualifications should highlight your skills and accomplishments that benefited previous employers. We recommend that you present this content in the form of a bulleted list (see Figure I.4).

In addition to basic job skills, it is important to let potential employers know about your cultural, language, and communication talents. While being multilingual may not be a requirement for a position, it is certainly a nice bonus that may get you noticed. Being willing to relocate may allow you to be considered for a wider range of jobs in an organization. Be decisive about what you want to do and showcase your skills whether they have been gained in the classroom, through life experiences, travel, or on the job.

Figure I.4

Objective and Summary
Examples

	Entry-level Objective Statement
Objective	Public accounting auditor position in the Midwest capitalizing on internal and external audit experience gained in a four-month PricewaterhouseCoopers internship. Familiar with payroll, tax, and general ledger processing. Multilingual and willing to travel.
	Entry-level Objective Statement with Summary
Objective Summary	Public accounting auditor position in the Midwest. Accounting coursework and internships • PricewaterhouseCoopers auditor internship with four months of experience in both internal and external general ledger audit techniques • Bookkeeping and coursework experience with payroll, cost, and tax accounting • Spanish fluency gained through extensive travel in Mexico and South America • Willing to travel and relocate

FEEDBACK, FEEDBACK, FEEDBACK!

As you probably learned in every course you've taken, it is important to proofread and obtain feedback before submitting written work. This is even more essential for projects as important as your job search e-portfolio. Either formally or informally, create a group of two to three people who will provide constructive feedback throughout the remainder of your e-portfolio development.

1. Begin by each discussing your overall career goals and your work to date on this module.

2. Test your 30-second commercial on the group and solicit feedback.

3. Test your objective on the group and solicit feedback.

4. Discuss the other sections needed for your résumé and how to make your content employer centered.

5. Repeat steps 2 through 4 for the other group members.

Regardless of whether you are writing an objective statement, keywords, or a summary of qualifications, write for your audience, or, in other words, write from the hiring organization's perspective. Remember to state *what you can do for the organization* that hires you using the industry jargon and skill keywords you uncovered through networking, self-assessment, and research. Do not use words that indicate that you are not competent at a skill, such as "entry level" or "beginner."

Avoid statements that appear self-centered or self-serving. For instance, do not mention money or promotions. Instead state that you are willing to accept increasing levels of responsibility. Money and promotions benefit you, while increasing your responsibility *benefits the organization*. Do not include statements with "I," "my," or "me," since these personal pronouns focus on you rather than on the organization.

Stay away from canned or hyped phrases normally associated with résumé writing. For example, a "position with a progressive company" and "opportunity for advancement" are commonly seen in résumés but don't communicate anything important about the applicant. Write honestly about your abilities and skills in a way that demonstrates your value to employers.

Most people reviewing résumés visually scan the objectives and summary of qualifications to determine whether or not to review the remaining résumé content. If you do not have enough skills to create competitive objective and summary statements, create a plan to acquire them.

OTHER VALUABLE RÉSUMÉ SECTIONS

Most résumés should include sections outlining your education and work experience. Place the section most important to your marketable skills first. Within each section, organize the information to best present your skills. In general, hiring organizations prefer chronological presentations because they are traditional and easy to follow, but other styles can be effective as long as it does not appear that you are trying to hide or omit anything.

Use the same writing techniques outlined for creating a powerful objective statement to describe and demonstrate your relevant coursework and job skills. It is not enough to list course and job titles. Include descriptions documenting relevant skills and their organizational benefit using jargon relevant to the position and industry. For example, "responsible for coding and testing Visual Basic applications" is an adequate job description for a programmer but "coded Visual Basic applications consisting of thousands of executable lines to solve complex business problems, manage system throughput, and improve end-user satisfaction" demonstrates both the level of skill being offered and how the organization benefited from them.

On most résumés, the last section should present information on references. Commonly this section contains a single statement, "References available upon request." This is common nomenclature to use since references are not needed until you are actually being considered for a position or going through the interview process.

Other sections to consider include Awards, Publications, Personal Information, and anything specific to the particular job being applied for. For example, a "Statement of Belief" could be important when applying for a job with a religious organization but probably should not be included otherwise. Personal information can be troublesome. When applying for a position with a formal organization, too much personal information can make you look informal. However, the same information can make you look like a good fit in a less formal institution. Use your research to determine what to include and what to omit.

In summary, no résumé is likely to rise to the top of the stack without the following elements:

- **Contact information.** At the very least include your name, phone number, and an e-mail address.
- **Objective.** Describe your purpose for seeking a particular job.
- **Qualifications.** List your abilities and skills that pertain to the job.
- **Education.** Include the name and location of the school(s) you attended, and diploma(s), degree(s), and honors received.
- **Work experience.** Include the name and location of the company, how long you worked there, and your job responsibilities.
- **Activities.** List volunteer activities, organization memberships, and leadership roles.
- **Style.** Use standard fonts, such as 12 point Times, Arial, or Helvetica.
- **Correct spelling and grammar.** Proofread very carefully. Use your word processor's spell-checker, but do *not* rely on it solely. Ask someone you trust to proofread too.
- **Clarity.** Use clear, concise, professional language.

SHOW ACTION

Finally, use action verbs to describe your work experiences powerfully. And avoid being "wordy." Instead of saying that you "participated in the organization of work teams," say that you "organized work teams." Action verbs should be used abundantly throughout your résumé to promote your talents, skills, and achievements. They help make a strong impression. Action verbs can bring your résumé to life. The intent is to indicate that you are a person of action, a "take charge and get the job done" person. Refer to Figure I.5 for a list of powerful action verbs.

Figure I.5

Action Verbs

Accelerated	Accomplished	Achieved	Acted
Adapted	Addressed	Administered	Advanced
Advised	Allocated	Analyzed	Appraised
Approved	Arranged	Assembled	Assigned
Assisted	Attained	Audited	Authored
Automated	Balanced	Broadened	Budgeted
Built	Calculated	Catalogued	Chaired
Clarified	Classified	Coached	Collected
Compiled	Completed	Composed	Computed
Conceptualized	Conducted	Consolidated	Contained
Contracted	Contributed	Controlled	Coordinated
Corresponded	Counseled	Created	Critiqued
Cut	Decreased	Delegated	Demonstrated
Designed	Developed	Devised	Diagnosed
Directed	Dispatched	Distinguished	Diversified
Drafted	Earned	Edited	Educated
Enabled	Encouraged	Engineered	Enlisted
Established	Evaluated	Examined	Executed
Expanded	Expedited	Explained	Extracted
Fabricated	Facilitated	Familiarized	Fashioned
Focused	Forecast	Formulated	Founded
Generated	Guided	Headed up	Identified
Illustrated	Implemented	Improved	Increased
Indoctrinated	Influenced	Informed	Initiated
Innovated	Installed	Instituted	Instructed
Integrated	Instigated	Interviewed	Introduced
Invented	Interpreted	Launched	Lectured
Led	Maintained	Managed	Marketed
Mediated	Moderated	Monitored	Motivated
Negotiated	Organized	Originated	Overhauled
Oversaw	Performed	Persuaded	Planned
Prepared	Presented	Prioritized	Processed
Produced	Programmed	Projected	Promoted
Provided	Publicized	Published	Purchased
Pursued	Recommended	Reconciled	Recorded
Recruited	Redesigned	Reduced	Referred
Regulated	Rehabilitated	Remodeled	Represented
Researched	Restored	Restructured	Retrieved
Revitalized	Saved	Scheduled	Schooled
Screened	Serviced	Shaped	Solidified
Solved	Sparked	Specified	Stimulated
Streamlined	Strengthened	Summarized	Supervised
Surveyed	Systemized	Tabulated	Tailored
Targeted	Trained	Translated	Taught
Upgraded	Validated	Wrote	Trimmed

ELECTRONIC FILE FORMATS

You should prepare your résumés in a variety of electronic file formats. Each format should be incorporated into your e-portfolio. Begin by building an unformatted résumé with solid content and then add formatting to create the other required formats.

Figure I.6

Electronic File Formats

Just a few years ago, a résumé referred only to a sheet or two of paper that listed your work experience, accomplishments, education, and a few other career details. Today, it also means an electronic document that can work for you in cyberspace 24 hours a day. There are three kinds of electronic résumés (these formats are displayed in Figure I.6):

- The *scannable (or ASCII) résumé* is a paper résumé that becomes electronic when it is scanned into a computer.

- The *portable document format résumé (PDF résumé)* is a standard electronic distribution format typically used for e-mailing.

- The *multimedia (or HTML) résumé* uses a multimedia format displayed on the Web for employers to explore at their convenience.

THE SCANNABLE RÉSUMÉ

Say you create a handsome paper résumé and mail it to a potential employer. Unbeknownst to you, the company has a computerized system for scanning résumés that reach the Human Resources department. Instead of a person reading your application and deciding how to forward or file it, someone will scan it into a computer. The type is converted into a text file that is stored in an electronic résumé database. The paper version will be filed or discarded.

A typical Fortune 1000 corporation processes as many as 2,000 electronic résumés a day. Approximately 25 percent come directly through the company's Web site; 25 percent come through major online job banks such as Monster.com; 20 percent arrive via e-mail; and the rest get entered into the company's résumé database through scanning devices.

Medium- and small-sized companies have also become increasingly dependent on the electronic transfer and storage of résumés, as they hook up to online résumé databases or outsource job fulfillment to recruiters who use résumé databases. Even nonprofit organizations receive more résumés through e-mail than ever before.

To design a scannable résumé that improves your hiring prospects, follow these basic guidelines (a demonstration of this format is displayed in Figure I.7):

- Create a text-only file. In Microsoft Word select **File** from the menu, click **Save As**, and then set the **Save As Type** to **Plain Text (*.txt)** or use Notepad to create your document.
- Use only Courier or Times New Roman 10 or 12 point font.
- Do not include character formatting such as bold, underline, italics, or text color.
- Do not center or tab-indent text (every line should be left justified).
- Press **Enter** at the end of each line. Line length should be between 65 and 70 characters.
- Do not include tables or graphics.
- Leave two blank lines between sections.
- Capitalize all letters in section headings.
- Use asterisks (*), dashes (—), or another standard keyboard character for bullets (do not use automated bulleted or numbered lists).

Figure I.7

Scannable Résumé Format

THE PDF RÉSUMÉ

When you type words onto a computer screen using word processing software, you are creating a "file" or "document." When you save that file, it includes special formatting such as fonts, margins, tab settings, and so on, even if you did not specifically add these. Each word processing program (e.g. WordPerfect, Microsoft Word, etc.) automatically saves files in its own native format, making the file readable only to those with the same software or a conversion program. To make sure your document can be read by everyone, ***Portable document format (PDF)*** is the standard electronic distribution file format. The benefit of PDF is that documents created in any application can be shared across platforms and still look exactly as designed. All fonts, indentations, graphics, links, tables, and alignment are retained. This format is widely used to distribute books and forms electronically. For example, most U.S. tax forms are available as PDF downloads from a Web site. To read a PDF file, all you need is a Reader. You can download Adobe Acrobat Reader free from www.adobe.com.

Once you convert your presentation résumé to a PDF format, anyone can view and print it exactly as you designed it (as shown in Figure I.8). You can easily distribute your PDF résumé as an e-mail attachment or a Web download. The process of creating a PDF file is simple but requires access to Adobe Acrobat software, which is available in several versions. Currently, a Create Adobe PDF Online link is available from www.adobe.com that will allow you to subscribe and create up to five free PDF files.

Figure I.8

PDF Résumé Format

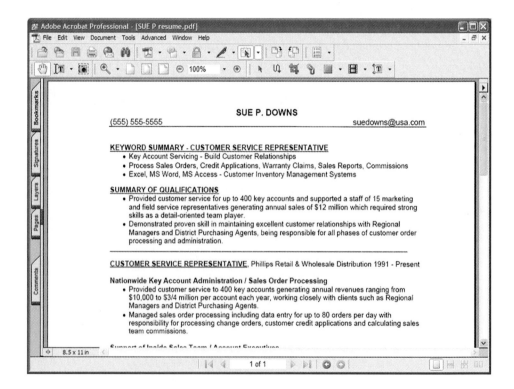

THE MULTIMEDIA (OR HTML) RÉSUMÉ

If you are a computer programmer, Web page developer, graphic designer, artist, sculptor, singer, dancer, actor, model, animator, cartoonist or other professional who would benefit from the photographs, graphics, animation, sound, color and movement possible with a multimedia résumé, then this is the format for you.

As you create and deliver Web content, you create files with either .htm or .html as the file extension. Within these files (called HTML documents), you use hypertext markup language (HTML) tags to provide document formatting instructions to Web browsers such as Microsoft Internet Explorer or Netscape Communicator (see Figure I.9).

A good e-portfolio Web site should include a home page that acts as a site overview and menu, all of your résumé text, and additional supporting materials using HTML tags to format attractive pages. Résumés and supporting content already formatted for other delivery modes (.txt, .pdf, .doc, .ppt, .xls, and so on) for other purposes are usually not converted to HTML. You should refer to *Extended Learning Module F* for using HTML to create a Web site and provide links to downloadable files. In the remainder of this module, we'll specifically address designing and building the pages of your e-portfolio.

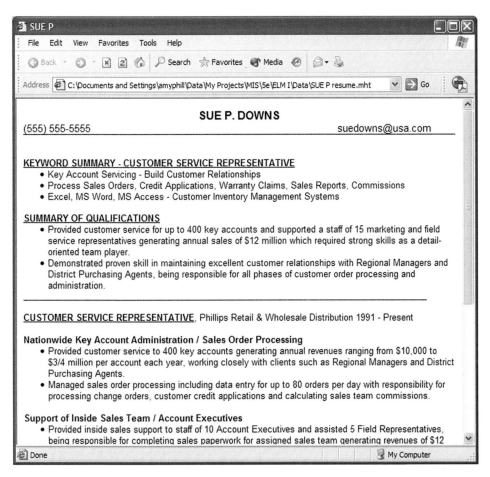

Figure I.9

Multimedia Résumé Format

WHAT IS THE RIGHT RÉSUMÉ STYLE?

Choose a résumé layout that fits your job history and target position (Figure I.10 displays two of these formats).

1. **Chronological.** You easily meet all skill, experience, and education requirements. A chronological résumé arranges work experiences according to time sequence. Generally, your most recent experiences are listed first. Use a chronological résumé:
   - When your work history occupies the same field.
   - When your job history shows real growth or advancement.
   - When your prior job titles and companies are impressive.
2. **Functional.** You are a new graduate, changing fields or industries. A functional résumé focuses on skills, abilities, volunteer experiences, and work experiences. It highlights what you can do. Use a functional résumé:
   - For your first job.
   - When your skills are more impressive than your work history.
   - When you've frequently changed employers or careers.
3. **Curriculum Vitae (or CV).** You are a scientist or educator. A CV is an academic résumé that you use to tell others about your academic qualifications. A CV needs to be as long as it takes to convey the information. For many fourth-year students, the document may be a page or so. For a tenured professor in a medical school, it may cover several hundred pages.

Figure I.10

Chronological and Functional Résumé Layout

Chronological Résumé Layout

Functional Résumé Layout

Developing Your Job Search E-Portfolio

Your job search e-portfolio is your living document on the Internet. More than just a homepage, more than just a résumé, the job search e-portfolio offers you a new, smarter model for self-marketing and networking.

You should design your job search e-portfolio (or what we will refer to as your e-portfolio) to provide everything that a prospective employer needs to evaluate your employment potential. That means that it should include several e-résumé formats, permanent contact information, and a gallery designed to demonstrate your skills.

An e-portfolio can be one of the most rewarding marketing tools you will ever use, because it can help you expand your reach in ways never before possible. It shows that you are up-to-date, gives you instant credibility, and expands your market globally and exponentially. But most important of all, your e-portfolio and the World Wide Web makes it possible to have access at anytime to examples of your work. Your prospective employers can get information when they need it without having to wait for you to send it, making it simple for anyone to evaluate you and satisfying the desire for instant gratification that is pervasive in our digital economy.

In this section we will examine several of the techniques you need to use to present yourself successfully, from a marketing point of view, on the Web. Whether you already have a Web site up and running or you are still in the preparation stages, this section will help you make your site one that will achieve your personal marketing goals.

An e-portfolio is one marketing tool that does not live on the back burner. In fact, the opposite is true. Many people have slapped their sites up without much planning, perhaps in preparation for an event or because a client says, "Give me your Web address," or maybe just because everyone else is doing it.

Some people put a site up quickly and then revamp it. In fact, many people who have already created an e-portfolio Web site have transitioned their presentation to a second or third iteration, as they have learned from the comments of visitors and from Web reports what works and what does not.

SELF-PROMOTION

Even if you have no gizmos to sell, the Internet is a powerful tool to get the word out and to increase your visibility. An e-portfolio is not the ultimate marketing tool, but it is an essential one in our digital economy. If you do not have an e-portfolio yet, here are four reasons why you should:

1. *An e-portfolio can give you instant credibility.* Because anyone anywhere can put up a Web site, you must use yours to establish your credibility. A list of projects, examples of your work, and your contact information will show potential employers who you are.

2. *A Web site provides access anytime to you and examples of your work.* Potential employers can go straight to your Web site and get the information they need when they need it.

3. *A Web site shows that you are current and up-to-date.* It is essential that you have either a Web site with your own domain name, or at the very least, an online presence (i.e., Web site) where your e-portfolio is posted.

4. *A Web site expands your exposure and increases your visibility worldwide.* That means your potential reach is wider than it has ever been before because people with whom it was once difficult to communicate are now just a click away.

One of the main principles of self-promotion is this: Self-promotion is not just about you; it is also about your prospective employers. Your e-portfolio materials should offer your solutions to *their* problems, and that applies to your Web site. So instead of focusing all your attention on how to show your work in the best light, ask yourself, "When they visit my site, what do they need to learn more about me and my work, in order to trust that I can do what they need done?"

GIVE THEM WHAT THEY WANT

Some of your future employers are visually oriented, and some are not. Some are Web savvy, and some are not. Some know what they are talking about when they use Internet jargon, and some do not. And yet, every one of them has an opinion and a perspective that matters. Here is what your future employers are looking for when they visit your Web site (see Figure I.11 for an example):

- *Lots of work.* When your future employers are in their moment of need, they want to see as much work as possible. And they want to see the quality of your work before they decide to invest the time to make contact.
- *Creativity.* Though it is very subjective, employers want creativity from the creative professionals they hire. Anything different or unusual—not boring or "industrial"—will make them stop and take notice.
- *Strategy.* Creativity alone is not enough. Future employers also want to see your marketing savvy. Use your Web site to show how your work will help add value to their business.
- *Good architecture.* Future employers do not have time to figure out your Web site, so make it easy to navigate and understand.

Figure I.11

An e-Portfolio Example

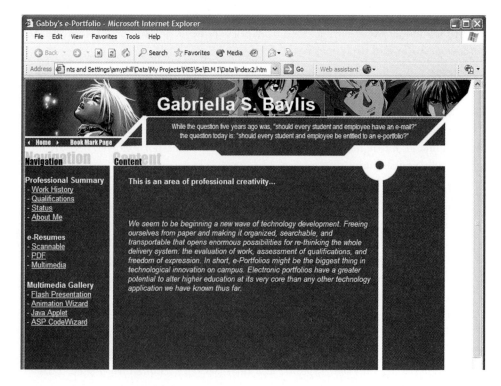

THE SHAPE OF AN E-PORTFOLIO

The e-portfolio has added a new step to the process of hiring online, a step that comes at the very beginning of the getting-to-know-you period and that makes everyone's life—yours and your prospective employer's—easier and more efficient. Your prospective employer can go to your e-portfolio (or Web site), and check you out before making contact, because even a simple online portfolio allows you to convey so much more about yourself and your services than the few examples of your work they would find in a creative directory. The goal of your e-portfolio then, is to provide enough of a taste of your work for a prospect to decide whether to take the next step: making contact.

When your online prospective employer arrives at your e-portfolio, the first thing they need to know is how to find the samples of your work. The easier an e-portfolio is to understand and navigate, the longer visitors will stay. And the more they see of your work, the more they will get to know you.

One strategy that helps to orient visitors quickly is to use a metaphorical interface that is familiar and intuitive. With that said, the simplest Web site must have at least:

1. **Biographical information.** Call it what you want—"Profile," "About Me," or "Who I Am"—but provide information about yourself.

2. **Examples.** First and foremost your visitors will be looking for examples of your work and information about your skills and talents. So give them a lot to look at and organize it in a simple way.

3. **Contact information.** Visitors will need to know how to contact you, so make it easy for them. Give them many options—phone, fax, e-mail—and make that information accessible from every page of your Web site.

E-GALLERY

Besides the ability to deliver your résumé in multiple formats, an e-portfolio provides you with the opportunity to demonstrate your skills through a gallery of works, called an **e-gallery** (see Figure I.12). Because the Web allows viewers to click on links to view

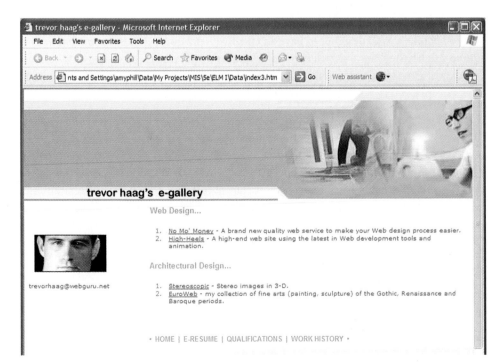

Figure I.12

An e-Gallery Example

materials that are of interest to them, there is no absolute limit to the number of supporting pages that you should develop.

The simplest way to compose an e-gallery is to make use of materials that you already have in hand. Remember that the gallery should display your skills, so consider including the following:

- Writing samples
- Spreadsheets or other application business tools
- Demonstrations of analytical, planning, or management skills
- Presentations that you have developed

Existing documents may need to be edited to remove confidential materials or to shorten the content. For example, you might include the introduction, problem analysis, and summary sections of a 30-page report since it is unlikely that anyone would read the entire report; they would thereby miss those sections that sufficiently demonstrate your talent. Do not include proprietary employer information or group projects without giving appropriate credit or obtaining permission.

If you do not have existing documents that sufficiently demonstrate your job skills, create them from scratch. This can be time-consuming, but they create a much stronger statement about your talent and dedication than just saying you can do the job. Start small and spend the time to do an excellent job. One of the biggest benefits of an e-gallery is that you can add and remove components at any time.

There are no hard-and-fast rules about what to include in your gallery, but remember to keep it focused on your goal of obtaining a job. Label and organize your gallery content so that viewers can click on only what they want to see. For example, provide links from your job and education descriptions to documents demonstrating related skills.

Web Design Considerations

Web design is the successful blending of text and graphics to create appealing and useable Web pages. Web design is also a complex art requiring technical knowledge, research, skill, and an understanding of your audience. The good news is that you do not have to become a Web designer to have an effective e-portfolio. The sections that follow outline a few basic rules that will help you organize your content.

BASIC WEB DESIGN PRINCIPLES

You need to take advantage of some tried-and-true Web design tips. We will address key Web page design issues and tactics, but with a small disclaimer, because first and foremost, designing Web pages is a creative endeavor. Understand that the parameters that we outline in this module are guidelines. If you search the Web for Web design principles, you will find many lists of suggestions that have only a few elements in common. Every Web design expert has an opinion about what makes a good Web site and so does everyone browsing the Web. Can they all be right? Probably yes, depending on the context. However, we will cover effective Web design principles for creating an e-portfolio.

The difference between content designed for printed viewing and content designed for electronic viewing on the Web is quite dramatic. You should keep in mind that good print layout does not translate effectively to good Web layout. There are many reasons for this; the primary reasons include:

- Printed pages are designed to be read, while Web pages are designed to be browsed.
- Printed pages are typically the same size, while Web pages are not. The viewable area of a Web page is also much smaller than a printed page.
- Printed pages stay visually the same, while Web page layout varies depending on the Web browser, screen resolution, operating system, and monitor being used.

Even with the improved resolution of today's monitors, it is more difficult to read from a computer screen than it is from a printed document. Few readers will actually read long passages online; they most often print it or skip it altogether. Consider breaking long text (three or more screens) up so that the user is presented with an overview and can then link to the details. If you need to present long text as a single unit, be sure that it is printer friendly by using the dimensions outlined in Figure I.13.

Web content must be concise, well labeled, and formatted for browsing. Every page needs to contain information about who, what, when, and where, so that a person who just "pops" into that page has a point of reference. The top of each page needs to contain a header that holds your name, logo (if you have one), and other identifying information. Including navigational links in the header is a common design element. The bottom of each page should contain a footer and the date the page was last updated. The middle of each page contains your content, which should be displayed in a manner that helps viewers find topics of interest.

Often the left-hand side of the content zone contains a menu of links. This is particularly important in large sites with long pages. Whether or not you add a menu column to the left of your content, white space to the left and right of your text will make it easier to read. Also, make sure to leave white space between headings and other page elements to avoid a cluttered look.

Figure I.13

Printer Friendly Web Page Dimensions

410 pixels

760 pixels

17–19 inch screen (800 × 600)
Browser safe area (760 × 410)

670 pixels

535 pixels

■ Use blue dimensions to fill the maximum safe area on most screens
■ Use red dimensions for pages that will print well

US Letter size page = 535 × 670 pixels safe area

AUDIENCE REIGNS SUPREME

Planning your Web site affects design in a couple of major ways. Specifically, before you design, you should consider your audience and organize your Web page layout and your Web site's structure.

You create and use a job search e-portfolio to market yourself for a job or ranges of related jobs to the hiring organizations of a particular industry. To make this clear, add the industry and job title(s) to your job search e-portfolio. In doing so, you have defined both your audience and your purpose. The key to developing a Web site that will appeal to your audience is to build what they like, not what you like. Again, your research should pay off. Think about the industry and business sites that you visited while researching your chosen career.

Some of the questions you can ask yourself to help gain insight into your target audience are:

- What is the average age of managers (the people who do the hiring)? Employees (the people you would work with)?
- How conservative is this industry?
- Are employees expected to be artistic?
- How will my audience view my page?
- What do the backgrounds, colors, graphics, and navigation of business sites in the industry look like?
- How does this industry promote itself?

There are no absolutes in e-portfolio design. A site that works well for an artist, while beautiful, would probably be inappropriate for an accountant. Remember that this is not a personal Web site. It should demonstrate your business personality without being too personal.

STORYBOARDING

After you identify your audience but before you start to create your Web pages, you should sketch your Web page's layout as well as any relationships among ancillary pages—this intended visual relationship is called a *storyboard.* In other words, you should illustrate the relationships among your site's pages to ensure that you have created a clear site layout that includes all the related information in an easily accessible format.

You will then need to figure out how best to present yourself electronically. For example, you can organize your site in any number of ways, including the following:

- Alphabetically
- Chronologically
- Graphically
- Hierarchically
- Numerically
- Randomly (not recommended)
- Topically

By far, most sites are organized hierarchically, that is, they present a homepage that contains catchy introductory text and links to the site's content.

SITE STRUCTURE

The structure of a Web site is how the various pages are linked together. There are two main schools of thought when it comes to Web page length: scrolling or clicking. Long pages of content require the viewer to scroll to see everything while short pages contain clickable links that provide the full content. Overall, Web users prefer small fast-loading pages that allow them to click directly to the desired content. In other words, most people prefer to click rather than scroll. It is not possible to avoid scrolling altogether, but try not to annoy your users by having them scroll too much.

To create a site of linked pages, you must segment or break your content into usable units. Each segment becomes a separate Web page in your site. Try to think of screens of text rather than pages of text. At 800×600 screen resolution, the average Web browser screen displays about one-half page of text when there is nothing else on the screen. The page title, navigation, and footer information can cut that to one-third of a page for text. So, to view one printed page of text, the person reading your e-portfolio would have to scroll down at least two screens. More than three screens of scrolling is beyond the tolerance of the average user unless the text is very interesting or must logically be presented as a unit.

Once you have determined your Web site segments, your next step is to determine how pages will be linked together. The homepage is the preferred entry point to your site and should start the navigation. Users should also be able to move from topic to topic in your site without returning to the *homepage*. Web sites can contain grid, Web, sequence, and hierarchical navigation (see Figure I.14). Linear sites, such as sequence and hierarchical, are the simplest to build and navigate but are appropriate only for sequential information such as a book. Grid structures are appropriate for sites with multiple topics or entry points.

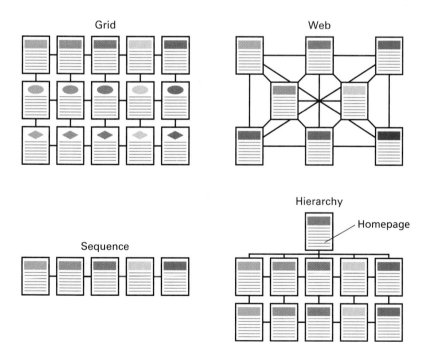

Figure I.14

Documenting Web Site Structure

BUILD YOUR RÉSUMÉS AND VISIT E-PORTFOLIO SITES

Although documents created in Microsoft Windows have filenames that are not case sensitive and handle spaces well (My Résumé.doc), more than likely your e-portfolio will be posted on a UNIX server. UNIX is the most common operating system for Web servers. Make your files UNIX friendly by using consistent capitalization and no spaces in the filenames (MyRésumé.doc). Open a Notepad or Microsoft Word document to create an ASCII résumé. Enter all of your résumé content without any formatting. Be sure to follow the guidelines outlined in the module text. If you use Microsoft Word, be sure to change the **Save As Type** to Plain Text (*.txt).

To create a presentation résumé, open your ASCII résumé in Microsoft Word and save it with a **Save As Type** of Word document (*.doc). Remove all of the extra hard returns (where you pressed Enter) in the document and then select **Theme** from the Format menu. Click the Style Gallery button and select one of the résumé templates. Update the text and formatting to create a résumé that can be printed in one or two pages.

Visit www.adobe.com and register to create free PDF files. Use this service to create a PDF version of your presentation résumé. Create a folder for your Web site development and place copies of all of your résumés there.

To enhance your understanding of job search e-portfolio content, segmenting, navigation, layout, and design, visit www.mhhe.com/haag and select the **XLM/I** link. Look through the available portfolios paying attention to the content, use of color, fonts, navigation, page layout, and graphics.

1. How important was color in your initial assessment of a site?

2. What attributes made it easy to move through a site?

3. What was your favorite site? Why? Evaluate the way that site content was segmented. Sketch out the navigation structure of this site.

4. What was your least favorite site? Why?

Because an e-portfolio has a structured entry point (the homepage), we recommend using some combination of the hierarchical and Web navigation. Simple Web sites can use a basic hierarchy with just two levels. The homepage would be the first level and all second-level HTML pages would be linked back to the homepage. More complex Web sites will need three hierarchical levels with the level under the homepage representing site topics. At least some of the third-level pages should link back to both the second and third levels, creating a Web hierarchy navigational structure. We do not recommend that your e-portfolio include more than three levels.

Regardless of how you structure your Web site, it is important for the navigation to be well marked and intuitive. Make sure to label your links descriptively and to group content together that logically belongs together. With few exceptions, each HTML page of a site should contain links to the homepage and other site topics. Non-HTML pages such as Word or Excel documents do not usually contain links. It is helpful that you create a Web site navigation chart to have a checklist of pages and links to build and test.

DESIGN YOUR HOMEPAGE

When designing a group of Web pages that are structured to work together, such as an e-portfolio site, it is critical that each page contain common color, font, navigation, and layout design elements. It should be obvious to a user who has clicked on a link to another Web page that he or she is still in your e-portfolio site. Similarly, someone who has clicked from another Web site into a subpage of your e-portfolio site should be able to easily navigate to content matching their interests. Design your opening or homepage and then apply those navigation, layout, font, and color elements throughout the remaining Web site pages.

COLOR

You need to pay considerable attention to your Web page's color scheme. A color scheme refers to your site's interface elements, such as title graphics, buttons, background, and text. Ideally, you should limit the number of colors used in your Web page's interface to three colors. The key is to use contrasting colors, especially if you are using a colored background.

Color impacts the look and feel of your site. We speak of colors as being warm, cool, muted, light, dark, and garish. Decide what type of color description is appropriate for your audience and then select colors within that description. For example, mocha is a warm color while cyan is a cool color.

In Web page design, browser-safe colors are important since there are 216 different colors that can be displayed by both a PC and Apple computer. When a Web browser encounters a color that it cannot interpret, it substitutes a color that it knows, resulting in unpredictable Web page displays. For that reason, we recommend that you use **browser-safe colors** that can be displayed by all monitors and Web browsers. You can easily find a chart of browser-safe colors at http://www.lynda.com/hexv.html. Test your color selections on as many different computers as possible.

Overall, you should use your color scheme to create balance and unity through your site, but you should also use colors to draw attention to specific areas of your Web page.

FONTS AND FORMATTING

You have the power to control your text's size, color, formatting, and style. Almost universally, Web designers recommend that you use the default size for the main content. This allows viewers to choose the font size via their browser's default settings.

Even though thousands of font styles exist, all font styles can be categorized as either *serif* or *sans serif*. Serif fonts, such as Times, use "hooks" or short lines, on the ends of letters, whereas san serif fonts, like Arial, use plain-edged letters. We generally prefer to use sans serif fonts when creating Web pages because they are easier to read online and tend to be more visually appealing.

Regardless of your preference, you should stick with cross-platform fonts (those that are displayed similarly on a PC or Apple) to ensure that users see your text similar to how you designed your page. Cross-platform fonts include the following:

- Arial
- Arial Narrow
- Comic Sans
- Courier New
- Georgia
- Times New Roman (or Times)
- Trebuchet
- Verdana

Titling Images

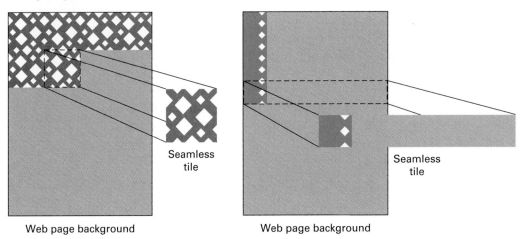

Web page background · Web page background

Titles for Web Pages

Initial Caps Cause Pointless Bumps

Start cap with bold omits pointless bumps

Figure I.15

Backgrounds and Titles

As we have already mentioned, reading is more difficult on a computer monitor than on paper. To simplify reading, headings should be easily identified and use sentence case, not title case as they would in a written document. Title case causes unnecessary bumps in a line of text as we show in Figure I.15.

Use tables, bulleted lists, and   (the HTML equivalent to a space) to control the layout of your pages. Tables can provide white space, make columns, and control the placement of graphic elements. For both print and screen reading, three-inch lines of text provide the best readability, so columns are an effective design tool. Bulleted lists make items under a heading easy to identify. The   instruction adds a space to your page and is the most effective way to indent a first line of text. Use the <BLOCK-QUOTE> tag to indent the left (and on some browsers the right) margin of a block of text. Make sure that all the design elements you select work well to create the desired visual impact.

GRAPHICS

Web graphics look fairly similar to print graphics, but some Web-specific factors are relevant when you are creating and using graphics on the Web. Specifically, Web graphics require you to consider color limitations, file formats, and files sizes as well as possible transparency, downloading, and animation issues. You should adhere to the following four practices when using graphical elements on the Web:

1. Avoid large graphics that seem to take days to download on a modem. You might try using *thumbnails* where appropriate. A thumbnail is a small picture that links to a larger image. This gives viewers the choice of viewing the small image or clicking on the thumbnail to view the larger image.

2. Do not use meaningless graphics. Make sure you use graphics that contribute to the user's experience.

3. Ensure that every graphical link has a text link equivalent.

4. Create either GIF (Graphics Interchange Format) or JPEG (Joint Photographic Expert Group) images. These are standard formats used pervasively on the Web.

TEXTUAL ELEMENTS OF YOUR HOMEPAGE

The content for your Web site needs to be segmented into logical units that will become the pages of your Web site. The opening or homepage is the entrance to your Web site and deserves special attention. If at all possible, this page should all be displayed on one screen at 800×600 screen resolution. The goal is to load fast and provide the viewer with enough information to assess the site and navigate to pages of interest. Remember that each Web page should include who, what, when, and where.

Recall that each page of your site should contain the same footer. This is the easiest content to develop. At a minimum, your footer should include your name, e-mail address, and the last time the page was updated.

Each page of your site should also contain a header or title bar. The header needs to include your name and contact information. If you have a business logo or graphic relevant to your job search, you can incorporate it in your header.

Although it is uncommon to include a personal photograph in a printed résumé, many people include a high-quality business attire photo in their e-portfolio Web site. However, there is no need to include your photo in the header that will appear on every page of the site, since that would appear egotistical.

Page content is displayed between the header and footer, often with a menu bar down the left-hand side. Since you are developing an e-portfolio site, your objective statement, a description of your ultimate job, or a summary of skills can be effective homepage content. Avoid uninformative text such as "Welcome to my e-Portfolio." Overall, your homepage should be both inviting and informative (refer back to Figure I.11).

DOCUMENT THE SITE DESIGN

After designing your homepage, you should have a good idea of how to segment and link (organize) your remaining e-portfolio content. Ideally, you should create logical groupings of content so that you have no more than eight links on your homepage. For example, you could create a résumé page that, in turn, links to your "30-second commercial" presentation, PDF, and scannable résumés. Similarly, you might provide an e-gallery page with links to your work.

Be sure that your Web site segments account for all of your e-gallery content and all résumé file formats before developing a navigational or hierarchy chart. The navigational chart will document the content of each page and how it is linked to the other pages of the site. You will use it to determine the content and links to place on each page during development and then to test each link once you build the site.

The various résumé formats (ASCII, PDF, and HTML) that you have already developed should be placed on the Web site as is, so that potential employers have access to all formats. The navigation chart makes this distinction by including the file extension (.txt, .pdf, .html, and so on) that identifies the file format. You can also place much of the content of your e-gallery in its native formats since your goal is to demonstrate your skills.

Figure I.16

Sample e-Portfolio
Navigation Chart

Links using the anchor <A HREF="filename"> tag can link to all of these file formats. We do not recommend that you provide links from these documents back to your e-portfolio site since your site viewers will most likely save them. The navigation chart shows a link to these non-HTML files, but provides no return link (see Figure I.16).

Preparing Web Content

Use the navigation chart (shown in Figure I.16) first to develop and link each page of your site. Begin by placing your existing résumé and gallery files in a site folder and then create an abbreviated HTML document for each HTML Web site page in the same folder. Each abbreviated HTML page should contain a word or two that describes what the page will hold once you fully develop it. You will use these "dummy" pages to test your links on each page as you finish developing them.

One of the trickiest parts of developing a Web site is writing the text and choosing the photos and graphics. This material—the site content—needs to be succinct, informative, and well presented; otherwise you risk being seen as an amateur.

Here are some tips for preparing your Web content:

- Gather all the material you have been preparing through this module, such as your objective statement, résumé formats, and e-gallery examples. It is very helpful to have a printed copy of all these materials.

- Write one key sentence of no more than 30 words describing the essence of your e-portfolio. This could be used to describe who your are when your site is listed in a search directory or even as an introduction element on your homepage.

- Write down at least 10 single keywords and 10 key phrases of two to three words that could be used to reference the site and attract people entering those keywords or phrases into a search engine.

- If you have a special logo, or professional photograph, find the cleanest and largest possible version of it for scanning. You want a physical image that is focused and has an excellent definition of color. Create a digital image of your logo or photograph making sure that you use the highest resolution possible for high definition. You will be able to resize this according to Web standards later.

- Look at other e-portfolios on the Web. Go to a good search engine, such as www.google.com, and enter into the search field the words you would expect someone to use if they were trying to find someone with your skills, talents, and interests. Look at some of the sites that this search produces, and see how they are designed and the words they use. Some will be great, some awful—examine the good ones for ideas.

HTML VERSUS GENERATED CODE

Overwhelmingly, when you are creating your Web pages, you will be spending the greatest amount of time interacting with a text editor or an HTML editor. You can use editors to create HTML files that contain display tags for Web browsers which hold the content of your Web page. When you use an editor, you have the option of working with HTML code manually or using a more advanced what-you-see-is-what-you-get (WYSIWYG) editor which will autogenerate your HTML code while you type, insert images, and drag elements around in a Web page layout view.

When you use a basic text editor, you type in all the HTML commands into a blank document. The most basic of the text editors is Notepad that comes with the Microsoft Windows operating system. Hand-coding Web pages is still considered a feasible option for the following reasons:

- Control
- Quick fixes
- Clean code
- Fine-tuning

In general, we believe it is a good idea to get comfortable with some basic HTML before using an HTML editor so that you are familiar enough with the code to read it and apply simple changes manually. Refer to *Extended Learning Module F* for an introduction to building a Web page with HTML.

WEB DESIGN TOOLS

HTML editors enable you to create and edit Web pages by using a graphical interface that will also allow you to view and edit your HTML source code. Although Web authoring software can simplify many tasks, there may be a learning curve to become efficient in their use. Additionally, Web authoring software can generate unnecessary code, making it more difficult for you to make manual modifications and slowing page load time. Sometimes the Web site management portion of this software can introduce errors in Web page links through the default settings and assumptions. A list of the more popular HTML editors are:

- Dreamweaver (www.macromedia.com)
- Microsoft FrontPage (www.microsoft.com/frontpage, see also *Extended Learning Module L*)
- NewObjects Fusion (www.netobjects.com)
- Adobe GoLive (www.adobe.com)
- HotMetal Pro (www.hotmetalpro.com)

Figure I.17

Sample HTML Code in
Notepad

```
index4.htm - Notepad
File  Edit  Format  View  Help
<html>
<head>
<meta name="keywords" content="e-portfolio, organizational development, project management
<title>Stacy Liebson e-Portfolio</title>
</head>
<link rel=StyleSheet href="mycss.css" type="text/css" media=screen>
<body background="stacy images/bg.gif">
  <table border="0" width="700" height="438" cellspacing="0" cellpadding="0" bgcolor="#cc6
    <tr>
      <td width="140" rowspan="2" valign="top">
              <img border="0" src="stacy images/wwwball.jpg" width="170" height="140"><b
        <img border="0" src="stacy images/line.jpg" width="170" height="54"><br><br>
        <table width=130 cellpadding=4 cellspacing=4 align=right>
              <tr><td align=center class="button"><b><a href="index.htm">Home</a></b></t
              <tr><td align=center class="button"><b><a href="index.htm">About Me</a></b
              <tr><td align=center class="button"><b><a href="bg.gif">e-Resume</a></b></
              <tr><td align=center class="button"><a href="index.htm"><b>Publications</b
              <tr><td align=center class="button"><b><a href="index.htm">e-Gallery</a></
              <tr><td align=center class="button"><b><a href="index.htm">Contact Me</a><
        </table><br>
      </td>
      <td width="560" height="84" valign="top" align="left">
        <table width=100% height=100% boder=0 cellpadding=0 cellspacing=0>
              <tr>
              <td width=97 valign="top" align="left">
                    <img border="0" src="stacy images/corner.jpg" width="97" height="8
              <td width=302 align=center><h3>Stacey Liebson</h3>
                    <div>Tel: 915.888.8888<br>
                    Email: <a href="mailto:me@me.com">sliebson@wwwaccess.org</a></div>
              </tr>
              <td width=131 align=center> </tr>
        </table>
      </td>
    </tr>
    <tr>
      <td width="560" height="354" valign=top>
```

You can create or generate HTML code to build Web pages in many ways. In the short history of the Web, the tool that has gained the greatest universal acceptance is Notepad. On the Macintosh, the equivalent tool is called Teach Text or Simple Text. These simple text editing tools are easy to use and are still relied upon by HTML authors as displayed in Figure I.17.

Many of the latest office applications now convert documents to HTML. For example, you can create your résumé in Microsoft Word and export it to create your e-résumé, an HTML page. You can even create a slideshow for an e-gallery in Microsoft PowerPoint and export that to HTML.

The Web page creation capabilities of Microsoft FrontPage are designed for both experienced and beginning Web site developers with a simple yet powerful tool for designing and building great looking, easy-to-navigate Web pages. Microsoft FrontPage is a full-featured HTML editor that uses a number of Web page elements including:

- Button rollover effects
- Image maps
- Marquee text
- Thumbnails
- Counter

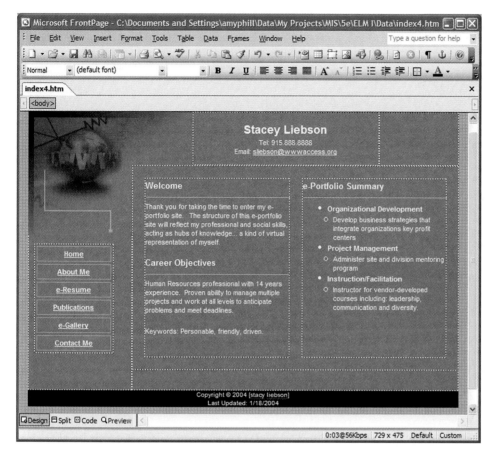

Figure I.18

Sample of FrontPage Interface

With Microsoft FrontPage, you will create Web pages almost as if you were creating them in a word processing environment, with no programming knowledge required (see Figure I.18). For example, formatting attributes such as fonts, borders, and bulleted lists look very close to the way they display in your browser, and many features and options are available using familiar elements such as toolbars, dialog boxes, and templates. Microsoft FrontPage offers two key types of functionality:

- *Web page creation.* Microsoft FrontPage allows you to create and edit Web pages without needing to know HTML or other programming languages. FrontPage includes many features that make Web page creation easy, such as templates, graphics, and more.
- *Web site management.* Microsoft FrontPage allows you to view Web pages, publish them to the World Wide Web, and manage existing Web sites. Using FrontPage, you can test and repair hyperlinks on a Web page, view all of the files and folders on a site, and import image files, to name just a few features.

Figure I.19

Sample of Web Page
Created in FrontPage
Imported in Word

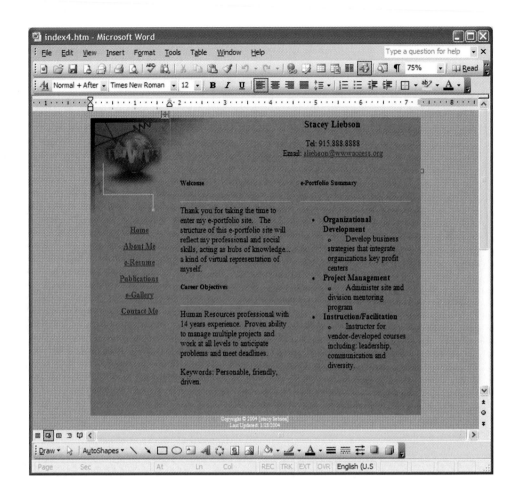

Microsoft Office Web components are not a new technology. Microsoft introduced them in Office 2000. The latest release 2003, however, brings great improvements in the areas of usability, ease of development, and more formatting and functionality. Figure I.19 shows an example of the Web page built in FrontPage that has been imported into Microsoft Word. Because we used Cascading Stylesheets, the formatting is not imported into Word. However, had we used Microsoft Word from the beginning, the formatting would be exactly the same as we intended. We suggest you visit *Extended Learning Module L*, FrontPage, for more detail.

TEST, TEST, TEST

A word of caution: It is critical that you test your Web site many times and from multiple platforms and devices. Statistics gathered in August 2005 indicate that 75 percent of people browsing the Web use Microsoft Internet Explorer (www.w3schools.com). That being the case, 21 percent of your audience is using another Web browser. In addition, about 3 percent of Internet users have an Apple. At a minimum, view your site in multiple versions of Internet Explorer, Mozilla Firefox, and Netscape Communicator to get a feel for how most people will see it.

It is also best to develop your site in its own folder to make it easier to move from your PC as a development platform to an online Web server. The folder should contain all gallery files, HTML pages, and graphics from your site.

Move your Web site (all files, pages, and graphics) to another computer and test it again. Often links that work on your development computer may not work when pages

E-Portfolio HTML Code in
TextPad

E-Portfolio Design in
FrontPage

Completed E-Portfolio in Browser

Figure I.20

View of HTML,
FrontPage, and Browser
of e-Portfolio Site

are moved. These are called broken links and you should definitely repair them before placing your site on a Web server or "going live." Testing on multiple computers will also let you see color and resolution variances that your viewers will experience.

Finally, when you place your site on a Web server, test it again. Most Web servers use the UNIX operating system. UNIX is case sensitive and prefers filenames without spaces or special characters (!@#$%^&*,. and so on). Microsoft Windows is not case sensitive and accepts filenames with spaces. This is an important difference because Web sites that work on your local computer running a version of Windows may not work when placed in a UNIX environment, mainly due to filename discrepancies. For example, in Windows a link to Page2.htm will work when the file is actually named page2.htm; in UNIX it will not (case sensitivity being the issue).

That ends our module on how to build an e-portfolio. If you have been working through the projects in this module and you complete the assignments and exercises to follow, you will be well on your way to developing an effective e-portfolio (see Figure I.20).

As a final note, we highly recommend that you have several people—including classmates, your instructor, and people from your school's career placement center—view your e-portfolio before you send it to the Web for everyone else to see. An effectively designed and well-worded e-portfolio can indeed help you find a really great job. On the other hand, an ineffectively designed and poorly worded e-portfolio can be disastrous. Take some extra time to have other people review your e-portfolio before placing it on the Web for potentially millions of people to see and scrutinize. And by all means—test, test, test.

Summary: Student Learning Outcomes Revisited

1. **Describe the types of electronic résumés and specify when each is appropriate.** The three types of electronic résumés presented are *scannable* (also called *ASCII*), *portable document format (PDF)*, and *multimedia (HTML)*. A scannable résumé can be submitted in print or electronically to organizations using skills extraction software. A PDF résumé is a version of your presentation résumé that can be delivered electronically (via e-mail or a Web page link) without impacting your formatting. A job search e-portfolio contains a multimedia (HTML) résumé, content, and a gallery supporting your skills designed for Web delivery.

2. **Discuss networking strategies you can use during a job search.** Because up to 80 percent of jobs are in the *hidden job market,* networking is critical to a successful job search. Networking involves contacting people and asking them to help you to uncover hidden jobs. Both electronic and face-to-face contacts are necessary to optimize your job opportunities. Strategies involve creating a contact list, developing a 30-second commercial, setting a weekly contact goal, joining *mailing lists,* tracking responses, and following up.

3. **Explain how self-assessment is valuable to résumé writing.** Employers want to hire employees who are focused. Employees want a job that not only produces an income but is satisfying. A good self-assessment will clarify the skills you have to offer an employer, the work environment that best suits you, and employment qualities that lead to your satisfaction.

4. **Use the Internet to research career opportunities and potential employers.** The World Wide Web offers a wide array of tools that can help you research your chosen career. Effective career research should make use of area-specific search engines, job boards, newsgroups, media sites, government statistics, and employer sites. By combining the information provided by these resources, you should be able to get a complete picture of the employment market you wish to enter and the *skill words* that should be included in your résumé.

5. **Develop powerful job search e-portfolio content.** Powerful job search e-portfolio content is employer-centered and documents the skills that will make you an attractive employee. Quality research and self-assessment are critical to developing content centered on the skills employers want and the benefits these skills provide in an easy-to-use Web site. All traditional résumé content should be developed with these requirements in mind in a manner that does not appear self-centered. Additional e-portfolio content to demonstrate your skills is included as a gallery for potential employers to peruse.

6. **Document effective Web site structure and design components.** Documenting effective Web site structure involves segmenting Web site content and outlining what will be presented on each site page. A navigation chart is developed showing how the various pages of the site will be linked together. Each page of the site should use the same design components outlining the who, what, when, and where of the site. Select a *browser-safe color* scheme for effective viewing by the widest possible audience and use standard content in the header and footer of each page to create a site identity.

7. **Create a job search e-portfolio Web site and place it on an Internet server.** A job search e-portfolio consists of anything that will help a potential employer evaluate your worth as a potential employee. Use the site navigation chart to develop HTML pages displaying traditional résumé content and linking to your ASCII résumé, PDF résumé, and a gallery of works that demonstrate your skills to allow the evaluator to see how effective you could be in their organization. Once all of your content (HTML pages, supporting documents, résumés, and graphics) has been stored in a folder and tested locally, it can be moved to a Web server. The site should be tested again from the Web.

Key Terms and Concepts

Browser-safe colors, 481
E-gallery, 475
Electronic job market, 455
Electronic portfolio (e-portfolio), 455
Hidden job market, 457
Mailing list, 458
Multimedia (HTML) résumé, 468

Portable document format (PDF), 470
Portable document format résumé (PDF résumé), 468
Résumé, 461
Scannable résumé (ASCII résumé), 468
Skill words, 459
Storyboard, 478

Short-Answer Questions

1. What is the main purpose of a scannable résumé?
2. How is designing a Web page different from designing a print document?
3. Why should multiple résumé formats be included in a job search e-portfolio?
4. What elements of a Web site homepage should be carried throughout the rest of the site pages? Why?
5. Why is the gallery of a job search e-portfolio as important as a well-written and researched résumé?
6. What factors do you believe contribute to 80 percent of available jobs never being publicized?
7. Why is it important to include job and industry-specific skill words in the content of your résumé?
8. What important audience preferences should you consider when designing a job search e-portfolio?
9. Why should a Web site that works on your computer be retested after it is placed on a Web server?
10. How do you know what skill words to include in your résumé? Where do you put these skill words?
11. How do you determine how much content to put on a single Web page?
12. Why is it important to view a newly developed Web site on multiple computers using a variety of browsers?
13. Why should you consider using browser-safe colors on your e-portfolio site?
14. How does the hidden job market complicate the job search?
15. Visit the job board www.monster.com and review the site content. Is this a site that you would recommend for first-time job hunters? Why or why not?

Assignments and Exercises

1. **DESCRIBE YOUR CAREER** Using the research methods we have outlined in the module, locate information about your career. Document your findings in a paper, being sure to include job title synonyms, educational standards, work environment, job forecast statistics, normal work week, and any other pertinent information. Cite your sources.
2. **DEVELOPING JOB CONTACTS** Begin to build a list of job contacts. Consider it a running list. Create a list of your friends; your business associates; teachers; adults in your immediate and extended family; acquaintances; and people who are in the field that interests you.
3. **OCCUPATIONAL OUTLOOK** One important resource you can find online is the *Occupational Outlook Handbook.* Go to the *Occupational Outlook Handbook* Web site www.bls.gov/oco/ and look through the index to get an idea of the many jobs that people actually do. Select three to five jobs from the index that

interest you. Write a brief description of each, including as much information as you can find on what kind of work the job involves; working conditions; qualities and skills you need to get the job; job outlook; earnings; related occupations, including advanced positions; and sources you can contact for more information.

4. **VISIT INDUSTRY WEB SITES** Using the research methods we have outlined in the module, locate and visit at least three business Web sites in the industry you've selected. For each site document the page layout, the colors, and the formality of the site. Did you find press and news releases? If so, what did they tell you about the company? Did you find recruitment pages? If so, what types of positions are available? What skill words did you find on these sites that should be included in your résumé?

5. **ENTRY-LEVEL JOB POSTINGS** Visit www.collegegrad.com and search for entry-level job postings in your area of interest. How many postings did you find? Are you qualified, or will you be qualified for the available positions when you complete your current educational goals? Are the listings for a geographic location that you would consider? What skill words should you include in your résumé to be considered for these positions?

6. **FINALIZE YOUR RÉSUMÉS** If you compiled your résumés as you completed the module, review them for presentation effectiveness and content. If you did not build your résumés as you went through the module, do so now. Start by building all of the content in an unformatted document and then create scannable, PDF, and HTML versions. Unless you have sufficient business experience to use a Summary of Qualifications section, use an objective statement that includes the job title, industry, your best skill words, and the benefit you could provide to the hiring organization. In addition to the objective statement, include Work, Education, and References sections. Other sections can be included to suit your background and career. Solicit feedback from at least one classmate.

7. **SELECT CONTENT FOR YOUR E-PORTFOLIO GALLERY** Look through the files on your computer for work that represents your current skills and could be of interest to a potential employer. Create a list of at least three files that would be appropriate for a job search e-portfolio along with a short description of the skills the files exhibit. What other skills should you develop documents to demonstrate? What types of documents would best showcase these skills?

8. **SEARCH THE WORLD WIDE WEB** Use search tools to locate e-portfolios that have already been posted on the Web. How many e-portfolios did you locate? How many of these e-portfolios were designed for a job search? Pick the best e-portfolio you located and critique its content and design.

9. **BUILD YOUR E-PORTFOLIO SITE** Use either a text editor or Web authoring software to build the HTML pages of your job search e-portfolio Web site. Do not use office productivity software such as a word processor. Include a minimum of three HTML pages, your ASCII résumé, your PDF résumé, and three gallery pages using another document format such as Word or PowerPoint.

EXTENDED LEARNING MODULE J

IMPLEMENTING A DATABASE WITH MICROSOFT ACCESS

Student Learning Outcomes

1. IDENTIFY THE STEPS NECESSARY TO IMPLEMENT THE STRUCTURE OF A RELATIONAL DATABASE USING THE DATA DEFINITION LANGUAGE PROVIDED BY MICROSOFT ACCESS.

2. DEMONSTRATE HOW TO USE THE DATA MANIPULATION SUBSYSTEM IN ACCESS TO ENTER AND CHANGE INFORMATION IN A DATABASE AND HOW TO QUERY THAT INFORMATION.

3. EXPLAIN THE USE OF THE APPLICATION GENERATION SUBSYSTEM IN ACCESS TO CREATE REPORTS AND DATA ENTRY SCREENS.

Taking Advantage of the CD

In Chapter 3 we discussed the important role that databases play in an organization. We followed that with *Extended Learning Module C,* in which you learned how to design the correct structure of a relational database. That module includes four primary steps. They are:

1. Defining entity classes and primary keys.
2. Defining relationships among entity classes.
3. Defining information (fields) for each relation (the term relation is often used to refer to a file while designing a database).
4. Using a data definition language to create your database.

In *Extended Learning Module C,* you followed the process through the first three steps above. In this module, we'll take you through the fourth step—using a data definition language to create your database—by exploring the use of Microsoft Access, today's most popular personal database management system package (it comes as a standard part of Microsoft Office Professional suite).

You'll find this extended learning module on the CD that accompanies this text. In this module, we've included coverage of

- Creating a simple query using one relation
- Creating an advanced query using more than one relation
- Generating a simple report
- Generating a report with grouping, sorting, and totals
- Creating a data input form

We believe this material is vitally important. As the business world increasingly moves toward empowering employees with technology tools, you'll be better prepared for the job market if you know how to design, implement, and access a database. Module C covered how to design a database, and this module covers how to implement and access a database using Microsoft Access.

If you need proof of the growing importance of databases, just connect to any job database Web site and enter "Microsoft Access" as a search term. We did that at Monster.com (www.monster.com) and found over 550 job listings requiring expertise in Microsoft Access. Some of the job titles included

- Financial Analysis Manager
- Education Administrator
- Logistics Engineer
- Military Intelligence
- Corporate Trust Administrator
- Market Research Analyst
- Medical Finance Coordinator
- Guest Satisfaction Agent
- Training Coordinator
- Data Consumption Analyst
- Project Manager
- Retail Support Analyst
- Quality Engineer
- Reinsurance Accountant

If you look carefully at the above list, you'll see that not a single job title is IT-specific. Rather, they represent job openings in such areas as finance, hospitality, logistics, retail sales, medicine, and insurance.

We applaud you for popping in the CD and reading this module.

EXTENDED LEARNING MODULE K

CAREERS IN BUSINESS

Student Learning Outcomes

1. IDENTIFY THE CAREER FIELD AND BUSINESS SPECIALIZATION IN WHICH YOU ARE INTERESTED.

2. PROVIDE TYPICAL JOB TITLES AND DESCRIPTIONS FOR YOUR CAREER FIELD.

3. LIST AND DESCRIBE THE IT SKILLS YOU NEED TO GAIN WHILE IN SCHOOL.

Taking Advantage of the CD

In the business world, you need to be "a jack of all trades and a master of one." That means that you need to excel in a particular business functional area (or specialization), such as finance, accounting, marketing, or any of the other many business specializations. It also means that, while your expertise lies within one functional area, you need to be competent in all the other functional areas.

Think about majoring in marketing, for example. You need expertise in consumer behavior, marketing strategies, branding techniques, and many other marketing-oriented concepts. But as a marketing analyst, you need other skills to be successful. You need knowledge of accounting and finance so you can put together a budget and monitor expenses. You need team and employee management skills so you can work effectively in a group and manage other people. You need knowledge of production and operations management so you can understand works-in-progress information and transportation optimization algorithms.

No matter what your career choice, you need knowledge of information technology tools that will allow you to perform your tasks more efficiently and effectively. This textbook isn't about trying to get you to major in information technology or choose MIS as a career. It's about informing you of the role of information technology and MIS in an organization and enabling you to select and use the right IT tools to carry out your tasks.

In this module, we want to explore with you many of the career specializations in business, including:

- Accounting
- Finance
- Hospitality and tourism management
- Information technology
- Management
- Marketing
- Production and operations management
- Real estate and construction management

At your school, there are probably departments devoted to providing degrees in these specializations. While titles and nomenclatures may differ (e.g., production and operations management is often called management science, operations research, statistics and operations technology, or some other variation), those specializations represent the major functional areas in a typical business.

After providing you with a brief introduction to each specialization, we include the following information:

- List of typical job titles and their descriptions
- IT tools you should focus on learning while in school
- Statistics concerning the job market

It is our hope that, after reading this module, you will come to understand that IT and MIS are important no matter what your career choice. You may be taking this class because it's a required part of the business curriculum. It's required because, no matter what career you choose, you need knowledge of IT and MIS. It's similar to taking a human resource management class. While you may not be majoring in human resource management, you will at some time in your career have to manage people. Knowing how to manage them effectively is a career opportunity for you.

Take the time to pop in the CD that accompanies this textbook and read about careers in business.

EXTENDED LEARNING MODULE L

BUILDING WEB SITES WITH FRONTPAGE

Student Learning Outcomes

1. DESCRIBE THE DIFFERENT KINDS OF WEB SITES THAT YOU CAN BUILD USING FRONTPAGE.

2. DESCRIBE THE DIFFERENT WAYS TO NAVIGATE IN FRONTPAGE.

3. EXPLAIN THE DIFFERENT FRONTPAGE VIEWS.

4. DESCRIBE AND BUILD A WEB SITE USING FRONTPAGE.

5. DESCRIBE AND BUILD A WEB PAGE USING FRONTPAGE.

6. DEMONSTRATE THE METHOD USED TO INSERT A GRAPHIC INTO A WEB PAGE USING FRONTPAGE.

7. DESCRIBE AND CREATE THE DIFFERENT TYPES OF HYPERLINKS YOU CAN CREATE USING FRONTPAGE.

8. CREATE A LIST AND TABLE IN A WEB PAGE USING FRONTPAGE.

9. DEFINE THE BENEFITS OF USING THEMES WHEN DEVELOPING A WEB PAGE.

Taking Advantage of the CD

Microsoft **FrontPage** is *Web authoring* software. Web authoring software helps you design and develop Web sites and pages that you publish on the Web. FrontPage allows people with limited Web page design experience to create, modify, and maintain full-featured, professional-looking pages without having to learn how to code all the functions and features from scratch.

Using FrontPage, you can create Web pages, complete with formatted text and graphics, tables, buttons, animations, and sound. You can add frames, borders, and hyperlinks to connect the pages into a Web site, or connect the pages to other Web sites. In FrontPage, you create Web pages in much the same way as you create documents using word processing software. By using the FrontPage menus and toolbar buttons, you enter and format text, pictures, and other page elements in much the same way as you enter and format these items in Word.

Hypertext markup language (HTML) is the language you use to create a Web page. HTML allows you to specify the content of your Web site and format the content such as adding bold, underline, and numbered lists. FrontPage generates the HTML tags in the background, so you need never concern yourself with them. However, if you want to go into the HTML view and make changes, you can do that as well. We covered HTML in *Extended Learning Module F (Building a Web Page with HTML),* so we won't deal with that here. As a refresher, you may want to review that material before beginning this module.

You can use FrontPage to build many different kinds of Web sites:

- *Personal Web site*—A popular type of public Internet site, the personal Web site is all about you. It can describe your interests, your friends, and your family, or offer hyperlinks to your favorite Web sites. Many Web development professionals started by creating a personal Web site. The personal Web site is a chance to be creative.

- *Small business Web site*—If you have a home-based or small business and your advertising budget is small, a Web site is a great way to spread the news about your product or service. By making use of the FrontPage templates, you can set up a professional storefront without having to spend months learning techniques and technologies.

- *Corporate Web site*—Large companies want their Web sites to provide product information, customer support, consumer relations information, and even online shopping. FrontPage is useful in a corporate setting because its powerful tracking features make it possible for more than one person to make changes and updates to Web site pages. FrontPage is compatible with and can be integrated with many other software products, such as Microsoft Excel and Microsoft PowerPoint.

- *Corporate intranet*—A corporate intranet is an internal company network that employees can surf in the same way that they surf the Internet. A Web site on an intranet is like a Web site on the Internet except for the fact that it is available only to employees who can access the company network. Because an intranet is protected from curious Web surfers, internal company information such as sales figures, human resources communications, and department resources can be transmitted company wide. FrontPage has tools for creating customized intranets.

We definitely believe that it is worth your time and energy to pop in the CD and read this module. In it, you'll learn many things including:

- Web sites, Web pages, and HTML
- Understanding the interface
- FrontPage views
- Creating a Web Site with Templates
- Creating a Web Site with a Wizard
- Creating an Empty Web Site

- Building a Web page
- Working with graphics
- Including hyperlinks
- Presenting information in lists and tables
- Formatting pages

EXTENDED LEARNING MODULE M

PROGRAMMING IN EXCEL WITH VBA

Student Learning Outcomes

1. EXPLAIN THE VALUE OF USING VBA WITH EXCEL.

2. DEFINE A MACRO.

3. BUILD A SIMPLE MACRO USING A SUB PROCEDURE AND A FUNCTION PROCEDURE.

4. DESCRIBE AN OBJECT.

5. EXPLAIN THE DIFFERENCE BETWEEN A COMMENT, A VARIABLE, AND A CONSTANT.

6. LIST THE VARIOUS VISUAL BASIC APPLICATION DATA TYPES AND OPERATORS.

7. DESCRIBE AND BUILD A MACRO THAT USES THE *IF-THEN-ELSE, FOR-NEXT, DO-UNTIL, DO-WHILE,* AND *SELECT CASE* STRUCTURES.

Taking Advantage of the CD

VBA, which stands for *Visual Basic for Applications*, is a programming language developed by Microsoft. Excel, along with the other members of Microsoft Office, includes the VBA language. VBA extends and customizes Excel, allowing you to do things that Excel itself is not able to do, such as calculating values in cells based on user input values.

Excel VBA is a programming application that allows you to use Visual Basic code to run the many features of Excel, thereby allowing you to customize your Excel applications. Units of VBA code are often referred to as *macros*. Although this module covers more formal terminology, the term macro will be used as a general way to refer to any VBA code. It is not essential to make a further software purchase in order to learn the elements of Visual Basic programming. Excel VBA comes free with Excel (97, 2000, 2002, 2003, etc.) and provides a great deal of the functionality (which happens to be the topic of this module).

One of the great advantages of Excel VBA is the macro recorder. The *macro recorder* is a software tool that will let you record a sequence of commands in Excel and save them as a macro. This is invaluable if you are struggling with some programming syntax. Just get the recorder to do it for you and then view the code to see how it is done.

Excel programming terminology can be a bit confusing. For example, VBA is a programming language, but it also serves as a macro language. A ***macro language*** is a programming language that includes built-in commands that mimic the functionality available from menus and dialog boxes within an application. What do you call something written in VBA and executed in Excel? Is it a macro or is it a program? Excel's Help system often refers to VBA procedures as macros. A ***macro*** is a set of actions recorded or written by a user. For instance, you can create a macro that always prints your name in bold on a spreadsheet. You can name it PrintName and then reuse the PrintName macro in any spreadsheet. This term means that a series of steps is completed automatically. For example, if you write a macro that adds a background color to some cells and then prints the worksheet, you have automated those two steps.

People use Excel for thousands of different tasks, such as:

- Budgeting and forecasting
- Analyzing data
- Creating invoices and other forms
- Developing charts from data

One thing virtually every user has in common is the need to automate some aspect of Excel. For example, you might create a VBA macro to format and print a month-end sales report. You can execute the macro with a single command, triggering Excel to automatically perform many time-consuming tasks, such as inserting your name at the top of every spreadsheet you create, specifying which rows are to be repeated at the top of each printed page, adding information in the footer area, and so on.

We definitely believe that it worth your time and energy to pop in the CD and read this module. In it, you'll learn many things including:

- VBA in a Nutshell
- The Visual Basic Editor
- The Visual Basic Editor Tools
- The Visual Basic Editor Module Code
- Elements of VBA Programming
- The If-Then Structure
- Using ElseIf
- The Select Case Structure
- Looping

→

CASE 1:
ASSESSING THE VALUE OF CUSTOMER RELATIONSHIP
MANAGEMENT

TREVOR TOY AUTO MECHANICS

Trevor Toy Auto Mechanics is an automobile repair shop in Phoenix, Arizona. Over the past few years, Trevor has seen his business grow from a two-bay car repair shop with only one other employee to a 15-bay car repair shop with 21 employees.

Trevor wants to improve service and add a level of personalization to his customers. However, Trevor has no idea who his best customers are, the work that is being performed, or which mechanic is responsible for the repairs. Trevor is asking for your help. He has provided you with a spreadsheet file, **TREVOR.xls**, that contains a list of all the repairs his shop has completed over the past year including each client's name along with a unique identifier. The spreadsheet file contains the fields provided in the table below.

Column	Name	Description
A	CUSTOMER #	A unique number assigned to each customer.
B	CUSTOMER NAME	The name of the customer.
C	MECHANIC #	A unique number assigned to the mechanic who completed the work.
D	CAR TYPE	The type of car on which the work was completed.
E	WORK COMPLETED	What type of repair was performed on the car.
F	NUM HOURS	How long in hours it took to complete the work.
G	COST OF PARTS	The cost of the parts associated with completing the repair.
H	TOTAL CHARGE	The amount charged to the customer for the repair.

Your analysis should include (1) Trevor's best customers (top 10 in terms of volume and revenue); (2) Trevor's worst customers (bottom 10 in terms of lowest volume and lost revenue); and (3) the mechanics that perform the repairs for each customer.

SOME PARTICULARS YOU SHOULD KNOW

1. As you consider the information provided to you, think in terms of what information is important. You might need to use the existing information to create new information.

2. In your analysis, provide examples of the types of marketing campaigns Trevor should offer his most valuable customers.

3. Upon completing your analysis, please provide concise yet detailed and thorough documentation (in narrative, numeric, and graphic forms) that justifies your recommendations.

4. File: **TREVOR.xls** (Excel file).

CASE 2:
ANALYZING THE VALUE OF INFORMATION

AFFORDABLE HOMES REAL ESTATE

In late 1995, a national study announced that Eau Claire, Wisconsin, was the safest place to live. Since then, housing development projects have been springing up all around Eau Claire. Six housing development projects are currently dominating the Eau Claire market: Woodland Hills, Granite Mound, Creek Side Huntington, East River Community, Forest Green, and Eau Claire South. These six projects each started with 100 homes, have sold all of them, and are currently developing phase 2.

As one of the three partners and real estate agents of Affordable Homes Real Estate, it is your responsibility to analyze the information concerning the past 600 home sales and choose which development project to focus on for selling homes in phase 2. Because your real estate firm is so small, you and your partners have decided that the firm should focus on selling homes in only one of the development projects.

From the Wisconsin Real Estate Association you have obtained a spreadsheet file that contains information concerning each of the sales for the first 600 homes. It contains the following fields:

Column	Name	Description
A	LOT #	The number assigned to a specific home within each project
B	PROJECT #	A unique number assigned to each of the six housing development projects (see table to follow)
C	ASK PRICE	The initial posted asking price for the home
D	SELL PRICE	The actual price for which the home was sold
E	LIST DATE	The date the home was listed for sale
F	SALE DATE	The date on which the final contract closed and the home was sold
G	SQ. FT.	The total square footage for the home
H	# BATH.	The number of bathrooms in the home
I	# BDRMS	The number of bedrooms in the home

The following numbers have been assigned to each of the housing development projects:

Project Number	Project Name
23	Woodland Hills
47	Granite Mound
61	Creek Side Huntington
78	East River Community
92	Forest Green
97	Eau Claire South

It is your responsibility to analyze the sales list and prepare a report that details which housing development project your real estate firm should focus on. Your analysis should cover as many angles as possible.

SOME PARTICULARS YOU SHOULD KNOW

1. You don't know how many other real estate firms will also be competing for sales in each of the housing development projects.

2. Phase 2 for each housing development project will develop homes similar in style, price, and square footage to their respective first phases.

3. As you consider the information provided to you, think in terms of what information is important and what information is not important. Be prepared to justify how you approach your analysis.

4. Upon completing your analysis, please provide concise, yet detailed and thorough, documentation (in narrative, numeric, and graphic forms) that justifies your decision.

5. File: **REALEST.xls** (Excel file).

CASE 3:
EXECUTIVE INFORMATION SYSTEM REPORTING

POLITICAL CAMPAIGN FINANCE

When it comes to campaign finance, Americans want a system that minimizes the influence of "fat cats" and organized money, that keeps campaign spending at sensible levels, that fosters healthy electoral competition, that doesn't take advantage of wealthy candidates, and that doesn't require candidates to spend all of their waking hours raising money.

Indeed, the much maligned congressional campaign finance system we have now is itself a product of well-intended reform efforts, passed by Congress in 1974 to achieve these ideals. Dozens of new reform plans have emerged during the 1990s that also reach for these goals. Yet, no reform scheme, however well intended, is likely to produce a perfect congressional campaign finance system.

The city of Highlands Ranch, Colorado, wishes to organize its campaign contributions records in a more strategic format. The city council is considering various executive information system packages that can show them overall views of the contribution information as well as give them the ability to access more detailed information. You have been hired to make recommendations about what reports should be available through the soon-to-be-purchased executive information system.

The table below is a list of the information that will be the foundation for the reports in the proposed executive information system. To help you develop realistic reports, the city has provided you with a spreadsheet file that contains specific contributions over the last six months.

Column	Name	Description
A	DATE	The actual date that the contribution was made
B	CONTRIBUTOR	The name of the person or organization that made the contribution
C	DISTRICT	The district number that the councilperson belongs to
D	AMOUNT	The amount of the contribution
E	TYPE	The description type of where the contribution amount was given
F	COUNCILPERSON	The councilperson's name
G	PARTY	The councilperson's political party

What the city council is most interested in is viewing several overall reports and then being able to request more detailed reports. So, as a consultant, your goal is to develop different sets of reports that illustrate the concept of drilling down through the information provided. For example, you should develop a report that shows overall campaign contributions by district (each of the eight different districts) and then also develop more detailed reports that show contribution by political party and contribution by type.

SOME PARTICULARS YOU SHOULD KNOW

1. The council would much rather see information graphically than numerically. So, as you develop your reports, do so in terms of graphs that illustrate the desired relationships.

2. As you consider the information provided to you, think in terms of overall views first and then detailed views second. This will help you develop a logical series of reports.

3. If you wish, you can explore a variety of software tools or functions to help you create the reports. Then prepare your presentation using a presentation graphics package that lets you create a really great presentation of your recommendations.

4. Again, your goal is not to create reports that point toward a particular problem or opportunity. Rather, you are to design a series of logical reports that illustrate the concept of drilling down.

5. File: **CONTRIBUTE.xls** (Excel file).

CASE 4:
BUILDING VALUE CHAINS

HELPING CUSTOMERS DEFINE VALUE

StarLight is a Denver-based retailer of high-quality apparel, shoes, and accessories. In 1915, with money earned in the Colorado gold mines, Anne Logan invested in a small downtown Denver shoe store. A few years later, Anne expanded her business by adding fine apparel. Today, StarLight has 97 retail stores and discount outlets throughout the United States. Since the beginning, StarLight's business philosophy has reflected its founder's beliefs in exceptional service, value, selection, and quality. To maintain the level of service StarLight's customers have come to expect, the company empowers its employees to meet any customer demand, no matter how unreasonable it may seem. With so many stores, it's difficult for Cody Sherrod, StarLight's vice president for Business Information and Planning, to know the level of service customers receive, what customers value, and what they don't. These are important questions for a retailer striving to provide the finest customer experience and products while keeping costs to a minimum.

Cody decided a value chain analysis would be helpful in answering these questions. So, customer surveys were designed, distributed, completed, collected, and compiled into a database. Customers were asked to value their experience with various processes in the StarLight value chain. Specifically, for each value chain process, customers were asked whether this area added value to their experience or reduced the value of their experience. Customers were asked to quantify how much each process added or reduced the value of the services they received. Using a total of 100 points for the value chain, each customer distributed those points among StarLight's processes. The survey results in the database consist of the fields shown in the following table.

Field Name	Description
Survey ID	An ID number uniquely identifying the survey
VA/VR	A field that identifies whether the current row of information reflects a value-added response or a value-reducing response
Date	Survey response date
Mgmt/Acctg/Finance/Legal	Customer value experience, if any, with management, accounting, finance, and the legal departments
HR Mgmt	Customer value of the attitude and general personnel environment
R&D/Tech Dev	Customer perceived value of the quality of research and technology support
Purchasing	Customer value placed on the quality and range of product selection
Receive and Greet Customers	Customer value placed on initial contact with employees
Provide Direction/Advice/Info	Customer value placed on initial information provided by employees
Store Location/Channel Availability & Convenience	Customer value placed on location, availability, and convenience
Product Display/Site or Catalog Layout	Customer value placed on aesthetic appeal of merchandise display and layout
Sales Service	Customer value placed on quality of service provided by sales associates
Marketing	Customer value placed on the effectiveness of marketing material
Customer Follow-up	Customer value placed on postsales service and follow-up

Cody has asked you to gather the raw survey material into two value chains, the value-added chain and the value-reducing chain. You'll create chains that summarize the survey information and size the process areas proportionately as described in Chapter 2. Specifically, your job is to perform the following:

1. Create queries or reports in the provided database to summarize the value-added amounts and the value-reducing amounts for each process.
2. Draw two value chains using that summary information to size the depicted area for each process. Use the value chains in Chapter 2 as reference.
3. Compare the value-added and value-reducing process percentages. Do they correlate in any way? If so, why do you think that is? If not, why not?
4. In the table description provided, a dashed line is drawn between the "purchasing" process and the "receive and greet customers" process. Processes above the line are considered support processes, while processes below are considered primary processes. Create a database query to compare how customers value the total of support processes versus primary processes. Do this for both value-added and value-reducing processes. Do the results make sense or are they surprising? Explain your answer.

SOME PARTICULARS YOU SHOULD KNOW

1. Remember that the total value-added/value-reducing amount for each process must equal 100 percent.
2. The survey values in the database are not percentages although the sum of all responses for a given survey equals 100.
3. File: **STARLIGHT.mdb** (Access file).

CASE 5:
USING RELATIONAL TECHNOLOGY TO TRACK PROJECTS

FOOTHILLS CONSTRUCTION

Foothills Construction Company is a Denver-based construction company that specializes in subcontracting the development of single family homes. In business since 1993, Foothills Construction Company has maintained a talented pool of certified staff and independent consultants allowing the flexibility and combined experience required to meet the needs of its nearly 300 completed projects in the Denver metropolitan area. The field of operation methods that Foothills Construction is responsible for as it relates to building include structural development, heating and cooling, plumbing, and electricity.

The company charges its clients by billing the hours spent on each contract. The hourly billing rate is dependent on the employee's position according to the field of operations (as noted below).

Figure GP.1 shows a basic report that Foothills Construction managers would like to see every week concerning what projects are being assigned as well as a summary of assignment hours and changes. Foothills Construction organizes its internal structure in four different operations: Structure (500), Plumbing (501), Electrical (502), and Heating and Ventilation (503). Each of these operational departments can and should have many subcontractors who specialize in that area.

Figure GP.1

Foothills Construction Project Detail

FOOTHILLS CONSTRUCTION PROJECT DETAIL

PROJECT NAME	ASSIGN DATE	EMP LAST NAME	EMP FIRST NAME	JOB DESCRIPTION	ASSIGN HOUR	CHARGE/HOUR
Chatfield						
	Thursday, February 10, 2005	Jones	Anne	Heating and Ventalation	3.4	$84.50
	Thursday, February 10, 2005	Sullivan	David	Electrical	1.8	$105.00
	Friday, February 11, 2005	Frommer	Matt	Plumbing	4.1	$96.75
	Saturday, February 12, 2005	Newman	John	Electrical	1.7	$105.00
	Saturday, February 12, 2005	Bavangi	Terry	Plumbing	4.1	$96.75
Summary of Assignment Hours and Charges					15.10	$1,448.15
Evergreen						
	Thursday, February 10, 2005	Smithfield	William	Structure	3.0	$35.75
	Thursday, February 10, 2005	Newman	John	Electrical	2.3	$105.00
	Thursday, February 10, 2005	Nenior	David	Plumbing	3.3	$96.75
	Friday, February 11, 2005	Marbough	Mike	Heating and Ventalation	2.6	$84.50
	Saturday, February 12, 2005	Johnson	Peter	Electrical	2.0	$105.00
	Saturday, February 12, 2005	Newman	John	Electrical	3.6	$105.00
	Saturday, February 12, 2005	Olenkoski	Glenn	Structure	1.9	$35.75
Summary of Assignment Hours and Charges					18.70	$1,543.65
Roxborough						

Page: 1

Because of the boom in home sales over the last several years, Foothills Construction has decided to implement a relational database model to track project details according to project name, hours assigned, and charges per hour for each job description. Originally, Foothills Construction decided to let one of its employees handle the construction of the database. However, that employee has not had the time to completely implement the project. Foothills Construction has asked you to take over and complete the development of the database.

The entity classes and primary keys for the database have been identified as the following:

Entity	Primary Key
Project	Project Number
Employee	Employee Number
Job	Job Number
Assign	Assign Number

The following business rules have also been identified:

1. A job can have many employees assigned but must have at least one.
2. An employee must be assigned to one and only one job number.
3. An employee can be assigned to work on one or more projects.
4. A project can be assigned to only one employee but need not be assigned to any employee.

Your job is to be completed in the following phases:

1. Develop and describe the entity-relationship diagram.
2. Use normalization to assure the correctness of the tables (relations).
3. Create the database using a personal DBMS package (preferably Microsoft Access).
4. Use the DBMS package to create the basic report in Figure GP.1.

SOME PARTICULARS YOU SHOULD KNOW

1. You may not be able to develop a report that looks exactly like the one in Figure GP.1. However, your report should include the same information.
2. Complete personnel information is tracked by another database. For this application, include only the minimum employee number, last name, and first name.
3. Information concerning all projects, employees, and jobs is not readily available. You should, however, create information for several fictitious systems to include in your database.
4. File: Not applicable.

CASE 6:
BUILDING A DECISION SUPPORT SYSTEM

CREATING AN INVESTMENT PORTFOLIO

Most experts recommend that if you're devising a long-term investment strategy you should make the stock market part of your plan. You can use a DSS to help you decide what stocks to put into your portfolio. You can use a spreadsheet to do the job. The information you need on 10 stocks is contained in a Word file called **STOCKS.doc**. This information consists of

1. Two years of weekly price data on 10 different stocks.
2. Stock market indices from
   - The Dow Jones Industrial Average
   - NASDAQ Composite
3. Dividends and cash flow per share over the last 10 years (Source: Yahoo Finance).

Using this information, build a DSS to perform stock analysis consisting of the following tasks:

1. Examine Diversification Benefits
   A. Calculate the average return and standard deviation(s) of each of the 10 stocks.
   B. Form six different portfolios: two with two stocks each; two with three stocks each; two with five stocks each.

   Answer the following questions using your DSS:

   - How does the standard deviation of each portfolio compare to the (average) standard deviation of each stock in the portfolio?
   - How does the average return of the portfolio compare to the average return of each stock in the portfolio?
   - Do the benefits of diversification seem to increase or diminish as the number of stocks in the portfolio gets larger?
   - In the two-stock and five-stock portfolios what happens if you group your stocks toward similar industries?

2. Value Each of the Stocks

   A. Estimate the dividend growth rate based on past dividends.
   B. Estimate next year's dividend using this year's dividend and the estimated growth rate.
   C. Generate two graphs, one for past dividends and one for estimated dividends for the next five years.

SOME PARTICULARS YOU SHOULD KNOW

1. When performing your calculations, use the weekly returns. That is, use the change in the price each week rather than the prices themselves. This gives you a better basis for calculation because the prices themselves don't usually change very much.
2. File: **STOCKS.doc** (Word file).

CASE 7:
ADVERTISING WITH BANNER ADS

HIGHWAYSANDBYWAYS.COM

Business is booming at HighwaysAndByways, a dot-com firm focusing on selling accessories for car enthusiasts (e.g., floor mats, grill guards, air fresheners, stereos, and so on). Throughout the past year, HighwaysAndByways has had Web site management software tracking what customers buy, the Web sites from which customers came, and the Web sites customers went to after visiting HighwaysAndByways. That information is stored in a spreadsheet file and contains the fields in the accompanying table. Each record in the spreadsheet file represents an individual visit by a customer that resulted in a purchase.

HighwaysAndByways is interested in determining three items and has employed you as a consultant to help. First, HighwaysAndByways wants to know on which Web sites it should purchase banner ad space. Second, HighwaysAndByways wants to know which Web sites it should contact to determine if those Web sites would like to purchase banner ad space on the

Column	Name	Description
A	CUSTOMER ID	A unique identifier for a customer who made a purchase
B	TOTAL PURCHASE	The total amount of a purchase
C	PREVIOUS WEB SITE	The Web site from which the customer came to visit HighwaysAndByways
D	NEXT WEB SITE	The Web site the customer went to after making a purchase at HighwaysAndByways
E	TIME SPENT	The amount of time that the customer spent at the site

HighwaysAndByways Web site. Finally, HighwaysAndByways would like to know which Web sites it should develop reciprocal banner ad relationships with; that is, HighwaysAndByways would like a list of Web sites on which it would obtain banner ad space while providing banner ad space on its Web site for those Web sites.

SOME PARTICULARS YOU SHOULD KNOW

1. As you consider the information provided to you, think about the levels of information literacy. In other words, don't jump to conclusions before carefully evaluating the provided information.
2. You don't know if your customers made purchases at the Web site they visited upon leaving HighwaysAndByways.
3. Upon completing your analysis, please provide concise yet detailed and thorough documentation (in narrative, numeric, and graphic forms) that justifies your recommendations.
4. File: **CLICKSTREAMS.xls** (Excel file).

CASE 8:
ASSESSING THE VALUE OF OUTSOURCING INFORMATION TECHNOLOGY

CREATING FORECASTS

Founded in 1992, Innovative Software provides search software, Web site accessibility testing/repair software, and usability testing/repair software. All serve as part of its desktop and enterprise content management solutions for government, corporate, educational, and consumer markets. The company's solutions are used by Web site publishers, digital media publishers, content managers, document managers, business users, consumers, software companies, and consulting services companies. Innovative Software solutions help organizations develop long-term strategies to achieve Web content accessibility, enhance usability, and comply with U.S. and international accessibility and search standards.

Innovative Software has a 10-year history of approximately 1 percent in turnover a year and its focus has always been on customer service. With the informal motto of "Grow big, but stay small," it takes pride in 100 percent callbacks in customer care, knowing that its personal service has been one thing that makes it outstanding.

Innovative Software has experienced rapid growth to six times its original customer-base size and is forced to deal with difficult questions for the first time, such as, "How do we serve this many customers? How do we keep our soul—that part of us that honestly cares very much about our customers? How will we know that someone else will care as much and do as good a job as we have done?" In addition, you have just received an e-mail from the company CIO, Sue Downs, that the number of phone calls from customers having problems with one of your newer applications is on the increase.

As customer service manager for Innovative Software, your overriding goal is to maintain the company's reputation for excellent customer service, and outsourcing may offer an efficient means of keeping up with expanding call volume. Innovative Software is reviewing a similar scenario, that of e-BANK, which outsourced its customer service in order to handle a large projected number of customers through several customer interaction channels. Although e-BANK had excellent people, it felt that its competencies were primarily in finance, rather than in customer service and that it needed to have the expertise that a customer-service-focused company could offer. e-BANK also discovered that it was cost effective to outsource its customer service center.

Additionally, the outsourcing approach was relatively hassle-free, since e-BANK did not have to set up its own call center.

SOME PARTICULARS YOU SHOULD KNOW

1. Create a weekly analysis from the data provided in **FORECAST.xls**.
2. The price of the products, the actual product type, and any warranty information is irrelevant.
3. Develop a growth, trend, and forecast analysis. You should use a three-day moving average: a shorter moving average might not display the trend well and a much longer moving average would shorten the trend too much.
4. Upon completing your analysis, please provide concise yet detailed and thorough documentation (in narrative, numeric, and graphic forms) that justifies your recommendations.
5. File: **FORECAST.xls** (Excel file)

CASE 9:
DEMONSTRATING HOW TO BUILD WEB SITES

WITH HTML

Building a good Web site is simple in some respects and difficult in others. It's relatively easy to learn to write HTML code. Building an effective and eye-catching Web site is a horse of a different color. That is to say, there is a stretch between just using the technology and using the technology to your best advantage.

Your task in this project is to build a presentation (using presentation graphics software such as Microsoft PowerPoint) that achieves two goals. First, your presentation should show your audience how to write simple HTML code to create a Web site. Your presentation should include the HTML code for

- Text formatting (bold, italic, and the like)
- Font families and sizing
- Font colors
- Background colors and images
- Links
- Images
- Numbered and bulleted lists

Next, your presentation should provide the audience with a list of guidelines for creating an *effective* Web site. For this, you should definitely embed links into your presentation that go to Web sites that illustrate good Web site design, displaying examples of both effective and ineffective designs.

SOME PARTICULARS YOU SHOULD KNOW

1. In a file called **HTML.doc**, we've provided many links to Web sites that teach you how to write HTML code.
2. In a file called **DESIGN.doc**, we've provided many links to Web sites that teach you how to design Web sites effectively.
3. Files: **HTML.doc** and **DESIGN.doc** (Word files).

CASE 10:
MAKING THE CASE WITH PRESENTATION SOFTWARE

INFORMATION TECHNOLOGY ETHICS

Management at your company is concerned about the high cost of computer crime, from lawsuits over e-mail received to denial-of-service attacks and hackers breaking into the corporate network to steal information. You've been asked to make a presentation to inform your colleagues of these issues. Develop a presentation using a presentation package such as Microsoft's PowerPoint.

You can choose your presentation's emphasis from the following topics:

- Ethics as it relates to IT systems
- Types of crime aimed at IT systems (such as viruses)
- Types of crime that use IT systems as weapons (such as electronic theft of funds from one account to another)
- Security measures, how good they are, what they cost, how expensive they are to implement
- Electronic monitoring of employees (from employer and employee standpoints)
- Collection and use of personal information on consumers

SOURCES OF INFORMATION

- In the file **ETHICS.doc**, you'll find sources for the topics listed above.
- The Web is a great place to find lots of information.
- Most business publications, such as *Business Week, Information Week, Fortune,* and *The Wall Street Journal,* frequently have good articles on ethics, cybercrime, and security. You can get some of these articles on the Web.
- General news publications such as *Newsweek* and *USA Today* print articles on these topics.

Your task is to weave the information you find into a coherent presentation using graphs and art where appropriate.

SOME PARTICULARS YOU SHOULD KNOW

1. Content Principles
   - Each slide should have a headline
   - Each slide should express one idea
   - Ideas should follow logically

2. Design Principles
   - Follow the "Rule of 7," which is no more than 7 lines per slide and 7 words per line
   - Keep it simple
   - Keep it organized
   - Create a path for the eye
   - Divide space in an interesting way
   - Use at least 30-point type
   - Use color and graphics carefully, consistently, and for a specific purpose
   - Use high-contrast colors (black/white, deep blue/white, etc.)
3. File: **ETHICS.doc** (Word file)

CASE 11:
BUILDING A WEB DATABASE SYSTEM

WEB-BASED CLASSIFIED SYSTEM

With the emergence of the Internet as a worldwide standard for communicating information, *Gabby's Gazetteer,* a medium-size community newspaper in central Colorado, is looking to enter the electronic commerce market.

In the listing of classified ads, advertisers place a small ad that lists items they wish to sell and provide a means (e.g., telephone number) by which prospective buyers can contact them.

The nature of a sale via a newspaper classified system goes as follows:

- During the course of the sale, the information flows in different directions at different stages.
- First, there is a downstream flow of information (from seller to buyer)—the listing in print on the newspaper. (Thus, the classified ad listing is just a way of bringing a buyer and seller together.)
- When a potential purchaser's interest has been raised, then that interest must be relayed upstream, usually by telephone or in person.
- Finally, a meeting should result that uses face-to-face negotiation to finalize the sale—if the sale can be agreed upon.

By placing the entire system on the Internet, the upstream and downstream communications are accomplished using a Web browser. The sale becomes more of an auction, because many potential buyers, all with equal status, can bid for the same item.

Any user who is trying to buy an item can

- View items for sale
- Bid on an item they wish to purchase

Any user who is trying to sell an item can

- Place a new item for sale
- Browse a list of the items that he or she is trying to sell, and examine the bids that have been made on each of those items
- Accept a bid on an item that he or she is selling

This system should also allow users to do some very basic administrative tasks, such as

- Browse the listings to see what is for sale
- Register with the system (users can browse without registering; but they must register if they want to sell an item or bid for an item)

Figure GP.2

Gabby's Gazetteer Classified Registration System

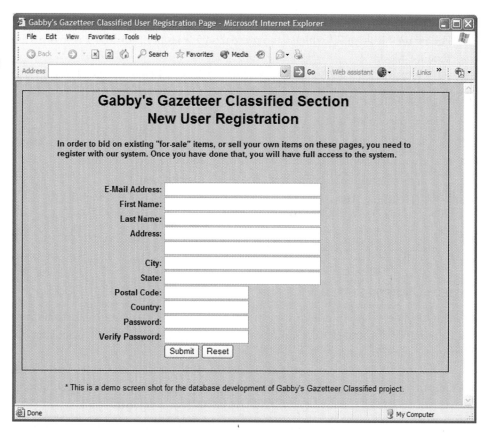

- Log on to the system
- Change their registration details

Your job will be to complete the following:

1. Develop and describe the entity-relationship diagram for the database that will support the above activities.

2. Use normalization to ensure the correctness of the tables.

3. Create the database using a personal DBMS package.

SOME PARTICULARS YOU SHOULD KNOW

1. Use Figure GP.2 as a baseline for your database design.

2. File: Not applicable.

CASE 12:
CREATING A DECISION SUPPORT SYSTEM

BUY VERSUS LEASE

A leading supplier of grapes to the wine-producing industry in California, On the Vine Grapes, wants to expand its delivery services and expand its reach to market by increasing its current fleet of delivery trucks. Some of the older vehicles were acquired through closed-end leases with required down payments, mileage restrictions, and hefty early termination penalties. Other vehicles were purchased using traditional purchase-to-own loans, which often resulted in high depreciation costs and large maintenance fees. All vehicles were acquired one at a time through local dealers.

On the Vine Grapes has asked you to assist in developing a lease/buy cost analysis worksheet in order to make the most cost-effective decision. Currently the director of operations, Bill Smith, has identified a 2005 Ford F-550 4x2 SD Super Cab 161.8 in. WB DRW HD XLT as the truck of choice for the business. This vehicle has a retail price of $34,997.00 or a lease price of $600/month through Ford Motor Credit Company.

Here are some basic fees and costs that you need to factor in:

1. **Lease Costs**

Refundable security deposit	$500
First month's payment at inception	$500
Other initial costs	$125
Monthly lease payment for remaining term	$600
Last month payment in advance	No
Allowable annual mileage	15,000
Estimated annual miles to be driven	20,000
Per mile charge for excess miles	0.10

2. **Purchase Costs**

Retail price including sales taxes, title	$34,997
Down payment	$4,000
Loan interest rate	8.75%
Will interest be deductible business or home equity interest?	Yes
Is the gross loaded weight of the vehicle over 6,000 lbs?	Yes

3. **Common Costs and Assumptions**

Total lease/loan term	36
Discount percent	8.75
Tax bracket—combined federal and state	33%
Business use percentage	100%

SOME PARTICULARS YOU SHOULD KNOW

1. In the file **BUYORLEASE.xls** is a template you can use to enter the information above. There is also a sheet that has been developed to assist you with the annual depreciation for an automobile.
2. Create a detailed summary sheet of the lease/buy option for On the Vine Grapes.
3. File: **BUYORLEASE.xls** (Excel file).

CASE 13:
DEVELOPING AN ENTERPRISE RESOURCE PLANNING SYSTEM

PLANNING, REPORTING, AND DATA PROCESSING

The State Annual Report on Enterprise Resource Planning and Management was developed to provide a comprehensive view of the management and use of technology by the Higher Educational System of Colorado. This report shows the statewide issues surrounding information technology, priorities for the ensuing two years, initiatives and projects, performance management, and the information technology resources utilized to support the business processes of Higher Education during fiscal year 2004–2005. A comparison report is also generated to produce a percentage change in funds from fiscal year 2003–2004 and fiscal year 2004–2005.

Chief information officer (CIO) for the Department of Higher Education, David Paul, was required to report the estimated expenditures for technology across five appropriation categories: Employee Salaries/Benefits, Other Personal Services (OPS—noncareer service employees with no permanent status), Expenses (all hardware purchases under $1,000, travel, training, and general office expenses), Operating Capital Outlay (OCO), and Data Processing Services. Most of these performance management initiatives have been measured using manual processes. Several reporting units documented the need for automated measurement tools in the future to take advantage of the full opportunities for improvement. David Paul has asked you to assist him in organizing this information and calculating some of the requirements established by the State Board of Education. Along with the appropriation categories mentioned above, each institution is categorized according to status (2 Year, 4 Year Public, or 4 Year Private). This will aid in the overall analysis for current and future resource planning.

SOME PARTICULARS YOU SHOULD KNOW

1. You need to create a detailed report for:
   a. Summary of overall change from 2003–2004 fiscal year (FY) and 2004–2005 FY
   b. Percentage of budget allocated to data processing services
   c. Percentage of 2 year, 4 year public, and 4 year private institutions allocating resources to data processing services
2. Develop a graphical representation of the percentage of 2 year, 4 year public, and 4 year private institutions allocating resources to data processing services
3. File: **COLORADOHIGHERED.xls** (Excel file)

CASE 14:
ASSESSING A WIRELESS FUTURE

EMERGING TRENDS AND TECHNOLOGY

"Intelligent wireless handheld devices are going to explode, absolutely explode over the next several years."—Steve Ballmer, CEO, Microsoft.

Wireless, mobility, small form factor, pervasive computing, the anytime network—whatever name you choose—it's here. The price of easy-to-handle devices which provide access to a variety of applications and information is rapidly falling while the efficiencies of such devices are increasing. More and more, the business user is looking to use mobile devices to perform tasks that previously could be handled only by the desktop PC. End user adoption is skyrocketing. The next 18 months will demonstrate a true growing period for mobile computing as the world changes to one characterized by the mobile user.

As this market sector grows, software and information companies are evolving their products and services. Wireless mobility and associated functionality provide new market opportunities for both established companies and new entrants to increase efficiency and take advantage of new revenue possibilities. The services to Internet-enabled mobile devices create a vast array of new business opportunities for companies as they develop products and services that utilize location, time, and immediate access to information in new and innovative ways.

Some of the lower profile topics that are currently being developed at this time include:

- Hard drives for wireless devices
- Global-roaming movement
- Mobile power supplies that run on next-generation fuel cells.

All three could bring about significant changes in the wireless space.

You have been asked to prepare a presentation using a presentation package such as Microsoft's PowerPoint. Using the list of wireless solution providers and manufacturers provided in WIRELESS.htm, select at least two developers and create a presentation that will emphasize the following topics:

1. What are the current products or services under development?
2. What is the target market for that product or service?
3. What are the key features that product or service will bring to the wireless industry?
4. Which provider/manufacturer/developer seems to be the first to market with their product?
5. How is the wireless product or service content being delivered?
6. Are the products or services able to deploy interactive multimedia applications to any digital wireless device, on any carrier, or across any type of network?
7. Are there any new privacy concerns that are being discussed in relation to the new products or services? (These can include concerns from being able to track users' preferences, purchasing history or browsing preferences, or the capability to track a user's physical location while using a wireless device.)
8. How does this product or solution affect the global marketplace?
9. What is the current retail price for the wireless products or solutions?
10. Is current bandwidth available to the wireless industry a concern?

Your task is to weave the information you find into a coherent presentation using graphs and art where appropriate.

SOME PARTICULARS YOU SHOULD KNOW

1. Content Principles
   - Each slide should have a headline
   - Each slide should express one idea
   - Ideas should follow logically
2. Design Principles
   - Follow the "Rule of 7"—no more than 7 lines per slide and 7 words per line
   - Keep it simple
   - Keep it organized
   - Create a path for the eye
   - Divide space in an interesting way
   - Use at least 30-point type
   - Use color and graphics carefully, consistently, and for a specific purpose
   - Use high-contrast colors (black/white, deep blue/white, etc.)
3. File: **WIRELESS.htm** (html file)

CASE 15:
EVALUATING THE NEXT GENERATION

DOT-COM ASPS

E-business is creating a new set of challenges for not only dot-com start-ups but also well-established brick-and-mortar companies. Driven by the need to capture increasing shares of business online, IT managers take the first step by deciding on a commerce application. Then they face the most important decision: whether to assign implementation, deployment, and application hosting to internal IT resources or to contract for these services with an ASP.

A few years ago, no one had even heard the term *application service provider (ASP)*. Now the ASP market is a certified phenomenon. In the short space of two years, the concept of leasing applications to businesses has grown to an interesting but unproven proposition in an ever-expanding industry.

You have been hired by Front Range Car Rental, a major car rental company in Colorado, to research ways to use technology to leverage more business. The company needs a Web service written which transacts reservations on its back-end mainframe system. This Web service will need to be made available to airline partners to integrate the travel booking process. When consumers book a flight, they are also given the option to reserve a car from the airline site. The rental details will need to be captured and transported to the car rental company's Web service, which processes the reservation. This new capability will help the car rental company to drive more bookings and achieve a competitive advantage in a highly commoditized market.

The major task that Front Range Car Rental needs you to research is what the cost benefits would be for in-house implementation and an ASP deployment. You have been given an analysis spreadsheet, **DOTCOMASP.xls**, with all the detailed information; however, you will need to use the Internet in order to find current price information. Another file, **DOTCOMASP_SEARCH .htm**, has been developed for you with a list of search engines that will provide you with a focal point for your research.

SOME PARTICULARS YOU SHOULD KNOW

1. All ASPs are not created equal. Here are some questions to help you identify their strengths, weaknesses, capabilities, and core competencies.
   - Does the ASP offer full life-cycle services, including proof-of-concept, installation, operations, training, support, and proactive evolution services?
   - What is the ASP's depth and breadth of technical expertise? What are the company's specialties?
   - Where and how did key technical staff obtain their expertise?
   - Does the ASP have actual customers online and if so, what results have they achieved?
   - Does the ASP offer service-level agreements and what are the penalties for SLA violations?
   - Specifically, how does the ASP's infrastructure deliver:
     High availability (uptime)?
     Assured data integrity?
     Scalability?
     Reliability?
     High performance?
     Security and access control?
   - Does the ASP offer 24 × 7 technical support to end users? Escalation procedures? High-priority problem resolution? Dedicated account managers?
   - Can the ASP provide development expertise to customize the applications?
   - How does the ASP handle updates? Adding product modules?
   - Is the ASP capable of assisting with add-on projects such as bringing a new factory online or adding a new supplier?
   - Can the ASP provide a comprehensive suite of integrated applications (versus a single application)?

2. File: **DOTCOMASP.xls** (Excel File) and **DOTCOMASP_SEARCH.htm** (html file)

CASE 16:
ANALYZING STRATEGIC AND COMPETITIVE ADVANTAGE

DETERMINING OPERATING LEVERAGE

Pony Espresso is a small business that sells specialty coffee drinks at office buildings. Each morning and afternoon, trucks arrive at offices' front entrances, and the office employees purchase various beverages with names such as Java du Jour and Café de Colombia. The business is profitable. But Pony Espresso offices are located to the north of town, where lease rates are less expensive, and the principal sales area is south of town. This means that the trucks must drive cross-town four times each day.

The cost of transportation to and from the sales area, plus the power demands of the trucks' coffee brewing equipment, is a significant portion of the variable costs. Pony Espresso could reduce the amount of driving—and, therefore, the variable costs—if it moves the offices much closer to the sales area.

Pony Espresso presently has fixed costs of $10,000 per month. The lease of a new office, closer to the sales area, would cost an additional $2,200 per month. This would increase the fixed costs to $12,200 per month.

Although the lease of new offices would increase the fixed costs, a careful estimate of the potential savings in gasoline and vehicle maintenance indicates that Pony Espresso could reduce the variable costs from $0.60 per unit to $0.35 per unit. Total sales are unlikely to increase as a result of the move, but the savings in variable costs should increase the annual profit.

You have been hired by Pony Espresso to assist in the cost analysis and new lease options to determine a growth in profit margin. You will also need to calculate a degree of operating leverage to better understand the company's profitability. Degree of operating leverage (DOL) will give the CEO of Pony Espresso, Darian Presley, a great deal of information for setting operating targets and planning profitability.

SOME PARTICULARS YOU SHOULD KNOW

1. Consider the information provided—especially look at the change in the variability of the profit from month to month. From November through January, when it is much more difficult to lure office workers out into the cold to purchase coffee, Pony Espresso barely breaks even. In fact, in December of 2005, the business lost money.

2. First, develop the cost analysis on the existing lease information using the monthly sales figures provided to you in the file **PONYESPRESSO.xls**. Second, develop the cost analysis from the new lease information provided above.

3. You need to calculate the variability that is reflected in the month-to-month standard deviation of earnings for the current cost structure and the projected cost structure.

4. Do not consider any association with downsizing such as overhead; simply focus on the information provided to you.

5. You will need to calculate the EBIT—earnings before interest and taxes.

6. Would the DOL and business risk increase or decrease if Pony Espresso moved its office? *Note:* Variability in profit levels, whether measured as EBIT, operating income, or net income, does not necessarily increase the level of business risk as the DOL increases.

7. File: **PONYESPRESSO.xls** (Excel file).

CASE 17:
BUILDING A DECISION SUPPORT SYSTEM

BREAK-EVEN ANALYSIS

Ski-YA! is a Colorado-based company that sells high-performance ski equipment. When it comes to the serious business of sliding downhill, the Ski-YA! dudes of Colorado don't trouble themselves with petty categories; to them, all alpine snow equipment is summed up in one word, AWESOME!

This season's offerings at Ski-YA! are no exception. Skis continue to grow wider for better flotation beyond the groomers, and the sidecuts, the stick's hourglass shape designed to help a skier turn, now reflect the needs of terrain skiers. Even bindings have been rejiggered: forget the drill and screwdriver; the latest fittings snap or slide into place, extending ski life and improving energy transfer.

The Ski-YA! company wants to begin selling a new pair of skis, labeled the Downhill Demons, in the upcoming ski season. It wants to know how many skis it will have to sell in order to break even on its investment in materials and equipment. The chief financial officer has provided the following information:

Fixed Costs

Metal molding machine:	$200,000
Milling machine:	$150,000
Sander and grinder:	$10,000
Presses:	$25,000
Silkscreen machine:	$50,000

Variable Costs (per Unit)

Packaging material	$5.00
Raw material	$100.00
Shipping	$20.00

The marketing department estimates that it can sell the new skis for $400.00 per unit. Further projections estimate that an average of 200 units will be sold per month. The goal is that the skis will break even and start to earn a profit within the first year. Ski-YA!'s target profit level for the end of the first fiscal year is $100,000.

SOME PARTICULARS YOU SHOULD KNOW

1. First, create a break-even analysis where your goal is to determine how many units you must sell to recover all of your fixed costs.

2. Then create a target profit analysis where your goal is to determine how many units you must sell to reach a predefined profit level. The difference between the two is that at breakeven your target profit is zero, whereas when you specify a target profit that is greater than zero, you are setting your goal above the break-even point.

3. You will want to create a table sheet that contains the data used to generate the break-even/target profit chart. This includes 10 data points on either side of the break-even/target profit point.

4. Finally create a chart where you can visually measure your break-even or target profit level along with total fixed and variable costs. If you choose to calculate the number of months before you reach a break-even or target profit, those numbers will be reported here.

5. File: **SkiYA.xls** (Excel file).

CASE 18:
CREATING A FINANCIAL ANALYSIS

QUALIFICATION AND AMORTIZATION WORKSHEETS

The Foothills Savings Bank (FSB) is a federally insured stock savings bank which was organized in 1982 as a privately insured savings and loan association in Denver, Colorado. It received federal insurance in 1985 and a federal savings bank charter in 1986. FSB is a member of the Federal Home Loan Bank (FHLB) system and its deposits are insured by the Federal Deposit Insurance Corporation (FDIC) to the maximum amount provided by law.

The Foothills Savings Bank offers loans for owner-occupied properties, second homes, and investment homes. FSB offers first trust residential conventional fixed rate and ARM (adjustable rate mortgage) loans. Conventional financing is any mortgage that is not insured or guaranteed by federal, state, or local governments. FSB is now offering an online prequalification worksheet for its customers or prospective customers to use. FSB requires a minimum of 10 percent down, which is generally required for conventional financing.

It is your responsibility to complete a mortgage qualification worksheet and then create a mortgage amortization analysis worksheet from the data in the mortgage qualification worksheet.

SOME PARTICULARS YOU SHOULD KNOW

1. A template for the mortgage qualification worksheet has been created; however, you need to complete the formulas.
2. The Qualifying Section:
   - The first qualifying number needs to calculate the maximum monthly payment, assuming there are no long-term debts. It is computed by multiplying the total income by the housing cost ratio and dividing the result by 12.
   - The second qualifying number takes into account the monthly debt payments, applying the total debt service ratio. It is calculated by multiplying the total debt by the debt service ratio and dividing the result by 12.
   - Mortgage companies usually qualify people for monthly payments that are no higher than the lesser of the two results.
   - By default, your worksheet should assume a housing cost ratio of 0.28 and a total debt service ratio of 0.36, which are standards often used for conventional mortgages.
3. The Loan Amount Section:
   The table created below the qualifying section calculates the amount of a loan you might qualify for with the monthly payment. Depending on the circumstances, some or all of the following will be true:
   - In all cases, the monthly payment will include principal and interest payments.
   - In most cases, it will include a monthly escrow deposit to cover taxes and mortgage insurance, if any. In some cases, homeowner's insurance is also included in this calculation. Use your best guess estimates for these figures.
   - If the customer is buying a condominium or co-op unit, the monthly payment figure may also include the homeowner's dues and/or maintenance fees. You will need to estimate these monthly costs and type them into the appropriate cells.
4. Creating an amortization analysis worksheet:
   - Use the data from the mortgage qualification worksheet to create an amortization table. You will need to calculate beginning balance, principal paid, interest paid, total principal, total interest, and ending balance per payment period for the life of the loan.
5. File: **Mortgage.xls** (Excel file).

CASE 19:
BUILDING A SCHEDULING DECISION SUPPORT SYSTEM

AIRLINE CREW SCHEDULING

Rockies Airline is a new airline company that maintains a schedule of two daily flights between Salt Lake City, Denver, and Chicago. Rockies Airline took to the air on February 11, 2004, with the inauguration of service between Denver International Airport and Salt Lake City. Every Rockies Airline aircraft is outfitted with roomy all-leather seats, each equipped with 24 channels of DIRECTV programming.

Rockies Airline must strategically position itself as a low-cost provider in a very volatile industry. Therefore, it must work toward finding a minimum cost assignment of flight crews to a given flight schedule while satisfying restrictions dictated by the Federal Aviation Administration. Rockies Airline needs to solve the crew scheduling problem that is an involved and time-consuming process.

To begin, you will want to figure out all the possible crew rotations. You will want to find an approximate expected cost of each combination and then solve the traditional crew scheduling problem by using these costs. Second, you will want to calculate the crew constraints in order to determine the decision variables, constraints, and objectives.

You have been given Rockies Airline flight schedule as follows:

From	To	Departure	Arrival	Departure	Arrival
Salt Lake City	Denver	9:00 AM	12:00 PM	2:00 PM	5:00 PM
Salt Lake City	Chicago	10:00 AM	2:00 PM	3:00 PM	7:00 PM
Denver	Salt Lake City	8:00 AM	11:00 PM	2:00 PM	5:00 PM
Denver	Chicago	9:00 AM	11:00 PM	3:00 PM	5:00 PM
Chicago	Salt Lake City	8:00 AM	12:00 PM	2:00 PM	6:00 PM
Chicago	Denver	10:00 AM	12:00 PM	4:00 PM	6:00 PM

SOME PARTICULARS YOU SHOULD KNOW

1. A crew that leaves a city in the morning has to return there at night.
2. The crew can be brought back on another airline. This would always be on an 8 PM flight. There are 6 airplanes in use.
3. When a crew is flying, the cost is $200 per hour.
4. When a crew is waiting or being flown back, the cost is $75 per hour.
5. How should the company schedule its crews to minimize cost?
6. *Hint:* You will want to install the Solver Add-in to assist with this.
7. File: **CREWSCHEDULING.xls** (Excel file).

CASE 20:
CREATING A DATABASE MANAGEMENT SYSTEM

MOUNTAIN BIKE RENTALS

Vail Resort in Vail, Colorado, is internationally known as one of the best places in North America for mountain biking. Since 1973, Slopeside Bike Rentals has been a tradition in the area. At Slopeside Bike Rentals customers will find the largest selection of bikes, parts, accessories, books, maps, clothing, shocks, helmets, eyewear, shoes, car racks, and touring gear in the area with everything you need for on and off the road. Its state-of-the-art demo and rental program has everything from premium dual suspension to kids' bikes and trailers.

You have been employed for the past three summers by Slopeside Bike Rentals. Recently, there has been a surge in business and the owners need a more accurate way to manage the rental business. You have decided to create a database to help the owners keep track of the bike rentals, who the customers are, amount paid, and any damage to the bikes when they are rented. Currently Slopeside Bike Rentals owns 13 mountain bikes in its fleet of rentals. The bikes vary in type, size, and parts. When customers rent bikes, they are required to leave their driver's license number and to give you a home address, phone number, and credit card number.

You have designed the entity classes and primary keys for the database as the following:

Entity	Primary Key
Bike	Bike_ID
Customer	Customer_ID
Rental	Rental_ID

You have also identified the following business rules:

1. Rentals can have many customers assigned but must have at least one.
2. A bike must be assigned to one and only one rental type.
3. A customer can rent one or more bikes at one time.
4. A bike can be assigned to only one customer but need not be assigned to any customer.

Your job is to be completed in the following phases:

1. Develop and describe the entity-relationship diagram.
2. Use normalization to assure the correctness of the tables (relations).
3. Create the database using a personal DBMS package (preferably Microsoft Access).
4. Slopeside Bike Rentals has the following fee structures for its 13 bike rentals:

Description	Cost Per Hour
Specialized Rockhopper	$12
Specialized Rockhopper	$12
Trek Fuel 70	$12
Trek Fuel 80	$15
Trek Fuel 80	$15
Trek Fuel 90	$16
Marin Downhill FRS	$16
Marin Downhill FRS	$16
Marin Downhill FRS	$16
Specialized Stumpjumper FSR	$18
Specialized Stumpjumper FSR	$18
Specialized Stumpjumper FSR	$18
Specialized Stumpjumper Hardtail	$20

Slopeside Bike Rental Report

Description	Date	Last Name	First Name	Amount Paid
Specialized Rockhopper				
	5/30/2005	Smith	Sue	$24.00
	6/2/2005	Smith	Sue	$42.00
	7/5/2005	Dunn	David	$72.00
Summary for Specialized Rockhopper (3 detail records)				$138.00
Trek Fuel 70				
	6/29/2005	Myers	Mike	$24.00
	6/30/2005	Myers	Mike	$24.00
Summary for Trek Fuel 70 (2 detail records)				$48.00
Trek Fuel 80				
	7/5/2005	Elliott	Raymond	$30.00
	7/7/2005	Elliott	Raymond	$15.00
	7/11/2005	Lapierre	Lynne	$225.00
	7/12/2005	Lapierre	Lynne	$37.50
Summary for Trek Fuel 80 (4 detail records)				$307.50
Trek Fuel 90				
	7/1/2005	Smith	Sue	$48.00
	7/11/2005	Dunn	David	$32.00
Summary for Trek Fuel 90 (2 detail records)				$80.00
Grand Total				$573.50

5. Use the DBMS package to create the basic report in Figure GP.3.

SOME PARTICULARS YOU SHOULD KNOW

1. You may not be able to develop a report that looks exactly like the one in Figure GP.3. However, your report should include the same information.
2. One of your tables will need a composite primary key.
3. File: Not applicable.

CASE 21:
EVALUATING THE SECURITY OF INFORMATION

WIRELESS NETWORK VULNERABILITY

Empty cans of Pringles could be helping malicious hackers spot wireless networks that are open to attack. Security companies have demonstrated that a directional antenna made with a Pringles can most often significantly improves the chances of finding wirelessly networked computers. An informal survey carried out by i-sec (an Internet security research company) using the homemade antenna found that over two-thirds of the networks surveyed were doing nothing to protect themselves. Known as the "PringlesCantenna," these are rapidly becoming popular because they are cheap (under $10) and easy to set up.

Not surprisingly, wireless network security, particularly regarding wireless local area networks (WLANs), is the number one concern of network managers, and an entire industry has grown to serve the ever-changing demands of wireless-network-based information integrity. As companies and home users have gradually adopted wireless technology, special security precautions are required to deal with the unique nature of wireless communications. After all, wireless purposely puts information out on the airwaves, and anyone within range and equipped with an appropriate receiver (e.g., PringlesCantenna) would be able to grab this information and put it to all kinds of questionable use. Since this is the case, many wireless networks implement inherent authentication and encryption mechanisms to provide basic assurance to wireless users that their information will at least be difficult to decrypt and their networks at least challenging to crack.

SOME PARTICULARS YOU SHOULD KNOW

1. Create an analysis report based on a thorough Internet search that discusses the tips, techniques, and best practices to protect against this type of amateur hacking.
2. Include a summary of the types of detection and prevention technology available, specifically the use of firewalls and intrusion detection software.
3. In your analysis report, include the current statistics on identity theft, the number of times networks are hacked, and the total annual cost of online security breaches to corporations.
4. During your research, you might also consider finding statistics on the percentage of companies that have yet to implement adequate security measures and the percentage of companies that spend 5 percent or less of their IT budgets on security for their networks.
5. File: Not applicable.

CASE 22:
ASSESSING THE VALUE OF SUPPLY CHAIN MANAGEMENT

OPTIMIZING SHIPMENTS

One of the main products of the Fairway Woods Company is custom-made golf clubs. The clubs are manufactured at three plants (Denver, Colorado; Phoenix, Arizona; and Dallas, Texas) and are then shipped by truck to five distribution warehouses in Sacramento, California; Salt Lake City, Utah; Albuquerque, New Mexico; Chicago, Illinois; and New York City, New York. Because shipping costs are a major expense, management is investigating a way to reduce them. For the upcoming golf season, an estimate has been created as to the total output needed from each manufacturing plant and how much each warehouse will require to satisfy its customers. The CIO from Fairway Woods Company has created a spreadsheet for you, **FAIRWAYS.xls**, of the shipping costs from each manufacturing plant to each warehouse as a baseline analysis.

SOME PARTICULARS YOU SHOULD KNOW

1. The problem presented involves the shipment of goods from three plants to five regional warehouses.
2. Goods can be shipped from any plant to any warehouse, but it costs more to ship goods over long distances than over short distances.
3. The challenge presented is to determine the amounts to ship from each plant to each warehouse at a minimum total shipping cost in order to meet the regional demand, while not exceeding the plant supplies.
4. Specifically you need to focus on:
   a. Minimizing the total shipping cost.
   b. Total shipped must be less than or equal to supply at plant.
   c. Totals shipped to warehouses must be greater than or equal to demand at warehouses.
   d. Number to ship must be greater than or equal to 0.
5. File: **FAIRWAYS.xls** (Excel file).

GLOSSARY

1-tier infrastructure   the most basic setup because it involves a single tier on a single machine.

2-tier infrastructure   the basic client/server relationship.

3-tier infrastructure   the most common approach used for Web applications today.

A

Ad hoc (nonrecurring) decision   decision you make infrequently (perhaps only once) and for which you may even have different criteria for determining the best solution for each time.

Adware   software to generate ads that installs itself on your computer when you download some other (usually free) program from the Web.

Affiliate program   an arrangement made between two e-commerce sites that directs viewers from one site to the other.

Agent-based modeling   way of simulating human organizations using multiple intelligent agents, each of which follows a set of simple rules and can adapt to changing conditions.

Agile methodology   a form of extreme programming that aims for customer satisfaction through early and continuous delivery of useful software components.

Analysis phase   of the systems development life cycle involves end users and IT specialists working together to gather, understand, and document the business requirements for the proposed system.

Anonymous Web browsing (AWB) service   hides your identity from the Web sites you visit.

Anti-spyware software   utility software that detects and removes spyware and other unwanted software that can track every electronic move you make.

Anti-virus software   detects and removes or quarantines computer viruses.

Application generation subsystem   of a DBMS contains facilities to help you develop transaction-intensive applications.

Application service provider (ASP)   supplies software applications (and often related services such as maintenance, technical support, and the like) over the Internet that would otherwise reside on its customers' in-house computers.

Application software   the software that enables you to solve specific problems or perform specific tasks.

Architecture   the blueprint for translating a business strategy into a plan.

Arithmetic logic unit (ALU)   a component of the CPU that performs arithmetic, as well as comparison and logic operations.

Artificial intelligence (AI)   the science of making machines imitate human thinking and behavior.

ASCII (American Standard Code for Information Interchange) the coding system that most personal computers use to represent, process, and store information.

Authenticity   of information, means that it really came from the source it claims to come from.

AutoFilter function   filters a list and allows you to hide all the rows in a list except those that match criteria you specify.

Automatic speech recognition (ASR)   a system that not only captures spoken words but also distinguishes word groupings to form sentences.

B

Back office system   used to fulfill and support customer orders.

Backup   the process of making a copy of the information stored on a computer.

Bandwidth   capacity of the communications medium, refers to the amount of information that a communications medium can transfer in a given amount of time.

Bar code scanner   reads information that is in the form of vertical bars, where their width and spacing represent digits (often used in point-of-sale [POS] systems in retail environments).

Basic formatting tag   HTML tag that allows you to specify formatting for text.

Benchmarking   a process of continuously measuring system results, comparing those results to optimal system performance (benchmark values), and identifying steps and procedures to improve system performance.

Benchmarks   baseline values a system seeks to attain.

Binary digit (bit)   the smallest unit of information that your computer can process.

Biochip   a technology chip that can perform a variety of physiological functions when inserted into the human body.

Biometrics   the use of physiological characteristics—such as your fingerprint, the blood vessels in the iris of your eye, the sound of your voice, or perhaps even your breath—to provide identification.

Biometric scanner   scans some human physical attribute, like your fingerprint or iris, for security purposes.

Biomimicry   learning from ecosystems and adapting their characteristics to human and organizational situations.

Black-hat hacker   a cyber vandal.

Bluetooth   a standard for transmitting information in the form of short-range radio waves over distances of up to 30 feet, used for purposes such as wirelessly connecting a cell phone or a PDA to a computer.

Bot   computer program that runs automatically.

Broadband   connection that is a high-bandwidth (high-capacity) telecommunications line capable of providing high-speed Internet service.

Broadband (home) router   a device to connect several computers together to share a DSL or cable Internet connection in a home or small office.

Browser-safe colors   215 colors that can be viewed by all browsers and computers.

Business intelligence (BI) knowledge—knowledge about your customers, your competitors, your business partners, your competitive environment, and your own internal operations—that gives you the ability to make effective, important, and often strategic business decisions.

Business intelligence (BI) system the IT applications and tools that support the business intelligence function within an organization.

Business process standardized set of activities that accomplishes a specific task, such as processing a customer's order.

Business process outsourcing (BPO) using a contractual service to completely manage, deliver and operate one or more (typically IT- or call center–intensive) business processes or functions.

Business process reengineering (BPR) the analysis and redesign of workflow within and between enterprises.

Business requirement a detailed set of knowledge worker requests that the system must meet to be successful.

Business to Business (B2B) e-commerce when a business sells products and services to customers who are primarily other businesses.

Business to Consumer (B2C) e-commerce when a business sells products and services to customers who are primarily individuals.

Buyer agent or **shopping bot** an intelligent agent on a Web site that helps you, the customer, find the products and services you want.

Buyer power in Porter's Forces Model it is high when buyers have many choices from whom to buy, and low when their choices are few.

Byte a group of eight bits that represents one natural language character.

C

Cable modem a device that uses your TV cable to deliver an Internet connection.

Capacity planning determines your projected future IT infrastructure requirements for new equipment and additional network capacity.

Cat 5 (Category 5) cable a better-constructed version of twisted-pair phone cable.

CAVE (cave automatic virtual environment) a special 3-D virtual reality room that can display images of other people and objects located in other CAVEs all over the world.

CD-R (compact disc—recordable) an optical or laser disc that you can write to one time only.

CD-ROM (compact disc—read-only memory) an optical or laser disc whose information cannot be changed. A CD stores up to 800 Meg of information.

CD-RW (compact disc—rewritable) an optical or laser disc on which you can save, change, and delete files as often as you like.

Central processing unit (CPU) the hardware that interprets and executes the system and application software instructions and coordinates the operation of all other hardware.

Centralized infrastructure involves sharing of information systems in one central area or one central mainframe.

Chief information officer (CIO) responsible for overseeing every aspect of an organization's information resource.

Chief privacy officer (CPO) responsible for ensuring that information is used in an ethical way and that only the right people have access to certain types of information such as financial records and payroll.

Chief security officer (CSO) responsible for the technical aspects of ensuring the security of information such as the development and use of firewalls, intranets, extranets, and anti-virus software.

Choice the third step in the decision-making process where you decide on a plan to address the problem or opportunity.

Class contains information and procedures and acts as a template to create objects.

Click-and-mortar refers to those organizations that have a presence in the physical world such as a building you can visit and also a presence in the virtual world of the Internet.

Click-and-order (pure play) an organization that has a presence in the virtual world but no presence in the physical world.

Clickstream a stored record about your Web surfing session, such as which Web sites you visited, how long you were there, what ads you looked at, and what you bought.

Click-through a count of the number of people who visit one site, click on an ad, and are taken to the site of the advertiser.

Client/server infrastructure (client/server network) a network in which one or more computers are servers and provide services to the other computers, called clients.

Coaxial cable (coax) one central wire surrounded by insulation, a metallic shield, and a final case of insulating material.

Cold site a separate facility that does not have any computer equipment but is a place where the knowledge workers can move after the disaster.

Collaboration system a system that is designed specifically to improve the performance of teams by supporting the sharing and flow of information.

Collocation facility available to a company that rents space and telecommunications equipment from another company.

Communications medium the path, or physical channel, in a network over which information travels.

Communications protocol (protocol) a set of rules that every computer follows to transfer information.

Communications satellite microwave repeater in space.

Communications software helps you communicate with other people.

CompactFlash (CF) card a flash memory card that is slightly larger than a half-dollar, with a capacity of up to 6 gigabytes.

Competitive advantage providing a product or service in a way that customers value more than what the competition is able to do.

Competitive intelligence (CI) business intelligence focused on the external competitive environment.

Composite primary key   consists of the primary key fields from the two intersecting relations.

Computer crime   a crime in which a computer, or computers, played a significant part.

Computer forensics   the gathering, authentication, examination, and analysis of electronic information for presentation in court.

Computer network (network)   two or more computers connected so that they can communicate with each other and share information, software, peripheral devices, and/or processing power.

Computer virus (virus)   software that is written with malicious intent to cause annoyance or damage.

Conditional formatting   highlights information in a cell that meets some criteria you specify.

Confidentiality   means that information can be obtained only by those authorized to access it.

Connectivity software   enables you to use your computer to dial up or connect to another computer.

Constant   a named element whose value doesn't change.

Control unit   the component of the CPU that directs what happens in your computer, sends to RAM for instructions and the information it needs.

Conversion rate   the percentage of potential customers who visit your site who actually buy something.

Cookie   a small record deposited on your hard disk by a Web site containing information about you.

Copyright   the legal protection afforded an expression of an idea, such as a song, video game, and some types of proprietary documents.

CPU cache   a type of memory on the CPU where instructions called up by the CPU wait until the CPU is ready to use them.

CPU clock   a sliver of quartz that beats at regular intervals in response to an electrical charge.

CPU (machine) cycle   consists of retrieving, decoding, and executing the instruction, then returning the result to RAM, if necessary.

Cracker   a hacker for hire; a person who engages in electronic corporate espionage.

Crash-proof software   utility software that helps you save information if your system crashes and you're forced to turn it off and then back on again.

Critical success factor (CSF)   a factor simply critical to your organization's success.

Crossover   the process within a genetic algorithm where portions of good outcomes are combined in the hope of creating an even better outcome.

CRT   a monitor that looks like a traditional television set.

CRUD (Create, Read, Update, Delete)   the four procedures, or ways, a system can manipulate information.

Custom AutoFilter function   allows you to hide all the rows in a list except those that match criteria, besides "is equal to," that you specify.

Customer relationship management (CRM) system   uses information about customers to gain insights into their needs, wants, and behaviors in order to serve them better.

Customer self-service system   an extension of a TPS that places technology in the hands of an organization's customers and allows them to process their own transactions.

Cyberterrorist   one who seeks to cause harm to people or destroy critical systems or information.

D

Data   raw facts that describe a particular phenomenon.

Data administration   the function in an organization that plans for, oversees the development of, and monitors the information resource.

Data administration subsystem   of a DBMS helps you manage the overall database environment by providing facilities for backup and recovery, security management, query optimization, concurrency control, and change management.

Data definition subsystem   of a DBMS helps you create and maintain the data dictionary and define the structure of the files in a database.

Data dictionary   contains the logical structure for the information in a database.

Data management   component of a DSS that performs the function of storing and maintaining the information that you want your DSS to use.

Data manipulation subsystem   of a DBMS helps you add, change, and delete information in a database and query it for valuable information.

Data mart   a subset of a data warehouse in which only a focused portion of the data warehouse information is kept.

Data-mining agent   an intelligent agent that operates in a data warehouse discovering information.

Data-mining tool   a software tool you use to query information in a data warehouse.

Data warehouse   a logical collection of information—gathered from many different operational databases—used to create business intelligence that supports business analysis activities and decision-making tasks.

Database   a collection of information that you organize and access according to the logical structure of that information.

Database administration   the function in an organization that is responsible for the more technical and operational aspects of managing the information contained in organizational information repositories (databases, data warehouses, and data marts).

Database management system (DBMS)   helps you specify the logical organization for a database and access and use the information within a database.

DBMS engine   accepts logical requests from the various other DBMS subsystems, converts them into their physical equivalent, and actually accesses the database and data dictionary as they exist on a storage device.

Decentralized computing   an environment in which an organization distributes computing power and locates it in functional business areas as well as on the desktops of knowledge workers.

Decentralized infrastructure   involves little or no sharing of information systems.

Decision support system (DSS)   a highly flexible and interactive IT system that is designed to support decision making when the problem is not structured.

Demand aggregation   the combining of purchase requests from multiple buyers into a single larger order, which justifies a discount from the business.

Denial-of-service (DoS) attack   floods a server or network with so many requests for service that it slows down or crashes.

Design   the second step in the decision-making process, where you consider possible ways of solving the problem, filling the need, or taking advantage of the opportunity.

Design phase   of the systems development life cycle builds a technical blueprint of how the proposed system will work.

Desktop computer   the type of computer that is the most popular choice for personal computing needs.

Desktop publishing software   extends word processing software by including design and formatting techniques to enhance the layout and appearance of a document.

Development phase   of the systems development life cycle takes all your detailed design documents from the design phase and transforms them into an actual system.

Digital camera   captures still images or video as a series of 1s and 0s.

Digital cash (electronic cash, e-cash)   an electronic representation of cash.

Digital dashboard   displays key information gathered from several sources on a computer screen in a format tailored to the needs and wants of an individual knowledge worker.

Digital still camera   digitally captures still images in varying resolutions.

Digital Subscriber Line (DSL)   a high-speed Internet connection using phone lines, which allows you to use your phone for voice communications at the same time.

Digital video camera   captures video digitally.

Digital wallet   both software and information—the software provides security for the transaction and the information includes payment information (for example, the credit card number and expiration date) and delivery information.

Direct materials   materials that are used in production in a manufacturing company or are placed on the shelf for sale in a retail environment.

Directory search engine   organizes listings of Web sites into hierarchical lists.

Disaster recovery cost curve   charts (1) the cost to your organization of the unavailability of information and technology and (2) the cost to your organization of recovering from a disaster over time.

Disaster recovery plan   a detailed process for recovering information or an IT system in the event of a catastrophic disaster such as a fire or flood.

Disintermediation   use of the Internet as a delivery vehicle, whereby intermediate players in a distribution channel can be bypassed.

Disk optimization software   utility software that organizes your information on your hard disk in the most efficient way.

Distributed denial-of-service (DDoS) attack   attack from multiple computers that floods a server or network with so many requests for service that it slows down or crashes.

Distributed infrastructure   involves distributing the information and processing power of IT systems via a network.

Distribution chain   the path followed from the originator of a product or service to the end consumer.

Domain name   (technical name for a Web site address) identifies a specific computer on the Web and the main page of the entire site.

Dot pitch   the distance between the centers of a pair of like-colored pixels.

DS3   a high-speed business network circuit running at 44.736 Mbps.

DVD-R or DVD+R (DVD—recordable)   a high-capacity optical or laser disc to which you can write one time only.

DVD-ROM   a high-capacity optical or laser disc whose information cannot be changed.

DVD-RW or DVD+RW   (depending on the manufacturer) a high-capacity optical or laser disc on which you can save, change, and delete files.

E

E-gallery   electronic gallery of works that demonstrates your skills.

Electronic Bill Presentment and Payment (EBPP)   a system that sends bills (usually to end consumers) over the Internet and provides an easy-to-use mechanism (such as clicking on a button) to pay them if the amount looks correct.

Electronic check   a mechanism for sending money from your checking or savings account to another person or organization.

Electronic commerce (e-commerce)   commerce, but it is commerce accelerated and enhanced by IT, in particular the Internet.

Electronic data interchange (EDI)   the direct computer-to-computer transfer of transaction information contained in standard business documents, such as invoices and purchase orders, in a standard format.

Electronic government (e-government)   the use of digital technologies to transform government operations in order to improve efficiency, effectiveness, and service delivery.

Electronic job market   consists of employers using Internet technologies to advertise and screen potential employees.

Electronic marketplace (e-marketplace)   an interactive business providing a central space where multiple buyers and sellers can engage in e-commerce and/or other e-commerce business activities.

Electronic portfolio (e-portfolio)   collection of Web documents used to support a stated purpose such as demonstrating writing, photography, or job skills.

E-mail (electronic mail) software   enables you to electronically communicate with other people by sending and receiving e-mail.

Encapsulation   information hiding.

Encryption   scrambles the contents of a file so that you can't read it without having the right decryption key.

End-user development (EUD)   the collection of techniques and methodologies for the creation of nontrivial software applications by end users.

Enterprise resource planning (ERP) system   software system for business management, supporting areas such as planning, manufacturing, sales, marketing, distribution, accounting, finance, human resource management, project management, inventory management, service and maintenance, transportation, and e-business.

Enterprise system (ES)   a large software application that companies use to manage their operations and to distribute information of all kinds to their workforce, to their suppliers, and to their customers.

Entity class   a concept—typically people, places, or things—about which you wish to store information and that you can identify with a unique key (called a primary key).

Entity-relationship (E-R) diagram   a graphic method of representing entity classes and their relationships.

Entry barrier   a product or service feature that customers have come to expect from organizations in a particular industry and that must be offered by an entering organization to compete and survive.

Ethernet card   the most common type of network interface card.

Ethical (white-hat) hacker   a computer security professional who is hired by a company to break into its computer system, so as to find security lapses.

Ethics   the principles and standards that guide our behavior toward other people.

Executive information system (EIS)   highly interactive IT system that allows you to first view highly summarized information and then choose how you would like to see greater detail, which may alert you to potential problems or opportunities.

Expandability   refers to how easy it is to add features and functions to a system.

Expansion bus   the set of pathways along which information moves between devices outside the motherboard and the CPU.

Expansion card (board)   a circuit board that you insert into the expansion slot on the motherboard and to which you connect a peripheral device.

Expansion slot   a long skinny socket on the motherboard into which you insert an expansion card.

Expert system (knowledge-based system)   an artificial intelligence system that applies reasoning capabilities to reach a conclusion.

External information   describes the environment surrounding the organization.

Extraction, transformation, and loading (ETL)   a process in which you specify what information you want from each database, how that information is to be associated, and what rules to follow in consolidating the information to ensure its cleanliness in a data warehouse.

Extranet   an intranet that is restricted to an organization and certain outsiders, such as customers and suppliers.

Extreme programming (XP) methodology   breaks a project into tiny phases and developers cannot continue on to the next phase until the first phase is complete.

F

F2b2C (Factory to business to Consumer)   e-commerce business model in which a consumer communicates through a business on the Internet that directly provides product specifications to a factory that makes the customized and personalized product to the consumer's specifications and then ships it directly to the consumer.

Facial recognition software   software that provides identification by evaluating facial characteristics.

Fair Use Doctrine   allows you to use copyrighted material in certain situations.

Feature analysis   captures your words as you speak into a microphone, eliminates any background noise, and converts the digital signals of your speech into phonemes (syllables).

Feature creep   occurs when developers add extra features that were not part of the initial requirements.

File transfer protocol (ftp)   communications protocol that allows you to transfer files of information from one computer to another.

Financial cybermediary   an Internet-based company that makes it easy for one person to pay another person or organization over the Internet.

Financial EDI (financial electronic data interchange)   an electronic process used primarily within the Business to Business e-commerce model for the payment of purchases.

Firewall   software and/or hardware that protects a computer or network from intruders.

Firewire (IEEE 1394 or I-Link) port   fits hot-swap, plug-and-play Firewire connectors and you can connect up to 63 Firewire devices to a single Firewire port by daisy-chaining the devices together.

Five Forces Model   helps business people understand the relative attractiveness of an industry.

Flash memory card   has high-capacity storage units laminated inside a small piece of plastic.

Flash memory device (jump drive, thumb drive)   a flash memory storage device that is small enough to fit on a key ring and plugs directly into the USB port on your computer.

Flat-panel display   thin, lightweight monitor that takes up much less space than a CRT.

Foreign key   a primary key of one file (relation) that appears in another file (relation).

Forensic image copy   an exact copy or snapshot of the contents of an electronic medium.

Front office system the primary interface to customers and sales channels.

FrontPage Web authoring software.

Ftp (file transfer protocol) server maintains a collection of files that you can download.

Function procedure a VBA macro that returns a single value.

Fuzzy logic mathematical method of handling imprecise or subjective information.

G

Game controller used for gaming to better control screen action.

Gamepad a multifunctional input device with programmable buttons, thumb sticks, and a directional pad.

Gaming wheel a steering wheel and foot pedals for virtual driving.

Gas plasma display sends electricity through gas trapped between two layers of glass or plastic to create a screen image.

Genetic algorithm an artificial intelligence system that mimics the evolutionary, survival-of-the-fittest process to generate increasingly better solutions to a problem.

Geographic information system (GIS) a decision support system designed specifically to analyze spatial information.

Gigabyte (GB or Gig) roughly 1 billion bytes.

Gigahertz (GHz) the number of billions of CPU cycles per second that the CPU can handle.

Glove an input device that captures and records the shape and movement of your hand and fingers and the strength of your hand and finger movements.

Government to Business (G2B) the electronic commerce activities performed between a government and businesses for such purposes as purchasing direct and MRO materials, soliciting bids for work, licensing applications, meeting equal employment opportunity regulations, and so on.

Government to Consumer (G2C) the electronic commerce activities performed between a government and its citizens or consumers including paying taxes, registering vehicles, and providing information and services.

Government to Government (G2G, intra-G2G) the electronic commerce activities performed within a single nation's government.

Graphical user interface (GUI) the interface to an information system.

Graphics software helps you create and edit photos and art.

GUI screen design the ability to model the information system screens for an entire system.

H

Hacker a knowledgeable computer user who uses his or her knowledge to invade other people's computers.

Hacktivist a politically motivated hacker who uses the Internet to send a political message of some kind.

Haptic interface uses technology to add the sense of touch to an environment that previously had only visual and auditory elements.

Hard disk magnetic storage device with one or more thin metal platters or disks that store information sealed inside the disk drive.

Hardware the physical devices that make up a computer (often referred to as a computer system).

Hardware key logger a hardware device that captures keystrokes on their journey from the keyboard to the motherboard.

Heading tag HTML tag that makes certain information, such as titles, stand out on your Web site.

Headset (head-mounted display) a combined input and output device that (1) captures and records the movement of your head, and (2) contains a screen that covers your entire field of vision.

Help desk a group of people who respond to knowledge workers' questions.

Hidden job market the collective term used to describe jobs that are not advertised.

Holographic device a device that creates, captures, and/or displays images in true three-dimensional form.

Holographic storage device stores information on a storage medium that is composed of 3-D crystal-like objects with many sides or faces.

Horizontal e-marketplace an electronic marketplace that connects buyers and sellers across many industries, primarily for MRO materials commerce.

Horizontal market software application software that is general enough to be suitable for use in a variety of industries.

Hot site a separate and fully equipped facility where the company can move immediately after the disaster and resume business.

Hot swap an operating system feature that allows you—while your computer is running—to unplug a device and plug in a new one without first shutting down your computer.

HTML document a file that contains your Web site content and HTML formatting instructions.

HTML tag specifies the formatting and presentation of information on a Web site.

Hub a device that connects computers together and passes messages by repeating all network transmissions to all the other computers.

Hypertext markup language (HTML) the language you use to create a Web site.

Hypertext transfer protocol (http) the communications protocol that supports the movement of information over the Web.

I

Identity theft the forging of someone's identity for the purpose of fraud.

Image scanner captures images, photos, text, and artwork that already exist on paper.

Implant chip a technology-enabled microchip implanted into the human body that stores important information about you (such as your identification and medical history) and that may be GPS-enabled to offer a method of tracking.

Implementation the final step in the decision-making process where you put your plan into action.

Implementation phase   of the systems development life cycle distributes the system to all the knowledge workers and they begin using the system to perform their everyday jobs.

Information   data that have a particular meaning within a specific context.

Information age   a time when knowledge is power.

Information agent   intelligent agent that searches for information of some kind and brings it back.

Information decomposition   breaking down the information and procedures for ease of use and understandability.

Information granularity   the extent of detail within the information.

Information-literate knowledge worker   can define what information they need, know how and where to obtain that information, understand the information once they receive it, and can act appropriately based on the information to help the organization achieve the greatest advantage.

Information technology (IT)   any computer-based tool that people use to work with information and support the information and information-processing needs of an organization.

Information view   includes all of the information stored within a system.

Infrared, IR, or IrDA (infrared data association)   uses red light to send and receive information.

Infrastructure   a relative term meaning "the structure beneath a structure."

Inheritance   the ability to define superclass and subclass relationships among classes.

Inkjet printer   makes images by forcing ink droplets through nozzles.

Input device   tool you use to enter information and commands.

Insourcing   using IT specialists within your organization to develop the system.

Instance   an occurrence of an entity class that can be uniquely described with a primary key.

Integrated collaboration environment (ICE)   the environment in which virtual teams do their work.

Integration   allows separate applications to communicate directly with each other by automatically exporting data files from one application and importing them into another.

Integration testing   verifies that separate systems can work together.

Integrity   in information, means that the information has not been altered.

Integrity constraint   rule that helps ensure the quality of the information.

Intellectual property   intangible creative work that is embodied in physical form.

Intelligence   the first step in the decision-making process where you find or recognize a problem, need, or opportunity (also called the diagnostic phase of decision making).

Intelligent agent   software that assists you, or acts on your behalf, in performing repetitive computer-related tasks.

Interface   any device that calls procedures and can include such things as a keyboard, mouse, and touch screen.

Inter-modal transportation   the use of multiple channels of transportation—railway, truck, boat, and so on—to move products from origin to destination.

Internal information   describes specific operational aspects of an organization.

International Government to Government (inter-G2G)   the electronic commerce activities performed between two or more governments including providing foreign aid.

Internet   a vast network of computers that connects millions of people all over the world.

Internet backbone   the major set of connections for computers on the Internet.

Internet server computer   computer that provides information and services on the Internet.

Internet service provider (ISP)   a company that provides individuals, organizations, and businesses access to the Internet.

Intersection relation (composite relation)   a relation you create to eliminate a many-to-many relationship.

Intranet   an internal organizational Internet that is guarded against outside access by a special security feature called a firewall (which can be software, hardware, or a combination of the two).

Intrusion detection system (IDS)   software and/or hardware that watches network traffic for intrusion attempts, reports them, and optionally takes action against them.

Intrusion-detection software   looks for people on the network who shouldn't be there or who are acting suspiciously.

IRC (Internet Relay Chat) server   supports your use of discussion groups and chat rooms.

J

Joint application development (JAD)   occurs when knowledge workers and IT specialists meet, sometimes for several days, to define and review the business requirements for the system.

Joystick   vertical handle with programmable buttons that controls action.

Just-in-time (JIT)   an approach that produces or delivers a product or service just at the time the customer wants it.

K

Key logger (key trapper) software   a program that, when installed on a computer, records every keystroke and mouse click.

Keyboard   the most often used input device for desktop and notebook computers.

Knowledge-based system (expert system)   an artificial intelligence system that applies reasoning capabilities to reach a conclusion.

Knowledge management (KM) system   an IT system that supports the capturing, organization, and dissemination of knowledge (i.e., know-how) throughout an organization.

Knowledge worker a person who works with and produces information as a product.

L

Language processing attempts to make sense of what you're saying by comparing the word phonemes generated in step 2 with a language model database.

Laser printer forms images using the same sort of electrostatic process that photocopiers use.

Legacy information system (LIS) represents a massive, long-term business investment; such systems are often brittle, slow, and nonextensible.

Link (hyperlink) clickable text or an image that takes you to another site or page on the Web.

Linux an open-source operating system that provides a rich operating environment for high-end workstations and network servers.

Liquid crystal display (LCD) makes the screen image by sending electricity through crystallized liquid trapped between two layers of glass or plastic.

List a collection of information arranged in columns and rows in which each column displays one particular type of information.

List definition table a description of a list by column.

Local area network (LAN) a network that covers a building or buildings in close proximity, such as one campus of a university or corporation.

Logical view focuses on how you as a knowledge worker need to arrange and access information to meet your particular business needs.

Looping repeating a block of statements or code numerous times.

Loyalty program rewards customers based on the amount of business they do with a particular organization.

M

Mac OS Apple's operating system.

Macro a set of actions recorded or written by a user.

Macro language a programming language that includes built-in commands that mimic the functionality available from menus and dialog boxes within an application.

Macro virus spreads by binding itself to software such as Word or Excel.

Mail server provides e-mail services and accounts.

Mailing list discussion groups organized by area of interest.

Mainframe computer (mainframe) a computer designed to meet the computing needs of hundreds of people in a large business environment.

Maintenance phase of the systems development life cycle monitors and supports the new system to ensure it continues to meet the business requirements.

Maintenance, repair, and operations (MRO) materials (indirect materials) materials that are necessary for running a modern corporation, but do not relate to the company's primary business activities.

Malware software designed to harm your computer or computer security.

Malware bot bot that is used for fraud, sabotage, DoS attacks, or some other malicious purpose.

Management information systems (MIS) deals with the planning for, development, management, and use of information technology tools to help people perform all tasks related to information processing and management.

Marketing mix the set of marketing tools that your organization will use to pursue its marketing objectives in reaching and attracting potential customers.

Mass customization the ability of an organization to give its customers the opportunity to tailor its product or service to the customers' specifications.

M-commerce the term used to describe electronic commerce conducted over a wireless device such as a cell phone, PDA, or notebook.

MD5 hash value a mathematically generated string of 32 letters and digits that is unique for an individual storage medium at a specific point in time.

Megabyte (MB or M or Meg) roughly 1 million bytes.

Memory Stick Media card elongated flash memory card about the width of a penny developed by Sony with capacities up to 512 megabytes.

Message how objects communicate with each other.

Metropolitan (municipal) area network (MAN) a set of connected networks all within the same city or metropolitan area, but not in immediate proximity to each other.

Microphone captures audio for conversion into electronic form.

Microsoft Windows XP Home Microsoft's latest personal computer operating system designed specifically for home users.

Microsoft Windows XP Professional (Windows XP Pro) Microsoft's latest personal computer operating system with enhanced features to support home users and business users.

Microwave transmission a type of radio transmission.

Minicomputer (mid-range computer) a computer designed to meet the computing needs of several people simultaneously in a small to medium-size business environment.

Mobile computing broad general term describing your ability to use technology to wirelessly connect to and use centrally located information and/or application software.

Mobile CPU a special type of CPU for a notebook computer that changes speed, and therefore power consumption, in response to fluctuation in use.

Mobisode short one-minute video clips of TV shows designed for viewing on a small cell phone screen.

Modeling the activity of drawing a graphical representation of a design.

Model management component of a DSS that consists of both the DSS models and the DSS model management system.

Monitoring-and-surveillance agent (predictive agent) intelligent agent that constantly observes and reports on some entity of interest, that could, for example, be a network or manufacturing equipment.

Mouse   a pointing device that you use to click on icons or buttons.

Multi-agent system   system in which groups of intelligent agents have the ability to work independently and interact with each other.

Multidimensional analysis (MDA) tool   slice-and-dice technique that allows you to view multidimensional information from different perspectives.

Multifunction printer   a printer that can scan, copy, and fax, as well as print.

MultiMediaCard (MMC)   flash memory card that looks identical to an SD card (but SD cards have copy protection built-in), is a little larger than a quarter, and is slightly thicker than a credit card.

Multimedia (HTML) résumé   a multimedia format displayed on the Web for employers to explore at their convenience.

Multi-state CPU   works with information represented in more than just two states, probably 10 states with each state representing a digit between 0 and 9.

Multitasking   allows you to work with more than one piece of software at a time.

Mutation   the process within a genetic algorithm of randomly trying combinations and evaluating the success (or failure) of the outcomes.

N

Nearshore outsourcing   contracting an outsourcing arrangement with a company in a nearby country.

Network access point (NAP)   a point on the Internet where several connections converge.

Network hub   a device that connects multiple computers into a network.

Network interface card (NIC)   an expansion card for a desktop computer or a PC card for a notebook computer that connects your computer to a network and provides the doorway for information to flow in and out.

Network service provider (NSP)   such as MCI or AT&T, owns and maintains routing computers at NAPs and even the lines that connect the NAPs to each other.

Neural network (artificial neural network or ANN)   an artificial intelligence system that is capable of finding and differentiating patterns.

Nonrecurring (ad hoc) decision   one that you make infrequently (perhaps only once) and you may even have different criteria for determining the best solution each time.

Nonstructured decision   a decision for which there may be several "right" answers and there is no precise way to get a right answer.

Normalization   process of assuring that a relational database structure can be implemented as a series of two-dimensional tables.

Notebook computer   a small, portable, fully functional, battery-operated computer.

N-tier infrastructure   balances the work of the network over several different servers.

O

Object   an instance of a class.

Objective information   quantifiably describes something that is known.

Object-oriented approach   combines information and procedures into a single view.

Object-oriented database   works with traditional database information and also complex data types such as diagrams, schematic drawings, video, and sound and text documents.

Object-oriented programming language   a programming language used to develop object-oriented systems.

Offshore outsourcing   contracting with a company that is geographically far away.

Online ad (banner ad)   small advertisement that appears on other sites.

Online analytical processing (OLAP)   the manipulation of information to support decision making.

Online training   runs over the Internet or off a CD or DVD.

Online transaction processing (OLTP)   the gathering of input information, processing that information, and updating existing information to reflect the gathered and processed information.

Onshore outsourcing   the process of engaging another company in the same country for services.

Open-source software   software for which the source code (how the software was actually written) is publicly available and free of charge.

Operating system software   system software that controls your application software and manages how your hardware devices work together.

Operational database   a database that supports OLTP.

Operational management   manages and directs the day-to-day operations and implementations of the goals and strategies.

Optical character reader   reads characters that appear on a page or sales tag (often used in point-of-sale [POS] systems in retail environments).

Optical fiber   uses a very thin and flexible glass or plastic fiber through which pulses of light travel.

Optical mark reader   detects the presence or absence of a mark in a predetermined spot on the page (often used for true/false and multiple choice exams answers).

Optical storage media   plastic discs on which information is stored, deleted, and/or changed using laser light.

Output device   a tool you use to see, hear, or otherwise recognize the results of your information-processing requests.

Outsourcing   the delegation of specific work to a third party for a specified length of time, at a specified cost, and at a specified level of service.

P

Parallel implementation   using both the old and new system until you're sure that the new system performs correctly.

Parallel port   fits parallel connectors, which are large flat connectors found almost exclusively on printer cables.

Pattern classification   matches your spoken phonemes to a phoneme sequence stored in an acoustic model database.

PC Card   the expansion card you use to add devices to your notebook computer.

PC Card slot   the opening on the side or front of a notebook, where you connect an external device with a PC Card.

Peer-to-peer collaboration software   permits users to communicate in real time and share files without going through a central server.

Performance   measures how quickly an IT system performs a certain process.

Personal digital assistant (PDA)   a small handheld computer that helps you surf the Web and perform simple tasks such as note taking, calendaring, appointment scheduling, and maintaining an address book.

Personal finance software   helps you maintain your checkbook, prepare a budget, track investments, monitor your credit card balances, and pay bills electronically.

Personal information management software (PIM)   helps you create and maintain (1) to-do lists, (2) appointments and calendars, and (3) points of contact.

Personal productivity software   helps you perform personal tasks—such as writing a memo, creating a graph, and creating a slide presentation—that you can usually do even if you don't own a computer.

Phased implementation   implementing the new system in phases (e.g., accounts receivables, then accounts payable) until you're sure it works correctly and then implementing the remaining phases of the new system.

Phishing (carding or brand spoofing)   technique to gain personal information for the purpose of identity theft, usually by means of fraudulent e-mail.

Physical view   deals with how information is physically arranged, stored, and accessed on some type of storage device such as a hard disk.

Pilot implementation   having only a small group of people using the new system until you know it works correctly and then adding the remaining people are added to the system.

Pirated software   the unauthorized use, duplication, distribution or sale of copyrighted software

Pivot table   enables you to group and summarize information.

Pixels (picture elements)   the dots that make up the image on your screen.

Planning phase   of the systems development life cycle, you create a solid plan for developing your information system.

Plotter   form output by moving a pen across the surface of a piece of paper.

Plug and play   an operating feature that finds and installs the device driver for a device that you plug into your computer.

Plunge implementation   discarding the old system completely and immediately using the new system.

Pointing device   a device that is used to navigate and select objects on a display screen.

Pointing stick   a little rod (like a pencil-top eraser) used almost exclusively on notebook computers.

Polymorphism   to have many forms.

Pop-under ad   a form of a pop-up ad that you do not see until you close your current browser window.

Pop-up ad   small Web page containing an advertisement that appears on your screen outside the current Web site loaded into your browser.

Port   a place on your system unit, monitor, or keyboard through which information and instructions flow to and from your computer system.

Portable document format (PDF)   standard electronic distribution file format.

Portable document format (PDF) résumé   a standard electronic distribution format typically used for e-mailing.

Presence awareness   a software function which determines whether a user is immediately reachable or is in a less-available status.

Presentation software   helps you create and edit information that will appear in electronic slides.

Primary key   a field (or group of fields in some cases) that uniquely describes each record.

Privacy   the right to be left alone when you want to be, to have control over your own personal possessions, and not to be observed without your consent.

Procedure   manipulates or changes information.

Procedure view   contains all of the procedures within a system.

Program   a set of instructions that, when executed, cause a computer to behave in a specific manner.

Programming language   the tool developers use to write a program.

Project manager   an individual who is an expert in project planning and management, defines and develops the project plan, and tracks the plan to ensure all key project milestones are completed on time.

Project milestone   represents a key date by which you need a certain group of activities performed.

Project plan   defines the what, when, and who questions of systems development including all activities to be performed, the individuals, or resources, who will perform the activities, and the time required to complete each activity.

Project scope   clearly defines the high-level system requirements.

Project scope document   a written definition of the project scope and is usually no longer than a paragraph.

Proof-of-concept prototype   a prototype you use to prove the technical feasibility of a proposed system.

Prototype   a smaller-scale representation or working model of the user's requirements or a proposed design for an information system.

Prototyping   the process of building a model that demonstrates the features of a proposed product, service, or system.

PS/2 port   fits PS/2 connectors, which you often find on keyboards and mice.

Public key encryption (PKE)   an encryption system that uses two keys: a public key that everyone can have and a private key for only the recipient.

Push technology   an environment in which businesses and organizations come to you with information, services, and product offerings based on your profile.

Q

Query-and-reporting tool   similar to a QBE tool, SQL, and a report generator in the typical database environment.

Query-by-example (QBE) tool   helps you graphically design the answer to a question.

R

Random access memory (RAM)   a temporary holding area for the information you're working with as well as the system and application software instructions that the CPU currently needs.

Rapid application development methodology (RAD, rapid prototyping)   emphasizes extensive user involvement in the rapid and evolutionary construction of working prototypes of a system to accelerate the systems development process.

Recovery   the process of reinstalling the backup information in the event the information was lost.

Recurring decision   a decision that you have to make repeatedly and often periodically, whether weekly, monthly, quarterly, or yearly.

Relation   describes each two-dimensional table or file in the relational model (hence its name relational database model).

Relational database   uses a series of logically related two-dimensional tables or files to store information in the form of a database.

Repeater   a device that receives a radio signal, strengthens it, and sends it on.

Report generator   helps you quickly define formats of reports and what information you want to see in a report.

Request for proposal (RFP)   a formal document that describes in detail your logical requirements for a proposed system and invites outsourcing organizations (or "vendors") to submit bids for its development.

Requirements definition document   defines all the business requirements and prioritizes them in order of business importance.

Resolution of a printer   the number of dots per inch (dpi) it produces.

Resolution of a screen   the number of pixels it has.

Résumé   summary of your qualifications.

Reverse auction   the process in which a buyer posts its interest in buying a certain quantity of items with notations concerning quality, specification, and delivery timing, and sellers compete for the business by submitting successively lower bids until there is only one seller left.

RFID (radio frequency identification)   uses a microchip (chip) in a tag or label to store information, and information is transmitted from, or written to, the tag or label when the microchip is exposed to the correct frequency of radio waves.

Risk assessment   the process of evaluating IT assets, their importance to the organization, and their susceptibility to threats to measure the risk exposure of these assets.

Risk management   identification of risks or threats, the implementation of security measures, and the monitoring of those measures for effectiveness.

Rivalry among existing competitors   in the Five Forces Model is high when competition is fierce in a market, and low when competition is more complacent.

Robot   a mechanical device equipped with simulated human senses and the capability of taking action on its own.

Router   a device that passes network traffic between smaller subnetworks (or subnets) of a larger network.

S

Sales force automation (SFA) system   automatically tracks all of the steps in the sales process.

Satellite modem   modem that allows you to get Internet access from your satellite dish.

Scalability   refers to how well your system can adapt to increased demands.

Scannable (or ASCII) résumé   a paper résumé without any formatting that becomes electronic when it is scanned into a computer.

Scanner   used to convert information that exists in visible form into electronic form.

Scope creep   occurs when the scope of the project increases beyond its original intentions.

Script bunny (script kiddie)   someone who would like to be a hacker but doesn't have much technical expertise.

Search engine   a facility on the Web that helps you find sites with the information and/or services you want.

Secure Digital (SD) card   flash memory card that looks identical to an MMC card (but SD cards have copy protection built-in), is a little larger than a quarter, and is slightly thicker than a credit card.

Secure Electronic Transaction (SET)   a transmission security method that ensures transactions are legitimate as well as secure.

Secure Sockets Layer (SSL)   creates a secure and private connection between a Web client computer and a Web server computer, encrypts the information, and then sends the information over the Internet.

Security auditing software   checks out your computer or network for potential weaknesses.

Selection   the process within a genetic algorithm that gives preference to better outcomes.

Selling prototype   a prototype you use to convince people of the worth of a proposed system.

Shared information   an environment in which an organization's information is organized in one or more central locations, allowing anyone to access and use it as he or she needs to.

Sign-off   the knowledge workers' actual signatures indicating they approve all the business requirements.

Skill words   nouns and adjectives used by organizations to describe job skills which should be woven into the text of an applicant's résumé.

Slack space   the space left over from the end of the file to the end of the cluster.

Smart card   a plastic card the size of a credit card that contains an embedded chip on which digital information can be stored and updated.

SmartMedia (SM) card   flash memory card that's a little longer than a CF card and about as thick as a credit card with capacities of up to 512 megabytes.

Social engineering   conning your way into acquiring information that you have no right to.

Social network system   an IT system that links you to people you know and, from there, to people your contacts know.

Software   the set of instructions that your hardware executes to carry out a specific task for you.

Software-as-a-service (SaaS)   delivery model for software in which you would pay for software on a pay-per-use basis instead of buying the software outright.

Software suite   bundled software that comes from the same publisher and costs less than buying all the software pieces individually.

Spam   unsolicited e-mail (electronic junk mail) from businesses that advertises goods and services.

Spam blocker software   utility software that filters unwanted e-mail from your inbox.

Spoofing   the forging of the return address on an e-mail so that the e-mail message appears to come from someone other than the actual sender.

Spreadsheet software   helps you work primarily with numbers, including performing calculations and creating graphs.

Spyware (sneakware, stealthware)   malicious software that collects information about you and your computer and reports it to someone else without your permission.

Steganography   the hiding of information inside other information.

Storage area network (SAN)   an infrastructure for building special, dedicated networks that allow rapid and reliable access to storage devices by multiple servers.

Storage device   a tool you use to store information for use at a later time.

Storyboard   a visual representation illustrating relationships of objects on a Web page.

Strategic management   provides an organization with overall direction and guidance.

Structure tag   HTML tag that sets up the necessary sections and specifies that the document is indeed an HTML document.

Structured decision   a decision where processing a certain kind of information in a specified way so that you will always get the right answer.

Structured query language (SQL)   a standardized fourth-generation query language found in most DBMSs.

Stylus   penlike device used to write or draw on a PDA or tablet PC.

Sub procedure   computer code that performs some action on or with objects.

Subjective information   attempts to describe something that is unknown.

Supercomputer   the fastest, most powerful, and most expensive type of computer.

Supplier power   in the Five Forces Model is high when buyers have few choices from whom to buy, and low when their choices are many.

Supply chain management (SCM)   tracks inventory and information among business processes and across companies.

Supply chain management (SCM) system   an IT system that supports supply chain management activities by automating the tracking of inventory and information among business processes and across companies.

Swarm (collective) intelligence   collective behavior of groups of simple agents that are capable of devising solutions to problems as they arise, eventually leading to coherent global patterns.

Switch   a network device that connects computers and passes messages by repeating each computer's transmissions only to the intended recipient, not to all the computers connected.

Switching cost   a cost that makes customers reluctant to switch to another product or service supplier.

System bus   electrical pathways that move information between basic components of the motherboard, including between RAM and the CPU.

System software   handles tasks specific to technology management and coordinates the interaction of all technology devices.

System testing   verifies that the units or pieces of code written for a system function correctly when integrated into the total system.

Systems development life cycle (SDLC)   a structured step-by-step approach for developing information systems.

T

T1   a high-speed business network circuit typically used for business connections, running at speeds up to 1.544 Mbps (1.544 million bits per second).

Tablet PC   a pen-based computer that provides the screen capabilities of a PDA with the functional capabilities of a notebook or desktop computer.

Tactical management   develops the goals and strategies outlined by strategic management.

TCP/IP (Transport control protocol/Internet protocol)   the primary protocol for transmitting information over the Internet.

Technical architecture   defines the hardware, software, and telecommunications equipment required to run the system.

Technology-literate knowledge worker   person who knows how and when to apply technology.

Telecommunications device   tool you use to send information to and receive it from another person or computer in a network.

Telecommuting   the use of communications technology (such as the Internet) to work in a place other than a central location.

Telephone modem (modem)   a device that connects your computer to your phone line so that you can access another computer or network.

Terabyte (TB)   roughly 1 trillion bytes.

Test conditions   the detailed steps the system must perform along with the expected results of each step.

Testing phase   of the systems development life cycle verifies that the system works and meets all the business requirements defined in the analysis phase.

Threat of new entrants   in the Five Forces Model is high when it is easy for new competitors to enter a market, and low when there are significant entry barriers to entering a market.

Threat of substitute products or services   in the Five Forces Model is high when there are many alternatives to a product or service, and low when there are few alternatives from which to choose.

Thrill-seeker hacker   a hacker who breaks into computer systems for entertainment.

Tiered infrastructure (layer infrastructure)   the IT system is partitioned into tiers (or layers) where each tier (or layer) performs a specific type of functionality.

Top-level domain   extension of a Web site address that identifies its type.

Touchpad   the little dark rectangle that you use to move the cursor with your finger, often found on notebook computers.

Trackball   similar to a mechanical mouse, but it has a ball on the top.

Traditional technology approach   has two primary views of any computer-based system—information and procedures—and it keeps these two views separate and distinct at all times.

Transaction processing system (TPS)   a system that processes transactions within an organization.

Trojan horse software   software you don't want hidden inside software you do want.

Trojan horse virus   hides inside other software, usually an attachment or download.

True search engine   uses software agent technologies to search the Internet for key words and then places them into indexes.

Twisted-pair cable   a bundle of copper wires used for transmitting voice or data communications; it comes in several varieties.

U

Ubiquitous computing   computing and technology support anytime, anywhere with access to all needed information and access to all business partners, both internal and external to the organization.

Unallocated space   the set of clusters that have been set aside to store information, but have not yet received a file, or still contain some or all of a file marked as deleted.

Uniform resource locator (URL)   an address for a specific Web page or document within a Web site.

Uninstaller software   utility software that you can use to remove software from your hard disk that you no longer want.

Unit testing   tests individual units or pieces of code for a system.

USB (universal serial bus) port   fits small flat plug-and-play, hot-swap USB connectors, and, using USB hubs, you can connect up to 127 devices to a single USB port on your computer.

User acceptance testing (UAT)   determines if the system satisfies the business requirements and enables knowledge workers to perform their jobs correctly.

User agent (personal agent)   an intelligent agent that takes action on your behalf.

User documentation   highlights how to use the system.

User interface management   component of a DSS that allows you to communicate with the DSS.

Utility software   software that provides additional functionality to your operating system software.

V

Value chain   views your organization as a chain—or series—of processes, each of which adds value to your product or service for your customers.

Variable   a place to store a piece of information.

Vertical e-marketplace   an electronic marketplace that connects buyers and sellers in a given industry (e.g., oil and gas, textiles, and retail).

Vertical market software   application software that is unique to a particular industry.

View   allows you to see the contents of a database file, make whatever changes you want, perform simple sorting, and query to find the location of specific information.

Viewable image size (VIS)   the size of the image on a monitor.

Viral marketing   encourages users of a product or service supplied by a B2C e-commerce business to encourage friends to join in as well.

Virtual private network (VPN)   uses encryption to protect the confidentiality of *all* network transmissions between two endpoints.

Virtual reality a three-dimensional computer simulation in which you actively and physically participate.

Virtual team a team whose members are located in varied geographic locations and whose work is supported by specialized ICE software or by more basic collaboration systems.

Virus (computer virus) software that is written with malicious intent to cause annoyance or damage.

Visual Basic Editor (VBE) a separate application where you write and edit your Visual Basic macros.

VoIP (Voice over Internet Protocol) allows you to send voice communications over the Internet and avoid the toll charges that you would normally receive from your long distance carrier.

W

Walker an input device that captures and records the movement of your feet as you walk or turn in different directions.

Waterfall methodology a sequential, activity-based process in which one phase in the SDLC is followed by another from planning through implementation.

Wearable computer a fully equipped computer that you wear as a piece of clothing or attached to a piece of clothing similar to the way you would carry your cell phone on your belt.

Web authoring software helps you design and develop Web sites and pages that you publish on the Web.

Web browser software enables you to surf the Web.

Web log consists of one line of information for every visitor to a Web site and is usually stored on a Web server.

Web page a specific portion of a Web site that deals with a certain topic.

Web portal a site that provides a wide range of services, including search engines, free e-mail, chat rooms, discussion boards, and links to hundreds of different sites.

Web server provides information and services to Web surfers.

Web site a specific location on the Web where you visit, gather information, and perhaps even order products.

Web site address a unique name that identifies a specific site on the Web.

Web space storage area where you keep your Web site.

Webcam captures digital video to upload to the Web.

White-hat (ethical) hacker a computer security professional who is hired by a company to break into its computer system, so as to find security lapses.

Wide area network (WAN) a set of connected networks serving areas or buildings not in immediate proximity to each other.

WiFi (wireless fidelity or IEEE 802.11a, b, or g) a standard for transmitting information in the form of radio waves over distances up to about 300 feet.

Wired communications media transmit information over a closed, connected path.

Wireless access point (WAP) a device that allows a computer to use radio waves to access a network.

Wireless communications media transmit information through the air.

Wireless Internet service provider (wireless ISP) a company that provides the same service as a standard Internet service provider except that the user doesn't need a wired connection for access.

Word processing software helps you create papers, letters, memos, and other basic documents.

Workflow defines all of the steps or business rules, from beginning to end, required for a business process.

Workflow system facilitates the automation and management of business processes.

Workshop training held in a classroom environment and is led by an instructor.

World Wide Web (Web) a multimedia-based collection of information, services, and Web sites supported by the Internet.

Worm a type of virus that replicates and spreads itself, not just from file to file, but from computer to computer via e-mail and other Internet traffic.

X

xD-Picture (xD) card flash memory card that looks like a rectangular piece of plastic smaller than a penny and about as thick, with one edge slightly curved.

NOTES

CHAPTER 1

1. Duarat, Cecile, "Blockbuster Drops Late Fees," *The Denver Post,* December 14, 2004, pp. 1C, 5C.

2. "Highlights from VSDA's 2004 Annual Report on the Home Entertainment Industry," Video Software Dealers Association, 2004, www.vsda.org/Resource.phx/vsda/publications/2003annualreport/index.htx, accessed December 15, 2004.

3. Kirsner, Scott, "An ATM Approach to Renting Movies," *The Boston Globe,* December 13, 2004, www.boston.com/business/technology/articles/2004/12/13/an_atm_approach_to_renting_movies, accessed December 15, 2004.

4. Zuckerman, Mortimer, "America's Silent Revolution," *U.S. News & World Report,* July 18, 1994, p. 90.

5. McGann, Rob, "U.S. Online Travel Market to Soar," ClickZ Network, November 10, 2004, Jupitermedia Corporation, www.clickz.com/stats/sectors/travel/article.php/3433881, accessed December 15, 2004.

6. "Home-Based Telework by U.S. Employees Grows by 40% Since 2001," from www.telecommute.org/news/pr090403.htm, accessed December 23, 2003.

7. Charles Schwab at www.schwab.com, accessed January 23, 2004.

8. Low, Lafe, "How Citigroup Measures Up," CIO.com Special—Performance Management, *CIO Magazine* of CXO Media Inc., April 15, 2004, www.cio.com/archive/041504/citigroup.html, accessed December 15, 2004.

9. "Big Y Foods," a company success story provided by Cognos Inc. at www.cognos.com/company/success/big_foods.pdf, accessed December 16, 2004.

10. Smalley Bowen, Ted, "The Career Path of the Complete CIO," CIO Magazine Hot Seat, *CIO Magazine* of CXO Media Inc., October 1, 2004, www.cio.com.archieve/100104/hs_verdict.html, accessed December 16, 2004.

11. Kallman, Ernest, and John Grillo, *Ethical Decision Making and Information Technology* (San Francisco: McGraw-Hill, 1993).

12. Peyser, Marc, and Steve Rhodes, "When E-Mail Is Ooooops Mail," *Newsweek,* October 16, 1995, p. 82.

13. Global Online Populations, Internet.com, at http://cyberatlas.internet.com/big_picture/geographics/article/0,1323,5911_151151,00.html, accessed January 23, 2004.

14. Donker, Anne, "Less Taxing at the IRS," *Optimize,* November 2004, pp. 40–42.

15. "Enabling the Collaborative Enterprise," a company success story provided by Open Text Corporation at www.opentext.com/customers/index.html, accessed December 18, 2004.

16. Perez, Juan Carlos, "Update: AOL Launches New Bill-Paying Tool," *TheStandard,* March 16, 2004, www.thestandard.com/article.php?story=20040316172813723, accessed April 7, 2004.

17. Wehner, Ross, "Sweeping Spies from the Net," *The Denver Post,* December 15, 2004, pp. 1, 10C.

18. "Losses from Identity Theft to Total $221 Billion Worldwide," *CIO Magazine,* May 23, 2003, at www2.cio.com/metrics/2003/metric551.html, accessed April 16, 2004.

19. "Accenture: Customer Satisfaction Driving Egovernment," from www.nua.com/surveys/index.cgi?f=VS&art_id=905358759&rel=true, accessed December 2, 2003.

20. Greenspan, Robyn, "U.S. Web Usage and Traffic, August 2004," ClickZ Network, Jupitermedia Corporation, September 21, 2004, at www.clickz.com/stats/sectors/traffic_patterns/print.php/3410151, accessed February 26, 2005.

21. "Benchmarking E-Government: A Global Perspective," United Nations Division for Public Economics and Public Administration, released May 2002, available at www.unpan.org.

CHAPTER 2

1. Miami Dolphins, a customer success story from Hyperion Solutions, at www.hyperion.com/customers/miami_dolphins.cfm, accessed May 1, 2005.

2. Beth, Scott, et al., "Supply Chain Challenges: Building Relationships," *Harvard Business Review,* July 2003, pp. 65–73.

3. Edwards, Owen, "Bow Tech: ASAP Case Study," *Forbes ASAP,* June 3, 1996, pp. 54–58.

4. "Configuring 9 500 Percent ROI for Dell," i2 White Paper, at www.i2.com/customer/hightech_consumer.cfm, accessed May 5, 2004.

5. Malykhina, Elena, "Order-Management Software Brings Automation to Online Florist," *InformationWeek,* February 23, 2005, at www.informationweek.com/shared/printableArticleSrc.jhtml?articleID=60402303, accessed February 28, 2005.

6. Navas, Deb, "Supply Chain Software Stands Tough," *Supply Chain Systems Magazine,* December 2003, at www.scsmag.com/reader/2003/2003_12/software1203/index.htm, accessed June 10, 2004.

7. "Websmart 50," *BusinessWeek,* November 24, 2003, p. 96.

8. Koudal, Peter, et al., "General Motors: Building a Digital Loyalty Network through Demand and Supply Chain Integration," Stanford Graduate School of Business, Case GS-29, March 17, 2003.

9. Schuster, Roy, "Nine Steps to Make the CRM Case," CRMIQ 2004, at www.crmiq.com/resources/tips/148-CRMIQ_shortcuts.html, accessed May 5, 2004.

10. Greenspan, Robyn, "Behavioral Targeting Study Reveals CPM Life," Jupitermedia Corporation Advanced technology, August 17, 2004, at www.clickz.com/stats/sectors/advertising/article.php/3396431, accessed February 17, 2005.

11. Dragoon, Alice, "Business Intelligence Gets Smart(er)," *CIO Magazine*, September 15, 2003, at www.cio.com/archive/091503/smart.html, accessed June 10, 2004.

12. Gray, Paul, "Business Intelligence: A New Name or the Future of DSS?" in T. Bui, H. Sroka, S. Stanek, and J. Goluchowski (eds.), *DSS in the Uncertainty of the Internet Age* (Katowice, Poland: University of Economics in Katowice, 2003).

13. Willen, Claudia, "Airborne Opportunities," *Intelligent Enterprise* 5, no. 2 (January 14, 2002).

14. Gray, "Business Intelligence."

15. Bosavage, Jennifer, "BI Helps H&B Hit Business Targets," *InformationWeek* Business Intelligence Pipeline, February 22, 2005, at www.bizintelligencepipeline.com/showArticle.jhtml?articleID=60402524, accessed March 1, 2005.

16. Rudin, K., and D. Cressy, "Will the Real Analytics Applications Please Stand Up," *DM Review* 13, no. 3 (2003).

17. Stodder, D., "Enabling the Intelligent Enterprise: The 2003 Editor's Choice Awards," *Intelligent Enterprise* 6, no. 2 (2003).

18. "From Germany to America: SiteScape Connects Siemens AG, a Fortune Global 50 Organization," from SiteScape Testimonial, 2004, at www.sitescape.com/next/test_siemens.html, accessed June 10, 2004.

19. GlaxoSmithKline, customer case study, Groove Networks, at www.groove.net/index.cfm?pagename=CaseStudy_GSK, accessed April 31, 2005.

20. Surmacz, Jon, "Collaborate and Save: Collaboration Technology Can Save Big Money for the Oil and Gas Industry," *CIO Magazine*, November 5, 2003, at www2.cio.com/metrics/2003/metric625.html, accessed June 19, 2004.

21. Davenport, Thomas, and Laurence Prusak, "What's the Big Idea?: Creating and Capitalizing on the Best Management Thinking" (Boston: Harvard Business School Press, 2003).

22. "Social Networks," *New York Times Magazine*, December 14, 2003, p. 92.

23. Malykhina, Elena, "Retailers Take Stock," *InformationWeek*, February 7, 2005, at www.informationweek.com/shared/printableArticleSrc.jhtml?articleID=59301319, accessed March 3, 2005.

24. Levinson, Meredith, "The Brain Behind the Big, Bad Burger and Other Tales of Business Intelligence, *CIO Magazine*, March 15, 2005, at www.cio.com/archive/031505/intelligence.html, accessed May 1, 2005.

CHAPTER 3

1. "Krispy Kreme—Driving Growth through Content Management," Customer Success Stories from Open Text Corp., at www.opentext.com/customers/success-stories.html (Krispy Kreme), accessed February 21, 2005.

2. Watterson, Karen, "A Data Miner's Tools," *BYTE,* October 1995, pp. 170–72.

3. Cash, James, "Gaining Customer Loyalty," *InformationWeek*, April 10, 1995, p. 88.

4. Marlin, Steven, "County in Washington State Expands GIS Capabilities," *InformationWeek,* May 2, 2005, at www.informationweek.com/story/showArticle.jhtml?articleID=162100493, accessed May 19, 2005.

5. "Britannia Airways—Keeping the Crews Flying High," Customer Success Stories from Open Text Corp., at www.opentext.com/customers/success-stories.html (Britannia Airways), accessed May 5, 2005.

6. Anthes, Gary, "Car Dealer Takes the Personal Out of PCs," *Computerworld,* August 14, 1995, p. 48.

7. Hulme, George, "Hospital Secures Wireless Network," *InformationWeek,* December 8, 2004, at www.informationweek.com/story/showArticle.jhtml?articleID=55300433, accessed February 17, 2005.

8. "Laurentian Bank Creates Online Scoring Models for Dealer Financing," customer success story from SAS Corporation, at www.sas.com/success/laurentian.html, accessed April 21, 2005.

9. Maselli, Jennifer, "Insurers Looks to CRM for Profits," *InformationWeek,* May 6, 2002, www.informationweek.com/story/IWK20022050250007, accessed March 1, 2005.

10. Kling, Julia, "OLAP Gains Fans among Data-Hungry Firms," *Computerworld,* January 8, 1996, pp. 43, 48.

11. Hutheesing, Nikhil, "Surfing with Sega," *Forbes,* November 4, 1996, pp. 350–51.

12. LaPlante, Alice, "Big Things Come in Smaller Packages," *Computerworld,* June 24, 1996, pp. DW/6–7.

13. "Customer Success: Land O'Lakes," from Informatica at www.informatica.com/Customers/Customer+Success/landolakes.htm, accessed January 2, 2004.

14. Doble, Curt, "Land O'Lakes Unscrambles Enterprise Content Management," *Optimize Magazine,* December 2004, at www.optimizemag.com/article/showArticle.jhtml, accessed May 12, 2005.

15. Bernard, Allen, "Majority of IT and Business Plans Still Not Linked," ClickZ of Jupitermedia Corporation, at www.clickz.com/stats/sectors/professional/print.php/3305971, accessed May 2, 2005.

16. Schlosser, Julie, "Tech@Work," *Fortune,* March 3, 2003, www.fortune.com/fortune/subs/print/0,15935,427294,00.html?cookie=1l1073974157, accessed January 10, 2004.

17. Whiting, Rick, "Analysis Gap," *Informationweek,* April 22, 2002, www.informationweek.com/story/IWK20020418S0007, accessed April 24, 2004.

18. "Bigelow Teas," Customer Spotlight from Business Objects, at www.businessobjects.com/company/customers/spotlight/bigelow.asp, accessed May 17, 2005.

19. "Red Robin International," company success story from Cognos at www.cognos.com/company/success/ss_entertainment.html, accessed January 13, 2004.

20. "Mining the Data of Dining," *Nation's Restaurant News,* May 22, 2000, pp. S22–S24.

21. Brown, Erika, "Analyze This," *Forbes,* April 1, 2002, pp. 96–98.

22. Levinson, Meredith, "The Brain Behind the Big, Bad Burger and Other Tales of Business Intelligence, *CIO Magazine,* March 15, 2005, at www.cio.com/archive/031505/intelligence.html, accessed May 1, 2005.

CHAPTER 4

1. Kolbasuk McGee, Marianne, "Mayo Builds toward Customized Medicine," *InformationWeek,* August 9, 2004, p. 24.

2. Gambon, Jill, "A Database That 'Ads' Up," *InformationWeek,* August 7, 1995, pp. 68–69.

3. Simon, Herbert, *The New Science of Management Decisions,* rev. ed. (Englewood Cliffs, NJ: Prentice Hall, 1977).

4. Sullivan, Laurie, "Take a Bite Out of High Gas Costs," *InformationWeek,* October 25, 2004, p. 60.

5. Kauderer, Steven, and Amy Kuehl, "Adding Value with Technology," *Best's Review,* October 2001, p. 130.

6. "M/W Planning: It's All in the Data," *Railway Age,* January 2001, pp. 60–61.

7. Marlin, Steven, Cristina McEachern, and Anthony O'Donnell, "Cross Selling Starts with CRM System," *Wall Street & Technology,* December 2001, pp. A8–A10.

8. "Software Integration from Down on the Farm," *Fleet Equipment,* April 2004, pp. 8–10.

9. Davis, David, *GIS for Everyone,* 3rd ed. (Redlands, CA: ESRI Press, 2003).

10. Smelcer, J. B. and E. Carmel, "The Effectiveness of Difference Representations for Managerial Problem Solving: Comparing Tables and Maps," *Decision Sciences,* 1997, pp. 391–420.

11. Brewin, Bob, "IT Helps Waste Hauler Handle Anthrax Safely," *Computerworld,* November 12, 2001, p. 8.

12. Johnson, Robert, "AM/FM/GIS Moves to the Web," *Transmission & Distribution World,* October 2001, pp. 52–57.

13. Dunkin, Amy, "The Quants May Have Your Numbers," *BusinessWeek,* September 25, 1995, pp. 146–47.

14. Port, Otis, "Computers That Think Are Almost Here," *BusinessWeek,* July 17, 1995, pp. 68–71.

15. Williams, Fred, "Artificial Intelligence Has Small but Loyal Following," *Pensions & Investments,* May 14, 2001, pp. 4, 124.

16. Stuart, Ann, "A Dose of Accuracy," *CIO,* May 15, 1996, pp. 22–24.

17. Blair, Robin, "From Opaque to Crystal Clear," *Health Management Technology,* January 2004, pp. 38–39.

18. Kay, Alexx, "Artificial Neural Networks," *Computerworld,* February 12, 2001, p. 60.

19. Ibid.

20. Perry, William, "What Is Neural Network Software?" *Journal of Systems Management,* September 1994, pp. 12–15.

21. Port, Otis, "Diagnoses That Cast a Wider Net," *BusinessWeek,* May 22, 1995, p. 130.

22. Baxt, William G., and Joyce Skora, "Prospective Validation of Artificial Neural Network Trained to Identify Acute Myocardial Infarction," *The Lancet,* January 6, 1997, pp. 12–15.

23. McCartney, Laton, "Technology for a Better Bottom Line," *InformationWeek,* February 26, 1996, p. 40.

24. Whiting, Rick, "Companies Boost Sales Efforts With Predictive Analysis," *InformationWeek,* February 25, 2002.

25. Hoffman, Thomas, "Users Tap Energy Management Systems to Reduce Power Costs," *ComputerWorld,* February 24, 2003, p. 18.

26. Harvey, Martin, "Keeping the Lights On," *InformationWeek,* August 9, 2004, pp. 34–39.

27. Whiting, Rick, "Companies Boost Sales Efforts With Predictive Analysis."

28. Punch, Linda, "Battling Credit Card Fraud," *Bank Management,* March 1993, pp. 18–22.

29. "Cigna, IBM Tech Tool Targets Health Care Fraud," *National Underwriter Property & Casualty—Risk & Benefits,* October 1994, p. 5.

30. Anthes, Gary H., "Picking Winners and Losers," *Computerworld,* February 18, 2002, p. 34.

31. Johnson, Colin, "Breeding Programs," *Financial Management,* February 2001, pp. 18–20.

32. Ruggiero, Murray, "Enhancing Trading with Technology," *Futures,* June 2000, pp. 56–59.

33. Patrick, C., L. Hui, S. F. Frency, Keith Ng, and C. C. Chan, "A Study of the Roll Planning of Fabric Spreading Using Genetic Algorithms," *International Journal of Clothing Science & Technology,* 2000, pp. 50–62.

34. Begley, S., "Software au Naturel," *Newsweek,* May 8, 1995, pp. 70–71.

35. Goldbert, David E., "Genetic and Evolutionary Algorithms Come of Age," *Communications of the ACM,* March 1994, pp. n113–119.

36. Baumohl, Bernard, "Can You Really Trust Those Bots?" *Time,* December 11, 2000, p. 80.

37. Thibodeau, Patrick, "Agents of Change," *Computerworld,* September 6, 2004, p. 24.

38. Hill, Alice, "Google Inside Out," *Maximum PC,* April 2004, pp. 44–48.

39. Dobbs, Sarah Boehle Kevin, Donna Gordon Goldwasser, and Jack Stamps, "The Return of Artificial Intelligence," *Training,* November 2000, p. 26.

40. Totty, Patrick, "Pinpoint Members with New Data-Mining Tools," *Credit Union Magazine,* April 2002, pp. 32–34.

41. Wolinsky, Howard, "Advisa Helps Companies Get More from Their Data: Helps Managers to Understand Market," *Chicago Sun-Times,* December 20, 2000, p. 81.

42. Anthes, Gary H, "Agents of Change," *Computerworld,* January 27, 2003, pp. 26–27.

43. Bonabeau, Eric, "Swarm Intelligence," O'Reilly Emerging Technology Conference, April 22–25, 2003, Santa Clara, CA.

44. Ibid.

45. Fredman, Catherine, "Lessons from the Ant Farm," *Chief Executive,* January/February 2003, pp. 42–46.

46. Bonabeau, Eric, and Christopher Meyer, "Swarm Intelligence: A Whole New Way to Think about Business," *Harvard Business Review,* May 2001, pp. 107–14.

47. Bonabeau, Eric, Marco Dorigo, and Guy Theraulaz, *Swarm Intelligence: From Natural to Artificial Systems* (London: Oxford University Press, 1999).

48. Brewin, Bob, "IT Goes on a Mission: GPS/GIS Effort Helps Pinpoint Shuttle Debris," *Computerworld,* February 10, 2003, pp. 1,6.

49. Ursery, Stephen, "Chattanooga, Tenn., Builds Tree Inventory," *American City & County,* July 2003, p. 18.

50. "Transit Agency Builds GIS to Plan Bus Routes," *American City & County,* April 2003, pp. 14–16.

51. Sharp, Charles, "Fire Screen," *Best's Review,* October 2004, pp. 120–22.

52. "Weblining," *BusinessWeek Online,* April 3, 2000, at www. businessweek.com, accessed May 29, 2005.

53. Llewellyn, Mike, "Check One, Two," *Dealerscope,* March 2005, p. 82.

CHAPTER 5

1. Perez, Juan Carlos, "Update: AOL Launches New Bill-Paying Tool," *TheStandard,* March 16, 2004, www.thestandard.com/article. php?story=20040316172813723, accessed April 7, 2004.

2. AOL Bill Pay Help, America Online, Inc., at http://billpay.aol.com/ bpweb/help/index.html, accessed May 29, 2005.

3. McGann, Rob, "Active Home Web Usage by Country, February 2005," March 16, 2005, Jupitermedia Corp., at www.clickz.com/stats/sectors/ geographic/article.php/3490516, accessed April 24, 2005.

4. Burns, Enid, "Firefox Market Share Gains Continue," Jupitermedia Corp., April 26, 2005, at www.clickz. com/stats/sectors/traffic_patterns/ article.php/3500691, accessed May 1, 2005.

5. Kerner, Sean Michael, "Bricks-and-Mortars Retailers See Lower Online Conversion Rates," Jupitermedia Corp., April 11, 2005, at www.clickz. com/stats/sectors/retailing/article. php/3496786#table1, accessed June 1, 2005.

6. McGann, Rob, "Generation Y Embraces SMS," Jupitermedia Corp., March 14, 2005, at www.clickz.com/ stats/sectors/wireless/article.php/ 3489776, accessed May 29, 2005.

7. "Top 50 Internet Advertisers in April," Jupitermedia Corp., May 26, 2005, at www.clickz.com/stats/ sectors/advertising/article.php/ 3507981, accessed May 29, 2005.

8. McGann, Rob, "Majority of Searchers Use Multiple Search Engines," Jupitermedia Corp., February 28, 2005, at www.clickz. com/stats/sectors/search_tools/ article.php/3486206, accessed May 30, 2005.

9. www.epinions.com/about/, accessed April 5, 2004 and June 1, 2005.

10. Violine, Bob, "The Global 50," *Optimize,* April 2005, pp. 41–50.

11. Hulme, George, "Supply-Chain Software Cuts Costs for Auto-Parts Firm," *InformationWeek,* May 6, 2005, at www.informationweek. com/story/showArticle.jhtml? articleID=162800199, accessed May 30, 2005.

12. "Global eXchange Services and ChinaECNet Establish B2B Exchange for China's $80 Billion Electronics Industry," Global eXchange Services, Inc., www.gxs.com/gxs/ press/release/press20040318, accessed April 4, 2004.

13. "Introduction to China eHub System," ChinaECNet Organization, at www.chinaecnet.com/eng/eHub/ int.asp, accessed May 30, 2005.

14. "The President's Management Agenda," Executive Office of the President Office of Management and Budget, Summer 2001, at www.whitehouse.gov/omb/budget/ fy2002/mgmt.pdf, accessed May 30, 2005.

15. Thomas, Owen, "How to Sell Tech to the Feds," *Business 2.0,* March 2003, pp. 111–12.

16. Hofmann, Martin, "VW Revs Its B2B Engine," *Optimize,* March 2004, pp. 22–30.

17. Hansen, Meike-Uta, "Volkswagen Drives Supply-Chain Innovation," *Optimize,* April 2005, at www. optimizemag.com/showArticle. jhtml;jsessionid=AWFT0BGTAWLIQQ SNDBCSKHSCJUMEKJVN?articleID= 159904448, accessed May 29, 2005.

18. "eBags.com Celebrates Five Years of Helping Consumers Find the Perfect Bag Online," eBags.com, www. ebags.com/info/aboutebags/index. cfm?Fuseaction=pressitem&release_ ID=102, accessed April 6, 2004.

19. "Awards," eBags.com, www.ebags. com/info/aboutebags/index.cfm? Fuseaction=awards, accessed May 30, 2005.

EXTENDED LEARNING MODULE E

1. "How to Revitalize Host Systems for Client/Server Computing Today and Tomorrow," *Datamation,* April 1, 1995, pp. S1–S4.

CHAPTER 6

1. Roth, Sabine, "Profile of CAS Software AG," March 29, 2005, www.cas.de/English/Home.asp, accessed June 9, 2005.

2. "Boise Office Solutions," boise.bc.com/office, accessed June 8, 2005.

3. "Business Technology Optimization," www.mercuryinteractive.com, accessed June 11, 2004.

4. Barnes, Cecily, "More Programmers Going 'Extreme'," April 9, 2001, www.news.com, accessed June 1, 2005.

5. "Who We Are," www.agilealliance.org, accessed June 2, 2005.

6. "Industry Associations," connextions.net/IndustryAssoc.asp, accessed June 1, 2005.

7. "Outsourcing's Next Wave," July 15, 2004, www.fortune.com, accessed June 2, 2005.

8. "Survey Reports," January 31, 2005, www.pwcglobal.com, accessed June 3, 2005.

9. Cohen, Peter, "*Twelve* Technical and Business Trends Shaping the Year Ahead," May 6, 2004, www.babsoninsight.com, accessed June 2, 2005.

10. "Statistics Related to Offshore Outsourcing," May 2005, www.rttsweb.com, accessed June 1, 2005.

11. Miller, Jim, "A Call to India," December 22, 2004, www.computerworld.com, accessed June 2, 2005.

12. "Offshore Services: Maximizing the Benefits for Financial Institutions," April 4, 2005, www.eds.com, accessed June 3, 2005.

13. "Agile Development," www.versionone.net/customers.asp, accessed June 3, 2005.

14. "The Pace of Research at St. Jude," www.borland.com, accessed June 3, 2005.

15. Malykhina, Elena, "Behind the Numbers," May 23, 2005, www.informationweek.com, accessed June 9, 2005.

16. "News Release," February 23, 2005, www.sears.com, accessed June 9, 2005.

17. "Life after Outsourcing," May 15, 2004, www.jnpconsortium.com, accessed June 9, 2005.

CHAPTER 7

1. "Company Profile," www.delmonte.com, accessed May 16, 2005.

2. "Industry Implementations," www.dmreview.com, accessed May 16, 2005.

3. Rashid, Mohammad, et al., "The Evolution of ERP Systems: A Historical Perspective," www.idea-group.com, accessed May 11, 2004.

4. "President Bush's Proposed FY06 Budget Represents Growth in IT Spending for Federal Government," February 8, 2005, www.bitpipe.com, accessed May 19, 2005.

5. "ERP Outsourcing Picks Up and Takes Off," www.outsourcing.com, accessed May 19, 2005.

6. Stedman, Craig, "Failed ERP Gamble Haunts Hershey," November 1, 1999, www.computerworld.com, accessed on May 20, 2005.

7. "Tools and Resources," www.cfo.com, accessed May 20, 2005.

8. "Abercrombie & Fitch Ace the Basics of Selling Lifestyle Online," www-3.ibm.com, accessed June 10, 2004.

9. "Fact Gap Fuels ERP Investments," www.techexchange.com/, accessed May 20, 2005.

10. Harris, Rob, "Make It Automatic," April 1, 2005, www.cfo.com, accessed May 19, 2005.

11. "News and Events," www.computerworld.com, accessed May 20, 2005.

12. "News and Events," www.scandoil.com, accessed May 20, 2005.

13. "Business Technographics," www.forrester.com, accessed May 19, 2005.

14. Bushell, Sue, "From Zero to One Hundred," June 10, 2004, www.cio.com, accessed May 22, 2005.

15. Walter, Mark, "Harnessing the Value of Multiple Content Repositories Across a Large Enterprise," November 15, 2004, www.gilbane.com, accessed May 19, 2005.

16. "CBS SportsLine.com Tips Off March Mayhem Coverage," March 11, 2002, about.sportsline.com, accessed May 22, 2005.

17. "The Gap Inc," www.corba.org, accessed June 10, 2004.

18. Wildstrom, Stephen, "Linux for the Desktop: It's a Contender," January 31, 2005, *BusinessWeek,* February 2004, www.businessweek.com, access June 10, 2004.

19. Null, Christopher, "How Netflix is Fixing Hollywood," *Business 2.0,* July 2003, www.business2.com, accessed June 10, 2004.

CHAPTER 8

1. Behar, Richard, "Never Heard of Acxiom? Chances Are It's Heard of You," *Fortune,* February 23, 2004, pp. 140–48.

2. Herman, Josh, "Marketing News: Albany, N.Y., Reflects True Test Market," *Marketing News,* February 1, 2004.

3. "American Banker: TransUnion Teams with Acxiom on Anti-Fraud Tool," *American Banker,* February 23, 2004 from www.acxiom.com, accessed May 27, 2005.

4. Bleed, Jake, "Acxiom Thrives on Sorting Bank Megamergers," *Arkansas Democrat-Gazette,* February 8, 2004, from www.acxiom.com, accessed May 27, 2005.

5. Pliagas, Linda, "Learning IT Right from Wrong," *InfoWorld,* October 2, 2000, pp. 39–40.

6. Fogliasso, Christine, and Donald Baack, "The Personal Impact of Ethical Decisions: A Social Penetration Theory Model," Second Annual Conference on Business Ethics Sponsored by the Vincentian Universities in the United States, New York, 1995.

7. Jones, T. M., "Ethical Decision-Making by Individuals in Organizations: An Issue-Contingent Model," *Academy of Management Review,* 1991, pp. 366–95.

8. Kallman, Ernest, and John Grillo, *Ethical Decision-Making and Information Technology* (San Francisco: McGraw-Hill, 1993).

9. Zhivago, Kristin, "Et Tu Enron?" *AdWeek Magazine's Technology Marketing,* April 2002, p. 33.

10. Baase, Sara, *The Gift of Fire: Social, Legal and Ethical Issues in Computing* (Upper Saddle River, NJ: Prentice Hall, 1997).

11. Jonietz, Erika, "Economic Bust Patent Boom," *Technology Review,* May 2002, pp. 71–72.

12. Stevens, Tim, "Cashing In on Knowledge," *Industry Week,* May 2002, pp. 39–43.

13. Moores, Trevor, "Software Piracy: A View from Hong Kong," *Communications of the ACM,* December 2000, pp. 88–93.

14. Software and Information Industry of America, at www.siaa.net/sharedcontent/press/.2000/5-24-00.html, accessed May 31, 2005.

15. Rittenhouse, David, "Privacy and Security on Your PC," *ExtremeTech,* May 28, 2002, from www.extremetech.com, accessed May 31, 2005.

16. Russell, Kay, "Phishing," *Computerworld,* January 19, 2004, p. 44.

17. DeBaise, Colleen, and Jochi Dreazen, "Ring of Identity Thieves Is Broken," *The Wall Street Journal,* November 26, 2002, p. A3.

18. Scalet, Sarah, "5 Ways to Fight ID Theft," *CSO,* March 2004, pp. 46–52.

19. BBC NEWS Story, January 11, 2005 from http://news.bbc.co.uk/go/fr/-/1/hi/world/americas/4163237.stm), accessed May 27, 2005.

20. Tam, Pui-Wang, Erin White, Nick Wingfield, and Kris Maker, "Snooping E-Mail by Software Is Now a Workplace Norm," *The Wall Street Journal,* March 9, 2005, pp. B1, B3.

21. Corbin, Dana, "Keeping a Virtual Eye on Employees," *Occupational Health & Safety,* November 2000, pp. 24–28.

22. Pliagas, "Learning IT Right from Wrong."

23. Sanders, Peter, "Casinos Bet on Radio-ID Gambling Chips," *The Wall Street Journal,* May 13, 2005, pp. B1, B7.

24. Vaught, Bobby, Raymond Taylor, and Steven Vaught, "The Attitudes of Managers Regarding the Electronic Monitoring of Employee Behavior: Procedural and Ethical Considerations," *American Business Review,* January 2000, pp. 107–14.

25. Parker, Laura, "Medical-Privacy Law Creates Wide Confusion," *USA Today,* October 17–19, 2003, pp. 1A, 2A.

26. Medford, Cassimir, "Know Who I Am," *PC Magazine,* February 7, 2000, pp. 58–64.

27. Charters, Darren, "Electronic Monitoring and Privacy Issues in Business-Marketing: The Ethics of the DoubleClick Experience," *Journal of Business Ethics,* February 2002, pp. 243–54.

28. Naples, Mark, "Privacy and Cookies," *Target Marketing,* April 2002, pp. 28–30.

29. Higgins, Michelle, "A Back-Seat Driver for Your Teen's Car," *The Wall Street Journal,* February 23, 2005, pp. D1, D4.

30. Forelle, Charles, "IBM Embraces Bold Method to Trap Spam," *The Wall Street Journal,* March 22, 2005, pp. B1, B2.

31. Angwin, Julia, "Elusive Spammer Sends Web Service on a Long Chase," *The Wall Street Journal,* May 7, 2003, pp. A1, A10.

32. Graven, Matthew P., "Leave Me Alone," *PC Magazine,* January 16, 2001, pp. 151–52.

33. Mirsky, Dara, "Tap Your Web Site's Log Files to Improve CRM," *Customer Inter@action Solutions,* May 2001, pp. 42–43.

34. Baase, *The Gift of Fire.*

35. Rittenhouse, "Privacy and Security on Your PC."

36. Soat, John, "IT Confidential," *InformationWeek,* June 3, 2002, p. 98.

37. Salkever, Alex, "A Dark Side to the FBI's Magic Lantern," *BusinessWeek Online,* November 27, 2001, at www.businessweek.com, accessed May 14, 2005.

38. Lefler, Dion, "'Erasing' Data Often Does No Such Thing," from www.kansas.com/mld/kansas/news/special_packages/btk/11037867.htm March 3, 2005, accessed May 27, 2005.

39. Manning, Carl, "KSU Professor Sentenced for Murder," *Morning Sun* (Pittsburg, KS), May 7, 2005, from www.morningsun.net, accessed May 27, 2005.

40. Bank, David, "Keeping Information Safe," *The Wall Street Journal,* November 11, 2004, pp. B1, B2.

41. Delaney, Kevin, "In 'Click Fraud,' Web Outfits Have a Costly Problem," *The Wall Street Journal,* April 6, 2005, pp. A1, A6.

42. Conley, John, "Knocking the Starch out of White Collar Crime," *Risk Management,* November 2000, pp. 14–22.

43. Radcliff, Deborah, "Hackers, Terrorists, and Spies," *Software Magazine,* October 1997, pp. 36–47.

44. Hulme, George V., and Bob Wallace, "Beware Cyberattacks," *InformationWeek,* November 13, 2000, pp. 22–24.

45. "Europe Plans to Jail Hackers," from zdnet.com/2100-11105-889332.html, April 23, 2002, accessed May 31, 2005.

46. Meyer, Lisa, "Security You Can Live With," *Fortune,* Winter 2002, pp. 94–99.

47. "Fast Times," *Fortune,* Summer 2000, pp. 35–36.

48. "Tech-Savvy Blackmailers Hone a New Form of Extortion," *The Wall Street Journal,* May 5, 2005, pp. B1, B3.

49. Zemke, Ron, "Tech-Savvy and People-Stupid," *Training,* July 2000, pp. 16–18.

50. Venetis, Tom, "Companies Urged to Use Security to Improve Productivity," *ComputerWorld,* May 20, 2005, at www.computerworld. com, accessed May 31, 2005.

51. Brooke Paul, "How Much Risk Is Too Much?" *InformationWeek,* November 6, 2000, pp. 116–24.

52. Radcliff, Deborah, "Beyond Passwords," *Computerworld,* January 21, 2002, pp. 52–53.

53. Eyres, Patricia, "Legal Traps for Unwary Managers during Corporate Criminal Investigations," *Business Credit,* February 2005, pp. 62–63.

54. Berman, Dennis, "Online Laundry: Government Posts Enron's E-Mail," *The Wall Street Journal,* October 6, 2003, pp. A1, A12.

55. Jaikumar, Vijayan, "Breach of Credit Data May Have Broad Scope," *ComputerWorld,* April 18, 2005, p. 6.

56. "Data Security Breaches Lead to Calls for Legislation," *ABA Bank Compliance,* March 2005, p. 7.

EXTENDED LEARNING MODULE H

1. Garretson, Cara, Jim Duffy, "Cybercrime: The Story behind the Stats," *Network World,* November 29, 2004, pp. 42–44.

2. Hanna, Greg, "Preventing Computer Fraud," *Strategic Finance,* March 2005, pp. 30–35.

3. Pack, Thomas, "Virus Protection," *Link-Up,* January/February 2002, p. 25.

4. Meserve, Jason, "People around the World Bitten by 'Love Bug,'" *Network World,* May 8, 2000, pp. 14, 28.

5. Zemke, Ron, "Tech-Savvy and People-Stupid," *Training,* July 2000, pp. 16–18.

6. York, Thomas, "Invasion of Privacy? E-Mail Monitoring Is on the Rise," *InformationWeek,* February 21, 2000, pp. 142–46.

7. Meserve, "People around the World Bitten by 'Love Bug.'"

8. Harris, Shane, "SoBig: A Look Back," *Government Executive,* November 2003, p. 72.

9. Babcock, Charles, "Fast-Moving Virus Slams E-Mail Systems," *InformationWeek,* August 2003, p. 22.

10. Roberts, Paul, "The Year Ahead in Security," *InfoWorld,* January 2004, p. 17.

11. Kirkpatrick, David, "Taking Back the Net," *Fortune,* September 29, 2003, pp. 117–22.

12. Luhn, Robert, "Eliminate Viruses," *PC World,* July 2002, p. 94.

13. Landolt, Sara Cox, "Why the Sky Isn't Falling," *Credit Union Management,* October 2000, pp. 52–54.

14. "Hackers Attack *USA Today* Web Site," *Morning Sun* (Pittsburg, KS), July 13, 2002, p. 6.

15. Hulme, George, "Vulnerabilities Beckon Some with a License to Hack," *InformationWeek,* October 23, 2000, pp. 186–92.

16. Bischoff, Glenn, "Fear of a Black Hat," *Telephony,* September 3, 2001, pp. 24–29.

17. Kornblum, Janet, "Kournikova Virus Maker: No Harm Meant," *USA Today,* February 14, 2001, p. 3D.

18. "Firms Increasingly Call on Cyberforensics Teams," cnn.com, January 16, 2002, accessed March 18, 2004.

19. "*USA Today* Says Writer Made Up Part of Stories," *Dallas Morning News,* March 20, 2004, p. 11A.

20. Kruse, Warren G., and Jay G. Heiser, *Computer Forensics: Incident Response Essentials* (New York: Addison-Wesley, 2002).

CHAPTER 9

1. Ward, Mark, "Hacking with a Pringles Tube," BBC News, March 8, 2002, http://news.bbc.co.uk/1/hi/sci/tech/1860241.stm, accessed April 15, 2004.

2. www.intenseschool.com/bootcamps/security/hacking/default.asp?mc=ggass_hacking&GTSE=goog&GTKW=hacking, accessed April 15, 2004.

3. Lu, Stephen C-Y, "Process Planning as Negotiation—A Step toward F2B2C Ecommerce," STC/O CAPP Working Group, January 24, 2001, at www.3s.hmg.inpg.fr/ci/GAMA/01Lu.pdf, accessed June 6, 2005.

4. Corcoran, Elizabeth, "The Next Small Thing," *Forbes,* July 23, 2001, pp. 96–106.

5. Center to Integrate Nanotechnologies, United States Department of Energy, at http://cint.lanl.gov/, accessed June 1, 2005.

6. Adams, Nina, "Lessons from the Virtual World," *Training,* June 1995, pp. 45–47.

7. Flynn, Laurie, "VR and Virtual Spaces Find a Niche in Real Medicine," *New York Times,* June 5, 1995, p. C3.

8. Chabrow, Eric, "Facial-Recognition Software Gives a Better Picture," *InformationWeek,* March 13, 2003, www.informationweek.com/story/showArticle.jhtml?articleID=8700238, accessed April 13, 2004.

9. www.businesswire.com/webbox/bw.050201/211220321.htm, accessed May 2, 2002.

10. Bonsor, Kevin, "How Facial Recognition Systems Work," HSW Media Network, at www.howstuffworks.com/facial-recognition.htm, accessed June 2, 2005.

11. Weikle, Bobbie, "Riding the Perfect Wave: Putting Virtual Reality to Work with Disabilities," from www.pappanikou.uconn.edu/weikle.html, accessed April 14, 2004.

12. McConnaughey, Janet, "Virtual Reality Used to Treat Autism," *Denver Post,* October 20, 1996, p. 39A.

13. www.nytimes.com/2002/05/30/technology/circuits/30TEEN.html, accessed June 7, 2002.

14. Ouchi, Monica Soto, "Wildseed: A Start-up on the Cusp of Success with Teens," *Seattle Times,* January 12, 2004, seattletimes.nwsource.com/html/businesstechnology/2001834588_ces12.html, accessed April 15, 2004.

EXTENDED LEARNING MODULE A

Photo A.1a, page 39, Courtesy of Veo Intl.

Photo A.1b, page 39, Photo Courtesy of Kensington Technology Group (www.kensington.com).

Photo A.1c, page 39, © 2005 SANYO North America Corporation. All Rights Reserved.

Photo A.1d, page 39, Photo courtesy of Fossil.

Photo A.1e, page 39, Used with permission of Eastman Kodak Company.

Photo A.1f, page 39, Gateway, Inc.

Photo A.1g, page 39, Courtesy of Apple.

Photo A.2a, page 40, Image courtesy of Microsoft Hardware.

Photo A.2b, page 40, © Precise Biometrics.

Photo A.2c, page 40, © Nance S. Trueworthy.

Photo A.2d, page 40, Image courtesy of NVIDIA Corporation.

Photo A.2e, page 40, Photo courtesy of Intel Corporation.

Photo A.2f, page 40,© 2005 Dell Inc. All Rights Reserved.

Photo A.2g, page 40, Courtesy of Linksys.

Photo A.4a, page 43, Treo 650 smartphone by palmOne.

Photo A.4b, page 43, Image reprinted with permission from ViewSonic Corporation.

Photo A.4c, page 43, Photo courtesy of Overdrive PC.

Photo A.4d, page 43, © 2005 Dell Inc. All Rights Reserved.

Photo A.5a, page, 44, Courtesy, Hewlett-Packard Development Company, L.P.

Photo A.5b, page 44, Courtesy of International Business Machines Corporation. Unauthorized use not permitted.

Photo A.5c, page 44, Photo Courtesy of Cray Inc.

Photo A.9a, page 52, Courtesy, Hewlett-Packard Development Company, L.P.

Photo A.9b, page 52, Image courtesy of Microsoft Hardware.

Photo A.9c, page 52, Photo used with permission from Plantronics, Inc.

Photo A.9d, page 52, Courtesy of Belkin Corporation.

Photo A.9e, page 52, Courtesy of Micro Innovations.

Photo A.9f, page 52, Courtesy of Logitech.

Photo A.12a, page 55, Courtesy of Apple.

Photo A.12b, page 55, © Copyright 2005 Samsung Electronics America. All Rights Reserved.

Photo A.12c, page 55, Image reprinted with permission from ViewSonic Corporation.

Photo A.13a, page 55, Courtesy of Epson America, Inc.

Photo A.13b, page 55, Courtesy, Hewlett-Packard Development Company, L.P.

Photo A.13c, page 55, Courtesy of Epson America, Inc.

Photo A.15a, page 57, © Nance S. Trueworthy.

Photo A.15b, page 57, Spencer Grant / PhotoEdit Inc.

Photo A.16a, page 58, SanDisk Corporation.

Photo A.16b, page 58, SanDisk Corporation.

Photo A.16c, page 58, Image courtesy of Kingston Technology.

Photo A.16d, page 58, SanDisk Corporation.

Photo A.16e, page 58, Viking InterWorks A Sanmina-SCI Company. www.vikinginterworks.com

Photo A.17a, page 59, Photo Courtesy of Intel Corporation.

Photo A.17b, page 59, Image courtesy of Kingston Technology.

Photo A.20a, page 62, Courtesy, Hewlett-Packard Development Company, L.P.

Photo A.20b, page 62, © Crutchfield Corporation.

Photo A.20c, page 62, Photo by R.D. Cummings, Pittsburg State University.

Photo A.20d, page 62, © Crutchfield Corporation.

Photo A.20e, page 62, Courtesy of Belkin Corporation.

Photo A.20f, page 62, Courtesy of Belkin Corporation.

Photo A.22, page 64, FirewireDirect.com www.firewiredirect.com.

CHAPTER 9

Photo 9.5a, page 432, Euan Myles / Getty Images.

Photo 9.5b, page 432, Andersen Ross / PhotoDisc / Getty Images.

Photo 9.5c, page 432, © Stockbyte.

Photo 9.8a, page 437, © FORESTIER YVES / CORBIS SYGMA.

Photo 9.8b, page 437, Lara Jo Regan / Liaison / Getty Images.

Photo 9.8c, page 437, Courtesy Xybernaut Corporation © Xybernaut Corporation 2002.

Photo 9.10, page 441, Image is the property of Texas Instruments Inc. All rights reserved.

INDEX

1-tier infrastructure, 336
2-tier infrastructure, 336
3-tier infrastructure, 336

A

A/L. *See* Arithmetic/logic unit
Abercrombie & Fitch, 329
Accenture, 32
Access to data, 326–327. *See also* Availability of data
    authentication for, 380–381
ACFE. *See* Association of Certified Fraud Examiners
Action verb list, 467
Acxiom Corp., 355, 384
Ad hoc decisions, 182
Administration
    data, 146
    database, 146
Advantage, competitive, 18, 21–24, 71, 94
Adware, 370–371
AFC Enterprises, 152
Affiliate program, 251, 267
Affordable Homes Real Estate, 503–504
Agent-based modeling, 209
    and multi-agent systems, 204–208
Agile Alliance, 290
Agile IT systems, 326–328, 330
    accessibility of data, 326–327
    availability of data, 326
    capacity planning, 327
Agile methodology, 290
AI. *See* Artificial intelligence
AirFortress, 139
Alliance partnership, 89
Allstate Insurance, 202
Amazon.com, 20–21
America Online (AOL), 26, 239
American Express, 244
American Management Association, 366
American Production and Inventory Control Society (APICS), 320
Analysis phase, 282–283, 408
ANN. *See* Artificial neural networks
Anonymizer, 371
Ant colonies, and swarm intelligence, 204–207
Anthrax scare of 2001, 189
Anti-spyware software, 50
Anti-virus software, 50, 383
AOL, 26, 116
    Advertising.com, 83
    Bill Pay, 26, 239
Application generation subsystems, 136, 149
Application service providers (ASP), 425–426
Application software, 16, 41–42, 45–50
Archinfo, 210
Architecture
    IT, 329
    technical, 284–285

ARGUS system, 434
Arithmetic/logic (A/L) unit, 60
Artificial intelligence (AI), 23–24, 189–190, 209
Artificial neural networks (ANN), 193, 209
ASCII (American Standard Code for Information Interchange), 51
ASCII résumés, 468
Ask Jeeves, 200, 375
ASP. *See* Application service providers
ASR. *See* Automatic speech recognition
Assessment, of risk, 383
Association of Certified Fraud Examiners (ACFE), 376
ATMs, 19
Audiogalaxy, 370
Australian P&C Direct, 124
Authentication, 406–407
    of access, 380–381
Autism, 444
AutoFilter, 220, 222–226
    custom, 224–226
Automatic speech recognition (ASR), 429, 446, 450
Availability of data, 326

B

Back office systems, 84, 319
Backups, 136, 337, 339, 344, 383
Bank of America, 385
Bank One, 355
Banner ads, 509–510
Bar code scanner, 53
Bargain hunting online, 203
Bayer AG, 360
B&B Travel Consultants, 237
Behavioral marketing technology, 83
Ben & Jerry's, 150–151
Benchmarking, 327
BI. *See* Business intelligence
Binary digits (bits), 51
Biochips, 435, 450
Biometric borders, 383
Biometric processing, integrating with transaction processing, 433–435
Biometric processing systems (BPSs), 434
Biometric scanner, 54
Biometric security, 433
Biometrics, 380–381, 383, 432–435, 446
Biomimicry, 204
BKD, LLP, 417
Black-hat hackers, 377, 401, 418
Blackmail online, 378
Blaster worm, 396, 399
Blockbuster late fees, 3
Blue Mountain Arts, 251
Bluetooth, 63
Book intelligence software, 71
Bookmarks.list, 106
Books and music, buying on the Internet, 100

Booz Allen Hamilton, 19
BPO. *See* Business process outsourcing
BPR. *See* Business process reengineering
BPSs. *See* Biometric processing systems
Brand spoofing, 363
Break-even analysis, 520
Britannia Airways, 137
British Columbia Milk Marketing Board, 187
British Telecom (BT), 386
Browser-safe colors, 481
BT. *See* British Telecom
BTK strangler case, 373
Build vs. buy, 304
Bureau of Labor Statistics, 201
Burlington Northern and Santa Fe (BNSF) railroad, 184
Buses
    expansion, 63
    system, 60
Business Commerce Limited, 252
Business geography, 189
Business intelligence (BI), 6, 85–88, 124, 149
    IT support for, 87–88
    software for, 87
    strategic and competitive opportunities with, 86–87
Business intelligence (BI) systems, 71, 85, 94
Business on the Internet
    competitive intelligence, 274
    storefront software, 274–275
Business partnerships and alliances
    customer relationship management systems, 81–85
    sales force automation systems, 82
    supply chain management systems, 24, 78–81
Business process outsourcing (BPO), 297–298, 305
Business process reengineering (BPR), 341
Business requirements, 282, 309
Business-to-business (B2B) e-commerce, 242, 247–266
    horizontal versus vertical, 248–249, 266
    MRO versus direct, 247–248, 266
Business-to-consumer (B2C) e-commerce, 242, 245–247, 266
    commoditylike and digital, 245–246
    convenience versus specialty, 245
    mass customization, 247, 266
BusinessObjects, 150–151
BusinessWeek, 103
Buyer agents, 200–201, 209
Buyer power, 73, 93
Buying products and services on the Internet, 100–101
    automobiles, 101
    books and music, 100
    clothing and accessories, 100–101
    Internet auction houses, 101

Buying versus leasing, 514–515
Bytes, 51

C

Cable modems, 116, 119
Cache, CPU, 60
Cadbury Schweppes, 10
CAN-Spam Act, 369, 374
Capacity planning, 327, 328
Capital One Financial Corporation, 355
Carding, 363
Career issues, 26–27, 144–145, 154–155, 417
Carlson Restaurant Worldwide, 96–97
CAS Software AG, 279
Casual Male retail group, 95
Catalina Supermarkets, 212
CAVEs (cave automatic virtual environments), 431–432, 446
CD-ROMs (compact disc—read-only memory), 57
CD-Rs (compact disc—recordable), 57
CD-RWs (compact disc—rewritable), 57
CEH (Certified Ethical Hacker), 423
Cell phone technology, future in, 439–440
Cell phones, 99
    Web-enabled, 68
Census Bureau, 201, 373
Central processing unit (CPU), 16, 41, 59–60, 65
    cache, 60
    clock, 60
    cycle (machine), 59
Centralized infrastructure, for information technology, 333–334, 343
Certificates, digital, 403
CF. See CompactFlash card
Change management facilities, 139
Charmed Technologies, 437
Chattanooga, Tennessee, 210
Check the Grid, 349
Chevron Corp., 14, 365
Chicago Police Department, 194
Chief information officers (CIO), 146
Chief privacy officers (CPO), 146
Chief security officers (CSO), 146
ChinaECNet, 252
Choice, 181
ChoicePoint, 384–385
Chronological résumés, 472
CI. See Competitive intelligence
CIGNA HealthCare, 191
CIO. See Chief information officers
Citibank, 194
CKE Restaurants, 96
Classification, in data mining, 202, 211–213
Clean Harbor, 189
Cleveland Clinic, 179
Click-and-mortar, 261
Click-and-order (pure play), 263
Click-throughs, 251
Client computer, 113
Client/server networks, 333–335, 343
Clock, CPU, 60

CNN, Custom News bots, 201
Code Red, 398–399
Cognos Business Intelligence, 152
Cold sites, 338
Collaboration systems, 22, 94, 98
Collection phase, of computer forensics, 405–407
Collective intelligence, 204–207, 209
Collocation facility, 338
Columbia spacecraft, 210
Columbus Regional Healthcare System, 139
Combination worm/DoS attacks, 398–399
Coming Attractions Web site, 349
Common cookies, 368
Communications media
    wired, 61–62
    wireless, 63–64
Communications protocols, 118
CompactFlash (CF) card, 58
Competitive advantage, 18, 21–24, 71, 94
Competitive intelligence (CI), 86, 274
Competitors, rivalry among existing, 75–76
Composite primary keys, 169
Composite relations, 169
Compressing a file, 414
Computer-aided decision-making tools, 179
Computer Associates (CA), 383
Computer crime, 418
    combination worm/DoS attacks, 398–399
    denial-of-service attacks, 377, 382, 397, 418
    distributed denial-of-service attacks, 397
    inside the company, 403
    outside the organization, 392
    the players, 400–402
    stand-alone viruses, 396
    Trojan-horse viruses, 396, 418
    virus hoaxes, 396–397
    viruses, 377, 382, 393–396
    Web defacing, 399–400
Computer Ethics Institute, 359, 387
Computer forensics, 403–408, 418–419
    analysis phase, 408
    the authentication and preservation process, 406–407
    collection phase, 405–407
    forensic hardware and software tools, 407
    reactive, 416–417
Computer forensics experts, 415–418
Computer hardware. See Hardware
Computer monitors, 68
Computer printers, 55–56
Computer Sciences Corporation (CSC), 147
Computer Security Institute survey, 376
Computer software. See Software
Computer viruses, 377, 382, 393–396, 418
Computers
    desktop, 43–44
    Internet server, 112–113, 118
    mainframe, 45
    mid-range, 44–45
    minicomputers, 44–45, 64
    notebook, 43, 60, 64
    personal digital assistants, 42

Computers—Cont.
    supercomputers, 45
    wearable, 437–438, 446
    Web-enabled, 68
Computing
    decentralized, 17
    intellectual, 428
    mobile, 18
    ubiquitous, 17
Concurrency control facilities, 138
Conditional formatting, 226–228, 236
Connecting devices, 61–64
Connectivity software, 115, 119, 319–320
Consolidated sales information, 10
Content management database solutions, 137
Control unit, 59
Convenience merchandise, 245
Conversion rates, 251
Cookies, 368
    unique, 368
Cooking from the Internet, 350
Copyrights, 359–360, 382, 386
Costs
    of disaster recovery, 338
    of switching, 74
Covisint, 249
CPU. See Central processing unit
Crackers, 377, 401, 418
Crash-proof software, 50
Credit card companies, 212
CRM. See Customer relationship management system
Crossover, 198, 209
CRTs, 54
CRUD (Create, Read, Update, and Delete), 148
Curriculum Vitae (or CV), 472
Custom AutoFilter function, 224–226, 236
Custom News bots, 201
Customer relationship management (CRM)
    systems, 81–85, 94, 324
        invasiveness of, 93
        IT support for, 84
        opportunities with, 83–84
Customer relationship management systems, 71
Customer self-service system, 19
Customers
    affiliate programs for, 251
    e-mail and viral marketing to, 251
    gaining loyalty of, 95
    identifying, 244–245
Customization, 67
    mass, 247, 266
Cut and paste functionality, for Microsoft Word, 285
Cyberterrorists, 377, 401–402, 418

D

Data, 6
    access to, 326–327, 380–381
    availability of, 326
    versus information, 6

Data administration, 146
Data administration subsystems, 136–139, 149
    backup and recovery facilities, 136
    change management facilities, 139
    concurrency control facilities, 138
    query optimization facilities, 137
    reorganization facilities, 138
    security management facilities, 137
Data cleansing, 327
Data definition subsystems, 131–132, 149
Data dictionaries, 126, 175
Data management, 186
    of external information, 186
    of organizational information, 186
    of personal information, 186
Data manipulation subsystems, 132–136, 149
    query-by-example tools, 135
    report generators, 134
    structured query language, 136
    views, 133
Data marts, 86, 143–144
Data-mining agents, 202–203, 209
Data-mining techniques, 179
Data-mining tools, 141–143
    intelligent agents, 142
    multidimensional analysis tools, 142– 143
    query-and-reporting tools, 142
    statistical tools, 143
Data processing, for higher education, 515–516
Data warehouses, 86, 140–141, 149
    considerations in using, 145–146
    data marts, 86, 143–144
    mining, 141–143, 146
    up-to-date information, 146
Data warehousing/business intelligence (DWBI), 324
Database administration, 146
Database administrators (DBA), 155
Database management systems (DBMS), 130, 175
    example of, 522–524
    software for, 20–21
Databases, 123–157
    for business intelligence, 126
    implementing with Microsoft Access, 494–495
    and information ownership, 147
    multidimensional, 140
    operational, 124, 149
    primary keys, foreign keys, and integrity constraints in, 129–130
    relational, 126–130
    security for, 139
DBA. *See* Database administrators
DBMS. *See* Database management systems
DBMS engines, 130, 149
DBMS tools, 131–132
    application generation subsystem, 136
    data administration subsystem, 136–139
    data definition subsystem, 131–132
    data manipulation subsystem, 132–136
DDoS. *See* Distributed denial-of-service attacks
Decentralized computing, 17

Decentralized infrastructure, for information technology, 332–333, 343
Decision analysis with spreadsheet software, 219–238
    AutoFilter, 222–226
    conditional formatting, 226–228
    custom autofilters, 224–226
    lists, 220–221
    pivot tables, 228–235
Decision making, 181
    integration, 339–340
Decision support, 178–215
    and artificial intelligence, 189–190
    bargain hunting online, 203
    classifying people, 194
    expert systems, 190–197
    finding investment opportunities, 217–218
    genetic algorithms, 197–200
    geographic information systems, 187–189
    intelligent agents, 200–203
    neural networks, 193–197
    traffic light example, 193
Decision support systems (DSS), 183–186, 208, 323, 514–515
    building, 508–509
    data management component, 186
    model management component, 184, 186
    user interface management component, 186
Decision support team, 520
Decisions
    nonrecurring, 182
    nonstructured, 182
    recurring, 182
    structured, 182
Del Monte Foods, 317
Deleted files and slack space, 409–411
Dell Computer Corp., 78–79, 247, 291, 324
Demand aggregation, 247–248
Denial-of-service (DoS) attacks, 377, 382, 397, 418
    distributed, 397
Deregulation, and outsourcing, 292
Design, 181
Design phase, 283–284
Designing databases
    creating an intersection relation, 114, 171
    defining the cardinality among entity classes, 168
    designing and building a relational database, 161–175
    and entity-relationship diagramming, 164–167, 176
Desktop computers, 43–44
Development phase, 284–285. *See also* Systems development methodologies
Diesel-fuel prices, 183
Digital camera, 54
Digital cash (electronic cash, e-cash), 436–437, 446
Digital dashboards, 88
Digital divide, 271
    closing, 442–443
Digital merchandise, 246

Digital signatures and certificates, 403
Digital still camera, 54
Digital Subscriber Lines (DSL), 116–119
Digital video camera, 54
Digital wallet, 255, 267
Dining data, mining, 152–153
Direct materials, 248, 266
Directory search engines, 108–110, 118
DIRECTV programming, 522
Disaster recovery plans, 337–338
    cost curves for, 338
Disk optimization software, 50
"Disruptive technologies," 3
Distance learning, 5
Distributed denial-of-service (DDoS) attacks, 397
Distributed infrastructure, for information technology, 334, 343
Distribution chains, 78–79
Document management systems, 89–90, 94
Domain names, 104, 118
Domains, 190–191
DoS. *See* Denial-of-service attacks
Dot-bombs, 103
Dot pitch, 55
DoubleClick, 368
Dow Chemical, 324
Dr Pepper, 10
DSL. *See* Digital Subscriber Lines
DSS. *See* Decision support systems
Du Pont, 360
DVD-ROMs, 57
DVD-Rs, 58
DVD-RWs, 58
DVD+RW, 58
DWBI. *See* Data warehousing/business intelligence (DWBI)

E

E-cash, 436
E-classified@GabbyGazetteer.com, 513–514
E-commerce, 238–275
    business models, 242
    eBags, 269–270
    new F2b2C business model for, 426, 446
E-commerce payment systems, financial cybermediaries, 254
E-government, 261
    broadening of, 261–266
    career opportunities in, 264, 417
    exploring the world of, 265
E-learning management system, 12
E-mail
    confiscation by regulators, 383–384
    misleading, 396–397
    software, 14, 115, 118
E-portfolio building, 454–492
    careers, industries, amid companies, 459
    content, 473–476
    developing, 473–476
    the electronic job market, 455–457
    feedback, 465
    file formats, 467–471

E-portfolio building—*Cont.*
    HTML versus generated code, 484–488
    networking, 457–458
    research, 461
    self-assessment, 459–460
    Web content, 484–489
    Web design tools, 485–488
    your commercial, 458
    your objective, 463
    your résumé, 480
E-R. *See* Entity-relationship diagrams
Earth Observing-1 (EO1) satellite, 201
Eastman Kodak Chemical Co., 360
eBags.com, 326
eBay, 25, 247, 256, 448
EBPP. *See* Electronic Bill Presentment and
    Payment
Economic growth, and outsourcing, 292
eCRM. *See* Electronic customer relationship
    systems
EDI. *See* Electronic data interchange
Education. *See* Higher education; Training
Einstein/Noah Bagel, 153
EIS. *See* Executive information systems
Electronic Bill Presentment and Payment (EBPP),
    254–255, 267
Electronic checks, 267
Electronic Communications Privacy Act of 1986,
    366
Electronic customer relationship (eCRM)
    systems, 367
Electronic data interchange (EDI), 256–258
Electronic job market, 455–457
Electronic marketplace (e-marketplace), 248, 266
Electronic savings bonds, 264
Employees, privacy of, 364–367
EnCase, 413
Encryption, 258–259, 267, 381, 383, 413, 419
End-user development (EUD), 302–304, 309
Energizer, 291
Engineering, social, 401
Enron, 359, 383–384
Enterprise resource planning (ERP), 203, 298
    implementing, 317
Enterprise resource planning (ERP) systems,
    320–323, 343
    advantages of, 322
    dilemma of, 324
    disadvantages of, 322
    evolution of, 323–324
    vendors and market trends, 324–326
Enterprise systems (ES), 318–326, 343
    defining, 318–320
Entertainment industry, 345–346
Entity classes, 163–171, 176
Entity-relationship (E-R) diagrams, 164–167, 176
EPC (electronic product code), 442
Epinions.com, 243
Erased information, 412
Ernst & Young, 376
ERP. *See* Enterprise resource planning
Errors, spotting early, 283
Ethical hackers, 401

Ethics, 13, 27–28, 29, 356–361, 382
    deciding ethical issues, 357–358
    guidelines for ethical computer system use,
        358–359
    intellectual property, 359–360
ETL. *See* Extraction, transformation, and loading
    process
EUD. *See* End-user development
Evaluating software suites, 49
Evolutionary processes, 197, 200
Executive information systems (EIS), 21–22, 323,
    504–505
Expandability, 63–64
Expansion buses, 63
Expansion cards, 63
Expansion slots, 63
Expedia, 389
Expert systems, 190–197, 209
    capabilities of, 192–193
External information, 9, 29, 34
Extraction, transformation, and loading (ETL)
    process, 148
Extreme programming (XP) methodology,
    289–290, 304–305
Eye scanning, 383

F

FaceIt, 434
Facial recognition software, 381, 434–435
Fair and Accurate Credit Transactions Act, 374
Fair Use Doctrine, 359, 382
Faulty software, 287
Favorites list, 106
F2b2C (Factory to business to Consumer) e-
    commerce, 426, 446
FBI. *See* Federal Bureau of Investigation
FDIC. *See* Federal Deposit Insurance Corporation
Feature analyses, 429
Feature creep, 281
Federal Aviation Authority, 388
Federal Bureau of Investigation (FBI), 372, 374,
    376
    Computer Security Institute, 376
Federal Deposit Insurance Corporation (FDIC),
    521
Federal Energy Regulatory Commission (FERC),
    383–384
Federal Trade Commission (FTC), 362
FEDI. *See* Financial EDI
FERC. *See* Federal Energy Regulatory
    Commission
FERRET (Federal Electronic Research and
    Review Extraction Tool), 201
FiberMark North America, 85
File transfer protocol (ftp), 113–114, 118
Financial cybermediaries, 254, 267
Financial EDI (FEDI), 258, 267
Financial Executives International (FEI), 147
Financial Services Modernization Act, 373–374
Financing, 521
Fingerhut, 195
Fingerprint scanners, 381

FIPS (Federal Information Processing Standards),
    139
Firewall Guide Web site, 380
Firewalls, 380, 383
Firewire (IEEE 1394 or I-Link) port, 62
First Union Bank, 211
Five Forces Model, 72–76, 81, 92–93
    buyer power, 73, 93
    rivalry among existing competitors, 75–76,
        94
    supplier power, 73, 94
    threat of new entrants, 75, 94
    threat of substitute products or services, 74,
        94
Flash memory cards, 58
Flash memory device, 58
Flat panel displays, 54
FleetBoston Financial Corp., 195
Flexibility, data, 327
Foothills Savings Bank (FSB), 521
Forbes, 103
Ford Motor Co., 257
Foreign keys, 128–129, 169, 176
Forensic hardware and software tools, 407
Forensic image copies, 405, 419
Formatting, conditional, 226–228, 236, 523
Forrester Research Inc., 306
Fortress Technologies, 139
Fortune magazine, 103
"Fraudulent clicking," 375
FreeMerchant.com, 274
Freeware and shareware on the Internet, 311–312
    creating and posting electronic résumés,
        36–37
    customer information, 158
    demographics, 158
    financial aid resources, 157
    job databases, 36
    learning about investing, 217
    libraries, 157
    locating internships, 37
    protecting your computer investment,
        311–312
    real estate, 158
    researching the company behind the stock,
        217–218
    retrieving stock quotes, 218
Front office systems, 84, 319
FrontPage, 487, 498–499
FSB. *See* Foothills Savings Bank
FTC. *See* Federal Trade Commission
ftp. *See* File transfer protocol
Fulfillment, 80
Functional résumé, 472
Fundamental research, 217
Fuzzy logic, 197, 209

G

Gallery, 475 476, 492
Game controllers, 53
Gamepad, 53
The Gap, 341

Gartner Research, 87
Gas plasma display, 54
Gates Rubber Company, 244, 257
GB. *See* Gigabytes
General Electric (GE), 256
General Motors (GM), 25, 257
Genetic algorithms, 23, 197–200, 209
Geographic information systems (GIS), 132, 187–189, 209–210, 213
GHz. *See* Gigahertz
Gigabytes (GB or Gig), 57
Gigahertz (GHz), 59
GIS. *See* Geographic information systems
GlaxoSmithKline (GSK), 89
Global eXchange Services (GXS), 256
Global information technology, 34
Global positioning system (GPS), 210, 271–272
Global reach, collocation facilities, 338
Global Technology Ventures (GTV), 360
Globalization, and outsourcing, 292
Glove, 430
GMAC, 25
Google, 110, 197, 200, 375
Government-to-business (G2B), 261–263, 267
Government-to-consumer (G2C), 261, 263, 267
Government-to-government (G2G), 261–262, 267
    international, 261, 264, 267
GPS. *See* Global positioning system
Granularity, of information, 9
Graphical user interface (GUI), 284
Groove Workspace, 89, 91, 98
GTV. *See* Global Technology Ventures
GUI. *See* Graphical user interface
GUI screen design, 284
GXS. *See* Global eXchange Services

H

Hackers, 376–377, 400–401, 418
    black-hat, 377, 401, 418
    ethical, 401
    thrill-seeking, 400, 418
    white-hat, 377, 401, 418
Hactivists (cyberterrorists), 377, 401–402, 418
The Happy Hacker, 154
Haptic interfaces, 430, 442
Hard disks, 57
Hardee's, 96
Hardware, 15–16, 29, 40–41, 51–64
    buses, expansion slots, and expansion cards, 61–64
    categories of computers by size, 42–45
    characteristics of CPUs and RAM, 59–60
    connecting devices, 61–64
    desktop computers, 43–44
    forensic tools for, 407
    input devices, 15, 41, 52–54, 65
    minicomputers, mainframe computers, and supercomputers, 44–45
    monitors, 54–55
    notebook computers, 43, 60, 64
    output devices, 16, 41, 54–56, 65
    personal digital assistants, 4

Hardware—*Cont.*
    printers, 55–56
    a quick tour of technology, 40–42
    scanners, 53–54
    storage devices, 4, 16, 56–58, 65
Hardware key logger, 366
Harrah's Entertainment, 152
Headset, 430
Health Insurance Portability and Accountability Act (HIPAA), 139, 373
HealthShare, 191
Help desk, 287
    outsourcing, 291, 295
Hershey Foods, 324
Hewlett-Packard (HP), 90
Hidden job market, 457, 490
Hiding information, 412–414
    compressing the file, 414
    encrypting the file, 413
    making the information invisible, 413
    protecting the file with a password, 413
    renaming the file, 412–413
    using steganography, 413–414
    using Windows, 413
Higher education, planning and data processing for, 515–516
Higher education through the Internet, 452–453
    graduate school information and tips, 453
    MBA programs, 452
    specialized MBA programs, 452
    tele-education, 453
Hoaxes, virus, 396–397
Holographic storage devices, 431, 438, 446
Home appliances, "intelligent," 450
Homeland Security Act, 374
Honeybees, work allocation system of, 208
Horizontal e-marketplace, 248, 266
Horizontal market software, 26, 46, 65
Hosting services, 275
Hot sites, 338
Hot swapping, 61
HTML. *See* Hypertext markup language
HTML code, 486
http. *See* Hypertext transfer protocol
Hunt Transportation Inc., 183
Huntington National Bank, 307
Hurricane Andrew, 187–189
Hyperion Solutions, 71
Hyperlinking, 105, 386
Hypertext markup language (HTML), 480
    building Web pages with, 314–315, 499
Hypertext transfer protocol (http), 105, 114, 118

I

i-sec, 423
IBM, 90, 360
ICEs. *See* Integrated collaboration environments
Identity theft, 28, 362–364
Identity Theft and Assumption Deterrence Act of 1998, 374
IDSs. *See* Intrusion-detection systems
IEEE 802.11a, b, or g, 63

IG2G. *See* International government-to-government business
Image scanner, 53
Implant chips, 435, 450
Implementation phase, 181, 286
Incident response, reactive, 416–417
Informatica, 144
Information, 6
    assessing the value of, 502–504
    cleanliness of, 148
    external, 9, 29, 34
    the form dimension, 8
    hiding, 412–414
    internal, 9, 29, 34
    the location dimension, 7
    objective, 9, 29, 34
    the organizational dimension, 8–10
    ownership of, 146–148
    the personal dimension, 6–7, 30–31
    security of, 524–525
    shared, 17
    sharing responsibly, 147–148
    stray, 409–411
    subjective, 9, 29, 34
    the time dimension, 6–7
    what information describes, 9–10
Information Age
    changing the face of business, 2–37
    decentralized computing and shared information, 17
    information as a key resource, 6–10
    people as a key resource, 10–13
Information flows, 8–9
Information granularity, 9
Information-literate knowledge workers, 11–12, 29
Information systems infrastructure, 328–331
Information technology infrastructure, 332–339
    centralized, 333–334
    client/server network for, 334–335
    decentralized, 332–333
    distributed, 334
    supporting, 337–338
    tiered, 335–336
Information technology (IT), 4, 14–18, 39–40, 64. *See also* IT infrastructures
    careers, 26–27, 264, 417
    for competitive advantage, 71
    creating the business vision for, 18–26
    ethics, security, and privacy, 27–28
    in life, 26–28
    spending by the U.S. government on, 264–266
Information theft, 385, 418. *See also* Identity theft
Infrared (IR), 63
Infrastructures. *See also* IT infrastructures
    importance of, 330–331
    for information systems, 328–331
    for information technology, 332–339
    investment in, 336–337
Inkjet printers, 56
Input devices, 15, 41, 52–54, 65
Instances, 163, 176

Instant Messaging (IM) technology, 90–91
Integrated collaboration environments (ICEs),
 88–92, 94
  IT support for, 90–92
Integration, 339–340, 344
  benefits of, 342
  motives of, 341–342
  necessity of, 340–341
  obstacles to, 342–343
  testing, 286
Integrity constraints, 129–130
Intellectual computing, 428
Intellectual interface, 45–50
Intellectual property, 359–360, 382
Intelligence, 181
Intelligent agents, 142, 150, 200–203
  components of, 209
  data-mining agents, 202–203
  monitoring-and-surveillance agents,
   201–202
  types of, 209
  user agents, 203
Intelligent home appliances, 450
Inter-modal transportation, 79–80
Interfaces, intellectual, 45–50
Internal information, 9, 29, 34
Internal Purchasing Agent Desk (iPAD), 268
Internal Revenue Service (IRS), 372
  now more "customer-oriented," 19
International Data Corporation (IDC), 294
International government-to-government (IG2G)
  business, 261, 264, 267
Internet, the, 102–121, 319, 425–428. See also
  Life on the Internet; Monitoring-and-
  surveillance agents
  communications protocols, 113–114
  communications software, 115–116
  connecting to, 114–117
  directory search engines, 108–110
  evaluating ISP options, 116
  finding and using search engines, 108–111
  freeware and shareware on, 311–312
  higher education through, 452–453
  investment opportunities on, 217–218
  job searches on, 36–37
  making travel arrangements on, 388–389
  offering software-as-a-service (SaaS),
   425–426
  ordering products and services on, 100–101
  and outsourcing, 292
  search engines, 108–110
  telecommunications hardware, 116–117
  true search engines, 108, 110
Internet Age, the five forces model, 72–76
Internet backbone, 111, 118
Internet Explorer, 113
Internet Movie Database, 350
Internet server computers, 113, 118
Internet servers, 112–113
Internet service providers (ISP), 26, 112, 116,
 118

Internet technologies, 111–114
Internet telephony. See Voice over Internet
  Protocol (VoIP)
Intersection relations, 169
Interviewing, 37
Intranets, 7, 319
Intrusion-detection software, 381–383
Intrusion-detection systems (IDSs), 383
Investment opportunities on the Internet
  learning about investing, 217
  researching the company behind the stock,
   217–218
  retrieving stock quotes, 218
iPAD. See Internal Purchasing Agent Desk
IRC (Internet relay chat) servers, 113, 118
IrDA (infrared data association) ports, 63
IRS. See Internal Revenue Service
ISP. See Internet service providers
IT. See Information technology
IT infrastructures, 328–331
  backup/recovery, 337, 339, 344
  disaster recovery plan, 337–338
  and the real world, 338–339
  sponsoring, 347
IT system agility
  accessibility, 326–327
  availability, 326
  capacity planning, 328
  flexibility, 327
  performance, 327
  reliability, 327
  scalability, 327

J

J. B. Hunt Transportation Inc., 183
J. P. Morgan, 355
JAD. See Joint application development
JIT. See Just-in-time
Job boards, 461
Job market
  electronic, 455–457
  hidden, 457, 490
Job searches on the Internet, 36–37
  creating and posting electronic résumés,
   36–37
  job databases, 36
  locating internships, 37
Joint application development (JAD), 282
Joystick, 53
Just-in-time (JIT), 79

K

Kazaa Media Desktop, 370
Kelley's Blue Book, 350
Key logger software, 362, 396
Key trapper software, 362, 396
Keyboards, 52
KM. See Knowledge management system
Knowledge-based systems, 190, 209

Knowledge management (KM) system, 22, 90, 94
Knowledge workers, 4
  information-literate, 11–12
  technology-literate, 11
Krispy Kreme Doughnuts, 123

L

Land O'Lakes, 144
Lands' End, 184
Language processing, 429
Las Vegas casinos, 367
Laser printers, 56
lastminute.com, 299
Late fees, dropped at Blockbuster, 3
Laurentian Bank, 142
Layer infrastructure, for information technology,
 335
LeadBack behavioral marketing technology, 83
Legacy information system (LIS), 320
Leverage, operating, 519
LEXIS-NEXIS, 157
Life on the Internet, 349–350
  cooking from the Internet, 350
  online magazines, 349
  online movie listings and reviews, 349
Links, 105
Linux, 48, 344–345
Liquid crystal display (LCD), 54, 438
List definition tables, 221
Lists, 220–221
Livelink, 137
Local Number Portability (LNP), 74
Logical view, 130
Logistics, 80
Lotus, 90
Love Bug worm, 377, 395
Loyalty programs, 73

M

M. See Megabytes
M-commerce, 18, 271–272
Mac OS, 48
Machine cycle, 59
Macro viruses, 393
Mail servers, 113
Mailing lists, 458
Mainframe computers, 45, 64
Maintenance, repair, and operations (MRO)
  materials (indirect materials), 247–248, 266
Maintenance phase, 286–287
Malware, 393, 399
Management
  of data, 186
  of models, 184, 186
  operational, 8
  of risk, 379, 382–383
  strategic, 8
  tactical, 8
  of user interfaces, 186

Management information systems (MIS), 4
Management systems
    database, 130, 175
    supply chain, 78–81
Manufacturing Resources Planning (MRPII), 323
Market segmentation, 212
Marketing, mix of, 250, 266
Mass customization, 247, 266
Materials Requirement Planning (MRP), 323
Mayo Clinic, 179
MB. *See* Megabytes
MD5 hash value, 406–407, 419
MDA. *See* Multidimensional analysis tools
Media, adding to presentation software, 68
Megabytes (MB or M or Meg), 57
Memory Stick Media card, 58
Mercedes-Benz, customer advisory system, 279
Merrill Lynch, 298
Miami Dolphins, 71
Miami Herald, 187–189
Microphones, 54
Microsoft Access, implementing a database with, 494–495
Microsoft Corp., 90, 325, 365
Microsoft Excel, 220. *See also* Visual Basic for Applications
Microsoft Windows XP Home, 48
Microsoft Windows XP Professional, 48
Microsoft Word, cut and paste functionality for, 285
Mid-range computers, 44–45, 64
Mind support, 10
Minicomputers (mid-range computers), 44–45, 64
MIS. *See* Management information systems
MMC. *See* MultiMediaCard
Mobile computing, 18
Mobile CPUs, 60
Mobility, increasing in the future, 435–438
Model management, 184, 186
Modeling, 284
Modems, 116–117, 119
    cable, 116, 119
    satellite, 116, 119
    telephone, 116, 119
Monitoring-and-surveillance agents, 201–202, 209
Monitoring technology, 365–367
Monitors, 54–55, 68
Monster.com, 244, 253
Mountain Bike Rentals, 522–524
Mouse, 52
Movex software, 203
Movie Database, 349
Movie Review Query Engine Web site, 349
Moviefone Web site, 349
Multi-agent systems, and agent-based modeling, 204–208
Multi-state CPUs, 437, 446
Multidimensional analysis (MDA) tools, 142–143, 150
Multidimensional databases, 140
Multifunction printers, 56
Multimedia (HTML) résumé, 468–471, 490

MultiMediaCard (MMC), 58
Multitasking, 48
Murder investigations, 373
Music store, 214
Mutations, 198, 209
MySimon.com, 200

N

n-tier infrastructure, 336
Nanotechnology, 429
NAP. *See* Network access points
Napster, 370
NASA, 201
NASD. *See* National Association of Securities Dealers
NAT. *See* Nutrition Analysis Tool
National Association of Securities Dealers (NASD), 217
National Crime Information Center (NCIC), 371–372
NCIC. *See* National Crime Information Center
Nearshore outsourcing, 294, 305
Negotiating, 37, 268
Netflix, 345–346
Network access points (NAP), 111, 118
Network basics, 276–277
Network service providers (NSP), 111–112, 118
Network Services, 12
Networks, neural, 179, 193–197, 209, 211–212
Neugent, 202
Neural networks, 179, 193–197, 209, 211–212
    layers of, 196
NextPage, 91
Nielsen Net Ratings, 32
Nonrecurring decisions, 182
Nonstructured decisions, 182
Normalization, 169, 176
Notebook computers, 43, 60, 64
Novell, 90
NSP. *See* Network service providers
Nutrition Analysis Tool (NAT), 350

O

Object-oriented (OO) technologies, 352–353
Objective information, 9, 29, 34
Occupational Outlook Handbook, 491
Offshore outsourcing, 294, 305
OLAP. *See* Online analytical processing
OLTP. *See* Online transaction processing
OMR. *See* Optical mark recognition
"1-Click ordering," 20
100 Top Companies, 35
Online ad (banner ad), 250, 266
Online analytical processing (OLAP), 21, 124–125
Online banking and bill paying, 4, 19–20
Online blackmail, 378
Online purchases. *See* Buying products and services on the Internet
Online training, 286
Online transaction processing (OLTP), 21, 124–125, 141, 154, 378

Onshore outsourcing, 293, 305
OO. *See* Object-oriented technologies
Open-source software, 50
Open Text Corporation, 137
Operating leverage, analyzing, 519
Operating system software, 16, 42, 48, 50, 65. *See also individual programs*
Operational databases, 124, 149
Operational management, 8
Optical character reader, 53
Optical mark reader (OMR), 53
Optical storage media, 56
Order-management software, 80
Ordering online. *See* Buying products and services on the Internet
OrderMotion order-management software, 80
Output devices, 16, 41, 54–56, 65
Outsourcing, 290–298, 305
    advantages of, 295–296
    better predicting future costs, 296
    developing a request for proposal, 292–293
    disadvantages of, 296–297
    exploiting the intellect of another organization, 295
    improving performance accountability, 296
    increasing dependency on other organizations, 297
    increasing vulnerability of strategic information, 296–297
    nearshore, 294, 305
    onshore, 293, 305
    reducing costs, 296
    reducing degree of control, 296
    reducing technical know-how for future innovation, 296
Outsourcing information technology, 510–511
Outsourcing Research Council, 291
Ownership of information, 146–148
    sharing responsibly, 147–148
    strategic management support for, 146–147

P

PageRanking process, 201
Parallel implementation, 286
Parallel port, 62
Passwords
    figuring out, 413
    making up, 402
Pattern classification, 429
PayPal, 25, 255, 267
PC Card, 64
PC Card slot, 64
PC Magazine, 16, 242, 368
PDA. *See* Personal digital assistants
PDF. *See* Portable document format
Peer-to-peer collaboration software, 91
People as a key resource
    ethical responsibilities of, 13
    information and technology literacy of, 10–12
Performance, 327
Personal agents, 203, 209

Personal digital assistants (PDA), 42, 64
  software for, 68
Personal productivity software, 45–47, 65
Phased implementation, 286
Phishing, 363–364
Physical view, 130
Piedmont Hospital, 190
Pierce County, Washington, 132
Pilot implementation, 286
Pirated software, 382
Pivot tables, 228–235
Pixels (picture elements), 55
Pizzeria Uno, 152
PKE. *See* Public key encryption
Planning phase, 280–282
  for higher education, 515–516
Plotters, 56
Plug and play, 61
Plunge implementation, 286
PMA. *See* President's Management Agenda
Point-of-sale (POS) transactions, 152
  data from, 123
Pointing devices, 52–53
Political campaign finance consultants, 504–505
Polo Ralph Lauren, 385
Pony Espresso, analyzing operating leverage, 519
Pop-under ads, 250–251, 266
Pop-up ads, 250, 266
Portability, increasing in the future, 435–438
Portable document format (PDF), 468, 470, 490
Porter's Five Forces Model, 72–76, 81, 92–93
Ports, 61–63
POS. *See* Point-of-sale transactions
Predictive agents, 201–202, 209
Presence awareness, 90
Presentation software
  adding media to, 68
  making the case with, 512–513
Preservation process, 406–407
President's Management Agenda (PMA), 32, 261
PricewaterhouseCooper, survey of CEOs, 291
Primary keys, 128, 163–164, 176
Pringles, 423
Printers, 55–56
  resolution of, 55
Privacy, 27–28, 361–374, 382, 444–445
  adware and spyware, 370–371
  of consumers, 367–373
  of employees, 364–367
  and government agencies, 371–373
  and law enforcement, 371–372
  monitoring technology, 365–367
Prodigy, 386
Production
  costs of, 80
  problems with, 236
Products, value as perceived by the customer, 245–261
Professional services consulting firms, 22
Profit, 80
Profit maximization, 199
Project manager, 282
Project milestones, 282

Project plan, 281, 309
Project scope, 281
  documents regarding, 281
Proof-of-concept prototypes, 299
Protecting people and information, 355–401
  ethics, 356–361
  security, 374–382
Protocols, 113–114
Prototypes
  proof-of-concept, 209
  selling, 299
Prototyping, 289, 298–302, 305, 309
  advantages of, 301
  disadvantages of, 301–302
  encouraging active knowledge worker participation, 301
  failing to indicate performance under operational conditions, 301
  giving knowledge workers a feel for the final system, 301
  helping to determine technical feasibility, 301
  helping to resolve discrepancies among knowledge workers, 301
  helping to sell the idea of a proposed system, 301
  inducing the project team to forgo proper testing and documentation, 302
  leading people to believe the final system will follow shortly, 301
Prototyping process
  developing the initial prototype, 300
  identifying basic requirements, 300
  knowledge worker reviewing, 300
  revising and enhancing the prototype, 300
Protx, 378
PS/2 port, 62
Public key encryption (PKE), 258–259, 267, 381
Pure play, 263
Purina Mills, 144
Push technology, 426–427, 446

Q

QlikView, 85
Query-and-reporting tools, 142, 150
Query-by-example (QBE) tools, 135
Query optimization facilities, 137
Quick View Plus, 407

R

RAD. *See* Rapid application development
RAM (random access memory), 16, 41, 59–60, 65
Rapid application development (RAD), 279, 288–289, 304
Reactive computer forensics, 416–417
Recovery, 136, 337, 344, 409–414
  and computer forensics experts, 415–418
  places to look for useful information, 409–412
  ways of hiding information, 412–414
Recurring decisions, 182

Red Robin International, 152
Redlining, 212
Registry files, 411
Relational database model, 126–130, 149, 161
  built-in integrity constraints, 129–130
  collections of information, 126
  created with logical structures, 126–128
  logical ties within the information, 128–129
Relational databases
  defining entity classes and primary keys, 163–164
  defining information (fields) for each relation, 172–174
  defining relationships among the entity classes, 164–171
  designing and building, 161–175
  using a data definition language to create, 176
Relational technology, tracking projects with, 507–508
Relations, 126, 252
Reliability, data, 327
Renaming a file, 412–413
Reorganization facilities, 138
Report generators, 134
Request for proposal (RFP), 292–293
Requirement definition documents, 282
Research, fundamental, 217
Resolution
  of a printer, 55
  of a screen, 55
Résumé content
  important contact information, 462
  powerful objective statements, 463–465
  valuable sections of, 465–466
  your objective, 463
Revenue, 80
Reverse auctions, 248
RFID (radio frequency identification) chips, 440–442, 446, 450
  embedded into gaming tokens, 367
  future of, 441–442
RGT. *See* "Run-Grow-Transform" framework
Richmond, Virginia, City of, 210–211
  sniper attacks in, 210–211
Risk assessment, 379, 383
Risk management, 379
Ritz-Carlton Hotel, 130
Rivalry among competitors, 75–76, 94
Robots, 189–190
Rockies Airline, 522
Ruby Tuesday, 97
"Run-Grow-Transform" (RGT) framework, 25–26, 72, 83, 92

S

Sales force automation (SFA) systems, 82
SAN. *See* Storage area network
Sarbanes-Oxley Act of 2002, 374, 417
SAS, 142
Satellite modems, 116, 119
Scalability, 327

Scannable résumés, 468–470
Scanners, 53–54
Scheduling, 522
SCIP. *See* Society for Competitive Intelligence Professionals
SCM. *See* Supply chain management systems
Scope creep, 281
Screen resolution, 55
Script bunnies (script kiddies), 402, 418
SD. *See* Secure Digital card
SDLC. *See* Systems development life cycle
Search engines, 118
    directory, 108–110, 118
    true, 108, 110, 118
Searching online databases and information repositories
    customer information, 158
    demographics, 158
    financial aid resources, 157
    libraries, 157
    real estate, 158
Sears, Roebuck & Co., 306–307
Secure Digital (SD) card, 58
Secure Electronic Transactions (SETs), 259, 267
Secure Sockets Layer (SSL), 259, 267
Security, 27–28
    access authentication, 380–381
    anti-virus software, 379
    backups, 379
    and employees, 374–376
    encryption, 258–259
    firewalls, 380
    intrusion-detection and security auditing software, 381–383
    for people and information, 374–382, 524–525
    precautions, 378–382
    types of cyber crime, 377–378
Security-auditing software, 381–383
Security management facilities, 137
Selection, 198, 209
Self-assessment, 459–460, 490
Self-promotion, 473–474
Selling prototypes, 209
Servers
    ftp, 113
    IRC, 113
    mail, 113
    Web, 113
Service providers, Internet, 112, 116
Services, value as perceived by the customer, 245–261
SETs. *See* Secure Electronic Transactions
7 Up, 10
SFA. *See* Sales force automation systems
Shared information, 17
Shareware. *See* Freeware and shareware on the Internet
Shopping bots, 200–201, 209
Siemens AG, 88–89
Sign-off, 282–283
Signatures, digital, 403
Sinclair Knight Merz, 22

SiteScape Forum, 88–89
Ski-YA!, 520
Skill words, 459–460, 490
Slack space, 409–411, 419
Slammer worm, 395
SM. *See* SmartMedia
Small Business Administration (SBA), loans from, 263
Smart cards, 255
SmartMedia (SM) cards, 58
Sneakware, 27, 370
Sniper attacks in, Richmond, Virginia, 210–211
SoBig virus, 395
Social engineering, 401
Social network systems, 90, 94
Society, technology for the betterment of, 444
Society for Competitive Intelligence Professionals (SCIP), 86
Software, 15–17, 29, 40, 45–50
    anti-spyware, 50
    anti-virus, 50, 379, 383
    application, 16, 41–42, 45–50
    for business intelligence, 87
    connectivity, 115, 119
    crash-proof, 50
    for database management systems, 20–21
    development of, 305–306
    disk optimization, 50
    e-mail, 115, 118
    facial recognition, 434–435
    faulty, 287
    forensic, 407
    horizontal market, 46, 65
    intrusion-detection, 381–383
    key logger, 362, 396
    key trapper, 396
    open-source, 50
    operating system, 16, 42, 48, 50, 65
    order-management, 80
    peer-to-peer collaboration, 91
    for personal digital assistants, 68
    personal productivity, 45–47, 65
    pirated, 382
    presentation, 512–513
    security-auditing, 381–383
    spam blocker, 50
    spyware, 370
    system, 42, 48–50, 65
    Trojan-horse, 370
    understanding the complexity of, 67–68
    uninstaller, 50
    utility, 16–17, 42, 50, 65
    vertical market, 46, 65
    Web browser, 106, 115
Software-as-a-service (SaaS), the Internet offering, 425–426, 445
Software suites, 47, 49
    evaluating, 49
Solomon Enterprises, 125–128, 131–133, 161–163, 170–175
Southwest Airlines, 206–207
Spam blocker software, 50
Spam Buster, 369

Specialty merchandise, 245
SPIN. *See* Supply Partner Information Network
Spoke, 91–92
Spoofing, 256, 363, 396
SportsLine.com, 338
Spyware, 27, 370
SQL. *See* Structured query language
SSA Global, 324–325
SSL. *See* Secure Sockets Layer
St. Jude Children's Research Hospital, 302
Stand-alone viruses, 396
Staples, 95–96
Star Sales and Services, 249
Statistical tools, 143, 150
Stealthware, 27, 370
Steganography, 413–414, 419
Still camera, digital, 54
Stolen identities, 365. *See also* Identity theft
Storage area network (SAN), 337
Storage devices, 16, 41, 56–58, 65
Storyboarding, 478
Strategic and competitive opportunities
    ordering products and services on the Internet, 100–101
    using IT for competitive advantage, 70–101
Strategic management, 8
Stray information, 409–411
    in deleted files and slack space, 409–411
    in unallocated disk space, 412
    to unused disk space, 412
Structured decisions, 182
Structured query language (SQL), 136
Stylus, 52
Subjective information, 9, 29, 34
Subsystems
    application generation, 136, 149
    data administration, 138–139, 149
    data definition, 131–132, 149
    data manipulations, 132–136, 149
Supercomputers, 45, 64
Supplier power, 73, 94
Supply chain management (SCM) systems, 24, 78–81, 94, 324
    for competitive advantage, 24
    strategic and competitive opportunities, 80–81
Supply Partner Information Network (SPIN), 123
Support, for an IT infrastructure, 337–338
Sutter Health, 7
Swarm (collective) intelligence, in ant colonies, 204–207, 209
Switching, costs of, 74
Symantec Corp., 247
System buses, 60
System integration, 339–340, 344
System software, 42, 48–50, 65
System testing, 286
Systems. *See also* Subsystems
    back office, 84
    collaboration, 22
    customer relationship management, 81–85
    database management, 130, 175
    decision support, 183–186, 208

Systems—*Cont.*
    document management, 89–90
    expert, 190–197, 209
    front office, 84
    geographic information, 187–189, 209
    knowledge-based, 190, 209
    management information, 4
    sales force automation, 82
    supply chain management, 24, 78–81
    transaction processing, 19
    workflow, 89
Systems development life cycle (SDLC),
    280–287, 295, 304, 308
    analysis phase, 282–283
    building the database and software, 285
    building the technical architecture, 284
    design phase, 283–284
    development phase, 284–285
    help desk, 287
    implementation phase, 286
    maintenance phase, 286–287
    planning phase, 280–282
    test conditions, 285
    testing phase, 285–286
    training, 286
    user documentation, 286
Systems development methodologies, 287–290,
    304
    agile methodology, 290, 305
    extreme programming methodology,
        289–290, 304–305
    rapid application development, 288–289,
        304
    waterfall methodology, 288, 304
SYSTRAN Enterprise, 7

T

Tablet PCs, 42, 64
Tactical management, 8
Talbott neckties, 77–78
TB. *See* Terabytes
TCP/IP (transport control protocol/Internet
    protocol), 114, 118
"Team & Task" IT collaboration tool, 87
Team collaboration
    in document management systems, 89–90
    in workflow systems, 89
Technical architecture, 284–285
Technologies, "disruptive," 3
Technology, and outsourcing, 292
Technology for the betterment of people and
    society, 444
Technology Issues for Financial Executives
    survey, 147
Technology-literate knowledge workers, 11, 29
Technology metrics, 31–32
Telecommunications devices, 16, 41, 65
Telecommuting, 5
Telephone modems, 119
Terabytes (TB), 57
Test conditions, 287
Testing phase, 285–286

TFAK. *See* Trojan First Aid Kit
Thin wallet, 255
Threats
    of new entrants, 75, 94
    of substitute products or services, 74, 94
Thrill-seeking hackers, 400, 418
Thumbnails, 482
TicketMaster, 71
Tiered infrastructure, for information technology,
    335–336
Top-level domain, 105–106, 118
Top line, versus bottom line, 18–20, 81, 92
Touchpads, 53
TPSs. *See* Transaction processing systems
Tracert function, 361
Trackballs, 53
Traffic light expert system, 192–193
Training, 286
Transaction processing, integrating with biometric
    processing, 433–435
Transaction processing systems (TPSs), 19, 434
Transferable skills, 460
Transportation, inter-modal, 79–80
Travel arrangements on the Internet, 388–389
    air travel, 388
    rental cars, 389
TreasuryDirect, 264
Trends for the future
    automatic speech recognition, 429
    broadening of e-government, 261–266
    CAVE automatic virtual environments,
        431–432
    closing the great digital divide, 442–443
    continuing your education through the
        Internet, 452–453
    digital cash, 436–437
    exchanging privacy for convenience,
        444–445
    explosion of C2C e-commerce, 439
    increasing portability and mobility, 435–438
    necessity of technology, 443
    new physiological interactions, 428–435
    push, not pull technologies, and
        personalization, 426–427
    technology for the betterment of people and
        society, 444
    virtual reality, 429–432
    wearable computers, 437–438
Trevor Toy Auto Mechanics, 502
Trojan First Aid Kit (TFAK), 371
Trojan horse software, 370
Trojan horse viruses, 396, 418
Truck Online Configurator (TOC), 279
True search engines, 108, 110, 118
TRUSTe, 34
Twentieth Century Fox, 212

U

UAT. *See* User acceptance testing
Ubiquitous computing, 17
Unallocated space, 412, 419
Unemployment lows, and outsourcing, 292

Uninstaller software, 50
Unique cookies, 368
Unit testing, 286
UrbanFlorist, 80
URL (uniform resource locator), 104–105, 118
U.S. Department of Commerce, 190
U.S. Department of Justice, 400
U.S. government, 32–33
    spending on information technology,
        264–266
U.S. News & World Report, 452
US West, 199
USA Patriot Act, 374
USA Today, 104–105
USB (universal serial bus), 61
User acceptance testing (UAT), 286
User agents, 203, 209
User documentation, 286
User interface management, 186
Utility software, 16–17, 42, 65

V

Vail Resort, 522
Value chains, 76–78, 81, 92–94, 99
    building, 505–507
    identifying processes that add value, 77
    identifying processes that reduce value,
        77–78
VBA. *See* Visual Basic for Applications
Vertical e-marketplace, 249, 266
Vertical market software, 26, 46, 65
Video camera, digital, 54
Video rental business, 75, 154, 177
Viewable image size (VIS), 55
Views, 133
    logical, 130
    physical, 130
Viral marketing, 251, 267
Virtual reality, 429–432, 444, 446
Virtual teams, 89
Virus hoaxes, 396–397
Viruses, 377–378, 382, 393–396, 418
    macro, 393
    stand-alone, 396
    Trojan-horse, 396, 418
VIS. *See* Viewable image size
Visa, 212
Visual Basic for Applications (VBA), with Excel,
    501
Voice over Internet Protocol (VoIP), 331, 428,
    446
Volkswagen AG, 203, 267–268
Vulnerability, of WLANs, 524

W

Wal-Mart, 98–99, 215
Walker, 430
Wall Street Journal, 457
Waterfall methodology, 288, 304
Wearable computers, 437–438, 446, 450
Web. *See* World Wide Web

Web browser software, 106
Web computers, 68
Web defacing, 399–400
Web design considerations, 476–484
    background color, 481–482
    basic Web design principles, 476–480
    color, 481
    defining the audience and purpose, 478
    designing your home page, 481–484
    documenting the site design, 483–484
    fonts and formatting, 481–482
    graphics, 482–483
    home page content, 483
    site structure, 479–480
    testing, 488–489
Web logs, 371
Web pages, 104, 118
    browser software for, 115
    building with HTML, 314–315
Web servers, 113, 118
Web site addresses, 104, 118
Web sites, 104, 118
    demonstrating how to build, 511–512
Web space, 114
Webcam, 54

WebFocus, 87
Wells Fargo Bank, 81
Westminster, California, City of, 194
Weyerhaueser Corp., 212
"Where's My Refund?", 19
White-hat hackers, 377, 401, 418
White River Valley Electric Cooperative
    (WRVEC), 189
WiFi (Wireless Fidelity), 63
Wildseed, 446–448
Wired communications media, 61–62
Wired magazine, 242
Wireless communications media, 63–64
Wireless future, 439–442, 516–517
    in cell phone technology, 439–440
Wireless local area networks (WLANs), 524
    vulnerability of, 524
WiSE (Worldwide information Sharing
    Environment), 22
WLANs. *See* Wireless local area networks
Work allocation, system of honeybees, 208
Workflow, 89, 94
    reorganizing, 208
    systems for, 89
Workshop training, 286

World Bank, 336
"World of TUI" group, 137
World Wide Web (Web), 87, 104–107
    understanding addresses, 105–106
    using a Web portal, 113
    using Web browser software, 106
    Web sites, addresses, and pages, 104–105
Worms, 393–396. *See also* Combination
    worm/DoS attacks
    the Love Bug, 393–395

X

xD-Picture (xD) card, 58
Xybernaut, 437

Y

Yahoo!, 109, 247, 375

Z

ZoneAlarm, 380–381